MONEY AND POWER

ALSO BY THE AUTHOR

The Last Tycoons

House of Cards

WILLIAM D. COHAN

DOUBLEDAY   New York   London   Toronto   Sydney   Auckland

MONEY AND POWER

HOW
GOLDMAN
SACHS
CAME
TO RULE
THE
WORLD

Copyright © 2011 by William D. Cohan

www.doubleday.com

Portions of this work were previously published in *Vanity Fair*.

Grateful acknowledgment is made to the Columbia University Oral History Research Office Collection.

Book design by Maria Carella
Jacket design by John Fontana
Jacket illustration by Serial Cut™
Title page photograph by Marco Di Fabio / Flickr / Getty Images

Cataloging-in-Publication Data is on file with the Library of Congress.

ISBN 978-0-385-52384-4

PRINTED IN THE UNITED STATES OF AMERICA

10 9 8 7 6 5 4 3 2 1

First Edition

TO QUENTIN, DEB, AND TEDDY

CONTENTS

PROLOGUE / The Pyrrhic Victory   1

CHAPTER 1 / A Family Business   25

CHAPTER 2 / The Apostle of Prosperity   41

CHAPTER 3 / The Politician   62

CHAPTER 4 / The Value of Friendship   85

CHAPTER 5 / "What Is Inside Information?"   109

CHAPTER 6 / The Biggest Man on the Block   138

CHAPTER 7 / Caveat Emptor   154

CHAPTER 8 / The Goldman Way   190

CHAPTER 9 / A Formula That Works   214

CHAPTER 10 / Goldman Sake   237

CHAPTER 11 / Busted   250

CHAPTER 12 / Money   276

CHAPTER 13 / Power   302

CHAPTER 14 / The College of Cardinals   314

CHAPTER 15 / $10 Billion or Bust   357

CHAPTER 16 / The Glorious Revolution   381

CHAPTER 17 / It's Too Much Fun Being CEO of Goldman Sachs   414

CHAPTER 18 / Alchemy   465

CHAPTER 19 / Getting Closer to Home   489

CHAPTER 20 / The Fabulous Fab   508

CHAPTER 21 / Selling to Widows and Orphans   528

CHAPTER 22 / Meltdown   547

CHAPTER 23 / Goldman Gets Paid   571

CHAPTER 24 / God's Work   596

ACKNOWLEDGMENTS   611

NOTES   615

INDEX   631

MONEY AND POWER

THE PYRRHIC VICTORY

Wall Street has always been a dangerous place. Firms have been going in and out of business ever since speculators first gathered under a buttonwood tree near the southern tip of Manhattan in the late eighteenth century. Despite the ongoing risks, during great swaths of its mostly charmed 142 years, Goldman Sachs has been both envied and feared for having the best talent, the best clients, and the best political connections, and for its ability to alchemize them into extreme profitability and market prowess.

Indeed, of the many ongoing mysteries about Goldman Sachs, one of the most overarching is just how it makes so much money, year in and year out, in good times and in bad, all the while revealing as little as possible to the outside world about how it does it. Another—equally confounding—mystery is the firm's steadfast, zealous belief in its ability to manage its multitude of internal and external conflicts better than any other beings on the planet. The combination of these two genetic strains—the ability to make boatloads of money at will and to appear to manage conflicts that have humbled, then humiliated lesser firms—has made Goldman Sachs the envy of its financial-services brethren.

But it is also something else altogether: a symbol of immutable global power and unparalleled connections, which Goldman is shameless in exploiting for its own benefit, with little concern for how its success affects the rest of us. The firm has been described as everything from "a cunning cat that always lands on its feet" to, now famously, "a great vampire squid wrapped around the face of humanity, relentlessly jamming its blood funnel into anything that smells like money," by *Rolling Stone* writer Matt Taibbi. The firm's inexorable success leaves people wondering: Is Goldman Sachs better than everyone else, or have they found ways to win time and time again by cheating?

But in the early twenty-first century, thanks to the fallout from

Goldman's very success, the firm is looking increasingly vulnerable. To be sure, the firm has survived plenty of previous crises, starting with the Depression, when much of the firm's capital was lost in a scam of its own creation, and again in the late 1940s, when Goldman was one of seventeen Wall Street firms put on trial and accused of collusion by the federal government. In the past forty years, as a consequence of numerous scandals involving rogue traders, suicidal clients, and charges of insider trading, the firm has come far closer—repeatedly—to financial collapse than its reputation would attest.

Each of these previous threats changed Goldman in some meaningful way and forced the firm to adapt to the new laws that either the market or regulators imposed. This time will be no different. What is different for Goldman now, though, is that for the first time since 1932—when Sidney Weinberg, then Goldman's senior partner, knew that he could quickly reach his friend, President-elect Franklin Delano Roosevelt—the firm no longer appears to have sympathetic high-level relationships in Washington. Goldman's friends in high places, so crucial to the firm's extraordinary success, are abandoning it. Indeed, in today's charged political climate, which is polarized along socioeconomic lines, Goldman seems particularly isolated and demonized.

Certainly Lloyd Blankfein, Goldman's fifty-six-year-old chairman and CEO, has no friend in President Barack Obama, despite being invited to a recent state dinner for the president of China. According to *Newsweek* columnist Jonathan Alter's book *The Promise,* the "angriest" Obama got during his first year in office was when he heard Blankfein justify the firm's $16.2 billion of bonuses in 2009 by claiming "Goldman was never in danger of collapse" during the financial crisis that began in 2007. According to Alter, President Obama told a friend that Blankfein's statement was "flatly untrue" and added for good measure, "These guys want to be paid like rock stars when all they're doing is lip-synching capitalism."

Complicating the firm's efforts to be better understood by the American public—a group Goldman has never cared to serve—is a long-standing reticence among many of the firm's current and former executives, bankers, and traders to engage with the media in a constructive way. Even retired Goldman partners feel compelled to check with the firm's disciplined administrative bureaucracy, run by John F. W. Rogers—a former chief of staff to James Baker, both at the White House and at the State Department—before agreeing to be interviewed. Most have likely signed confidentiality or nondisparagement agreements as a condition of their departures from the firm. Should they make themselves available, unlike bankers and traders at other firms—where self-aggrandizement in the press at the expense of colleagues is typical—Goldman types stay firmly on the message that what matters most is the Goldman team, not any one individual on it.

"They're extremely disciplined," explained one private-equity executive who both competes and invests with Goldman. "They understand probably better than anybody how to never take the game face off. You'll never get a Goldman banker after three beers saying, 'You know, listen, my colleagues are a bunch of fucking dickheads.' They just don't do that the way other guys will, whether it's because they tend to keep the uniform on for a longer stretch of time so they're not prepared to damage their squad, or whether or not it's because they're afraid of crossing the powers that be, once they've taken the blood oath . . . they maintain that discipline in a kind of eerily successful way."

***

ANYONE WHO MIGHT have forgotten how dangerous Wall Street can be was reminded of it again, in spades, beginning in early 2007, as the market for home mortgages in the United States began to crack, and then implode, leading to the demise or near demise a year or so later of several large Wall Street firms that had been around for generations—including Bear Stearns, Lehman Brothers, and Merrill Lynch—as well as other large financial institutions such as Citigroup, AIG, Washington Mutual, and Wachovia.

Although it underwrote billions of dollars of mortgage securities, Goldman Sachs avoided the worst of the crisis, thanks largely to a fully authorized, well-timed proprietary bet by a small group of Goldman traders—led by Dan Sparks, Josh Birnbaum, and Michael Swenson—beginning in December 2006, that the housing bubble would collapse and that the securities tied to home mortgages would rapidly lose value. They were right.

In July 2007, David Viniar, Goldman's longtime chief financial officer, referred to this proprietary bet as "the big short" in an e-mail he wrote to Blankfein and others. During 2007, as other firms lost billions of dollars writing down the value of mortgage-related securities on their balance sheets, Goldman was able to offset its own mortgage-related losses with huge gains—of some $4 billion—from its bet the housing market would fall.

Goldman earned a net profit in 2007 of $11.4 billion—then a record for the firm—and its top five executives split $322 million, another record on Wall Street. Blankfein, who took over the leadership of the firm in June 2006 when his predecessor, Henry Paulson Jr., became treasury secretary, received total compensation for the year of $70.3 million. The following year, while many of Goldman's competitors were fighting for their lives—a fight many of them would lose—Goldman made a "substantial profit of $2.3 billion," Blankfein wrote in an April 27, 2009, letter. Given the carnage on Wall Street in 2008, Goldman's top five executives decided to eschew their bonuses. For his part, Blankfein made do with total compensation for the year of $1.1 million. (Not to worry, though; his 3.37 million Goldman shares are still worth around $570 million.)

Nothing in the financial world happens in a vacuum these days, given the exponential growth of trillions of dollars of securities tied to the value of other securities—known as "derivatives"—and the extraordinarily complex and internecine web of global trading relationships. Accounting rules in the industry promote these interrelationships by requiring firms to check constantly with one another about the value of securities on their balance sheets to make sure that value is reflected as accurately as possible. Naturally, since judgment is involved, especially with ever more complex securities, disagreements among traders about values are common.

Goldman Sachs prides itself on being a "mark-to-market" firm, Wall Street argot for being ruthlessly precise about the value of the securities—known as "marks"—on its balance sheet. Goldman believes its precision promotes transparency, allowing the firm and its investors to make better decisions, including the decision to bet the mortgage market would collapse in 2007. "Because we are a mark-to-market firm," Blankfein once wrote, "we believe the assets on our balance sheet are a true and realistic reflection of book value." If, for instance, Goldman observed that demand for a certain security or group of like securities was changing or that exogenous events—such as the expected bursting of a housing bubble—could lower the value of its portfolio of housing-related securities, the firm religiously lowered the marks on these securities and took the losses that resulted. These new, lower marks would be communicated throughout Wall Street as traders talked and discussed new trades. Taking losses is never much fun for a Wall Street firm, but the pain can be mitigated by offsetting profits, which Goldman had in abundance in 2007, thanks to the mortgage-trading group that set up "the big short."

What's more, the profits Goldman made from "the big short" allowed the firm to put the squeeze on its competitors, including Bear Stearns, Merrill Lynch, and Lehman Brothers, and at least one counterparty, AIG, exacerbating their problems—and fomenting the eventual crisis—because Goldman alone could take the write-downs with impunity. The rest of Wall Street squirmed, knowing that big losses had to be taken on mortgage-related securities and that they didn't have nearly enough profits to offset them.

Taking Goldman's new marks into account would have devastating consequences for other firms, and Goldman braced itself for a backlash. "Sparks and the [mortgage] group are in the process of considering making significant downward adjustments to the marks on their mortgage portfolio esp[ecially] CDOs and CDO squared," Craig Broderick, Goldman's chief risk officer, wrote in a May 11, 2007, e-mail, referring to the lower values Sparks was placing on complex mortgage-related securities. "This will potentially have a big P&L impact on us, but also to our clients due to the marks and associated margin calls on repos, derivatives, and other products. We need to survey our clients and take a shot at determining the most vulnerable clients, knock on implications, etc. This is getting lots of 30th floor"—the executive floor at Goldman's former headquarters at 85 Broad Street—"attention right now."

Broderick's e-mail may turn out to be the unofficial "shot heard round the world" of the financial crisis. The shock waves of Goldman's lower marks quickly began to be felt in the market. The first victims—of their own poor investment strategy as well as of Goldman's marks—were two Bear Stearns hedge funds that had invested heavily in squirrelly mortgage-related securities, including many packaged and sold by Goldman Sachs. According to U.S. Securities and Exchange Commission (SEC) rules, the Bear Stearns hedge funds were required to average Goldman's marks with those provided by traders at other firms.

Given the leverage used by the hedge funds, the impact of the new, lower Goldman marks was magnified, causing the hedge funds to report big losses to their investors in May 2007, shortly after Broderick's e-mail. Unsurprisingly, the hedge funds' investors ran for the exits. By July 2007, the two funds were liquidated and investors lost much of the $1.5 billion they had invested. The demise of the Bear hedge funds also sent Bear Stearns itself on a path to self-destruction after the firm decided, in June 2007, to become the lender to the hedge funds—taking out other Wall Street firms, including Goldman Sachs, at close to one hundred cents on the dollar—by providing short-term loans to the funds secured by the mortgage securities in the funds.

When the funds were liquidated a month later, Bear Stearns took billions of the toxic collateral onto its books, saving its former counterparties from that fate. While becoming the lender to its own hedge funds was an unexpected gift from Bear Stearns to Goldman and others, nine months later Bear Stearns was all but bankrupt, its creditors rescued only by the Federal Reserve and by a merger agreement with JPMorgan Chase. Bear's shareholders ended up with $10 a share in JPMorgan's stock. As recently as January 2007, Bear's stock had traded at $172.69 and the firm had a market value of $20 billion. Goldman's marks had similarly devastating impacts on Merrill Lynch, which was sold to Bank of America days before its own likely bankruptcy filing, and AIG, which the government rescued with $182 billion of taxpayer money before it, too, had to file for bankruptcy. There is little doubt that Goldman's dual decisions to establish "the big short" and then to write down the value of its mortgage portfolio exacerbated the misery at other firms.

———

UNDERSTANDABLY, GOLDMAN DOES not like to talk about the role it had in pushing other firms off the edge of the cliff. It prefers to pretend—even in sworn testimony in front of Congress—that there was no "big short" at all, that its marks were not much lower than any other firm's marks, and that its profits in 2007 from its mortgage trading activities were *de minimis,* something on the order of $500 million, Blankfein later testified, which is chump change in the world of Goldman Sachs. (Goldman officials preferred to talk about their mortgage business as having lost $1.7 billion in 2008, and therefore for the two-year period, Goldman lost $1.2 billion in its mortgage business.) Rather than crow—as would be typical on Wall Street—about its trading prowess in 2007, a prowess that probably saved the firm, Goldman has been taking the opposite tack in public lately of obfuscating and suggesting that it was just as stupid as everyone else. For a firm where Blankfein once said of his job, "I live ninety-eight percent of my time in the world of two-percent probabilities," this argument may seem counterintuitive. But in a political and economic environment where the repercussions of the financial crisis are still reverberating and blame is still being apportioned, Goldman's preference for appearing dumb rather than brilliant may be the best of its poor options.

Consider this exchange, from an April 27, 2010, U.S. Senate hearing, between Senator Carl Levin, D-Michigan, the chairman of the Permanent Subcommittee on Investigations, and Blankfein:

LEVIN: The question is did you bet big time in 2007 against the housing mortgage business? And you did.
BLANKFEIN: No, we did not.
LEVIN: OK. You win big in shorts.
BLANKFEIN: No, we did not.

This disconnect with Senator Levin had followed Blankfein's opening statement, where he denied the firm had made a bet against the housing market in 2007. "Much has been said about the supposedly massive short Goldman Sachs had on the U.S. housing market," he said. "The fact is, we were not consistently or significantly net-short the market in residential mortgage-related products in 2007 and 2008. Our performance in our residential mortgage-related business confirms this. During the two years of the financial crisis, while profitable overall, Goldman Sachs lost approximately $1.2 billion from our activities in the residential housing market. We didn't have a massive short against the housing market, and we certainly did not bet against our clients."

In a separate interview, Blankfein said the decision to mitigate the firm's risk to the housing market in December 2006 has been "overplayed" and was just a routine decision. "It's what you do when you're managing risk, and a huge part of risk management is scouring the P&L every day for aberrations or unpredicted patterns," he said. "And when you see something like that, you call the people in the business and say, 'Can you explain that?' and when they don't know, you say, 'Take risk down.' That's what happened in our mortgage business, but that meeting wasn't significant. It was rendered significant by the events that subsequently happened."

In fact, Goldman's decision to short the mortgage market, beginning around December 2006, was anything but routine. One former Goldman mortgage trader said he does not understand why Goldman is being so coy. "Their MO is that we made as little money as possible," he said. "[So,] anything that makes it look like they didn't make money or they lost money is good for them, right? Because they don't want to be seen as benefiting during the crisis."

For his part, Senator Levin said he remains mystified by Blankfein's denials when the documentary evidence—including e-mails and board presentations—points overwhelmingly to Goldman having profited handsomely from the bet. "I try to understand why it is that Goldman denies, to this day, making a directional bet against the housing market," he said in a recent interview. "They don't give a damn much about appearances, apparently, on a lot of things they did, but at any rate, I don't get it. Clearly [Goldman] made a directional bet and . . . they lied. The bottom line: They have lied. They've lied about whether or not they made a directional bet." He said his "anger" about Goldman is "very deep" because "they made a huge amount of money betting against housing and they lied about it, and their greed is incredibly intense."

———

DESPITE HAVING "the big short," Goldman and Blankfein could not avoid the tsunami-like repercussions of the crisis. On September 21, 2008, a week after Bank of America bought Merrill and Lehman Brothers filed for bankruptcy protection—the largest such filing of all time—both Goldman and Morgan Stanley voluntarily agreed to give up their status as securities firms, which required increasingly unreliable borrowings from the market to finance their daily operations, to become bank holding companies, which allowed them to obtain short-term loans from the Federal Reserve but, in return, required them to be more heavily regulated than they had been in the past. Goldman and Morgan Stanley made the move as a last-ditch, Hail Mary pass to restore the market's confidence in their firms and stave off their own—once unthinkable—bankruptcy filings. The plan worked. Within days of becoming a bank-holding company, Goldman raised $5 billion in equity from Warren Buffett, considered one of the world's savviest investors—making Buffett the firm's largest individual investor—and another $5.75 billion from the public.

Weeks later, on October 14, Treasury Secretary Paulson summoned to Washington Blankfein and eight other CEOs of surviving Wall Street firms, and ordered them to sell a total of $125 billion in preferred stock to the Treasury, the funds for the purchase coming from the $700 billion Troubled Asset Relief Program, or TARP, the bailout program that Congress had passed a few weeks earlier on its second try. Paulson forced Goldman to take $10 billion of TARP money, as a further step to restore investor confidence in the firms at ground zero of American capitalism. Paulson's evolving thinking, which was shared by both Ben Bernanke, the chairman of the Federal Reserve Board, and Timothy Geithner, then president of the Federal Reserve Bank of New York and now Paulson's successor at Treasury, was that the economic status quo could not be restored until Wall Street returned to functioning as normally as possible. "We were at a tipping point," Paulson said in a speech a few weeks later. Paulson's idea was that the banks receiving the TARP funds would make loans available to borrowers as the economy improved.

Blankfein never believed Goldman needed the TARP funds—and perhaps unwisely said so publicly, earning him Obama's ire. Exacerbating the concerns of the banks that received the TARP money was the fact that Obama had appointed Kenneth Feinberg as his "pay czar" and gave him the mandate to monitor closely—and limit if need be—the compensation of people who worked at financial institutions that received TARP money. Wall Street bankers and traders like to think their compensation potential is unlimited, and so the idea of having Feinberg as a pay czar did not sit well. At the earliest opportunity, which turned out to be July 2009, Goldman—as well as Morgan Stanley and JPMorgan Chase—paid back the $10 billion, plus dividends of $318 million, and paid another $1.1 billion to buy back the warrants Paulson extracted from each of the TARP recipients that October day as part of the price of getting the TARP money in the first place.

"People are angry and understandably ask why their tax dollars have to support large financial institutions," Blankfein wrote in his April 27 letter. "That's why we believe strongly that those institutions that are able to repay the public's investment without adversely affecting their financial profile or curtailing their role and responsibilities in the capital markets are obligated to do so." He made no mention of pay caps as influencing his decision to repay the TARP money or that the TARP money was supposed to be used to make loans to corporate borrowers. Instead, Goldman likes to boast that for the nine months that it had the TARP money it said it didn't want or need, American taxpayers received an annualized return of 23.15 percent.

Ironically, no one seemed the slightest bit grateful. Rather, there was an increasing level of resentment directed at the firm and its perceived arrogance. The relative ease with which Goldman navigated the crisis, its ability to rebound in 2009—when it earned profits of $13.2 billion and paid out bonuses of $16.2 billion—and Blankfein's apparent tone deafness to the magnitude of the public's anger toward Wall Street generally for having to bail out the industry from a crisis of largely its own making made the firm an irresistible target of politicians looking for a culprit and for regulators looking to prove that they once again had a backbone after decades of laissez-faire enforcement of securities laws. Aiding and abetting the politicians in Congress, and the regulators at the U.S. Securities and Exchange Commission, were scornful and wounded competitors angry that Goldman had rebounded so quickly while they still struggled.

Those who believe, like Obama, that the steps the government took in September and October 2008 helped to resurrect the banking sector, and Goldman with it, point to a chart of the firm's stock price. Before Thanksgiving 2008, the stock reached an all-time low of $47.41 per share, after trading around $165 per share at the start of September 2008. By October 2009, Goldman's stock had fully recovered—and more—to around $194 per share. "[Y]our personally owned shares in Goldman Sachs appreciated $140 million in 2009, and your options appreciated undoubtedly a multiple of that," John Fullerton, a former managing director at JPMorgan and the founder of the Capital Institute, wrote to Blankfein on the last day of 2009. "Surely you must acknowledge that this gain, much less the avoidance of a total loss, is attributable directly to the taxpayer bailout of the industry."

James Cramer, who worked as a stockbroker in Goldman's wealth management division before starting his own hedge fund and then a new career on CNBC, said it is patently obvious that without the government's bailout Goldman would have been swept away, along with Bear Stearns, Lehman Brothers, and Merrill Lynch. "They did not get it and they still don't," he said of Goldman's comprehension of the help the government provided. He then launched into a Socratic exposition. "How did the stock go from fifty-two dollars back to a hundred and eighty dollars?" he wondered. "Is it because they worked really hard and did better? Was it because they had a good investor in Warren Buffett? Or was it because the U.S. government did its very best to save the banking system from going to oblivion, to rout the people who had been seriously shorting stocks, to be able to break what I call the *Kesselschlacht*—the German word for battle of encirclement and annihilation—against all the different banks that had been going on? Who ended that? Was it Lloyd? Was it Gary Cohn [Goldman's president]? No. It was the United States government." Cramer said, "It did not matter" at that moment "that Goldman was better run than Lehman." What mattered was "the Federal Reserve decided to protect them and the Federal Reserve and Treasury made it be known you're not going to be able to short these stocks into oblivion and we're done with that phase."

WHEN, IN 2009, Congress and the SEC started investigating Goldman's business practices leading up to the crisis and how it had managed to get through it intact, they found much unappealing—and perhaps fraudulent—behavior. In April 2010, Congress and the SEC started making their findings public, and as the slings and arrows of outrageous fortune began to fly, one wound after another opened up on Goldman's corpus, handing Blankfein a series of Job-like tests that he never anticipated and that, for all his smarts, he may ultimately prove incapable of handling.

Blankfein now had the burden of the firm's history on his shoulders. He is a somewhat perplexing fellow, whose balding pate and penchant for squinting and raising his eyebrows at odd moments give him the appearance of the actor Wallace Shawn in the 1981 Louis Malle film *My Dinner with Andre*. He has been described as looking "like a chipper elf, with a round, shiny head, pinchable cheeks, and a megawatt smile." But for a Wall Street titan, he is also surprisingly quick-witted, self-aware, and thin-skinned. "Of course I feel a huge responsibility to address the assault on Goldman Sachs's reputation," he said recently in the comfort of his spare, fairly modest office on the forty-first floor of Goldman's new forty-three-story glass and steel $2.1 billion skyscraper in lower Manhattan. "Of course it's not relaxing. Of course I think about this all the time. Of course it takes a toll. I think it takes a toll on the people around me, which in turn takes a further toll on me."

———

THE FIRST ACID TEST for Blankfein came on April 16, 2010, when, after a 3–2 vote along party lines, the SEC sued Goldman Sachs and one of its vice presidents for civil fraud as a result of creating, marketing, and facilitating, in 2007, a complex mortgage security—known as a synthetic CDO, or collateralized debt obligation—that was tied to the fate of the U.S. housing market. The CDO Goldman created was not composed of actual home mortgages but rather of a series of bets on how home mortgages would perform. While the architecture of the deal was highly complex, the idea behind it was a simple one: If the people who took out the mortgages continued to pay them off, the security would keep its value. If, on the other hand, home owners started defaulting on their mortgages, the security would lose value since investors would not get their contracted cash payments on the securities they bought.

Investors who bought the CDO were betting, in late April 2007, that home owners would keep making their mortgage payments. But in an added twist of Wall Street hubris, which also serves as a testament to the evolution of financial technology, the existence of the CDO itself meant that other investors could make the opposite bet—that home owners would not make their mortgage payments. In theory, it was not much different from a roulette gambler betting a billion dollars on red while someone else at the table bets another billion on black. Obviously, someone will win and someone will lose. That's gambling. That's also investing in the early twenty-first century. For every buyer, there's a seller, and vice versa. Not surprisingly, plenty of other Wall Street firms were manufacturing and selling these exact kinds of securities.

But in its lawsuit, the SEC essentially contended that Goldman rigged the game by weighting the roulette wheel in such a way that the bouncing ball would have a very difficult time ending up on red and a much easier time ending up on black. What's more, the SEC argued, the croupier conspired with the gambler betting on black to rig the game against the fellow betting on red. If true, that would not be very sporting, now would it?

Specifically, the SEC alleged that Goldman and Fabrice Tourre, the Goldman vice president who spent around six months putting the

CDO together, made "materially misleading statements and omissions" to institutional investors in arranging the deal by failing to disclose that Goldman's client—hedge-fund manager John Paulson, who paid Goldman a $15 million fee to set up the security—was not only betting home owners would default, but also had a heavy hand in selecting the mortgage-related securities that the CDO referenced specifically because he hoped the mortgages *would* default. The SEC further alleged that Goldman had represented to ACA Management, LLC, a third-party agent responsible for choosing the mortgage securities referenced by the CDO, that Paulson was *actually* betting the CDO would perform well, when in fact he was betting the opposite.

Adding credibility to the SEC's argument of fraud was the fact that some six months after the completion of the deal—known as ABACUS 2007-AC1—83 percent of the mortgage securities referenced in ABACUS had been downgraded by the rating agencies—meaning the risks were increasing so rapidly that they would default. By mid-January 2008, 99 percent of the underlying mortgage securities had been downgraded. In short, John Paulson's bet had paid off extravagantly—to the tune of about $1 billion in profit in nine months.

On the losing side of the trade were two big European commercial banks: the Düsseldorf-based IKB Deutsche Industriebank AG, which lost $150 million, and ABN AMRO, a large Dutch bank that had in the interim been purchased by a consortium of banks led by the Royal Bank of Scotland, which then hit trouble and is now 84 percent owned by the British government. ABN AMRO got involved in the deal when it agreed—for a fee of around $1.5 million a year—to insure 96 percent of the risk ACA Capital Holdings, Inc., an affiliate of ACA Management, assumed by investing $951 million on the long side of the deal. In other words, ABN AMRO had insured that ACA Capital would make good on the insurance it was providing that ABACUS would not lose value. When ACA Capital went bust in early 2008, ABN AMRO—and then Royal Bank of Scotland—had to cover most of ACA's obligation regarding ABACUS. On August 7, 2008, RBS paid Goldman $840.9 million, much of which Goldman paid over to Paulson.

Goldman itself lost $100 million on the deal—before accounting for its $15 million fee—because the firm got stuck holding a piece of ABACUS in April 2007 that it could not sell to other investors besides ACA and IKB. Nevertheless, the SEC claimed that Goldman and Tourre "knowingly, recklessly or negligently misrepresented in the term sheet, flip book and offering memorandum for [ABACUS] that the reference portfolio was selected by ACA without disclosing the significant role in the portfolio selection process played by Paulson, a hedge fund with financial interests in the transaction directly adverse to IKB, ACA Capital and ABN. [Goldman] and Tourre also knowingly, recklessly or negligently misled ACA into believing that Paulson invested in the equity of [ABACUS] and, accordingly, that Paulson's interests in the collateral selection process were closely aligned with ACA's when in reality their interests were sharply conflicting." The SEC asked the United States District Court in the Southern District of New York to find that both Goldman and Tourre violated federal securities laws, to order them to disgorge "all illegal profits" they obtained from "their fraudulent misconduct," and to impose civil penalties upon them.

Goldman at first seemed flat-footed in reacting to the filing of the SEC complaint, in part because it took Goldman almost completely by surprise—itself a highly abnormal turn of events for the ultimate insider firm. Blankfein told Charlie Rose, on April 30, 2010, that he got the news of the SEC's civil suit "in the middle of the morning" coming across his computer screen. "I read it and my stomach turned over," he said. "I couldn't—I was stunned. I was stunned, stunned."

During the summer of 2009, Goldman had received a so-called Wells notice from the SEC and, in September, Sullivan & Cromwell, Goldman's longtime law firm, had provided the SEC with lengthy responses to its inquiries in hopes of being able to persuade it not to the file the civil charges against Goldman. But then the SEC stopped responding to S&C and to Goldman, which tried again to contact the SEC during the first quarter of 2010 to see if a settlement could be reached. The next communication from the SEC came with the filing of the complaint on April 16, which happened to be the same day the SEC inspector general issued a critical report about the SEC's bungling of its investigation into the Ponzi scheme perpetrated by Bernard Madoff.

The news media—understandably—focused on the fraud charges against Goldman, rather than the SEC's poor handling of the Madoff case, a fact Goldman noted in its communications with journalists. When Goldman eventually responded to the SEC's complaint, it denied all allegations. "The SEC's charges are completely unfounded in law and fact and we will vigorously contest them and defend the firm and its reputation," Goldman said initially. A few hours later, the firm offered a more elaborate defense: its disclosure was adequate and appropriate, the investors got the risks they wanted and bargained for, and, in any event, everyone was a big boy here. Moreover Goldman claimed it "never represented to ACA that Paulson was going to be a long investor." Besides, Goldman ended up losing money. "We were subject to losses and we did not structure a portfolio that was designed to lose money," the firm said.

Goldman also provided some background about the deal. "In 2006, Paulson & Co. indicated its interest in positioning itself for a decline in housing prices," the firm explained. "The firm structured a synthetic CDO through which Paulson benefited from a decline in the value of the underlying securities. Those on the other side of the transaction, IKB and ACA Capital Management, the portfolio selection agent, would benefit from an increase in the value of the securities. ACA had a long established track record as a CDO manager, having 26 separate transactions before the transaction. Goldman Sachs retained a significant residual long risk position in the transaction." Goldman's responses did little to stem the carnage the SEC's complaint caused in the trading of Goldman's stock, which lost $12.4 billion in market value that day.

The SEC's case against Goldman was no slam dunk. For instance, ACA was no innocent victim but rather had transformed itself in 2004 from an insurer of municipal bonds to a big investor in risky CDOs after getting a $115 million equity infusion from a Bear Stearns private-equity fund, which became ACA's largest investor. Furthermore, documents show that Paolo Pellegrini, John Paulson's partner, and Laura Schwartz, a managing director at ACA, had meetings together—including on January 27, 2007, at the bar at a ski resort in Jackson Hole, Wyoming—where the main topic of conversation was the composition of the reference portfolio that went into ABACUS. Reportedly, in his deposition with the SEC, Pellegrini stated explicitly that he informed ACA of Paulson's intention to short the ABACUS deal and was not an equity investor in it. (Pellegrini did not respond to a request to comment and his deposition is not available to the public.) Other documents show Paulson and ACA together agreeing on which securities to include in ABACUS and seem to call into question the SEC's contention that ACA was misled.

Another e-mail, sent by Jörg Zimmerman, a vice president at IKB, on March 12, 2007, to a Goldman banker in London who was working with Fabrice Tourre on ABACUS, revealed that IKB, too, had some say in what securities ABACUS referenced. "[D]id you hear something on my request to remove Fremont and New Cen[tury] serviced bonds?" Zimmerman asked, referring to two mortgage origination companies then having severe financial difficulties (and which would both later file for bankruptcy) and that Zimmerman wanted removed from the ABACUS portfolio. "I would like to try to [go to] the [IKB] advisory com[m]i[t]tee this week and would need consent on it." The final ABACUS deal did not contain any mortgages originated by Fremont or New Century. (Zimmerman did not respond to an e-mail request for comment.) A former IKB credit officer, James Fairrie, told the *Financial Times* that the pressure from higher-ups to buy CDOs from Wall Street was intense. "If I delayed things more than 24 hours, someone else would have bought the deal," he said. Another CDO investor told the paper, though, that IKB was known to be a patsy. "IKB had an army of PhD types to look at CDO deals and analy[z]e them," he said. "But Wall Street knew that they didn't get it. When you saw them turn up at conferences there was always a pack of bankers following them."

The judge in *SEC v. Goldman Sachs* gave Goldman an extension until July 19 to file its response to the SEC complaint. On July 14, five days early, and as expected, Goldman settled the SEC's case—without, of course, admitting or denying guilt—and agreed to pay a record fine of $550 million, representing a disgorgement of the $15 million fee it made on the ABACUS deal and a civil penalty of another $535 million. About as close as Goldman got to admitting any responsibility for its behavior was to state that it "acknowledges that the marketing materials for the ABACUS 2007-AC1 transaction contained incomplete information. In particular, it was a mistake for the Goldman marketing materials to state that the reference portfolio was 'selected by' ACA Management LLC without disclosing the role of Paulson & Co. Inc. in the portfolio selection process and that Paulson's economic interests were adverse to CDO investors. Goldman regrets that the marketing materials did not contain that disclosure." The firm also agreed to change a number of its regulatory, risk assessment, and legal procedures to make sure nothing like the disclosure snafus in the ABACUS deal happens again.

Despite the settlement of the SEC's case against Goldman—its case against Tourre, the Goldman vice president, continues and, in January 2011, an ACA affiliate sued Goldman in a New York State court, accusing the firm of "egregious conduct" and seeking damages of a minimum of $120 million—some usually sober voices have raised questions about Goldman and its alleged behavior. The critics lament that the ABACUS deal represents the loss of the once quasi-sacred compact between a Wall Street firm and its clients. "The SEC's complaint against Goldman raises serious issues about the level of integrity in our capital markets," John C. Coffee Jr., the Adolf A. Berle Professor of Law at Columbia University Law School, testified before Congress on May 4, 2010. "The idea that an investment banking firm could allow one side in a transaction to design the transaction's terms to favor it over other, less preferred clients of the investment bank (and without disclosure of this influence) disturbs many Americans. . . . Such conduct is not only unfair, it has an adverse impact on investor trust and confidence and thus on the health and efficiency of our capital markets. . . . Once, 'placing the customer first' was the clearly understood norm for investment banks, as they knew they could only sell securities to clients who placed their trust and confidence in them. That model was also efficient because it told the client that it could trust their broker and did not need to perform due diligence on, or look between the lines of, the broker's advice. But, with the rise of derivatives and esoteric financial engineering, some firms may have strayed from their former business model."

Michael Greenberger, a professor at the University of Maryland School of Law and a former director of trading and markets at the Commodity Futures Trading Commission, believes the day the SEC filed its suit against Goldman is akin to the U.S. victory in the Battle of Midway, in 1942. "What has been a great awakening is this idea that, 'Look, we have loyalties to no one but ourselves. We can be advising both sides of the bet, that the bet is good and that's perfectly within the mainstream of the way we do business,'" Greenberger explained. "That has . . . more than anything else, very badly hurt Goldman." Goldman is not alone in creating these products, he said, "but the blatancy of it and refusal to acknowledge a problem with it has really been very, very sobering to a much broader audience than was there before the case."

Added John Fullerton, the former banker at JP Morgan, in a blog post, "At its core, Wall Street's failure, and Goldman's, is a failure of moral leadership that no laws or regulations can ever fully address. *Goldman v. United States* is the tipping point that provides society with an opportunity to fundamentally rethink the purpose of finance."

———

THE SECOND BODY blow Goldman suffered began to be felt on April 24, 2010—a Saturday—when Senator Levin announced that on April 27 Goldman would be the subject of the fourth hearing of his Permanent Subcommittee on Investigations, which had been studying the causes of the financial crisis. That Levin's subcommittee was looking into what role Goldman, specifically, had played in causing the financial crisis had been a closely guarded secret for months, and the news brought more unwanted attention to the firm. "Investment banks such as Goldman Sachs were not simply market-makers, they were self-interested promoters of risky and complicated financial schemes that helped trigger the crisis," Senator Levin wrote in his April 24 press release. "They bundled toxic mortgages into complex financial instruments, got the credit rating agencies to label them as AAA securities, and sold them to investors, magnifying and spreading risk throughout the financial system, and all too often betting against the instruments they sold and profiting at the expense of their clients." (Levin had actually made the statement publicly at the end of the ratings agency hearing the day before, earning him a sharp rebuke within hours from a Goldman lawyer at O'Melveny & Myers.)

Levin also released a taste treat of sorts: a set of four internal Goldman e-mails—out of millions of documents the subcommittee had examined and out of the nine hundred or so pages of documents Levin planned to release at the hearing—that appeared to contradict the firm's public statements that it did not make much money in 2007 betting against the housing market, when in fact the firm made around $4 billion on that bet.

One of those e-mails, sent on July 25, 2007, by Gary Cohn, Goldman's co–chief operating officer at the time, to Blankfein and Viniar noted that the firm had made $373 million in profit that *day* betting against the mortgage market and then took a $322 million write-down of the firm's existing mortgage-securities assets, netting a one-day profit of $51 million. This calculus—that Goldman was able to make millions even though it had to write down further the value of its mortgage portfolio—prompted Viniar to talk about "the big short" in his response. "Tells you what might be happening to people who don't have the big short," Viniar wrote. Another of the e-mails, from November 18, 2007, let Blankfein know that a front-page *New York Times* story would be coming the next day about how Goldman had "dodged the mortgage mess." Blankfein, a careful reader of articles written about himself and the firm, was not above chastising journalists for them. "[O]f course we didn't dodge the mortgage mess," Blankfein replied a few hours later. "We lost money, then made more than we lost because of shorts"—the firm's bet the mortgage market would collapse. "Also, it's not over, so who knows how it will turn out ultimately."

Unlike Goldman's response after the filing of the SEC lawsuit, this time the firm seemed more prepared—even aggressive—in its response, releasing that same Saturday twenty-six documents designed to counter the tone and implication of Levin's statements. Included in the Goldman cache were many e-mails and documents that Levin's committee did not intend to release. Among them were four highly personal e-mails that Fabrice Tourre, the Goldman vice president fingered by the SEC in its lawsuit, had written to his girlfriend in London, who also happened to be a Goldman employee in his group. Goldman also released personal e-mails Tourre wrote to another woman, a PhD student at Columbia, that seemed to suggest Tourre was cheating on his girlfriend in London.

The juiciest parts of Tourre's e-mails were written in French—Tourre and the two women are French—but for some reason Goldman's attorneys at Sullivan & Cromwell provided the English translation of them to the news media. "Those are insane," one of Tourre's former colleagues said about the e-mails. "Goldman put those out, that's the incredible thing." Such a move seemed to violate Goldman's self-proclaimed commandment promoting teamwork and team spirit.

That Goldman would go to such trouble to embarrass Tourre—whom the firm has placed on paid "administrative leave" from his position in London pending the resolution of the SEC lawsuit, while also paying for his attorneys—had many people puzzled and wondering about the ethics of the decision. Goldman's ethics code states the firm expects "our people to maintain high ethical standards in everything they do" but also includes the following language: "From time to time, the firm may waive certain provisions of this Code." (The firm denies issuing a waiver to its ethics code in deciding to release Tourre's e-mails.)

At the April 27 hearing, Senator Tom Coburn, a physician and a Republican from Oklahoma, asked Tourre about the e-mails and how he felt upon learning that Goldman had released them. Tourre didn't specifically address Senator Coburn's question about Goldman's behavior, preferring to focus on his own. "As I will repeat again, Dr. Coburn, I regret, you know, the e-mails," he said. "They reflect very bad on the firm and on myself. And, you know, I think, you know, I wish, you know, I hadn't sent those." A few hours later, Senator Coburn asked Blankfein about Goldman's decision to release Tourre's personal e-mails. "Is it fair to your employee?" he wondered. "Why would you do that to one of your own employees?" After Blankfein fumbled his answer, Senator Coburn repeated, "If I worked for Goldman Sachs, I'd be real worried that somebody has made a decision he's going to be a whipping boy, he's the guy that's getting hung out to dry, because nobody else had their personal e-mails released." Blankfein answered anew: "I think what we wanted to do . . . was to just get it out so that we could deal with it, because at this point—and I think you are aware that the press was just very—and maybe even the press—I don't know where they came from. But I don't think we added, to the best of my knowledge—but I don't know—I don't think we added to the state of knowledge about those e-mails which our employee addressed, and I think needed to address."

———

AT SENATOR LEVIN'S hearing, which lasted eleven hours, a parade of seven current and former Goldman executives, including Blankfein and Viniar, as well as the three traders who created "the big short"—

Sparks, Birnbaum, and Swenson—were alternately ridiculed and bludgeoned, and prevented from going to the bathroom. The ostensible reason for the hearing was to investigate the role investment banks played in causing the financial crisis. But very little of the actual hearing seemed to pertain to the role Goldman may or may not have played in exacerbating the financial crisis by aggressively lowering the marks on its mortgage-related securities—a topic rife with possibility—and instead focused on the type of synthetic CDO deals at the heart of the SEC's lawsuit and the inherent conflict of interest that many senators believed such securities embody. (Senator Levin termed the timing of SEC's lawsuit a "fortuitous coincidence" with his hearing but "it was a coincidence." The SEC's inspector general investigated the timing of the filing of the SEC's lawsuit to see if there was a political element to it and concluded there was not.) For instance, no senator asked Craig Broderick, Goldman's chief risk officer who was impaneled with Viniar, about his May 11, 2007, memo about Goldman's fateful decision to lower its CDO marks, a missed opportunity for sure.

In his opening remarks, Senator Levin excoriated Goldman. While noting that "when acting properly," investment banks have an "important role to play" in channeling "the nation's wealth into productive activities that create jobs and make economic growth possible," he then proceeded to lay out his case against the firm. "The evidence shows that Goldman repeatedly put its own interests and profits ahead of the interests of its clients and our communities," Senator Levin said. "Its misuse of exotic and complex financial structures helped spread toxic mortgages throughout the financial system. And when the system finally collapsed under the weight of those toxic mortgages, Goldman profited in the collapse." He then wondered why Goldman's executives continued to deny that it had profited when the "firm's own documents show that while it was marketing risky mortgage-related securities, it was placing large bets against the U.S. mortgage market. The firm has repeatedly denied making those large bets, despite overwhelming evidence that [it] did so."

"Why does that matter?" Senator Levin wondered. "Surely, there's no law, ethical guideline or moral injunction against profit. But Goldman Sachs—it didn't just make money, it profited by taking advantage of its clients' reasonable expectation[s] that it would not sell products that it did not want to succeed and that there was no conflict of economic interest between the firm and the customers that it had pledged to serve. Those were reasonable expectations of its customers, but Goldman's actions demonstrate that it often saw its clients not as valuable customers, but as objects for its own profit. This matters, because instead of doing well when its clients did well, Goldman Sachs did well when its clients lost money." He said Goldman's "conduct brings into question the whole function of Wall Street, which traditionally has been seen as an engine of growth, betting on America's successes, and not its failures."

Senator Levin was particularly exercised about one e-mail—he brandished it like a stiletto throughout the day—because it crystallized for him how rife with conflicts of interest Goldman seemed to be. It was written by Thomas Montag, then a Goldman partner, to Dan Sparks about another Goldman synthetic CDO named Timberwolf—a $1 billion deal put together in March 2007 by Goldman and Greywolf Capital, a group of former Goldman partners—that lost most of its value soon after it was issued. "[B]oy that [T]imberwo[l]f was one shitty deal," Montag wrote to Sparks in June 2007. The two Bear Stearns hedge funds bought $400 million of Timberwolf in March before being liquidated in July. A hedge fund in Australia—Basis Yield Alpha Fund—bought $100 million face value of Timberwolf for $80 million, promptly lost $50 million of it, was soon insolvent, and has since sued Goldman for "making materially misleading statements" about the deal. A Goldman trader later referred to March 27—the day Timberwolf was sold into the market—as "a day that will live in infamy."

Relatively early in the hearing, Senator Levin asked Sparks about Montag's e-mail. (Montag, meanwhile, now a senior executive at Bank of America, was never asked to appear before Senator Levin's committee.) When Sparks tried to explain that "the head of the division"—Montag— had written the e-mail and not "the sales force," Senator Levin seemed uninterested and reiterated that the e-mail was sent from one Goldman executive to another and the sentiment was readily apparent. When Sparks tried to provide "context," Senator Levin cut him off. "Context, let me tell you, the context is mighty clear," Senator Levin said. "June 22 is the date of this e-mail. 'Boy, that Timberwolf was one shitty deal.' How much of that 'shitty deal' did you sell to your clients after June 22, 2007?" Sparks said he did not know but that the price at which the securities traded would have reflected both the buyers' and sellers' viewpoints. "But . . . ," Senator Levin replied, "you didn't tell them you thought it was a shitty deal." Observed one Goldman partner: "Having the senior person at Goldman Sachs calling the deal 'shitty,' when so many people lost money, it's not great." According to someone familiar with his thinking, Montag has said he was "joking around" with Sparks but in retrospect wished he hadn't used the word "shitty." "Does he wish he would have said that was one *bad* deal?" this person said. "Yeah, just so that wouldn't have happened, but other than that, he's not, like, 'Oh, God, I wish I'd never said it was a bad deal.' Of course it was a bad deal. It was a bad deal because it performed poorly and, by the way, [the politicians] didn't care what the answer was, they just wanted to make hay out of it."

The legal claim made by Basis Yield Alpha Fund in its complaint against Goldman was that had Goldman informed the fund that it thought Timberwolf was "one shitty deal," the fund would never have bought the securities in the first place, even at the discounted price. "Goldman deliberately failed to disclose this remarkably negative internal view about Timberwolf," the complaint stated. "Instead, Goldman falsely represented to [the hedge fund] that Timberwolf was designed for 'positive performance.'" (Goldman called the lawsuit "a misguided attempt by Basis . . . to shift its investment losses to Goldman Sachs.")

Senator Levin then directed Sparks toward a series of internal Goldman e-mails about the importance of selling off the Timberwolf securities into the market. He wanted to know from Sparks how Goldman could do that after Montag had made his observation about Timberwolf. Sparks started to explain about how the price of the security drives demand and even a security sold at a discount can attract buyers. But Senator Levin was not much interested. "If you can't give a clear answer to that one, Mr. Sparks, I don't think we're going to get too many clear answers from you," Senator Levin concluded.

When Viniar, Goldman's CFO, testified later in the day, Senator Levin asked him about Montag's e-mail, too. "Do you think that Goldman Sachs ought to be selling that to customers—and when you were on the short side betting against it?" he asked. "I think it's a very clear conflict of interest, and I think we've got to deal with it . . ." Before Viniar could answer, Senator Levin interjected: "And when you heard that your employees in these e-mails, in looking at these deals said, 'God, what a shitty deal. God, what a piece of crap.' When you hear your own employees and read about those in e-mails, do you feel anything?"

For the first—and perhaps only—time during the hearing, Viniar's answer strayed from the script. "I think that's very unfortunate to have on e-mail . . . ," he said. "I don't think that's quite right."

"How about feeling that way?" Senator Levin shot back.

"I think it's very unfortunate for anyone to have said that in any form," Viniar replied, backtracking.

"How about to believe that and sell that?" Senator Levin asked.

"I think that's unfortunate as well," Viniar said.

"No, that's what you should have started with," Senator Levin replied.

"You are correct," Viniar said.

When Blankfein finally appeared, after cooling his heels for most of the day, Senator Levin asked him about Montag's e-mail, too. "What do you think about selling securities which your own people think are crap?" he asked Blankfein. "Does that bother you?" Blankfein seemed a bit confused and wondered if perhaps Montag's comment was hypothetical. When Senator Levin assured him the e-mail was real, and that Montag had written "this is a 'shitty' deal, this is crap," Blankfein seemed off-balance. He tilted his balding head to one side and squinted his eyes, something he has been doing since he was a youth—but which left many people thinking he was being evasive. "The investors that we are dealing with on the long side or on the short side know what they want to acquire," he responded, and then added, "There are people who are making rational decisions today to buy securities for pennies on the dollar, because they think [they] will go up. And the sellers of those securities are happy to get the pennies, because they think they'll go down."

Blankfein's perfectly rational response about the way markets work—where for every buyer there must be a seller and vice versa at various prices up and down the spectrum—had little or no impact on Senator Levin's growing anger with Goldman and Blankfein. "I happen to be one that believes in a free market," Levin said near the end of the long day. "But, if it's going to be truly free, it cannot be designed for just a few people to reap enormous benefits, while passing the risks on to the rest of us. It must be free of deception. It's got to be free of conflicts of interest. It needs a cop on the beat and it's got to get back on Wall Street." Shortly after the hearing, along with Senator Jeff Merkley (D-Oregon), Senator Levin introduced an amendment to the huge financial reform bill that would prevent Wall Street firms from engaging "in any transaction that would involve or result in any material conflict of interest with respect to any investor" in an asset-backed security, such as a CDO. A version of the amendment was included in the Dodd-Frank Act President Obama signed on July 21, 2010.

The senators raised a good question. How could Goldman keep on selling increasingly dicey mortgage-related securities, even though sophisticated investors wanted them, at the same time the firm itself had pretty much become convinced—and was betting—the mortgage market would collapse? And, frankly, why did synthetic CDOs exist at all, given how rife with conflicts of interest they seemed to be? Are these kinds of securities too clever by half? For that matter, how could Goldman get comfortable, in January 2011, with offering its wealthy clients as much as $1.5 billion in illiquid stock of the privately held social-networking company Facebook—valued for the purpose at $50 billion—while at the same time telling them it might sell, or hedge, at any time its own $375 million stake and without telling them that its own private-equity fund manager, Richard A. Friedman, had rejected the potential investment as too risky for the fund's investors?

In a way that he was unable to articulate at the Senate hearing, in his spiffy but simple new office overlooking New York Harbor, Blankfein mounted a spirited defense of synthetic securities. He gave the example of an investor, with a portfolio of mortgage securities heavily weighted toward a certain year or a certain region of the country, looking to diversify the portfolio or the risk his portfolio contained. "It's just like any other derivative," he said. "If there are willing risk takers on both sides, you could diversify your portfolio with a 'synthetic'—which is just another word for a 'derivative'—on those securities. We could run the analysis and could take away or add to some of your exposure to this state or region, this vintage, this credit. We could be on one side of the transaction, which is what we do as a market maker—a client would ask us to do that—or source the risk from someone else or some combination. We might source some, not all, of that risk, or we might substitute it by trying to replicate a physical portfolio. That, to me, serves a purpose just like any other derivative helps sculpt a portfolio in order to give an institution the exposure or lack thereof they desire." He is not blind, though, to the risks such complexity creates. "There could be trade-offs," he continued. "If the securities and the risks created are too hard to analyze or too illiquid or too this or too that, you can well decide that those type of transactions shouldn't be done. But that's a very different calculation from saying derivatives serve no social purpose."

But Senator Levin remained unimpressed by Blankfein's argument. He believed that once Goldman made the decision to short the market in December 2006, the firm should have stopped selling mortgage-related securities, such as ABACUS or Timberwolf or other mortgage-backed securities, and let its clients know it was increasingly worried. "As a lawyer"—like Blankfein, Senator Levin is a graduate of Harvard Law School—"who's trained that you've got a client and that your duty is owed to that client—and I know there's various degrees of duty, and I understand that—but the duty here clearly was violated, to me, in the most fundamental sense," he said in an interview. "And that's what got me so really, really disturbed at that hearing was when they didn't get it. They did not understand how wrong it is to package stuff, which they're trying to get rid of, which they internally described as 'crap' or 'junk' or worse, [and sell] that to a customer. And then bet heavily against it. And make a lot of money by betting against it. They don't get it. To me, the underlying injury is the conflict itself—is selling something that you then go out and bet against. But adding insult to the injury is when you are selling something, which you internally believe is junk that you want to get rid of, and describe it as such to yourself, knowing that . . . you're aware of it. The underlying injury, to me, is the conflict whether or not it's described that way."

In his opening remarks, Blankfein told Senator Levin's committee that April 16—the day the SEC filed its lawsuit—"was one of the worst days in my professional life, as I know it was for every person at our firm." He then continued, "We believe deeply in a culture that prizes teamwork, depends on honesty and rewards saying 'no' as much as saying 'yes.' We have been a client-centered firm for 140 years and if our clients believe that we don't deserve their trust, we cannot survive."

No company likes to see the word "fraud" in headlines next to its name or to have its top executives endure a public flogging. Goldman Sachs—where a pristine reputation is the sizzle it has been selling for decades—is no exception. Will Rogers's adage that "it takes a lifetime to build a good reputation but you can lose it in a minute" seemed to be playing out in slow motion for Blankfein during the eleven-day stretch that started with the filing of the SEC lawsuit and ended with the Senate hearing.

Blankfein, focused on the particulars and steeped in the Goldman worldview, was convinced the firm was unfairly vilified. His failure to see the larger picture, his inability to understand the outrage at Goldman's huge profits in the face of widespread economic misery have much to do with the insularity of Wall Street, and especially Goldman's view of itself as the elite among the elite—smarter, and better, than anyone else. Indeed the story of Goldman's success and long history underscore one of the great political truths: the scandal is not what's illegal, it's what's legal. And no firm, through many crises and decades, had developed more skill in walking that fine line. Goldman certainly succeeded because it consistently hired and promoted men (and an occasional woman) of intelligence and acumen and because it created an environment that rewarded them lavishly for their risk taking. But it also succeeded by creating an unparalleled nexus between the canyons of Wall Street and the halls of power—a nexus known as "Government Sachs." That nexus was finally coming unglued as the world markets teetered on the edge of the financial abyss now known as the Great Recession.

CHAPTER 1

A FAMILY BUSINESS

What became Goldman Sachs opened its doors in 1869. Like many of his fellow European Jewish immigrants who later went on to become successful bankers, when Marcus Goldman first came to the United States in 1848 from a small village in central Germany, he became a clothing merchant. This was the way the Lazards started in New Orleans in 1848, and how the Lehmans started in Montgomery, Alabama, in 1844. There was no surprise in this, of course, since owning a store was considered an "appropriate" occupation for a Jewish immigrant, whereas the banking profession was reserved for the established—non-Jewish—elites.

Marcus Goldman first arrived from Burgpreppach, Germany, in New York City but, according to Stephen Birmingham, the author of *Our Crowd*, "he quickly set off for the area that, rightly or wrongly, young German Jewish immigrants had heard was the peddlers' paradise, the coal hills of Pennsylvania." He made the journey from Germany when he was twenty-seven years old. At first, Goldman was a peddler, with a horse-drawn cart. But by 1850, according to the U.S. Census data, Goldman was in Philadelphia, where he owned a clothing store on Market Street and rented a "comfortable house" on Green Street. By then, he had met and married Bertha Goldman (no relation), who had also emigrated from Bavaria in 1848 and settled in Philadelphia with her relatives. Bertha "had supported herself quite nicely," according to Birmingham, "doing embroidery and fine needlework for Philadelphia society women." The Goldmans were married when Bertha was nineteen. By 1860, Goldman had become a merchant, according to the census data, and had fathered five children, Rebecca, Julius, Rosa, Louisa, and Henry. He listed on the census the value of his real estate at $6,000 and the value of his personal estate at $2,000. The Goldmans also employed two servants.

In 1869 Marcus Goldman moved with his family to New York City.

One of the main reasons for the move was that Bertha Goldman had had about as much of Philadelphia as she could stand and urged her husband to move them all north. They settled at 4 West Fourteenth Street. By this time, Goldman had decided to abandon the clothing business, as had a number of his Jewish peers, and decided to do what he could to get into the money business.

He started a sole proprietorship, at 30 Pine Street, focused on buying and selling IOUs from local businessmen. The idea was to help these small operations turn their accounts receivable into cash without having to make the arduous trip uptown to a bank. Goldman's office was in the cellar of the building, next to a coal chute and, according to Birmingham, "in these dim quarters he installed a stool, a desk and wizened part-time bookkeeper (who worked afternoons for a funeral parlor)." The name on the door: "Marcus Goldman, Banker and Broker."

Despite the humble office space, Goldman made sure he looked the part of an aristocrat. "In what was the standard banker's uniform— tall silk hat and Prince Albert frock coat—Marcus Goldman started off each morning to visit his friends and acquaintances among the wholesale jewelers in Maiden Lane, and in the 'Swamp,' where the hide and leather merchants were located," Birmingham wrote in *Our Crowd*. "Marcus carried his business in his hat. He knew a merchant's chief need: cash. Since rates on loans from commercial banks were high, one means New York's small merchants had of obtaining cash was to sell their promissory notes or commercial paper to men like Marcus at a discount." In his telling, Birmingham likened the "commercial paper" of the day— unsecured short-term debts—to a postdated check that could only be cashed six months in the future. Based on prevailing interest rates and the "time value" of money concept—the idea that one dollar in hand today is worth more than one dollar in hand six months from now, because presumably you could invest the money in the interim and earn a return on it—investors such as Marcus Goldman would buy the IOU for cash at a discount today knowing that, all things being equal, over time he could get face value for the paper.

According to Birmingham, the commercial paper of these small businesses in lower Manhattan would be discounted at between 8 to 9 percent. Goldman bought the discounted notes in amounts ranging from $2,500 to $5,000 and then "tucked the valuable bits of paper inside the inner band of his hat for safekeeping." Throughout his morning, as he bought more and more notes at a discount from these merchants, Goldman's "hat sat higher and higher above his forehead." In this way, Goldman could keep score against the likes of his fellow ambitious Jewish bankers: Solomon Loeb, the Lehmans, and the Seligmans. The higher the hat on the forehead in the morning, the more business being done. In the afternoon, Goldman would make his way uptown to visit the commercial banks—Commercial Bank on Chambers Street, the Importers' and Traders' Bank on Warren Street, or the National Park Bank on John Street—where he would see a "cashier, or perhaps the president," according to Birmingham, "deferentially remove his hat, and they would begin to dicker" about what price the bankers would pay for the notes Goldman had in his hat. The difference between the buying and selling—not unlike what his descendants would do with mortgage-backed securities 140 years or so later—would be Marcus Goldman's profits. Right away, according to Birmingham, Goldman was able to buy and sell some $5 million worth of this commercial paper a year. Assuming he could clear, say, five cents on every dollar, he may well have been making some $250,000 a year—a tidy sum indeed in 1869.

The Goldmans quickly improved their lifestyle. The family moved to a four-story brownstone at 649 Madison Avenue, some twenty-five feet wide and ninety feet tall. Bertha was able to afford one of the "sumptuous turnouts"—a carriage—"with liveried servants" to go about her morning errands and shopping sprees. Around this time, on a passport application, Marcus Goldman was described as five foot, three inches tall, with a gray beard, fair complexion, and an oval face. His forehead was described as "high."

For some thirteen years, unlike his peers who had a number of partners in their businesses—mostly siblings or in-laws—Goldman took in no partners, and his personal wealth grew, as did the capital of his firm, which stood at $100,000 in 1880, all of it belonging to Marcus Goldman. But, in 1882, at age sixty, at which point he was buying and selling around $30 million of commercial paper per year, he decided the time had come to bring a partner into the firm. In typical fashion, Goldman chose to invite a family member—in this case, his son-in-law, Samuel Sachs, the husband of his youngest daughter, Louisa—into the business. Not only would a family member be easier to control and to trust, but also in an era of quasi-arranged marriages, the Goldmans had already decided that the Sachses, also immigrants who came to the United States in 1848, possessed the right stuff.

Samuel Sachs's father, Joseph, was a poor tutor and the son of a saddle maker from outside Würzburg. As a teenager, the Baer family—the father of which was a wealthy goldsmith from Würzburg—asked Joseph Sachs to tutor their beautiful daughter, Sophia. Against the wishes of the Baers, of course, "in a fairy-tale way, the poor young tutor and the lovely young merchant princess fell in love," according to Birmingham. They decided to elope and take the next schooner for America (although where they got the cash from is not clear; Birmingham suspects Sophia Baer "pocketed some of her father's gold" on the way out of town).

The Sachses raised five children in Baltimore and Boston before moving, after the Civil War, to New York City, where Joseph—who had been both a teacher and a rabbi—opened a school for boys named the Sachs Collegiate Institute, in 1871, on West Fifty-ninth Street. Their oldest son, Julius, ran the Sachs school and went on to become a well-regarded educator. "Herr Docktor Sachs was a stern, Old World schoolmaster whose uniformed boys, in smart black suits and starched stand-up collars, were seldom spared the rod," according to Birmingham. He emphasized discipline and classicism and spoke nine languages fluently, including Sanskrit. Sachs Collegiate Institute quickly became the school of choice for other aspiring Jewish immigrants with names such as Lehman, Cullman, Goldman, and Loeb. The idea was to get these boys—it was an all-boys school then—"ready for Harvard at the age of fifteen," Birmingham wrote.

By arrangement, Julius Sachs married the Goldmans' daughter, Rosa, a combination that worked out sufficiently well that the parents arranged for Louisa to marry Sam, who had already started his working life—as a bookkeeper—at the age of fifteen after his parents' untimely death.

In 1882, when Sam Sachs was thirty-one, his father-in-law invited him into his business. This required Sam to sell his small dry-goods business one piece of clothing at a time, and to do this, according to Birmingham, Goldman loaned Sachs fifteen thousand dollars, which was to be repaid in three annual payments over three years. As agreed, Sachs repaid ten thousand dollars over two years. On May 28, 1884, the Sachses' third son, Walter, was born, and in recognition of the birth of yet another grandchild, Marcus Goldman agreed to forgive his son-in-law's third and final installment of the original fifteen-thousand-dollar debt. In Goldman's "old-fashioned German script," according to Birmingham, he acknowledged his son-in-law's "energy and ability" as a partner, thus relieving him of his final portion of the debt. Louise Goldman Sachs had kept her father's letter to her husband plus a copy of the canceled note. "And thus," Walter Sachs said later in an oral history of his life after seventy-two years as part of his father's and grandfather's firm (he died in 1980, age ninety-six), "it appeared that on the very first day of my entrance into the world, I concluded my first business deal for Goldman, Sachs."

With Samuel Sachs's arrival, Marcus Goldman's business began to look more like the other small, Jewish Wall Street partnerships that had evolved from their roots as merchants. The firm became known as M. Goldman & Sachs. Not everything went as swimmingly, of course, as the various accounts of the firm's history would have one believe. For instance, in February 1884, one of the pieces of paper Marcus Goldman carried around in his hat went awry. A Mr. Frederick E. Douglas has purchased a $1,100 note from Goldman & Sachs, written on the account of an "A. Cramer" and endorsed by "Carl Wolff." Goldman was selling the six-month note for Wolff, with Douglas being the buyer. But, it turned out, Cramer's signature had been forged, Wolff ran away, and the note became worthless. Douglas sued the firm in superior court on the grounds that it "had, by implication, guaranteed the note to have been made by Cramer." This certainly was one of the first legal examinations of the role of the responsibility of a financial intermediary in a transaction between a buyer and a seller. Would the jury hold Goldman & Sachs responsible for the IOU as if it had been an underwriter of the paper— the role of an underwriter of a security being one that Goldman Sachs would soon pioneer at the beginning of the twentieth century—or would the jury hold Goldman blameless and rely on the tried-and-true concept of caveat emptor, or buyer beware? A Judge Freedman instructed the jury to find for Douglas "if they believed the defendants to have been acting as brokers for Wolff at the time of the sale of the note." In the end, "the jury found a verdict for the defendants" and the new firm was spared liability for the fraud. Had the jury found differently in March 1886, the tantalizing possibility exists that the Goldman Sachs we know today might have been an early victim of the plaintiffs' bar.

Relieved of that potential legal burden for the moment, M. Goldman & Sachs plowed ahead. In 1885, Goldman asked his son Henry and son-in-law Ludwig Dreyfus to join the firm and, as a result, it became formally known as Goldman, Sachs & Co. (It was also briefly known as Goldman, Sachs & Dreyfus.) The partners lived near one another in town houses on the Upper West Side of Manhattan. Marcus Goldman gave up his house on Madison Avenue and moved to West Seventieth Street. Sam Sachs bought the town house next door. Harry Sachs, Sam's brother, bought a town house on West Seventy-fourth Street, and Henry Goldman, Marcus's son, bought "an even larger one" on West Seventy-sixth Street.

In December 1893, the growing firm narrowly avoided losing $22,500—some 5 percent of its capital—lent to N. J. Schloss & Co., a small manufacturer of boys' clothing on lower Broadway. It turned out the company's bookkeeper had embezzled $50,000 and, when caught, tried to commit suicide by lying down on a hotel bed—where he had registered under an assumed name—with the gas on. Goldman got its money back as a preference to other creditors because it had made a short-term loan to the manufacturer.

In 1894, Harry Sachs, Sam's brother, joined the firm and the five partners, ten clerks, and a handful of messengers settled into second-floor offices at 43 Exchange Place. At that time, Goldman Sachs had $585,000 in capital and an annual profit of $200,000, a return on equity of an astounding 34.2 percent and an early indicator of how profitable the business could be when managed properly. In 1896, Goldman Sachs joined the New York Stock Exchange. By 1898, the firm's capital stood at $1.6 million and was growing rapidly.

At that time, the firm also decided to open a foreign exchange department and by June 1899 had sent $1 million worth of gold coins to Europe. Some dealers thought the firm had mispriced the shipment and lost $500, but Marcus Goldman said that it was "a regular and profitable operation" and done because gold coins "were cheaper" than bills of exchange. During the next few years, Goldman Sachs—along with Lazard Frères & Co., another small banking partnership with a Wall Street business—were among the largest in the business of importing and exporting gold bullion. It wasn't all business at Goldman Sachs either: Goldman's employees—with last names like Gregory, Hanna, Odz, Keiser, and Morrissey—were also regular tenpin bowlers in the Bank Clerks' League.

Marcus Goldman was also developing a reputation as a small-scale philanthropist, especially for causes involving the "Hebrews," as Jewish immigrants to the United States were then known. In 1891, Goldman was part of leading an appeal—apparently the first of its kind—for general succor, "irrespective of creed or religion" of the donors, to Jewish Russian immigrants to New York City who had arrived in the United States "well nigh penniless." Some 7,500 Russians were then coming to Ellis Island monthly, "not willingly, nor even as did the Pilgrim Fathers, preferring liberty to persecution for conscience's sake. They are given no choice, but are driven forth relentlessly from a land in which they have been settled for hundreds of years." According to the *New York Times* article about the appeal, Jews, "always charitable to a degree, and famous for the care of the poor of their race, the Hebrews, now find themselves confronted with a task that is beyond them to carry out unaided."

As their wealth grew, the Goldman Sachs partners soon joined the "ghetto" of well-to-do Jewish bankers that had begun flocking to the New

Jersey coastal towns of Elberon, Long Branch, Deal, and Sea Bright about ninety miles south of New York City. At a time well before the Hamptons became the place for rich Wall Streeters to preen, the Jewish bankers were simply mirroring, in their way, the exclusive weekend retreats that the WASP bankers had established in Newport, Rhode Island. Indeed, Elberon and its environs became known as the "Jewish Newport." Newport was akin to Fifth Avenue, according to Stephen Birmingham, and Elberon was akin to Central Park West, a distinction without much substance except for the obvious implications of the exclusionary aspects of each community. Peggy Guggenheim called Elberon "the ugliest place in the world. Not one tree or bush grew on the barren coast."

Samuel Sachs's house in Elberon was a grand adaptation of an Italianate palazzo "of white stucco, with a red-tiled roof and fountains and formal gardens," and according to Birmingham "adopted from Versailles." The Loebs, Schiffs, and Seligmans had homes in and around Elberon. "Certainly at some point during these great Elberon years," Birmingham observed, "New York's German Jewish financiers and their families had begun to think of themselves as an American aristocracy of a certain sort. With their moral tone and their emphasis on family, they had begun to regard themselves as perhaps just a little bit 'better' than 'the butterflies' of Newport." On July 20, 1904, Marcus Goldman, whose health had been failing for a "long time," according to the *New York Times,* died at his daughter and son-in-law's Elberon home, where he had spent the summer. A few weeks earlier, Sam Sachs's sons, Arthur and Paul, had joined Goldman Sachs shortly after graduating from Harvard University.

THE FIRM Marcus Goldman bequeathed to his son Henry Goldman and to his son-in-law Samuel Sachs was in fine form and was nothing less than the leading commercial paper house on Wall Street. But Goldman, Sachs & Co. had greater ambitions than just trafficking in commercial paper and precious commodities such as gold. Goldman Sachs wanted to become part of the banking elite that raised debt and equity capital for American companies. Still in its infancy at the start of the twentieth century, the task of raising capital—dubbed "underwriting"—became one of the most crucial roles Wall Street would perform for corporate clients eager to expand their workforces and their factories, and led to the creation of American capitalism, one of the country's most important exports.

Henry Goldman, who ironically had dropped out of Harvard without a degree because he had trouble seeing, had a vision of Goldman

Sachs as a leading securities underwriter. He had been a traveling salesman after leaving Harvard but had joined the family business at age
twenty-eight and would help lead a transformation of the firm into the
underwriting business, which meant taking calculated risks for short
periods of time by buying the debt or equity securities of its corporate
clients before turning around and quickly selling these securities to
investors who had been previously identified and were eager to buy them,
assuming they had been priced correctly. The idea of the business was
that Goldman would get a fee for providing the capital to its clients and
would unload its risk as rapidly as possible by selling the securities to
investors. Usually, when markets were functioning properly—and
investor panic was not an issue—the process of underwriting worked
smoothly, seeming almost risk free and allowing the underwriter to perform what appeared to be an act of magic or one of alchemy. But, at other
times, if the securities were poorly priced or investor fear was palpable,
underwriters could get left holding huge amounts of the securities without a buyer in sight. Such misjudgments happened only rarely, of
course—the spring of 2007 and the ensuing financial crisis being one
particularly acute recent example of this phenomenon—but the consequences could be devastating for underwriters and investors alike.

The brothers-in-law Sam Sachs and Henry Goldman were said to
be "a study in contrast." Sachs was conservative both in his risk taking
and in his formal attire: even on the hottest days of the year he was said
to wear "a thin alpaca office coat." He also wanted to build the partnership based upon its past successes—a responsible enough approach to
preserving his capital. His son, Paul Sachs, once remarked about his
father's satisfaction that a deal the firm was working on with a partner
they did not know particularly well had fallen through. Their first impression of the potential partner had been negative. "From the very first
moment," Paul Sachs revealed, "[we were] disturbed by the moral[ity] of
these men and while I do not deny that the business might have proved
satisfactory enough, we are as a matter of fact glad to have seen it fall
through because as we progressed our first unfavorable impression was at
every meeting strongly emphasized." Goldman, by contrast, worked in his
shirtsleeves and often would tell his nephew Walter Sachs, "Money is
always fashionable" and relished trading railroad and utility bonds—
usually at a profit—but risking his partners' capital nonetheless. The tension between Goldman and Sachs—between prudent risk taking and
preservation of capital—would from then on become an integral part of
the firm's DNA.

As with other Wall Street firms started during this era, using the actual DNA of the Goldman senior partners to perpetuate the firm became essential, too. Walter Sachs, for one, was part of that grooming from a relatively early age. After graduating from Harvard College in 1904 and then enduring a year of Harvard Law School, Walter joined Goldman in 1905 as a clerk, going from office to office around the firm doing the menial tasks asked of him. The following spring, he accompanied his father, then the senior partner of the firm, on a trip to Europe, where he served as secretary: sending cables and dispatches and writing letters for his father's signature. When Samuel Sachs returned to the United States that summer, and to Goldman's downtown offices, Walter Sachs stayed behind in Paris, on sanctioned leave from Goldman, in order to receive some additional real-world experience working as an unpaid intern in the offices of two French banks. In early 1907, Walter Sachs continued his banking education in Berlin. He returned to New York at the end of 1907. While in the midst of this banking whirlwind—which was not uncommon for the sons of banking patriarchs looking to educate their children in the ways of the banking system—Samuel Sachs had promised Walter Sachs a trip around the world once he had completed his various tours of duty. Unfortunately, fate intervened in the form of the Panic of 1907, and Samuel Sachs cabled his son in London: "My boy, you come home and go to work." Walter Sachs's full-time career at Goldman, Sachs & Co. began on January 2, 1908. He was told to sell commercial paper to New York, Philadelphia, and Hartford banks. After his first day, he came home with the paper unsold and decided he must be a failure.

In addition to encouraging sons to join the family business, Goldman, Sachs & Co. also sought alliances with other banking partnerships, and particularly with Lehman Brothers, a successful family-run business with origins in retail merchandising and cotton trading in Montgomery, Alabama. As it turned out, Henry Goldman's best friend was Philip Lehman, one of the five Lehman brothers who ran Lehman Brothers when Emanuel Lehman died in January 1907.

As they took control of their firms after the deaths of their fathers, the two friends began to discuss ways to expand their businesses. Philip Lehman suggested to Henry Goldman that the two firms think seriously about getting into the underwriting business together. Indeed the two men even considered starting a new firm—Goldman & Lehman—dedicated solely to underwriting corporate securities. "But," according to Birmingham, "the pressures, both practical and sentimental, not to abandon their respective family firms were strong, and so at last they decided to collaborate in underwriting as a side line. Each house would continue with its specialty—Lehman with commodities, Goldman, Sachs with commercial paper—and the two friends would go in as partners in underwriting ventures, splitting the proceeds fifty-fifty."

Goldman already had had a taste of the underwriting business in April 1906, when the United Cigar Manufacturers' Corporation asked the firm to raise $4.5 million through the selling of preferred stock. On May 3, Goldman and three other firms underwrote an unspecified amount of 4 percent, fifty-year bonds for the state of Alabama. By the time Philip Lehman broached the idea with Henry Goldman of the underwriting joint venture, Goldman Sachs knew it was a business it wanted to be in.

Then the firm had a bit of good fortune. Thanks to the marriage of a distant relative to Samuel Hammerslough, a former peddler who had moved to Springfield, Illinois, to become a men's clothing merchant, Goldman met Hammerslough's cousin, Julius Rosenwald. Rosenwald had a successful clothing manufacturing business that was merged into Sears, Roebuck. In June 1906, he approached Henry Goldman, his "cousin" and friend from his days living in New York, and asked him whether Goldman would be willing to lend Sears $5 million. Sears had just built a new manufacturing facility and needed money for working capital to make the company's investment worthwhile. Legend has it that Goldman had a better idea for Rosenwald: Why not take Sears public, through an underwritten offering of equity by the new Goldman and Lehman joint venture? Rosenwald would get rich in the process and the business would be financed with equity, rather than with debt. While if the equity performed well—which it certainly did for the longest time— equity would be more expensive than debt, it would also put the company less at risk in the near term should the economy falter (which it did during the financial panic of 1907). Before making the suggestion about the IPO, which could prove risky for his firm if the deal did not go well, Goldman had the good sense to review Sears's financial performance. In 1904, Sears generated $27.6 million in revenue and $2.2 million in net income; in 1905, the numbers improved to $37.9 million in revenue and $2.8 million in net income. Considering that in 1897, Sears had a net worth of $237,000, the company had grown exponentially in fewer than ten years. In short, Sears was a great candidate for an IPO.

The offering would be unusual on a number of fronts. First, it would be the first large IPO Goldman and Lehman would lead together. There had been plenty of IPOs in the previous years—for steel companies, railroads, and oil companies—but rarely, if ever before, had a retail mail-order business ventured into the public markets. As a Jewish firm,

Goldman had not previously had much success breaking into the ranks of the underwriters for the big industrial companies that were run by old-line WASP executives such as Andrew Carnegie and John D. Rockefeller Jr. The Sears IPO would bring together, for one of the first times, Jewish bankers willing to underwrite the securities of a Jewish-owned, prominent national business. It was Henry Goldman's good fortune to be friendly with Julius Rosenwald at the very moment Goldman Sachs was venturing into the underwriting business.

Together, Goldman and Lehman underwrote $30 million of Sears's common stock and $10 million of Sears's preferred stock, with a 7 percent dividend. Goldman priced the IPO at $97.50 per share. "It was more or less blazing a trail . . . ," Walter Sachs said in 1964 of the Sears offering. "[T]his type of business, to my mind, was really a creative invention of my uncle, Henry Goldman. I think he was one of the two or three geniuses in our firm over a period of a hundred years."

Before long, according to Birmingham, the Goldman-Lehman underwriting partnership was the "hottest young underwriting team." Goldman had also enlisted Kleinwort, Sons & Co., a British merchant bank, to help underwrite these deals and to sell the securities to investors in Europe. Together, they underwrote fourteen major offerings, including those for Underwood Corporation, in 1910; what became May Department Stores, in June 1910; Studebaker Corporation, in February 1911; F. W. Woolworth Company, in 1912; B. F. Goodrich Company, in 1912; Diamond Rubber Company, in 1912; and Continental Can Company, in 1913. Goldman also helped to finance B. F. Goodrich's acquisition of Diamond Rubber Company, also in 1912. "That Sears business was the thing that began to give us this very great reputation in industrial securities," according to Walter Sachs. Goldman's financing of Woolworth also enhanced the firm's reputation. "Frank Woolworth all of a sudden became a very rich man," Sachs said. He built the Woolworth Building, in Manhattan, then the tallest building in the world. The architect was Cass Gilbert. After the building opened, Woolworth gave a celebratory dinner. "The story goes that Gilbert was on Woolworth's left hand, and Goldman was on Woolworth's right hand," Sachs remembered, "and he stood up and asked them to stand, and he put his right arm on Goldman and his left arm on Gilbert, and he said, 'These are the two men who have made this wonderful building possible.'"

HENRY GOLDMAN'S GROWING stature on Wall Street was such that his views were sought—along with those of J. P. Morgan himself—in January 1914 by the two cabinet members in the Wilson administration tasked with designing the architecture of the Federal Reserve System after the passage of the Federal Reserve Act in 1913. Here, at the inception of the government's regulation of Wall Street, Goldman Sachs was already advising politicians how to do the job. In a hearing in New York on January 6, Henry Goldman told the secretary of the treasury, William G. McAdoo, and the secretary of agriculture, David F. Houston, that New York City needed to have the most powerful and well-capitalized Federal Reserve bank in the system. He thought the New York Federal Reserve Bank should be on a par with the Bank of England, given that New York was the credit capital of the country. He told the Reserve Bank Organization Committee that unless the New York Federal Reserve Bank was made supremely important, "it will do no more exchange business with New York than at present unless the New York bank is strong enough to handle it." Morgan concurred with Goldman's view—and, of course, the New York Federal Reserve Bank did become the most powerful reserve bank in the system, and Goldman Sachs remains to this day one of the bank's most important affiliations. (The current president of the New York Fed, William Dudley, is a former Goldman partner.)

But Henry Goldman's conversation with the two secretaries that day also revealed additional morsels about Goldman's character and the DNA of the firm he had helped to create. First, he referred to himself— quite proudly—to the secretary of the treasury as a commercial banker, saying that commercial banking was his principal business and specifically, "commercial banking all over the world, issuing credits to commerce and industry in this country and abroad, to merchants in this country for use abroad." He made no mention of his firm's growing prowess in the underwriting of debt and equity securities. From a very early stage the firm wished to be seen as a solid pillar of capitalism, not as an engine of speculation.

Goldman also seemed acutely—and presciently—aware of the risks local banks faced from a confidence perspective if they turned to a reserve bank as a source of liquidity other than in the normal course of business. While it was true that the Federal Reserve System was being created, in part, to combat the causes of the Panic of 1907, Goldman seemed to have had an intuitive sense of the risks posed by actually turning to a reserve bank in an hour of need. "The word 'aid' should be banished from our minds," he told the secretaries. " 'Get aid.' That means alarm. . . . It ought to be perfectly normal for a bank to go to a Reserve Bank and take discount, not in the sense of it being 'aid.' "

After discussing what exact cities Goldman thought should house the reserve banks, McAdoo and Goldman returned one final time to the subject of the Fed providing liquidity in a time of crisis. It is easy to imagine that instead of McAdoo and Goldman speaking in January 1914, it was Paulson and Blankfein speaking in September 2008. "The reserve power that [the reserve banks] have through their ability to secure or to convert their resources into money when required, that is into circulating notes, is a power of transcendent importance here," McAdoo told Goldman.

Goldman agreed with the secretary that the power to provide that liquidity was essential, and then returned to the idea he mentioned before about the message that tapping a reserve bank for that liquidity would send to the market. "I do believe that in business there are psychic factors which are so old and so ingrained in the human mind that no system can set them aside, and one is [the] capital strength of an institution," he said.

———

NOTWITHSTANDING THESE CLEVER insights into the verities of a banking system built upon the confidence placed in it—is there any other kind?—by August 1914 and the outbreak of World War I, Henry Goldman's views in support of Germany's increasingly aggressive behavior were quickly becoming a problem for Goldman, Sachs & Co. For instance, when he had been vacationing in England before the start of the war, Sam Sachs—Henry's brother-in-law—had reassured Goldman Sachs's underwriter partners at Kleinwort that the firm "stood firmly behind Great Britain," only to discover, upon his return to New York, that Henry had become increasingly outspoken in his pro-German commentary. "He quoted Nietzsche to anyone who would listen," Birmingham wrote of Henry Goldman.

The long-simmering tensions between Sachs and Goldman—once limited to their differences about business strategy and risk—now burst onto the public stage. The catalyst for the rupture between the two Goldman partners was a $500 million bond issue that Wall Street's bankers had pledged to raise for the Allied war effort (the United States, of course, did not enter the war until 1917). The original plan called for the Wall Street firm Kuhn, Loeb to head up the effort to underwrite the war bonds. But when its pro-German leader Jacob Schiff said the Allies would have their money only if the finance ministers in France and England gave him their personal assurance that "not one cent of the proceeds of the loan would be given to Russia," all hell broke loose. Of course, neither France nor England could offer Schiff this guarantee in the time of war—especially since Russia was part of the Allied effort—and a Kuhn,

Loeb partners' meeting was quickly held to decide how to proceed. "I cannot stultify myself by aiding those who in bitter enmity have tortured my people and will continue to do so, whatever fine professions they may make in their hour of need," Schiff said. "I cannot sacrifice my profoundest convictions. This is a matter between me and my conscience."

While Schiff's partners were sympathetic to his strongly held views about the Russian leadership that had persecuted so many Jews for so long, the American press was outraged. "Kuhn Loeb, German Bankers, Refuse to Aid Allies," the headlines screamed. With Schiff's decision, the responsibility for raising the $500 million fell to J. P. Morgan, and soon one Wall Street firm after another lined up to take part of the debt offering. At Goldman, Sachs, the partners had a rule that no underwriting could be undertaken or any amount of capital committed unless the partners were unanimous in their agreement that the deal should proceed. Given his outspoken views, it was no surprise that Henry Goldman nixed his firm's participation in the bond deal. "An intense, high-strung and didactic man, when Henry's partners and sisters begged him to modify, or at least conceal, his feelings, he refused," Birmingham wrote, "and his public utterances became more frequent and startling." Goldman, Sachs became lumped into the same category as Kuhn, Loeb—an advocate for an anti-Allied, pro-German stance on the growing conflict. "But my father walked over to J. P. Morgan and Company and put in a personal subscription for himself and personal subscription for my uncle Harry Sachs, so as to go on the record as to where we stood," Walter Sachs observed. Nevertheless, the firm's decision not to participate in the bond offering would not be good for business.

As the United States' effort to aid the Allies ratcheted up in the ensuing years, the Goldman partners stepped up their own involvement. Howard Sachs, Henry Goldman's nephew, was on active duty with the Twenty-sixth Division. Paul Sachs, Sam's son, was a member of the Red Cross in France. "Other members of the joint families were selling Liberty Bonds, winding bandages, and appearing at rallies to 'bury the Kaiser,'" Birmingham wrote. Henry Goldman did not relent. When finally the partners at Kleinwort, in London, cabled Goldman Sachs in New York with the news that Goldman was "in danger of being blacklisted," Henry Goldman finally got the message. "Well, I guess I am out of step," he said. "I guess I'd better retire." He agreed to retire from Goldman Sachs on December 31, 1917, eight months after the United States entered the war. "I am not in sympathy with many trends which are now stirring the world and which are now shaping public opinion," he wrote his partners on company letterhead, accompanied by the words "Save &

Serve, Buy Liberty Bonds!" "I retire with the best of feeling towards the firm (and all of its members) with which I have been associated for thirty-five years and to which I have given all there is in me."

In the midst of the war, Goldman Sachs paid out Henry Goldman's capital contribution to the firm. At first, Goldman kept a desk at the office and agreed "to give his services to the firm in an advisory capacity." But this soon proved untenable and he left the firm altogether and set himself up in an office in midtown Manhattan. Of course, Goldman took with him his sizable chunk of the firm's capital, a not inconsiderable number of clients, plus his general prowess for bringing in new business. He made "two or three investments that stood him in enormous stead," Walter Sachs wrote. Goldman had large, personal equity stakes in CIT Financial, a lender to small businesses, in May Department Stores, and in Sears, Roebuck. Concluded Sachs: "Over the years he probably died a richer man than if he'd stayed in the investment banking business, because those were very successful investments."

Henry Goldman continued to support Germany after he retired from Goldman. He was made an honorary citizen in 1922, although later the Nazis would humiliate him. "Being a Jew, he was actually, I believe . . . subject to the indignity of being stripped and searched to see whether he was doing anything against Hitler's Germany," Walter Sachs wrote. "I would say that he died a disillusioned and unhappy man."

Goldman's retirement from the firm started by his father left a hole that would be difficult to fill. "Henry Goldman was an extraordinary personality, and there's no question that he made the first great imaginative contribution to the growth of the firm—not that my father didn't do his share," Walter Sachs observed. "My father had the dream of making this small commercial paper business an international banking business, and it was he that formed in the early stages the relationships with these various banking houses in the various foreign money centers. It was Henry Goldman who did the first financing of concerns, set up the first financing of concerns like Sears, Roebuck and Woolworth and Continental Can. So you can see this was a great time." But the families' relationship would not outlast the political divisions between the partners.

The Goldmans never again had a role in the firm and never again would Henry Goldman speak to the Sachses. He never again spoke with his sister Louise, who was Samuel Sachs's wife. The firm fell on hard times, relatively speaking, and would not begin to recover until after the war. The underwriting partnership with Lehman was an early casualty of the split, since it was so heavily driven by the friendship between Henry Goldman and Philip Lehman. "Lehman Brothers and Goldman, Sachs continued to try to collaborate on underwriting issues," Birmingham wrote, "but the relationship between the two firms was not what it had been. There were frequent arguments. Why, the Lehmans demanded, did Goldman, Sachs take all the credit, with their name showily at the top of the ads, for ventures for which Lehmans had supplied the money? Goldman, Sachs in turn asked why the Lehmans expected half the profits on deals originated by Goldman, Sachs. The arguments frequently disintegrated into angry name-calling. 'They were both too ambitious,' one banker has said, 'to stay married.' " A formal memorandum ended the relationship and at the same time divided their sixty clients between those where Goldman had the "prime relationship" and those where Lehman did. Not for the last time, Goldman got the better end of the deal: forty-one of the sixty companies went into Goldman's column, including—of course—Sears.

Indeed, at first, Lehman may have been the better off of the two firms, what with the departure of Henry Goldman from Goldman, Sachs and the dissolution of the Lehman underwriting partnership. After Goldman's retirement, left behind as partners were five members of the Sachs family: Sam, Harry, Arthur, Walter, and Howard, plus Sam's brother-in-law Ludwig Dreyfus and Henry S. Bowers, who lived in Chicago and ran the firm's office there. Bowers was the first partner from outside the family and the first non-Jewish partner when he joined the firm in January 1912.

Taking Goldman's place in the partnership—and replenishing a portion of the capital Goldman took with him—was Waddill Catchings, a "suave and polished Southerner," who was then president of the Sloss-Sheffield Steel & Iron Company and the chairman of the Committee on Co-operation with the Council of National Defense of the United States Chamber of Commerce. He was also increasingly well known, post World War I, for a series of books he co-wrote with names such as *Money, Profits,* and *Road to Plenty* that extolled the "increasingly rosy future" for America after the war. Catchings, a friend and Harvard classmate of Arthur Sachs, thus became the second partner from outside the families to join Goldman but the first one to be based in New York with real authority at the firm and a penchant for hucksterism. It would be a fateful decision.

CHAPTER 2

THE APOSTLE OF PROSPERITY

Waddill Catchings, born in Sewanee, Tennessee, was the son of Silas Fly Catchings and Nora Belle Waddill. He graduated from Harvard in 1901 and Harvard Law School in 1904. He has been described, by the *New York Times,* as a "tall, slender, unassuming man with a full head of thick, white hair and a trace of the South in his speech." In 1907, for the princely sum of ten dollars a week, he joined Sullivan & Cromwell, the whitest of the white-shoe law firms on Wall Street. At Sullivan & Cromwell, Catchings rode the wave of bankruptcies that followed the Panic of 1907 and proved himself adept at restructuring these forlorn companies and getting himself named the receiver—and getting well paid for his efforts—under the auspices of the bankruptcy court.

In June 1907, soon after Catchings arrived at Sullivan & Cromwell, Milliken Brothers, one of the country's largest steel-construction contractors, filed for bankruptcy protection with $6.5 million in liabilities, including a $3 million bond issued the year before. Milliken, based in New York City, had used the proceeds of the bond issue to build a steel foundry on Staten Island—the only steel mill in New York City—in an effort to become less dependent on the major steel companies in and around Pittsburgh, Pennsylvania. Unfortunately for Milliken, the Staten Island plant ended up costing the firm $1.35 million more than planned. For a generation the Milliken name had been "as good as gold" in the credit markets, and the new leaders at Milliken had decided that the company would finance the extra cost of the Staten Island plant itself, figuring the firm's long-standing reputation would allow it to replenish the funds as needed. That turned out to be a bad bet as the credit markets deteriorated in the spring of 1907, and the venerable company was forced into bankruptcy.

One of the receivers—August Heckscher, an industrialist from Long Island—was a friend of Catchings and eventually asked him to become involved in the Milliken matter, where he was described as one of the "active managers" of the proceedings. In 1909, Heckscher and Catchings successfully proposed a restructuring plan for Milliken, reorganizing the company's debts and allowing it to emerge from bankruptcy.

In February 1910, one of the companies in Heckscher's sprawling empire—the Central Foundry Company—filed for bankruptcy due, Heckscher allowed, to a "lack of adequate banking facilities and working capital. The result is an embarrassment we believe to be temporary." Catchings was named as the receiver for the Central Foundry bankruptcy and promptly assured the markets that the company would continue operating as normally as possible. "Although there is little cash on hand, the accounts receivable are substantial and the collections should, to a great extent, supply the necessary funds for the continued operation of the business." Catchings eventually became president of Central Foundry and a director of many of the companies that he guided through the bankruptcy process.

During the First World War, Catchings worked for Edward Stettinius, a partner at J. P. Morgan & Co., in the effort to supply the Allies with everything needed to wage a world war. "For the next three years Mr. Stettinius conducted the most magnificent shopping campaign in the world's history," *Time* magazine observed. "He put food, clothes, guns, explosives where the Allies put soldiers. He put them there good enough, cheap enough, soon enough, to win the War." In March 1917, Catchings became the president of the Sloss-Sheffield Steel & Iron Company, based in Birmingham, Alabama. In July 1917, Catchings—in his role as the chairman of a committee of the Chamber of Commerce—urged the federal government to create a Board of National Defense with the authority to negotiate contracts with American businesses to procure the supplies needed to fight the war.

Catchings became increasingly outspoken about the economic cycles and the prospects for American prosperity. Part of his philosophy of business was forged soon after he graduated from Harvard and discovered the harsh realities faced by companies such as Milliken Brothers and Central Foundry. His Harvard professors, he lamented, "had casually explained that their theories would hold true in the long run. But what people are interested in is the short, not the long, run. So I made up my mind that as soon as I had enough money I would set about reconciling these two phases of business—theory and practice." Together with his Harvard classmate William Trufant Foster he created the Pollak Foundation for Economic Research and then set about publishing a number of books that espoused the idea that the future was rosy as long as businesses focused on "money and profit" and kept production humming at all costs. "If business is to continue zooming," he once wrote, "production must be kept at high speed, whatever the circumstances. . . . Production would bring about consumption. Consumers would find work and spend money which would eventually accrue to the producers." In a phrase that would echo throughout the American economy at the end of the twentieth century, Catchings declared that the "business cycle was dead."

This was the profile of the man the Sachses invited to join Goldman Sachs on January 1, 1918. "Catchings was a brilliant person," Walter Sachs wrote of him years later, "but I've always used this term in regard to him: 'Most men can stand adversity and very few men can stand success.' In my estimation, he was the second genius in the firm," after Henry Goldman. The war had been tough on Goldman's business. "Things came to a stop," Sachs observed. "It was impossible to issue securities in the ordinary way. There was relatively little done. We carried on, but it was more or less just carrying on without moving forward." Catchings's arrival at the firm coincided with the end of the war and the resumption of the issuance of corporate securities. He "played an amazingly constructive part in that," Walter Sachs said, but added that despite his brilliance "very often when men are your partners you don't know everything about them. You only find out things after they cease to be your partners."

———

WITH A SENSE of renewed optimism in the possibilities that the banking business afforded in the postwar era, the Goldman Sachs partners decided to abandon their offices at 60 Wall Street in 1920 and purchased, for around $1.5 million, a twelve-story "fireproof" office building at 30–32 Pine Street, built on the site where Marcus Goldman had first started his firm.

Business boomed at Goldman Sachs in the postwar years. Sachs credited Catchings with creating "such great companies" as National Dairy Products Corporation—a combination of Hydrox in Chicago, Sheffield Farms in New York, and Rieck McJunkin Dairy Company in Pittsburgh—that later became Kraft Foods. He also helped to create what became the General Foods Corporation by combining the Postum Cereal Company, Maxwell House Coffee, Jell-O, and many others.

These companies, and others that Catchings helped to create, remained clients of Goldman Sachs for generations, and Goldman partners took their turns, seriatim, on their boards of directors, further cementing the ongoing and close relationships.

With Catchings's enormous commercial success at Goldman Sachs came a corresponding increase in his desire for more power and authority at the firm, in the enduring Wall Street fashion. Catchings's friend and classmate Arthur Sachs was spending more and more time in Europe to tend to the firm's business there, and the two men drifted apart. Arthur Sachs thought Catchings had become a bit of a rogue and a charlatan and should not have the greater partnership share he was demanding. But Arthur Sachs was away in Europe, in an era when communication was by cable and was slow at best. Walter Sachs was left to contend with Catchings and his power grab. "In those days," Sachs said of Catchings, he was "a handsome, attractive, slim person of great charm of personality. But as he became successful, he became more and more difficult."

Walter Sachs struggled with what to do about Waddill Catchings. "Our business had grown so, and the load was tremendous," he observed. "The burden was just too much for me." In the end, Walter Sachs acceded to Catchings's demands for greater control of the firm. "I thought that was the wise decision, and I very soon found out that I was wrong," Sachs said. "But I made that decision." He observed that it was a "question of partnership relationships and percentages and so forth, and dominancy in the partnership. Arthur was very unhappy about that, but I thought at the time it was the wise thing to do." By 1928, Catchings was the Goldman partner with the largest stake in the firm, and his power became increasingly absolute at the very moment when a degree of caution would have been a far more appropriate response to a time of rapidly increasing stock prices. Those prices were going up because, it was said, "there weren't enough [stocks] to go around, and, accordingly, they had acquired a 'scarcity value,'" according to John Kenneth Galbraith in his landmark history of the Depression, *The Great Crash*. This would be a time when the Goldman partnership would not display a high degree of competence regarding risk control.

RANK SPECULATION BY greedy investors is nothing new, of course. It was not new in the first decade of the twenty-first century, nor was it new in the late 1920s. Human beings' enduring infatuation with climbing aboard one freight train of get-rich-quick schemes after another has rarely ended well and always provides invaluable fodder for financial journalists and historians. Why we never seem to learn from the problems caused by our own ongoing reckless behavior is mysterious and unexplainable. According to Galbraith, "Historians have told with wonder of one of the promotions at the time of the South Seas Bubble," which—you will no doubt recall—was what happened when the South Sea Company agreed to refinance the £10 million of British debt incurred during the course of the War of the Spanish Succession, which ended in 1713. The British government agreed to grant the South Sea Company exclusive trading rights to all South American countries in exchange for South Sea's agreement to refinance the government war debt. Investors in South Sea would receive annual 6 percent interest payments—paid by the British government after taxing goods South Sea imported from South America—as well as stock in the company. The parties repeated this seemingly innocuous deal several times in the decade, with disastrous results. One such South Sea capital-raising exercise, according to Galbraith, was "for an undertaking which shall in due time be revealed." The historian noted with some understatement, "The stock is said to have sold exceedingly well."

Galbraith likened the investment trust Catchings and Goldman Sachs—and many others—created in December 1928 to the opportunities the South Sea Company offered investors in the early 1700s. "As a promotion the investment trusts were, on the record, more wonderful," he wrote. "They were undertakings the nature of which was never to be revealed, and their stock also sold exceedingly well." Investment trusts were just another in a long line of clever Wall Street innovations designed to separate investors from their money. The idea was to create a shell company, or holding company, that would sell debt and equity securities to the public and then invest that money—less management fees, of course—into the shares of other publicly traded companies. The thinking was that professional managers had special insight into the vicissitudes of markets and could pick outperforming stocks. An investment trust was akin to what a publicly traded individual mutual fund might look like if it also piled on the leverage to maximize potential returns (and magnify potential losses). In short, these investment trusts looked a lot like the hedge funds of today with far fewer sophisticated investment strategies. The best modern analogy, although imperfect, might be the few publicly traded hedge funds—such as Fortress Investment Group and Och-Ziff Management Group (both run by ex–Goldman partners)—that seem to be offering investors the chance to invest with self-proclaimed financial geniuses who have figured out a way to make a silk purse from a sow's ear.

Another analogy might be what has become known as a SPAC—special purpose acquisition corporations—which were all the rage a few years ago. Investors would give money to supposed experts in the art of acquiring companies using leveraged-buyout techniques—chiefly paying for the company with borrowed money—and then through the use of financial alchemy, spinning it all into gold. For whatever reason, people never seem to lose their infatuation with giving their hard-earned money away to other people who they are convinced will be better at investing it than they could themselves. In periods of market frenzy and irrational exuberance—the 1920s, the 1980s, the 1990s, the middle part of the first decade of the 2000s—these kinds of opportunities seem to make all the sense in the world to investors. This notion was reinforced by how these holding companies and empty shells trade in the market after their IPOs, increasing in value by leaps and bounds for no apparent reason—until the schemes fall apart, of course, which is an inevitable aspect of the narrative arc, all too easy to see in hindsight.

In fairness, Goldman was late to this particular party. Investment trusts had been floating around capitalist societies since the 1880s in England and Scotland, where small investors would invest their meager savings into these trusts that promised the opportunity to invest in a diversified array of other companies. "And the management of the trusts could be expected to have a far better knowledge of companies and prospects in Singapore, Madras, Capetown and the Argentine, places to which British funds regularly found their way, than the widow in Bristol or the doctor in Glasgow," Galbraith wrote. "The smaller risk and better information well justified the modest compensation of those who managed the enterprise." Soon the idea was exported to the United States, primarily under the guise that this was a financial innovation worth imitating, lest Wall Street be seen as falling behind the City of London as a repository of brilliant new ideas.

At first, the trickle of such trusts to the New World was slow. In 1921, an SEC report of the phenomenon put the number at "about forty." At the beginning of 1927, the same report noted there were 160 such trusts, and another 140 were established during the course of the year. During 1928, an estimated 186 investment trusts were established. By the first months of 1929, these trusts were being created at the rate of approximately one each business day, and a total of 265 made their appearance during the course of the year. As in any period of financial frenzy where salesmen are hawking the latest innovation—say, junk bonds, Internet IPOs, or mortgage-backed securities—some of the peddlers were honest and reputable—J. P. Morgan & Co. for example—and some were not. But when the market for innovation seems at its most indiscriminate and with prices investors are willing to pay only rising, it becomes increasingly difficult to tell the charlatans from the honest brokers. Worse, it may not even matter at such moments. Warren Buffett, the legendary investor with a knack for homespun observations about markets and human behavior, once observed, presciently, that it is "only when the tide goes out do you find out who is not wearing a bathing suit."

In March 1929, Paul C. Cabot, one of the founders of State Street Investment Corporation, a treasurer of Harvard University, and a highly respected observer of the financial scene, wrote in *The Atlantic Monthly* what amounted to a clarion call to the investing public about the dangers lurking inside investment trusts. He recounted in some detail the troubles trusts experienced in England "because I strongly believe that unless we avoid these and other errors and false principles, we shall inevitably go through a similar period of disaster and disgrace." He then explained that a few months prior to writing his article, he had testified before a New York Stock Exchange committee investigating the efficacy of the investment trusts. The committee wanted to know what Cabot thought of the phenomenon. "My reply was: 1) dishonesty. 2) inattention and inability. 3) greed."

Indeed, Cabot's chief criticism of the investment scheme—"All the profits go to the promoters and managers"—bears an eerie resemblance to the criticism of the 2008 financial crisis, right down to the leverage used to amplify supposed returns. Cabot explained that the managers of the trusts got paid only when they had paid off the senior-most securities in the structure. "[T]he compensation is dependent on the success of the enterprise," he wrote. "But the difficulty is that the management or promoters have put up only a very small percentage of the total funds. If the enterprise is a complete failure, they have little or nothing to lose. It is natural, therefore, that they should take the attitude of 'Let's either win big or win nothing.' This they accomplish by a very heavy pyramiding process. I do not believe there are many people who with only $100 equity would, as a general practice, proceed to borrow anywhere from $800 to $1000 worth of securities, and yet this exactly what many investment trusts are doing to-day."

Not surprisingly, this was exactly the approach taken by Waddill Catchings, the senior partner of Goldman Sachs, in structuring and marketing the Goldman Sachs Trading Corporation. Goldman may have been late to the party—the trust began operation on December 4, 1928, less than a year before the stock market crash—but it joined in with great enthusiasm. "[R]arely, if ever, in history has an enterprise grown as the

Goldman Sachs Trading Corporation and its offspring grew in the months ahead," Galbraith wrote. The idea of the company was not to own the shares of companies for the longer term but rather to trade in and out of them to make money for shareholders.

At first, things started off modestly enough. In a typical underwriting, Goldman bought all 1 million shares of the Trading Corporation at $100 per share—raising $100 million—and then turned around and resold 90 percent of its stock to investors at $104 per share, generating proceeds of $93.6 million, making a cool $4 million profit—some on paper, some in cash—in the process. Two months later, the Trading Corporation sold another 125,000 shares publicly at around $126 each, raising another $15.75 million in the process. Of course, the value of Goldman's remaining 100,000 shares kept trading higher as well. Goldman kept control of the management of the company—of which now it owned less than 10 percent of the shares—through management and investment contracts. Indeed, all of the partners of Goldman Sachs were the directors of the Goldman Sachs Trading Corporation, and the partners of Goldman had to approve any and all directors of the Trading Corporation.

By February 2, 1929, shares in the Trading Corporation had increased to $136.50 each, and by February 7, they were trading at $222.50, approximately double the value of the underlying securities the trust had bought with the original $100 million of investor proceeds. "This remarkable premium was not the undiluted result of public enthusiasm for the financial genius of Goldman, Sachs," Galbraith deadpanned.

———

IT TURNED OUT that Goldman had been buying the shares on the open market, driving the price farther upward in order to benefit Goldman Sachs, among other shareholders. And, if the subsequent voluminous 1932 congressional report on the factors that led to the 1929 Crash is to be believed, Goldman's determined efforts to drive the price of Trading Corporation's stock higher in anticipation of a merger between Trading Corporation and another trust, the Financial and Industrial Securities Corporation, can only be described as one of the first recorded instances of insider trading by Goldman's partners. While trading on material nonpublic inside information in early 1929 might not then have been a criminal offense—it was not even banned in the United States until 1934 and not criminalized until decades later—the actions taken by both senior partner Waddill Catchings and his then colleague Sidney

Weinberg to manipulate the stock of the Trading Corporation do not add up to the dictionary definition of moral rectitude either.

The day before Christmas 1925, Ralph Jonas and his partners organized the Financial and Industrial Securities Corporation to hold the stock they had amassed in several large banks and insurance companies, by far the largest holding of which was a 32 percent stake in Manufacturers Trust Company, a New York–based commercial bank. Jonas owned 45 percent of the outstanding shares of the Financial and Industrial Securities Corporation. In September 1928, Sidney Weinberg told Nathan Jonas, the president of Manufacturers Trust and the brother of Ralph Jonas, that Goldman would "like to take an interest" in the bank—this being in the years before Congress prevented the intermingling of commercial and investment banks through the Glass-Steagall Act. Nathan referred Weinberg to his brother Ralph, who in turn suggested that Goldman consider instead taking a stake in Financial and Industrial, which owned a 32 percent stake in the bank "sufficient to constitute working control" of it according to the report. But Weinberg decided not to pursue the Jonas brothers' suggestion that Goldman take a stake in Financial and Industrial "on the ground that it preferred to form its own investment company."

So on December 4, 1928—some two months later—Goldman created the Goldman Sachs Trading Corporation, including a ten-year exclusive right for Goldman and its partners to manage the business. According to the prospectus, the purpose of the trust was plenty amorphous: to "buy, sell, trade in or hold stocks and securities of any kind." Subsequent communications between Goldman and the trust's underwriters as well as with the New York Stock Exchange made clear that the purpose of the Trading Corporation was to "trade in securities." In later testimony, Catchings said the purpose of the Trading Corporation was to "give the clients and customers of Goldman, Sachs & Co. the same kind of opportunity of making money which Goldman, Sachs & Co. as a firm had given to its clients and customers in previous years." He added that "other banking houses had formed investment and trading companies and more were doing it, and we felt it was a wise thing for Goldman, Sachs & Company, as a firm, to afford to its clientele the same type of investment opportunities and service which every other house was affording to their clientele." And Catchings was not shy about testifying about Goldman's prowess, either. "Throughout the whole period of time of ins and outs and ups and downs of business, Goldman Sachs & Company had managed to select for issue to the public securities which on the whole had turned out to be very satisfactory investments, and it was the opinion of the firm that if an investment and trading company was formed which would engage in somewhat the same kind of investment policies as large individuals engaged in connection with securities issued by Goldman Sachs, it would be a beneficial thing to do."

After the IPO of Trading Corporation, Goldman owned 100,000 shares for which it had paid $1 million, or $10 per share. Considering that the public bought the same shares in the IPO for $104 per share, Goldman's profit was both immediate and immense. As part of the plan to offer shares in Trading Corporation at a discount to Wall Street dealers involved in the IPO syndicate, Financial and Industrial also bought 49,000 Trading Corporation shares at $102 per share, at a cost of nearly $5 million.

Despite the statements that the purpose of the Trading Corporation was to trade securities, one month after the IPO, Catchings approached Ralph Jonas again to try to negotiate a merger between the two trusts. The idea of the merger, he later testified, was for Goldman to get its hands on the large equity stakes that Jonas had acquired in his trust and to "build them up" through "trading" and then to "resell a large proportion of such stock at a profit after the earnings of the companies had increased as a result of the efforts of The Goldman Sachs Trading Corporation and of Goldman, Sachs & Co."

Investigators, though, had their doubts that this was Catchings's sole motivation for merging with Financial and Industrial. They suspected that Goldman coveted the controlling stakes in the banks and insurance companies in Financial and Industrial's portfolio because they were large buyers of the debt and equity securities that Goldman was in the business of underwriting and selling. Why not, the logic went, get control of companies that bought an awful lot of what Goldman manufactured? While in his later testimony Catchings conceded that Manufacturers Trust "might possibly at times have been a large buyer of securities" and that insurance companies "are what you would call 'big purchasers' of securities," he denied that getting access to them was the motivating factor for his second approach to Jonas in January 1929. He testified such an idea "was not even remotely" in his and his partners' thinking. (Unfortunately, the facts did not support Catchings's contention. In 1929, after Goldman did get control of Financial and Industrial, the companies in the portfolio—Manufacturers Trust, National Liberty Insurance Company, Baltimore American Insurance Company, and People's National Fire Insurance Company—were regular buyers of the securities Goldman sold during the year, in the amount of approximately $20 million. At the beginning of 1929, the investment portfolios of Liberty Insurance and Baltimore American consisted primarily of the stock of Manufacturers Trust Company. By the end of 1929, these two insurance companies had bought the securities of twenty-four companies who were also banking clients of Goldman.)

In January 1929, the negotiations between Catchings and Jonas once again foundered—as merger discussions often do—over the matter of price. After more than three years as a public company, including impressive earnings along the way of around $60 million, Financial and Industrial traded—understandably—at a higher multiple to the underlying value of the stocks in the portfolio than did Goldman's trust, which had been in business all of two months and had yet to have a public report of its financial performance. (Why holding companies whose assets are shares in other companies trade at a premium to the value of those underlying shares remains a bit of an ongoing mystery but can be explained, in part as Catchings did, by the chance to invest alongside other supposedly more savvy investors, much the way people today invest in Berkshire Hathaway to get Warren Buffett.)

In January 1929, Goldman's Trading Corporation stock was trading at around $136 per share (up from $104 at the IPO) and the underlying assets were worth around $108 per share, a multiple of 1.26. Financial and Industrial, on the other hand, was trading at around $143 per share and had an asset value of around $80 per share, a market trading multiple equal to 1.78 times its asset value. Constructing a stock-for-stock merger based upon the public trading of the two stocks—which is normally how it is done—would have worked to Jonas's advantage since Financial and Industrial's stock traded at a premium to Goldman's stock. Catchings wanted no part of that deal and insisted, instead, that the negotiations for the merger—in effect who controlled the resulting company and how many shares of the new company their respective shareholders owned—would have to be "predicated upon asset values" rather than market values, a measure that would favor Goldman over Jonas.

The discussions broke off again over whether to value the companies based on market trading or based on underlying asset values. But by the end of January 1929, Jonas had caved. "[A]fter discussing the matter with my associates," Jonas said, "we felt that it would be desirable even on the basis of an asset position to make a combination of interests" between the two companies. Part of his logic for moving forward on Goldman's terms was Jonas's belief—severely ill-placed, it turned out—

that Goldman Sachs would "materially aid the growth and profits" of both Manufacturers Trust and the National Liberty group of insurance companies, which, if true, would benefit the shareholders of Financial and Industrial, of which Jonas was by far the largest individual shareholder. The other part of the logic stemmed from Jonas's ebbing enthusiasm for continuing to manage his business and a desire to secure a new management team to do it. In addition, other members of Jonas's small, overtaxed management team appeared to be in ill health. "Two of my associates have broken down under the strain," Jonas wrote to his shareholders in February 1929 to explain his decision to sell the company to Goldman. "A third is now ill and I myself have not had a day's vacation in two and a half years. It is not prudent to trust new associates with large responsibilities until they have been tried. Under these circumstances it seemed easier to combine with some existing organization of standing and tried and trusted ability and success." Goldman Sachs Trading Corporation was all of three months old at that moment and its management "untried," according to the subsequent report about the 1929 Crash.

After less than a week of negotiations, on February 3, 1929, Jonas and Goldman Sachs reached a "tentative oral agreement" to merge the two trusts. Under the February 3 plan, Goldman would end up owning 4.4 percent of the stock of the combined company and Jonas, the largest shareholder, would own 16.6 percent of the combined company. Despite this obvious discrepancy, Goldman would be running the show. It entered into a new management agreement for ten years, and of the seven directors of the new company, six would be Goldman's partners—including Catchings and Weinberg—and the final director's seat would belong to Jonas. Given that Jonas had agreed to sell his company to the Trading Corporation, his shareholders would have to vote to approve the deal.

Catchings admitted that this would be new territory for him and his Goldman partners. Although he said Goldman had "done a great deal of business" that was "very similar to commercial banking," Catchings agreed that except for the "iron business" and "a few other businesses" he had "never actually been in any other kind of business, [but] I have been combating the point of view that you are presenting to me for a great many years, and I have discovered that in the shoe business, in the iron business and the department store business, the executive problems are very much the same." For his part, Jonas explained that he didn't know much about Goldman's business and instead was relying on Catchings's feeling that Goldman's "prestige and standing and fifty years of existence . . . at least equaled or offset the good will that we had in Financial and Industrial."

Still, Jonas faced a problem with his own shareholders, who, under the February 3 agreement, were to get one Trading Corporation share worth around $68 per share (accounting for the two-for-one split) for each of their Financial and Industrial shares, then worth $145 a share. This would certainly be a tough sell once the deal was announced.

Meanwhile, to help insure the likelihood that the remaining non-Goldman shareholders of the Trading Corporation voted for the merger, in the days after the handshake with Jonas, but before any public announcement of the deal, Goldman Sachs—through a new partnership that it controlled—set about aggressively and systematically buying the shares of the Trading Corporation, effectively driving up the shares' price and rewarding existing Trading Corporation shareholders for just holding on. An increase in the Trading Corporation share price would also, presumably, make a merger of equals between the Trading Corporation and Financial and Industrial more palatable to Financial and Industrial shareholders—once it was announced—if Trading Corporation's stock was not trading at such a discount to Financial and Industrial's stock. Goldman and Jonas quickly concluded that an increase in the Trading Corporation's share price would make the merger far more likely to be approved by both sets of shareholders.

As part of the February 3 agreement—documented on February 4, still before any public announcement had been made—an account was created to trade in the stocks of both Trading Corporation and Financial and Industrial. The owners of the account were the Goldman Sachs Trading Corporation (controlled by Goldman Sachs) and Delmar Capital Corporation (controlled by Ralph Jonas). According to the agreement between the two, "in connection with the proposed acquisition by Goldman Sachs Trading Corporation of the assets of Financial and Industrial Securities Corporation, this is to confirm our understanding that we both deem it expedient to arbitrage in the stock of these two companies." The account would be operative for thirty days, with all the profits and losses from the account accruing to the Trading Corporation. If the deal had not closed after thirty days, the account would continue to function with the profits and losses shared equally by the two companies. Goldman would manage the account and "in its uncontrolled discretion" would have full power to buy, sell, and trade in the two stocks. (In the end, the deal closed within thirty days and all the stock in the account went to Goldman.)

In fact, during the weeks the account was open, no arbitrage of the stocks—buying one stock and selling the other to lock in the spread between them—occurred. Rather, all that happened was that Goldman bought the shares of Trading Corporation in a thinly concealed effort to drive the stock price higher and higher in order to make the deal more palatable to the shareholders of both companies. Most of this trading by Goldman in the joint account was done prior to any public announcement about the deal. On February 2, 1929, the Trading Corporation's stock closed at $136.50. The next day, the two firms set up the joint trading account. On February 4, a "leak" from an undisclosed source about the combination of the two companies created "a tremendous hullabaloo" in the market.

The Trading Corporation's stock did not open until 11:00 a.m., and the indications were that it would open at $175 per share, up nearly 40 points from the previous close. Instead of selling at these prices—a big increase—Goldman, acting for the joint account of which Goldman was the beneficiary, put in a buy order for 53,000 shares of its own stock, or 54 percent of the total trading for the day. The stock closed at $178 per share. The next day, Goldman bought another 42,300 shares, or 76 percent of the total volume, and the stock closed at $179.625. Goldman sold no shares of Trading Corporation stock that day. This continued for the next few days, until the price of Trading Corporation's stock closed at $221 per share, up from $136.50 in less than a week. Goldman spent $33,325,000 buying Trading Corporation's stock—constituting 64 percent of the total volume during those four days—raising the price of the stock to double the value of the underlying assets and on par with the premium placed on Financial and Industrial's stock. With the extraordinary increase in the shares of Trading Corporation, the plan Catchings and Jonas reached on February 3—and still not disclosed publicly—was abandoned since the original ratio of one stock to the other no longer made sense. Instead, in effect, the stocks were exchanged based on equal market value as well as equal asset value (after a dividend of $4.5 million was made to the Trading Corporation's shareholders so that each company's assets would be $117.5 million).

On February 7, Catchings and Jonas recut their deal, and it was announced publicly four days later, on February 11. Goldman Sachs Trading Corporation agreed to issue 1.125 million new shares to the holders of Financial and Industrial, with shareholders' meetings set for February 21 to vote on the deal—in the case of Goldman's shareholders, the vote would authorize the new shares to be issued; in the case of the Financial and Industrial shareholders, they would vote to sell the company to Goldman. The revised deal was made possible through the extensive buying of the Trading Corporation's stock in the secret account that had driven the price of the stock dramatically higher than it had been a week earlier. "[I]t is apparent that the Goldman Sachs Trading Corporation's activities in its own stock were the substantial factor in the establishment and maintenance of the market value of its shares at a price equal to the market value of the shares of Financial and Industrial Securities Corporation on the basis of the ratio in which the shares of the two companies were to be exchanged under the final plan for the combination of the two companies," according to the Crash report. "However, in none of the public announcements of the impending combination of the two companies was there any reference either to the existence of, or to the trading activities in the stock of both companies conducted by the joint account."

The report went on to criticize Jonas for not disclosing in a letter to his own shareholders—a minority of whom were vociferously opposed to the combination with Goldman Sachs Trading Corporation—that by the terms of the joint-account agreement, his overriding incentive was to make sure his shareholders voted for the deal at the shareholders meeting on February 21. By around this time, the joint account had spent close to $50 million—a substantial sum at the time—buying the stocks of the two merger partners; if the shareholders did not approve the merger, Jonas would have been on the hook for half—$25 million—of the cost of the stock that had been bought. "Mr. Jonas thus possessed a special pecuniary interest in facilitating the sale," the report observed. In Jonas's letter to his shareholders he made the affirmative statement— albeit untruthful—that "I have never personally owned nor has anyone owned for me, a single share of Goldman Sachs Trading Corporation." Under later "interrogation," Jonas justified his decidedly misleading statement by claiming his obligation would only kick in had the merger not been approved. "I never regarded that we had a commitment except the one commitment on the merger not going through," he said.

On February 21, both sets of shareholders approved the merger, and the Trading Corporation issued 2.25 million shares of its own stock, valued at $235 million, to the holders of the Financial and Industrial Securities Corporation, which had assets of $117.5¹ million. Goldman paid this premium using its own stock, which it had inflated through its robust purchases during the previous weeks. "The market value for its own stock . . . was almost exclusively the creation of the Goldman Sachs Trading Corporation itself," the subsequent report concluded. When asked about the manipulation later, Weinberg conceded that "buying actually improves the market, we know that," but little else.

As for Catchings, he was even more dishonest than Weinberg.

"I tell you with great positiveness," he testified, "that the account was not formed for the purpose of putting up stock and that it was not formed for the sake of manipulating the market but was formed for the purpose of being active in the market during the time until the stock reached its natural level," which Catchings believed would be $220 per share "by the mere force of the agreement of the two companies to combine."

With tongue in cheek, Galbraith took note of all this activity at Goldman. "The spring and early summer were relatively quiet for Goldman, Sachs, but it was a period of preparation," he wrote. With the Financial and Industrial deal closed, in April 1929, Catchings and his editorial sidekick, William Trufant Foster, lashed out at the Federal Reserve Board in a statement printed in the *New York Times,* claiming that it "had gone outside its legitimate functions" in seeking to regulate the flow of credit into the stock market. Instead of accommodating business, they declared, the board had kept business in a "state of growing uncertainty and apprehension." The pair warned the Fed not to try to thwart the "confidence in the soundness of American business," a confidence that was "warranted by the facts." Not for the first time would a Wall Street figure guilty of rank speculation—and possibly insider trading—attack the government, even the weak government of the time, for trying to protect the public.

———

ON JULY 26, Catchings decided to ratchet up Goldman's exposure to its high-flying investment trust. Together with another sponsor, Goldman launched the Shenandoah Corporation by selling $102.5 million of securities to the public. The deal was said to be seven times oversubscribed and included layers of additional leverage that the original Goldman Sachs Trading Corporation did not have. The Trading Corporation bought 2 million of the 5 million Shenandoah shares offered, and Goldman partners took seats on its board. Goldman sold through a public offering the Shenandoah stock at $17.50 and it closed at $36 per share at the end of its first day of trading, up more than 100 percent on the day. Some twenty-five days later, Catchings struck again, this time selling $142 million of shares in yet another trust, the Blue Ridge Corporation— the board for which was identical to Shenandoah's. Of the 7.25 million shares Blue Ridge offered to the public, Shenandoah bought all but 1 million of them. "Goldman Sachs by now was applying leverage with a vengeance," Galbraith observed.

And why not? At the time of the Blue Ridge offering, according to the *New York Times,* Goldman Sachs Trading Corporation was worth $500 million, up fivefold in nine months, and Shenandoah had doubled in value in less than a month. Blue Ridge had the additional financial innovation that it allowed investors to exchange shares in a select group of twenty-one other blue-chip New York Stock Exchange companies—among them AT&T and General Electric—at fixed prices for shares in Blue Ridge. Why anyone would want to do this was not made clear, of course, especially if the fixed price offered for, say, a share of General Electric by Blue Ridge was less than where GE was trading in the market. It is often the case that Wall Street's shenanigans are not readily apparent. After the Blue Ridge deal, Goldman Sachs had created well over $1 billion in market value—actually $1.7 billion—in about nine months, as impressive an act of financial alchemy as had ever been achieved. "[T]he nearly simultaneous promotion of Shenandoah and Blue Ridge was to stand as the pinnacle of new era finance," Galbraith wrote. "It is difficult not to marvel at the imagination which was implicit in this gargantuan insanity. If there must be madness something may be said for having it on a heroic scale."

It was not much of an excuse, but the Sachses—Walter and Arthur—were in Europe during the summer when Catchings constructed and sold Blue Ridge. Walter Sachs was in Merano, Italy, up north, with his wife when he received a cable informing him of the Blue Ridge deal. "Well, this is just absolutely crazy," he said to her, and then he stayed up all night worrying about what might come of the deal. When Sachs returned to New York in September, he made a beeline to Catchings's apartment at the Plaza Hotel and told him he thought "this thing was crazy" and that he "didn't agree with it." Sachs remembered precisely what Catchings responded. "The trouble with you, Walter, is that you've got no imagination."

In the end, the entire enterprise collapsed, and Goldman lost nearly its entire $10 million investment plus another $3 million from other associated liabilities in the Goldman Sachs Trading Corporation—a meaningful chunk of capital in those days and of Goldman's. The other shareholders had lost hundreds of millions of dollars more.

Of the Crash itself, Sidney Weinberg later told the writer Studs Terkel, "I remember that day very intimately. I stayed in the office a week without going home. The tape was running. I've forgotten how long that night. It must have been ten, eleven o'clock before we got the final reports. It was like a thunder clap. Everybody was stunned. Nobody knew what it was all about. The Street had general confusion. They didn't understand it any more than anybody else. They thought something would be announced." Weinberg said he remembered that John D. Rockefeller Jr. stood on the steps of the J. P. Morgan building on Wall Street to announce that he and his sons were buying stock. "Immediately the market went down again," Weinberg said. "Pools combined to support the market, to no avail. The public got scared and sold. It was a very trying period for me." Weinberg blamed the Crash on "over-speculation" and a "reckless disregard of economics." He said he doubted those people who claimed to have gotten their money out of the market before it collapsed and saw many people scarred psychologically by what happened. "I don't know anybody that jumped out of the window," he said. "But I know many who threatened to jump. They ended up in nursing homes and insane asylums and things like that. These were people who were trading in the market or in banking houses. They broke down physically, as well as financially."

A couple of months after the Crash of 1929, Catchings headed out west, to Reno, Nevada, to "secure a divorce from his first wife." One day while Catchings was on the West Coast as the markets were, according to Walter Sachs, "beginning, in 1930, to show some improvement," Catchings called his partner Sidney Weinberg from San Francisco and said, "We owe $20 million to the banks and we have certain other obligations, amounting to about $10 million. We ought to fund this debt into a two-year convertible note. We ought to sell $50 million of two-year convertible notes" and take the balance of the proceeds—$20 million or so—and give it to Frank Taylor, an investment manager affiliated with the firm, to invest. "Frank Taylor can make a world of money," Catchings told Weinberg.

Walter Sachs and Sidney Weinberg thought perhaps that Catchings had lost his mind. How in the world, a mere three months after the most devastating financial crisis in American history, did Catchings think Goldman would be able to issue $50 million in new risky securities? "Weinberg and I talked together," Sachs said. "We spent practically the whole night talking about this thing. At first we said, 'We can't sell a note like that.'" Sachs then said to Weinberg, "Well, either you and I are crazy, or this man Catchings is crazy, and of course it can't be done."

The next morning, when Walter Sachs went into the office—"and this was not an easy thing to do," he said—he found his brother, Arthur, and admitted to him that he had been right about Catchings all along. "Arthur, you have been right about this man Catchings and I have been wrong," he told his brother. "The sooner we mend our fence the better." It fell to Walter Sachs to arrange for Catchings to meet him in Chicago shortly thereafter. "In those days we didn't fly very much," Sachs said. "I took the Century"—a cross-country luxury train—"in the afternoon and got there the next morning." Sachs and Catchings spent the whole morning "closeted" together at the Chicago Club discussing recent events at the firm. First, Sachs told Catchings that his idea for the $50 million of financing would not be done and made no sense. He also said the firm was going back "to the old principle of agreement on the part of all partners if anything was undertaken." In recounting the meeting some twenty-six years later, Sachs said he "took a position of clipping his wings, and he took it." A newly contrite Catchings got the message. "Walter, I cannot imagine ever making a decision again without your agreement," Catchings told him. Catchings went back to Reno; Sachs returned to New York.

But the real work of digging Goldman out of its sizable financial hole had just begun. The Sachs brothers realized that the only way out of the Goldman Sachs Trading Corporation fiasco was to sell as many of the assets it had—the shares of other companies—as quickly as possible, especially since the markets had improved in the spring of 1930. "Those were the days when I worked every night till nine or ten o'clock at night," Sachs said. "Then I'd go home and fall into bed and I'd sleep until perhaps four in the morning. Then I'd wake up and have to face the world with a smile." After the Crash, the stock of the Trading Corporation hit $32 a share—its all-time high was $326 a share—and fell steadily until reaching its low of $1.75 per share in 1931. On January 1, 1932, Goldman announced a deal with the Atlas Corporation, an investor in distressed securities, whereby Atlas would become the largest shareholder in the Trading Corporation and then buy it out completely and run it. The full acquisition by Atlas took place in April 1932. And eventually Atlas sold off the remains of the Trading Corporation at a modest profit—for Atlas. "[W]e could hold up our heads," Walter Sachs remembered, "because we never sold a share of stock until finally a merger took place with the Atlas Corporation"—why he felt vindicated even though investors lost many millions is not mentioned—"and then we turned over the management, and we certainly as far as I'm concerned will never run an investment trust again."

By then, not surprisingly, the Sachses had decided Catchings had to go. Walter Sachs said that in 1929 Catchings "just went haywire" and reluctantly noted that he and his brother had done nothing to stop him. "We weren't smart enough perhaps—or perhaps we were too greedy too—but anyway, we didn't stop it in time." By the early summer of 1930, "as things became clearer and clearer to us, we made up our minds that we were going to call it a day with Catchings." The partnership had a contract with him that terminated at the end of 1930, but the Sachses decided they could not wait until then. "[W]e had made up our minds to ask him to retire . . . ," Walter recalled. "This was because it had become clear to us that we just didn't think alike, that he had come as near ruining the name and the reputation of the firm as any man could do."

When Catchings—whom *Time* magazine referred to as "the loudest prophet of the New Era"—returned to New York from Reno, fresh from his divorce, the Sachs brothers decided *les jeux sont faits*. Despite Catchings conceding in Chicago that he could not "imagine" making a decision ever again without Walter Sachs's assent, there was no second chance for him at Goldman Sachs. "Well, that was very nice," Walter Sachs said of Catchings's Chicago mea culpa, "but it was too late." Despite the $13 million of losses that came out of their collective hides, the partners decided to pay Catchings $250,000 to cancel his contract seven months early. The Sachses decided to name Sidney Weinberg the firm's senior partner. "I was too egotistical to refuse it," Weinberg said with a smile some thirty-seven years later. At that moment, he had been getting paid one-third of the firm's profits annually. His role in the Trading Corporation fiasco seemed to have no effect on his rise to power at Goldman Sachs.

Unfortunately, Catchings's departure from Goldman did not prevent a flood of litigation against the firm for its role in sponsoring, underwriting, and managing the failed trusts. "There were all kinds of stockholders' suits," Walter Sachs allowed. "Everybody had them. Our great trouble was that in good faith we had called our investment trust the Goldman Sachs Trading Corporation, while others called theirs things like 'the United Corporation.' J. P. Morgan and Company created that. That's why this stigma clung to us." Investors who lost money charged Goldman with "neglect and with fraud," according to Sachs. With Sullivan & Cromwell at its side, Goldman headed off the vast majority of the suits—the last one of which did not get settled until 1968—by compromising and settling.

One lawsuit, involving comedian and movie star Eddie Cantor, rattled the firm's partners especially, not only because Cantor asked for a huge sum in damages—$100 million—but also because Cantor made the firm a punch line in his stand-up routines, not unlike the way *Saturday Night Live* made fun of Goldman in November 2009 for being given doses of the swine flu vaccine before those perceived to be more in need. Or the way Jon Stewart did in January 2011 when he wondered in the wake of Goldman's investment in Facebook, which some claimed helped Facebook bend SEC rules that require companies to be public if they have more than five hundred shareholders, "Oh Goldman, is there any regulation's intent you can't subvert?" In one of Cantor's bits, he would be onstage with a stooge who tried to squeeze juice from a dry lemon.

"Who are you?" Cantor would ask the fellow.

Without missing a beat, the stooge would reply, "The margin clerk for Goldman Sachs."

CHAPTER 3

THE POLITICIAN

With Catchings gone, the Trading Corporation heading to the dustbin of history, and the Depression in full swing, Goldman Sachs began what Walter Sachs described as the firm's "great rehabilitation." In the aftermath of the Trading Corporation debacle, the firm was somehow able to retain all of its clients except for Warner Bros. and the Pet Milk Company of St. Louis. "Don't imagine for a moment that other banking houses weren't shooting at our relationships . . . ," Sachs wrote. "[Y]ou may be sure that these relationships with National Dairy and General Foods and Sears and all these companies were great crumbs for other banking houses." These were difficult times for the Goldman Sachs partnership. Indeed, according to *Fortune,* "In the '29 crash the name Goldman, Sachs emerged as a sort of symbol of everything that was bad and ill-fated about Wall Street."

One way the firm pulled through was by marking down the value of the securities it owned, selling them into a depressed market, and raising cash—the very strategy Blankfein, Viniar, et al. used starting in December 2006 to begin to reduce the firm's exposure to the mortgage markets that would tear asunder so much of Wall Street in the following years. "We faced the music," Sachs said. "We got ourselves as rapidly as we could, not only at the cost of profits but even of taking losses, into a solid position. We had to take losses to get the firm into a strong cash position." The firm had also fortunately, Sachs said, taken the position of not providing margin loans on the Trading Corporation shares, which cost it some profits in the boom years but probably saved the firm from even bigger losses when the market crashed.

In the middle of the years of financial struggle—March 1935—Sam Sachs died. "His mind began to fail with age," his son observed. "He thought he knew what was going on, but he always said to me, 'So long as the name isn't hurt.' But poor man, he didn't know—thank fortune, he didn't realize—that in 1932, 1933, along in there, the name had been hurt."

To survive, the firm appealed to its bankers—at National City Bank, at Guaranty Bank, and at Bankers Trust Company—to keep providing short-term loans, so that Goldman could keep doing business, in an era before the U.S. government would play the role of lender of last resort for Wall Street. "I was perfectly frank with them," Sachs said. "I showed them the situation, showed them what the picture was, and they knew I was telling the truth. They knew what the reputation of the firm was. They knew what our standing was. And that pulled us through." There were five very bleak years—until 1935—when the firm's capital continued to be reduced by losses and a dearth of business. "We lost money for several years," he continued. "Still, we knew what we had in the way of clientage, and we knew that when the turn came, we'd come back. There were lots of other people in the same position. That's what we mean by the [G]reat Depression."

The key to Goldman keeping the bulk of its clients rested squarely on two facts. First, "that people began to realize that we may have made errors in judgment, but that we had stood our guns, and we had not sold out on people," Sachs wrote. The second reason—and by far the more important—was because of a gnome of a man named Sidney Weinberg, who joined the firm as an office clerk in 1907, rising mightily through the ranks to become a redwood, a giant among Wall Street men.

———

THE LEGENDARY *New Yorker* writer E. J. Kahn Jr. compared Sidney Weinberg to a "kewpie doll" who "at five feet four inches tall, with legs only twenty-six inches long" seemed "in constant danger of being swallowed whole by executive-size chairs." In a gargantuan two-part *New Yorker* profile of the Goldman partner that appeared in September 1956, Kahn also described the nearsighted Weinberg as "irrepressibly antic and unabashedly outspoken, he affects a brassy impudence that many of his staid associates appear to find refreshing." Kahn compared Weinberg to Bernard Baruch, the legendary Wall Street financier and statesman. "Though largely unknown to the man in any street but Wall," Weinberg was "among the nation's most influential citizens. In his role as a power behind the throne, he probably comes as close as Bernard Baruch to embodying the popular conception of Bernard Baruch."

Sidney James Weinberg, born on October 12, 1891, "hustled his way to eminence from slum beginnings" in the Red Hook section of Brooklyn, New York, according to the *Times*. He was the third of eleven children of the Polish-born Pincus Weinberg, a wholesale liquor dealer and bootlegger who later became a small-time stockbroker. He once noted that his grandfather lived to be ninety years old and drank "half a pint of whisky a day." The family's economic prospects were at first so dismal that the children "used to sleep three to a bed," and Sidney was "obliged to fend for himself as soon as he graduated from grammar school." Before he was ten, Weinberg sold the evening papers at the Hamilton Avenue terminal for the Manhattan-Brooklyn ferry. (From this, he apparently earned scars on his back from knife fights.) He also shucked oysters for a local fish vendor. Weinberg was a fan both of Horatio Alger—of whose books he was an avid reader—and of Abraham Lincoln.

In the summer of 1905, he got himself a job as a runner for one brokerage firm—John H. Jacqueline—and "finding this no strain" also got hired to do the same job at Charles M. Schott & Co. and then De Coppet & Doremus. Everything was fine until a bank clerk recognized his various, conflicting associations, a violation—understandably—of stock exchange rules. "Then he lost all three jobs when a bank teller caught on to his duplicity, or triplicity," E. J. Kahn observed. (This failure of judgment was airbrushed out of all the later profiles of Weinberg.)

Weinberg's formal education more or less ended after he completed the eighth grade at Public School 13, in June 1906. His last teacher, Jennie C. Cooke, wrote a brief and succinct letter of recommendation for Weinberg—"To whom it may concern"—as he set off into the world to seek his own version of Algeresque success. "It gives me great pleasure to testify to the business ability of the bearer, Sidney Weinberg," she wrote. "He is happy when he is busy and being always ready and willing to oblige, we believe he will give satisfaction to anyone who may need his services." Years later—in an October 1953 *Fortune* profile—after Weinberg's numerous accomplishments over thirty years had reached legendary proportion, the writer Robert Sheehan observed that Cooke's inchoate "profile" of Weinberg would be difficult to embellish "for accuracy, succinctness, and prophetic understanding." The same could be said—in many ways—for the firm that he resurrected from the ashes of the Great Depression and remade in his image, a firm where the underdog ambitious overachiever felt at home and was always "ready and willing to oblige" not only the needs of clients but its partners' and employees' seemingly insatiable appetite to get richer and richer.

Despite his renown, Weinberg remained devoted to his Brooklyn school and would occasionally remind people, "I'm just a dumb guy from P.S. 13." Once Paul Cabot, then head of State Street Bank and the treasurer of Harvard—he and Weinberg became friends after his prescient warning about investment trusts in *The Atlantic*—invited Weinberg to join him for dinner. Weinberg—who liked to pronounce his name "Wein-*boig*"—told Cabot that he "already had an engagement for an academic evening" because he had agreed to go back to P.S. 13 to see a fellow classmate whom no one had seen in twenty-five years. When Cabot inquired where the fellow had been, Weinberg replied, "In Sing Sing," referring to the upstate New York prison. "He shot our teacher for giving him a lousy mark." Such was Weinberg's reverence for his grade school that in 1954, a group of Weinberg's high-powered friends—including the executives from the companies where he was a director and a World War II general—arranged for the principal of P.S. 13 to give him an honorary postgraduate degree, the only one the school ever bestowed, at a surprise party held in his honor at the '21' Club, on West Fifty-second Street, for years a favorite Goldman haunt. "Sometimes you don't know whether you're talking to a street urchin, a comedian or a banker," explained one of Weinberg's "blue-blooded" Wall Street competitors.

In 1907, Weinberg got a job—for two dollars a week—as a "feather horse," which he explained once was "a kid who delivered millinery," or women's hats. To make his way to work delivering the hats, Weinberg used to cadge a ride with a friend on the back of a horse-drawn freight wagon, in exchange for watching the horse and the wagon's contents while the driver made his early morning deliveries. One day, in 1907, when his friend—who was a runner at the brokerage firm J. S. Bache & Co.—told Weinberg there was a panic on Wall Street, he wondered, "What's a panic?" His friend's explanation didn't mean much to him, but one thought did stick in his head: that people were scared and wanted their money out of their banks. He figured he could make a little money of his own—said to be five dollars a pop (and later embellished to ten dollars a pop)—by standing in the long lines that were forming at the entrance of the Trust Company of America bank, putting in the hours needed to make it to the front, and then selling his coveted space in line to a panicked depositor in a hurry. On his first day in this endeavor—around October 23, as the panic was at its peak—he sold his space in line twice. The next day, he sold it once. By his third day, the panic had subsided, but by then, he "had given his heart to Wall Street forever," or so the myth surrounding him goes. That day, instead of showing up at Trust Company and standing in line, he decided to take the elevator to the top floor of 43 Exchange Place, in the heart of the financial district and then Manhattan's tallest building at twenty-five stories, and knock on the doors of one small office after another to see if anyone needed help. "Do you need a boy?" he wanted to know.

When he made his way down to the building's third floor—to the offices of Goldman, Sachs & Co.—he asked his question. "No," came the reply, "but we need someone to help Jarvis, the colored porter." "I'll take it," Weinberg said immediately and thus began his three-dollar-a-week job as the assistant to Jarvis, Goldman's janitor. (References to Jarvis's race are often removed from Weinberg profiles.) The first task assigned to him at the firm was to polish a brass spittoon, which he later kept in his office as a memento of that assignment. In addition to cleaning the partners' cuspidors, he also brushed their silk hats and polished their galoshes. "Weinberg remained an inconsequential cog in this rapidly accelerating machine," Kahn wrote, noting that he not only placed tacks on the chairs of the firm's clerks but once also inserted an ad into a local newspaper advertising—falsely—that Samuel Sachs was looking for chorus girls to hire for a Broadway show. Candidates were to report to 43 Exchange Place to be interviewed, the ad said, and that is exactly what happened during the subsequent week.

Weinberg's big break so to speak came two years later, when partner Paul Sachs—before he left for Harvard—asked the diminutive Weinberg to lug a flagpole up to Sachs's house on 138th Street, in Manhattan. "Ever try to carry a flagpole on a trolley car?" he asked rhetorically years later. "It's one hell of a job." But lug it he did and went further by then assembling the flagpole in its designated place at Sachs's home and raising the American flag up it. The two men—the partner and the clerk—got to chatting while Weinberg was toiling away and Sachs told him he had a bright future at the firm and so should think about beefing up his education, at night. By then, Weinberg had been taking—for fifty dollars—an accounting class at Browne Business College, in Brooklyn. (One version of the same story has Weinberg taking a stenography class.) But at Sachs's urging—and based on his willingness to foot the twenty-five-dollar bill—Weinberg began a course of study at night at New York University. Sachs hadn't told the boy what to study. "One course they offered was investment banking," Weinberg recalled later. "I knew Goldman, Sachs was in the investment banking business, so I took that course." He also took some classes—briefly—in foreign exchange at Columbia. "Paul Sachs was the first partner who ever really gave me a second glance," he told Kahn. "Until he took me in hand, I was an awful kid—tough and raw." Such was what passed for progress in those days that Weinberg made twenty-eight dollars a week trolling for new commercial paper accounts at Goldman Sachs.

During World War I, Weinberg enlisted in the navy and convinced the recruiter to make him an assistant cook, even though he couldn't see or cook particularly well. He served in this capacity aboard the boat owned by Henry Goldman Jr., which had been converted into a submarine chaser for the war. He grew thin from malnutrition. Desperate for a change of venue, he tried to become an officer and took the officer's exam, which had been designed for college graduates. He got a zero. But he could organize things and seemed to have a penchant for "knowing everybody," a combination that finally caught the attention of his military superiors, who decided to transfer him to the Office of Naval Intelligence in Norfolk, Virginia. His job there was to inspect the cargo of all ships using the port. "He has since become almost as proud of having been an enlisted man as of having gone to P.S. 13," Kahn observed.

After the war, he returned to Goldman, where the partners were glad to see him but had no job for him. "Unless you can make one," they told him. Put to this new challenge, Weinberg convinced the Goldman partners to make him a trader in the firm's fledgling bond department for the same twenty-eight dollars per week he had been making before he enlisted. "Within a matter of months, he was doing most of the work on one corporate-financing job after another," the *Times* reported later. "He was so astute in his pricing recommendations that he was given participation in the profits" of the firm equal to one-eighth of 1 percent. In 1920, Weinberg married Helen Livingston, a talented amateur pianist and the daughter of a dress manufacturer. They rented a small house in Woodmere, Long Island, and in 1923 bought the same not-quite-so-small house in Scarsdale, New York, that they lived in for the rest of their lives. He was then making around five thousand dollars a year. The Weinbergs had two sons, John L. and Sidney Jr., both of whom went to Deerfield, Princeton, and Harvard Business School, bearing full witness to the ability of hard work and ambition to make a powerful difference in the space of a single generation to the lives of one poor family from Brooklyn.

Around this time, Goldman Sachs left the New York Stock Exchange—after Harry Sachs sold his seat—and a joint stock association was formed. Weinberg then bought his own seat on the exchange and formed his own, new firm. In April 1925, after he bought himself a seat on the New York Stock Exchange for $104,000, Weinberg then proposed forming Weinberg & Co. as part of the New York Stock Exchange with himself, Catchings, the five Sachses, Henry Bowers, and Clarence Dauphinot as partners. But this did not happen, and in December 1926 he rejoined Goldman Sachs as a partner and the firm rejoined the New York Stock Exchange—after a four-year absence—using Weinberg's seat. "He will be the youngest member of an international banking firm in the Wall Street district," the *Times* observed. The $100,000 he invested as his capital contribution came entirely from his own pocket. "It was my own money, which I earned," he said. Such was his good fortune at the time that he famously won *five* automobiles in a single night, in May 1928, at the annual Wall Street bond club dinner.

Despite his partnership status and his growing importance at the firm, Weinberg, of course, did nothing to stop Waddill Catchings, whose assistant he had once been, from creating and promoting Goldman Sachs Trading Corporation. He could poke fun at it, though. "I just wasn't very bright," Weinberg told *Fortune* of his role in inflating the Trading Corporation bubble; "[let] it go at that." One day while Weinberg was playing golf at the Greenbrier, in White Sulphur Springs, West Virginia, he asked his caddy, who appeared to him to be particularly weathered, how old he was. When the caddy responded that he was only thirty-six, he replied, "I guess you must have run an investment trust."

Although he got his start at Goldman trading bonds, Weinberg never considered himself even remotely a trader. Instead he was, proudly, an investment banker. Of course, in the context of the era, his preference for investment banking—financing and advising growing American businesses—rather than trading securities—with undercapitalized counterparties in an undeveloped marketplace—made tremendous sense. Like any ambitious young man in New York City, he wanted to be where the action was. "I'm an investment banker," he said in 1967. "I don't shoot craps. If I had been a speculator and taken advantage of what I knew, I could have had five times as much as I have today." Despite not slowing Catchings in any way, Weinberg's career at Goldman benefited directly from Catchings's self-destruction. Not only did he become the senior partner at Goldman in the wake of Catchings's firing, he also inherited nine of Catchings's eighteen corporate board seats and then proceeded to use his position as an insider to—naturally—generate investment banking business for Goldman Sachs.

Once upon a time on Wall Street, a widely shared aspiration for investment bankers was to be asked to serve on the boards of directors of public corporations. While there was some potential liability to serving as a board member—they could be sued, of course, for perceived grievances, although it was exceedingly rare for any negative judgment to be visited upon an individual director personally—the potential benefits far outweighed them. Sure there were the stipends directors were paid to attend board meetings—in the years before 1933, when America went off the gold standard, directors would often be paid in twenty-dollar gold coins; their stipends now consist of cash or stock totaling hundreds of thousands of dollars a year. But the real payoff came—and still comes—because corporations were ongoing sources of fees for investment bankers, whether from raising debt or equity capital for them, for advising on their mergers and acquisitions, or for managing their pension assets. A board member becomes privy to the internal machinations of a corporation and when and whether it intends to raise capital, seek a merger, or sell a division or some other asset. A board member who was also an investment banker would be in the best possible position year after year to capture the vast majority of this business; hence the role was much coveted. (And remained so until the passage of the Sarbanes-Oxley Act of 2002, which acknowledged the conflicts inherent in such a role.)

No investment banker—not Bobbie Lehman, not André Meyer, not Felix Rohatyn, not Bob Greenhill—was more expert than Sidney Weinberg at winning the confidence of corporate management throughout his long—sixty-two years—career on Wall Street. In short order he became known as "Mr. Wall Street," and at his most fecund, he served on the almost incomprehensible number of thirty-one boards at one time, and some thirty-five different corporate boards in total. "Let's ask Sidney Weinberg" became the mantra not only of his Goldman partners but also of many a corporate executive and government leader. The fees that flowed through Goldman Sachs as a result and into the pockets of the firm's partners account in large part for why Weinberg was not only the senior partner but its biggest beneficiary, helping himself to one-third of the annual profits.

It didn't take long for Weinberg to make an impact at the companies on whose boards he served. For instance, at B. F. Goodrich Company, the tire maker in Akron, Ohio, where Weinberg took over as a director from Catchings, he was at a meeting in 1931 when he became aware of a run on the local Akron banks. The failure of these banks would not have been good news for the town, for Goodrich, or for its thousands of employees. Taking a page from J. P. Morgan's playbook, Weinberg decided to hunker down in Akron, to study the banks' books for ten days, and then to craft rescue financing for them. He called back to New York frequently and "on his say-so alone," a group of friendly financiers arranged for and sent to Akron the money needed to help the banks stay open. "[T]he funds of Goodrich and its employees remained intact, and Weinberg came back to New York, another little job out of the way," Kahn wrote.

Weinberg was not only a ubiquitous presence in corporate boardrooms. Goldman's resurrection was not hurt by Weinberg's considerable political connections in Washington—setting firmly in place another one of the firm's DNA strands. Weinberg had been a "clubhouse Democrat," according to *Fortune,* from when he was a boy in Brooklyn, and he had the prescience—or just the good common sense—to befriend the governor of New York, Franklin Delano Roosevelt, during his one term in that office. As a "practical liberal," Weinberg was one of a "handful of Wall Streeters" who worked for Roosevelt during the 1932 presidential campaign. "The Street was against Roosevelt," he told Terkel. "Only me and Joe Kennedy, of those I know, were for Roosevelt in 1932." He served as a member of the Democratic National Campaign Executive Finance Committee, assistant treasurer to be precise. "I cannot tell you how delighted I am about the sweeping victory that you had at the polls yesterday," Weinberg wrote to the president-elect, in Albany, one day after the November 1932 election, "and I hasten to offer you my most sincere congratulations." He wrote that he was "very glad to do my small part in promoting your election" and signed off on his Goldman, Sachs & Co. letterhead, "With kind regards, believe me."

Roosevelt replied to Weinberg on January 12, 1933. "My dear Mr. Weinberg," the president-elect wrote, "I have been overlong in thanking you for your fine message of congratulation and good wishes for the future. However, my delay now gives me an opportunity to add to this expression of appreciation my heartiest greetings for the New Year." A week or so later but before Inauguration Day, Weinberg sent Roosevelt a copy of a photograph "you might wish to have" that had been taken at a recent dinner honoring three top Roosevelt campaign aides, including Louis Howe, who went on to become Roosevelt's powerful first chief of staff. When the answer to Weinberg came—more than a month later—it was Howe who replied. "He was pleased to have this," Howe wrote on the president's behalf. Weinberg had previously been corresponding with Howe about the possibility of introducing Howe to Charles McCain, Weinberg's "intimate friend" and "also a good Democrat" who happened also to be the chairman of the board of Chase National Bank. "He happened to mention that he had not had the pleasure of meeting you and would like to do so," Weinberg wrote to Howe. "I wonder whether it would be possible for you to come down"—to Goldman's office at 30 Pine Street—"some day and have luncheon with me and meet him."

In addition to this political hobnobbing, Weinberg was also working on a set of principles that he believed corporate directors should study and observe throughout their service on boards. He considered being a corporate director akin to public service and, unlike almost every other director out there, seemed determined to professionalize the job. In June 1933, Weinberg descended the mountain with his eleven commandments. "The problem comes down to the question of the extent and quantity of information which a corporation ought to provide each director regularly and in a satisfactory manner in order to enable him to exercise the reasonable care of a prudent man in the discharge of his duties," he wrote. His prescription ranged from the utterly mundane—how many times a corporate board should meet annually and what a meeting agenda should contain—to how much information a director should have (Weinberg preferred more to less) and to such sensitive matters as whether a corporation should make a loan to a director or officer (no) and the amount of management bonuses. "Questions of bonuses and profit sharing should be discussed and approved by the board with only those directors voting who do not share in such bonuses or profit sharing," he wrote.

Occasionally, Weinberg would get hoisted on his own petard. For instance, he was a director of the McKesson & Robbins Corporation during the years it was run by a man Weinberg knew as F. Donald Coster, M.D. *and* PhD. In fact, Coster was actually Philip Musica, a clever swindler who was twice convicted of fraud before his thirtieth birthday. Using an alias, in 1919, Musica founded Adelphia Pharmaceutical Manufacturing Company to create high-alcohol liquid hair and grooming products to sell to bootleggers eager to distribute booze during Prohibition. (The bootleggers would extract the alcohol from the hair products and resell it.)

In 1925, according to Paul Clikeman, a University of Richmond professor who has studied con men, Musica—claiming to be Coster—used his profits from Adelphia to buy McKesson & Robbins, a publicly traded and respectable drug distribution company that sold milk of magnesia, cough syrup, and quinine. Musica's con this time was to inflate McKesson's assets by creating phony invoices, purchase orders, and shipping statements and making it look like a newly created dummy company—W. W. Smith & Co.—was buying various products from McKesson. To make the scam work, Musica enlisted the help of his three brothers, and together they took a 0.75 percent commission on all the sales—of around $21 million (a tidy sum in those days)—to W. W. Smith & Co., enabling them to benefit personally from the scam while inflating McKesson's stock price from the phony revenue. The con worked brilliantly for thirteen years. In the logbook on Coster's yacht, Weinberg had written, "I'm for McKesson & Robbins and Coster, that's all." The company's directors and auditors had completely missed the fraud.

The deceit began to be revealed in 1938, thanks to the curiosity of Julian Thompson, McKesson's treasurer. He became suspicious about why McKesson was paying all this money on a regular basis to W. W. Smith & Co. To satisfy the auditors about the viability of W. W. Smith & Co., the Musica brothers had concocted Dun & Bradstreet credit reports. Thompson showed the dummy reports to a D&B representative, who told Thompson he did not know where they had come from but that they surely had not been the work of D&B. On December 6, 1938, the SEC started an investigation into McKesson's relationship with W. W. Smith & Co. and suspended the trading in McKesson's shares. One week later, Coster was arrested. He was fingerprinted and released on bail. From the fingerprints, the FBI figured out that Coster was really Musica, the convicted felon. The authorities ordered Musica rearrested. But before that could happen, he put a gun in his mouth and pulled the trigger. That same day, the McKesson & Robbins board was meeting to fire Coster when it received word of the man's suicide. After a "moment of grim silence," Weinberg piped up: "Well, come on, gentlemen, let's fire him for his sins anyway."

To avoid potential costly litigation against the directors for their obvious negligence, the men decided to chip in some $600,000 to the McKesson & Robbins coffers, including $75,000 from Weinberg alone. He remained on McKesson's board for years after the scandal. During the SEC's investigation, Weinberg testified, and his correspondence with Coster/Musica combined with his previously published polemic about the responsibilities of directors and officers "gave Sidney some uncomfortable moments in the witness chair," *Fortune* reported. When the SEC's attorney wondered why he had failed to act in accordance with his treatise, Weinberg "pointed out to him that Moses had brought down the Ten Commandments from Mount Sinai, that we all believed in them, but that unfortunately few of us live in accordance with all of them."

Mostly, though, Weinberg was a corporate juggernaut, which greatly benefited Goldman Sachs, and Weinberg himself. "My partner, Sidney Weinberg, is supposed to be the finest professional director in the country," Walter Sachs said in 1956, with a noticeable level of resentment about what that meant for him in terms of having to run the firm day to day. "He devotes more time to it than I do. His theory is a little different, and that's all right, I don't quarrel with it. He wants to be on the executive committee. He wants to get his finger into every question. And he's been a very valuable director to the companies he's on, no question about that." Sachs conveniently overlooked Weinberg's omissions during the McKesson & Robbins scandal. "I would say 90 percent of his activity has been in his director relationships," Sachs continued, "and that's been very valuable to Goldman, Sachs and Company, and has led to a lot of business. He's done more of it—I mean, consciously more of it—than I have because I've had to watch administrative work in the firm."

The occasional sniping aside, the consensus seemed to be that Weinberg's genius was essential to the revival of Goldman Sachs's fortunes. "Sidney Weinberg has this alchemy—there is no other word for it—of converting an ordinary business relationship into a very real and abiding friendship," Robert Sheehan wrote in *Fortune*. "He is not, as the surface facts might suggest, a mere trader of favors. He is, rather, a gregarious, accessible and outgiving man who has soaked up a tremendous knowledge of the business world and the people who make it, and who finds his greatest pleasure in life in putting that singular knowledge at the disposal of others. Of course, as with the Biblical bread, all this has come back to him manifold. As an underwriting technician, Weinberg is top flight, but no better, perhaps, than a dozen other bankers in the Street. But a vast amount of business flows into Goldman, Sachs as an almost unsolicited gesture of goodwill to Sidney."

Even if he merely just showed up at the board meetings and told a joke—he had by all accounts a fine sense of humor—his weekly workload would have defied imagination. But Weinberg was an extraordinarily devoted and engaged board member, in part because of his manifesto on corporate director responsibilities, in part because it was (very) good for Goldman's business, and in part because he believed passionately in this kind of service. Of course, as his eighth-grade teacher at P.S. 13 observed, "He is happy when he is busy." Quite simply, Weinberg's willingness to serve on corporate boards, while time-consuming, was vital to resurrecting the firm's public image in the wake of the Goldman Sachs Trading Corporation disaster and Eddie Cantor's ongoing efforts to make the firm the butt of his jokes. "Once into this activity, however, he made such a job of it as few individuals before him ever attempted," *Fortune* reported in October 1953. "Of each company he requested in advance an agenda of the directors' meeting, and full sets of figures pertinent to the issues to be discussed. He put his boys at Goldman, Sachs to work analyzing those figures, and set up an office on the top floor of his Scarsdale home where he devoted his weekends to preparing for board sessions. As word of these conscientious practices got around, the presence of Weinberg on the board became a point of pride with many companies."

THERE IS NO question that Weinberg, and Goldman, were aided immeasurably in their efforts to win new business by Weinberg's decades-long involvement in national politics, his years in public service—including when he took two separate leaves of absence from

Goldman during World War II and a third as the Korean War was unfolding—and the lifelong friendships with important businessmen and politicians he made along the way. "Sidney's a sucker for anything patriotic," is how one of his friends described him. Writers have variously described him as having a "gourmand's appetite for public service" and as "an ambassador between financiers and politicians."

In what seemed to be a fairly typical pattern on Wall Street, especially these days, as Weinberg's importance at—and to—Goldman Sachs increased in the wake of Waddill Catchings's escapades at Goldman, Weinberg ratcheted up his dealings with politicians, especially those in Washington. He was the assistant treasurer of the Democratic National Committee—and one of its most able fund-raisers—in both the 1932 and 1936 presidential elections. In April 1933, he wrote to Roosevelt asking him to make a radio address referencing the embargo on gold, and he shared his views on the proposed federal Securities Act. In July 1935, Roosevelt invited Weinberg and a dozen or so other business leaders to join him, the vice president, the Speaker of the House, five cabinet members, and eight senators for the weekend at the Jefferson Islands Club, in Chesapeake Bay. The previous year, the club built a lodge for Roosevelt's exclusive use for fishing, hunting, and "exceptional social companionship." The purpose of the July 1935 weekend was supposed to be fishing. "But observers here found it hard to believe that two score leading Democrats could get together without considerable discussion of the program and tactics to be pursued during the remainder of the Congressional session," the *Times* reported.

Weinberg was in attendance at the April 1937 funeral of W. Forbes Morgan, the former treasurer of the Democratic National Campaign Committee, when he was buried at Arlington National Cemetery. Morgan was related by marriage to Eleanor Roosevelt. His funeral was a big event, and all the New Dealers turned out for it. A photograph that appeared the next day featured Roosevelt's key advisers, including Cordell Hull, the secretary of state; James Roosevelt, the administrative assistant to the president and his oldest son; Edward J. Flynn, the New York secretary of state; Joseph T. Robinson, then Senate majority leader; Alben Barkley, soon to be the Senate majority leader (and later vice president under Truman)—and in the middle of them all, Sidney J. Weinberg. No less a master politician than President Roosevelt himself referred to Weinberg as "the Politician." Indeed, "many grimly intransigent members of the business community" at the time "were fully convinced that nothing but Weinberg's temperate advice to the Roosevelt administration was saving the capitalistic system from annihilation."

In exchange for this advice, Roosevelt offered Weinberg not only access to him—as long as it was properly scheduled, of course—but also various positions in his government. In June 1934, along with the CEOs of Sears and IBM, Weinberg was rumored to be among those Roosevelt would appoint to the first board of the U.S. Securities and Exchange Commission.

Weinberg was also reported to have been offered a cabinet post and several undersecretary slots. Then, in the summer of 1938, Roosevelt offered Weinberg the chance to succeed his friend Joseph Davies as the U.S. ambassador to the Soviet Union. Davies had already offered Weinberg the position, and the Soviets had already approved the choice. It was a done deal, notwithstanding the U.S. Senate had not yet voted to approve the appointment. The problem was Weinberg didn't want the job. Not only was there no one at Goldman of his stature and business-getting prowess around in 1938 to take over for him; as Goldman's largest shareholder, his entire net worth was on the line at the firm and he likely had little interest in being forced to sell his stake to take the ambassador-ship or to leave others to manage the firm—and his fortune—without him. There was also the small matter that his two sons were both in mid-dle school, and educating them in the Soviet Union or being thousands of miles apart was not particularly appealing. In addition, there was the issue of Weinberg being Jewish at a time when anti-Semitism was on the rise throughout Europe and the Soviet Union. His reasons for not accept-ing the post were "entirely personal," Weinberg wrote to Stephen Early, Roosevelt's press secretary. To the outside world, Weinberg said simply, "I don't speak Russian. Who the hell could I talk to over there?"

On July 5, 1938, Weinberg wrote to Roosevelt. "Ever since Joe Davies on your behalf offered me the Ambassadorship to Russia, I have intended to thank you for this honor, and tell you how deeply apprecia-tive I am of your confidence in me, as evidenced by your consideration of me for this important post . . . ," he wrote. "I did want you to know how grateful I am to you for this distinction, as well as other evidences of friendship which you have shown to me during the past several years." The president wrote Weinberg back that "I fully understand" and that he hoped to see him again soon "after I get back from my cruise."

By this point, President Roosevelt was not an easy man for a Wall Street banker to like, or to support financially. Toward the end of 1936, as he was campaigning for his second term as president, Roosevelt earned the endearing enmity of many on Wall Street by speaking often about "business and financial monopoly, speculation, reckless banking." Roosevelt knew he was making Wall Street angry but said, "I welcome their hatred." Weinberg stayed by Roosevelt's side through the 1936 election and continued to raise impressive amounts of money for him. At one point, Weinberg acknowledged what Roosevelt had done to begin to repair the battered economy through both his Keynesian approach to fiscal policy and his panoply of new regulations covering Wall Street's behavior. "FDR saved the system," Weinberg said. "You could have had a rebellion; you could have had a civil war."

On September 1, 1939, the German army marched into Poland, marking the start of World War II. Weinberg, vacationing with his family in Nantucket, cabled Roosevelt. "I offer you my services in any capacity during these critical times," he wrote. That same day, Edwin Watson, secretary to the president, wrote back, "The President has asked me to acknowledge your telegram . . . and to assure you of his deep appreciation of your kind offer of service."

At first, the letters on both sides seemed gratuitous, in part because Roosevelt probably wasn't sure what role Weinberg could play or what that role should be, and in part because Weinberg had started to question whether he wanted to support Roosevelt's bid for an unprecedented third term. In the end, Weinberg pulled back from Roosevelt after concluding that a third term would be "unsound" and threw his considerable fund-raising muscle behind lawyer Wendell Willkie, the Democrat turned Republican from Indiana. "I did not support him after the first two terms," Weinberg recalled. "I had a great argument with him. I didn't think any man should serve more than two terms. I was getting a little tired, too, of all the New Deal things." Weinberg joined the short-lived Democrats for Willkie organization, whose members decided to back Willkie because they feared electing Roosevelt for a third term would be a dangerous precedent and one that could lead to dictatorship. Although Willkie received more popular votes—22 million—than any previous Republican candidate for president, Roosevelt thrashed him, receiving 27 million votes and 449 of the 531 votes in the electoral college.

Weinberg quickly fell back in line supporting Roosevelt, his president, during wartime. On April 20, 1941, he joined a committee of other bankers, chaired by Robert Lehman at Lehman Brothers, to raise money for the Royal Air Force Benevolent Fund of the United States of America. Then, nine days later, on April 29, Roosevelt appointed Weinberg as a special consultant in the purchasing division in the Office of Production Management, or OPM, which Roosevelt had created in January 1941 "to increase production for the national defense through mobilization of material resources and the industrial facilities of the nation."

Weinberg, along with eight other men, was appointed by Roosevelt that day, all earning one dollar per year plus their living expenses. They became known as the "dollar-a-year men," a precedent that would be revived during the financial crisis of 2008 (and many of the men receiving the dollar a year would be, coincidentally—or not so coincidentally— former Goldman partners).

On May 5, Donald Nelson, the director of purchases at the Office of Production Management and a former vice president of Sears, Roebuck (technically, Weinberg was once his boss since he was on the Sears board), announced Weinberg's appointment as "a consultant on various industry problems" who "would report for duty" on May 15. This, of course, meant taking a leave of absence from Goldman Sachs and leaving behind—for the time being—his board seats at twelve companies (including Sears). With Weinberg's leave of absence, Walter Sachs took over the day-to-day management of Goldman, a position, he explained, he had occupied "for a great many years" anyway.

For his part, Sachs knew "Frank" Roosevelt from Harvard—they worked on the *Crimson* together—and found him to be "a man of great charm, there's no question about that," but they were not close socially or politically. Sachs, whose "father was a stricter man," lived in simpler student housing in Harvard Yard, where there was no running water in the rooms and showers had to be taken in the basement. "And it was pretty damn cold . . . ," Sachs said, "and we had no running water, and the water would be frozen in the pitcher in the morning and it had to thaw out before we could wash." On the other hand, Roosevelt lived on the "Gold Coast" of Cambridge, on Mount Auburn Street, in Claverly Hall, "one of those private dormitories where men lived whose families had a certain amount of money, and were more social, more elegant."

As Weinberg did, Sachs also wrote a letter to Roosevelt after his election in 1932. Roosevelt sent back a letter "in which he thanked me and said he wanted all the advice he could get from his friends." In the early days of the Roosevelt administration when he closed the banks, Sachs urged caution. "I remember telling people that I might have been wrong about this man and to give him a chance," Sachs explained. But he quickly parted ways with his Harvard classmate. He hated the New Deal. "I felt there were a great many things that were just a great, great mistake," he wrote. "What I probably resented, and we'll look at the psychological aspect of it, that when one talks about driving men out of the temple, I couldn't help but think, Franklin Roosevelt knew Arthur Ballantine"—the founder of the law firm Dewey Ballantine—"me, Eugene

Thayer"—the president of the Chase bank—"and others like us, and he classed us altogether. There were the passions of the times, and I was against him."

While admitting he was a "dyed-in-the-wool Republican" he was also "resentful" of Roosevelt's "attitude" toward bankers and Wall Street in 1929. "Not that I didn't realize as much as any man the errors in judgment and mistakes that were made," but Roosevelt "knew enough men" on Wall Street that "his shattering attack on business as a whole, I thought, was entirely unjustified." Sachs said Roosevelt "must have known in his heart of hearts" that the men on Wall Street, many of whom Roosevelt knew from school and elsewhere, "may have been subject to poor judgment or been carried away by waves of the speculative era, but he must have known that we meant to do the right thing. Those are the things that I couldn't quite forgive him."

Reflecting back, though, Sachs said "maybe it was partly my own fault" and "maybe I should have sought him out the way my partner Weinberg did, who was a Democrat for a while." These choices made, Weinberg went to Washington to help Roosevelt with the war effort and Sachs stayed in New York to hunker down and to run Goldman Sachs—not that there was much business to be done during America's involvement in the Second World War, or in the year or so leading up to it.

In short order, Weinberg took on more and more responsibility at the OPM, becoming head of the OPM Industry Advisory Committee designed to help streamline the process of manufacturing goods needed in the war effort. But he also came in for his share of partisan criticism. *Time* magazine accused him of being "small" and "gossipy" and complained he was "Wall Street's Walter Winchell," the creator of the gossip column. In February 1942, the *New York Times* profiled Weinberg in a more laudatory way, suggesting that his appointment as Nelson's aide was "tantamount to a guarantee that if finance and industry really want to do a job they will receive a fair hearing." The newspaper recounted his Horatio Alger rise to fame and riches at Goldman and described how his collection of the letters, documents, and pictures of Abraham Lincoln— "one of the largest private collections"—that was kept "in the vaults of Goldman, Sachs & Co." kept him busy "in spare time, if he has any." (He also had a collection of Roosevelt campaign buttons that he later gave the president.) The *Times* explained how Weinberg was now "hustling around for the War Production Board just as he did in private life for his own organization."

For much of Weinberg's time in Washington, there was considerable confusion about just what his responsibilities were first at the OPM and then at its successor, the War Production Board, or WPB. "Every time I went to a meeting with Nelson, this fellow would be there," according to Weinberg's friend General Lucius D. Clay. "He had no apparent responsibility, and I kept wondering why Nelson had him around. Then I realized he was acting as a counsellor and adviser—as a Minister without portfolio, you might say. That's the way Sidney likes to operate—in a little back office, as somebody's assistant."

Despite his efforts to stay in the background, Weinberg did—briefly—get a dose of unwanted attention when Senator Harry S. Truman (D-Missouri) accused him of favoring the big corporations—where he had served as a director—in the procurement and production process over smaller businesses. Weinberg told Roosevelt he "resented" Truman's accusations and "having his motives impugned" and was "going to quit." But Roosevelt talked him off the ledge. "That's ridiculous," he told Weinberg. "Look at what they say about me every day. *I* don't quit."

His plumage back in place, Weinberg returned to his position at the WPB with renewed enthusiasm. His most crucial role in government, it turned out, was to recruit other businessmen—who would not normally be sympathetic to Roosevelt's call—to Washington to help with the war effort. He became known as the Body Snatcher. Not surprisingly, given his bias toward persistence, he could be quite persuasive with those executives reluctant to abandon their cushy posts and join the WPB. He would route his calls through the White House switchboard to give them a heightened air of importance. He would also bad-mouth in the business community those executives who tried to avoid his calls or public service. Since business executives generally viewed Weinberg with great respect and affection, this ill will had the desired effect—rather quickly in fact—of getting the recalcitrant executives to return Weinberg's calls and to enlist in the war effort.

Weinberg's greatest recruiting coup, many thought, was his snatching of Charles "Electric Charlie" Wilson away from his position as president of General Electric to join the WPB in 1942. Wilson, who barely knew Weinberg and who had been in his position at GE for only two years, was reluctant to give up the post and move to Washington. Wilson also believed that GE was already so actively involved in war production that his highest and best use during the war would be to stay put, overseeing GE's work. But after a meeting in Washington with the secretaries of war and of the navy, Owen Young, the retired chairman of the GE board, told Wilson, "Somebody's put the finger on you." When Young relayed to Washington Wilson's preference for staying at GE, the message came back that Roosevelt wanted to meet with Wilson at the White

House. That did it. Wilson signed up. "Sidney Weinberg never material-ized in any of the negotiations involving me," Wilson said later. "But I could see that *somebody* had put the heat on, and I knew from conversa-tions I had later with Roosevelt and members of the Cabinet that Sidney had had a hell of a lot to do with it. I wasn't in Washington very long before I realized that a good many other people around were there because of Sidney, too."

After Independence Day 1943, Weinberg submitted his resignation to Nelson, effective August 1. Without elaboration, Nelson told the *New York Times* that Weinberg resigned "on the advice of physicians who have ordered [him] to obtain rest and medical treatment." He returned to New York and to his post at Goldman.

Whether Weinberg was genuinely ill or whether this was a cover to allow him to pursue his next assignment for the U.S. government is not clear. On November 5, 1943, at the request of William J. Donovan, the New York lawyer and head of the Office of Strategic Services, Roosevelt approved the appointment of Weinberg to go to "Russia openly as the representative of the OSS," assuming "Mr. Weinberg can be persuaded to go." Roosevelt initialed Donovan's request—"O.K. FDR—11/5/43"—and returned the memo to Donovan. Even though Weinberg was Jewish and spoke no Russian, or so he had earlier claimed, this time he took on the assignment. What he did in the Soviet Union for the U.S. government—and how long he was there—is not known. The CIA, the successor to the OSS, did not respond to a Freedom of Information Act request seeking information about Weinberg's mission. One of his grand-sons, Peter Weinberg, a former Goldman Sachs partner and the founder of Perella Weinberg, a boutique investment bank, was not aware of what his grandfather did in the Soviet Union during the war or even that he had gone there.

Regardless of his secret mission and what he did on it, Weinberg returned, apparently at the request of Roosevelt, to the WPB—this time as vice chairman—in June 1944, eleven months after he left, supposedly for health reasons. His job this go-around was to handle "special prob-lems" for Nelson and to once again act as the Body Snatcher to fill exec-utive positions at the WPB. But his true mission was to see if he could end the public feuding between his two former clients—"Electric Char-lie" Wilson and Donald Nelson. The two men's public disagreements stemmed from a dispute about when to reconvert the country's industrial production to public consumption from wartime consumption. Thinking the war almost won, Nelson wanted to revert back to manufacturing for consumers. Wilson, citing the judgment of the Joint Chiefs of Staff that an ammunitions shortage was looming, wanted to keep the country's industrial production focused on the war.

Weinberg sided with his friend Wilson over his friend Nelson and then was criticized for "stabbing his old friend Don Nelson in the back," according to *Fortune*. "Not so, states Weinberg. What he thought of Nelson's actions, in this instance, he told him, in anguish and bald Brooklynese, to his face." By August 31, Weinberg's latest mission was over. "I have just learned, with real regret, of your resignation from the War Production Board," Roosevelt wrote to him. "I am indeed sorry to see you go and I want to send you this little personal note to tell you how very much I appreciate the many sacrifices you have made in order to serve the Government during these trying days. You have done a grand job and I am grateful to you." Weinberg later made light of the dispute with Nelson and chalked up his departure to boredom. "There was less and less real work for me to do," he said. "In the winter I was reading important papers until eight p.m. Last spring, I'd be finished by three. When I was done by ten a.m., I knew it was time to resign in Washington and return to New York." Just over two years later, in September 1946, President Truman awarded Weinberg the Medal for Merit for "outstanding services" for his role working at the War Production Board.

––––––

BY THEN, WEINBERG had returned to Goldman, just in time for the firm to celebrate its seventy-fifth anniversary. To mark the occasion, the firm held a dinner at the Pierre Hotel on Fifth Avenue (now the Pierre) for the partners and employees. At that time, Goldman had eleven partners, including Walter and Howard Sachs and Weinberg, and branch offices in Boston, Philadelphia, Chicago, and St. Louis. Despite the firm's many successes to that point—many of them thanks to Weinberg's perspicacity and determination—Goldman was still a firm on the outside of Wall Street looking in, like many of the predominantly Jewish firms.

Anti-Semitism continued to complicate the calculus of doing business. But mores were changing, too, albeit slowly. One morning after Weinberg's friend Paul Cabot had dinner with Weinberg and another man at the exclusive Brook, a club on East Fifty-fourth Street, the acting president of the club came over to Cabot's table as he was eating breakfast to tell him it had been "inappropriate what he had done the night before."

"Did we speak in too-loud voices?" Cabot asked him, knowing full well to what the man was referring.

"Oh, no, it wasn't that," came the reply. "It was the *individuals* at your table."

"What's your exact meaning?" Cabot demanded to know.

"You know we don't accept Jews at the Brook," the man said.

"Well," Cabot replied, "I've read the by-laws and there's nothing on the subject there. . . . If that's the way this club is to be run, you can stick your club you know where. You will have my resignation this very morning."

After the dispute with Nelson, Wilson went back to General Electric as a top executive. Weinberg's reward for his loyalty to Wilson was nearly immediate when GE appointed him to its board of directors in June 1945. No board was more prestigious at that time, but it would be years before his spot there would translate into business for Goldman Sachs.

The Korean War further enhanced the relationship between Wilson and Weinberg. In 1950, President Truman asked Wilson to head up the Office of Defense Mobilization, a new version of the WPB. Once again, Wilson was reluctant to give up his post at GE because he felt if he left again he would have to leave the company for good, in fairness to the management team. He asked Weinberg, the board director and Wilson's friend, what to do. "Sidney spoke right up, as he always does," Wilson recalled. " 'Hell you're going to go,' he told me. 'Of *course,* you'll go. And I'll go with you.' That made up my mind." Once again, Wilson and Weinberg returned to Washington—for six months—to remobilize America's war machine.

But this time, the country was less passionate about the war effort, as Wilson and Weinberg figured out quickly. On their first day in Washington for the new assignment, in December 1950, there was no one around to let them into their offices at the Old State Department Building. So they pulled up a couple of chairs and sat in the corridor outside their offices and began to sketch out the plan for the defense mobilization effort. For months, they were inseparable, sharing a suite at the Shoreham Hotel and having lunch together in a small private dining room near their offices. But "it was a tougher task than either of them experienced in World War II," *Fortune* reported. "The political atmosphere was hostile, the press was waspish, the response of industry was somewhat grudging." They had their victories—for instance, the decision to produce more than just weapons—but "this whole chapter seems, in some strange way, to have slipped off the pages of history."

In 1952, Weinberg had once again changed his political leanings and agreed to serve as the treasurer of the Citizens for Eisenhower-Nixon. This was a splinter group, especially when compared with the powerful Republican National Committee. At one point, Weinberg and

John Hay Whitney, another leader of the citizens committee, agreed to a rapprochement with the RNC. To get the deal done, Whitney—who had been meeting with the party's leaders in Cleveland—called Weinberg at home at two-thirty in the morning seeking his advice on some concession or other. Weinberg advised Whitney to make the deal. "Jock, if they cut us down, we got to go along," Weinberg told him. "I learned long ago that if you're born a pygmy, you got to live a pygmy."

It was a good deal for the Republicans, given the staggering amount of money Weinberg was able to raise. "Without any doubt, Sidney is the best money-getter I've ever seen," Whitney said. "He'll go to one of his innumerable board meetings—General Foods, or General Electric, or General Whatever—and makes no bones about telling everybody there what he wants. Then he'll say, 'Come on boys, where is it?'—and up it comes." In return for all this fund-raising, Weinberg got what he really craved—unlimited access to power.

After Eisenhower's election, the president-elect surrounded himself with three trusted advisers: Sherman Adams, Herbert Brownell, and General Lucius Clay. Weinberg, of course, knew Clay from the Second World War, when Clay was in charge of procurement for the army. In 1950, Weinberg had also recommended Clay to be the chairman and CEO of Continental Can Company, where Weinberg had been a director since 1930. Early one afternoon after the 1952 election, Adams, Brownell, and Clay were meeting together at the Commodore Hotel, in New York, for the sole purpose of figuring out whom they should recommend to Eisenhower for treasury secretary. By three o'clock that afternoon, after going around and around making little progress, Clay called Weinberg in his Goldman office at 30 Pine Street and begged him to recommend someone in the next two hours. Weinberg no doubt had already been giving the matter some thought and continued his thinking as he hopped on the subway—his preferred mode of transportation—to meet the men at the Commodore, on Forty-second Street. (Weinberg used to proudly tell his partners he saved five dollars a week by taking the subway.)

"I didn't have any clear idea of the matter when I got on the train," Weinberg recounted later. "Then I began thinking about Clay. I'd been against him in a number of fights about war production, but I'd always thought this, this Clay fellow could run anything. The trouble is he's not a fiscal expert, of course." At about Fourteenth Street, still on the subway, Weinberg had an insight. "I suddenly said to myself, 'George Humphrey's like Clay! Goddam it, why not George Humphrey? I've always said he's one of the ablest fellows I know in industry.'" By the time he arrived at the hotel, Weinberg had convinced himself that Humphrey, a steel executive, should be Eisenhower's treasury secretary. He quickly convinced Eisenhower's advisers of his belief as well and then introduced Humphrey to the president. The two men had never met, and Eisenhower did not know of Humphrey. He served Eisenhower for more than four years and became a powerful force in the cabinet. "When George speaks, we all listen," Eisenhower used to say. Naturally, after Humphrey's appointment, he and Weinberg spoke regularly about the economy and fiscal policy to the point where if the two men did not speak in a given day, Weinberg would worry about the machinations going on at Treasury. The irony, of course, was that had Weinberg wanted the job—or likely any other cabinet post by that point—he could have easily had it, but he chose instead his preferred path of being a power behind the throne.

CHAPTER 4

THE VALUE OF FRIENDSHIP

W einberg wanted to get back to Goldman and reap what he had been sowing during the war years. With America's enormous productive capacity turned back again toward meeting fifteen years of pent-up consumer demand, Weinberg had figured correctly that Goldman was in position to make vast profits by providing capital to meet those needs. After years of Weinberg's politicking and public service, it was time for Weinberg and Goldman Sachs to make some serious money.

After he was elected to the board of General Electric in 1945, no small accomplishment for a Jewish banker from Brooklyn, GE's board chairman, Philip D. Reed, asked Weinberg to address a group of company executives at a banquet at the Waldorf-Astoria hotel on Park Avenue in Manhattan. In introducing his new director, Reed felt certain Weinberg's comments would be enlightening, but in any event he assumed that Weinberg felt as Reed did that GE "was the greatest outfit in the greatest industry in the greatest country in the world." Most Wall Street bankers would hit that softball out of the park by sycophantically agreeing with the boss. Not Weinberg. "I'll string along with your chairman about this being the greatest country," Weinberg told the crowd, "and I guess I'll even buy that about the electrical industry being a pretty fair industry. But as to GE's being the greatest business in the field, why, I'm damned if I'll commit myself until I've had a look-see." He then sat down abruptly and reveled in the warm applause from the stunned group.

Such antics were typical of Weinberg and merely endeared him further—for reasons not entirely clear—to his fellow board members. In 1953, for instance, at a GE board meeting, there was a proposal for the directors to consider about awarding women employees, or the wives of the male employees, five shares of GE stock should they happen to give birth to a child during the year, which also happened to be the company's seventy-fifth anniversary. "His lips characteristically pursed," Weinberg bided his time after considering the proposal and then offered his fellow board members—not a young man among them—one hundred shares of GE stock if any of them again became a father. "The others could barely wait to get out of the room and broadcast this—to them—hilarious proposition among their friends," according to one account of the meeting.

No doubt his fellow board members enjoyed Weinberg's levity because he also was plenty serious about the business at hand. As Walter Sachs had observed, Weinberg liked to be part of the board committees—for instance, the Executive Committee, the Compensation Committee, or the Audit Committee—where the real work of the corporation got done. Thanks to his weekend sessions at his home in Scarsdale, he was always well prepared—the McKesson debacle notwithstanding—and therefore could be a real ally, assuming he agreed, to a chief executive looking to pursue a particular path. After World War II, for instance, GE's executives wanted to spend several hundred million dollars pursuing an aggressive expansion program to take advantage of what they perceived to be—correctly—a coming boom in demand among Americans for GE's products. But the amount of capital to be committed was not trivial, and Charles E. Wilson, GE's president, was not certain the board would go along. "Sidney had done his homework, and that was all I needed," Wilson recounted a few years later. "He seconded my proposals in his inimitably persuasive fashion, and after that there was nothing to it. He's a great man to have on your board."

It wasn't until 1956—eleven years after Weinberg's appointment to the board—that Goldman joined Morgan Stanley as the lead underwriter of a $300 million bond issue for General Electric. "That, as Bobby Lehman was good enough to say, is a great triumph for the firm," Walter Sachs recalled. "I told him when he called me at the hospital that I thought it was a great triumph for Sidney Weinberg, which it is." As Sachs pointed out, the "Morgans have always been the bankers for General Electric." It was "through Sidney's relationship with Charlie Wilson and his work during the War, the Second World War, on W.P.B., [that] they became good friends."

———

EVEN IF WEINBERG was not on a company's board, he was still able to figure out a way for Goldman Sachs to benefit from his relationships. In 1949, Weinberg's son, Jimmy, began working at Owens-Corning Fiberglas, which was a joint venture between the Owens-Illinois Glass Company and Corning Glass Works and the Houghton family, the high WASPs of Corning, New York. Two years later, Jimmy Weinberg married Elizabeth Houghton, itself a bit of a coup, but nothing—it turned out—

compared to the refinancing Weinberg arranged for Owens-Corning Fiberglas. The same month that Jimmy Weinberg married into the Houghtons, Harold Boeschenstein, the CEO of Owens-Corning Fiberglas, contacted Weinberg about how the company might raise some additional capital. The two parent companies, which together owned 84 percent of Owens-Corning, were not permitted by the Justice Department to own any more of the company and so could not invest anything additional.

There were any number of possible solutions to the question of what Owens-Corning should do, of course, including obtaining a bank loan, or selling corporate bonds, or issuing equity publicly for the first time in an IPO. Of the three options, the most lucrative for Goldman Sachs from a fee perspective was the IPO—but it was the most risky. Even though Weinberg was in the Presbyterian Hospital, in New York, for surgery and "flat on his back," he gave the matter of how Owens-Corning should raise the needed capital some considered thought. He was not alone in thinking through this issue, of course, as the proposed financing was one of the most coveted assignments on Wall Street at the time. Not being on the board of Owens-Corning at first seemed like a disadvantage for Goldman Sachs and Weinberg, notwithstanding the business of the royal nuptials. While he was recuperating in the hospital from his surgery, Weinberg wrote Boeschenstein a memorandum recommending that Owens-Corning raise the needed capital through an IPO.

Fortune, in its profile of Weinberg, made much of the fact that he was not on the Owens-Corning board of directors and that Goldman had never before done any business with the company. But it made clear that Weinberg had relationships all around it: without mentioning the (plenty important) familial relationship, *Fortune* reported that both Amory Houghton, the chairman of Corning Glass, and William Levis, chairman of the Executive Committee of Owens-Illinois, were said to be "really good friends" of Weinberg's from their days together on the War Production Board; that Boeschenstein also knew Weinberg from the War Production Board; that Keith Funston, the president of the New York Stock Exchange and a member of the Owens-Corning board, also knew Weinberg from the War Production Board; and that another Owens-Corning board member, Robert Stevens, then the secretary of the army, was also Weinberg's "very good friend." Both Funston and Stevens, it turned out, served together with Weinberg on the board of General Foods, and this bit of serendipity proved to be essential in getting Weinberg the hearing with Boeschenstein after Funston and Stevens relayed to the Owens-Corning CEO some of the details of a supposedly masterful piece of financing that Goldman and Weinberg had executed for General Foods. When Boeschenstein heard of this, the decision was made to "ask Sidney about this." When Boeschenstein asked the Goldman senior partner what he thought his company's stock was worth, Weinberg reportedly "gave him a figure off the cuff that was practically the price at which the stock was ultimately offered." This insight combined with Weinberg's extensive personal connections to the decision makers was the key to Goldman being selected as the lead underwriter of the IPO. "Such is the familiar pattern—the threads of Weinberg's three lives interweaving to produce a beautiful piece of business," *Fortune* observed.

Any solution for Owens-Corning was further complicated by the New York Stock Exchange rules, which required that companies listed on the exchange be widely held, meaning that more than 50 percent of the stock of the company be owned, after the IPO, by the public. This was potentially problematic for Owens-Corning because the two partners—Corning Glass and Owens-Illinois—together owned 84 percent of the company and were not so keen on selling down to below the 50 percent threshold level. But this is where Weinberg's skills as a banker—and a diplomat—were thrust into sharp relief. Not only did he convince his friend Funston at the New York Stock Exchange (how convenient) to relax the rules about how widely held the stock issue needed to be—the 50 percent rule was reduced to 20 percent, at least in this case—he also convinced his pals at Owens-Illinois and Corning Glass to sell more stock than they initially wanted to so that after the IPO the public owned the 20 percent that Funston had agreed to. These compromises resulted in a bigger IPO—ultimately it was $22.5 million, $15.5 million of which went to Owens-Corning itself—and more fees for the underwriters, $866,000, led by Goldman Sachs. One admiring competitor of Weinberg's said of him after the successful Owens-Corning IPO, "Sidney is a wizard at reconciling groups with different objectives. In the Owens-Corning deal, as in so many others, he made all the rival interests end up thinking that they'd won the day."

———

BY THE TIME the blockbuster opportunity to underwrite the initial public offering of the Ford Motor Company popped up onto the radar screens of every investment banker on Wall Street in October 1953, all the pieces of the puzzle were in place for Weinberg and Goldman Sachs to be selected as the lead underwriter of one of the most prestigious and important financings of all time. Not only was Weinberg close with "Electric Charlie" Wilson, the chairman of the finance committee of the Ford Foundation—one of two major Ford shareholders looking to sell stock (the other being the Ford family, of course)—but he also had long known the Ford family's matriarch, Mrs. Edsel Ford. As for her son, Henry Ford II, who became president of the company in 1945, Weinberg had known him since 1947, when he became a member of the Business Advisory Council of the U.S. Department of Commerce.

Weinberg helped to organize the Business Advisory Council in 1933 in order to increase communication between the Commerce Department and the business community and, of course—in time-honored tradition— as a way for powerful businessmen to influence government officials. The council met with the secretary of commerce several times a year, either in Washington or in resorts such as the Greenbrier, in West Virginia, or Sea Island, Georgia, or Sun Valley, Idaho. (Just how cozy these businessmen were with the government became the subject of a congressional investigation, led by Brooklyn congressman Emanuel Celler, in July 1955.)

Weinberg's courting of Henry Ford II was not nearly as seamless as his other personal and professional triumphs. Part of the problem may have stemmed from the fact that Henry Ford—the patriarch and Henry Ford II's grandfather—was notoriously and grotesquely anti-Semitic. Ford's *Dearborn Independent,* which once had a circulation of more than seven hundred thousand readers, began attacking Jews in May 1920— after the end of World War I—and kept at it for years. Sadly, the diatribes were collected, bound, and published as *The International Jew: The World's Foremost Problem.* A small sample of Ford's thinking suffices to convey his ignorance. "The Jew is the world's enigma," Ford's surrogates wrote in the *Independent.* "Poor in his masses, he yet controls the world's finances. Scattered abroad without country or government, he yet presents a unity of race continuity which no other people has achieved. Living under legal disabilities in almost every land, he has become the power behind many a throne. There are ancient prophecies to the effect that the Jew will return to his own land and from that center rule the world, though not until he has undergone an assault by the united nations of mankind. The single description[,] which will include a larger percentage of Jews than members of any other race is this: he is in business. It may be only gathering rags and selling them, but he is in business. From the sale of old clothes to the control of international trade and finance, the Jew is supremely gifted for business."

After the death of Edsel Ford, the old man's son, in 1943, an ailing Henry Ford Sr. took back the reins of the company for two years before elevating his grandson, Henry Ford II, to run the company. Weinberg first met Henry Ford II the same year—1947—that Henry Ford Sr. died. Soon thereafter, the chatter began on Wall Street that the Ford Motor

Company would consider an IPO as a way for the family's heirs to diversify their holdings.

There was also the feeling that Henry Ford Sr.'s hatred of Jews, and Jewish bankers, made him opposed to doing business with Wall Street, including going there to discuss an IPO. But his grandson shared no such reluctance, and so he was sympathetic when, in October 1953, "Electric Charlie" Wilson told him that the Ford Foundation wanted to hire Weinberg and Goldman Sachs as the foundation's adviser on the IPO. "You can't have Weinberg," Ford told Wilson. "We want him as an adviser to the family." Not surprisingly, the Ford family—not the Ford Foundation—got Weinberg as their adviser, and the foundation had to make do with three advisers where one Weinberg would have sufficed. When Weinberg asked Ford how long the assignment would last, Ford responded that he had no idea, which was good enough for Weinberg, who gladly took it—as would any investment banker worth his salt—spending nearly half his time during the next two years, working largely in secret, to get the deal completed.

In many ways, the Ford IPO was a mirror image of the Owens-Corning deal. On one side were the Ford Foundation, which owned 88 percent of Ford's shares, and Ford's outside directors and some company management, who together owned another 2 percent of the shares. The Ford family owned the other 10 percent of the Ford shares—but, importantly, all of the voting rights to them that allowed for ultimate decisions for how the company would be run and when it would go public as well as other essential corporate governance decisions. "The big problem," E. J. Kahn Jr. wrote in *The New Yorker,* "was to get all hands to agree on how much money the Fords should get for transferring a part of their voting rights in the company to the shares the Foundation wanted to sell." This bit of shuttle diplomacy and alchemy was left to Weinberg. He had to find a solution that satisfied the New York Stock Exchange, which required that the shares the foundation was selling have voting rights; that satisfied the Ford family, in that the value conveyed to them for sharing their voting rights could not be a taxable event; that satisfied the Ford Foundation, which could not lose its tax-exempt status; and, of course, that satisfied the IRS, which had to somehow bless the deal as a tax-free transaction.

Weinberg worked in secret on more than fifty different proposals on how the financial reorganization of Ford and the Ford Foundation might be structured in order to satisfy all concerned. Once, during the process, when Henry Ford was traveling in Europe and Weinberg wanted to communicate with him by cablegram without giving away any of the confidential details of the plan, he created an alphabet soup of names to cover his tracks, including such charming pseudonyms as "Alice" for Henry Ford and "Ann" and "Audrey" for his two brothers. Ford, the company, was "Agnes," although at other times it was simply "X." "Cable offices here and abroad soon found themselves handling messages that read like passages from Louisa May Alcott," according to one account. (Code names for Wall Street deals soon thereafter became standard practice.) The solution that Weinberg hit on that worked for all involved the Fords increasing their equity stake in the company by 1.74 percent (after the IPO that extra bit of ownership was worth some $60 million to the family). For Weinberg's advice, Goldman received a fee said to be "as high as a million dollars," which would certainly have been a milestone in the early 1950s. Goldman also participated as an underwriter of the huge Ford Foundation offering, which added millions more to Goldman's coffers, even if this risked conflicts of interest (concern about which the Goldman partners somehow overcame).

The first inkling the world got that the Fords were cooking up an IPO came in March 1955, when Henry Ford and Weinberg decided to attend a charity event together in Palm Beach—after working all day—and they were spotted by a society columnist when Ford brought Weinberg over to say hello to the Duke and Duchess of Windsor. Weinberg was mildly offended that his cover had been blown. "How could you keep anything confidential under those conditions?" he wondered later. Of course, he almost blew it on his own, when that same year he had traveled by private plane to Detroit for a clandestine meeting with Mrs. Ford and her children and left behind on a newsstand at the airport the only copy of the company's confidential financial report outside the family's hands. At the time, he had traveled to Detroit with his associate, John Whitehead, and when later, after they had left the airport in the limousine Ford had sent for them, Weinberg discovered that he no longer had in his possession the leather briefcase with the confidential papers, he nearly exploded. "John, John, where in hell did you put my portfolio?" he demanded to know. Weinberg ordered the car turned around to return to the newsstand. Fortunately for Weinberg—and no doubt Whitehead, too—the briefcase was sitting right where Weinberg had left it. "If you fellas hadn't come soon for those papers, I'd've tossed 'em away," the vendor told the two men.

On November 9, 1955, the Ford Foundation announced that it had hired seven investment banks, led by Blyth & Co., to manage the sale of close to 10.2 million shares of Ford stock—22 percent of the foundation's holdings—in the largest IPO ever to that time. Goldman was one of the seven lead underwriters selected, although no mention was made of Weinberg and Goldman's unique role advising the Ford family. At that time, press reports listed Goldman's capital at $9.2 million and explained how the firm had lead-managed $27 million worth of securities in 1954. The entire syndicate of underwriters for the Ford offering—which was priced at $64.50 a share and generated $642.6 million of proceeds on January 17, 1956, with the balance of $15.3 million going in fees to the underwriters—totaled 722 investment houses, in large part because the stock was sold to retail investors generally in chunks of no more than one hundred shares at a time. At a meeting before a large percentage of the underwriters, Henry Ford II tried to tamp down the increasing enthusiasm for the deal. "I think some people are indulging in wishful thinking about their chances for fast and fabulous gains," he said. Ford's stock closed at $70.50 on its first day of trading on the New York Stock Exchange, a respectable 9.3 percent increase on the day.

In addition to Goldman's advisory fee, Henry Ford sent Weinberg a handwritten letter, which he had framed and kept in his office at Goldman. "Without you, it could not have been accomplished," the letter said, in part. Weinberg used to tell visitors to his office that the letter was "the big payoff as far as I'm concerned." The deal was a huge coup for Weinberg and Goldman.

In August 1956, Ford asked Weinberg to become a director of the Ford Motor Company, the first—and only—automobile company board on which he served. Until then, Weinberg owned a Cadillac and an Oldsmobile—two cars made by General Motors, where he had many friends among the executives. He made sure his own GM cars had either Goodrich or Sears tires (companies where he was also a director, although he resigned from the Sears board in 1953 after a federal judge ruled he had to give up the seat at either Sears or Goodrich). But after getting the call from Ford to serve on the board of directors, out went the Cadillac and the Oldsmobile, replaced by a shiny new Lincoln and by a shiny new Mercury, both made by the Ford Motor Company.

––––––

NOT BEING ON the Sears board any longer did not seem to hinder Weinberg's ability to generate business from the company. Indeed, some two years after engineering his Ford coup—the largest equity deal of all time to that point—he and Goldman also structured and sold a $350 million debt deal for Sears, its first in the public markets since 1921 and the largest public debt deal up to that time. As a result, the *New York Times* referred to Weinberg as a "financial Alexander the Great," meaning that Weinberg was "very nearly left without any new worlds of securities to conquer." Asked whether he and Goldman could top their current successes in the future, Weinberg replied to the paper, "Maybe we'll be asked to sell bonds for the United States Government," a tongue-in-cheek response because the U.S. government required no underwriter to help it sell its securities. He said that some Wall Street competitors had "jokingly suggested" that Goldman "might be able to help the Treasury." To which, Weinberg reportedly quipped, "We would consider it for a fee."

By this time, Goldman had busted out of its 30 Pine Street headquarters and had moved into a new "ultra-modern" building at 20 Broad Street, just a stone's throw from the New York Stock Exchange. The most striking innovation of the new building, according to the *Times*, was the introduction of sixteen turret-style, vertical telephone boxes at each trading desk, which gave Goldman 1,920 private-access lines to the firm's traders at any time. The New York Telephone Company designed the new phone system especially for Goldman and its traders so that it could handle more client calls, more seamlessly than before. The other innovation worth mentioning was a vertical document filing system, which slid on tracks on the floor and comprised one thousand square feet, one-third of the space devoted to business files at Pine Street.

———

GIVEN GOLDMAN'S INCREASING prowess in the business of underwriting debt and equity securities for its growing stable of clients (thanks in large part to Weinberg's connections and board seats), it was not particularly surprising that the firm found itself enmeshed in a massive antitrust lawsuit brought by the U.S. government in October 1947 against Wall Street's seventeen most influential firms. In its complaint, the government alleged that between 1915 and 1947, these firms created "an integrated, over-all conspiracy and combination" starting in 1915 "and in continuous operation thereafter, by which" the banks " 'developed a system' to eliminate competition and monopolize 'the cream of the business' of investment banking." Indeed, even though Goldman was far from the largest or most successful of the seventeen securities firms named in the complaint—that honor probably belonged to Morgan Stanley & Co., which was listed as the lead defendant—and even though the Goldman partners did not believe the government's allegations were true, the firm was pleased nonetheless to be among those deemed to be the most powerful Wall Street firms. To have been excluded from the lawsuit—as were, say, Merrill Lynch & Co., Lazard Frères & Co., and Halsey Stuart & Co., then the largest bond underwriter—would have been worse, or so the convoluted logic went around the firm.

The crux of the government's case was that these seventeen firms conspired against the rest of the investment banking industry and their corporate clients to control the fees and other financial benefits that could be gained through the underwriting of the debt and equity securities of their corporate clients. As to the fact that executives at the corporations issuing the securities would be able to decide, at their sole discretion, which banks to hire and fire and when, the complaint alleged that to "preserve and enhance their control over the business of merchandising securities," the banks kept "control over the financial and business affairs of the issuers, by giving free financial advice to issuers, by infiltrating the boards of directors of issuers, by selecting officers of issuers who were friendly to them [and] by utilizing their influence with commercial banks with whom issuers do business."

Regarding the last point, it is essential to keep in mind that the Glass-Steagall Act of 1933 required the separation of commercial banking from investment banking by June 16, 1934. On that date, most investment banking firms, such as Goldman Sachs, chose to remain in the investment banking business. They either had very little in the way of consumer deposits—which they quickly got rid of—or had no interest in that kind of business. Those firms that were decidedly more integrated, and thus more powerful in the market—such as J. P. Morgan & Co.— were forced to choose between the two sides of the business. J. P. Morgan chose to stay in the commercial banking business and to remain a depository institution.

The other stinging allegation—that these seventeen firms used their seats on the boards of directors of their clients to win and control investment banking business—hit particularly hard at Goldman Sachs and Sidney Weinberg, who had more directorships than any other banker on Wall Street. The complaint alleged that when a banker from "one of the 17 defendant banking houses becomes a director of an issuer, this is understood by all the rest to be the equivalent of 'raising a red flag,' and thus warning the others to keep off."

These practices were said "to have gone on for almost forty years," U.S. Circuit Court judge Harold R. Medina wrote in his February 1954 ruling, "in the midst of a plethora of congressional investigations, through two wars of great magnitude, and under the very noses of the Securities and Exchange Commission and the Interstate Commerce Commission, without leaving any direct documentary or testimonial proof of the formation or continuance of the combination and conspiracy." As if his judicial leanings weren't already clear by this obvious tone of incredulity—found just nine pages into his extraordinary 417-page ruling—he added flatly, in the next sentence, "The government case depends entirely on circumstantial evidence."

———

ON SEPTEMBER 22, 1953, Judge Medina dismissed all the charges "on merits and with prejudice," effectively barring the government from further litigation against the seventeen securities firms. Medina threw the case out after hearing only the government's side, after the defense had made summary judgment motions before him to do so. A few weeks later, on October 14, he published his complete ruling, an important—if rarely viewed—distillation, preserved in amber, of the investment banking business in the United States from its origins through the first half of the twentieth century. "The best description of the business that I know of is Judge Medina's opinion," Walter Sachs said later. "That was a remarkable document. It's a document that any author of investment banking history will want to study very carefully."

Judge Medina's opinion is indeed a remarkable document. It demonstrated in vivid detail how investment banks garner business. Medina ruled that the investment banking firms did not violate the law. But his lengthy analysis raised the question of whether Wall Street's practices at that time furthered its ostensible mission—to help companies raise capital for growth—or whether much of the banks' activity was designed to increase the bank accounts of their senior partners. An activity may be legal, but is it just?

Although Goldman was not the main defendant, the antitrust case laid bare how the firm used its connections to get deals. The government's charge that these firms put their partners on the boards of directors of their clients to insure control over their future investment banking business was particularly germane to Goldman. To try to get a handle on whether these banker-directors influenced their clients' decisions over where to direct investment banking business, Judge Medina looked at all 1,117 underwritten securities issues from 1935 to 1949. The first observation he made was that a mere 140 of these underwritings, or 12.5 percent, were from issuers during this period where a partner from an investment banking house sat on the board. He further found that most of these 140 issues were underwritten by Goldman, Lehman, and Kuhn, Loeb, "the older firms who had in the early days become more or less accustomed to have a partner on the board of an issuer because of their sponsorship of the issue, and as a measure of protection for the investors to whom the securities were sold."

Medina's chart did show that of the fifty issues Goldman underwrote for its clients during this fifteen-year period, some twenty-seven of them, or 55 percent, were for clients where a Goldman partner was on the board of directors, by far the most of any of the seventeen defendants. But the judge remained unconvinced by either the government's documentary evidence or these numbers that any conspiracy existed.

As evidence for his conclusion, he cited the example of the extraordinary lengths Goldman and a smaller, regional Minneapolis investment bank, Piper, Jaffray & Hopwood, went to keep another competitor, White Weld, out of a financing for Pillsbury, the Minneapolis-based food company, a battle that lasted almost ten years. Both Piper and Goldman—in the person of Henry Bowers—had a partner on Pillsbury's board. Goldman and Piper had been "in privity with Pillsbury" according to Medina since 1927, when the two firms worked together on a financing for the company. Seven years later, in 1934, Pillsbury was thinking about refinancing $6 million of 6 percent first mortgage bonds, and quite naturally Goldman and Piper expected to win the mandate to do it and began proposing ideas for it in early 1935.

The complicating factor, though, was that Harold B. Clark, or Ben as he was known, a senior partner at White, Weld, had become a "close friend" of John S. Pillsbury, the chairman and largest shareholder of the company. Pillsbury had asked Clark to serve as a trustee for his children's trust fund, consulted him about where the boys should go to school, and kept a bunch of his money in an account—and "a very valuable one"—at White, Weld and sought his advice on a myriad of other financial matters.

Goldman fought this threat to their business ferociously, using Bowers's position on the board as a cudgel and issuing not-so-subtle threats to White, Weld.

At one point, Bowers telephoned a White, Weld partner, Faris Russell. "[A] neat little sparring match ensued," Medina observed, and then quoted from Bowers's account of the conversation from a letter that same day that Bowers wrote to Piper. "He and Benny Clark are friends of John," Bowers wrote. "I told him, of course, John would talk with him, *as with everybody,* but that I was absolutely confident that you and we could hold the business and all that White, Weld would do would be to bother us and make us do the business on a closer basis than was fair; that if White, Weld, who claimed to be high-toned people, felt that that was a sound and fine action to take in competing with other friendly houses, members of whom were on the Board of Pillsbury, it would be a surprise to me. I tried to put a little shame into him, and to leave him with a feeling that his conscience would have to be his guide." While it is rare to get a ringside seat into how the sausage is made inside an investment bank—and rarer still in 1935, no less—it is worth recalling how desperate Goldman Sachs must have been at that time to win a meaningful piece of new business in the middle of the Great Depression and in the years after the firm's reputation had been so badly sullied by the collapse of the Goldman Sachs Trading Corporation.

The battle raged on. More than two years later the deal had still not been done and Goldman and Piper were still fighting for it and trying to keep White, Weld out. On June 8, 1938, Bowers wrote to Piper that he had spoken to Pillsbury and learned that Ben Clark had introduced Pillsbury to Thomas Parkinson, the president of the Equitable Life Assurance Society, which was looking to provide Pillsbury the capital needed to refinance the mortgage securities. This was a serious threat to Goldman and Piper, for if Pillsbury ended up doing the deal with the Equitable, and Clark had provided the introduction to the Equitable, Goldman and Piper would be hard-pressed to make the case for a fee. Bowers recounted to Piper that Pillsbury "went on . . . to state that he wouldn't think of doing anything more than explain to the Equitable President your position and my position on the board, the idea being that if they do anything, or could do anything with an insurance company, we should arrange it for the Company. He asked the direct question, how could it be worked out that a refunding be arranged with an insurance company or companies and you and I be taken care of?"

In the end, Pillsbury met with Parkinson, and the Equitable refinanced Pillsbury's mortgage bonds. Unfortunately—much "to the amazement and disappointment" of Clark—White, Weld got nothing for its effort, and Goldman and Piper, Jaffray split the fee for the private placement between Pillsbury and the Equitable. The power of being in the Pillsbury boardroom for both Goldman and Piper can clearly be seen in an October 1939 letter from Bowers to Piper where he laments the possibility—being then discussed—that either Piper or Bowers, or both, might be removed from the Pillsbury board. Bowers expressed the view that he wanted to remain on the Pillsbury board "not only from my own personal point of view, but from the point of view of what seems best for the interests of G.S. & Co." and that if both he and Piper remained "we can do some more good, constructive work." Judge Medina deemed this outcome legal and fair.

In a later episode, in August 1944, Pillsbury was thinking about selling equity. Once again, White, Weld sought a piece of the action, and once again, Henry Bowers at Goldman tried to shut them out.

This time White, Weld did get an allocation of the 75,000-share equity offering—a mere 2,000 shares, or a 2.7 percent slice. From this ten-year saga at one company in the Midwest, Judge Medina concluded that this was normal, fierce competition on Wall Street. "It was downright competition of the most ruthless variety," Medina wrote.

FAR MORE COMPLICATED for Medina to parse and to defend—for it did look for a time like downright collusion—was the eighteen-year arrangement that Goldman had with Lehman Brothers for the underwriting of equity offerings. Although the explicit arrangement ended in the 1920s, they came to an "amicable" agreement in January 1926 about how the firms would split fees and clients in the future.

The document was extraordinary in that it existed at all. The idea that Goldman Sachs and Lehman Brothers—fierce competitors and archrivals for much of the second half of the twentieth century and for the first eight years of the twenty-first—would have an underwriting joint venture for so many years was a testament to the difficulty these two predominantly Jewish firms had in breaking into the established order on Wall Street at the time.

Except for a brief exchange of letters toward the end of January 1926, where Catchings, for Goldman, and Philip Lehman, for Lehman Brothers, did some tweaking to the language about how the two firms' trading accounts were exempt from the agreement, this reconfigured arrangement lasted another ten years, until it blew up in spectacular fashion. The proximate cause of the "acrimonious discussions" between the two firms, according to testimony Walter Sachs gave in July 1951, was the "division of the management fee" between them after an underwriting. The management fee was a relatively new phenomenon among underwriters, following the passage of the Securities Act of 1933, and was designed to compensate the lead underwriter for the additional work required to comply with the SEC requirements.

In a February 6, 1936, letter to "Messrs. Goldman, Sachs & Co," Lehman partner John Hancock made it clear he believed Goldman had breached their revised agreement. After referring to the written agreements from the 1920s, Hancock asserted, "We believe we have proceeded completely in accordance with these memoranda and their spirit." Then, citing recent financings Goldman had done for Brown Shoe, National Dairy, and Endicott-Johnson, Hancock wrote that they "indicate clearly that you have not felt bound by your agreements with us, in spite of the fact that no notice has as yet been given us of the termination of the arrangement to which both firms were parties. In view of the situation, we see no alternative for us but to inform you that inasmuch as the arrangement has not been controlling on you for some time, we cannot accept any longer any commitment inherent within our written arrangements which we have always assumed as controlling upon us. We feel that we have done our utmost to fulfill an arrangement which both of us had decided to continue; but we feel also that you have made further continuance of our arrangement no longer possible."

The next day, Goldman responded in writing. "We find ourselves unable to agree with the statement of the facts contained herein, but we cannot see that it will serve any useful purpose to enter into a discussion of these issues which are apparently highly controversial," Sidney Weinberg wrote on behalf of his partners. "Therefore we shall content ourselves with saying that while we cannot accept your statement of the premises upon which your action is based, we, nevertheless, accept your conclusion that the arrangement between us has been terminated."

The antipathy between the two firms reached a nadir of sorts on February 18, 1936, when Herbert Lehman, a partner at Lehman Brothers, wrote to Thomas H. McInnerney, the CEO of National Dairy Products Corporation, tendering his resignation as board member of the company and then lashed into McInnerney and the company for siding with Goldman Sachs on which firm would lead an upcoming financing. The following year, Lehman and Goldman had a similar dispute over a piece of business involving Cluett, Peabody, which Goldman also won.

In his July 1951 testimony during the antitrust trial, Sachs also described how during a discussion with General Foods about a financing, the two firms once again were acrimonious about roles and the splitting of the management fee. "This controversy annoyed the executives of the issuer," Sachs said, "who threatened to take their business elsewhere unless GS and LB got together, and may have even gone to the extent of having preliminary discussions with other bankers." Sidney Weinberg was on the board of General Foods at that time. "In the interests of peace," Sachs said, "the General Foods issue was done jointly by GS and LB."

In order to stanch the increasing animosity between the two firms, Sachs sought out William Hammerslough, a Lehman partner, to try to figure out a way of preventing future public displays of animal spirits. A new memorandum, dated June 30, 1938, divided up a new list of forty-two companies between Goldman and Lehman and parsed how they would allocate underwriting fees between the two of them should they be lucky enough to win financing business from these companies in the future. This memorandum was an effort to avoid another public incident similar to the National Dairy dispute. "The inclusion of a second house"—be it either Goldman or Lehman, depending on the client—"in a particular piece of business, and if included, its position in such business, is subject to acquiescence on the part of the Company involved and subject to pre-existing rights of any other house," the memo declared. "Both houses are to use their best efforts so that the basis of mutual participation may be as set forth above [in the memo]." The term of the new arrangement was to be a mere six months, until January 1, 1939, unless extended by the parties. The agreement was largely adhered to subsequently, with the lone exception of a financing that Goldman and Dillon, Read underwrote, in 1945, for B. F. Goodrich, the tire manufacturer, without Lehman.

Despite all of these agreements—both oral and written—between Goldman and Lehman during the thirty-two-year period, Judge Medina found "nothing in these agreements to support the government's claims of an over-all, integrated conspiracy and combination, as there is no evidence that any of the other defendant firms were parties to the arrangements between Lehman Brothers and Goldman Sachs, or that they knew of the existence of these memoranda."

Notwithstanding Medina's conclusion about this arrangement, Walter Sachs, at Goldman, and John Hancock, at Lehman Brothers, found themselves having to defend publicly the arrangement and explain to a skeptical public why they weren't conspiring together to hurt corporations seeking to finance their businesses.

In his opening statement to Judge Medina, in room 1505 of the federal courthouse in Foley Square, Henry V. Stebbins, the special assistant to the attorney general who argued the case, suggested—eerily reminiscent of words Senator Carl Levin would utter five decades later—that these bankers were playing on both sides of the ball to the detriment of their clients. "They sit on one side of the table and advise their clients on what they should sell and the price at which they should sell it," he said. "Then they go around to the other side of the table and buy it."

Stebbins's opening statement lasted four and a half days. Then Arthur Dean, a partner at Sullivan & Cromwell representing five of the defendants, including Goldman Sachs, took center stage and immediately cast doubt—as one would expect—on the government's assertions. He said he welcomed the trial because for years bankers had been essentially demonized by Congress without having a forum for presenting their side of the story.

So when Dean finally got his chance, he pushed for a dismissal of the charges against Goldman Sachs and defended the firm's honor at every opportunity. "Early in this century, automobiles, rubber tires and wheels without spokes came on the scene," he said. "Women, although they did not get the vote until 1920, were going into offices and businesses and had less time and inclination for knitting, for making their own clothes, baking, and putting up preserves. Food and meat had to be processed, canned and distributed in new ways. Store-bought clothing, including hosiery and shoes, were being produced by machine. . . . Our society was changing and Goldman, Sachs & Co. helped finance the change."

Walter Sachs, who had long worked behind the scenes at Goldman Sachs while Sidney Weinberg basked in much of the firm's glory, was the partner whose job it was to make sure Goldman did not get convicted in the antitrust trial. In December 1948, over the course of four days, he gave a lengthy deposition—running to some four hundred pages—to government attorneys during the pretrial phase of the case.

Early on in the deposition, Sachs offered an illuminating description of just how Goldman viewed an investment banker's job circa 1948. "I think that the investment banker should be a man who, by reasons of his experience and his training and his knowledge, should be in a position to give sound advice to companies, issuers, on the intricacies of finance," he said. "And he should be in a position, by reason of all these qualifications, to give sound investment advice to institutional or individual investors." The "professional" aspects of the business had led investment bankers to serve on the boards of directors of their clients and to seek out "men who are trained in such institutions" as Harvard Business School. At industrial companies, he continued, "the problems are very real: The problems of merchandising, the problems of markets. There are constantly very real problems that are coming up, and in my opinion one can only have a better knowledge and judgment as to a company's problems if you are in constant contact with them over a period of time as a director. I think it is preferable from the company's point of view and from the investing public's point of view."

Sachs explained that Goldman was very much a new-business machine. "I don't want to be facetious," he testified, "but I will say this— we have members of our organization who devote themselves almost exclusively to ferreting out opportunities of doing new business, and I would also say that of course a major part of the activity of our partners, or many of our partners, is to originate or ferret out and get new business, and we all do it at one time or another." While this seems like an obvious point—salesmen must always be selling, to paraphrase David Mamet in *Glengarry Glen Ross*—at this time on Wall Street a much preferred new-business strategy at many other firms could best be summarized as "waiting for the phone to ring" or for the business "to float in over the transom." This was not Goldman's strategy, and the firm used a series of offices outside of New York—in Chicago, in Boston, in St. Louis, and in Philadelphia, as well as having representatives in Detroit, Albany, and Buffalo—to keep in regular touch with businessmen in much of the country.

Needless to say, and despite the government's allegations in the antitrust case, there was pretty stiff competition among the various investment banking firms for business. And Goldman lost its share, despite using its growing set of connections. Indeed, in an effort to show Judge Medina that Goldman could not have colluded with the other defendants to restrain trade, during Sachs's cross-examination, Arthur Dean, his attorney at Sullivan & Cromwell, peppered him with questions about one failed underwriting after another. Remember that $75 million issue of Michigan Bell Telephone bonds from October 1948? "After the public offering price, they went down very substantially," Sachs said. "A very unfortunate incident occurred there." Goldman decided to market and sell the bonds right after AT&T had announced a $150 million bond deal at roughly the same time. Suddenly, there was too much supply and not enough demand. Many investors "sold out at a depressed price and lost quite a bit of money," he said. There was a disastrous preferred stock offering for Pure Oil in August 1937, and another "very unsuccessful" $48 million bond issue for Bethlehem Steel, and a failed September 1948 preferred stock issue for Reynolds Tobacco Company.

Generally, though, through ongoing trial and error—and through friendships honed and burnished over many years—Goldman Sachs proved itself to be masterful at exploiting its corporate relationships and turning them into substantial profits over many years for the firm's partners. Take, for instance, the firm's long association with Merck, the big German drug company. Goldman's relationship with Merck began after World War I, around 1919, when the Alien Property Custodian's office had seized the German Merck family's shares in the company and was "developing plans to dispose of those shares to American interests." With the legal advice of Alfred Jaretzki, the senior partner of Sullivan & Cromwell, George Merck, the founder of the company, worked out a plan to divest his shares through a public stock offering, which also allowed the American branch of the Merck family to get more control of it. Jaretzki brought the deal to his firm's best client, Goldman Sachs. In 1920, Goldman underwrote a successful preferred stock offering to bring the firm public. At the time, Waddill Catchings went on the board of directors of Merck (he would be replaced by Sachs in 1930). Merck remained a loyal and, as it grew, very lucrative client for Goldman.

Goldman's relationship with the May Department Stores Company was also a long and fruitful one. Sachs joined the board of the company in 1919. As a result of that assignment, he made regular trips—two or three times a year—to St. Louis in search of business opportunities at May and at other important St. Louis companies. Along with the executives at May, Sachs had also become friendly with the executives at Kaufmann Stores—a similar upscale department store chain based in Pittsburgh—and run by Edgar Kaufmann. "It was always in the back of my head that the Kaufmann Store was a store very similar in type . . . to the May Stores, and that it was geographically situated so that it was a natural thing to bring the two together," Sachs testified. For some ten years, Sachs had talked to Kaufmann about his idea of merging the two companies together. Before speaking with Kaufmann, Sachs had received the go-ahead from May, and so he knew May was interested in such a deal if he was able to interest Kaufmann. But Kaufmann had a son—Edgar Jr.—whom he wanted to have run the business and keep it independent, and so for the longest time Sachs's idea went nowhere. "Well, they cannot pay me anywhere near what I am willing to take, I am sure," Kaufmann Sr. told Sachs.

Some time later, Sachs heard that Edgar Jr. had been named an assistant curator at the Museum of Modern Art, in New York, and figured that the young man's interests had changed. When Sachs arrived at the office that morning he told his colleagues, "Here is the chance to do this deal that I have been dreaming about because he won't have that ambition anymore." Sachs's timing was perfect. There was general agreement that both sides would be interested in a deal if the parameters could be worked out.

A long negotiation ensued. "Figures were exchanged finally," Sachs recalled, "were weighed in the balance, and, in conjunction with us and with protracted discussions, an equation was finally worked out to which the two men . . . agreed in so far as they could." The deal was then brought to the respective boards of directors of the two companies. Of course, since Sachs was on the board of the May Company and Goldman was to receive a fee for its advice in crafting and negotiating the deal, Sachs recused himself from the board vote. He stayed for only the first part of the board meeting "in which I gave certain expression to my reasons for thinking this was a constructive thing." Once both boards approved the deal, "[t]hen came our share of the work," he said, "in seeing that all the mechanics were carried out correctly." Goldman continued to advise May on other acquisitions as well as other financings but, Sachs testified, in the long history of the relationship between the two firms, it wasn't until Goldman received its fee for the Kaufmann merger that the account had been a profitable one.

Turns out, this kind of thing was not atypical, a fact the government lawyers found hard to fathom. Sachs explained that often he and his partners would give advice in passing to company executives—free of charge—in anticipation of winning an M&A (mergers and acquisitions) assignment or underwriting in the future. These kinds of off-the-cuff conversations happened frequently, especially when the Goldman partner in question served on many boards at the same time, as did Sidney Weinberg and Henry Bowers. The compensation for serving on a board at that time was around fifty dollars a year. The government lawyers responded to these observations by wondering how Goldman could remain in business without getting paid for its advice. "From time to time, financing does take place with these companies," he explained, "and we make every effort to retain the relationship that we have by giving them good advice, by being sound advisers. And then when it comes time for an issuance of securities, why, we hope to be favored with it, of course."

Then, clearly playing to the audience—this was a deposition in anticipation of a serious antitrust trial after all—he said, "I cannot emphasize too strongly, perhaps, the fact that in Goldman, Sachs & Company's history there has never been an agreement of any kind as to a potential right to a future piece of financing—never."

Sachs made much of the idea that unless and until there was a "chink in the armor" of a firm's relationship with its client there often was not much sense in trying to steal clients away. This didn't mean there was any kind of tacit understanding between bankers about such things, he allowed, but rather that there was simply a well-honed sense that existing relationships between bankers and companies develop over many years and often involve close personal relationships so that it just often is not worth the precious time it would take to pry loose a potential client if there was not otherwise a reason to try to do so.

There were, of course, a number of examples where other firms tried to dislodge Goldman Sachs from its perch at a given company, only to have the Goldman partners—quite understandably—go to the greatest lengths to prevent that from happening. In one instance, in 1930, Sachs used all his muscle to prevent Dillon, Read & Co. from making inroads into Goldman's—albeit at that time, apparently still unprofitable—relationship with May Department Stores. Dillon, Read had financed Commercial Investment Trust—now known as CIT, the large consumer lender—and was close to Henry Ittelson, the CIT CEO. (This was the same CIT that Henry Goldman had invested in after he retired from the firm.) Ittelson had started in business at May, and the May family was a big investor in CIT, which was also based in St. Louis at the time.

Five years later, in 1935, Sachs had to defend Goldman again from a rear-guard action by a competitor seeking to make inroads with Brown Shoe Company, another St. Louis–based client where Sachs was on the board. This time the incursion came from Stifel, Nicolaus & Co. Brown Shoe was considering doing a financing and had approached other under-writers about their interest in potentially leading such a deal for the company. "I think it was about this time that I jumped on a train and went out there," Sachs said, "and used every effort to persuade the Brown Shoe Company to do business with us rather than with someone else. I might amplify that statement by saying that in the depth of the depression they were one of the concerns that were very restive in their relationship with us, and I at that time, and subsequently, and I think successfully, made every effort to keep their business." In the end, Goldman and Lehman did the $4 million bond deal alone, without Stifel, Nicolaus.

In May 1951, Sachs took the stand after the government entered large swaths of his deposition into the court record.

Sachs considered himself "in a rather conceited way" a good wit-ness on behalf of Goldman. He enjoyed watching Judge Medina up close and considered him "very intelligent," in effect someone he thought Wall Street could do business with and therefore was worth betting on to do the right thing and find in its favor. "My own position, Sidney Weinberg's position, our firm's position was absolutely adamant from the word go," he said. "I never for a moment was willing to listen to any question of a consent decree. . . . I took the position that the relationship between a banking house and its clients was of a quasi-professional nature. As I say, I would never listen to the question of any compromise." He said that he and Weinberg used to tell the firm's associates as well as bankers at other firms, "We will never submit to this." Goldman, though, was prepared to continue fighting the government if Medina ruled against the industry. Not only would Goldman pursue an appeal, Sachs allowed, but he also said Goldman had asked its clients to testify on its behalf—and the clients had agreed to do it.

The antitrust trial against Wall Street lasted some three years, more than 309 courtroom days. The trial transcript ran to nearly 24,000 pages and contained nearly 6 million words. Some 108,000 pages were printed related to the case. To defend themselves, the seventeen firms spent mil-lions on legal fees, estimated by the *New York Times* to be $6 million. (The government reportedly spent around $3 million.) First Boston alone spent $1 million on its lawyers; according to Walter Sachs, Goldman spent $700,000 for Sullivan & Cromwell—at a time when the firm's total capital was around $6 million, a tidy percentage indeed. Goldman never considered settling with the government or discussing the possibility of signing a consent decree. Goldman, Sachs said, was "absolutely firm because we thought [settling] would be a mistake. We felt confident that having a highly intelligent judge, the question would be presented properly and clearly and he would understand, and that the result would be the result that, as we saw it, should have been."

Goldman Sachs made a smart bet. Indeed, Medina ended up announcing his decision at a procedural hearing because he feared that his written opinion—at that moment nearly 80 percent complete—would leak out. So at the hearing, he took out a yellow legal pad and his fountain pen and sketched out his decision. He surprised the forty or so people in the courtroom that day. "I have come to the settled conviction and accordingly find that no such combination, conspiracy and agreement as is alleged in the complaint, nor any part thereof, was ever made, entered into, conceived, constructed, continued or participated in by these defendants, or any of them," he wrote on his legal pad in throwing out the case. "Since there was no combination, the monopoly charges fall of their own weight."

Needless to say, Wall Street breathed a collective sigh of relief that Medina had ruled in its favor. Despite the years of headlines and the huge number of documents produced, some of them unflattering, there would be no changes—zero—to the way investment bankers performed the business of financing the exploding postwar growth of American industry. As for Goldman, Medina found the firm pursued "a competitive policy which was in every sense of the term aggressive" and then found, explicitly, that it "was at no time a party to any scheme or plan involving deferring to any other investment banking house, or holding off because of 'satisfactory relations' between an issuer and any of the defendant firm or any other firm named or not named as an alleged co-conspirator. . . . On the contrary, there are indications that Goldman Sachs even transcended the bounds of reasonable competitive effort in its endeavor to get every piece of business it could possibly secure, within the limits of its personnel and its resources."

SACHS WAS CONVINCED that the trial had vindicated the investment banking profession, that its future was exceedingly bright, and that it would continue to attract the best and the brightest from the nation's top business schools. "I think there's a realization . . . that the investment banking community, the profession, performs a perfectly enormous service for American industry," he said.

More to the point, he contended, in an argument familiar to modern ears, "the industry today earns every dollar that it gets," an idea he put forth "without fear of contradiction." "You have to maintain an organization year in and year out of highly trained experts," he said. "[Y]ou have to pay selling commissions to your sales force." He said much was made in the press about the seemingly high fees—"of four or five hundred thousand dollars"—an investment banker received for underwriting a deal, but that ignores that the banker has "paid selling commissions. They've paid printing expenses. They've paid for telegraph and telephone. They've paid for these highly trained men who've come out of the Harvard Business School, or I trust, out of the Columbia Business School, or the Wharton School—men who are career men, men who are highly paid."

Sachs noted that after the Depression, graduates of Harvard Business School "turned away from Wall Street" and sought jobs instead in corporate America. "Now, of course, in the more recent active years, they're coming back. We've gotten many of our most able men from the Harvard Business School. We get every year men from the top third. Many of them have stayed to become partners." Others stayed at Goldman for a number of years and then went into other corporations, where they often showed loyalty to Goldman, resulting in new business for the firm. "Needless to say, there's friendship there for Goldman, Sachs and Company, because they got this training with us."

He assumed Goldman would continue to attract the best and the brightest—men. "It's a wonderful field for young men, it seems to me," he said, "just as chemistry is a wonderful field and a lot of other things are wonderful fields. He told these young men, using a homely phrase that my uncle Henry Goldman [used]: 'Money is always fashionable.' That was one phrase, and the other was, 'You must do what is fashionable.' By that he meant that you must gear your financing to what is the order of the day."

And that business would boom, with the next ten years being "enormously active years in investment banking." Sachs said in April 1956, "[A]nd it's easy to see why. You only have to read the daily press to see the enormous amounts of money that industry requires for the building of plants and for development." But the boom would not be uninterrupted. "We're sure to have that," he continued. "I don't believe—and I may be wrong—that we're going to have a 1929, 1930 debacle or depression. But business surges up and business surges back somewhat. I don't think there's any doubt about that. [T]he greatest factor is the continued growth in population, and the growth in population means that more consumer goods are wanted, and if more consumer goods are wanted, you've got to build factories to produce those consumer goods. It's just as simple as that, it seems to me." He said the "reason for 1929 was easy to see—[t]here was cheap money, and it was profitable from a tax point of view for people to create debt. Now, you go along that road up to a certain point, but that takes care of itself in a certain way, because if your debt, in relation to your assets, gets too high, you have to take another route." At that end of World War II, Goldman had more equity capital—$6.5 million—than all but seven other investment banks. Merrill Lynch had the most capital—$11.4 million—followed by Wertheim & Co., with $10.6 million, and Loeb, Rhoades, with $10.3 million. Lehman Brothers had $9.9 million; Bear Stearns had $6.9 million, just above Goldman. After Goldman on the list was Lazard Frères & Co., with $6.447 million. Morgan Stanley, twenty-sixth on the list, had $2.9 million of its partners' capital in the firm. Sachs had a view about how Goldman would capture more of the pie. Sachs's aim, essentially, was to find companies where competitors did not already have a toehold and then provide the best-quality service possible, ensuring the firm would have the best chance of winning business and then repeat business. "Industrialists naturally go back to banking houses that have done a good job . . . ," he said. "If you have a lawyer or a doctor that has served you well, you're not going to go around and have one man compete against another. You're pretty apt to go back to the same lawyer. You're pretty apt to go back to the same doctor. And in the same way, you're pretty apt to go back to the same banker." At the same time that Goldman "tried to keep our own fences well mended," he said, it tried to exploit weaknesses at other firms. "We are constantly on the look-out for weaknesses."

In Sachs's 1956 musings about how to win investment banking business and its future emerge the first stirrings of a way of doing business—call it this notion of being "long-term greedy"—that would form the bedrock of the Goldman Sachs partnership for the next fifty years, even as it transformed itself into a global behemoth that would be unrecognizable to Sidney Weinberg and Walter Sachs.

CHAPTER 5

"WHAT IS
INSIDE INFORMATION?"

On April 1, 1957, when Goldman moved to 20 Broad Street, the *New York Times* also included a large photograph of the firm's latest technological acquisition—the previously mentioned telephone-turret trading desk designed especially for the firm by New York Telephone. Essentially, the innovation was little more than a group of bulky, vertical rotary phones with 120 different access lines and the ability—by pushing a button—to tap into the conversations of any of their fellow traders on the desk "for greater flexibility in transacting business." This was a material innovation at the time. In the picture, thirteen Goldman traders can be seen sitting at their "turrets," and every one of them has on his suit jacket. Standing behind one of the traders and dressed elegantly in a suit and pocket square, with a tight-collared shirt and a tie bar under the knot of his tie and slicked-back black hair, was Gustave Lehmann Levy, forty-seven years old, and the partner then in charge of the firm's fledgling trading efforts. The athletic, nearly six-foot-tall Levy was looking particularly patrician that day. Although he was anything but that, there was no mistaking his importance to Goldman Sachs. A year earlier, during one of his "reminiscences" about his banking career, Walter Sachs had described Levy as the firm's "new brilliant genius" with "a great flair for the security business" and then added that Levy was "the fourth genius in the firm."

Despite Levy's appearance in that cleverly staged photo, there was nothing the slightest bit polished about his upbringing. Born in May 1910 in New Orleans, Levy was the only son of Sigismond, known as Sigmund, Levy, a box manufacturer, and Bella Lehmann Levy. Somehow the fact of Levy's father being a box manufacturer got transformed over the years. "His father was a middle-class doctor," was what L. Jay Tenenbaum, who for years worked directly for Levy at Goldman, remembered being told.

In June 1924, Sigmund Levy died at age forty-seven. Sigmund Levy's death brought some insurance money to the family, and Bella moved them to Paris, where Gus attended the American School. "She wanted to show the people in New Orleans that the Levys were some-body," Tenenbaum said when asked why the family moved to Paris. He said Bella was trying to marry off one of the daughters to European roy-alty, but that did not go so well. She was "sort of an ugly sister to tell you the truth . . . ," Tenenbaum said. "Gus spent six months going to bars and doing nothing," which was quickly decided was not best for him. "He was unsupervised and undisciplined," according to *The New Crowd*, Judith Ramsey Ehrlich and Barry Rehfeld's 1989 book about Jewish bankers on Wall Street. "His favorite pastime was skipping off to the racetrack instead of attending school." In 1927, the family moved back to New Orleans, at least in part so that Levy could attend Tulane University, where he tried out for the football team. But Gus was not much of a stu-dent and his mother could not afford the tuition. "His mother was a real flake," according to Betty Levy Hess, Levy's daughter. "He had to go to work to support the family. His father had died . . . and his mother took the kids to Europe and spent all the money." Levy left Tulane after three months and headed to New York City in 1928 to find work if he could. His mother became a seamstress and lived in the Bronx. Levy lived at the Young Men's Hebrew Association on Ninety-second Street and Lexing-ton Avenue and was so poor that at one point he stiffed the Y on a two-dollar balance. Tenenbaum remembered Levy always telling him, "I had two dollars in my pocket. That's all I had, that's all I had was two dollars and lived at the Y."

His first job in New York was as a runner on Wall Street in Novem-ber 1928. "It was the thing to do in those days," he told the *Times* in a 1961 interview. The writer then added the thought—which obviously had come from Levy—"His decision to make Wall Street his career is not too surprising, since he is distantly related to the Lehman family." (His mother was not, in fact, related to the Lehman Brothers clan.) He started as a runner at Newborg & Company, a small brokerage located on Broad-way, but quickly worked his way up to being an assistant in the firm's arbitrage department as well as a trader. He attended New York Univer-sity at night but never graduated from there or from any college. He later told a *New York Times* reporter he was one of the few people not to lose money in the 1929 Crash. "I didn't have any money to lose," he said. The 1930 census showed that Bella, Gus, and Rose, his sister, lived in Man-hattan and that Gus, age twenty, was a "broker" in "art" and "bronze," but without any elaboration.

In 1931, in the aftermath of the Crash, Newborg's trading department went out of business, and Levy left to join a "two-man shop in Wall Street" named Pringle & Company, where he stayed "for about a year" and worked as a securities trader. He also told the newspaper that this was when he roomed at the Y. "It may be emotion," Levy said, "but the Y gave me more than a room. It gave me friendship and confidence in myself at a time when I needed it badly." In 1933, he heard that Goldman—still reeling from the Trading Corporation scandal—was looking for a young trader, a job that paid $27.50 per week, or $1,400 a year. "With a friend's help," the *Times* reported, Levy "landed it." He began at Goldman on the foreign bond desk and then moved over to the arbitrage desk, working for Edgar Baruc, a cousin of Bernard Baruch, under Walter Sachs, where he contributed a "wealth of ideas" and "added substantial profits to what would have been otherwise very lean years." His job was to buy and sell foreign securities. "I was known as a foreign arbitrageur," he explained. The next year, Levy married Janet Wolf, a chorus girl and the daughter of Alec Wolf, a limited partner at Goldman from 1935 to 1945. They had two children, Peter and Betty.

Walter Sachs put Levy in charge of the firm's relationships with the New York Stock Exchange as well as its arbitrage business, which the legendary mergers and acquisitions banker at Lazard, Felix Rohatyn, described to Congress in 1969 as a business "age-old in concept and execution [that] represents essentially the hedged short-term investment of funds at fairly high risk with commensurate rewards."

According to *The New Crowd*, "Arbitrage as a form of trading had a long history dating back to medieval times, when Venetian merchants traded interchangeable currencies to profit from price differentials." Ehrlich and Rehfeld wrote that Levy "led the way from traditional to risk arbitrage," where "arbs" bought "shares in companies being reorganized or merged into other companies, based on the premise that if the transaction was completed, they would be holding a new stock worth considerably more than their investment. It was not a game for the timid, but the payoffs could be huge." In his congressional testimony, Rohatyn described how the game was played. "The classic example in present-day markets is the arbitrage of a merger between two publicly traded companies after the exchange values have been announced," he said. "Theoretically, since one security is soon to be exchanged at a specific ratio for other securities, the two values should be identical but for reasons enumerated later they are not." Among these reasons, he explained, were "abrupt changes in securities and money markets," "various warranties and other 'outs' in the merger agreement," "governmental opposition," and "shareholder opposition." He continued, "The arbitrageur is willing to take the risk that the transaction will go through and to profit by the difference between the present market and the ultimate realized value."

According to Charles Ellis in his book about the firm, by the end of the 1930s, Levy had already made his first million dollars. "Despite a distinctive lisp that complicated the bayou drawl," Ellis wrote, Levy used his "aptitude for math, extraordinary memory, ability to connect with many, many people, and capacity for long hours of highly concentrated hard work" to get ahead at the firm in the years after the Trading Corporation scandal. With the advent of World War II in Western Europe "and the opportunities in arbitraging of foreign bonds diminished," the *Times* wrote, "Mr. Levy became active in arbitraging of railroad reorganization securities and of convertible debentures."

While largely profitable, Levy's focus on trading in risky railroad and utility bonds was not a business with which Sidney Weinberg, or Goldman Sachs for that matter, had much familiarity or interest. Levy "had collected a group of rough-and-tumble entrepreneurial clients that Weinberg thought of as ragtag," according to former partner Roy Smith. Levy's bets also required capital—and tied it up for potentially long periods of time—unlike an equity or debt underwriting, which generally used capital only sparingly (during the short period between purchasing the securities from an issuer and then selling them to investors), or advising on a merger or an acquisition, which required no capital whatsoever. Since Goldman's capital at the time was modest—around $9 million in the early 1950s—and it came from the partners' wallets, there was necessarily plenty of caution about how and when it was used and for what purposes. This led to a natural tension between Weinberg, the ultimate investment banker, and Levy, the younger, equally ambitious and hardworking trader and arbitrageur. For instance, in an interview Weinberg gave in 1967, he noted that the $100,000 in capital he invested when he became a Goldman partner in early 1927 came from the money he had earned as a banker. "None of it was from trading," he said. "I never traded." He then proudly reiterated that he was an "investment banker."

Sandy Lewis—a onetime Wall Street arbitrageur and the son of Salim L. "Cy" Lewis, a longtime senior partner at Bear Stearns & Co.—knew Gus Levy from the time he was a child growing up in Park Avenue splendor. Gus Levy and Cy Lewis were very close friends, in large part because they shared many of the same interests, whether playing golf or bridge, supporting Jewish philanthropic causes around New York City, or making money through arbitrage.

Cy Lewis's big break at Bear Stearns came after the bombing of

Pearl Harbor, when the United States decided the time had come to enter World War II. "The war came and Roosevelt needed to arm the nation and deliver whatever he needed to the factories and then take the product to the ports and get it out of here," Sandy Lewis said. "He was trying to produce airplanes, tanks, trucks, millions of things. They had to seize the railroads and force traffic over the railroads and make sure that the railroads were working just for the government to move product. You had to make sure you got it when you needed it. This was war. They broke the railroads. They put credit controls on. You couldn't borrow money." Cy Lewis noticed that before Roosevelt commandeered the railroads for the war effort, railroad bonds were trading at par because interest payments were still being made. "But, all of a sudden, they can't pay the coupon," Sandy Lewis said. "So they start trading what is called 'flat.' You can buy and sell a rail bond any way you please, but the coupon's not accruing. It's dead. . . . If you buy it, you can call it a future and maybe it'll be worth something someday." With these railroad bonds no longer paying interest, they were trading as low as five cents on the dollar. Lewis started to think about whether to buy the bonds at these severely depressed prices. He figured either Armageddon was imminent—in which case nothing much would matter—or the United States would end up winning the war and the country would desperately need its railroads back to rebuild and supply the victorious nation. In the latter instance, railroad bonds bought at a steep discount during the war would be worth a fortune.

Cy Lewis had a great influence on Gus Levy. He encouraged Levy to trade in distressed railroad bonds and in other forms of arbitrage, including so-called block trading—the buying and selling of large blocks of stock, ideally at a profit—and in so-called merger arbitrage, which as Rohatyn described was the trading in the stocks of companies involved in corporate mergers, generally after the mergers had been announced publicly.

Many institutional shareholders that owned the shares of companies involved in mergers often chose to sell those shares into the market—shares would trade up to near the offer price after a merger had been announced—since the time and risk involved in waiting often many months for a merger to close to get slightly more cash or stock was not generally worth doing. Merger arbs were willing to buy the stock being sold quite simply because they hoped to make an attractive return on the money invested. They were willing to take the chance a deal might not close, or the financial consideration might change unfavorably, in the hope of making money on their bet. There were risks, of course—if they bought the stock of a company being taken over and then the deal failed to close, such a mistake could be devastating financially. But such mishaps were rare, and experts in the art of merger arbitrage did their best to avoid them.

Why Cy Lewis would give away one valuable trading idea after another to a competitor—albeit someone who was also a friend—may never be known for sure. Perhaps it was just friendship, perhaps it helped create a market for the products Lewis was selling.

In 1941, with the United States on the verge of entering World War II, Levy was anxious to see action. He did not have to go to war because by then he had two children. But he was determined to do it. "I'm goin' in," he reportedly told his wife, and then he arranged to become a mission observer in the Civil Air Patrol. Levy was a pilot who used to fly his own Stinson Voyager single-engine plane. He hoped that experience would get him a gig flying fighter planes during the war. But it was not sufficient. "I didn't have enough experience to qualify as a pilot," he once told the *New York Times,* "and at thirty-two, I was too old for training. I ended up as a lieutenant colonel in the ground office of the Air Force in Europe." He was in the war for twenty-six months.

While Levy was off at war, his colleague in the arbitrage department, Baruc, remained behind at Goldman to try to keep whatever meager business the firm had moving along. When Levy returned to Goldman after the war, in November 1945, he and Baruc resumed their work together in the firm's arbitrage department and, according to Walter Sachs, "built one of the most active over-the-counter trading departments on Wall Street." Levy became a Goldman partner on January 1, 1946. Al Feld, who started working at Goldman as an office boy in July 1933, recalled how skillful Levy was at making money from trading railroad and utility bonds. "Gus was very smart, and an innovator," he told Ellis. "He built a good business because he recognized the opportunity in all the when-issued paper that came out on the big railroad and public utility financings of the 1940s. And he built a reputation for making good markets—in size. And if he had to take a loss, he took it."

Among Levy's best clients when he returned to Goldman after the war were two Dallas, Texas, brothers, the Murchisons—John D. and Clint W. Jr.—heirs to a Texas oil fortune established by their father, Clint W. Murchison Sr. Levy and Goldman's involvement with the Murchison brothers had its origins in the March 1933 bankruptcy filing of the Missouri Pacific Railroad.

The Missouri Pacific bankruptcy went on for twenty-three years, making it one of the longest running on record. During that time, investors could buy and sell its debt or buy and hold it, with an eye toward getting control of the company when Missouri Pacific emerged from bankruptcy in the hands of its former creditors. Sometime after the war, the Murchison brothers became the principal owners of the general mortgage bonds of Missouri Pacific. They were recommended to Levy and Goldman Sachs since they "were seeking the assistance of a Wall Street arbitrageur . . . ," the *Times* reported, "and Mr. Levy . . . is generally regarded as tops in the field." The article then explained that "an arbitrageur is one who deals in equivalents of currencies, securities and the like. He stands between the two parties in transactions involving equivalents and guesses"—guesses!—"how the opinions that each man has of what the other man wants will vary. If he guesses right he can make a great deal of money. If he guesses wrong he doesn't stay in the arbitrage business very long because the sums involved generally are too large." The paper noted that Levy had been an arbitrageur since he joined Goldman in 1933 and "by guessing right he has made a great deal of money."

The *Times* observed that during the long pendency of the Missouri Pacific bankruptcy, there "were plenty of opportunities for arbitrage transactions in the securities" since the railroad's bonds "were to be exchangeable for other securities of the to-be reorganized company. Because of the uncertainty that the reorganization would be effected as proposed[,] the bankrupt railroad's bonds often sold at a variance from" what the financial experts involved with the bankruptcy predicted they might be worth when, and if, the company ever emerged from bankruptcy. "The Murchisons and other investors all the through the years were quick to take advantage of the price differences . . . whenever it appeared to be to their advantage." Levy helped the Murchisons with their buying and selling and with their analysis—guessing—about the value of the railroad's bonds.

As would be expected from a good client, after their success trading the Missouri Pacific bonds, the Murchison brothers stayed in touch with Levy and Goldman Sachs. Soon, they had teamed up again in the quest of a bigger prize: the Murchisons wanted to get control of Allegheny Corporation, and they asked Levy to help them pull it off. There was nothing the slightest bit friendly about the Murchisons' proxy battle for control of Allegheny, and Levy and Goldman were right in the middle of it. (A decade or so later, in the early 1970s, Goldman would often proclaim that it would never get involved in a hostile takeover. "We've got a policy that we don't participate in unfriendly takeovers, as either a manager or as a consultant," Levy told *Institutional Investor* in November 1973, as if the Allegheny battle had never happened. Or as if Levy had never been elected to the board of Hunt Foods in August 1963 and then advised its chairman, Norton Simon, on his 1964 unfriendly effort to get a seat for Levy on the board of ABC, the television network, after Simon bought one hundred thousand shares of ABC stock.)

Allegheny was owned by two financiers, Robert R. Young and Allan P. Kirby, who wrested control of the company from the Ball family in 1942. The *Times* described Allegheny as "a heap of du——, with a jewel or two hidden in the debris."

Young and Kirby had used proceeds from asset sales to diversify Allegheny's holdings, including buying control of the New York Central Railroad, the nation's second largest, and Investors Diversified Services, Inc. (IDS), the Minneapolis-based mutual fund business. Allegheny also owned 51 percent of Missouri Pacific's Class B stock— postreorganization—and had a $20 million investment in Webb & Knapp, Inc., a real-estate company. "The Murchison-Kirby relationship," the *Times* noted, "began on a note of hearty common interest" during Kirby's proxy battle, in 1954, against the Vanderbilt family for control of the New York Central Railroad. Young and Kirby asked Clint Murchison Sr. and his longtime partner, Sid Richardson, to buy eight hundred thousand shares of New York Central and vote them in favor of the Young and Kirby takeover. Murchison and Richardson complied. In return for their support, or so it seemed, in 1955 the two Murchison brothers "obtained control" of IDS through a stock deal with Allegheny engineered by Young and Kirby.

But in January 1958, using a 20-gauge shotgun in the billiard room of his twenty-five-room oceanfront Palm Beach mansion, the "flamboyant" Young committed suicide. He was sixty years old and said to be suffering from "melancholy and depression" brought on by the recession of 1957, which had hurt Allegheny's businesses. Holding the shotgun with his knees, he had fired both barrels at his head at around 10:00 a.m., two hours after eating his normal breakfast. The mansion's staff, which had not heard any shots fired, became concerned about Young's whereabouts after he failed to show up for an appointment. Five days later, Kirby took control of Allegheny. In 1959, Allegheny's public shareholders filed suit, arguing that control of IDS had been given to the Murchison brothers "for the favors rendered by their father to Mr. Young and Mr. Kirby."

To settle the lawsuit, the Murchisons agreed to return control— through a 47.5 percent stake—of IDS to Allegheny. The Murchisons retained a 17 percent stake in IDS. The Murchisons, Kirby, and the Young estate paid another $3 million together to Allegheny. But, after the settlement, the Murchisons found themselves suddenly "frozen out" of the affairs of IDS, and they were not pleased. In an effort to strengthen their hand, the Murchisons paid Young's widow $10.2 million for the estate's stake in Allegheny. The Murchisons thought owning a large stake in Allegheny would get them more influence on IDS. But Kirby, resentful of the Murchisons' hostile act, started an investigation into the way they had managed IDS and asked for their cooperation in the investigation. When the Murchisons refused to help, Kirby kicked them off the IDS board.

Incensed, the Murchisons with Levy's help began a hugely public and hostile proxy fight in September 1960 to seize control of Allegheny from Kirby. According to the *Times*'s account of the nine-month proxy battle, Levy was the Murchisons' "principal banker-adviser" and played a "quiet, powerful role" in the fight. In the end, despite the Murchisons' owning only 2 million of the 9.8 million Allegheny shares outstanding— and Kirby owning 3 million shares—the Murchisons were able to get other shareholders, including no doubt Goldman Sachs, to vote in their favor in sufficient numbers to get an 855,000-vote majority. In May 1961, the Murchisons took control of Allegheny after getting five shareholder votes for every four votes received by Kirby and his supporters. The fight was believed to be one of the largest and most contentious to have occurred to that time.

After taking control of Allegheny, the Murchisons relieved Kirby of his duties as the company's chairman and CEO. Kirby left with a fortune estimated at $300 million, making him one of the wealthiest men in America.

Kirby, then sixty-nine years old, could have simply retired to his twenty-seven-room mansion in Harding Township, New Jersey, or to his "chateau" in Easton, Pennsylvania, or to "any of his other three homes," but instead he set about trying to regain control of Allegheny. After all, he still owned 31 percent of the company. Two years and another $10.5 million spent buying up more Allegheny shares, Kirby succeeded in getting back control of the company from the Murchisons with the help of well-placed allies. Of the then 6.7 million outstanding Allegheny shares, Kirby had control of 5.9 million after the votes in another proxy fight had been tallied. When asked why he had bothered, he told a reporter for the *New York Times,* "Pride. Family pride. As nearly as I can remember until the proxy fight with the Murchisons in 1961, I never got licked. I was very upset."

———

EDGAR BARUC—Levy's original mentor in the arbitrage business at Goldman—had died suddenly in 1952, leaving Levy on his own to run the group. By then, though, Levy had more than surpassed Baruc as a revenue generator and in importance to the Goldman partnership. Over time, Baruc had become Levy's assistant. When Baruc died, Levy quickly concluded he needed new help and set about hiring someone from the outside to work with him.

Around that time, Levy was playing golf in Boca Raton, Florida, with Harry Tenenbaum, who along with Paul Peltason had started Peltason Tenenbaum Company, a small brokerage in St. Louis, and Levy told Tenenbaum that he needed an assistant. "I offered the job to John Weinberg, Sidney's son, but he turned me down," Levy told Tenenbaum. "He wants to stay in his dad's end of the business, in investment banking." Tenenbaum asked Levy if he would be interested in hiring his son, L. Jay.

"Don't you want him?" Levy asked.

"Not if he can work for you," Tenenbaum said.

"Send him in," Levy replied.

L. Jay Tenenbaum studied mechanical engineering at Vanderbilt, but in 1943 he enlisted in the army and went through infantry school. He became a second lieutenant, was sent immediately overseas, and served with the Tenth Mountain Division, which was comprised of soldiers with expertise in skiing and surviving in winter terrain. Tenenbaum became a leader and had, at one point, forty men reporting to him. He was twenty-one years old. At the beginning of 1945, he saw action but soon the war was over. "I was in combat for six, seven months," he said. "I ended up with two Purple Hearts, a Bronze Star and a Silver Star."

When he got out of the army, he was stationed at Fort Ord, California, on the Monterey Peninsula. At that time, Tenenbaum was a scratch golfer—Fort Ord had one beautiful eighteen-hole course—and was playing the Pebble Beach course nearby. It was Christmastime and his parents were visiting him. After a round of nearly flawless golf, Tenenbaum told his father he wanted to join the PGA Tour. "He said, 'You damn fool. You can't beat anybody, all those guys, Snead, Demeret, Nelson, Hogan. You're going to go to work.'"

Tenenbaum had no idea what to do at Goldman Sachs, and Levy had neither the patience nor the interest in suggesting things for him to do, let alone teaching him the arbitrage business, Goldman Sachs style. "I joined him April 1, 1953," Tenenbaum said. "I found out I'm going to be his assistant. Well, I'd say, 'Gus, what could I do for you?' He said, 'L. Jay, leave me alone. I'm busy.' Then I didn't know what to do with myself." At one point, early on, Tenenbaum asked Levy if he could write a letter for him and Levy suggested that he "give a letter"—as they used to say in the old days—to his secretary, Charlotte Kamp. Tenenbaum took Levy's advice. "Charlotte, will you take a letter?" he asked her. "She said, 'Will you take a walk?'"

Tenenbaum's first break came when he ran into one of his parents' friends from Palm Beach at the Parke-Bernet Gallery, in New York. They talked for a bit and Tenenbaum said he was in the arbitrage department at Goldman. After a few more conversations, the friend agreed to give Tenenbaum $3 million to invest for him. He also introduced Tenenbaum to other wealthy Jewish refugees who were looking for a safe place to keep their money. "Instead of assisting Gus, I became a salesman because he gave me nothing to do," he said. "The reason was Gus absolutely had no what you'd call 'managerial experience.' He was a guy who could do things himself, and do them well, but no managerial experience." Tenenbaum became the second-best salesman at Goldman Sachs after Jerry McNamara, whose best client was the Catholic Archdiocese of New York. "I had all my Jewish refugees and I couldn't top him," he explained. "But, I was doing quite well. I was taking home two hundred and fifty, three hundred thousand dollars a year. I had a percentage of the arbitrage department."

In 1959, Sidney Weinberg decided unilaterally to make partners a number of men, including Tenenbaum, who had been assistants. Other firms weren't poaching them. They weren't producing huge amounts of revenue. One day they were assistants; the next day they were partners. "It was a Weinberg decision, I guess because he was the guy," Tenenbaum said. "It wasn't Gus . . . I was never told, 'L. Jay, you've earned it.' I wasn't even made a partner to do what I was doing. I was a salesman." By this time, Tenenbaum lived at 983 Park Avenue and had joined the Century Country Club, in Purchase, New York, a favorite of Levy and Weinberg's.

While Tenenbaum was no longer a scratch golfer—"I didn't carry scratch," he said—he was still very good. "I won the club championship a couple of times and was in the finals for about four or five times," he said. But given the way the economics worked—which was typical of Wall Street partnerships at the time—it turned out that making these men partners was a smart decision for the firm because Goldman was able to pay them less, as partners getting a slice of the profits, than as nonpartners getting a slice of the revenue they generated. "Now I become partner," Tenenbaum explained. "What was the deal? I got a salary of forty thousand dollars a year. I got one point five percent of Goldman's bottom line profits, which were what, ten million dollars? So, one point five percent is one hundred and fifty thousand dollars"—which had to be kept in the firm's capital account—"and forty thousand dollars to live on. And I'm making two hundred fifty, three hundred thousand dollars as a salesman. What kind of deal was that?" Levy once explained the Goldman partnership economics: "We've got a hard and fast rule. We pay salaries—modest by today's salary levels. On top of that, we pay six percent interest on capital. On the profit at the end of the year, we pay partners' taxes. The balance stays in the firm. That's been the success secret of the firm. It enabled us to go along without feeling a capital pinch, even after all the Sachses got out or died."

When asked about the apparent dichotomy between the "modest" salary and supposed glamour of Wall Street, and the perception that everyone there was—on a relative basis anyway—getting rich, Levy said, "But don't forget, the partners do have capital in the firm. They get their interest on that. So let's say a guy gets forty thousand dollars salary and has half a million in capital. On that he gets thirty thousand dollars interest. And the firm pays his taxes . . . that's money really net to him." He said Goldman partners were not allowed to trade securities on margin or sign for a loan and were not allowed to borrow money, except with the express permission of the firm's Management Committee and then only to buy a house or to buy insurance. "You cannot borrow money to buy stocks or for any other purpose," he said.

Tenenbaum was part of a group of five young men that included Jim Robertson, Chuck Grannin, Jim Callahan, and Arthur Altschul who were made partner seemingly overnight but saw their compensation cut. "I'm living on forty thousand dollars and borrowing money at 983 Park and borrowing money from my dad to live on," Tenenbaum said. "That went on for two years because at the end of two years they redo the partnership percentages."

When the two years was up, Sidney Weinberg called Tenenbaum to come see him in his office. "Sidney Weinberg was the omnipotent," he said. When Tenenbaum walked into the office, Weinberg had on his pince-nez glasses and, looking over them, told Tenenbaum that—thanks to Weinberg—he and his gang of five were going to have their partnership percentages increased to 2 percent, from 1.5 percent, a 33 percent increase. "What do you think of that?" Weinberg wanted to know. "Mr. Weinberg, I don't like it," Tenenbaum told him. "I'm either better than those four guys or I'm worse, but I ain't the same, and I don't like it." Understandably, Weinberg was taken aback. Nobody talked to him that way. But, to Weinberg's credit, he did not fire Tenenbaum on the spot. "He said to me, 'Keep your nose clean and see me in two years,'" Tenenbaum recalled. "In two years, I jumped all four of them."

Part of the way Tenenbaum was able to get ahead at Goldman was to be a self-starter and to make it up as he went along. Levy, as he certainly knew well by this point, was not going to give him any direction—certainly not on any consistent basis—leaving him to be opportunistic about getting his own clients and building a business, even though technically he was Levy's bag carrier in the arbitrage department. Occasionally, Levy would bark an order at him. "Gus says to me one day: 'We need an insurance stock trader.'" Tenenbaum recalled. "I said, 'We do?' He says, 'We do. What are you doing about it?' I said, 'Gus, I'm supposed to do something?' He said, 'What the hell am I paying you for?' So I went out and hired Rudy Russo. I got an insurance stock trader."

Another day, quite randomly, Levy asked Tenenbaum if he had seen the news about two companies that had agreed to merge. Levy wanted to know if Tenenbaum had figured out a way to make money arbitraging the deal, something he had never done to that point even though—again—he worked for Levy in the arbitrage department. "You usually do it," he told Levy.

"Can't you see I'm busy?" Levy barked. "I'm doing all these other things."

"You want me to do the arb?" Tenenbaum asked.

"Certainly I do," Levy replied.

"So now I find out I'm an arbitrageur guy," Tenenbaum said.

———

WHETHER TENENBAUM COULD see the bigger picture or not, clearly what was happening at Goldman in the late 1950s and early 1960s was that Weinberg was slowly coming to terms with his own mortality—which he never quite did, actually—and with the need to create a new generation of leaders at the firm. As much as Weinberg was reluctant to allow Levy's business of committing the firm's valuable capital to arbitrage deals, or for trading with clients, or for its own account, he was growing increasingly powerless to prevent Levy not only from pursuing that business but also from taking increasing charge of the firm. The truth was that Levy was making the firm good money by "guessing" correctly time and time again, and Weinberg's investment banking clients were not generating as much money for the firm as they once had done. Increasingly, Weinberg could not deny Levy, as painful as it was for him to admit. This same scenario has played itself out all over Wall Street, especially after World War II as firms started making more and more money and the generation that steered them through the Great Depression and the war began to think about retiring. Obviously if Levy was to be the firm's senior partner after Weinberg's departure, a group of younger men had to be put in place to carry on the business on a day-to-day basis. Hence, the Gang of Five's unexpected promotion to become Goldman partners.

Levy was a force of nature. "He was smart, quick, and extremely intuitive," Roy Smith explained. "He was the most intense man most intense men had ever met." Smith noted that Levy could not sit still—or stand still, for that matter—or listen to others. The coins jangling in his pocket announced his arrival around the office, which was rarely welcomed. Levy "was extremely tough on his subordinates," Smith noted, and "two or three quit the firm not long after becoming partners because of the incredible pressure they felt working under his constant gaze." He always wanted to know what everyone was working on but grew very impatient when the answers took longer than his short attention span could tolerate. "[W]e used to write out whatever we wanted to tell him as succinctly as we could," Smith continued, "with no excess words, and read it aloud to him. He always grasped everything immediately, even the complex parts. He was intimidating and frightened most of us as no one else did." Levy kept a frenetic pace at the office, "pacing back and forth, usually on the phone, in his cramped, glassed-in office in the center of the trading room, where he could watch the tape and yell at people for missing trades, without interrupting his telephone conversations." His two secretaries would simultaneously field an incoming call from a client while placing outgoing calls to others. There was very little wasted time. "If you had to see him about something, you just went down and stood around in his office until he noticed you," Smith observed, "and you made your ten-second report and then left after it was clear you were no longer being noticed."

At the same time that Levy's ascension at Goldman Sachs was looking increasingly inevitable, he was becoming more prominent around New York City, thanks in large part to his friend, Cy Lewis. Not only had Lewis managed Levy's money during the war, making him wealthier than he already had been, but he was also introducing Levy to important New York charities, where Jewish Wall Street could primp and preen while supporting a good cause. In 1954 and 1955, for instance, Levy served as chairman of the annual Federation of Jewish Philanthropies of New York campaign and was a vice president of the federation itself. (Cy Lewis was the federation's president.)

In 1955, Levy was honored at the benefit dinner, at the Plaza Hotel, where the federation announced it intended to raise $18.1 million for the year, of which $2.5 million had been raised at the dinner. In the quirky way that prominent New Yorkers agree to be "honored" at such dinners—and where expectations of a sizable donation are de rigueur as a result—the federation gave Levy an antique silver tankard and a book of testimonials, including one from Herbert Lehman, the former governor and then current senator from New York (and uncle of Goldman partner Arthur Altschul). According to the *Times,* the gifts were "in recognition of Mr. Levy's services to [the] federation and to local religious and nonsectarian causes." Cy Lewis spoke of the fact that "too many of our neighbors . . . were forced to wait too long for help from the time they first applied for services until the required help and treatment started." (Levy and Lewis weren't all business, though. In June 1956, they won the Candee Cup for Low Net golf tournament at the Bond Club of New York's annual field day at Sleepy Hollow Country Club.)

In April 1957, Levy succeeded Lewis as the president of the Federation of Jewish Philanthropies, for a three-year term. The funny thing was that Levy was not the slightest bit religious. He was agnostic, and his wife, Janet, was an atheist. "My mother never got me involved in anything religious, neither did my father," Peter Levy said. "My mother never believed in any kind of celebration of anything. No Christmas. No Hanukkah, nothing. No Passover, nothing, no God. No bar mitzvahs, no nothing."

Levy may not have been at all religious, but he was a prodigious fund-raiser, settling upon a technique of doing so through public peer pressure known as "calling the cards." The idea had originated with Cy Lewis, who decided the best way to raise money from his fellow Jewish bankers was to have a dinner and by going seriatim—out loud—through all the names of the attendees and asking them to make a donation for the year of more than they had made the year before. The problem was that Lewis did not like performing this public theater, so he got Levy to do it instead. "Hey you, you," Levy would stand up and say, with three-by-five note cards in hand, "You gave five thousand dollars last year. You've had a really good year this year, Joe. I know because I've talked to your partners and I know you're doing just fantastic. So what can we count on you for this year?" This went on hour after hour and was surprisingly effective both as entertainment and as fund-raising.

Even though Levy was a trader, not an investment banker, he was elected to numerous boards of directors, including for Diebold, Inc., the bank vault manufacturer; the Pacific Uranium Mine Company, in Beverly Hills, California; Witco Chemical Corporation, Inc.; and the New York Telephone Company. His board positions were in keeping with Goldman's philosophy—pioneered by Weinberg, of course—of seeking positions on the corporate boards as a way to give Goldman a better chance of winning banking and trading business.

In 1960, five of Goldman's partners, including both Weinberg and Levy, penned articles for the *Christian Science Monitor* about different aspects of the firm's business. The series, which amounted to free advertising, was highly unusual for both the fact that the newspaper ran the articles, uncritically, and that Goldman would choose to participate at all, thereby revealing a few kernels about its business. "Marcus Goldman could not have imagined the size, diversity, and leadership his investment banking firm would achieve by 1960 when he came to New York from Philadelphia in 1869 to buy and sell merchants' bills receivable," Weinberg wrote in the first installment. He explained that Goldman had more than five hundred employees in 1960, in nine separate U.S. offices—including Albany and Buffalo, of all places—and that the firm had "bought and sold" commercial paper worth in excess of $2 billion in 1959, making Goldman the "leading dealer" in the country. He also boasted about the $350 million bond issue for Sears in 1958 and the $637 million IPO for Ford in 1956.

Levy's article—about Goldman's over-the-counter trading and arbitrage departments—was the most revealing of all, mostly because one gets the sense he actually wrote it himself. He clearly was proud of the new trading desks—then three years old—and the nearly two thousand private telephone lines that traders could use. But he positively crowed about the firm's arbitrage department, "by far the most active of any in the country." After a quick description of what arbitrage entailed, he then shared two examples of recent profitable arbitrage opportunities, one involving the securities of AT&T and the other involving the convertible preferred stock of the Studebaker-Packard Company.

The Studebaker trade was the more complicated one. In that situation, Levy wrote, Goldman and three other firms formed a syndicate to buy 30,165 shares of the Studebaker convertible preferred stock for $11 million and in the process obtained around 1 million rights to buy Studebaker's "when issued" common stock at $11 per share. The Goldman syndicate then sold short 600,000 of the "when issued" shares at $12.75 a share and sold short the balance of 400,000 shares at a higher price, thus locking in around a $2 per share profit, or $2 million. "The arbitrage will be completed in January 1961, when the syndicate will convert its preferred shares and deliver the common against its short position," Levy wrote. While it would be hard to imagine the typical *Christian Science Monitor* reader comprehending Levy's trade—let alone wondering what it was doing in the paper at all—the fact that Goldman could make its share of $2 million in less than a year from that single trade showed why Levy was so important to the firm's finances. Whereas Weinberg worked for years on the Ford IPO to make the firm $1 million, Levy was able to make almost twice as much in far less time.

———

IN THE EARLY 1960s, Levy vastly increased his civic responsibilities. In August 1961, the B'nai B'rith Foundation named him the chairman of its 1961 fund-raising campaign. A few weeks later, New York governor Nelson Rockefeller—a close friend of Levy's—named him a member of a special investigating commission to study public welfare in the state. He was a member of the board of visitors at Tulane University and was the treasurer of Lincoln Center for the Performing Arts, in New York.

In October 1961, the American Stock Exchange named him chairman of a committee to study and investigate what changes the exchange needed to make following the expulsion of two members—a father and son—from both the exchange and from the securities business after having "willfully violated" securities laws, resulting in "millions of dollars of harm to unsuspecting investors." Soon enough, the SEC found that the American Stock Exchange had permitted "manifold and prolonged abuses" of trading rules by its members. As a result, the so-called Levy Committee, composed of a group of Wall Street executives led by Levy, took on added importance. During the five months ending in February 1962, Levy's committee issued three separate reports about how the rules governing the American Stock Exchange needed to be changed, and the exchange enacted many of them in April 1962.

Also that month, having just completed his three-year term as president of the Federation of Jewish Philanthropies, Levy was chosen to be the sixteenth president of Mount Sinai Hospital. He remained involved in a leadership role at Mount Sinai for the rest of his life and oversaw the establishment of the Mount Sinai School of Medicine, the achievement of a university affiliation, the $154 million fund-raising effort for the medical school building and endowment, and the planning and erection of the Annenberg Building, which contains the Gustave L. and Janet W. Levy Library, on One Gustave L. Levy Place in New York City.

In May 1963, he was elected a member of the New York Stock Exchange Board of Governors. (In 1950, Weinberg's seat on the New York Stock Exchange had been transferred to Levy.) Two years later, Levy was elected vice chairman of the stock exchange, becoming the first nonfloor governor in twenty-five years to take a leadership post. His election stirred conjecture that he would soon become chairman of the "33-man group ranking as the most powerful policymaking body on Wall Street." There was also some concern that the election of an office partner, working off the floor of the exchange as Levy did, would be the beginning of a shift of power at the exchange away from those people who actually worked on the floor and who had run the exchange for years. But one floor trader told the *Times* about Levy's appointment, "To be perfectly honest about it, the best managerial talent in this business is found not on the trading floors but in the offices. The office partners of the brokerage houses are the ones with the most organizational ability."

In April 1967, Levy was nominated to become the chairman of the New York Stock Exchange. "He was a very ardent, hardworking businessman," explained Walter Frank, his predecessor at the NYSE. "[A] good leader, respected for his ability rather than his school tie or clubs." Not only was he the first office partner to serve as chairman of the stock exchange in a generation, he was also the first Jewish chairman ever. "Gus was very proud" of becoming the first Jewish chairman of the exchange, his friend Tubby Burnham told Ellis; he added that he did not think Levy was a very good leader. "[H]e couldn't separate his thinking from what was in his firm's own interests," Burnham said. "He was always favoring Goldman Sachs." In a 1973 interview, though, Levy objected to the suggestion that he had ever put Goldman's interest ahead of the NYSE's interests. "As long as I am a governor of the stock exchange, I've got to speak as a governor of the stock exchange," he said. "I take the position that I cannot take any other point of view than that adopted by the board. But if I were to speak as a partner of Goldman, Sachs that would be a different matter." Indeed, he said he found his views and the exchange's views to be in sync. "It happens that none of the stock exchange's points of view so far support anything that would be harmful to Goldman, Sachs or the industry," he said. "If they did, I guess I would have to resign." In an oft-repeated pattern on Wall Street, someone in a position to benefit from a conflict of interest averred that being tempted by unethical behavior was impossible, since his own virtue was impeccable.

LEVY WAS PERIPATETIC. His day began—every day—at 5:30 a.m. with a fifteen-minute jog, and after getting cleaned up and dressed, "I say my prayers," he explained once to an interviewer. "I say prayers every day." (This despite his son's insistence he was an agnostic.) He never asked for anything in his prayers. "I just read a little book called the *Daily Word.*" His breakfast was usually fruit or a glass of juice, although sometimes he would eat leftovers. "I had crab meat for breakfast this morning," he once said. After reading the *Times* and the *Wall Street Journal,* he "got downtown" to Goldman's offices by 7:50 a.m. Once there, "I look over the trading sheets, transaction sheets, any mail that's left over from the last day and finish reading what's in my briefcase. Then I start mak-ing calls—at 8:30, or as soon as I can find somebody in."

He explained that he had some "early-bird clients" that he often called at home. "They're used to it by now," he said. "And then the boys start dribbling in about quarter to nine." Twice a week—on Tuesday and Thursday—his team came to his office for a meeting about "trends in the bond or the stock market," he said. Every Monday morning, there was a Management Committee meeting. "[T]hey were kept short, usually only fifteen minutes, and there was minimal discussion, no agenda, no minutes—and no chairs . . . ," Charles Ellis wrote. "Levy often took phone calls during the meetings to show how little importance he really gave to the committee." He also had a pocketful of coins and carried around worry beads, which he would rub constantly. The noise of the coins in his pocket would give him away when he started walking around the trading floor, looking for answers. Traders braced themselves for the Levy verbal assault.

He also became manic if he thought the firm had missed an arbi-trage opportunity or a block trade, which was a business that Lewis and Levy had pioneered, whereby Goldman or Bear Stearns would buy large blocks of stock—as principals—from the selling institutions, with the intention of breaking them up and selling them off to other investors in the market. Block trading was a great service to Goldman's clients, of course, because they could make a large sale in one fell swoop, but it meant that Goldman began taking increasing amounts of principal risk, although they generally made increasing amounts of profit doing so. That—and Levy's innate competitive spirit—made him nearly impossi-ble to be around if he thought a block trade had been missed or that Goldman had lost a piece of business. "Gus was always 100% commit-ted," explained Bob Menschel, an equity trader at the firm, "and that commitment could unnerve people or it could bring out the best in each person. He was so intent on doing every trade that he could get catatonic if he felt we'd missed one. Gus would be storming around, bemoaning our failures: 'We're losing out! We're not in the market anymore! We've lost it! We're not competitive anymore!' To build the business, we had to find ways to keep Gus calm—or at least at bay. . . . [O]riginating a trade is a lot like fly-fishing: Both take patience and quiet persistence to land the really big ones."

After Levy had lunch—usually at his desk—he spent the afternoon in "meetings, meetings, meetings" at his various philanthropic or civic organizations. "I normally get home at around 7:00," he said. "I love three or four drinks in the evening but I never drink during the day, so I am not an alcoholic." When he drank, though, his lisp and his southern accent became more pronounced and he would get silly. He had business meetings "practically every evening," he said, "every evening, September through May, I have business of one kind or another. I'm either taking out a client—usually to [the] '21' [Club, on West Fifty-second Street]— or going to one of those damn testimonial dinners, most of them philanthropic, where some guy's being honored or one of the banks is giving a dinner for some prominent citizen. My wife is very understanding."

"I can't say I ever really got to know him," Betty Levy said of her father. "We didn't spend that much time together. He tried to be a good father, but he didn't know how." She said he was either working or playing golf and didn't have much time for his children. She and Peter used to wish they had more in common with their father. "But we didn't have much to talk about," she said. "It was hard to talk to him." Every year, he and Cy Lewis, as well as Levy's friends Ray Kravis, a highly sought after Tulsa, Oklahoma, oil and gas consultant, and George Buchanan, another oil executive from Cody, Wyoming, would go off together for golf vacations in Scotland and other places around the world.

Levy expected Goldman's employees to share his devotion to the firm. When asked about the fact that many at Goldman felt the pressure Levy put on them was too much, he replied, "Well, we do demand a full day. But I think we've got as low a turnover as any place in the Street— certainly in key personnel. We think the secret of the business is not only to be bright but to be consistent. And the only way to be consistent is to make your calls and do your job and be constantly on the doorstep of your current and prospective customers. But I think we are a pretty happy firm and I've never heard of anyone complain of overwork here." How about Goldman's high divorce rates? "I don't know about that," Levy replied. "But it is true that someone who works here is married to Goldman, Sachs as well as his wife. We have a real spirit. We love to do business. We get a kick out of it and it's fun. And while none of us wants to deprive a guy of a family life and a home, we want to make Goldman, Sachs a close second to his wife and family. A very close second."

Tenenbaum seemed to echo this sentiment, although soon enough he would burn out at Goldman and leave the firm in his early fifties. "Gus Levy ruined my first marriage," he would tell people when explaining why he left. "I wasn't going to let him ruin my second." Before then, though, he spoke of the firm like a family. "The thing about Goldman Sachs, it was not only a place where you work with people," he said. "They became your lifelong friends. This was much more of a social type situation. Guys go into a factory and work in an office, and they have their own lives. That isn't the way it was. We were all very close."

As LEVY SPENT more and more of his time running the firm and managing his extracurricular activities, Tenenbaum began to take on more responsibility and more initiative in building Goldman's arbitrage business.

One way that the arbitrage business became more complex was that as the M&A business began to pick up in the 1960s, Goldman would "arb" the deals by buying and selling stock in the companies involved in a deal—usually after the deal had been announced publicly. In this new frontier of merger arbitrage—known among arbitrageurs as "event driven" arbitrage—information was power and could mean the difference between making a lot of money or losing a lot of money. The people with the information about M&A deals were, of course, the people responsible for putting the deals together in the first place—the corporate executives, the investment bankers, and the lawyers—and arbitrageurs would think nothing of "making the call"—as arbs referred to the practice—to these groups of insiders to try to glean whatever bits of information they could that would give them a trading advantage. Since there were often months between when a deal was announced and when it closed—the time that was needed for regulatory approvals, either by the Justice Department or the Federal Trade Commission or the SEC, and to file proxy statements and obtain shareholder votes—and the stocks of the companies involved in a deal continued to trade during this period of uncertainty, arbs put themselves in the position of either making or losing vast amounts of money based on subtle or not-so-subtle changes in the deal along the way. For instance, if an arb knew that the Justice Department was going to block an announced merger on antitrust grounds before it was announced publicly, he stood to make money based on that information that others in the market did not have. And so, in the event-driven arbitrage business, the ethos became all about making the calls to get information others did not have. (While the rules about insider trading were in their infancy during the 1960s—and not nearly as black and white as they are today—it was a good bet that trading the stock of a company involved in a merger *before* the deal was announced based on nonpublic material information was an easy way to court regulatory scrutiny.)

For instance, Tenenbaum explained, soon after a merger was announced, he needed to figure out whether it would be reviewed by the Justice Department, which had the power to block a deal on antitrust grounds, or the Federal Trade Commission, which did not have injunctive power. If an arb found out that the FTC was going to get the deal, he knew the deal would not get blocked and he could make money on the spread between where the price of the company being bought would trade for in the market and where it would trade—generally higher—when the deal ultimately closed. If the arb found out that the Justice Department would be reviewing the deal—raising the possibility it could be terminated on antitrust grounds—an arb would trade the stocks a different way. "If you found out that Federal Trade is going to get it"—and here Tenenbaum clapped his hands together—"it was a goddamn good spread there hanging over the market," he said.

In an effort to improve the quality of the information he was getting, Tenenbaum decided to hire a Washington law firm, Jacobs & Rowley, consisting of two attorneys, Heath Jacobs and Worth Rowley, who used to work in the antitrust division of the Justice Department. "I don't know how I found them, but I found them," he said. "They both had been with the Justice Department as agents, so they knew all the people in the department. They went to the right cocktail parties." After an announcement of a merger, Tenenbaum would call up the law firm. "Boys, is this a Federal Trade thing or is it Justice?" he'd want to know. Soon enough, the lawyers would call him back and share their opinion. "We think it's going to be Federal Trade," they would tell Tenenbaum and then would explain why they thought the way they did. "Fine," he would reply, "and I got it going." Was this inside information? "Well, inside information, call it whatever the hell you want," but he would get what he needed to know to make the trade more profitable for Goldman.

On tax matters, always a big part of mergers, he relied on tax lawyers he hired who also used to work in the Justice Department. "If there were tax cases, I wanted to know whether they were serious or not serious," he said. "I didn't use Sullivan & Cromwell, our lawyers, because they never thought there should be any antitrust. They were too right wing. I needed guys who knew the players, the line guys. I had good tax lawyers. I had good antitrust lawyers. I also was pretty good at talking to management and treasurers."

Tenenbaum thought nothing of calling up a company's executives and peppering them with questions about an announced deal. "When do you think you'll sign the agreement?" he would ask them. They would answer things like, "Well, we're about a month out." Tenenbaum said, "I kept a good calendar and called them in a month." The executives didn't mind the calls, Tenenbaum said. "I'd say, 'Did all the directors agree to it? Was it unanimous?' They were pretty happy to answer me. I didn't have any problem." He did draw the line, though, he said, and did not execute a trade when he would make a call and find out the merger agreement was going to be signed the next day. "I didn't buy a thing," he said. "That's shooting fish in a barrel. That was the way I designated. I never shot fish in a barrel."

That would be inside information, he believed, not seeing that perhaps also getting lawyers in Washington to provide nonpublic information about mergers could also be perceived as inside information. "The question is what is inside information?" Tenenbaum asked. "What is it? It's something that is special and is going to be an announcement. Now, if some guy says, 'We're signing the merger agreement in a month,' that's not inside information. It could be a month. It could be six weeks. It could never happen." He kept close tabs on what they told him, though, and if someone told him a merger would be announced in a few weeks, he would check back with them and ask how it was coming along. Making these kinds of calls were his "own instinct," he said, and were not done at the suggestion of Levy.

Levy also supported Tenenbaum's effort to hire more analysts and traders to grow the arbitrage business. Robert Lenzner was one of the more unusual people Goldman hired, as was the way in which Levy hired him. Lenzner's father was Levy's dentist, in New York, and one day he simply asked Levy if he would give his son a job. Bob Lenzner was highly credentialed but, unlike Tenenbaum, had no relevant experience in Wall Street, let alone in arbitrage. He graduated from Exeter in 1953, Harvard College in 1957, and attended Oxford University for a year after Harvard. In his senior year at Harvard, Lenzner was the business manager of the *Harvard Crimson*. He graduated from Columbia University's Graduate School of Business in 1961.

Levy hired Lenzner as his assistant in 1962. "Gus brought him in just like he brought me in for my dad," Tenenbaum said. "After Lenzner was in Gus's office as his assistant for six months, he says, 'You get that guy out of here.'" (Another version of the story has Levy telling Tenenbaum to get rid of Lenzner after *one* day.) The combination of the imperious Levy and the nervous Lenzner was not a good match. Levy did not want him around any longer. To appease Levy, Tenenbaum took Lenzner as his assistant. One of the first deals Tenenbaum and Lenzner worked on together involved Sinclair Oil's September 1963 agreement to buy Texas Gulf Producing Company for $252 million. Texas Gulf, which had oil and gas properties in Texas and Louisiana as well as production operations in Libya and Peru, had put itself up for sale the previous April. Texas Gulf's shareholders approved the sale to Sinclair in May 1964 but the deal could not close until the Libyan government signed off on the transfer of Texas Gulf's production facility in the country to Sinclair. Whether Libya would sign off was becoming a greater and greater threat to the deal's closing and for Goldman's arbitrage department a greater and greater concern. The firm had a bunch of money tied up in a bet the deal would close, but without the Libyan's government's sign-off it could not happen. Nerves were starting to fray on Broad Street.

In typical fashion, Tenenbaum had been in regular communication with Joe Dowler, the treasurer of Sinclair Oil. At one point, Lenzner asked Tenenbaum to let him help. "L. Jay, I know you're working with Dowler, but let me follow this thing," Lenzner told Tenenbaum. "I know all the stringers for the *New York Times* that are out in Libya. I can get us a lot of information because there's a feast of Ramadan, where nobody did anything, and I know what they're doing during Ramadan," which is the ninth month of the Islamic calendar and usually in the late summer. Lenzner spoke with the *Times* stringers in Libya and from them received "wonderful information," Tenenbaum said, which he then shared with Dowler. "I was able to feed it to Dowler and get into Dowler's good graces," he said. "This is what you did. You formed a friendship [based on] the fact that you were valuable to them. And you got stuff back from them. 'Joe, everything okay with this merger?' I would ask. He would reply, 'Fine.' "

Another important link in Goldman's information chain about pending deals—in addition to bankers, lawyers, and corporate executives—was other Wall Street arbitrageurs, the most prominent among them being Harold Cohen and Dicky Bear, at L. F. Rothschild, and George Soros and Arthur Klingenstein, at Wertheim & Company. For reasons not entirely clear—beyond allowing Goldman to make sure valuable information about deals was shared—Goldman had joint-account relationships with both L. F. Rothschild and Wertheim during this time, meaning that the firms would jointly arb certain deals together, sharing ratably in the profits and losses. Goldman and L. F. Rothschild were "joint account" on the Texas Gulf deal, for instance.

Having access to the intelligence Lenzner was uncovering in Libya was very helpful to Goldman, L. F. Rothschild, and Sinclair. "Lenzner's doing a beautiful job getting us information," Tenenbaum said. "One day he comes to me, very excited. He says, 'L. Jay, L. Jay, we've got a problem in Libya. I just heard that there may be an uprising in Libya, civil war, something in Libya. It's terrible.' I said, 'Oh, my God!' " It turned out there was some early uprising involving Libyan colonel Mu'ammar al-Gaddafi. Tenenbaum suggested to Lenzner that he call the Libyan ambassador to the United States and "check the story and see what it's about." Lenzner thought that was a great idea. "So, he goes away," Tenenbaum said. "An hour later, he comes back to me. He said, 'Oh, my god.

We're in trouble. We're in trouble.' I said, 'Bob, what's wrong? What's wrong?' He says, 'The Goldman Sachs's operator attached me to the *Liberian* ambassador, instead of the *Libyan* ambassador." Lenzner told the Liberian ambassador to the United States that there was "a revolution going on in your country." The ambassador said to Lenzner, "What are you talking about?" Lenzner said, "Well, I heard about it."

"My god," the ambassador said. "You're telling me there's a revolution in Liberia."

Lenzner replied, plenty flustered, "No, Libya. I don't know what . . . Oh, my god . . ." That's when Lenzner got off the phone and told Tenenbaum what happened. He realized quickly he had screwed up.

Tenenbaum called Dicky Bear, at Rothschild. "I said, 'You know what my nut's done now?' " Tenenbaum said. "I tell him the story."

After getting off the phone with Tenenbaum, Bear decided he was going to play a joke on Lenzner. He waited thirty minutes and went back to his office, where his private phone was, and called Lenzner. "Lenzner," Bear said, officiously, "John K. Smith with the U.S. State Department. We've just had a complaint from the Liberian people that you're spreading rumors of revolution in their country."

"Well, Lenzner goes bananas," Tenenbaum said. "Comes back and tells me."

Tenenbaum told Lenzner that the call was actually from Dicky Bear, who was pulling Lenzner's leg. "He grabbed everything on his desk and he swept the whole thing right off the desk," he said. "He says, 'God damn it.' He left the office and didn't come back for three days." In the end, the Libyan government approved the Texas Gulf deal in November 1964. The deal closed three weeks later, and Goldman made plenty of money.

Another time, David Henkel, a distinguished and very Waspy partner at Sullivan & Cromwell, came to Goldman to meet with Levy and Lenzner to discuss a legal concept related to arbitraging a deal. The three men met together in a small conference room. After about three minutes of listening to Henkel, Levy had had enough. "Gus suddenly becomes furious," Lenzner recalled. "In his inimitable New Orleans accent, he barks: 'I don't wanna hear what I CAN'T DO; I wanna hear WHAT I CAN DO!' And he bolts the room leaving me there to clean up. That's what I learned from six years under Gus Levy: 'I DON'T WANNA HEAH WHAT I CAN'T DO. I WANNA HEAH WHAT I CAN DO!' "

Around this time, Albert Feldman, Goldman's trader devoted to arbitrage, quit because Robert Mnuchin made partner and he didn't. Bruce Mayers, then an arb at a small Wall Street firm, had done some trading with Mnuchin at Goldman, and when Feldman quit, Mnuchin called up Mayers to see if he wanted to take the job that Feldman had vacated. Mayers, a graduate of Erasmus High in Brooklyn and the Wharton School in Philadelphia, had been content to make around thirty thousand dollars a year at Gregory & Sons, a small brokerage, doing little deals. "Which was *really* good money in those years," he remembered. Mayers was doing well at Gregory & Sons and had done well at his previous firm by making bits of money here and there, taking advantage of differences in the pricing of various securities. "I did some really very big deals which kind of made a name for myself, which is not meant in any way other than the fact that I was growing by devoting my time to one thing while the Goldman Sachses and the L. F. Rothschilds and Salomon Brothers of the world, which were the bigger names in arbitrage, had different parameters," he said.

He really did want to work at Goldman but felt an obligation to stay at Gregory & Sons because he had not been there very long. But in the wake of Feldman's departure, Tenenbaum and Mnuchin were increasingly anxious to find a trader to replace Feldman. "It got to the point one night where L. Jay said, 'Will no amount of money buy you?'" Mayers recalled. "Well, jeez, I had never heard that expression before." Goldman ratcheted up the pressure further on Mayers. "How would you like to make a hundred thousand dollars a year?" they asked him. "Jesus, that was *absolutely* mind-boggling to me," he remembered. "And I said, 'It's not the money. It's the fact that I have this obligation, a moral obligation, legal if you want but nothing in writing, to spend a year with Gregory & Sons.'" Tenenbaum told Mayers Goldman could not wait, and if he wanted the job he needed to decide sooner rather than later. Mayers went to see Hamilton W. Gregory III, the head of the firm, and told him he had an offer to go to Goldman. "Jesus, that's the Yankees of Wall Street," Gregory told him. They resolved that if he could find his own replacement—which he soon did—Gregory would release him from his moral obligation to stay at his firm.

Mayers started at Goldman on Valentine's Day 1966, and for the balance of the year, he received his pro rata for the time that year he worked at Goldman, or $87,500. As much as he loved working at Goldman, he noticed a few things right from the start that were troubling to him. First, even though some block trades were not particularly profitable, Levy wanted him to trade them anyway. "He would put his two cents in," Mayers remembered, "and he would say, 'I saw Morgan Stanley put this block of stock on. Did you have a chance to bid that?' I said, 'Yes, I got the call, it was from such-and-such a fund, but I didn't think the price was right. They wanted to sell it at thirty-two and that clearly wasn't worth taking on that.' And he would say, 'Brooth'—he had this lisp—'Brooth, that's a client of the firm's. You've gotta lift a leg a little bit to take care of what they want.'" Mayers said he learned to show a little leg. "It was not necessarily in my best interest as a trader," he said. "But in the long run, it was in the best interest of the firm to be identified with constantly doing the right thing. I understood that. But I was still person-ally motivated. I mean, I was motivated for Goldman, obviously, but I said, 'Jeez, why should I end up taking the loss and at the end of the year they're gonna say you lost a lot of money on this or whatever?' But I learned how to do that, [and] that was the whole basis of block trading. That was never a moneymaker."

Mayers also was uncomfortable with Levy's arrangements with L. F. Rothschild and Wertheim. "One of the things that really gripped me the wrong way at Goldman is that we did a lot of business, joint account, with Rothschild," he said, "so the relationship between Levy and Cohen was obviously a strong one." Mayers said he "fought it from day one" but soon enough decided, "What's the point?" since Levy was the boss and Levy liked the relationship the way it was and had no interest in changing it. Mayers remembered one arbitrage he did, in 1970, in some AT&T bonds where the issue of the joint accounts—in this instance, the issue involved Wertheim—"came to a head" with Levy. When he had the trade on, he discovered that when it came to AT&T arbitrage trades, Goldman was always joint account with Wertheim. This particular trade involved bonds that AT&T had issued with five-year warrants. Mayers called it the "spot-ted zebra" trade because it was "a unit of two totally diverse things" that lent itself to "terrific trading opportunities." He made $200,000 on the trade on the first day, which certainly caught Levy's attention.

During the few weeks the trade was on, though, Mayers knew that Wertheim had traded none of the units. Half of Goldman's profit went to Wertheim anyway. "That's great," Mayers told Levy. "I'm the arbitrageur and I'm stuck with doing business with Wertheim, who didn't do one trade during the three-week period, nothing." At Mayers's urging, Gold-man ended the deal with Wertheim. "I said, 'As long as we're doing this why don't you review what we're doing with L. F. Rothschild, too,'" he recalled. "And we did that and we parted amicably." Mayers got a plaque and a dinner from Goldman for creating one of the best arbitrage trades of the year.

Before receiving that modest accolade, though, Mayers had a major dispute with Levy about a trade he had made on the AT&T bonds. He had sold $4 million of the bonds, plus the attached warrants, to a very big trading account Goldman had. "I wouldn't want to use the name," he said. "But one of the largest accounts." He had offered the bonds at 94⅞ to 95, a very tight spread. But the client came back and said he wanted to buy them even tighter, at 94¹⁵⁄₁₆. Mayers was slightly perturbed that the guy was cutting it so close but he agreed to the deal. That was the end of the trade. Three hours later, Mayers got a call from an intermediary saying that the client wanted to cancel the trade. It turned out the price of the bonds had fallen to around 94½ in those few hours and the client wanted out. "It was an absolute idiotic reason," Mayers said. Mayers told the intermediary "a deal's a deal" and he would not rescind it. He hung up the phone. The ostensible reason he wanted to cancel the trade, Mayers was told, was because the client had "an obligation to trade with Morgan Stanley." Of course, Mayers knew that he had offered a better price than Morgan Stanley had. "I'm not canceling the trade," he said. "Click."

Ten minutes later, he heard tapping on the glass in Levy's office. "Which is twenty feet in back of me. 'Brooth! Brooth! You're having a trouble with Joe Jones at such-and-such?' "

Mayers told Levy he had done a trade with the client and that there "was no problem at all." But Levy told him he had to cancel the trade. "I said, 'No, Gus. I can't cancel the trade. A trade is a trade. I've arbitraged against it four million [dollars], a pretty reasonable size, not a small transaction,' " Mayers said. "He said—and to make a long story short—Gus said, 'They have indicated that they would take a big position in the Ford bonds that are coming out next week. And they need to cancel the trade.' I said, 'Gus, you're the boss. You can do whatever you want to do, but if you cancel the trade there's gonna be no integrity, there's gonna be no Bruce, there's gonna be no arbitrage, blah-blah-blah, and I'm outta here.' And he said, 'I have to cancel the trade.' I said, 'Good luck,' and I walked out. And I quit. I was just gone. I just left my positions, my stuff, and I was gonna come back in and pick up my stuff and get another job if I could. My whole life is exploding because of this one thing of morality, and of integrity."

Over the weekend, Mnuchin called him at home. They talked for two hours about what had happened and Mayers decided to return on Monday to Goldman. "But the trade was canceled," he said. "Don't misunderstand. I lost. Gus was the boss. He had the last say. The integrity was very important to me. I never made a trade that was not based on honesty or morality. It's one of the reasons I left my [previous] partnership because they did a trade once, which was very meaningless, because they had information that was public but very obscure and we saw it and the other guy didn't see it. And we—not me, but the firm—took advantage of this to make a half a point on a thousand shares or some ridiculous thing."

He said that, despite the incident, his opinion of Levy did not change. "He was running a business and I had always found him to be of the highest caliber," he said. "He was in a class by himself. I thought to myself, 'I guess there are certain things he has to do that are unpalatable to him but from a business point of view had to be done,' so I just let it go and that was the end of it." He thought that his stature at the firm might actually have increased as a result of the dispute. "It absolutely helped because everybody knew about it because I was goddamning it all over the place, which is my favorite thing to do, stomping around and saying, 'Goddamnit, how can they do this? It's Goldman Sachs, who cares about this other fucking firm!'" Mayers spent thirty years at Goldman Sachs but never became a partner. Robert Rubin, soon to be a major force at Goldman, used to say about Mayers that in "a fair world," he would have become a partner. But that didn't happen. He retired in 1995 and lives modestly in an apartment complex on Long Island.

CHAPTER 6

THE BIGGEST MAN
ON THE BLOCK

The Goldman arbitrage machine, like a shark, had to keep moving forward, and Tenenbaum needed a new assistant. He received a call from Martin Whitman, a fund manager, and he suggested that he consider hiring Robert E. Rubin, the son of Alexander Rubin, a lawyer whom Whitman had known in New York. Bob Rubin was then working at Cleary Gottlieb, a New York law firm, but was considering a move to Wall Street. Rubin had worked for Fowler Hamilton, one of Cleary Gottlieb's name partners, and a former antitrust lawyer in the Justice Department. Tenenbaum figured Rubin knew his way around antitrust procedures pertaining to mergers, an important skill in Goldman's prospering arbitrage department.

"There's only one problem," Whitman told Tenenbaum. "I think he's going to go work at Lazard for Felix Rohatyn." Tenenbaum called Rubin. "Marty Whitman called me," he said he told Rubin. "He's a good friend of your dad. I know you want to come to the Street. Give me a shot. Let's have lunch." Rubin agreed to have lunch with Tenenbaum at a restaurant near Wall Street.

Tenenbaum used the *idea* that Rubin might work for Rohatyn against the impressionable youth. "I hear you may work for Felix Rohatyn," Tenenbaum told Rubin. "I've known Felix a long time, extremely competent, really quite a big guy. Matter of fact, he's on four major corporate boards. You'll really be working for a very important guy. You'll carry his briefcase to every one of those meetings. That's what you'll be doing, but that's what he needs you for." Tenenbaum hoped his message was getting through to Rubin. "I lost my assistant," he continued, referring to Lenzner, who by then had left to work elsewhere. "I investigated four hundred and twenty-eight deals last year. I need somebody to investigate half of them. So, you work for me. You'd be your own man. You'd be investigating deals, which is right up your legal background. I think you'll have a lot of fun. You'll be working for Gus Levy.

He's a pretty big man, like Felix. It'll be more of a line job than an assistant to an important guy."

Reflecting on this moment many years later, Rubin wrote in his memoir, *In an Uncertain World*, "I was an odd choice for Goldman Sachs when the firm hired me, at the age of twenty-eight, to work in its storied arbitrage department. Nothing about my demeanor or my experience would have suggested I might be good at such work." The one thing that can unequivocally be said about Bob Rubin is that he has perfected the persona of the modest, self-deprecating man. From his conservative, somewhat threadbare attire to his stated preference for consensus building rather than to be seen taking unilateral action, to his penchant for seemingly random calls to journalists soliciting their views, he has come to embody Goldman's team-oriented approach to banking. One Bob Rubin story after another fits into the construct of the unassuming overachiever. Thinking he did not fit in at Goldman was in perfect keeping with his whole affect. "The stereotypical personality type of the arbitrageur was, in those days, forceful and confrontational," he continued. "I was then, as now, a low-key, not manifestly aggressive person. As for my qualifications, I don't think I'd ever heard the phrase 'risk arbitrage' before I started the job search that led to Goldman Sachs."

Morris Rubin, his paternal grandfather, born in 1882 in Minsk, Russia, came to Ellis Island in 1897 to avoid conscription into the czar's army. "As a young Jew," Rubin wrote of his paternal grandfather, "he didn't think the Russian military would be a terrific career choice." In 1906, he married Rose Krebs, a Polish immigrant. They settled in a tenement on the Lower East Side, where Morris was a milkman. Shortly after the birth of their first child, Alexander Rubin, in 1907, the family moved to Flatbush Avenue in Brooklyn, which Rubin described as a "step up" from the tenement. The Rubins' fortunes improved in Brooklyn, until Morris became gravely ill in the 1920s after developing an infection following a tonsillectomy.

On his doctor's advice that a warm, sunny climate would be Morris's best hope for recovery, the Rubins left Brooklyn for Miami. Miraculously, the climate change did the trick, and Morris's health improved, as did—for a time—his personal finances. Morris Rubin's arrival in Miami in the 1920s coincided with a wave of southern migration and land speculation that the businessman could not easily resist. "He quickly made a good deal of money speculating in real estate with large leverage," his grandson wrote. "For a short time in the 1920s, Morris Rubin was a wealthy man." But then, as a precursor to the Crash of 1929, the Florida land bubble burst, taking Morris Rubin's fortune with it. For several years thereafter—until he regained his composure—Morris Rubin seemed somewhat deranged.

By the time Rubin was born, living a mile away from his grandfather in Miami, Morris had regained his equanimity and learned to live with the money he had saved. He was never rich again.

Samuel Seiderman, his maternal grandfather, came from a power-house family in Brooklyn that had lived in the borough for generations. Seiderman was "a lawyer, an investor in real estate, a political activist, and a major figure in his Brooklyn world," Rubin wrote, and a big part of the Democratic Party machine in Brooklyn. "Family legend has my grandfather and his colleagues sitting around in the basement of what I remember as their enormous house at 750 Eastern Parkway"—in Brooklyn—"and choosing judges," Rubin wrote. Rubin's grandfather died in 1958, when Rubin was a sophomore at Harvard, but "his influence remained with me."

Rubin's parents met at a benefit dinner-dance at the Waldorf-Astoria in 1933. Alexander Rubin, who had graduated from Columbia Law School and was a property tax attorney, was at the benefit with a client who had made a large donation to a hospital and was being honored. During the course of the dinner, the client lamented that he had never married and urged Rubin not to make the same mistake. He suggested that his lawyer dance with one of the women seated nearby. After giving her the once-over, Rubin said he didn't feel like dancing, but he thought another woman he saw in the balcony was more his type. Sam Seiderman overheard Rubin's comment. "You'd like to dance with that young lady?" he said. "That's my daughter." They would be married for some seventy years.

The Rubins lived in Neponsit, Queens. Bob Rubin was born in 1938. When he was three, the family moved from Queens to an apartment on West Eighty-first Street, in Manhattan, across from the American Museum of Natural History. He went to the Walden School, around the corner on Central Park West. During World War II, Alexander Rubin offered to donate the family's money-losing mica mine—which was a remnant of Morris Rubin's business empire—to the U.S. government for the war effort. (Mica was used as a wire insulator for airplanes.) The government accepted the offer but then requested that Alexander run the mine. The family moved—briefly, it turned out—to Sylva, North Carolina, in the Great Smoky Mountains. "The people in the town called my father 'Jew man' and 'Mr. Jew,'" Rubin recalled. "It was a bit much for my mother, who felt as if she'd woken up in the wrong century." Rubin, his sister, Jane, and their mother moved back to New York, while Alexander stayed in Sylva and visited them every few weeks by train.

When Bob Rubin was nine, the family moved to Miami Beach to be closer to his grandfather and to allow his father to have a "calmer, more pleasant life." Alexander Rubin built a shopping center, continued to practice some law, and played golf, as did his wife, who had a "shelf full of local club trophies." On Bob Rubin's first day in fourth grade at North Beach Elementary, his teacher announced to the class, "Robbie Rubin has gone to a private school in New York and has never learned script. So let's all be very nice to him." That same day, over his protests, his classmates elected him class president. "I wasn't the class president type, but in a funny way the designation stuck with me," he wrote. "Though I was never a class leader, I held class positions intermittently throughout my school years."

In his autobiography, Rubin described a typical, idyllic boyhood in post–World War II America. He rode his bike to school every day, had a paper route, read Hardy Boys mysteries, developed a lifelong love of fishing, and tried not to be too heavily influenced by Rabbi Leon Kronish at the local temple. His parents had many friends, played golf and cards regularly, and hung out at the cabana club at the Roney Plaza Hotel. But, as he had briefly in North Carolina, Rubin again witnessed racial prejudice firsthand. He and his sister attended segregated schools, and the local Woolworth's had white and "colored" drinking fountains. Jane Rubin made a point of drinking from the "colored" drinking fountain and sitting in the back of the bus. Bob managed to thrive in that unsettling environment, partly by playing a fair amount of poker, at which he allowed he was "pretty good at."

Rubin has described his admittance to Harvard as both a matter of luck and, in keeping with the established pattern, his election as president of his high-school senior class. "My grades were good but not outstanding," he observed, "and I came from a regular public high school." But the critical factor, he maintained, was serendipity. At a Harvard Glee Club concert, Rubin's father saw a lawyer he knew whose friend—the Harvard College dean of admissions—happened to passing through Miami at the same time. One thing led to another, and Bob Rubin had a fortuitous interview with the dean.

As a member of the Harvard class of 1960, Rubin was overcome by a feeling of inadequacy. Despite taking four years of French in high school, he failed the test to release him from the entry-level course. He couldn't even get into the entry-level math course because he had not taken calculus in high school. On the first day of freshman orientation, in the fall of 1956, he took it to heart when the dean said that 2 percent of the class would flunk out. "I looked around and thought that everyone else was lucky," he later wrote, "because I was going to fill the entire quota by myself."

At the end of his first year, Rubin was doing fine at Harvard. Since law school seemed to be his ultimate destination, he started off as a government major. But then Rubin switched to economics, which was largely taught as a conceptual course of study, rather than with the mathematical rigor of subsequent decades. "I found it difficult but engrossing," he wrote. He worked with the Nobel Prize–winning economist Thomas Schelling on his—basically incomprehensible—125-page senior honors thesis, "Inflation and Its Relationship to Economic Development in Brazil." Schelling had just moved from Yale to Harvard, and Rubin was his only advisee. The subject appealed to him, Rubin later wrote, because it "seemed a potentially fruitful area for entrepreneurial involvement," whatever that means.

Atypically, Rubin spent the summer between his junior and senior years hanging around Cambridge "with no job, sleeping on a broken couch in the living room of a shared apartment, and working on my thesis to get a head start." Researching and writing the thesis "in the stacks of the Widener Library every day" turned out to be one of his best memories of Harvard, along with occasionally hanging out in coffeehouses in Harvard Square contemplating existentialism and the meaning of life.

Rubin didn't find his "sense of belonging" at Harvard until his senior year. He admitted that his early anxiety about whether he should be at the school was unrealistic but concluded that the paranoia spurred him on and was a "powerful driver" for him. "After thinking I wasn't going to cross the finish line," he wrote later, he managed to graduate from Harvard "with the unexpected distinctions" of Phi Beta Kappa, summa cum laude, and a "summa minus" on his Brazil thesis. He had applied—and was accepted—to Harvard Law School and the Harvard PhD program in economics. Apparently as a joke, after graduating from Harvard, Rubin sent a letter to the dean of admissions at Princeton, where he had been rejected four years earlier. "I imagine you track the people you graduate," he wrote. "I thought you might be interested to know what happened to one of the people you rejected. I just wanted to tell you that I graduated from Harvard summa cum laude and Phi Beta Kappa." He received a letter back. "Thank you for your note," the dean wrote. "Every year, we at Princeton feel it is our duty to reject a certain number of highly qualified people so that Harvard can have some good students too."

In the fall of 1960, Rubin showed up again in Cambridge but with little enthusiasm for gearing up anew for the rigors of law school. After three days, he went to see the assistant dean to tell him he was dropping out. The dean was unsympathetic. "You've taken a place somebody else could have had," he told Rubin.

"I told him that I was dropping out anyway," Rubin explained.

The dean told him that unless there were "extenuating circumstances," Rubin would not be readmitted to Harvard Law. They kept talking, though, and the dean said that if Rubin would go to a psychiatrist, get examined, and it was determined that he was making a reasonable decision, he would be readmitted the following year. The psychiatrist told Rubin that when he was about to start medical school, he took a year off instead. Rubin was fine, the psychiatrist told him, but "perhaps the dean ought to come see him if he found what I wanted to do so troubling." With a free option on Harvard Law School in hand, Rubin wondered how to spend his next year.

After realizing it was too late to apply to academic programs at Cambridge and Oxford, he ended up applying by cable to the London School of Economics, "emphasizing my Harvard credentials." The school cabled him back with an acceptance. Only then did Rubin tell his parents he was dropping out of Harvard Law School for the London School of Economics. Before he could head to London, though, Rubin had to return to Miami and get the approval of the local draft board to be deferred from the draft while studying abroad in graduate school, an acceptable option as long as the school was properly accredited. The Miami draft board rep had never heard of the London School of Economics. "The trouble with boys of your race is they don't want to go to war," he told Rubin. To get the draft board's approval, Rubin asked Arthur Smithies, the chairman of Harvard's economics department, to write a letter stating that the London School of Economics was the real deal. It worked.

Aside from a school trip to Cuba—when that was still possible—and a family trip to Mexico, Rubin had never been abroad before. His account of the year seems particularly self-indulgent. He was "an occasional student" at the school, "working toward a certificate rather than a real degree," allowing him to do what he pleased, which was pretty much what he did. "I spent most of my time talking to people," he wrote. "The sense of freedom was marvelous. In my lodgings on Earls Court Road, I could make dinner at midnight, sleep late, and then wake up and read all day if I felt like it."

Along with his traveling companion, David Scott, Rubin also indulged his wanderlust. He hitchhiked in England, albeit wearing a suit and a hand-lettered sandwich board with the plea "two Harvard students need ride" on it. He went skiing—for the first time—in Austria and spent six weeks in Paris, during Christmas vacation, living in a cheap hotel on the Left Bank reading Jack Kerouac and Arthur Miller. He spent Easter in Italy, and that summer drove around Denmark, Norway, and Sweden with Scott.

By then he could choose between either Harvard Law School or Yale Law School, where he had applied, and been accepted, in the interim. "I didn't necessarily want to be a lawyer," he wrote, "but law school seemed to keep a lot of options open." In the end, he chose Yale over Harvard because, he concluded, at Harvard "you sit around and discuss contracts," and at Yale "you sit around and discuss the meaning of good and evil." Rubin also, apparently, spent time debating the meaning of life, and he nurtured a skepticism that had initially been encouraged in him by his rabbi in Miami, Leon Kronish, and then again by a Harvard philosophy professor, Raphael Demos, who "burned into Rubin the necessity of challenging assumptions and beliefs."

WHILE AT THE London School of Economics, Rubin met Judy Oxenberg, who was a friend of a woman he had dated at Harvard. She was a junior at Wellesley College and Judy and his old girlfriend were passing through London on their way to spending the summer in France. He remembered being struck by Oxenberg's beauty when he saw her that night. During Rubin's second year at Yale Law School, the two started dating after Oxenberg showed up at Yale to study graduate-level French. She was also interested in classical music, theater, and dance. They shared, Rubin wrote, "a sense of curiosity about everything around us, from the people we knew to world affairs to the books the other person had read." By November of his final year at law school, the couple was engaged, and they were married the following March at the Branford Chapel at Yale.

Even though Rubin had some vague notion of returning to Miami and joining his father in the real-estate business, ultimately one does not spend three years at Yale Law School without some expectation of becoming a lawyer, even if it turns out to be for just a short period of time. After graduating from Yale Law, Rubin sought a job at a number of prominent New York City corporate law firms. In the end, he chose Cleary Gottlieb because "it had a more comfortable environment" and was smaller than other firms but equally "establishment." He and Judy lived in a basement apartment on Henry Street in Brooklyn Heights, with the rent subsidized by his parents. They commuted by subway to Manhattan: Rubin to offices on the southern tip of the island and Oxenberg to occasional acting gigs in and around the Broadway theaters.

Rubin liked the "cachet" of Cleary Gottlieb and "being part of an establishment organization" but doing research for major litigations or corporate matters or tax analysis on personal estates was not for him. Like many lawyers who work on Wall Street deals, Rubin marveled that the investment bankers seemed to be making the interesting business decisions and getting paid grand sums while the lawyers dutifully recorded the proceedings for (hefty) by-the-hour billings. "When I'm forty," Rubin thought, "I want to be doing what those guys are doing, not what we're doing."

But Rubin had no intention of waiting until he was forty to make the switch. After a couple of years at Cleary, he sent out a bunch of résumés to Wall Street firms, hoping to get into the deal business. "By sheer coincidence, two firms offered me jobs doing something I'd never heard of," he said. He chose Goldman over Lazard, he said, because it was "considered the top firm in the arbitrage field," thanks to Levy's skill and cunning and because "the pay was slightly higher." He joined Goldman in October 1966. But he worried he could not do what an arbitrageur was required to do: "get on the phone and interview executives at companies about transactions"—make the calls. "I wasn't sure I could be so audacious." His annual pay increased to $14,400 a year, from $13,000. He had heard from a variety of people that working at Goldman, as opposed to Cleary, "was a step down on the social scale."

One of Rubin's earliest deals, from September 1967, involved medical equipment manufacturer Becton, Dickinson's announced $35 million stock deal for Univis Lens Co., a maker of eyeglass lenses. Rubin set about making his calls. "The first order of business was rapid, intensive research," Rubin observed. "I had to examine all the publicly available information I could obtain. I had to talk to proxy lawyers and antitrust lawyers. Then I had to speak to officers at both companies, much as a securities analyst does. I almost never had all the information I would have liked. Seldom did I have enough time to think anything through." Unfortunately for Rubin, the merger fell apart.

By the end of January 1968, the first month of the new fiscal year, Rubin's bet had cost the firm $675,000. "That was a lot of money back then," Rubin wrote, "more than we made on any other arbitrage transaction that year and a noticeable slice out of the firm's yearly profits." Levy, whom Rubin described as having "terrific insight into deals in retrospect," was "furious" and "stalked around the trading room muttering that we should have known better than to think a merger like that would go through. . . . Anybody could have seen that was going to happen!"

While the loss had been sizable, Levy and Tenenbaum also knew that it was in the nature of the bets Goldman was making in merger arbitrage. Occasionally deals would fall apart and the bets would go awry but the odds—at least the way Goldman was calculating them—favored the firm the majority of the time. After all, most publicly announced deals do get completed in one form or another, and given the extent of the market intelligence Rubin and Tenenbaum and Mayers were picking up, chances were that Goldman would win more often than it would lose. "Having Gus Levy remind you of all the reasons you were a moron wasn't always the most pleasant way to begin a day," Rubin explained, "but not only could I live with the risk without becoming a nervous wreck[,] risk taking actually comported with my way of looking at the world." Although the antecedents aren't exactly clear, Rubin said he "took naturally to being rigorously analytical in weighing probabilities" and "described this as being like a mental yellow pad. Risk arbitrage sometimes involved taking large losses, but if you did your analysis properly and didn't get swept up in the psychology of the herd, you could be successful." While "flux and uncertainty made arbitrage quite nerve-wracking for some people," Rubin continued, "somehow or other, I was able to take it in reasonable stride."

The pressure to bet correctly was intense, even if Rubin preferred to minimize it and even though Goldman's market presence gave it some advantages.

––––––

IN MAY 1968, Levy was on the cover of *Finance* magazine, known then as "the magazine of money." The headline on the article, "The Biggest Man on the Block," was a reference to Levy's—and Goldman's—dominance of block trading. While Goldman was not known for its innovations, the introduction of block trading was one. The idea was that with the rise of institutional investors—mutual funds, pension funds, and their ilk—the willingness to buy big blocks of stock in one fell swoop from clients became a valuable service. Previously, large blocks of stock that a client wanted to sell would need to be broken up into smaller pieces that the market could absorb without moving the stock price materially (usually downward, as a result of more supply than demand). This would often take a long time and negatively affect the stock price, costing the client money. By agreeing to buy the block of stock from the client immediately, Goldman took the risk of selling it from the client, using its own capital, making the bet that later it would be able to sell the stock at a higher price. In any event, Goldman would also get the fees for buying and the fees for selling. All the risk is in the buying, which is why Levy coined the phrase, "Something well bought is half sold."

In 1968, for instance, almost half the volume of stock traded on the New York Stock Exchange came from institutional investors. "We, of course, know where all the big blocks are," Levy said in May 1968. Levy was the biggest block trader for Investors Diversified Services, or IDS, then the nation's largest mutual fund company, owned by Allan P. Kirby, Levy's old nemesis from his battle with the Murchisons. Goldman liked to be known at that time as "the biggest mover of stock on Wall Street." There was plenty of evidence to back up the claim. For instance, on October 31, 1967, Levy "crossed"—meaning he acted for both buyer and seller, and collected all associated fees—1,150,700 shares of Alcan Aluminum, at $23 per share, then the largest single individual trade ever. Levy was "so intrigued" by the trade that *Finance* reported that he went to the floor of the exchange himself to work with the specialist as the trade was crossing the tape.

The magazine allowed that as Levy was nearing his fifty-eighth birthday, he was "evolving" quickly from a "tough trader with [a] point-spread orientation" into a statesman of the financial community. "He wants to be Mr. Wall Street" just like Sidney Weinberg, said a friend of Levy's. For his part, Levy remarked one Saturday morning from his Sutton Place apartment, with stacks of work papers surrounding him and his multiline phone lighting up with calls time and time again, that he had been "working too hard," although he clearly loved doing so. His long-term ambition, he allowed, was to perhaps obtain "some Government job, appointive, not elected," although such a position was "down the line. I'm not ready for that yet."

Levy was really focused on consolidating his growing power at Goldman Sachs. His trading operation there in the late 1960s had become the profit engine of the firm. "More growth occurred during his period of leadership than during Sidney's period of leadership," John Whitehead observed. "Sidney saw to it that the firm survived and that its reputation reached a high level, but it was Gus who saw to it that the firm had the thrust and the drive to grow during this period."

Weinberg, then in his seventies, was still a force around the firm to be sure. But Levy and his minions—Tenenbaum, Rubin, and (until he left the firm) Lenzner—were the ones driving the firm's profits. "It was the only firm on the Street that was both a trading firm and an investment banking firm," Bob Rubin recalled of Goldman when he first got there. Rubin met Sidney Weinberg—"Mr. Weinberg" to one and all—only once, and that was as a result of writing a memo for him, at Levy's request, having to do with the Ford family's interest in possibly exercising some Ford stock options.

Rubin spoke on the phone with Weinberg and received his orders about what the memo should be about. "At some later point, Gus said that Mr. Weinberg said I did a good job," he continued. "And then one day, I was sitting in the trading room, and all of a sudden, L. Jay stood up. I was wondering what he was standing up for? And all of a sudden, this little man was walking in the door with a vest, and that was Sidney Weinberg, so I met him. That was the only time I met him." The reason that Rubin had only met Weinberg one time was that, thanks to Levy, Weinberg no longer had his office at 55 Broad Street. Levy had dispatched him to an uptown Goldman office at the Seagram Building at 375 Park Avenue in the mid-1960s. By the end, Weinberg and Levy didn't much like each other. "Sidney looked down his nose at Gus," Whitehead said. "But Sidney, I'm sure, acknowledged to himself that there was no other choice, and therefore selected Gus" to succeed him. "He preached mandatory retirement at age 65," the *Times* observed in 1971, "but he never quite practiced it." The paper continued that Weinberg's "semi-retirement" allowed Goldman to transform from what was a "one-man show to a more broadly based operation." It was highly unusual for a senior partner of a firm to be removed physically from the firm's offices, but without Weinberg at 55 Broad Street, Levy had a freer rein to run the firm the way he saw fit.

The story of how Levy engineered this move remains one of the more elusive in the Goldman lore. Neither of the previous two books about the firm mentioned the dispute between Levy and Weinberg that resulted in Weinberg moving his office to the Seagram Building. But there is no disputing Levy's desire to run the firm as he wanted, free of Weinberg's hugely conservative and controlling nature. "Sidney was a little jealous of his, I guess, priority," partner George Doty explained, "and he would step on Gus whenever he thought Gus was looming too large on the horizon. But Gus was a major moneymaker for the firm. So it was a love-hate relationship."

Levy saw that huge moneymaking opportunities existed in arbitrage, in block trading, and then in option and commodities trading. As an investment banker who had come from near poverty and lived through the Depression, Weinberg was highly risk averse, especially when it came to using the firm's scarce capital—which, after all, was nothing more than the partners' money—to make trading bets. Levy unleashed a wave of pent-up creative energy among the Goldman troops. "Gus was much more aggressive with an interest in getting new business and things like that," Alan Stein, a former Goldman partner, recalled. "And he also gave a lot more power to individuals to do their own thing, which Sidney never really liked to do. He was very much a control person." Doty was brought in from an accounting firm to try to counterbalance Levy's risk-taking tendencies. "Sidney and Walter Sachs used to be scared of Gus for taking them over the cliff because he was a better risk taker in the markets than they really had the stomach for," Doty said. "I was brought in at least partly as the counterbalance and to try and prevent us from getting too exposed."

Sandy Lewis had no knowledge of how Levy was able to get Weinberg to move uptown, either. But he was well aware of how important the move was to Gus Levy. "It was a cause for celebration between Dad and Gus," he said. "I can never remember such mirth. They were delighted to get him out of there. It's not that they didn't respect him. They did. But he was holding back principal trading. Not just getting agency business. That man did not want trading to get to be a big deal at Goldman Sachs. He hated it. He feared what it would do to the firm. He saw what happened in the Crash."

But as his influence grew at Goldman and on Wall Street, Levy—now known as "Mr. Wall Street"—decided that Weinberg had to go. Levy's succession of Weinberg was more akin to that between Weinberg and Waddill Catchings than the smooth, well-conceived leadership change the firm's image makers would have one believe. "Sidney Weinberg, like a lot of strong leaders, did not slip gently into the night when Gus Levy became senior partner," explained Peter Weinberg, Sidney's grandson. "In fact, I had always heard it was a hell of a challenge to get him out of the building up to 375 Park. I believe Sidney Weinberg felt he ran the firm until the day he died." Added Rubin, with typical understatement, "When Mr. Weinberg turned over the running of the firm to Gus, I think there was some stress there," he said. "Jimmy"—Weinberg, one of Sidney's two sons—"once said to me that Mr. Weinberg found it hard not running the firm." Even though Weinberg was not physically at Goldman's offices on Broad Street, he still retained for himself the power to set the partners' biannual profit percentages, which meant that Weinberg—not Levy—decided what partners got paid. On Wall Street, there was nothing more important. "Sidney, until the day he died . . . he was always the boss," Doty said. "He was the senior partner. I don't think Gus loved it. Gus had grown substantially in the public eye. He had become a very good investment banker. He had become chairman of the New York Stock Exchange. But Sidney never left any doubt in anybody's mind who was the senior partner of the firm."

In 1969, toward the end of the annual partners' dinner—often held at the '21' Club—Levy stood up to toast Weinberg. "Mr. Weinberg," he said, "even though your office is now uptown and we're downtown so we don't see you at the office anymore, we all want you to know that you are *always* in our thoughts and *always* in our hearts and we are so glad you are active and well and we just want you to know that never a day goes by without our thinking of you and how much we respect you. Wherever you are and wherever you go, Goldman Sachs is always with you—and you are always with Goldman Sachs." The other Goldman partners applauded Levy and his homage.

But Weinberg, at age seventy-seven, was not ready to go quietly. "Those are very nice thoughts, Gus, and I'm glad you feel as you say you do," he said in response. "But don't you ever forget this, Gus. No matter where I am, *I* am the senior partner of Goldman Sachs and *I* run this firm." Until the end, Weinberg remained a thorn in Levy's side. "While Sidney was alive he was a damper on Gus's business because he used to say that some of Gus's business was—'borderline' is the wrong word and I don't want to offend anybody by saying it—but he thought maybe some of Gus's business was 'too Jewish,' which is an expression he might have used," explained one former partner. "So when Gus was freed of Sidney, he could go after whatever business he thought was good for the firm. In the meantime Gus's own standards had developed. He had become more cautious of the firm's image and was less likely to try to go after business that was marginal."

———

ON JULY 24, 1969, after a short illness, Weinberg died at the Columbia-Presbyterian Medical Center. His lengthy obituary appeared on the front page of the *New York Times,* and in addition to recounting his hardscrabble upbringing in Brooklyn, and his investment banking prowess, there was also a recounting of his generally unknown role as a presidential adviser. In addition to working with and for President Roosevelt, he also advised—behind the scenes—Presidents Truman, Eisenhower, Kennedy, and Johnson. Although he voted for Democrats, he hedged his bets. His influence in the two Eisenhower administrations was said, by the *Times,* to be "enormous."

President Kennedy asked Weinberg for help on tax proposals and on how to create COMSAT, the Communications Satellite Corporation (the IPO of which Bob Rubin worked on as a lawyer). In 1964, Weinberg helped form a Johnson for President group that worked to get Johnson elected in his own right that year. He recommended both John T. Connor and Henry Fowler to Johnson, who chose both men for his cabinet—

Connor as secretary of commerce and Fowler as secretary of the treasury. (Fowler later became the first former government official to join Goldman as a partner.) Hubert Humphrey, the Minnesota senator, was the only presidential candidate Weinberg backed who ended up losing the presidency. At his death, Weinberg was on three corporate boards: Ford Motor Company, General Cigar Company, and the Corinthian Broadcasting Company.

But by the time of Weinberg's death, things were changing, even on the question of whether investment bankers should continue to sit on corporate boards. Increasingly, the SEC and the judicial system were reinterpreting securities laws pertaining to trading on inside information, making it increasingly less desirable from a legal point of view for investment bankers to continue to sit on the boards of their clients. In August 1968, a court of appeals ruled that senior officers of the Texas Gulf Sulphur Company had violated the law by trading in the company's stock without disclosing their knowledge of a big mineral discovery the company had made in Canada. Shortly thereafter, the SEC filed an administrative action against Merrill Lynch alleging that fourteen of its executives had passed inside information about an expected earnings decline at the Douglas Aircraft Company to fourteen other investment firms. (The case was settled with penalties all around.)

Then a small investor in the Penn Central Transportation Company, the nation's largest railroad, sued Howard Butcher III, a Philadelphia investment banker who served on the board of Penn Central and twenty-nine other companies, claiming he had "secret information" about the financial performance of the railroad and had urged his firm's customers to sell their stock in Penn Central, thereby depressing the stock price unfairly. Butcher promptly resigned from the boards of the thirty companies on which he served, with the lawsuit setting off a nationwide debate about whether investment bankers were using the information they learned while serving as corporate directors in an illegal way. For Butcher, "attitudes about the role of investment bankers" on the boards of companies had "change[d]." But John Loeb, the senior partner at Loeb, Rhoades & Co., disagreed. "If you take an ethical approach toward life, you're usually ahead of the rules," he told the *New York Times* in December 1968. Weinberg, not surprisingly, defended the practice. "I've been on boards for 40 years and there's no vice to having an investment banker on a board," he said. "Basically you've got to be honest"—invoking the familiar Wall Street refrain in matters related to potential conflicts of interest.

WITH WEINBERG'S PASSING, there was no question that Goldman Sachs was Levy's firm. When asked in a deposition when he became the senior partner of Goldman, Levy testified, "Since Mr. Sidney Weinberg's death in July of 1969." One of his first orders of business was to celebrate the firm's hundredth anniversary. This was done in a particularly low-key fashion, without any publicity, at a Bank of New York office building (for some unknown reason), on December 15, 1969. Along with speeches, the partners dined on shrimp cocktail, "assorted crackers," Duchess potatoes, and broiled Delmonico steak à la maître d'hôtel. For dessert, the group had lemon sherbet, Curaçao, and butter cookies.

In addition to the hundred-year-old firm, Weinberg had also bequeathed to Levy a passel of unexpected problems in Goldman's commercial paper business, the short-term, unsecured loans that had given Marcus Goldman his start in lower Manhattan. By 1969, Goldman was, by far, the largest commercial paper dealer on Wall Street and had proven itself expert at placing, for a fee, the short-term obligations of its clients with institutional investors, many of which were banks and insurance companies. The business was a low-margin, steadily profitable one and, since the Depression, had not posed any problems for Goldman since no companies had defaulted on their commercial paper obligations, in part because—generally speaking—by the late 1960s only the biggest companies with the best credit ratings had access to the market, given that the obligations were senior unsecured, low-yielding debt.

Suddenly this safe, boring business got scary. On the evening of December 27, word began to leak out that the Mill Factors Corporation, described as the "Tiffany" of finance companies and a "Cadillac" of its industry, was in serious financial difficulty—thanks to unexpectedly large losses in its loan portfolio—and would likely file for bankruptcy protection. The company, with grand offices at the New York Life Building on Madison Avenue, suggested that the losses in its loan portfolio would more than wipe out its profits for the year. Creditors were scrambling to figure out what the size of their losses would be. Other finance companies had already started circling the company to see if they could pick up its assets on the cheap.

Goldman Sachs had long been the chief commercial paper underwriter for Mill. Indeed, just three months before the calamitous announcement, Goldman had sold $1 million of the company's commercial paper to New York Life, which was not only Mill's largest single creditor (owed a total of $8.4 million) but also its landlord (owed nearly $100,000 in annual rent payments). Over the years, Goldman had placed some $7 million of the company's commercial paper with about fifty different investors. Most of that paper was then in default, meaning that Mill had stopped paying the interest on the IOUs in order to preserve cash. It turned out that of Mill's loan portfolio of $45 million, $35 million was suspect and unlikely to be paid back to Mill. This disaster, in turn, made it virtually impossible for Mill to make good on its own short- and long-term debt of more than $80 million. "There is no gainsaying the fact that there was mismanagement here," according to the company's special outside counsel, Charles Seligson. "You don't get a portfolio of $35 million in doubtful accounts out of a portfolio of $45 million unless somebody poorly managed the extension of credit."

Some of Mill Factors's creditors thought Goldman should have known about the company's problems before selling its commercial paper. Among them were Worcester County National Bank, in Worcester, Massachusetts, which bought $1.3 million in Mill's commercial paper on behalf of a number of charitable accounts it administered, and Alexander & Baldwin, a Hawaii-based diversified mini-conglomerate, which bought $1 million in Mill's commercial paper from Goldman. The Worcester bank's antipathy toward Goldman was such that it was the lone creditor holdout on a plan—which required unanimity from the creditors—to keep Mill out of bankruptcy and effect a sale of the company to another finance company. "Our position is that Goldman was negligent in recommending this paper to us and should make good the loss," John Hunt, a senior vice president of the bank, told the *Times*. Goldman refused to cover the losses—estimated at 60 percent of the original investment—for fear that a precedent would be set that it would have to follow in other bankruptcies where the commercial paper creditors suffered losses. In the end, while others in the case kicked in large sums to settle lawsuits—for instance, Mill's accounting firm, Lybrand, Ross Brothers & Montgomery, paid nearly $5 million—Goldman paid only $50,000 but denied "all liability" and agreed to settle the cases only "to avoid the time and expense" of protracted litigation.

Goldman was right to be worried about setting a precedent. The Mill Factors crash was merely an amuse-bouche for the collapse of the Penn Central Transportation Company, the nation's largest railroad, in June 1970. The Penn Central bankruptcy was then the largest in American corporate history, and Goldman's commercial paper business was at the center of the company's financial difficulties. Once again, Goldman Sachs was facing an existential threat. "Everyone hunkered down," Doty said. "We had a couple of difficult years."

CHAPTER 7

CAVEAT EMPTOR

Penn Central was formed, in February 1968, by the merger of the Pennsylvania and New York Central railroads to become the nation's largest railroad and one of its largest companies. Together, the two companies had some $1.2 billion in debt outstanding, spread out among more than fifty different bonds. After the merger, the company's executives sought to refinance and consolidate that debt. On July 29, 1968, the Interstate Commerce Commission, Penn Central's regulator, approved the company's request to issue commercial paper for the first time. On August 6, Goldman sold $35 million of Penn Central's commercial paper and expected to sell another $65 million by the end of the year. The offering was "very well received," Goldman said.

Fewer than two years later, Penn Central had filed for bankruptcy protection—allowing it to reorganize as a going concern, as opposed to being liquidated—in part because the company could not repay the minimum of $75 million in commercial paper outstanding it had to refinance by the end of June 1970. Penn Central had been negotiating with the U.S. government to provide it with loan guarantees, but those discussions did not come to fruition. The company operated 20,530 miles of track in sixteen states and two Canadian provinces and provided 35 percent of all railroad passenger service in the United States. The company also had substantial real-estate holdings, including Grand Central Terminal in New York, plus much of the land on Park Avenue between Grand Central and the Waldorf-Astoria hotel. Nevertheless, Penn Central ended up defaulting on $87 million of its short-term commercial paper. Sensing legal trouble, Levy dispatched John Weinberg, Sidney's son, to try to negotiate a deal with various holders of the Penn Central commercial paper whereby Goldman would buy back their paper at fifty cents on the dollar. Weinberg was not successful, and Goldman was soon facing serious problems.

Levy, meanwhile, was branching further out into public service, albeit in a behind-the-scenes role. In May 1970, New York governor Nelson Rockefeller appointed him to serve on the board of the powerful Port of New York Authority, which was responsible for overseeing the bridges, tunnels, and airports taking people into and out of the city. Soon enough, Levy was involved in getting his Wall Street buddies to pressure Rockefeller's successor, Governor Malcolm Wilson, to change his mind about raiding the authority's coffers to support mass transit, a move that really upset Lewis Kaden, then the counsel to Brendan Byrne, the governor of New Jersey, who wanted to use the money. "Levy is where the money is," Kaden told *New York* magazine.

Bob Rubin, meanwhile, who was still working for Tenenbaum in Goldman's arbitrage department, flirted with leaving the firm. Sandy Lewis, who ran White, Weld's arbitrage department, said Rubin called him about the possibility of getting a job working for Lewis there. Rubin had only been at Goldman for just over three years when he approached Lewis, at White, Weld, but clearly he was antsy.

According to Lewis, Rubin approached him in 1969. "Bob Rubin wanted to get out," Lewis said. He had grown disenchanted with Goldman and what he thought it took to succeed there. "It's a dishonest mess that's making honest people dishonest," Lewis said Rubin told him. He said Rubin complained about "making the calls" as well as the erratic behavior he witnessed day in, day out. "People were throwing books and chairs around," Lewis said Rubin told him. "There were lots of temper tantrums. But what's going on was to cover the kind of things they had to do that made them ashamed of themselves." (Sandy Lewis was convicted of federal charges of stock manipulation in 1989, pardoned by President Clinton in 2001, and had his lifetime trading ban overturned by the Securities and Exchange Commission in 2006.)

In his book, Rubin had a different version of his pursuit of the White, Weld offer. He wrote that a friend of his from law school, Eli Jacobs, worked at the firm and when "the fellow who ran its arbitrage department left"—Sandy Lewis, who was fired in December 1969— Jacobs called him to see if he would be interested. Paul Hallingby, the senior partner of White, Weld, offered to make Rubin a partner, at age thirty-two. Rubin was prepared to accept the White, Weld partnership. "I liked what I saw there," he said. He also assumed he would never become a partner at Goldman, and White, Weld was a good alternative, he thought, and in any event a certainty. "I never in a million years thought they'd offer me a partnership," Rubin said. Rubin went to Tenenbaum to tell him he was leaving Goldman for White, Weld. Tenenbaum went to see Levy, who, Rubin later wrote, "wasn't happy about having to deal with this problem." Tenenbaum said to Levy, "Gus, Hallingby offered Rubin a partnership. I think he's really valuable to us. He's a terrific kid. You know it and what he's like." Levy told Tenenbaum, "Okay. Tell him to keep his nose clean. At the end of the year, we'll put him up for partnership." What appealed to Tenenbaum and Levy about Rubin was, among other things, Tenenbaum recalled, "his pedigree of law. He'd been summa cum laude, and law degree, and the whole thing. He just was a bright kid, and careful." Tenenbaum said he did not mention it to Levy, but he was also impressed by Rubin's wife, Judy, who would eventually be named the New York City commissioner of protocol.

Based on Tenenbaum's representation about a Goldman partnership, Rubin told Hallingby he was staying at Goldman. True to Levy's word, he did put Rubin up for partner at the end of 1970. On December 30, Rubin became one of nine men to be named new general partners of the firm, along with H. Corbin Day, Eugene Mercy Jr., and Eric Sheinberg. "I was, to say the least, surprised," Rubin said, without explaining how he reconciled being surprised with what Levy had told him the year before. It was not lost on him, though, that he became a partner at Goldman in the middle of the Penn Central fiasco. "I thought to myself, 'This isn't very good, because there isn't going to be a firm'" of which to be a partner.

Rubin was onto something. By November, four investors in the Penn Central commercial paper sued the firm in federal court in Manhattan for more than $23 million, nearly half of the firm's capital. "The basic issue is this," the *Times* reported, "to what extent are commercial paper dealers, who have placed about $13 billion of the total [commercial] paper outstanding [of about $34 billion], responsible when one of the companies whose notes they are handling get into financial trouble." For Goldman, in 1970, this was not just a theoretical question but rather went to the heart of whether it would remain solvent. At that time, the firm had around $50 million in capital—all of it from its partners. Needless to say, if the holders of the full $87 million of the Penn Central commercial paper Goldman placed came after the firm, the effect could be devastating, especially since the Mill Factors case still loomed.

The plaintiffs in the lawsuit against Goldman were Fundamental Investors, a $1 billion mutual fund that held $20 million of Penn Central's commercial paper bought in a ten-day period near the end of 1969; C. R. Anthony, an Oklahoma City retailer with $1.5 million of the paper; Welch Foods, Inc., of Westfield, New York, the maker of Welch's grape juice, with a $1 million investment; and Younkers Inc., a Des Moines–based retailer, which bought $500,000 of the Penn Central notes. In their fifteen-page complaint, the creditors charged Goldman with "fraud, deception, concealment, suppression and false pretense" in the sale of the commercial paper to them. They claimed Goldman had "made promises and representations as to the future [of the company] which were beyond reasonable expectations and unwarranted by existing circumstances," had made "representations and statements which were false," that Goldman had represented that Penn Central was "prime quality," and that Goldman had made "an adequate investigation of, and kept under continuous current review, the financial condition of Penn Central." The plaintiffs also claimed that Goldman had agreed to buy back the commercial paper. "For the commercial paper holders this was an extremely big event," explained Daniel Pollack, the plaintiffs' attorney, about the Penn Central default. "For example, for the farmers at Welch's this was all their money. One bad harvest and the potential loss of cash equivalents was a potential catastrophic event for them."

Penn Central had been Gus Levy's client, but in the grand Wall Street tradition of success having many fathers and failure being an orphan, the firm's defense in the media was left to Robert G. Wilson, the partner in charge of Goldman's commercial paper business. "[T]here is absolutely no merit to the claims which have been made against Goldman Sachs," he told the *Times*. "We regret that anyone is facing a potential financial loss as a result of the unforeseen circumstances, but the action against Goldman Sachs has no basis in fact. We intend to resist it vigorously." He added that during the time that Goldman was selling Penn Central's commercial paper, "we were confident that the transportation company was credit worthy" and "had access to credit at least sufficient to cover its current obligations and repay commercial as it became due." He said that even in late May 1970—a few weeks before the company's bankruptcy filing—Wilson had "every expectation" that Penn Central would be able to get a government-guaranteed loan, which did not happen, despite the company's final appeals to Congress and to President Nixon.

A day after the Fundamental Investors suit, a subsidiary of American Express sued Goldman, too, for $2 million, as a result of sales of the Penn Central commercial paper, even though Goldman was also American Express's commercial paper dealer (American Express's claim was later increased to $4 million). Then, in February 1971, the Walt Disney Company sued Goldman for $1.5 million as a result of the collapse of Penn Central after Disney had bought $1.5 million of the commercial paper. A month later, the Mallinckrodt Chemical Works sued Goldman, among others, on account of its loss in the Penn Central commercial paper. In the end, some forty lawsuits were filed against Goldman.

THIS WAS YET another precarious time on Wall Street. The crux of the problem, which Wall Street historians have dubbed the "back-office crisis," was that during 1967 trading volumes on the major stock exchanges exploded, and the private, poorly capitalized Wall Street partnerships were ill equipped to handle the extensive paperwork involved with settling trades occasioned by the "sudden and unexpected upsurge" in volume. Many firms were slow to add the back-office personnel required to handle the new flow. Unfortunately, when the personnel were eventually hired—in a rush, of course—performance suffered. Some firms were drowning in a sea of unprocessed, and inaccurately accounted for, paper. But by the end of 1969, "the worst of the paperwork problems had been surmounted," according to Lee Arning, then a New York Stock Exchange executive.

The crisis, though, had just begun, for at the very moment that many brokerages had increased their personnel costs to scale the mountain of paper, the volume of business fell off a cliff. There was a feeling that 1970 was capitalism's most acute test since 1929. These were not Goldman's problems, though. The firm had virtually no retail customers and did not have the back-office problems experienced by retail brokers. Indeed, in 1970, the firm's profits "topped $20 million," Levy told the *Wall Street Journal,* the third highest in its 101-year history. The "gratifying" results came from Goldman's role in underwriting sixty-four debt and equity offerings, raising more than $3.5 billion, and an 80 percent increase in the volume of the firm's block trades. Goldman's capital increased to $49 million, from $46 million, and its leverage ratio— aggregate indebtedness to net capital—was 6.5, well within the 20:1 stock exchange regulations. But, thanks to the Penn Central bankruptcy, Goldman's problems were every bit as acute as those of its Wall Street brethren. Not that most people had any idea. For instance, in July 1971, despite the ongoing existential threat, Goldman appeared to get the full cooperation of John H. Allan, a Wall Street reporter at the *New York Times,* for a lengthy feature about the firm that discussed everything but Goldman's precarious legal and financial prospects. Goldman, Allan reported, was doing just fine.

The story was a coup for Edward Novotny, a young former journalist turned public-relations guru, who quietly started working for Goldman in 1970 and continued until his death in 2004. Over time, Goldman paid Novotny upward of $200,000 a year to manage its PR from his home office at Tudor Tower, on the east side of Manhattan. Goldman's aggressive public-relations efforts became part of its legend. "He was the invisible man," explained a former Goldman executive. "You dialed Ed Novotny's extension at the firm and it rang in his home office in Tudor Towers where it was, and he had a secretary in there, and he operated on a deep well of power." He said that Novotny's "whole thing" was "this incredible paranoia," where "the firm would never go on the record." If Novotny told a reporter something it would always be on "deep, deep, deep, deep, deep—five 'deeps' in a row—background," the former Goldman executive said. "Every time he would describe a reporter to me it would be he or she 'is *very, very, very* dangerous.' Even Bill Cunningham, the society photographer, was '*very, very, very* dangerous. So watch it.'"

The conceit of the *Times* article was that Goldman was unusual on Wall Street for having equally respected and profitable investment banking and trading operations under one roof, in this case with trading on the fourth floor of 55 Broad Street, "which rips with action," and banking one floor above, where the "atmosphere is subdued and Ivy League and the action more difficult to see." But, the *Times* reported, Goldman "seems to have no trouble at all in accommodating them under a single business roof and, in fact, has continued to look for more activities." The firm's next moves, the paper reported, would be in growing its bond underwriting and trading for both corporations and municipalities. Goldman was considering becoming a government bond dealer and was moving into real-estate finance, lease finance, and international markets. The goal was to boost profits beyond the $20 million Goldman made in 1970, an astounding almost 50 percent return on its $49 million in capital. By then, Goldman had opened its first foreign office—in London—as part of "a major international effort," Levy explained, which was separate from the alliance Goldman once had with Kleinwort Benson.

The *Times* article not only glorified Levy but also showcased the new generation of leaders at the firm. There was John Whitehead—a "49-year-old amiable, reflective investment banker" and graduate of both Haverford College and Harvard Business School—who was responsible for the firm's New Business Group within investment banking. Whitehead had taken to his role with such relish that not only had he identified the four thousand U.S. companies that made at least $1 million in profits a year, but he also had figured out which of Goldman's bankers would call on them and try to convince them to do business with Goldman Sachs.

The idea for a more systematic and aggressive calling effort came to Whitehead as Sidney Weinberg was getting older and Whitehead realized that Weinberg seemed like the only person at the firm capable of bringing in investment banking business, such as debt or equity underwriting or M&A deals. "Every single piece of investment banking business . . . every single one during at least a ten-year period, was produced by Sidney Weinberg," Whitehead said in a May 2003 speech. He wrote a confidential memo for Weinberg's eyes only about how a new group, inside investment banking, could be organized as a new business effort. "I knew the memo had to be approved by Sidney," Whitehead said, "so I wrote it in a delicate way. I said nobody will ever duplicate Sidney Weinberg—we don't have anybody here and couldn't get anybody, but if we could have ten people who each produced 20 percent of the business that Sidney Weinberg produces every year, our business would be twice as big as it is today." Weinberg stuffed the memo in his desk drawer and ignored it. One day, months later, after he had become a partner, Whitehead summoned the courage to ask Weinberg about his idea. He opened his desk drawer, looked at the forlorn document. "What a crazy idea," Weinberg responded. "We don't need anything like this. Do you really want to do it?"

Whitehead did. He had hoped to discuss the idea at the next partners' meeting. But "there weren't any partners' meetings," he said. "There never was a partner meeting. The only partner meeting was the annual event, which took place at various different exclusive places. And the year I first became a partner it took place in the private room of the '21 Club.' And the partners came. It was all in tuxedos." He later convinced the partnership to approve the plan by discussing it with them individually and getting their support. By July 1971, Whitehead was happy to report to the *Times* that, by his analysis, Goldman had made significant market share gains in investment banking. In 1968, Whitehead figured Goldman had 7.8 percent of the market—what he described as the "public and private financing we would have done if asked"—and that Goldman's share had increased to 11.6 percent in 1970 and so far in 1971 it was "higher still."

The *Times* article also featured John Weinberg, Sidney's son, and the continuity he provided at the firm with the Weinberg legacy, including the fact that John Weinberg took over his father's seat on nine corporate boards, including General Electric and B. F. Goodrich. Despite the controversy starting to percolate about the potential conflicts that emerge when investment bankers sit on corporate boards, the article made clear that Goldman Sachs and John Weinberg were outspoken believers that such conflicts could be managed. (At that time, Goldman partners sat on the boards of some seventy-five companies.)

Along with Levy, both Whitehead and Weinberg served on Goldman's six-man Management Committee, which ran the firm. The committee met at 9:00 a.m. every Monday morning for around an hour. The creation of the Management Committee was one of the prices that Sidney Weinberg extracted from Gus Levy when Levy moved Weinberg out of 55 Broad Street. The other members of the powerful committee were Howard "Ray" Young, head of Securities Sales; George Doty, a former senior partner at Coopers & Lybrand and head of the Administrative Department; Edward Schrader, head of the Buying Department. Levy described Whitehead as being the head of the New Business Group and John Weinberg as "free-lancing" with no specific departmental responsibility. This group was ably assisted, according to the article, by Tenenbaum and Robert Mnuchin, the block trader.

At the very end, Allan mentioned the problems in Goldman's commercial paper business and that Robert Wilson reported to his boss John Weinberg. "Unlike the founder of the firm," the *Times* observed, "Mr. Wilson does not scurry about the financial district stuffing notes in a stove-pipe hat, but instead he supervises a 46-man staff that raises as much as $40 billion a year in short-term funds for industry." As for the Penn Central lawsuits, Wilson said there was "absolutely no merit to the claims" and that the commercial paper business had picked up considerably since the credit freeze brought on by the collapse of Penn Central. While Allan noted that ongoing write-offs of commercial paper losses by big banks was the "chief potential trouble spot" at Goldman, he concluded by pointing out that Goldman had settled the claims against the firm in the Mill Factors matter by paying $50,000, a tiny fraction of the losses suffered by the buyers of the paper.

Unmentioned in the *Times* article was the fact that in March 1971, Goldman had decided to limit the liability of its partners to the amount of cash they had tied up in the company; formerly they had each been liable for their entire net worth. Although the *Wall Street Journal* reported that the move was "in line with a growing trend among many leading securities firms," which was true, one could not help thinking the move was also prompted by the severity of the Penn Central litigation against the firm. Also left out of the *Times* paean was the February 1971 news of yet another lawsuit—for $125 million—brought against Goldman and Sidney Weinberg Jr., known as "Jimmy," by American Cyanamid Corporation, the chemical manufacturer and consumer products company. American Cyanamid accused Goldman and Jimmy Weinberg of arranging to scuttle its deal to purchase Elizabeth Arden—which Goldman had been hired to sell—for $35 million by turning around and then encouraging Eli Lilly, a Cyanamid rival, to buy Elizabeth Arden for $38.5 million.

FAR LESS OF a coup for Novotny was a June 1972 *Wall Street Journal* article describing a racial discrimination lawsuit brought against Goldman by James E. Cofield Jr., a black Stanford University MBA, one of only two black students in his class. Two years earlier, according to Cofield's lawsuit, while Cofield was an MBA student at Stanford, he applied for a job at Goldman. Cofield had previously worked at the First National City Bank and Blair & Co., a regional brokerage. He was a graduate of the University of North Carolina and had attended Howard University's school of law. He first applied for a summer job at Goldman in March 1969, hoping to work in corporate finance. His résumé was sent to John Jamison, a partner in the firm's Corporate Finance Department, and who had been recruiting students at Stanford. Cofield wrote a follow-up letter to Jamison on March 18 and offered to meet with him when he was in New York on March 25. On April 11, Jamison wrote to Cofield that Goldman could not "work you into our operations this summer" and added, "[f]rankly, we have been so bust we haven't been able to spare the people over the last several years to develop or supervise a program that would be meaningful to any summer employee or useful to us." Jamison encouraged Cofield to "drop by to visit with us again if you get the chance." Cofield ended up working at Blair & Co. that summer.

The next year, Cofield tried again to get hired at Goldman. The dearth of blacks and Hispanics in white-collar jobs—and specifically on Wall Street—had been the subject of a series of hearings held by the Equal Employment Opportunity Commission between January 15 and January 18, 1968, in New York City. On January 15, partner George Doty testified before the commission on behalf of Goldman. In his opening statement, Doty explained that with the large increase in stock exchange trading volume, Wall Street firms, including Goldman, had been looking to hire more people, including by putting ads in the newspapers, talking to headhunters, and interviewing MBAs on college campuses. Nevertheless, he testified, "in the face of a very strong demand for qualified workers by ourselves and our competitors, the supply of Negroes or Spanish-Americans motivated to seek employment in our industry seems very small." He said Goldman had not had much success hiring blacks at the firm, despite interviewing at seventy-five schools and being willing to consider the applications of people who wrote to the firm unsolicited. Doty said Goldman saw "only one Negro student" in seventy-five schools and that he had not been aware of a "single write-in from a Negro."

On February 20, 1970, Cofield interviewed at Stanford with Jamison, who, according to Cofield, told him during the interview that his application for employment could not move forward because "of the negative view held by a senior partner regarding blacks." (In an interview, Cofield identified the partner as Richard Menschel.) "Jamison said that this particular partner . . . did not want any Blacks in the corporate finance department," according to a memo Cofield wrote on March 4 to a professor of finance at Stanford. "Thus he did not see how they could make me an offer." When Cofield asked Jamison who was responsible for hiring, Jamison told him "they would like to have a consensus of the key people in the department favoring the hiring of an individual before an offer was made" and that Jamison had "indicated" during the February 20 interview that Menschel "had refused to talk to me" and "of course, Jamison indicated that he was very sorry—his day was spoiled because he had to tell me this—that this was a very bad situation, and hopefully things would change over time. He felt that since the people at City Bank were pleased with me, I had beautiful opportunities there."

Cofield recalled "being stunned, really stunned when he dropped the bomb pretty early in our talk. I'd spoken to [Goldman] prior to that and I really thought I would be hired" because Jamison, without saying so, "sort of let on like I'd be hired. Like it sounds good and I'm really impressed by you." After making the statement about the "senior partner," Cofield said Jamison tried "to lessen the blow" by suggesting Goldman wasn't the right place for him anyway and that he "had some good opportunities" at First National City Bank. When Goldman denied Cofield a job in the firm's Corporate Finance Department, he asked for a job in another area of the firm but was also denied a chance to pursue that opportunity.

A day later, Jamison sent Cofield an Express Mail, handwritten, somewhat opaque note that he had written the day of the interview: "Your quiet reaction to our conversation this morning, I believe, belied your concern regarding it. I very honestly, but foolishly, allowed my frustrations to become yours. In fairness to the confidence of our conversation and what I have considered a valued personal relationship, I would hope that you would get in touch with me directly if your concern continues as mine does." Jamison gave Cofield his home and work telephone numbers and said he could call collect "anytime."

Cofield said that after the incident with Jamison, Goldman tried several times to offer him a job—doing what he was never sure—but he never thought the firm was serious about him or his career. "I really wanted to work in corporate finance," he said. "And I thought I was close to a job with Goldman. Then Jamison shared that point of view with me and it was all over." Cofield had grown up in Raleigh, North Carolina, and his mother was one of the first blacks to serve on both the Wake County Board of Education and the Wake County Board of Commissioners. He said he knew what to expect when it came to discrimination. "But this really surprised me," he said.

Cofield reported to his Stanford finance professor that he "place[d] no trust or confidence whatsoever in Jamison" and "if the situation were as Jamison described it on Friday he could override the bigot's decision and offer me a position anyway. It appears as though the main hiring responsibility for the department lays [sic] with Jamison."

The incident led to much consternation amond Cofield, Stanford, and Goldman. On February 27, Levy wrote to his friend Arjay Miller, the dean of the business school and a former president of Ford Motor Company. "I deeply regret that a misunderstanding has arisen regarding the employment practices at Goldman, Sachs & Co.," he wrote. "As a director of the New York Urban Coalition and one who has urged the employment of minorities both within my firm and the Stock Exchange community, it is embarrassing to feel the necessity of explaining our policies and outlining our performance in this regard." Levy attached a chart showing that of the firm's 1,505 employees as of May 1969, 201, or 13.4 percent, were blacks, women, "Oriental," "American Indian"—one man— or "Spanish Sur-Named Employees." He neglected to point out to Miller that there was only one black professional at Goldman and the other 94 blacks were clerical or janitorial employees.

On March 6, Robert Rosenzweig, Stanford's associate provost, met with Jamison—he referred to him as John "Jameson"—and H. Fred Krimendahl II, another Goldman partner and the head of the Buying Department, in New York, where he had been on other business. "I learned little that we did not already know," he wrote in a March 9 memo but then summarized that "Jameson and company would like very much to deny that anything happened. All that stands in the way are the facts." He said Goldman's "chief worry" was that Cofield "will bring an action against them, presumably for violation of one or another of the fair employment statu[t]es. Because of this fear, no one from Goldman, Sachs will speak directly to Cofield on the grounds—no doubt sound in the view of what they have already said—that more words mean more trouble." But this strategy "leaves them in a bind," Rosenzweig wrote, of being "solely at the mercy of Mr. Cofield's decision." Goldman wanted Stanford to mediate. "More specifically," Rosenzweig wrote, "they would like us to read Mr. Cofield's mind and advise them as to the best among the following courses: 1. Do nothing, if Cofield plans to do nothing; 2. Offer to bring Cofield to New York for an interview—their normal course for an applicant in whom they are interested, though they recognize that in this case it would be tantamount to offering him a job; 3. Just offer him a job."

Rosenzweig would have none of it. "I said we would not mediate, but that we would, of course, report to Cofield on our discussions with Goldman, Sachs, including this one, so that he would have all the evidence before him to aid him in deciding on a course of action," he wrote. In his memo to the file, Rosenzweig wrote that Stanford did not "want a fight with Goldman, Sachs or anyone else" and that if Cofield decided to "press the issue," the university would "stand with him based on the facts as we know them, since we want least of all to be in a position of aiding or being blind to discrimination." Rosenzweig sent a copy of the memo to Cofield, who later said in an affidavit that at this point Goldman "realized that they had blundered in rejecting me for racial reasons."

On March 16, he replied to Rosenzweig in preparation for a meeting he was having with him and other university officials that day: "Goldman, Sachs' discriminatory employment practices are symbolic of the injustices and discrimination Blacks have faced and continue to face. Although many Whites profess in their public life to denounce discrimination and urge equal treatment and opportunity for Blacks, their actions clearly indicate that they are racist." Cofield wrote that he would welcome the opportunity to discuss with Levy "the elimination of Goldman, Sachs' discriminatory employment practices" and invited him to Palo Alto "as soon after March 30th as possible." Without that discussion, he wrote, "we" would have "no choice" but to decide among four choices: that there be "an immediate cessation of all recruiting activities" by Goldman at Stanford; that Cofield sue Goldman privately; that he sue Goldman through the Justice Department based on equal employment statutes; or that a "sanction and redress" be undertaken by the New York Stock Exchange against Goldman.

During the meeting, Rosenzweig read Cofield's memo over the phone to Krimendahl. Stanford also sent a copy of the memo to Goldman in New York. On April 6, Krimendahl wrote to Cofield that Goldman now believed "it would be fruitful to hold further discussions with you relating to employment with our firm." Krimendahl offered Cofield an all-expense-paid trip to New York "at your earliest convenience" to "visit with members of our Buying Department as well as various partners of the firm." Cofield did not respond to Krimendahl's letter.

On April 27, Cofield filed a charge of discrimination against Goldman with the EEOC based on his February 20 interview with Jamison. He also filed a five-page affidavit that described what had transpired during the previous nine weeks. On June 10, Stanford's general counsel sent

Jamison a letter—again misspelling his name—describing that Stanford's president had asked that a study be conducted "to ensure that firms and companies which recruit here do not discriminate in hiring" and that in the "course of that study . . . the issues raised by Mr. Cofield will be considered fully." He wrote that pending the outcome of·the study Goldman would be barred from recruiting at Stanford, a ban that lasted five years. "There's not much more that Stanford could have done," Cofield said in a recent interview.

After graduating from Stanford, Cofield moved to Boston to take a job at Arthur D. Little & Co., the management consultants. One day, he got a call from Dick Menschel, whom Jamison had cited as the partner who raised the objection to Cofield's hiring, inviting him to dinner to talk "on a personal basis [about] what he thought were misunderstandings regarding Goldman Sachs." On August 17, Cofield filed a complaint with the New York State Division of Human Rights against Goldman, as well as, individually, Levy, Whitehead, Jamison, and Krimendahl, charging them with "unlawful discriminatory practice relating to employment by refusing to hire him because of his race and color." On August 28, Menschel and Cofield dined together at Locke-Ober restaurant—one of the toniest in the city—and Menschel assured Cofield he was not prejudiced against blacks and that Jamison had gotten it wrong. "Goldman Sachs does not have discriminatory hiring practices," Menschel told him. He also said he did not think Jamison was "a bigot" and that what Jamison said was not "a representation of his own views either." But the discussion steered clear of the actual words Jamison had used in the February 20 interview. A day earlier, Goldman would later claim, it offered Cofield a job—"a definite job offer," the firm said. Cofield denied any such offer had been made. On October 16, though, as part of "an investigatory conference" at the New York State Division of Human Rights, Goldman made "a definite offer of employment" to Cofield.

On December 16, 1970, the EEOC's acting district director in New York "found reasonable cause to believe" that Cofield's charges against Goldman were true and found "no concrete evidence to support Goldman's claims that it had 'actively recruited for executive personnel among minority groups as indicative of their commitment to the objective of providing equal employment opportunity to all qualified persons.'" There was an effort made at the end of December to settle the New York matter through a "proposed conciliation agreement" that included the agreement that Goldman would hire Cofield in Krimendahl's department.

But on January 16, 1971, Cofield rejected the settlement because he claimed he was never offered a job. "It is the practice of most firms to put an offer for employment in writing," he wrote. "This they have not done." He also objected to the settlement because there were no provisions in it to increase "the number of Black and other minority group employees in professional and executive positions." On June 16, the EEOC gave Cofield permission to bring a civil suit against Goldman in U.S. district court and told him he had thirty days in which to do so. If he failed to file, he would lose his right to sue. On July 2, the EEOC as a whole adopted the finding of the New York district office in Cofield's case and encouraged both Cofield and Goldman to "make proposals" on how to settle the matter. On March 6, 1972, Cofield and his lawyer, Clarence Dilday, of Owens & Dilday, in Boston, filed a suit against Goldman.

In the suit, which had the blessing of the Equal Employment Opportunities Commission and the New York State Division of Human Rights, Cofield sought a finding that Goldman violated the law and would be enjoined from doing so again. He also sought $100,000 personally and another $1 million from Goldman on behalf of other plaintiffs—the suit was given class-action status—"who might suffer from the firm's alleged discriminatory practices." But Cofield had filed the suit too late. On September 12, 1972, the U.S. District Court of the Southern District of New York found no "just cause for the delay" and dismissed Cofield's suit against Goldman.

Before the ruling against him in September, Cofield had taken the story to the *Wall Street Journal,* figuring he had missed the deadline and could not prevail. James Gilmour, Goldman's personnel manager, said the incident was a misunderstanding. "Somehow or other he felt we discriminated in our recruitment of college grads," he told the paper. "We tried to tell him that wasn't the reason and we've taken in blacks before." Gilmour said Cofield had wanted a job involving "risk capital," so the firm suggested he might have a better chance getting such a job somewhere else.

Cofield's brother, a student at Wharton at around the same time that Cofield had graduated from Stanford, remembered being at a Goldman Sachs recruiting event with John Whitehead, then on Goldman's Management Committee, when another student, who happened to be black, asked Whitehead about the incident with James Cofield at Stanford. Whitehead, who was busy touting Goldman's virtues to an eager audience, was left speechless by the question. In 1971, Goldman established the Goldman Sachs Fellowships at Harvard Business School, awarded annually to outstanding minority-group students.

DESPITE THE MISDIRECTION provided in the *Times* article, the Goldman partners were immensely fearful of what the potential consequences of the growing Penn Central lawsuits might be. "There was real fear that the liability for the Penn Central could put the firm under . . . ," Rubin explained. "People were really deeply worried that the firm and their net worths were going to be gone. They were surprised by the dangers lurking in the firm's commercial paper business. They weren't traumatized, but they were deeply worried. Deeply worried." Rubin elaborated in his book: "As a private partnership, we faced unlimited liability, and some people worried whether the firm would survive." In his memoir, Whitehead echoed Rubin's concerns. "It was scary for all of us, because the total claims at one point exceeded the firm's capital, and the partners would be personally liable for the remainder in the unlikely event that all the suits went against us." To try to provide some comfort, Sullivan & Cromwell wrote a letter to Levy that it didn't think the payments that Goldman would likely have to make to Penn Central's commercial paper creditors would "impair" Goldman's capital. "Gus carried it in his jacket pocket as a kind of talisman," Rubin wrote.

A comprehensive, eight-hundred-page report by the U.S. Securities and Exchange Commission, released in August 1972, made clear what Levy, Rubin, and their partners were so worried about. According to the report, not only had Goldman puts its own interests before those of its clients, but it had also continued to sell Penn Central's commercial paper to investors after learning that the company was in dire financial straits. The allegations were devastating, especially for a firm anxious to portray itself as in the vanguard of Wall Street. "Goldman Sachs continued to sell [Penn Central's] commercial paper after [it] had received information about the financial condition of the [company,] which should have raised serious questions as to the safety of an investment in the company's commercial paper, and Goldman, Sachs did not disclose such information to its customers," according to the report. "The information which Goldman, Sachs received should have put [it] on notice that a thorough examination of the financial condition of [Penn Central] would seem appropriate in order that [it], and through [it, its] customers would be apprised of the current position of [Penn Central]. Despite these warning signs, Goldman, Sachs made no meaningful investigation. Such an examination would have disclosed that the financial condition of the company was more serious than had been revealed to the public."

From the time the Interstate Commerce Commission, or ICC, authorized Penn Central to sell its commercial paper to investors, in July 1968, to the company's bankruptcy nearly two years later, Goldman had been the sole underwriter of the company's commercial paper. By the end of 1969, Goldman had sold $200 million of Penn Central's commercial paper. By the first half of 1970, the $200 million outstanding had been reduced to $83 million, held by seventy-two Goldman customers who had purchased the paper between November 1969 and May 1970. "As commercial paper is universally believed to be a very low-risk security, these customers were shocked to learn, prior to the maturity date of their paper, that the [Penn Central] had filed a petition in bankruptcy [court]," according to the SEC report. "Penn Central has repaid none of this indebtedness, and there is little likelihood of repayment."

Goldman's relationship with Penn Central originated with Levy's twenty-two-year friendship with David C. Bevan, Penn Central's longtime chief financial officer. By March 1968, months before the ICC approved Penn Central's application to issue commercial paper and after a round of meetings among Bevan, Levy, and Wilson, Goldman's head of commercial paper, Penn Central decided to hire Goldman to sell its commercial paper to investors.

According to Wilson, Goldman "followed its usual procedures for taking on a new issuer" but, apparently, these procedures did not include preparing any written reports about Penn Central's creditworthiness, according to the SEC. Jack Vogel, head of Goldman's commercial paper credit department, told the SEC that Goldman got one new commercial paper client a week and issued paper for some 250 separate companies. Vogel had a staff of four people to help him decide the creditworthiness of these companies and to help him review their prospects on an ongoing basis.

Within weeks of the ICC's decision to allow Penn Central to issue commercial paper, Goldman was busy flogging $100 million of it. Between September 1969 and May 1970, though, the SEC contended that Goldman "gained possession of material adverse information, some from public sources and some from nonpublic sources indicating a continuing deterioration of the financial condition of the [railroad]. Goldman, Sachs did not communicate this information to its commercial paper customers, nor did it undertake a thorough investigation of the company. If Goldman, Sachs had heeded these warnings and undertaken a reevaluation of the company, it would have learned that its condition was substantially worse than had been publicly reported."

From public information available in November 1969, Goldman should have known that Penn Central, the railroad (as opposed to the holding company, with other assets in it like Grand Central, Madison Square Garden, and a private-jet leasing business), had lost $40.2 million during the first nine months of 1969, $26.4 million more than the railroad lost in 1968. Also in November, Penn Central decided not to pay its quarterly dividend, often a sign of impending financial trouble. In his testimony at the time before the ICC, Penn Central's outside counsel explained the company was "having a very difficult time effecting the merger" of the two railroads. ("[M]anagement was very upset by this statement," the SEC reported.) "[T]his did not cause Goldman, Sachs to re-examine the financial condition of the company whose paper Goldman, Sachs was selling as prime rated commercial paper," the SEC found.

Goldman's Wilson had concerns about Penn Central. On September 3, 1969, he requested a meeting with the company's senior executives in the finance division. "[I]t had been a long time since we had gotten together to talk about the company," he wrote in an internal memo. "We have a lot of questions to ask about the merger, cash flow, and their long term financing plans." On September 19, Wilson and his Goldman colleagues met with Jonathan O'Herron, Penn Central's vice president of finance. O'Herron told Wilson that Penn Central's cash position in the first quarter of 1970 would be "very tight" and asked Goldman to sell "as much commercial paper as possible through April or longer." At that moment, lawyers would later argue, "Goldman Sachs was in possession of material, adverse non-public information about Penn Central which it failed to disclose." On October 22, O'Herron told Wilson that Penn Central would "show a small loss" in its third quarter but that the fourth quarter would improve and the company would be "in the black."

A week later, the ICC agreed to allow Penn Central to increase its commercial paper outstanding to $200 million, from $150 million. But the regulatory agency noted its concern that the company had a "deficit working capital situation" and seemed to be increasingly reliant on short-term financing—the commercial paper—to try to refinance long-term debt or to make capital expenditures. "The exhaustion of short-term credit to refinance maturing long-term debt or to finance long-term capital expenditures could expose a carrier to a serious crisis in the event of an economic squeeze, at which time a carrier may require short-term financing for traditional use," the ICC observed. "We are, therefore, concerned about the use of short-term financing for long-term purposes and feel that where necessary it should be resorted to cautiously."

According to the SEC, Goldman "never did explore in any depth" the topics Wilson said he wanted to investigate in his September memo, and the red flags raised by O'Herron and by the ICC "raised serious questions about the soundness" of Penn Central and "the safety of investing in its commercial paper." The observations "indicated that the company was experiencing a liquidity crisis and that it might find it extremely difficult in the future to meet its cash needs, thus jeopardizing commercial paper holders," according to the SEC. "A thorough study of the subject would have disclosed how much more damaging the information about the liquidity of the company and its ability to pay off commercial paper holders was." But Goldman did not "conduct any further investigation" and "made no disclosure of" the information "while continuing to actively promote the company's commercial paper. Customers were not told that the company expected to be in a tight cash position in the near future; were not told about the ICC order or the information about the deficit working capital situation or the fact that the company's commercial paper proceeds were being used for long-term financing."

But, according to the SEC, while Goldman did not share the bad news with its customers and continued to sell the increasingly squirrelly Penn Central commercial paper to them, it did use the public and non-public information to protect *itself* and its partners from having any of the paper on its own books. At the September 19 meeting, Wilson asked O'Herron to have Penn Central arrange for additional backup lines of credit from its banks to support the company's commercial paper program. In other words, Goldman wanted Penn Central to have another source of liquidity—banks—to borrow money from to make sure that its outstanding commercial paper, then around $200 million, could be paid off as it came due in the coming months. At that moment, Penn Central had already borrowed $250 million of its $300 million line of credit with a bank group, and O'Herron told Wilson the company intended to borrow the last $50 million to have in reserve to pay off the commercial paper if needed. Wilson asked O'Herron to get *another* $50 million as a backup for the commercial paper program. Even though Wilson did not like O'Herron's answer, O'Herron told him the company would not do it: "Penn Central already had a line of credit."

Throughout the first quarter of 1970, Goldman kept pushing Penn Central to increase its line of credit with its banks. "The management of the company was very reluctant to ask the banks for more line credit," the SEC found. "Although Goldman, Sachs never inquired too deeply into the reasons for the company's reluctance, it should have been apparent that the company had exhausted all credit." In his testimony to the SEC, Wilson conceded that such information "was information that investors would have considered important" but, according to the SEC, Goldman never disclosed it to its commercial paper customers. On February 5,

1970, O'Herron told Wilson that the company "could not raise any additional lines of credit," according to the SEC, which observed that "the inability of the company" to get the additional financing "as with other relevant information" was "not disclosed to customers."

February 5 turned out to be a busy day. Rather than the profit that Penn Central had earlier projected that the railroad would earn in the fourth quarter of 1969, the company announced that the railroad had lost $16 million, and lost $56 million for the full year. Wilson called O'Herron to set up a meeting to discuss the unexpected loss. The next day, Levy and Wilson met with Bevan and O'Herron. The company, Bevan explained, needed another $170 million for capital expenditures, which, combined with the expected loss, would bring its financing needs for the year to around $226 million. Bevan told Levy and Wilson that Penn Central had a variety of ideas about how to raise this additional financing, through a combination of a bridge loan, a Euro-dollar loan, and other financings. Levy and Wilson did not ask Bevan for the specifics of how he intended to raise this needed money. "I had complete confidence in Mr. Bevan's integrity," Levy told the SEC, "that he could do what he said he could do."

Goldman did not ask Bevan or O'Herron to provide any documentary evidence of Penn Central's financial situation for the coming year. "We had no reason to doubt him at that time," Wilson later said of Bevan, "and we were satisfied with the answers to the questions we asked in these areas." Vogel, the Goldman credit analyst, later told the SEC that the information obtained through these meetings "reassured" Goldman's executives that "the situation was one that was explainable, normal, and not of any problem."

Part of the reason why investors kept buying the Penn Central commercial paper that Goldman kept selling during this rocky financial period was that the rating agency—the National Credit Office—tasked with rating Penn Central's commercial paper kept giving the paper its "prime" rating, the highest available. After the fourth-quarter loss was announced on February 5, though, Allan Rogers, at National Credit Office, called Vogel at Goldman "to express concern over the sharply reduced earnings" at Penn Central. Vogel told Rogers that despite the earnings news Goldman was continuing to sell Penn Central's commercial paper, that Goldman felt Penn Central had enough ancillary assets that could be sold, and that he "was certain that something could be worked out should it ever become necessary." According to a memo Vogel wrote that day, "as a result of my comments," Rogers agreed to keep Penn Central as "a prime name," which it did until June 1. Wilson informed Levy that the National Credit Office, or NCO, would be keeping Penn Central as a prime name "as long as Goldman, Sachs was going to continue to handle the company's c/p [commercial paper]."

The circular nature of the relationship between Goldman and NCO—that NCO was continuing to rate Penn Central's paper as prime because Goldman was continuing to sell it and Goldman was continuing to sell it because NCO was rating it prime—infuriated the SEC. "As a result of this conversation with Rogers, Goldman, Sachs became aware of facts which undermined the value of the prime rating given by NCO to the company's paper and the independent nature of that determination," the agency observed. "Thus, from this point on it appears that NCO was not the thorough, independent rating service that Goldman, Sachs has represented to customers that it was. In addition, from this point on, Goldman, Sachs was aware that the 'prime' rating was based to a great extent on the fact that Goldman, Sachs was continuing to offer it." The SEC found the idea preposterous that Goldman would take comfort from asset sales worth multiples of the commercial paper outstanding—"which fact Goldman, Sachs had never investigated," the agency wrote—since "looking to liquidation as a means of determining credit-worthiness" meant that the "railroad clearly was no candidate for the 'prime' rating." Needless to say, the SEC continued, "Goldman, Sachs never disclosed to any customers any of these matters."

But the firm did take care of itself. "[O]n the very same day [it] learned of the first quarter losses, [it] contacted the company and got a commitment from the company to buy back $10 million of its commercial paper from Goldman, Sachs' inventory," the SEC wrote. Furthermore, from then on, Goldman "insisted" than any future commercial paper sales be sold on a "tap" arrangement, where Goldman would no longer underwrite the paper but rather agree to sell it only after it had found buyers in advance, "an arrangement involving no risk for Goldman, Sachs." Goldman had no exposure to Penn Central at the time of its bankruptcy but failed to share that fact with its customers or that the conditions under which it would sell the paper had changed. "Most customers believed that Goldman, Sachs maintained an inventory in all commercial paper which [it] offered for sale," according to the SEC report. "Many who purchased the company's paper after February 5, 1970, looked to the fact that Goldman, Sachs had an inventory of the company's paper as assurance that Goldman, Sachs felt the paper to be credit worthy." Pollack, the plaintiffs' attorney, remembered being appalled that Goldman had sold its Penn Central commercial paper back to the company at the same time Goldman continued to sell the paper to investors. "They did not view their inventory of Penn Central's commercial paper as something they owned as a security," he said. "They did not think they had an obligation to disclose their sales." He added, "While $10 million may seem like a rounding error, it was twenty percent of their capital at the time."

On March 23, O'Herron told Wilson that Penn Central's first quarter would "look terrible," but Goldman chose not to probe O'Herron about just how bad things were looking. Had Goldman done any research, it would have quickly discovered that Penn Central believed that it would have a $60 million loss in the first quarter. Apparently, instead of trying to figure out what was going wrong at Penn Central, Goldman was focused on selling another $17.3 million of the company's commercial paper to eighteen of its customers. "None of these customers were told about these expected terrible results for the first quarter," the SEC reported. On April 14, O'Herron reiterated his earlier view and told Wilson that Penn Central's first quarter would be "lousy" and the losses "staggering." The company's cash position, he said, was "in very serious shape."

Based on O'Herron's latest comments, Wilson told Levy that he no longer thought Goldman should offer Penn Central's commercial paper to its customers "until the current situation could be clarified." But in a meeting, Bevan downplayed the problems, and O'Herron apologized "for the casual nature of his remarks made earlier in the day." Bevan said the company would soon file for a new $100 million debt offering that he expected to complete "in early May." Bevan asked Wilson, Levy, and Goldman Sachs to continue to offer Penn Central's commercial paper for sale in the marketplace. According to the SEC, Bevan's comments assured Goldman that "there was no emergency at the Penn Central Transportation Company." The next day, Levy told O'Herron that Goldman would continue to deal the company's commercial paper.

Unfortunately for Goldman's commercial paper customers, "Bevan's statements at this meeting bore no resemblance to the reality of the situation," according to the SEC. During the eight days between the meeting with O'Herron and Bevan and the public announcement of the company's first-quarter losses, Goldman sold $300,000 of Penn Central's commercial paper to one customer. "This customer was told nothing of the first-quarter results," the SEC said.

Between April 22 and May 15, Goldman kept selling the Penn Central paper. On May 1, American Express bought $5 million of the commercial paper, a deal that would be the subject of the November 1970 lawsuit between the two firms. According to the SEC, American Express "had been reluctant to purchase the company's paper" but Jack

Vogel explained there were "adequate assets to back up" Penn Central's commercial paper "in order to persuade it to change its mind."

By mid-May "it was clearly impossible to sell any more of the company's paper," according to the SEC, and by "mutual agreement" Goldman and Penn Central decided to stop trying. One of the reasons Penn Central filed for bankruptcy in June 1970 was "its inability to roll over its commercial paper," which amounted to $117 million. Between November 1969 and May 1970, Goldman sold $83 million of Penn Central's commercial paper, none of which was repaid after the bankruptcy filing. According to the SEC, "Goldman, Sachs failed to disclose that [it] had reduced and [was] eliminating [its] inventory of the company's paper, that NCO had been induced to maintain the prime rating and that the company's paper was meeting strong resistance from customers."

A small college in Pennsylvania was one such Goldman customer, in late March 1970. The college already had invested $400,000 in Penn Central's commercial paper, and Goldman was hoping to sell it another $300,000 on March 30. When the school's treasurer asked the Goldman representative about Penn Central's latest financial performance, he was told the company had consolidated revenue of $2.3 billion compared to $2.1 billion the previous year and earnings of $4.4 million compared to nearly $87 million the year before. He was also told "there was no need for concern" because Penn Central had $6.5 billion in assets. "With some hesitancy," the college treasurer agreed to purchase another $300,000 of the Penn Central commercial paper for the school. Four days later, he received a letter of confirmation and the latest financial data about Penn Central. "I was dismayed to learn the information conveyed over the phone" was for the year ended 1968, not 1969.

Goldman's explanation for why it did what it did at the time sounds eerily familiar to the one it would give forty or so years later in the wake of the financial crisis of 2007 and 2008. First, the firm told the SEC, commercial paper sales were not profitable. While Goldman had sold an average of $4.7 billion of the product per year, its profits from doing so were only $435,000. Second, Goldman claimed the customers "were sophisticated investors" who were buying the stuff in $100,000 lots and "were capable of making their own investment decisions and did not have to rely on Goldman, Sachs' opinion." Furthermore, the firm "viewed itself as merely a conduit" selling the paper and "made no recommendations as to the quality" of it "or the credit-worthiness of the issuers." Goldman "merely" informed customers of "what paper was available and the customer would decide which paper it wished to purchase." Despite believing it had no obligation to assess the "credit-worthiness" of the issuers, Goldman did tell the SEC that it believed Penn Central "always" had "sufficient assets which could be liquidated should the need arise, which provided sufficient protection for commercial paper holders." Ultimately, Goldman argued, since Penn Central was a public company, required to file its financial statements with the SEC, there was plenty of information available to investors about Penn Central's financial condition. But Pollack said Goldman's argument amounted to a bunch of bunk. "Our clients were very much in need of [the information] and Goldman Sachs had represented the [Penn Central] commercial paper to be a cash equivalent," he said.

The release of the SEC's lengthy investigation into the collapse of Penn Central was big news, of course, but very little of the coverage focused on Goldman's role in selling the commercial paper that, in the end, could not be refinanced. Instead, the major newspapers focused on the juicier stories about how some fifteen top executives of Penn Central—including both Bevan and O'Herron—had, prior to the bankruptcy, sold about 70 percent of the stock they had received at the time of the merger a few years earlier. The stock sales, according to William J. Casey, then the chairman of the SEC, "were deemed to raise the most serious questions as whether [they] had been based on material inside information. . . . These officers had apparent access to information concerning the state of Penn Central's affairs which was reaching the public only with a serious amount of distortion."

On August 15, the *Times* editorialized about Casey's report and took Goldman to task. "Aware that new securities issues might expose the company to closer inspection by the financial community"—because new securities had to be registered with the SEC, while commercial paper did not—"Penn Central officers sought to keep afloat by borrowing and reborrowing hundreds of millions of dollars through the issuance of short-term commercial paper, exempt from government supervision. The marketing of this paper was handled by Goldman, Sachs & Co., which later insisted to the S.E.C. that it was 'merely a dealer and not an underwriter,' and therefore had no duties of disclosure to those who bought Penn Central paper."

THIS WAS THE worst kind of publicity for Goldman—and a headache for Novotny—especially with a rash of civil lawsuits pending that, if lost, could wipe out the firm's capital and the firm itself. The SEC's comprehensive report was not only devastating in the serious questions it raised about Goldman's behavior but also provided a potential legal road map for other litigants against the firm. There was also the growing risk that the SEC itself would sue the firm as a number of the newspaper stories were implying.

Novotny went to work. He arranged for Levy to be interviewed by Gilbert Kaplan, the founder and longtime editor of *Institutional Investor* magazine, for a long question-and-answer piece in the November 1973 issue of the magazine. "Gus Levy answers 132 questions about his firm, his business—and himself," read the headline. Fortunately for Goldman, not one of the 132 questions was about the mess at Penn Central or about Levy's and Goldman's role in it, or about any of the lawsuits swirling around the firm. Instead, readers were treated to a rare dish of Levy's humility and modesty. Asked about Goldman's vigorous competition with Salomon Brothers in block trading, Levy professed not to care. "They can't say they are No. 1 and we can't say we're No. 1 and I don't know a way to get the facts." As for his anger when someone at Goldman missed a block trade, Levy said, "I'm human. Obviously, if I hear X firm has done ten blocks and we've done only one in a day, it upsets me. So I go to our guys and suggest we try harder. But my real concern is Goldman, Sachs' profitability, rather than how much business we do."

Indeed, William "Billy" Salomon, one of the founders of Salomon Brothers, remembered once having lunch with Levy in a place where they could watch the broad tape from their table, and when Levy saw that a big block of three hundred thousand shares of stock had traded and Goldman wasn't the trader, he leapt up from the table and told Salomon he had to make a call. "Billy, I'll be gone for a few minutes," Levy told him. Levy went and called the seller of the stock, whom he knew, and berated him on the phone. "How could you give that trade to Bear Stearns!" he thundered. "I sold you that stock." "Sure enough," Salomon recalled, "Gus would get the next trade. But very few people at the time would have the audacity to even think of doing that. But Gus had no compunctions. And he hated to lose a trade." Salomon said people on Wall Street used to call Levy "the Octopus" because "he wanted to do every trade that was ever made on Wall Street."

———

LEVY WAS RIGHT to be concerned about the firm's profits in 1973, since there were none—an especially painful development since 1972 had been the best year the firm had ever had. The profits in 1972 "caused people to have a very positive feeling," Bob Rubin remembered. "They felt good. And then all of a sudden 1973 came and the market peak-to-trough was down forty-two percent and we really suffered." Roy Smith recalled, "[T]here was no money for bonuses in 1973." Rubin remembered the problem in 1973 was that the trading positions the firm had taken in its equities division—both in block trading and in arbitrage—went against the firm through the course of the year, with the firm losing money nearly every month. The collapse of the stock market also dried up much of the firm's investment banking business.

The next year was equally difficult. Goldman actually announced publicly that profits "rose" for 1974—without disclosing any actual data—but that they were less than the "unusually profitable" period from 1970 to 1972. Partners ended up taking money from their own pockets to pay employees' small bonuses. "This was hard on employees, who then, as now, received most of their income from bonuses, but few people left and hardly anyone was laid off," Smith observed. "Everyone weathered the storm with internal (and external) cost-cutting, and hoped for the best. But it was hard to be optimistic."

No doubt employee morale was taxed by the news, in April 1974, that the SEC was considering filing "fraud charges"—as a result of Penn Central's collapse—against both Bevan, the former chief financial officer, and Goldman. On May 2, the SEC dropped its bomb. In a civil suit filed in federal district court in Philadelphia, the agency charged two former Penn Central executives and three former directors with "making false and misleading statements about the carrier's financial condition to the S.E.C., to stockholders and to the investing public." Goldman avoided being cited in the SEC's complaint filed in Philadelphia, but the SEC filed a separate complaint on May 2 against Goldman in a Manhattan federal court. In it, the SEC alleged that from August 1968 to May 1970, in selling Penn Central's commercial paper, Goldman "has employed and is employing devices, schemes and artifices to defraud" and "has obtained and is obtaining money and property by means of untrue statements of material facts and omissions" and "has engaged in transactions, acts, practices and courses of business which have operated and are operating as a fraud and deceit upon purchasers of securities." Furthermore, the SEC contended, Goldman made "false and misleading statements of material facts and omitted to state material facts . . . concerning, among other things the financial condition of" Penn Central, the "financial prospects" of Penn Central, and "the risks of nonrepayment of the commercial paper of" Penn Central. The SEC sought a "permanent injunction restraining and enjoining" Goldman, and its employees, from continuing this deceptive behavior.

As was once typical, on the same day the SEC filed its complaint against Goldman, the two sides signed a consent decree, negotiated on Goldman's behalf by Michael Maney, a former CIA officer turned attor-

ney at Sullivan & Cromwell. In it, the firm—"without admitting or denying any of the allegations" in the SEC's complaint—agreed to be "perma-
nently restrained and enjoined" from continuing to sell Penn Central's
commercial paper and to implement, within sixty days, a new policy at
the firm regarding the marketing and sale of commercial paper. Hence-
forth, Goldman would be required to do what it should have done in the
first place: to wit, to perform due diligence about the financial efficacy of
the issuer of the commercial paper so that Goldman would have "reasonable ground" to expect the obligation would be repaid when it came due
and to disseminate that information on an ongoing basis to customers
who bought the commercial paper Goldman sold. This "new" policy was
required to be shared with the people in the commercial paper department and with partners of the firm. Goldman paid no fine as part of the
agreement.

"Within hours" of the agreement, the *Times* reported, Maney and
the SEC were bickering about what the two sides had agreed. Maney
argued that while Goldman had been charged under the SEC's antifraud
provisions, the firm "was charged only with negligence in failing to inform
itself and its customers of the actual state of financial affairs of Penn
Central." The SEC's counsel countered that "the intent of the complaint
was, indeed, to make the charge of fraud" under a part of the securities
act known as "Fraudulent Interstate Transactions." Goldman's in-house
counsel told the paper that Goldman's "decision to consent to the S.E.C.
injunction" was a "matter of business judgment."

The combination of the SEC's 1972 investigative report, the SEC's
civil lawsuit against the Penn Central executives and directors, and the
SEC's complaint and consent decree with Goldman conspired to ratchet
up the seriousness of the litigation still pending against Goldman from its
commercial paper customers. Levy figured out quickly that he needed to
put an end to the suits, if he could. John Weinberg's earlier gambit to settle with creditors at fifty cents on the dollar had failed, and the chances
of getting them to agree to a 2.2 percent settlement—the recovery that
the two creditors in Mill Factors had agreed to—seemed highly remote.
According to the SEC's 1972 investigation, several of the smaller
claimants against Goldman had settled with the firm for twenty cents on
the dollar; then it was revealed that in April 1972, Goldman had settled
$22 million of claims for $4.5 million—the twenty cents on the dollar—
with firms such as American Express (for $1 million), Norton Simon,
Inc. (for $600,000), and U.S. Steel (for $466,000). Walt Disney also settled with Goldman. At the time of the settlements, Goldman said the
payments were covered by its insurance. George Doty remembered that,

at one point, to try to put an end to the litigation, Levy wanted to buy the commercial paper back from his clients—many of whom were also his friends—at one hundred cents on the dollar. "I told him we would not do that," Doty said. "We couldn't really. We weren't going to bail out everybody that bought the paper. They were big adults. They bought. They knew everything we knew and I just as soon as hell was not going to jeopardize the firm to placate some of his best friend clients. So, he yielded."

But by the middle of 1974, following the signing of the consent decree with the SEC, Goldman still faced the looming lawsuit brought by Fundamental Investors, Welch's grape cooperative, and the two midwestern clothing stores. Goldman and Levy could not afford to lose that suit, especially since the plaintiffs were seeking 100 percent restitution. In July 1974, Levy decided to take matters into his own hands. He approached John Haire, the head of Fundamental Investors, to see if a settlement could be reached. He still kept that letter from Sullivan & Cromwell in his jacket pocket, after all, and he decided to see if he could prove its value as a harbinger.

With the case headed to a trial on September 5, the *Times* reported that in a deposition Levy gave on May 3, 1972—in which he was forced to admit Goldman had failed to reveal crucial information to its customers—he insisted that Goldman had "scrupulously observed the law and the highest principles of business and professional ethics." When the *Times* reporter called Levy at his office to get a comment about the deposition, Levy said it "stands on its own" and declined to elaborate. Novotny told the *Wall Street Journal* that the Levy deposition was "old news."

The next day, Goldman settled with Fundamental Investors for $5.25 million in cash plus some 75 percent of what, if anything, Goldman ended up receiving from Penn Central in the bankruptcy proceedings on its commercial paper claims. While the settlement with Fundamental, for around 26 cents on the dollar, eliminated a major threat to Goldman's capital, the deal did nothing to dissuade the other plaintiffs in the case—the two clothing stores and Welch's—to drop the lawsuit and to settle themselves. According to Charles Ellis, Welch's needed the money back because the co-op "had had a bad harvest" while the two retailers "saw the case as a matter of dishonest dealing and felt morally right in insisting on full recovery."

On September 9, the Welch's trial against Goldman began in southern Manhattan before a jury of three men and three women—said to all be "blue-collar" workers. As incredible as it may seem, Goldman allowed an extraordinary amount of dirty laundry to be aired in public, in front of a jury, over a $2.4 million dispute—the difference between the $3 million the plaintiffs sought (full restitution) and the $600,000 (twenty cents on the dollar) that Goldman likely would have offered. On the trial's first day, Pollack, a young lawyer for the plaintiffs then at his own firm, Pollack & Singer, told the jury, "The central point as the plaintiffs see it is simply this: They knew and they didn't tell." Pollack explained to the jury how Goldman had a system of various colored sheets of paper that would be used for memoranda sharing different kinds of information about the companies that it underwrote. For instance, "green sheets" were used to convey information to buyers that became available to Goldman from sources other than a company's public SEC filings, such as by having conversations with company management. Levy testified the green sheets were to "apprise" investors "of current information."

Then there were the blue sheets. "The blue sheets are secret memoranda in the files of Goldman Sachs, the credit files of Goldman Sachs recording contacts or conversations between Goldman Sachs and the issuer, in this case recording conversations between Goldman Sachs and Penn Central," Pollack said. "These blue sheets are profoundly important to this case because, in effect, they are like tracks in the snow. I think having read the blue sheets one would have very little doubt that Goldman Sachs possessed inside information. Having examined the witnesses, you will hear that they did not disclose to their customers the information in these blue sheets." The green sheets, Pollack said, were what "they told us"; the blue sheets were "what they knew."

The blue sheets in Goldman's files recorded everything from the key September 19, 1969, phone conversation between O'Herron, at Penn Central, and Vogel, at Goldman Sachs, where O'Herron told Vogel Penn Central would be "in a very tight cash position" in the first quarter of 1970. The blue sheets also recorded the Goldman partners' reaction to reading on the "broad tape," on February 5, 1970, that Penn Central had lost $56 million for 1969. "Mr. Wilson of Goldman Sachs put in a very hurried call to Mr. Levy of Goldman Sachs in St. Louis," Pollack recounted for the jury, "and Levy said, 'We've got to get them to a meeting in New York. Get Bevan and O'Herron too, to New York for a meeting. I will fly in from St. Louis.' " The blue sheets revealed that Wilson told O'Herron that Goldman would go to a "tap issue" basis for selling Penn Central's commercial paper, meaning it would no longer buy it until it knew it could off-load it immediately. Wilson also asked O'Herron to buy back Goldman's $10 million of Penn Central commercial paper, which he agreed to do on February 9. "This was right about the time when the sale to Younkers and the others occurred," Pollack told the jury. "They didn't tell us they were getting out while we were getting in, that they were bailing out."

Wilson then told O'Herron, "We're going to need a story to tell the purchasers." This set Pollack off. "Why did they need a story?" he asked the jury, rhetorically. "The fact of the matter is they should have told it straight."

One theme that "runs like a brook" through the entire Penn Central saga, Pollack told the jury, was Goldman's relentless push to get more and more banking business from the company after it became its exclusive provider of commercial paper. Pollack believed this ambition prevented Goldman from being objective about the company's financial danger. Goldman did not want to rock the boat. "Goldman Sachs was using commercial paper . . . as a door opener to other business," Pollack said. "They wanted to get in with Penn Central. They wanted to be their securities broker. They wanted to be their debentures underwriter. They wanted to do off-shore financing for them." He pointed out a telegram Levy sent to Bevan that "really tells something about [Goldman's] mentality" going into the relationship: "Tried to reach you on the telephone today to tell you how happy all of us at Goldman Sachs are that you are going ahead with $100 million of commercial paper and presume that we'll be the ones to do the job for you. Also hope that in the event of any debenture or convertible debenture financing of the company we will be the manager. Best regards, Gus."

Pollack was up against the Goliaths at Sullivan & Cromwell. Walter Sachs once described Goldman's relationship with the law firm as "always" an "intimate" one. Goldman had conducted "an adequate, proper and reasonable" analysis of Penn Central, William Piel Jr. told the jury, to "satisfy itself" and to "maintain its reputation as the leading commercial-paper dealer" in the country. Investors received the information that was "proper to give," Piel continued.

Piel told the jurors that to blame the Penn Central bankruptcy on Goldman Sachs was very much like "blaming the man who built his house because it got struck by lightning. It is something like that. We'll say how close it comes to that. We'll see what kind of disaster it was that hit the whole financial world like a thunder clap, a surprise and a shock—including [to] some of the officers of the railroad—as to what happened. So you must remember it is so easy with 20–20 hindsight to say that somebody who was trying to be aware of the things that might happen should have known that they were going to happen just because in hindsight we see that it did happen. That is the fix that Goldman Sachs is in."

Toward the end of his opening statement, Piel conceded that Levy and Weinberg knew little about Penn Central's commercial paper operations—even though Penn Central was Levy's client—and that this made perfect sense in a business, such as Goldman Sachs, that relied heavily on the confidence its customers put in it. "[W]hen you are running a business that is based on trust and confidence, you don't need— or you don't think you need—policemen to watch the policemen and then policemen to watch the policemen who are watching the policemen. What you think is that if you have a man who has the ability and responsibility and the honor to do the job, then you give him the job and trust him to do it."

Here, curiously, Sullivan & Cromwell and Goldman Sachs made this a case not about Gus Levy and John Weinberg but about Bob Wilson, the partner running the commercial paper department at Goldman. No matter what the jury decided, Piel seemed to be saying, the responsibility for what happened belonged solely to Wilson. "You will probably say to yourselves when he is on the stand he is a pretty young man to have had that responsibility for his firm, and it's true," Piel said, "but this is the age of able young men and women"—a curious comment indeed for an establishment attorney to make in 1969. "In a sense this is his case. It's the Welch Company and the Anthony Company and the Younkers Company against Bob Wilson, because he had the responsibility to his partners to make that decision and to make it on a sound basis." This maneuver—throwing a junior employee under the bus—would be revisited at Goldman with Fabrice Tourre in the wake of the 2007–2008 housing and mortgage-backed securities scandals.

On September 19, after the plaintiffs had rested their case, Goldman asked the court to throw out the case in its entirety. Goldman argued that the court lacked jurisdiction because the commercial paper was not sold through the use of interstate commerce or the mails, and thus was a state matter, not a federal matter. Goldman also argued that commercial paper was not a security as defined by the 1934 Securities Exchange Act. The judge ultimately rejected Goldman's argument, and Levy, Whitehead, Bevan, and the sacrificial lamb Wilson were forced to testify to embarrassing effect. Pollock made great sport of reading to the jury their previous depositions, which differed in substantial ways from their testimony in court.

Since Sullivan & Cromwell had made the case about Wilson— no doubt as a way of deflecting responsibility away from Levy and Weinberg—Pollack very cleverly hoisted Wilson on his own petard. He skillfully filleted Wilson—and many of the other Goldman witnesses—

by reading to the jury in his closing statement how he had answered a question one way in his deposition and how he answered the same question another way during the trial. For instance, in his trial testimony Wilson said he had regularly been kept apprised of Penn Central's creditworthiness. But in his deposition, when asked if he were focused on Penn Central's creditworthiness, he said, "No, there was no need in my mind because of, in our opinion, the tremendous underlying value of the assets in this [company]." When asked if anyone in his department was evaluating Penn Central on a weekly or monthly basis, Wilson responded, "Not that I am aware of." Which Pollack rightly found to be "a staggering admission for the head of the commercial paper department to make." Pollack said Wilson had no credibility as a witness.

After a long litany of Goldman's ongoing omissions and misrepresentations to his clients, Pollack referred to a blue memo written by John Whitehead, the partner in charge of Goldman's Corporate Finance Department. Whitehead wrote that he feared the commercial paper department "feels itself to be very much under the gun from the rest of the firm to produce instant profits at the maximum level possible for their department. Clearly this is not the proper objective and I think we should tell them so. Their job is to make the maximum possible contribution to the firm's overall profits, not just their own; to do it in the long run, not just immediately." Pollack said Whitehead was "perceptive" and saw "what was wrong" in the commercial paper department.

Pollack was brilliant right to the end. He said the case could be summarized simply: "When the company went under, Goldman Sachs, which for nearly two years had maintained an inventory [of Penn Central's commercial paper], was left with zero in its own position. These plaintiffs were left with $3 million."

On October 9, the federal jury reached a unanimous verdict against Goldman and ordered the firm to repay the $3 million, plus interest accrued since the filing of the lawsuit more than four years earlier, to the three plaintiffs. The *Times* called it a "landmark case" and the "first of its kind to go before a jury" and said that the verdict "could lay the groundwork" to resolve another thirty-five similar suits against Goldman, amounting to nearly $30 million. It was the first time a jury had extended securities law to commercial paper, which was a corporate IOU rather than technically a security.

The jury's verdict was a big blow—"epochal," Pollack said—to both Goldman's reputation and its traditional legal strategy of fighting claims against the firm rather than settling for reasonable amounts. The jury awarded the three plaintiffs one hundred cents on the dollar plus another $1 million in interest. Goldman could not afford to have the remaining Penn Central lawsuits against it go that direction. "This was not a minor event," Pollack said. "If you consider the fact that their total exposure was $82.5 million and they had total capital of $50 million, you can draw your own conclusions about whether this was an emergency for Goldman Sachs. It's fair to say they were on red alert."

In March 1975, Goldman settled with Getty Oil for $1.4 million, or seventy cents on the dollar. Some twenty lawsuits against Goldman remained outstanding, totaling around $20 million. According to a statement Novotny released, Goldman had "carefully prepared for any potential outcome of the remaining litigation to insure that these suits will not impair our capital." In December 1975, a federal judge ruled against Goldman and ordered the firm to pay $500,000, with interest, to Franklin Savings Bank, which had bought Penn Central commercial paper a few months before the bankruptcy. Even when Goldman appeared to win a suit, it ended up losing. For instance, in June 1976, a federal judge in St. Louis ruled in Goldman's favor against Alton Box Board Company, of Alton, Illinois, which was seeking $625,000. The judge found no "indication that the purchase was induced by any misrepresentation or omission of material fact" by Goldman and that Goldman "was warranted" in representing that Penn Central was "creditworthy" when it continued to sell its commercial paper. But Goldman lost Alton's appeal and, in November 1977, agreed to pay Alton $925,000, which was not only the original amount of the note, plus interest, but also Alton's attorneys' fees and court costs. In October 1976, a federal judge ruled that Goldman had to repay $600,000, plus interest, to the University Hill Foundation, a fund associated with Los Angeles's Loyola University. (In the end, Goldman ended up buying back enough of the Penn Central commercial paper to offset a portion of its losses when the company emerged from bankruptcy protection and revived. "The value of the paper subsequently rose when the railroad reorganized, limiting our losses some more," Whitehead observed.)

―――

IF ANY OF these ongoing legal judgments against Goldman affected Gus Levy, he did not let on. He ran into Pollack in 1976 at a public event, after not having spoken to him in six years. (They once served together on the board of the Foster Grant Corporation, a manufacturer of sunglasses.) The two men exchanged pleasantries about their health and their families. "He said he felt great," Pollack said of Levy. Nor did Levy seem fazed by L. Jay Tenenbaum's unexpected decision to retire from

Goldman in November 1975, after more than twenty-two years at the firm. At the time, he was the third or fourth highest paid partner at the firm, with a 3.5 percent share of the profits. But he was burned out. Additionally, he had just remarried—an airline stewardess—and he wanted to make sure his second marriage did not go the way of his first, which it very well might have had he stayed at Goldman Sachs. "L. Jay had *had* it," Peter Levy said. "There was a lot of pressure and he just wanted out." Ever diplomatic, Robert Rubin described Tenenbaum's departure from Goldman as a long-planned act of selflessness. "He was trying to clear the way for his own eventual retirement, even though he was only forty-four when he hired me."

When Tenenbaum retired, Ray Young, the partner in charge of equity sales, gave Rubin some unsolicited advice. Rubin had to make a choice, Young told him. He could continue to focus on event-driven arbitrage in a trading environment "focusing intently on my business, being short with people, and projecting an impersonal attitude," Rubin wrote, which would let him "continue as a successful arbitrageur." Or, Rubin could take Young's advice and "start thinking more about the people in the trading room and in sales—about their concerns and views—and how to enable them to be successful . . . [and] become more broadly involved in the life of the firm." Not surprisingly, soon after Tenenbaum's departure, Rubin took Young's advice and began to think more broadly about his role at the firm. "Ray Young's advice pointed me toward a whole new world that I hadn't thought much about," he conceded. Of course not.

Not only had Tenenbaum left behind at Goldman what could have become a major fortune, he also left behind the more enduring legacy of the people he hired, including Rubin, and the men who followed Rubin in the arbitrage department, Robert Freeman and Richard Perry among them. Tenenbaum also hired another young lawyer, Steve Friedman, who would become part of the firm's burgeoning M&A group.

As for Levy, there was not the slightest crack in his façade of invincibility. In April 1976, Levy gave an interview to a business writer for UPI, and the subsequent puff piece, which did not even mention Penn Central or the lawsuits against Goldman its bankruptcy had spawned, appeared in a number of local papers around the country. The article recounted Levy's rigorous work schedule, his extensive board seats—of "almost two dozen" American companies—and his vast philanthropic and political reach. It also pointed out how hard people at Goldman worked and conceded Levy was a "demanding" boss. "Sure, there's a lot of pressure here," Levy said. "But one secret of our success is to be consistent, and one way to be consistent is to make calls, do your job and be constantly in touch with current and prospective customers. I've never heard of anyone complain of overwork here." The article pointed out that Goldman had become a leader in providing advice to companies that were the subject of hostile advances from raiders and other corporations. Levy noted Goldman's "policy" of not "siding with firms that want to take over another company against its objections." He then added, "Sometimes it gets very messy."

When asked how he did it all, Levy responded, "I wish I knew" and complimented his wife as being "a very understanding woman." The article credited his lack of sleep—at most, five or six hours a night—with giving him the extra time he needed to get things done. "[T]he bags under his eyes to the contrary," Levy was, the writer pointed out, a "vigorous, lean, healthy-looking individual." Levy did not smoke and drank minimally, according to the article, notwithstanding his regular evening martinis. He exercised nearly every day, either on a machine in his apartment or by jogging in a nearby park. "I guess I just happen to have a better than average constitution," Levy explained.

Six months later, on October 26, while at a meeting of the commissioners of the Port Authority of New York and New Jersey, Levy suddenly put his head down, as if lost in deep thought. He seemed to be napping, which made perfect sense since he had taken the red-eye from Los Angeles the night before after attending a May Department Stores board of directors' meeting and then working a full day at Goldman. "Knowing of Levy's habit of intense concentration on something else," Roy Smith explained, "the other commissioners thought nothing of the fact that he had slumped down in his chair and seemed to be staring straight ahead. After a while someone asked if he was all right, and finding him not to be, called for an ambulance." He was sixty-six years old. Levy was taken to Mount Sinai Hospital, where he was still chairman of the board of trustees. Novotny told the *New York Times* Levy had suffered "a mild stroke," which was almost certainly inaccurate. That night, Levy was kept in the intensive care unit and his condition was listed as "stable," according to a brief article in the paper.

His son Peter, then a partner at Goldman, remembered being called after the meeting at the Port Authority. "He couldn't be seen that night," he said, "and the next day I went to see him. And he seemed okay. Actually he seemed fairly lucid and recognized me, and the next day he didn't. And then he went into a coma." Peter Levy sat with his father at Mount Sinai during much of the ordeal but he knew his father's prospects were grim when he asked the doctor about the prognosis and the doctor shrugged. "The worst thing you can do," he said. Gus Levy died on November 3.

The outpouring of accolades for him was one measure of his importance on Wall Street and in New York. "Gus Levy was a very special human being," the partners of Goldman allowed. "He was a generous man and devoted humanitarian, championing improved health care, increased educational opportunities, and the brotherhood of man. His untiring efforts on behalf of his clients, friends and associates and his achievements as a leader of the financial community rank him as a truly great man. All of us are richer for having known Gus Levy." The firm also published a long list of Levy's civic, philanthropic, and corporate associations, including his thirty-one board seats, his three honorary degrees, and his fourteen-year stint—who knew?—as treasurer of the International Synagogue at Kennedy Airport. Paid tributes in the *Times* came from his fellow Wall Street titans, including Laurence Tisch, and even a young Henry Kravis. On November 4, the NYSE observed one minute of silence in honor of Levy.

At a funeral service on the morning of November 7 at Temple Emanu-El, on Fifth Avenue, some two thousand people gathered to mourn Levy. Vice President Nelson Rockefeller, a longtime friend, delivered the principal eulogy. But even this moment was stage-managed; Novotny had written the words Rockefeller would utter, even retyping them on a special typewriter so that the vice president, who suffered from dyslexia, could read them. "What an extraordinary man," said Rockefeller, who had regularly sought out Levy for advice. Walter Frank, Levy's predecessor at the NYSE, said he was in "shock, shock" when he heard about Levy's death. "We lost a great man," Frank said. "He was a great man." (In 2002, Goldman acquired Frank's specialist firm.) Stopped by a reporter after the service, former New York City mayor John Lindsay said he was in a "state of shock" over Levy's death and that "in the years I was Mayor and in Congress, Gus Levy helped me beyond measure."

The next day, Levy's body was flown to New Orleans for burial at the Metairie Cemetery, on Pontchartrain Boulevard, in one of the above-ground crypts used in the city because it is below sea level. Nobody from Goldman went to the burial. Nor did Levy's wife or his two children. "I didn't go down," Peter Levy said. "None of the family went down. My mother said, 'There's no need to go down. We'll just mourn for him up here.'" Levy left an estate worth "millions," his son said, including a large apartment at 4 Sutton Place and a country estate—Apple Hill Farm—in Armonk, New York, next to the Blind Brook Club, where he played golf regularly; he was known to take the red-eye back from Los Angeles after a client meeting and head straight to the golf course.

Given the suddenness of Levy's death, Bob Rubin didn't get to say his good-byes, either. "After Gus died, I'd always regretted that I'd never asked him what he, driving himself all day long every day, thought life was all about," he wrote in his memoir. "I don't know if he would have had an answer, but one answer I don't think he would have given was money."

THE GOLDMAN WAY

T ime for reflection, or not, Levy's death caught everyone at Goldman by surprise. There was a firm to run, and there was no one to run it. "As you've all heard, Gus Levy died yesterday of a stroke," Bob Mnuchin told the troops on the morning call. "There'll be time to discuss his contributions at a later time. Right now, as he taught us so well, it's important that we all get on with our work and the job to be done today. That's what Gus would have wanted."

But what if Levy had somehow, somewhere left instructions about what was to happen if he were—metaphorically speaking—hit by a bus? There seems to be a fair amount of confusion about whether or not Levy had actually designated his successors. In his memoir, Rubin wrote that Levy was young enough when he died that "he'd been able to ignore the issue of succession at the firm." While, as one of the costs of getting Sidney Weinberg to move uptown to the Seagram Building, Levy had agreed to put together a Management Committee—the obvious place to look for new leaders—there was never any question that Levy was running Goldman with an iron fist and the other men on the Management Committee served at his pleasure. Levy's pleasure was to minimize their involvement in the overall management of the firm and leave things to him, alone.

According to Roy Smith, though, Levy's secretary "rummaging through his desk" found "an envelope addressed to the Management Committee," which contained a letter stating that "if anything happened to him," the Management Committee should "consider" replacing him with the "Two Johns"—John Whitehead, a patrician, silver-haired banker, then fifty-four years old, and John Weinberg, then fifty-one, one of Sidney's sons and also a banker, who had supposedly managed the firm's commercial paper business. Smith cited no source for the story about Levy's secretary finding the letter.

For his part, Rubin said that although he never saw the letter—"I'm not saying there wasn't one, I'm just saying nobody ever saw it," he explained—if such a letter existed, then it was George Doty who supposedly found it, not Levy's secretary, and that the letter contained the news that Levy was going to name the Two Johns as Goldman's *vice chairmen,* not as the next leaders of the firm. But the letter never materialized. Peter Levy said he "never was aware of the letter, although he certainly did appoint the Two Johns." Doty told Charles Ellis, "Gus would *never* have retired," adding some credence to the idea that Whitehead and Weinberg were to be named vice chairmen, although in his book Ellis ignored the controversy altogether and instead told a story of Levy's secretary finding in his desk a drawing of Levy—"a stick figure with a big cigar"—that one of his partner's sons had made on a Friday after Thanksgiving and given to Levy.

Doty, who is now in his nineties, said in an interview that there was never a letter, just Levy sharing with him his plans for the Two Johns in the weeks before his death. "Gus had spoken to me shortly before he had his stroke," Doty said. "He was perplexed by a problem: how to deal with the Two Johns. His solution was to make them both a vice chairman. He couldn't pick either one of them without creating a problem. It seemed logical enough to me. I don't think he was asking me for my agreement. He was telling me the way it was." In her Goldman book, Lisa Endlich wrote that while Levy had indicated publicly he had "heirs apparent" in mind, he had never named them. "Leaderless, the firm was left in turmoil," she wrote.

Three years earlier, in his November 1973 *Institutional Investor* interview, Gilbert Kaplan asked Levy about the future leaders at the firm. "I think the firm would be equally strong if I wasn't here," he said. "Mr. Weinberg created an aura of leadership, and he was a great leader. I hasten to add that I'm not in his class." He added that, under his leadership, Goldman had a Management Committee for the first time and worked in teams, with any number of senior people getting to know the firm's clients. "[I]n case I'm out of the country, or drop dead or something, these people know whom to call at Goldman, Sachs. We've got some wonderful young fellows coming along, and some who've come around already who could step into my shoes in a minute." When Kaplan asked directly if Levy had an heir apparent, Levy responded, "I wish you wouldn't ask me that question. It would cause too much trouble around here. But yes, there are heirs apparent." He said he would have considered it "a failure" to find a new leader for the firm from outside its own ranks.

When Whitehead heard the news about Levy's stroke, he tried to go see him at Mount Sinai but could not get in for a day or so. But when he did, Whitehead "could tell he was obviously a very sick man—weak, frail and ghostly pale. Even if he survived, I couldn't imagine he would ever come back to running Goldman Sachs. That was a terrible blow to the firm, as well as to me personally." According to Doty, "We had a partners meeting in which the subject of succession came up. And I told the partners what Gus had said to me. It wasn't the word of God, you know, but it was a leader who had thought about the subject and it was an acceptable solution. There was no better solution on the horizon anyway."

In Whitehead's version of events, "while Gus lay dying at Mount Sinai," he and John Weinberg "sat down together at the Goldman Sachs office to decide what to do." Whitehead made no mention of any letter stuffed in a desk. Rather, he observed, Levy "had made no such decision" about succession "because he had no thought of retiring." Whitehead decided, though, that since he and Weinberg were tied for second— behind Levy—for taking home the greatest percentage of the firm's profits, "it was clearly up to us to take strong leadership in this sudden crisis and make a clear recommendation to the management committee and all of the partners about who would succeed Gus."

Although Whitehead was three years older than Weinberg and had been at Goldman three years longer, they had both become partners on the same day in 1956, "moved up in the firm in lockstep," and received "identical increases in compensation at every stage." Apparently, they were also good friends. "We'd often have lunch together at Scotty's Sandwich Shop," Whitehead said. "Scotty's made the largest egg salad sandwich I had ever seen, and I ate my share of them. John and I would complain to each other about all the things wrong with Goldman Sachs, and talk about how things would go if we ever had a chance to run the firm."

Now that the opportunity was within their grasp, with Levy close to death, Whitehead "floated the idea" that he be the firm's chairman and that Weinberg be vice chairman. "John's face fell," Whitehead noted. "I could see he didn't take that too well. As Sidney's son, and a proud man in his own right, he was not inclined to settle for being my number two." John Weinberg had graduated from Princeton and, in World War II, joined the marines as a private and emerged from the war a second lieutenant. In the Korean War, he went in a first lieutenant and came out a captain. "My father was a very tough man," he once said, "but I had a gentle upbringing. The Marines were good for me." The Two Johns considered putting the matter to a vote of the Management Committee or to the entire partnership, but that "semipublic process" would have been "messy," Whitehead said, "with factions forming on each side" without producing the "united front the firm needed at such a difficult time." Additionally, according to Whitehead, neither John wanted to risk losing and having one John being hailed as the winner while the other John was labeled a loser.

Out of the conundrum came the unprecedented idea—at least on Wall Street—of having the two men share power as co-chairmen. "John and I were the logical choices," Weinberg said. "Gus had brought us along together and our perceptions and goals for Goldman had evolved according to our own thinking, which was done together." "After we'd decided, we both felt relieved," Whitehead wrote later. "Neither of us had to shoulder the entire responsibility of running Goldman Sachs alone, and neither of us had to settle for being number two. We'd each be free to travel without worrying too much about what was happening back at the office. The arrangement seemed ideal." The Two Johns also saw the marketing potential in the arrangement as clients often wanted to meet "with the top man," and now Goldman had two top men. "We could meet twice as many clients . . . ," Whitehead observed. "By pooling our abilities, we figured we would make the top of Goldman Sachs that much stronger." They decided to make sure to speak every day and have adjoining offices, with a shared conference room. Whitehead's former investment banking colleagues believed Whitehead made a major concession to John Weinberg. "I thought that John Whitehead would clearly have been chosen as the sole leader," recalled former partner Alan Stein, "but I think he decided, and I thought intelligently, that there was something to hold on to here in the Weinberg name." Over time, a revealing picture of Elizabeth Taylor appeared in the partners' bathrooms. "Two are better than one," read the caption.

After Levy's death, Whitehead and Weinberg told the—now eight-member—Management Committee of their decision. "The idea met with its approval," Whitehead said, "and so we informed the other partners." Doty said the idea just made sense. "John Weinberg was a great business getter and Whitehead was a better organizer," he said. "But Whitehead was not deeply loved by a great many people in the securities side of the business. And so it was a combination everyone could live with. Those two guys were sort of joined at the hip. It didn't seem unusual." Novotny also went to work, disseminating the news to the media. The Times, though, beat him to the punch and reported correctly two days after Levy's death that Whitehead and Weinberg would succeed him. Novotny denied that any decision had been made but the paper reported that the two men would be co-chairmen of the Management Committee and that they had "tremendous mutual respect for each other." Whitehead was described as a "planner and an organizer" while Weinberg, then head of the firm's fledgling fixed-income division, was known for "bringing in new business." The *Times*, kindly, reported a number of famous Goldman tropes, including that the "transition" from Levy's leadership to that of Whitehead and Weinberg would be a smooth one. "Among the 1,500 employees and at its 14 domestic and foreign offices, teamwork is a hallmark that built Goldman, Sachs to its present eminence in the competitive investment world."

———

BUT THE FACT that neither Whitehead nor Weinberg was a trader, or had trading experience, evoked considerable concern from Goldman's increasingly influential traders. Levy's death was "a tremendous shock," Rubin said, "because . . . I think a lot of us—I'll include myself in this—felt some degree of insecurity with respect, insecurity might be the wrong word, but uncertainty with respect to the question of would they"—Whitehead and Weinberg—"have the fortitude to live with what would inevitably be periodic downslides. But it turned out they were terrific."

In many ways, Whitehead was right out of Goldman's central casting department: although he was from a modest background, he was also bright, hardworking, tenacious, and ambitious. These, of course, were the very same qualities that made Sidney Weinberg and Gus Levy so successful. But unlike Weinberg and Levy, Whitehead was Episcopalian, not Jewish, and thus would be the first leader of Goldman—not counting the ill-fated tenure of Waddill Catchings—who was not cut from the firm's principal religious cloth. Not that any of Goldman's previous leaders were particularly religious—far from it—nor, by 1976, were Wall Street firms as strictly delineated by their religious orientation as had been the case earlier in the twentieth century, but it was still a momentous change. "To many people, Goldman Sachs was thought to be predominantly Jewish," Whitehead observed, "but I never sensed that anyone ever minded my being an Episcopalian." But he was not oblivious to the anomaly. Much was made around Wall Street of the news that Morgan Stanley had hired Lewis Bernard in 1963, the first Jew to work at the firm. In 1973, Bernard became the first Jewish partner at Morgan Stanley. At one point before Bernard became a partner, Morgan Stanley's senior partner, Perry Hall, called Weinberg and told him about Bernard being Jewish and his increasingly important role at Morgan Stanley. "Oh, Perry," Weinberg responded, "that's *nothing*. We've had them here for *years*." When Bernard became a partner at Morgan Stanley, Goldman tried to hire him away. But a senior executive at Morgan Stanley admonished the Goldman partners to leave him alone: "We finally make a Jewish partner and you guys want to hire him away! Forget it."

Whitehead was born April 2, 1922, in Evanston, Illinois, at four in the morning, he recalled with precision, "because my mother used to joke that she held me back for four hours so I'd avoid the embarrassment of being born on April Fools' Day." Whitehead's father, Eugene Cunningham Whitehead—born, bred, and reared in rural Georgia—had moved his family north so that he could learn how to climb telephone poles as a lineman for Western Electric. "Our stay in Evanston was brief," Whitehead explained, and the family soon moved to a second-floor apartment in Montclair, New Jersey, so that Eugene could take a job—and a promotion—as a junior manager at a Western Electric manufacturing plant in Kearny, near the Meadowlands. He would leave for work in his gray Dodge every morning at seven and returned home every night at six o'clock. Eventually the Whiteheads left the apartment for a small house near the center of Montclair, with a "little backyard" and a separate garage.

When the market crashed in October 1929, the Whiteheads were vacationing on the eastern edge of Nantucket. "It was remote enough that the city papers took several days to get there, so my father would listen to the radio every day to keep up with the news, and that's how he found out about the stock market collapse," Whitehead explained. Most of the family's savings were "carefully" invested in the stock market, with AT&T—the parent company of Western Electric—being his largest holding. Whitehead estimated his father had invested about $50,000 in the market—"perhaps the equivalent of $500,000 today"—and the loss of much of the family's savings hurt. They cut short the Nantucket vacation and returned home so that his father could "see to his investments." Compounding the stock market losses was the news that Western Electric had fired Eugene, who nevertheless still went off in his Dodge every day as if nothing had changed. Eugene never told his son that he had lost his job at Western Electric, and before long he landed a new job selling porch furniture on commission, door to door. Since there were monthly quotas to meet, the Whiteheads ended up with more than their fair share of the furniture. "I always thought that ours was the best-furnished porch in Montclair," Whitehead quipped.

During the Depression, the Whiteheads survived on macaroni and cheese and codfish cakes, recycled clothing, *Amos 'n' Andy*, *Jack Armstrong, The All-American Boy,* and Roosevelt's fireside chats. The family was able to spring for a new 1934 Model A Ford—cost: five hundred dollars. Like so many of his generation, living through the Depression seared in Whitehead an aversion to risk and borrowing money. "I don't even like credit cards!" he proclaimed. But he did not think of his family as poor "probably because we were no worse off than anyone else I knew."

Whitehead seemed to have a fairly normal childhood, collecting acorns, Indian-head pennies, and stamps. He weeded the lawn for pocket change, sang in the choir, and played the violin. But Whitehead also had a mischievous streak. At first, this meant launching paper airplanes in the choir loft while the reverend was delivering his lengthy sermons and drawing in crayon all over his aunt's wallpaper when he was supposed to be napping. Then he evolved to petty larceny by stealing freshly baked cookies from the window of Marker's Bakery, across the street from church where he sang in the choir on Sundays. The cops scared him straight, as did the lashing—with a switch taken from the backyard "switch bush"—he got from his father. "I tried hard not to cry," he said.

But it was the message that his mother delivered to him a few days later that once and for all set Whitehead on a very different path from the one he was on. After school, she went up to his bedroom, sat on his bed, took his hand, and told him the story of how a year after his parents were married, she had given birth to twin boys, who both died during childbirth. Worse, his mother's father was the doctor who delivered the twins. All of this was news to Whitehead. He never knew any of it, nor had he known that his grandfather had delivered him, too. "About two years later, you were born, a very healthy, normal little boy," his mother told him. "We were so grateful. Now, John, your father and I hope and pray every day that you will grow up to be a fine person and help us make up for our terrible loss." Holding back tears, Whitehead told her he would try.

In Whitehead's telling, there may never have been a more zealous convert. He became a devoted Boy Scout who "[n]ot satisfied with the twenty-one merit badges required by the Eagle rank, I kept going and earned fifteen more."

Then there was his apparently selfless effort, in 1939, to help his father defray the nine-hundred-dollar tuition for Whitehead to attend the prestigious Haverford College, outside of Philadelphia. He figured—but did not know for sure—that his father was earning about four thousand dollars a year then "and I didn't feel right about presenting him with such a large bill" but had no idea how he could ever earn enough in one summer to pay the tuition. He had made two hundred dollars as the assistant director of Camp Glen Gray and another two hundred dollars leading a canoe trip down the Delaware River. That left him needing five hundred dollars, with time running out before the start of school. Then he saw an ad in the Sunday *New York Times* offering jobs at the 1939 World's Fair, in Flushing Meadows, Queens (near today's LaGuardia Airport) and the opportunity to make at least a hundred dollars a week. He took the train there the next morning, from Montclair, to see if he could get hired. There was a "fairly seedy" Coney Island–style spread of concessions, carnival acts, and arcade games known as the "Great White Way." That's where Whitehead looked for a job. "To a boy like me from Montclair, it offered all the forbidden allure of the big city," he observed.

He ended up getting a job guessing people's weights. The way the game worked was that customers would pay twenty-five cents for "the privilege of having me guess his weight." If Whitehead could guess correctly within two pounds either way, he kept the quarter. If he guessed wrong, he still kept the quarter but had to fork over a stuffed animal—at a cost to Whitehead of twenty cents—to the fortunate customer. His obvious incentive was to lure as many people as possible to his arcade and guess their weight correctly. And the math was clear: correctly guessing the weight of two thousand customers would yield the five hundred dollars he needed. Although inherently shy—at that time—and without any previous experience hawking or guessing people's weights, Whitehead took quickly to the task at hand. "The trick is to ignore people's faces and concentrate on their waistlines, since that's where the pounds are," he allowed.

For the next six weeks, the seventeen-year-old Whitehead dedicated himself to the task. Twelve hours a day. Six days a week. "I scarcely returned home, and every night but Saturday I bedded down at a cheap motel nearby and, to cut expenses, just about lived on twenty-cent hot dogs and nickel Cokes." By the end of the summer, he had cleared the five hundred dollars he needed.

Whitehead's four years at Haverford were, apparently, similarly charmed. After a rocky first semester—he averaged a 79 and found he couldn't keep up with the "prep-schoolers"—he settled down and excelled at nearly everything, graduating Phi Beta Kappa, with a degree in economics. "I'd always been fascinated by money," he said. He played JV baseball and basketball, was the best high jumper on the track team, and was the director of intramural athletics. He also ran the International Relations Club and was president of student council.

To earn the money needed for tuition, Whitehead was part of the work scholarship program and had any number of odd jobs, from filling acid bottles in the chemistry labs, to updating encyclopedia entries for one professor, to grading economics exams for another. But, as he had working on the midway at the World's Fair, the way he made the bulk of the money he needed was by being entrepreneurial. At college, he and a friend started a company that controlled the business of setting up the pins at bowling alleys in and around Haverford. Whitehead called it a "near monopoly" and observed that by his senior year "the money flooded in" and he and his partner "scarcely had to lift a finger."

At graduation, in January 1943—the school had created a summer session to accelerate the class because of the war—Whitehead's ninety-nine fellow seniors voted him the most admired student in the class. He received a large carved ebony spoon and became known as the "Spoon Man," a title that Whitehead explained did not "reflect its great significance." The dean of admissions also offered him the position of assistant director of admissions at the college, with the idea that after five years Whitehead would succeed him. First, though, Whitehead was obligated to serve in the navy, something he had been keen on doing ever since the bombing of Pearl Harbor thirteen months before.

In June 1943, while awaiting the start of a ninety-day course in naval accounting being taught at Harvard Business School, the navy assigned him to be the commanding officer of the Brooklyn Navy Yard's Twentieth Street Pier. "Who knows why," he later wrote. "It was the first of many occasions—both in the Navy and out—when I would find myself in way over my head." As awkward as it was for a greenhorn college kid, without the slightest idea how to run a naval yard and with a Republican bent, to be in charge of the operation and its gruff, unionized workforce, Whitehead made the best of it. He befriended "Larry," a former longshoreman who ran the yard before Whitehead showed up, and slowly learned the ropes. He made suggestions to the navy brass about improving the efficiency of the operation, which were summarily ignored. But when he left after three months to head up to Harvard, his pier won an award for the most efficient pier in South Brooklyn. "I framed the certificate and hung it on the wall over Larry's desk."

After three months more in Cambridge, "spent learning how to fill out navy forms," a crashing bore, Whitehead eventually shipped out to Oran, Algeria, aboard the USS *Thomas Jefferson*. He was the ship's disbursement officer and assistant supply officer. The ship, a former luxury liner, was now responsible for transporting up to two thousand marines and army troops to combat situations in Europe. For the next two years, the "T.J.," as it was known, would be Whitehead's home.

Understandably, Whitehead's defining experience in World War II was his role in D-Day, the June 1944 invasion of Normandy. On the eve of the invasion, the T.J.'s captain, who Whitehead had never met or spoken to during his previous eight months on board, summoned him to his cabin. It seemed that one of the officers whose job it was to captain a landing craft known as an LCVP—"landing craft, vehicle, personnel"—had become ill and would have to leave the ship. The captain, having somehow noticed that Whitehead had a facility driving the LCVPs on occasion, ordered Whitehead into service as the captain of one of the LCVPs to be used to make the Normandy invasion.

In his memoir, Whitehead recounted the dramatic events of the invasion from his perspective—he ended up leading the five boats in his squadron—but his proudest moment appeared to be when he called an audible on the way to the beach at 6:00 a.m. on the crucial morning. One hundred yards from the beach, his boats confronted a string of heavy metal bars, or "Element C's," that were "angled menacingly" up at their boats. They had been warned to be alert for the Element C's but no one landing before Whitehead's squadron had encountered them. His orders were to plow straight ahead. But Whitehead decided to ignore his orders and send the LCVPs a hundred yards farther down the coast, where the boats could hit the beach without the danger of getting hung up on the metal obstructions. "This brought us well to the south of where we were supposed to be, but there was nothing to do about it," he said. "Actually, it proved to be a lucky break, for German mortar shells soon blasted the shoreline at the spot where we were supposed to have landed."

The T.J. had a string of other missions in the months that followed, in the south of France and then on to the Pacific theater, where it weathered fierce kamikaze attacks by the Japanese. Eventually Whitehead—now a lieutenant—was released to shore duty for the remainder of his service. His final year of military service, ironically, was spent teaching a new group of navy supply officers at Harvard Business School how to fill out the same dreaded military forms he had loathed.

Instead of taking up his post at Haverford, Whitehead decided to apply to Harvard Business School, where he was accepted. He found the curriculum more rigorous than he expected but ended up graduating with distinction, in the top 10 percent of the class. During business school, he met and married Helene "Sandy" Shannon, a Wellesley graduate who took a job as a dividend clerk at the John Hancock insurance company.

The remaining piece of Whitehead's puzzle was to figure out where he would work after Harvard. His plan was to end up at a big corporation, such as GE or DuPont, which would, he hoped, provide both security and a good outlet for the organizational skills he had perfected in the navy. Unsure he could land such a position directly from graduate school, he decided to go to Wall Street to learn additional skills that might enable him to go to a big corporation. Goldman was the only Wall Street firm interviewing at Harvard Business School that year and was interested in hiring only one graduate. He figured his chances were low—one out of twenty, in fact, since that is how many students signed up for interviews—but he decided it was worth a try. To his surprise, he was invited back to Goldman's office in New York for a further round of interviews. "Was it my grades?" he wondered. "My Navy career? Such were the secretive ways of Goldman Sachs that no one ever told me."

In New York, Whitehead met with the firm's "top brass" who "peppered" him with questions that often left him "tongue-tied." But, somehow, he was the one selected by Goldman and offered a job as an associate in Goldman's investment banking division. No doubt, Whitehead's self-deprecating manner appealed to the Goldman partners. He was the firm's only new hire that year.

Whitehead started at Goldman in October 1947, at an annual salary of $3,600. He and his wife left the Boston area, moved to Great Notch, New Jersey, near Montclair, and rented a house for $135 a month, more than half his monthly take-home pay from Goldman. At that time, Goldman was still leasing eight floors of 30 Pine Street, the top four and the bottom four. The twentieth floor was for the investment banking staff, all six of them. The floor had once been a squash court—"one of those luxuries which went by the boards" after the Crash, Whitehead said—and now six desks were squished into a space that was as high as it was wide, with only a tiny window high up on one side. A long pole was used to open and close the small window. Whitehead was the seventh member of the group. Much to the chagrin of his new colleagues, his desk was squeezed into the already cramped cube. "Without any heating vents (that we could find anyway) and certainly no air conditioning, the place had its Dickensian aspects," Whitehead recalled, "nippy in the winter and broiling in the summer." The associates were expected to keep their wool suit jackets on at their desks, all year round, even in the summer. "That was the Goldman Sachs way," according to Whitehead.

What was not the Goldman Sachs way was wearing a cotton seersucker suit in the hot and humid New York summer. One day, Whitehead bought himself such a suit and decided to wear it to the office. He got in the elevator in the morning and Walter Sachs followed him in. "Short, stocky, with a distinguished white beard, he inspired a certain awe, if not dread," Whitehead remarked.

He began to get nervous as Sachs eyeballed his suit.

"Young man, do you work at Goldman Sachs?" Sachs demanded.

"Yes sir, I do," Whitehead responded.

"In that case, I would suggest that you go home right now and change out of your pajamas," Sachs insisted.

———

WHITEHEAD STARTED AT Goldman trying to get the firm's clients to issue corporate debt that Goldman would then underwrite, for a fee, and sell to investors. The biggest issuers of corporate debt in those days were utility companies, busy building more plants and buying equipment to meet the postwar demand of a growing economy. Whitehead spent his time analyzing what the yield, or interest rate, should be on a particular bond being contemplated for issue and making recommendations about that yield to Goldman's senior executives, who would inform Walter Sachs, who, in turn, would be Goldman's representative at these syndicate meetings where the bond prices would be set and bids made to the issuing companies, which would then choose a syndicate to lead the offering. By his own admission, Whitehead was a "long way from the action" and his responsibilities amounted to "very dull work."

Indeed, there wasn't much investment banking business to be done in those days. Underwriting an equity offering was a rare event. As a result, writing the prospectus for an underwriting was "an arduous task," since "you didn't start by marking up the last prospectus. You started from scratch with a yellow pad" figuring out how best to describe the company whose securities were being sold. "Nobody quite knew what the SEC was looking for" in those days, Whitehead said. But Goldman had a rule: the firm would not underwrite any public offering unless the company was able to include a ten-year record of sales and earnings in the prospectus. "That was absolutely required . . . ," he said. "For many years, we wouldn't underwrite an offering unless there had been profits in each of the last three years, and particularly in the most recent year. We would never think of underwriting any offering for any company that didn't meet those standards."

A few months into his job, he picked up the *Times* one morning and saw that the Justice Department had sued much of Wall Street for alleged antitrust violations, claiming that they had colluded together. Whitehead read the story with interest, of course, but was among those at Goldman who were secretly pleased Goldman had been included in the lawsuit. "I thought it would have been a terrible embarrassment for the firm if Goldman Sachs had *not* been included in such a highly publicized list of Wall Street's leading firms," he said.

Increasingly, Whitehead came into the orbit of Sidney Weinberg. He is not certain how this happened exactly but suspected it had something to do with a combination of his Harvard Business School diploma—a pedigree of which Weinberg was secretly envious—and of his ability to use a slide rule with ease. Whitehead recalled how Weinberg would be meeting with "some important CEO" and making an observation about how much debt versus equity his company should have and what percentage the debt would be if the company issued it instead of equity. Whitehead would do the calculation on his slide rule during the meeting, and then whisper the percentage into Weinberg's ear. "Fifty-six percent, as a matter of fact," Weinberg would say, "and that's too damn much."

Duly impressed, Weinberg would ask Whitehead to come to his office and show him, once and for all, how to use the slide rule. Whitehead would explain how the scales worked and how to use them, along with the middle piece, to multiply numbers. One day, Whitehead showed Weinberg how to use the slide rule to show that two times two equaled four. "Get outta here," the senior partner told him. "I already know what two times two are. That's the damnedest stupidest thing." Back the slide rule would go into the desk, rarely to be heard from again.

Eventually, after one call after another on a variety of subjects became a flurry of regular calls, Weinberg asked Whitehead to move into his office with him—as his assistant—so that he would be more knowledgeable about whatever deal Weinberg needed his help with. Whitehead was a bit leery of the request, and of actually taking the job. "I was working on a variety of other matters," he observed, "and I didn't want to be just his assistant. Of course, if I had to be anyone's assistant, it would be best to be Sidney Weinberg's." He ended up taking the job but worried about the politics of aligning himself too closely with the senior partner—surely one of the oddest concerns a young banker could have.

Weinberg had a small table put in his office, across the room from his desk. This was where Whitehead sat. Then things got awkward. "There would be some telephone conversations that he didn't want me to overhear," he explained. Weinberg would then whisper into the phone, making it difficult for the person with whom he was talking to hear. "Sidney would have to repeat himself, louder, obviously to his annoyance," Whitehead observed. When clients would come to Weinberg's office, they never knew whether Whitehead was to be included in the conversation. If they did include him, Whitehead noticed that Weinberg would get nervous, as if somehow Whitehead was going to slip him a Mickey Finn and steal his clients and make them his own. "That's one quality I've noticed about the many powerful people I've known," Whitehead said. "They are often surprisingly insecure—afraid that someone is going to take away their position at any moment." Not surprisingly, after a few months, Whitehead went back to the squash court. "I think we were both relieved," he explained.

Whitehead's big break at Goldman came working with Weinberg on the Ford IPO. During the early 1950s, Whitehead stumbled upon the information that companies doing business in Massachusetts—even private ones, like Ford—were required to file a corporate balance sheet annually with the state. Whitehead took the train to Boston and rooted around in the state's files until he found the prized piece of paper showing Ford's 1952 net worth: it was in the billions of dollars, making Ford "the largest privately held company in the United States, and probably in the world," he thought. Weinberg was impressed, both "with the balance sheet" and, Whitehead thought, "my ability to get it," although the Goldman senior partner was "never particularly lavish with praise."

For two years, Whitehead worked with Weinberg—and various members of the Ford family and the Ford Foundation—on the Ford IPO. Not only was the IPO unusually complex—given the way Henry Ford had structured the voting rights of the various constituents—but it also had to be conducted in complete secrecy. The Ford IPO was a huge success, of course, raising millions for the Ford Foundation. "Getting Ford was a big, big event for Goldman Sachs," Whitehead wrote. "It put us on the map in a way that we weren't on the map before." The *New York Times* put the story on its front page, above the fold. "Goldman Sachs had arrived," Whitehead claimed. In the aftermath of the successful Ford IPO, Whitehead abandoned the idea of working for a big American corporation. "That seemed like small potatoes," he said. But he started getting inquiries from other firms. One that "intrigued" him particularly was the opportunity to become a partner at the elite venture-capital firm set up—with an initial stake of $10 million—by John Hay "Jock" Whitney, one of America's richest men. Whitehead had been at Goldman for nine years by that point—it was 1956—and had not been named a partner. "I was restless, and maybe a little resentful," he confided. He also worried he had become too closely associated with Sidney Weinberg in an era at the firm increasingly dominated by Gus Levy and his traders. He was invited to lunch in a regal dining room at the firm with Whitney, and despite Whitehead spooning his strawberries into a water bowl instead of his dessert bowl, by the end of the lunch Whitney offered Whitehead a partnership at his firm.

When he got back downtown, he marched right into Weinberg's

office and told him he would be leaving Goldman for Whitney. "Are you kidding me?" Weinberg responded, incredulous. He then "barked" at Mary Burgess, "his long-suffering secretary," and asked her to get him Whitney on the phone. Sitting in Weinberg's office, Whitehead remembered being "appalled" that Weinberg would have the nerve to do such a thing "but it was never possible to restrain Sidney once he'd gotten it in his mind to do something."

When Whitney got on the phone, Weinberg started barking at him: "Jock, I hear you've just offered my young assistant a job at J. H. Whitney. You can't do that, Jock. He's too important to me here, and I'm sorry, but I just can't spare him, and that's that." Whitehead was "astounded that even Sidney could be so brazen with such a man as Jock Whitney." But it worked. Whitney withdrew the offer. Goldman agreed to match the compensation Whitney had offered him and agreed to make him a partner at the end of 1956. Whitehead stayed. As promised, the firm promoted him to partner at the end of the year. He was paid a salary of $25,000 and one-quarter of 1 percent of the firm's profits. "It was the happiest day of my life, and a huge relief to me," he explained. "Being a partner at Goldman Sachs wasn't exactly lifetime tenure, but close. Now I figured that the only thing that would endanger my continued employment was the demise of the firm itself."

WHITEHEAD'S MAIN CONCERN, as Weinberg aged into his seventies, was the prospect of the firm's investment banking business withering away when Weinberg left the stage. Whitehead figured Weinberg's business-getting prowess could not be easily replaced, and he—alone, apparently—was increasingly worried about how the firm would carry on without its "ultimate rainmaker." Ironically, Whitehead reasoned, "it was apparent that our greatest strength was our greatest weakness."

It was this fear of failure that led Whitehead to devise his plan for a New Business Group—a group of ten or more senior bankers who would fan out across the country and touch base with one large company after another to see what, if anything, Goldman Sachs could do for them. Whitehead's thinking—Marketing 101, really—was highly Cartesian, logical, and totally radical for Wall Street at the time. "No one solicited business," he recalled. "That was undignified. The way to attract business was to act prestigious and important—and somehow that would lure the better sort of customer the investment banker was trying to attract. That was, in fact, the way Sidney did it. He established himself as the man to see for a corporation's financial needs. He rarely traveled, in fact, because everybody came to see him." What's more, Weinberg's most successful peers—André Meyer, Felix Rohatyn, and Bobbie Lehman, among them—did the exact same thing. Whitehead's organized calling effort was simply undignified.

Weinberg ignored Whitehead's "Blue Book," as his confidential report was dubbed (its cover was blue). Once he became a partner, though, he tried again and sent around the Blue Book to his fifteen other partners. Again, he heard nothing. A month later, he asked Weinberg if he had read the report. "Haven't read it," he told Whitehead. This prompted Whitehead to start lobbying his partners about the idea and to realize, albeit slowly, that while none of them was wildly enthusiastic, none of them wanted to thwart him either.

Whitehead took their silence as permission. He recruited three men from inside Goldman to be part of his team, and a hired a fourth, Dick Mayfield, from the outside. Mayfield had previously been a jazz pianist. They were all outgoing and gregarious, qualities Whitehead knew would be essential in selling the firm's services to new and existing customers. As innovative as this approach was to generating new investment banking business for the firm, Whitehead also insisted that if and when these men brought in a piece of business, they should waste no time executing it themselves but rather they should turn the assignment over to the firm's internal technicians to be executed. On so many levels, this was an even more radical idea, because few Wall Streeters were (or are) secure enough about their own standing at any given moment to remove themselves from a piece of business they brought in, let alone turn it over to a colleague (read: rival) who had no role in generating the business.

In his own quiet way, Whitehead was seeking to upset the entire investment banking gestalt. But his logic was impeccable. "I noted that at Procter & Gamble and other market-driven companies, the sales department and manufacturing plants were separate entities," he observed. "After making a sale, a Procter & Gamble salesman continued on his rounds to make another. He'd keep an eye on all his customers, to make sure they were happy, but not to the point of involving himself with actually making the soap. So we did the same thing at Goldman Sachs." The firm rolled out an aggressive new-business calling effort, the likes of which Wall Street had never before seen. Every large company in the country—and then the world, as the program expanded—heard from a Goldman banker. "Many had never been called on by an investment banker from a Wall Street firm before," he discovered.

In daylong seminars, Whitehead's team heard talks on "How to Get an Appointment with the CEO," "How to Treat the CEO's Secretary," "What to Talk About When You Do Get an Appointment," and how to answer such burning questions as, Should the new-business man give the CEO's secretary flowers to ingratiate himself? (It turned out the answer to this one was to let each man decide on his own.) But getting in the door to see the top executives of companies who had never heard of Goldman Sachs—a small, private partnership based in New York and only the fifteenth-largest Wall Street firm—was a daunting challenge. "[F]ew people outside of New York had even heard of us," Whitehead recalled.

To try to orient the bankers in the direction of profitable, repeat business, Whitehead penned a memo for them. It contained such gems as "When there's business to be done, get it!" and "Important people like to deal with other important people. Are you one?" He also threw in a few phrases akin to those that might appear in a Chinese fortune cookie, including "The respect of one man is worth more than acquaintance with 100" and "You can never learn anything when you're talking." As Whitehead and his gang of four kept showing up at companies, new-business assignments began to trickle Goldman's way. Of his baby, Whitehead later wrote, "It just showed the value of an organized, highly structured sales effort and a sensible delegation of responsibility for carrying out the project."

Whitehead's New Business Group at Goldman revolutionized the investment banking business on Wall Street. It took some other firms a generation to come to the realization that what Whitehead had unleashed on the rest of the industry gave Goldman a serious competitive advantage that would have to be emulated. The days of waiting for the phone to ring were largely over. To win new banking business on Wall Street in the wake of the Whitehead revolution meant calling on potential companies year after year with good ideas in the hope that when they decided to raise capital or do an M&A deal, they would call and hire your firm. Whitehead related the story of how J. Fred Weintz, one of his new-business partners, was so engrossed in a new-business call at a company in Cleveland—including staying on for lunch with the company's president at his club—that he completely forgot about his wife, who had been waiting for him in the car since ten in the morning. "That's the kind of new-business man we wanted," Whitehead said.

BUT WHITEHEAD did not consider this his most important contribution to the firm, or his greatest triumph. Rather, he appears to take greatest pride in having memorialized for future generations of Goldman employees and executives a code by which they should live and work. "I get too much credit," he said, "more than I deserve for having invented somehow the ethical considerations at Goldman Sachs." He took it upon himself to create the twelve commandments—which the firm's lawyers have since increased by two, to fourteen—that had made the firm so successful and would continue to make the firm successful, if they were followed. Whitehead, in effect, institutionalized what was—and remains—the "Goldman Way" and spawned a new generation of highly paid Wall Street soldiers, who have been called everything from "cyborgs" to "Stepford wives" to the "Manchurian bankers." But from their inception, the more cynical members of the Goldman army—not surprisingly—belittled Whitehead's efforts. "As a practical matter 14 is a lot," said one longtime Goldman partner. Around the water cooler, among those less willing to drink the Goldman Kool-Aid, bankers and traders had taken to quoting French leader Georges Clemenceau, who, after President Wilson showed up at Versailles at the end of World War I with his Fourteen Points, said, "Even Moses only had *ten* commandments."

But, again, Whitehead was ahead of the curve, and now nearly every Wall Street firm has principles by which it is supposed to live (although few actually succeed in adhering to them, of course). "I did it out of necessity," Whitehead explained. He said he believed that as Goldman got bigger and bigger in the 1960s, more new employees were joining the firm than "we could fully assimilate," and he fretted that they would not "get inculcated with the Goldman Sachs ethic" that "we old hands had learned over time by osmosis." He did not want the firm's "core values" to be lost to future generations. Nor did he want the principles to leak outside the firm. "It was not meant for external consumption," he said.

One Sunday afternoon at home, Whitehead sat down at his desk with a pen and yellow pad and created his list. He wanted to emphasize what made Goldman a "distinctive" and "unique place to work" without "sounding too schmaltzy." Although the original document has disappeared, much of what Whitehead wrote that afternoon remains both crucial and central—for instance, on the firm's website and in its public filings, despite his hope that the wisdom would not be disseminated to a wide audience—in propagating the timeless myths about the firm. And though many of Goldman's employees believe in—and try to adhere to—the principles, as the firm continued to grow during the next thirty years and became increasingly global, the behavior of its employees became harder and harder to control, despite the existence of a list of principles by which they were expected to live.

That Sunday afternoon, he originally wrote up ten principles. But when he showed them to one of his partners, he told Whitehead, "The Ten Commandments, John? Isn't there, in your religion, something about Ten Commandments and do you really want this to sound like it's the Ten Commandments?" Whitehead replied that he did not. "So I made it twelve," he said.

Whitehead's commandments seem like banal pabulum today, especially for a service-oriented business. At the time he wrote them they were nearly revolutionary. What Wall Street firm thought of itself as important enough to lay down principles of behavior for its employees? "Our clients' interests always come first," Whitehead put at the top of his list, understandably. "Our experience shows that if we serve our clients well, our own success would follow." He could have stopped there, of course, and, assuming he could get the troops to go along, be hailed a Wall Street hero.

But among those precepts that followed were some that sounded great on paper but were too easily violated, as was apparent at Goldman in the Trading Corporation and Penn Central scandals (and on others to come, in short order). "Our assets are our people, capital and reputation," Whitehead continued. "If any of these is ever diminished, the last is the most difficult to restore. We are dedicated to complying fully with the letter and spirit of the laws, rules, and ethical principles that govern us. Our continued success depends upon unswerving adherence to this standard." As a corollary to the importance Whitehead placed on ethical behavior at the firm, he added, "Integrity and honesty are at the heart of our business. We expect our people to maintain high ethical standards in everything they do, both in their work for the firm and in their personal lives."

Whitehead's remaining goals for the Goldman troops involved the expected exhortations on the importance of profitability, professionalism, creativity, and innovation. He also acknowledged how important recruiting had become to the firm. "Although our activities are measured in the billions of dollars, we select our people one by one," he wrote. "In a service business, we know that without the best people, we cannot be the best firm." He later elaborated on what he meant. His definition of "the best" was a combination of "brains, leadership potential and ambition in roughly equal parts." Brains, he allowed, could be determined easily enough from test scores and grades. Leadership was apparent from extracurricular activities and summer jobs. He always looked for "take-charge people," those with "energy and initiative, which are so critical to leadership." Ambition was essential. "We depended on people who were absolutely driven to succeed at everything they did." Whitehead also wanted to make sure the people Goldman recruited had the "opportunity to move ahead more rapidly than is possible at most other places. We have yet to find limits to the responsibility that our best people are able to assume." (This was one of the commandments that the lawyers seemed to get hold of, by adding that "[a]dvancement depends solely on ability, performance and contribution to the firm's success, without regard to race, color, religion, sex, age, national origin, disability, sexual orientation, or any impermissible criterion or circumstances," albeit too late for James Cofield.)

When Whitehead finished his list, he shared it with Goldman's Management Committee, which tweaked it and then approved its distribution to everyone at the firm. A copy was also sent to each employee's home "in hopes that the family would see it, too, and be proud of the firm where Dad (or in a few cases, Mom) worked, and spent so much of his time." Whitehead explained that "travel was pretty extensive in those days, especially for new businessmen" and he shared the principles with wives and children "to impress the families" that Dad "worked for a high-grade firm that did have high standards" and helped to "assuage our employees' feelings of guilt toward their families for their absenteeism by saying 'Look at the character of our firm.' " To Whitehead, the principles were "a big hit" and "respected throughout the firm." Indeed, managers were expected to meet with their groups—"including secretaries," he said—at least once a quarter for "at least an hour" to discuss the business principles and how they applied to the transactions the department was doing. "[T]he department heads were required to send in minutes of their meeting and what was raised and what questions came up about ethics," Whitehead said. "[The] management committee would look at that and contemplate whether or not there was a need to make some formal change in policies." These meetings continue at Goldman Sachs today.

———

WHITEHEAD'S OTHER PET project at Goldman was forcing the firm to expand internationally. He criticized both Levy and Sidney Weinberg for being painfully parochial. "Sidney Weinberg's contacts were all American and, later on, so were Gus Levy's," Whitehead explained. "I don't think Sidney ever left the United States, even for vacations." As for Levy, he observed, "When Gus had to fly to London one time for a business meeting, he flew back the next day. There was nothing more for him to do there."

During the more than forty years these two men ran Goldman there were a few stabs at being part of the international community. There was Goldman's long-standing "correspondence" relationship with Kleinwort Benson in London. But that was more of a relationship based on mutual favors. "If a client needed something done in London," Whitehead explained, "we always recommended Kleinwort." In return, Goldman expected Kleinwort to direct its U.K. clients to Goldman if they wanted to do something in the United States.

But Goldman's competitors were more aggressively establishing themselves in Europe. In the early 1960s, Morgan Stanley had opened an office in London. First Boston had an office in Europe. Merrill Lynch had several brokerage offices across Europe, and Salomon Brothers "was doing a brisk business in bonds overseas," Whitehead observed. Goldman had barely done anything. In 1967, General Electric's chairman called Sidney Weinberg and informed him that the company had hired Morgan Stanley to underwrite a bond issue for it in Europe. "[T]hat was a dark day for the firm," Whitehead allowed. "We had to get into Europe or else."

The next year, Henry Fowler, the outgoing treasury secretary, joined Goldman as a partner and as chairman of the firm's new International Advisory Committee. "I thought it would give our international efforts a great boost to have a former treasury secretary such as Joe"—as everyone called Fowler—"with us . . . ," Whitehead explained. "With his political and financial contacts around the world, Joe proved a tremendous asset." Fowler worked closely with Michael Coles, a British citizen and Harvard Business School graduate who Whitehead asked to move to London in early 1970 to open Goldman's first European office.

A few years later, Whitehead flew to Washington to try to persuade another former senior government official—Secretary of State Henry Kissinger—to join Goldman as a partner. At first, Kissinger demurred. But the Two Johns persisted and met with him "at least a dozen times to try and win him over," figuring he would be even a more valuable door-opener than Fowler. In the end, Kissinger opened his own consulting firm—Kissinger Associates—but agreed to consult with Goldman two days a month and become head of the International Advisory Committee. Kissinger provided Goldman with "tremendous advice about the political side of world affairs" and his judgment was "invariably sound." The relationship lasted eight years. The relationships with Fowler and Kissinger were further evidence of a key Goldman strategy of forging relationships with powerful government officials, one that would become increasingly crucial to the firm.

Slowly but surely, Goldman built up its London operations, staffing it with one ambitious man after another willing to call on British companies that for generations had never done any business with an American investment bank, let alone a Jewish firm like Goldman. (Even for long-established European firms such as Lazard Brothers—which was one of seventeen banks favored by the British government—doing business in London often proved difficult because of how recognizably "Jewish" it was.) Whitehead's tactic for making progress was very much the same one he pioneered in expanding Goldman's business in the United States: a concerted, organized calling effort by Goldman's best and brightest. But the process of winning new business in Europe was even more difficult than it proved to be at home, and many of Goldman's partners grumbled about the ongoing losses in London. But Whitehead rebuffed these concerns. Goldman had to make the investment in Europe "or the consequences for the firm would be dire." That's when he lighted on the idea of changing the way the losses in London were accounted for. Instead of treating London as a stand-alone business, he decided to net its investment banking losses against the overall investment banking profits. He made a similar calculation for the other business lines in London. All the expenses in London should be netted off against the gains in the United States, he reasoned, since "[w]hen you're starting a new activity in a new place you have to add people before you can expect revenues." He had learned that very lesson when he started the New Business Group, "which had taken a long time to produce a substantial return on our investment." Like magic, the attitudes toward the London office "swung around 180 degrees" since "every division head now felt some responsibility for what happened in London, and the results began to show it."

Notwithstanding the accounting change, Goldman's slog in Europe continued to be a tough one. The firm was competing not only against other upstart American firms but also against an entrenched establishment of British merchant banks, where corporate executives "were reluctant to change bankers for fear of offending some old classmate from Harrow or Eton who now worked at Morgan Grenfell or Schroders." But, according to Whitehead, the "different style" of Goldman's new-business bankers "began to catch on" in London because "[t]hey were younger, seemed brighter, were better informed, had new ideas," and "sometimes were a little brash but didn't waste time talking about their golf game." Word slowly got around that Goldman's bankers were worth talking to.

WHATEVER GOLDMAN WAS doing in the years after Levy's untimely death seemed to be working. After its record $50 million pretax earnings in 1977, the firm made $60 million pretax in 1978, a 20 percent increase. When asked about the increased earnings, Whitehead declined to comment, but the firm did allow—in what the *Wall Street Journal* described as an "understatement that has become something of an annual tradition"—that "[d]uring the past five years, the firm's net income before income taxes has averaged well over $25 million annually," putting Goldman in the same league—in terms of profitability—with the much larger retail-oriented firms Merrill Lynch and E. F. Hutton. In 1978, Goldman handled nearly 15 percent of the block trades—of ten thousand shares or more—on the New York Stock Exchange, indicating that Levy's competitive spirit lived on. It managed, or comanaged, eighty-seven corporate underwritings, totaling $7.6 billion. Goldman also managed $2.6 billion private-placement financings—those sold to specific institutional investors, not to the public—and raised some $16 billion for state and local governments.

In October 1980, such was Goldman's increasing prominence on Wall Street that the firm announced it was building a new twenty-nine-story, $100 million headquarters building at 85 Broad Street, down the street from the New York Stock Exchange. Skidmore, Owings & Merrill was the building's architect (although the nondescript brownish precast concrete façade was not one of the firm's proudest achievements). It was to be the first major office building built by a Wall Street firm in Manhattan in more than a decade. New York City gave Goldman ten years of tax abatements on the building, starting at a 50 percent annual abatement and decreasing by five percentage points each year thereafter. The Goldman partners had decided to build 85 Broad Street instead of one of the alternatives, which was to take a bunch of top floors in one of the World Trade Center towers.

But what made the new building controversial—at least from the Goldman partners' perspective—was that the firm decided it would *own* the building and the land itself, rather than just rent the space it needed, meaning the equity for it would come from the Goldman partners individually. In typical Goldman fashion, the Two Johns presented a united front about the decision to build and own a new headquarters building, but the reality was not so clear-cut. "There was a lot of debate about whether to build Eighty-five Broad Street," Bob Rubin recalled. The idea of sinking so much of their own net worth into a building in lower Manhattan did not sit well with many of the Goldman partners. But once the generals made the decision to proceed, the troops got in line. In the end, Goldman made the building work. "When we all first moved in there,

there were cigarettes at every table, in a silver holder," former partner Richard Witten recalled. "The chef was famous for his chocolate chip cookies, and they were served at every meal." According to the *New York Observer,* "A partner running a meeting got a button that looked like a garage door opener. It summoned the uniformed waiter."

CHAPTER 9

A FORMULA THAT WORKS

There was much less internal debate at Goldman, Rubin stated, not entirely accurately, about another momentous decision: to buy, in October 1981, J. Aron & Company, the nation's largest supplier of green coffee beans and a major trader of precious metals and commodities with more than $1 billion in revenues in 1980. Not only was the acquisition of J. Aron the largest in Goldman's history, but it was also the only major acquisition the firm had ever made, aside from buying one or two small, regional commercial paper providers at the time of the Great Depression. Nearly alone on Wall Street, Goldman had—to that point—shunned major acquisitions as a way to grow its business for fear of diluting its insular corporate culture and because of the inherent difficulties of integrating mergers under any circumstances.

The idea for the acquisition of J. Aron evolved as Goldman's arbitrage business became more and more sophisticated—and profitable—over time. As part of his job, Rubin was always on the lookout for arbitrage opportunities, and not necessarily those involving two merging companies. Sometimes two securities trading independently but linked through a derivative presented an arbitrage opportunity. After reading up on one such opportunity involving the warrants and equity of Phillips Petroleum, Rubin—then not a partner—wrote a long memo suggesting that the firm buy Phillips's common stock and sell its warrants (the right, but not the obligation, to buy Phillips's common stock). Rubin gave the memo to Tenenbaum, who passed it along to Levy. He called Rubin into his office. "Ahh, I don't want to do all that," Levy told Rubin. "Let's just go short the warrants."

"Gus," Rubin replied, "you know we have to be hedged."

But Levy had decided and couldn't care less if Rubin thought the firm should be hedged. "Gus responded with a five-word sentence conveying that he didn't care about hedging, didn't care about my memo, and didn't care about explaining the matter," Rubin explained, "because if I didn't know this stuff, I shouldn't be at the firm in the first place."

"I don't have time for on-the-job training," Levy told Rubin.

Rubin asked Tenenbaum what he should do since he suspected that constructing the trade the way Levy demanded would expose the firm to unnecessary risk. L. Jay told him that he should short the Phillips warrants, as Levy had said. Rubin did as told, and the firm made money. "[F]ortunately the stock didn't run up while we were holding the position," Rubin said.

Rubin's experience trading the Phillips warrants led him to explore whether money could be made exploiting the illiquidity that then existed in the over-the-counter trading of options, which were the right, but not the obligation, to buy specific amounts of stock in a company at a specific price by a specific time. In other words, buying and selling options was—and is—a form of legalized gambling. That was especially so in the 1960s and early 1970s before options began to be traded on an exchange—which began in 1973, with the creation of the Chicago Board Options Exchange, or CBOE—and were traded among less-than-reputable securities dealers. "Prices were not transparent, to say the least," Rubin explained, but he believed his arbitrage desk could make money trading them. Over time, Rubin came to the conclusion that Goldman could supplant the unsavory options dealers by trading options directly with its clients, other Wall Street firms and investors. There was money to be made.

But Rubin's proposal met with some initial resistance from his partners, who were well aware of Sidney Weinberg's dictum against trading options, a carryover from Weinberg's belief that options trading had been one of the causes of the problems Goldman had with the Goldman Sachs Trading Corporation. By the time Rubin proposed the idea to Levy, though, Weinberg was dead. "If you want to get involved with options, go ahead," Levy told him and then got the Management Committee to approve it. The creation of the CBOE allowed option trading to flourish by creating standardized terms for listed options and a clearing system—whereby there was a method to make sure one party to a trade did not welch on it—for secondary trading. Rubin remembered how Joe Sullivan, the founder of the CBOE, came to see him sometime in 1972 and explained how it was going to work. Rubin introduced Sullivan to Levy, "who listened to him and said, with a twinkle in his eye, that this was 'just a new way to lose money,' and then offered his support." Rubin went on the CBOE's founding board of directors. He remembered that before the first trade on the CBOE—on the morning of April 26, 1973—Sullivan called him with a concern that no one would show up to trade the options. Rubin had also hoped that Goldman could do the first trade. In the end, on that first day, 911 options contracts traded for sixteen underlying stocks. "[O]ptions trading turned into a genuinely liquid market and led to the creation of large markets in listed futures on stock indices and debt," Rubin explained.

Based on Goldman's success trading options, around 1978 Rubin pushed the firm to start trading commodities. "We're in the arbitrage business," he told George Doty. "We're in the options business. It's not that different than commodities. So why don't we go in the commodities business?" Doty agreed with Rubin. The firm decided to get into the commodities business "in a small way" by hiring Dan Amstutz, a grain trader at Cargill, to start trading agricultural commodities as part of Rubin's arbitrage department.

J. Aron had been a banking client of Goldman's for many years, and Goldman was J. Aron's futures broker. The company had been founded in New Orleans in 1898 by Jacob Aron as an importer of green coffee beans. In 1915, J. Aron opened an office in New York City at 91 Wall Street. The firm was conservatively run. Its principal business evolved into buying and selling commodities in different geographic markets— for instance, buying sugar or rubber in New York and selling in London— and capturing the price differential as profit. "Our plan of operation calls for being long or short up to a maximum of twenty seconds," Jack Aron, the company's chairman and Jacob's son, once said. Jack Aron had known Gus Levy for many years, and both were active in the Jewish community and in their support of Mount Sinai Hospital.

Occasionally, Aron would talk to Levy about the sale of the family's business. Whitehead was also part of the discussions. In 1979, with Aron looking to retire and take his money out—his sons were not interested in the business—Goldman came close to buying J. Aron. But the deal fell apart over how to handle the tax liability related to a major trading gain J. Aron had embedded in its balance sheet. Soon thereafter, Jack Aron decided to sell his stake in J. Aron to the other partners in the business, led by the shrewd Herbert Coyne, his brother Marty, and twelve other shareholders.

For his part, George Doty got to know J. Aron through work he was doing with the firm to help create tax-deferral schemes for Goldman's partners. As a result, he became an increasingly supportive proponent of seeing if Goldman could buy the business. In 1981, that chance came again when Coyne asked Goldman to help it find a buyer for J. Aron, as consolidation was rampant in the commodities trading business. J. Aron received a bid from Engelhard Minerals and Chemicals Corporation, a publicly traded company, but J. Aron did not want to be part of a public company for fear that competitors would learn just how obscenely profitable it had become. "Aron's philosophy was 'Never tell anybody how much money you make, just smile on the way to the bank,'" explained one former Aron partner. Coyne and his partners rejected the Engelhard offer.

That's when Whitehead, Doty, and Rubin got the idea that maybe Goldman should buy Aron. After all, Goldman was still private—thus eliminating the largest obstacle for a sale from the Aron perspective—and the business had been incredibly profitable, with return on equity in the range of 70 percent annually, well in excess of Goldman's business, in large part because J. Aron made more money than Goldman did on a per-employee basis. "These people seem to have the same culture we do, and it's a business we can understand," Rubin told Doty. "Maybe we should try to buy them." By then, Rubin had been appointed to Goldman's Management Committee after Young had retired. Whitehead and Weinberg were also on board for making the acquisition.

But not everyone thought buying J. Aron was a good idea. Whitehead had asked Steve Friedman to analyze the deal and make a recommendation. He did not see the fit between J. Aron and Goldman Sachs. "I looked at it and I basically thought, 'Culturally—I'm a merger guy, I know how difficult it is to make cultures work—I don't see this working culturally at the senior levels,'" Friedman said. "And we're paying a heck of a price, in terms of goodwill." Friedman had no problem with Goldman being in the commodities trading business but preferred the approach of finding the right people and building the business the Goldman way. Friedman thought that approach would be less costly—financially and culturally. Friedman wrote a memo to Whitehead arguing that Goldman should pass on the J. Aron deal and build a commodities trading group itself. "Whitehead was somewhat annoyed with me because he asked me to get involved and then I disagreed with his judgment," Friedman said.

Despite some internal opposition from other partners, at the end of October 1981, Goldman announced it was buying J. Aron, which had some $1 billion in annual revenue and $60 million in profits. In an interview with the *Times*, Whitehead declined to state the price Goldman paid, but the newspaper pegged it at "slightly more than $100 million," or nearly half Goldman's $239 million of capital (other estimates ranged from $120 to $135 million to as much as $180 million). One seat on Goldman's Management Committee went to a J. Aron partner, and six J. Aron partners became partners of Goldman, 10 percent of the partnership ranks—not one of which had been vetted in the traditional, rigorous Goldman way. "While we prefer not to discuss the price involved," Whitehead said, "we can say that the five top officers of J. Aron will become partners in our house"—it ended up being six partners—"and that J. Aron will continue to operate with its present staff" of around four hundred people "and company name, which is too well known around the world to change."

Goldman's acquisition was as much a reaction to what its competitors were doing as anything else. By 1981, Salomon Brothers had been acquired by Phibro Corporation (with the whole business later being renamed Salomon Brothers, Inc.), and Donaldson, Lufkin & Jenrette, or DLJ as it was known, the midsize but plenty savvy investment bank, had bought ACLI International, another large commodities trading business. At the same time as some Wall Street firms were getting into the commodity trading business in a big way, others were selling themselves outright: by then, American Express had bought Shearson Loeb Rhoades, Prudential Insurance had bought Bache Halsey Stuart Shields, and Sears, Roebuck, the longtime Goldman client, had bought Dean Witter.

Whitehead's vision for J. Aron was that it could vastly increase Goldman's reach into trading commodities and gold and would allow the firm to provide its clients with the opportunity to trade stocks and bonds in any currency anywhere around the world. Before J. Aron, he said, Goldman's clients would have to go to a commercial bank if they wanted to trade in, say, Swiss francs. He wanted to change that dynamic. "I saw huge moneymaking opportunities," he said, "for instance, if we could have bought the entire coffee crop of Brazil, in one transaction with the Brazilian government, at a fixed price, and then sell it simultaneously to the coffee makers in the United States." He said with J. Aron, Goldman could assume the responsibility for storing the coffee in Brazil, for putting it on ships, for bringing the ships to New York, for insuring it, and then for selling the coffee at the same time to the coffee companies. "We could have supplied them with all their coffee," he said, "ready to be ground, in a warehouse in New York for X dollars. I saw that as a big arbitrage opportunity. The efforts to do something like that in the first couple of years were unsuccessful by the Aron people. They weren't used to taking any positions at all, not a single dollar of risk. I saw this as a riskless transaction. We would get the insurance in advance, we would get the warehouse rented in advance, we would think of all the things that might happen and hedge ourselves against those and take them into consideration and still provide coffee beans in New York at a lower price than all the big coffee companies could buy them if they went on their

own. And so eventually it worked, but it only worked after Goldman people had taken over the management of J. Aron, which they basically did
within five years after we had acquired it. There were hardly any J. Aron
people left."

———

BUT MUCH AS some of the partners, especially Steve Friedman, had
feared, J. Aron was a near disaster for Goldman from the start. The six
J. Aron partners and their four hundred colleagues seemed like a poor fit
at the buttoned-down Goldman—"[I]t was something of a shock to find
a division full of people who would not have made the first cut," Lisa
Endlich wrote—and many of the younger, ambitious Goldman bankers
and traders were offended that six coveted partnership spots had been
ceded to the J. Aron crew, making their path to the top even more difficult than it already seemed to be. Such was the growing level of antipathy between the two groups that in the 1983 Goldman "annual review"
photograph, the former J. Aron employees—including Lloyd Blankfein—
wore red suspenders in order to mock the straitlaced Goldman bankers.
"J. Aron was a graft on the body which never took," according to one former Goldman partner.

But what led to near-open revolt at Goldman was the simple fact
that the J. Aron business stopped performing financially. "It was less than
six months after that that all of a sudden, instead of being this very profitable thing, they started not making money," Rubin explained. Part of
J. Aron's competitive advantages were lost when its competitors became
better capitalized after being bought by DLJ and Salomon, and part was
lost when those who left J. Aron after the Goldman acquisition took their
intellectual capital to other firms that could then compete more effectively against J. Aron. Whatever the reasons, J. Aron quickly became a
major problem for Goldman. In 1982, J. Aron's profits were half of what
they were the year before, and by 1983, the profits were gone. "You had
the combination of people not really blending well together," one former
partner of both firms said. "There was defensiveness on the part of the
Aron people. If you were making $50 million it would not have mattered
but we weren't making any money, we were just sort of surviving." He
recalled speaking with one of the senior Goldman partners. Echoing Walter Sachs, "He said, 'Anybody can be your partner when things are going
well. Now you'll find out who your good partners are and who are not.' I
have never forgotten that and I still think about it today. He was right."

Ironically, J. Aron, which was in the arbitrage business, found, in
short order, that its business had been arbitraged away. It remained an
open question whether J. Aron partners snookered Goldman at the

height of the market—the prices of gold and silver fell soon after the sale—and sold out because they knew it or whether the market just overwhelmed them, too. "I honestly don't know," Rubin said, "and you'll never find anybody who can tell you." But some J. Aron partners, anyway, realized what a great deal they had cut. "People thought we had made the sale of the century," one Aron partner recalled. "The price of silver peaked, I think, in January of 1982, and we sold the company at the end of October of 1981. With the benefit of hindsight, the way the business went sour, with all the people that we had, I don't know what would have happened. It would have been a very difficult time if we had not sold the company."

Then there was the internecine warfare between Goldman and J. Aron about who should run the firm's fixed-income business. "The three senior people from J. Aron got into a disagreement with the people at Goldman's fixed-income group about whether J. Aron should have its own fixed-income department or they should use the Goldman Sachs fixed-income department, which is what I thought they should do," Rubin explained. "I didn't really want two competing fixed-income departments. It would be chaotic. But it actually was a long dispute, with Weinberg and Whitehead having different views, which is what made it complicated. Ultimately, we decided to have one fixed-income department. In any event, the three guys running J. Aron left." Within a year of closing the acquisition, both Coyne and his partner Marvin Schur, who had been given the seat on Goldman's Management Committee, had left Goldman, complaining of chest pains and other ailments. "With chest pains and $40 million apiece in the bank, who wouldn't [leave]?" former Goldman partner Leon Cooperman wondered.

Doty then went to work, and for the first time in Goldman's history, the firm engaged in a mass firing, letting go nearly a quarter of the four hundred J. Aron employees. News of the "staff reductions" of some ninety people at J. Aron leaked out in August 1983, although Ed Novotny told the *New York Times* that the reports of that many firings were "vastly exaggerated" and that only "several employees" had been let go after a "study by J. Aron" determined that it could operate "as well as it had been with fewer personnel."

But that was only the beginning of the changes that were to come at J. Aron. After Doty had made these initial cuts, the Two Johns gave to Rubin the responsibility for fixing J. Aron and returning it to profitability. It was a complicated task that would likely mean more firings and, equally momentous, would require Goldman to reengineer the business to compete in a more complex environment. "I could have said to myself that this might not work and could upend my position at Goldman Sachs," Rubin explained, with typical self-effacement. "At the very least, I might have done some probabilistic analysis." Not Rubin. He did not "calculate," he said. "I wasn't all cocky about my ability to turn Aron around, but neither was I anxious. Once I had the job, I just focused on trying to do what needed to be done."

He quickly came to the realization that the Two Johns had given him an opportunity of a lifetime: if he could turn around Aron—the firm's largest acquisition that had quickly become a disaster—his future prospects at the firm would be virtually unlimited. Of course, such raw ambition was not something he could admit. Instead, he conceded, "I very much wanted the responsibility, because it was interesting and would enlarge my role at the firm." Moreover, since Aron was a "trading business, with a strong arbitrage bent," he felt "suited to the task." Before taking over at Aron, he spent two or three months just talking to the professionals there, making notes on his yellow legal pad and learning the business. He discovered, with some surprise apparently, that "the people doing the work had many thoughtful ideas about how to revise our strategy and move forward."

That's when Rubin made a wise decision and gave the day-to-day task of running J. Aron to Mark Winkelman, a Dutch former World Bank official who had almost quit the firm when he was surprised with the news that Goldman was buying J. Aron in the first place. Rubin chose Winkelman not only because he was "extremely sophisticated" about "relationship trading in bonds and foreign exchange" but also because he had the "substantive background" to understand Aron's problems and the "managerial skills to help set them right." Another reason for sending Winkelman to J. Aron, according to Doty, was so that the firm could make him a partner, "which he deserved to be. He was a really bright guy."

Rubin also likely figured that if Aron turned out to be hopeless, he would have one layer of insulation between him and the problem. Rubin turned out to be very demanding of Winkelman. Winkelman's first business plan for the newly revamped Aron would be for the firm to make $10 million, a meaningful rebound toward profitability after years of slippage. "Mark, ten million dollars is not why we bought J. Aron," Rubin told him. "Tell us what we need to do to make a profit of one hundred million dollars *this* year." Winkelman was reportedly "dumbfounded" by Rubin's demand and was not even sure he was serious. But, of course, he was.

Together, the two men determined that Aron needed to transform its business from one that took little or no risk—the firm would shut down during the middle of the day if it could not account for an extra hundred ounces of gold (then worth around $85,000)—into one that would take far more risk. Keeping in mind that the Goldman partners' net worths were on the line with every trade, Winkelman and Rubin transformed Aron into a business that took advantage of short-term price differentials between various commodities and securities tied to them. They also decided Aron needed to become a much bigger player in foreign exchange trading, by, for instance, helping clients hedge against currency risk, and in the trading of oil and other petroleum products. "That meant taking risks that the Aron people had always been proud of not taking, and with the firm's own money," Rubin explained. "The firm decided to abandon the sure thing that no longer existed in favor of calculated risk taking." For his part, Winkelman realized Aron "had to start over" and "risk our capital and work as dealers." Together, Rubin and Winkelman transformed Aron into a global force trading commodities on behalf of Goldman's clients and Goldman itself. And Doty took the brunt of much of his partners' ire for pushing the Aron deal. "I took tar and feathers from several of my partners," he said.

Although he makes no mention of Aron in his memoir, Whitehead—together with Weinberg—committed to their Goldman partners that they would "take care of this situation." They met with Winkelman weekly to review the emerging strategy for how to change Aron. "At first I thought it would be difficult, a real punishment," Winkelman recalled, "but soon I realized that it was a golden opportunity. . . . They got personally involved to be *sure* we would eventually solve the many problems at J. Aron—and there were *lots* of problems."

His first task was figuring out how many more people at Aron had to be fired. "J. Aron was in real trouble," he said. "Costs had to be cut back sharply, and cutting costs meant cutting people—something Goldman Sachs traditionally did not do." The Goldman brass decided the firings should occur in one day, with each person's boss informing him or her of the decision. Since Aron was still in a separate building, firing people there was not considered the same as firing people at Goldman. "We were fighting for our very existence," Winkelman continued, "and we had to cleanse the culture from a bootlicking family-run business." Not only did that mean firing those that no longer fit but also hiring new people into the business who were capable of executing the new business plan, as opposed to those people who were hired, according to Rubin, based on "horse sense" and who just might be decent traders.

Not surprisingly, Rubin described the firings at Aron more diplomatically than did Winkelman as "certain personnel changes" and a "most delicate undertaking." He and Winkelman concluded that while

Aron had "some extraordinarily capable people" who could clearly help to execute the new strategy, "some others were so steeped in the old, risk-free way of doing business" that they could not make the transition "to a risk-based approach." They would have to go. In the end, another 130 or so of the Aron employees were fired, leaving a smaller, core group out of the original 400 that Goldman would rely on to build the new business. "There is an incredible bitterness at the way the departures were handled," a former employee told *Institutional Investor*. "People who spent 28 years with the firm were fired."

One of the people who Winkelman decided to save was Lloyd Blankfein. The decision to keep him would be a fateful one for Goldman Sachs.

———

WHILE RUBIN AND Winkelman were preoccupied behind the scenes in trying to resurrect the nearly moribund J. Aron, Goldman—with the help of Novotny, the PR maestro—was busy helping the *Wall Street Journal* provide a December 1982 front-page advertisement for the firm's increasingly lucrative business of advising on mergers and acquisitions. Goldman's role in the burgeoning M&A business had been highlighted once before in the *Journal,* in September 1965, in another front-page article about how the use of "merger-makers" was greatly expanding in corporate America and "demand for their services is climbing sharply." In that article, John Weinberg, who founded Goldman's M&A department while at the same time supposedly "overseeing" the commercial paper department, was quoted as explaining that the "merger-makers" provided "the lubricant in the transaction" to get it done and could often make the extraordinary sum of $1 million for their work.

Seventeen years after that somewhat quaint description of M&A bankers, it seemed the supposedly press-shy Goldman partners were willing to make an exception for writer Tim Metz's 1982 page-one story, which portrayed the firm—virtually alone on Wall Street—as unwilling to represent a corporate raider in an unfriendly, hostile deal for a company. Whether intentional or not, in one fell swoop, Goldman had white-washed a meaningful chunk of Levy's role in the 1950s and 1960s on behalf of raiders—such as the Murchison brothers and Norton Simon—in mounting hostile takeover attempts. The *Journal*'s story would not only prove invaluable in marketing Goldman's M&A business but would also ratify what Levy had told *Institutional Investor,* in December 1973, that the firm would not work for corporate raiders on hostile deals. Indeed, the story's headline said it all: "The Pacifist: Goldman Sachs Avoids Bitter Takeover Fights but Leads in Mergers."

Metz's story explained how Goldman opted out of one of the most contentious hostile takeovers ever, then just finishing up on Wall Street: the 1982 fight for Bendix among Martin Marietta, Allied Corporation, and United Technologies. Bendix, led by its charismatic CEO, William Agee, took the offensive by launching a hostile offer for Martin Marietta, another aerospace company. Martin Marietta then partnered with United Technologies and countered with its own bid for Bendix. Ultimately, though, Allied won Bendix, but not before Bendix had acquired 70 percent of the public equity of Martin Marietta and Martin Marietta had acquired 50 percent of the public equity of Bendix. Allied ended up with Bendix and 38 percent of Martin Marietta. The two-month battle during the summer of 1982 played into the media's fascination with takeovers. There were the high-profile bankers, of course, but this mess had four huge corporations fighting a public war on multiple battlefields. There were more fronts than World War II. There was even the additional spice of the revealed affair between Agee and Mary Cunningham, one of his executives.

Goldman wanted no part of it. Indeed, it had been asked to represent at least one of the four combatants but declined because of "potential conflicts of interest," the paper reported. "Thank God we didn't have to get involved," Whitehead told Metz. Instead, during the summer of 1982 Goldman was busy advising *each* party in two separate mergers—the $4 billion merger between Connecticut General Corp. and INA Corp. (to create CIGNA, the global insurer) and the near $550 million merger of Morton-Norwich Products, Inc., and Thiokol Corp. to create Morton Thiokol Inc.—four fee-paying clients in all, a highly unusual turn of events fraught with potential conflicts. But Goldman was only too happy to crow about how it was able to manage the conflicts satisfactorily. The executives at the four companies "told us they couldn't think of anyone else they trusted as much as us," Geoffrey Boisi, Goldman's head of M&A, told the paper, which noted that Goldman ended up with only a $5 million fee in the CIGNA deal, despite representing both sides, while First Boston received $7 million representing Bendix, even though that merger was half the size of the CIGNA deal. (Left unsaid by Metz was that in the mid-1970s, Goldman got itself into a pack of trouble with one client—Booth Newspapers, Inc., in Michigan—when it greased media mogul Samuel I. Newhouse's purchase of big blocks of Booth's stock against the wishes of the Booth management. Newhouse's Advance Communications eventually bought Booth for $305 million in 1976.)

As was often the case in such articles, the *Journal* made sure to include a few arrows from Goldman's competitors. The firm's "pacifist stance" was "intensely irritating" to others on Wall Street, who claimed to dislike Goldman's "sanctimonious airs" and found its M&A advice to be of a "cookie-cutter fashion." There were also digs aimed at Goldman's hard-to-fathom tactic of not playing one bidder off against another in the selling of a company. Competitors claimed Goldman did its clients a disservice by not getting the highest possible price and gave the example of Goldman's sale of Marshall Field for $330 million to B.A.T. Industries, a British conglomerate. "The price they got for Marshall Field wasn't exactly mind-boggling," one of them said. But Boisi defended the practice. "If you know that you'll very probably have one chance and one chance only to put your bid in, then you are going to think long and hard about keeping any extra money in your pocket when you make that bid," he said. (Despite Boisi's explanation, it seems highly improbable that Goldman's M&A bankers would not have played one bidder off against another.)

Whitehead claimed to have originated the idea not to represent acquirers in a hostile situation. When he suggested it to the Management Committee, "I had a lot of opposition to that." There was concern about what Goldman would do if a "very good investment banking client" asked the firm to represent it in a hostile acquisition. Would Goldman have to say no? "Yes, that's what I mean," Whitehead told the Management Committee. "We have to try to dissuade them from going forward with this and explain to them why our experience showed that it would be unlikely that this unfriendly tender offer would turn out to be successful for them a few years later." Goldman did lose business, though, as a result. Just the price of leadership, Whitehead explained. "If you're the senior partner, your view has to prevail," he said. "Some people agreed and quite a few people did not."

Metz noted that at other leading investment banks, the M&A departments were run by "stars"—among them, Bruce Wasserstein and Joe Perella at First Boston, Felix Rohatyn at Lazard Frères & Co., and Bob Greenhill at Morgan Stanley—who "attract new business with their reputations as brilliant field marshals of past successful takeover battles." Wasserstein and Perella at First Boston, Metz noted, had raked in "well over $100 million" in M&A fees in the previous two years; before 1978, First Boston's M&A business had been "negligible." At Goldman, by design, the M&A bankers were anonymous executors of transactions, just as Whitehead had planned. "When you have superstars, you are going to have some clients disappointed when their projects aren't assigned to one of them," he explained to Metz. "When a client hires us, he gets the firm, not an individual."

And besides, the *Journal* explained, "[p]ersonal publicity of this sort is abhorrent to the reserved, somewhat austere men who run" Goldman's M&A group. Notwithstanding the observation, Metz, with Goldman's cooperation, did go out of his way to feature one those "austere" men: Steve Friedman, one of the founders of Goldman's M&A group and the architect of many of its business practices. Born in Brooklyn, Friedman grew up in Rockville Centre, on Long Island. His father and his uncle, together, had their own insurance brokerage, Friedman & Friedman, first in New York City and then on Long Island. Steve attended Oceanside High School, where he was a champion wrestler in the 157-pound weight class. "I was interested in girls and athletics," he said.

Indeed, Friedman was in the bottom half of his class academically in high school, after having flunked French. "Now at Oceanside High School, that was no mean achievement," he said. "I mean, we're not talking about a Groton here." He would sit in the back of his classes and read about Doak Walker, an All-American football player at Southern Methodist University. Such was Friedman's indifference to his studies that he didn't even realize he was performing so poorly until he went for an admissions interview at Yale, where he was finally informed about where he stood academically. The admissions officer thought he tested well and was an underachiever. He made Friedman a deal: he would get into Yale—he was a gifted high-school wrestler after all—if he could somehow average grades of 90 or better for the first semester of his senior year at Oceanside. His competitive juices unleashed (and with the help of a tutor), Friedman rose to the challenge. In the end, he said he was accepted at Harvard, Yale, and Cornell, among others, and decided to go to Cornell after a visit to the upstate New York campus and the promise from the university that he would have a chance to wrestle competitively on the collegiate level. (The $3.5 million Friedman Wrestling Center, at Cornell, the nation's first stand-alone building devoted to wrestling, is testament to Friedman's love of the sport.) He thinks he was the first person from Oceanside High School accepted at either Harvard or Yale.

After graduating from Cornell in 1959, as did his wife, Barbara Benioff—they had their honeymoon in Miami Beach; total cost: $129—Friedman went to Columbia Law School. There was no longer any ambiguity about his academic performance. Law school "was a great intellectual awakening," he said. "In law school you knew precisely where you stood. And if you were on the law review it was a great, great discipline. A time-consuming, detail-oriented pain in the ass, but it was a great discipline. It taught you a lot about precision with facts and being careful to double-check things and thinking things through." After graduating, he clerked for a judge and then headed to a midsize New York law firm, Root Barrett Cohen Knapp & Smith, where he practiced tax law.

But, after reading Joseph Wechsberg's *The Merchant Bankers* (published in January 1966), he wanted to go to Wall Street. He sent out a bunch of letters to investment banking firms but heard nothing back from any of them. This was not the kind of response the can-do Friedman expected. Around that time, he was visiting with one of his roommates from Cornell—"I'm mixing martinis and more loquacious than usual," he said—and he confided he wanted to leave the law for investment banking, if he could. His friend said, "Well, you really ought to meet my friend L. Jay Tenenbaum at Goldman Sachs. L. Jay is a terrific guy." Friedman told his roommate he was not interested in Goldman. "I hear it is very stuffy," Friedman said. But his friend persisted. "If nothing else you'll get good advice," he said. Friedman had lunch with Tenenbaum, setting in motion a process that resulted in Goldman hiring Friedman in 1966 to work with Corbin Day in building up an M&A department at Goldman.

One of Friedman's first assignments defending a company under attack from a hostile aggressor came in July 1974 when Friedman and his new colleague Robert Hurst, who had recently joined Goldman from Merrill Lynch, were hired by Electric Storage Battery Company, or ESB, in Philadelphia, to attempt to fend off the unwanted advance of International Nickel Company, which announced a $28-per-share cash bid and put ESB firmly in play.

Friedman and Hurst camped out in Philadelphia—buying new shirts and underwear at Brooks Brothers—hoping to devise a strategy to keep ESB, the maker of car batteries as well as the owner of Rayovac and Duracell consumer batteries, out of the hands of International Nickel. Friedman and Hurst contacted Harry Gray, the CEO of United Aircraft, and Gray started a bidding war for ESB. In the end, International Nickel offered $41 a share for ESB and bested Gray and United Aircraft. Although Goldman could not keep ESB from being sold, "our client won a major improvement in price," Friedman told Ellis, "and we got great press coverage for all the good work we'd done, plus a nice fee. And smart people in the marketplace got the crucial message: Goldman Sachs is a good firm to have in your corner when the going gets really tough," especially when wearing a white hat could also lead to a big fee.

They certainly did. By the time of Metz's article, Friedman had created an industry leader, and a much-envied juggernaut. He has been described as containing the "energy of a tightly coiled spring," a reflection of his cobralike reflexes derived from years of grappling. Goldman had even devised a rare advertising campaign based on just that notion of hiring their firm in the event of a hostile corporate takeover. "Who do you want in your corner?" the ad asked. Companies signed up "in droves," Whitehead said, paying a $50,000 annual retainer to have Goldman in its corner in case of a hostile attack. Friedman told the *Journal* that Goldman's refusal to represent "corporate raiders" actually enhanced the firm's "credibility" and "effectiveness," since Goldman would not even show a potential acquisition to a buyer unless the buyer agreed, in advance, that a hostile approach would not later be made. "That lets us approach just about anyone at any time and talk openly with them," he said. "You would be surprised at how frank they are with us, too, knowing that we won't be back later uninvited." (Of course, if the company was public that pledge would be a hollow one, since almost every public company can be bought if the price is high enough and appeals to shareholders, who ultimately have the final say about whether to sell their company; at a private company, the matter is moot.)

Friedman also pointed Metz to statistics that showed that "most often," in the end, a raider loses out to a third-party "white knight" that showed up to offer a higher price, in a friendlier way, to the company under assault. "Since [banking] fees are structured to reward success rather than failure, the investment bank loses out when its raider client loses out . . . ," he said. "If you are willing to turn down money and keep your ego in control, you can save yourself a lot of heartache in this business." (Of course, if the raider won—as happened more often than Friedman preferred to admit—the fees to the bankers were enormous, since fees for financing the deal plus the M&A advice were also included.) In any event, Friedman's M&A group was making plenty of money, about a third of Goldman's $250 million in pretax profit in 1982. Since Friedman had put the M&A group on a higher trajectory, it had raked in more than one-quarter of a billion dollars in fees. Goldman, meanwhile, was continuing to hit on all cylinders, posting, in 1982, its eighth consecutive year of higher revenues and pretax profits.

Despite the *Journal*'s article, which appeared to deify Goldman, others on Wall Street had also pursued the strategy of refusing to work with raiders and other hostile acquirers. One other who did was Marty Siegel, a Harvard Business School graduate who joined Kidder, Peabody & Co. in 1971, turning down Goldman in the process. After working on a few hostile takeovers at Kidder—for the raider—Siegel apparently found religion (or a more lucrative business plan) and started pushing companies to hire him and Kidder on the defense. At one point, he had

250 clients, each paying him around $100,000 a year. He became known as the "Secretary of Defense."

One of the secrets to Goldman's ability to increase revenues and profits year after year—according to Whitehead—was to get his partners to do a little bit of annual budgeting. Such behavior, a central part of life throughout corporate America, was anathema to bankers and traders on Wall Street and smacked too much of "management" for their entrepreneurial tastes. In most Wall Street firms at that time, there was no budget planning whatsoever. Once a fiscal year ended, the pretax profits—should there be any—were paid out to the partners based on a predetermined split. At Lazard, for instance, the partners divvied up 90 percent of the pretax profits in a given year, with the balance staying in their capital accounts at the firm. Come January, the cycle would begin anew, as would bankers' fears about whether they would ever again make any money.

At Goldman, not only were all the pretax profits kept within the firm and divided among the partners' capital accounts—with withdrawals possible only with Doty's approval, for instance—but Whitehead also insisted the partners do some annual planning. He had started the practice when he was running investment banking at the firm and then implemented it across the company. "It was even harder for the traders to forecast profits than it had been for investment bankers," he observed. Projecting expenses was easy; Whitehead wanted the Goldman partners to think hard about what revenue for the coming year would be and where it would be found. "When a department head accepted a higher goal, he worked harder and smarter to achieve success," he explained. "This was another way that accounting can change perception"—referring to his decision to net losses from international expansion into domestic profits—"[and] the move boosted revenues and margins substantially." (As with Whitehead's innovation to have bankers call on clients instead of waiting for the phone to ring, Wall Street firms nowadays routinely make annual forecasts by business line.)

Whitehead scheduled the budget sessions with the Management Committee on two successive weekends in January of each year. But by January 1984, Whitehead started to lose interest. "[F]or the first time," he recalled, "I could remember . . . feeling bored and tired." He was listening to a presentation from the head of Goldman's Detroit office, "whose annual revenues amounted to less than a tenth of one percent of the firm's total," and found himself becoming "uncharacteristically snappish." He thought to himself, "By God, I don't think I can do this one more time." That's when he first contemplated retiring from Goldman. At sixty-two, after thirty-seven years at the firm, he concluded, "I loved the work, but it was hard and intense, and it took every ounce of energy I had, and I was getting worn down. I'd also found myself saying no to people more often than ever before, and I sensed that my decision-making had turned cautious and conservative, and I didn't want to hold the firm back."

For the time being, he shared his thoughts with no one at Goldman. Indeed, in a comprehensive January 1984 cover story about the firm in *Institutional Investor,* Whitehead was front and center. Naturally, he and Weinberg were pictured sitting together at a highly polished, round conference table—"no one sits at the head, because there isn't any," a symbol of their "collegial, laissez-faire management style"—but Whitehead seemed to be the one doing most of the talking. The previous November, he had given out copies of the mega-bestseller *In Search of Excellence* to his seventy-five partners. "In many ways, it describes what we are trying to do at Goldman Sachs," he told the magazine. "There are some things about Goldman as an institution that make it unique: its team spirit, the pride in what we do, the high standard of professionalism, the service orientation. And in all modesty I like to think it is a well-managed organization. That's the essence of Goldman Sachs culture, the things that have made us what we are. And I would say the culture has been the key to our success."

The article's writer, Beth McGoldrick, knew she was drinking from the PR fire hose and allowed that some "[c]ynics can be forgiven a certain amount of chuckling," but "at Goldman they take the bromides seriously." Goldman's partners not only "extol these virtues," they "believe in them and act on them." One of the reasons why, of course, was that Goldman was making them very rich. What had been $250 million in pretax profits in 1982 was something on the order of $400 million in pretax profits in 1983, a 60 percent increase in profitability in one year. If true, that meant that each of the firm's seventy-five partners also took home, in addition to Tom Peters's book, on average more than $5 *million* in cash, an astounding per-person figure for that time. That level of profits was after paying out another $80 million—or $200,000 each—to the four hundred Goldman vice presidents who were below the partners in seniority at the firm. "They are the envy of all firms, both in organization and in execution, and they are a moneymaking machine," one competitor told McGoldrick.

She spent much of the long article analyzing how Goldman had become so successful, across so many different aspects of Wall Street's

businesses, from investment banking to trading to investment management. McGoldrick found six main factors for Goldman's prowess, with a
devotion to teamwork at the top of the list, followed by a laserlike focus
on the firm's clients. A third factor was Goldman's extreme reluctance to
hire from other Wall Street firms, preferring instead to recruit highly
selectively from the nation's top business schools—thirty MBAs a year
were hired from a pool of fifteen hundred—because "young MBAs have
a certain plasticity to their character," explained one partner. "We can
mold them more easily to our values than we can someone who's worked
somewhere else." Another factor McGoldrick cited for Goldman's success was the firm's willingness to let others innovate new products while
waiting to see how they played in the market before deciding to jump in
and emulate them.

McGoldrick also cited as factors contributing to Goldman's success
its decentralized management structure and its reluctance to focus on
what competitors were doing. "We don't need to know what other firms
are like," one Goldman banker told her. "We have a formula that works.
We are hugely successful. Other firms aren't. Why should we pay attention to what they are doing wrong?" While humble that sentiment was
not, it was hard to argue with.

Indeed, Goldman also had an extraordinarily low turnover rate,
despite demanding from employees and partners a near-total devotion to
the firm. "Why do I work until 2:30 in the morning and then come back
for breakfast at 8:00 a.m. almost every day?" asked one partner in 1984.
"Because I own a piece of this. We've built this, and I feel a tremendous
commitment to seeing it continued."

Could Goldman be for real? "If you polled people here and asked
them why they work so hard," one partner explained, "they would probably say it's because there is nothing else in their lives that gives them
nearly the charge work does." Or, perhaps they had better say something
along those lines. McGoldrick told the story of a Goldman associate who
scheduled his wedding date to coincide with the end of a project. "We
didn't tell him he couldn't get married," the partner said. "But we did suggest that the honeymoon not be contiguous with the wedding." And, the
article noted, for many years Goldman professionals had the highest
divorce rate on Wall Street, although the partner in charge of one particularly hard-charging group said, "[W]e haven't had a single divorce here
all year."

Also frowned upon was the slightest display of an individual's ego,
a staple at most other Wall Street firms. "If an unwise young person
walks in and starts telling me how well he did on such-and-such a deal, I

simply look at him sternly and remind him in no uncertain terms that what he thinks is *his* achievement was made possible by years of work and cooperation by everyone connected with this firm," explained one partner. "You can be sure he gets the message." Friedman was even blunter. At the conclusion of a successful deal, a client might think of the Goldman banker who worked on it as a "star," he said, but "in our eyes he's a utility infielder." Then there was Goldman's obsession with sharing information. "We have a mania for communication," Friedman explained, "always asking, 'Have you checked with so-and-so?' and 'Have you posted such-and-such?'" As technology evolved, Goldman professionals became obsessive about leaving one another voice mails with the latest scrap of information about a deal or to share credit for something good; then their collective obsession switched to e-mail.

Partners reinforced the officially condoned behaviors at Goldman through their daily interactions with others in the firm, happily delivering the sermonettes of perceived wisdom. After all, their livelihood depended on the machine remaining well oiled. For those below the partner level, Goldman used its compensation system to reward those who fell into line while banging down those who stuck out. For those below the partner level, compensation depended greatly on how well they played with others. Some 20 percent of the firm's profits in a given year were put into a pool that would be distributed to nonpartners based on a point system designed to judge compliance with preferred behavior. The more points one received, the more compensation. But Whitehead conceded that becoming a partner at Goldman was increasingly difficult, even for those who conform. "Our challenge is to keep those professionals who do not make partner happy—both financially and in terms of career development," he said. One example of how to do that was by creating a vice presidents' dining room, with the same food and service as the partners received in their dining room.

McGoldrick's article touched the third rail, apparently, of Goldman politics: trying to ferret out who the successors to the Two Johns might be was not something anyone at Goldman wanted to discuss. When she asked one partner about this, he "abruptly" ended their conversation and responded "snappishly" that "we just don't think in terms of 'heirs apparent' around here," which was ridiculous, of course. But reporters being pesky, she persisted nonetheless. McGoldrick reported that neither of the Two Johns would retire "for another four to six years," but then she added that Whitehead, who had been co-chairman of the Republican National Finance Committee, might be headed for "a top cabinet post" if President Reagan were reelected in November. If that were to happen, she wrote, Weinberg would lead the firm alone until he retired. Naturally, that led to speculation about who were the firm's likely next leaders. Her answer—Rubin and Friedman—was logical enough, given that they were the two rainmakers in the firm's two main businesses, investment banking and trading. "The two are undoubtedly stars among the field of driven achievers who are Goldman partners," she explained. Rubin, though, might have his own Washington aspirations. "[T]he top job at Goldman may not be Rubin's ultimate goal," she speculated. "One of the leading fund-raisers for Democratic presidential candidate Walter Mondale, Rubin himself might be headed for Washington."

That was as close as McGoldrick got to ferreting out that Whitehead had made the decision to leave Goldman. He kept his decision to himself "lest any rumors force my hand," he confided. In May 1984, Whitehead told Weinberg, who was taken by surprise. "He tried to talk me out of it," Whitehead explained, "but soon saw that I had really made up my mind." According to Whitehead, they decided that Weinberg would stay as sole chairman of the firm while Rubin and Friedman would become vice chairmen and, "in due course," co-chairmen. On August 15, Goldman announced Whitehead would step down on November 30 and that Weinberg, then fifty-nine, would "take the helm alone." No mention was made of Goldman's plans for Rubin and Friedman, both then forty-six, other than that they were among the names mentioned to potentially lead the firm in the future.

In a memo to the firm's 3,600 employees, Whitehead wrote that his job was "very demanding" and "it was time to do some other things in the non-profit sector which are important to me."

The next day, the *Times* profiled Weinberg, noting that he had "maintained a remarkably low profile in one of Wall Street's most visible firms," a degree of anonymity that would make a CIA boss "envious." During a "leisurely" and "rare" two-hour interview over lunch, Weinberg smoked one of his four daily cigars—"El Rope-O No. 2," he called them—and explained, "I don't let my ego get in the way" of work, the best of which, he said, was "anonymous." Then came the kind of high-profile public praise from a client that cannot be bought. "I could talk about him for a week," John F. "Jack" Welch, the chairman and CEO of GE, told the paper. "I'm really a fan; I think he's terrific. He's sensitive. The thing that distinguishes him is that he's not just a deal-maker for a deal's sake. He's interested in what's right for both parties. He cares about his clients and his own people in as sensitive a way as anybody in business."

There has always been speculation that one of the reasons Whitehead left Goldman in 1984 was that with the firm's profits and size growing rapidly, there was increasing pressure from his partners to take the firm public, as any number of other firms had done since Donaldson, Lufkin & Jenrette started the stampede in 1970. In 1983, Goldman's net income was around $400 million, and the firm's capital had grown to $750 million, $500 million of which had come from the partners themselves. When Whitehead and Weinberg became Goldman partners, in 1956, the firm's capital account stood at $10 million.

In a June 1987 interview in *Institutional Investor* with writer Cary Reich, Whitehead argued that other investment banking firms had gone public not because they needed capital, but because of a desire on the part of the partners to "cash in." He said that for a Wall Street firm, having limited capital was a good thing. "It forces you to make choices as to what businesses you engage in and don't engage in. Any business that has all the capital it could possibly need is in trouble, because nobody is there making choices as to how it uses its capital." Access to unlimited capital, he claimed, deprived firms of having to make the tough choices about what business lines to be in, or not. "But with limited capital, you have to analyze and make choices, and you pick the most profitable businesses to be involved in . . . ," he explained. "At Goldman we had a study going every year about whether or not we should go public or whether we should raise capital in some other way. But there was never any serious feeling that we needed to augment our capital very substantially." This view within Goldman would change soon enough.

In the first few months of his retirement, Whitehead appeared daily in his same office at Goldman and spent his time researching and writing a book he intended to title *The Social Responsibilities of Business,* about how companies were able to make money for shareholders while also "doing good works." McGraw-Hill had paid him a "modest retainer," as he referred to his advance, and he'd written one chapter by April 1985. He had also written an op-ed for the *New York Times* on the eve of his retirement where he observed, "It begins to appear that the tide of Soviet power, the principal threat to stability in the world for many years, has begun to ebb. Beset by aging, unstable leadership, serious internal economic problems, an embarrassingly unsuccessful war in Afghanistan, and recurring rebellion within its own orbit, Russia has lost its appeal to third world nations and may now be slipping backward. Over time, these developments may permit some moderation in the increase of defense expenditures and lead to a more easily balanced budget."

One late April afternoon, Whitehead's phone rang and, since his secretary had left for the day, he answered it himself. It was George

Shultz, the secretary of state. "Can you be in my office in Washington at eight tomorrow morning?" he asked.

"If you'd like me to be there, of course I'll come," Whitehead told Shultz, thinking that he might have to alter his long-existing plans for a trip to the Far East. "But George," he continued, "if you can tell me what it's about, I can be thinking about it overnight." Shultz wouldn't tell him anything. "It's not something I can discuss over the phone," he said before hanging up. Whitehead started to think about what Shultz could have wanted to see him about, and he decided it must have something to do with Latin America because the "whole region was beset with serious economic problems that had everyone on Wall Street concerned" because banks had made numerous loans in Argentina and Brazil that looked on the verge of default. Convinced that was the topic, he found a young assistant at her desk in the Goldman library and told her he needed the latest economic and financial news and data on Argentina and Brazil. He studied his briefing documents on the shuttle down to Washington and into the night at his hotel, the Madison.

As soon as he showed up in Shultz's office the next morning, Shultz greeted him briskly and told him they were going over to the White House to see the president. Whitehead thought the crisis in Latin America must be worse than he thought. Shultz said nothing to him during the car ride, preferring to stare out the window at the blooming cherry trees. They made their way to the Oval Office. Whitehead had met Reagan before when he had hosted a large dinner in New York during the 1980 election campaign. He had sat next to Reagan at that dinner and come away impressed by his "confidence and conviction." This time, Whitehead was meeting him as the president of the United States.

"Have you told him yet?" Reagan asked Shultz, who shook his head no.

"We understand you've retired from Goldman Sachs," Reagan began, "and we want you to come to Washington to join the State Department as deputy secretary of state." Shultz then looked at Whitehead and said, "I want you to be my partner."

Whitehead thought long and hard before agreeing to accept the post—an appointment that harkened back to Sidney Weinberg's long career as a behind-the-scenes presidential adviser but presaged something new. From then on, senior government service became part and parcel of a Goldman executive's mind-set and would forge increasingly close ties between money on Wall Street and power in Washington.

On April 19, the *Times* ran the announcement of Whitehead's appointment on its front page, along with his picture. In describing Whitehead's attributes for the job, Shultz noted that Whitehead was a member of the Council on Foreign Relations and had been a frequent dinner guest of Henry Kissinger's. The web of relationships that had begun with the hiring of former treasury secretary Henry Fowler was beginning to crystallize. Shultz also spoke approvingly of Whitehead's having been an investment banker. "Having had a little experience in that area, I noticed that investment bankers have all those characteristics that we need here and hope to have," Shultz said. "You've got to think pretty fast sometimes and you've got to keep cool and you've got to be able to bounce back a little." He added, "[O]perating at the strategic level, I think investment bankers tend to get involved when the big deals come along." He made no mention of Whitehead's role as finance co-chairman of the RNC, in which he raised millions of dollars for the president's party.

On July 8, by unanimous voice vote, Whitehead was confirmed as deputy secretary of state. His tenure at Goldman Sachs was officially over. He returned his book advance to McGraw-Hill. He never finished the book he set out to write about how corporations do well by doing good.

GOLDMAN SAKE

Very little changed at Goldman following Whitehead's retirement. "If anything did, I don't know what it would have been," Doty said. "John Weinberg continued in there. And he was placing more reliance on Rubin and Friedman." One of Weinberg's first decisions as sole head of Goldman was to take Rubin and Friedman out of their comfort zones—Rubin had been head of the firm's trading and arbitrage businesses (with the additional responsibility for J. Aron) and Friedman had been head of the firm's investment banking business—and make them co-heads of the firm's fledgling fixed-income division, which had been run for about eight years by Frank Smeal, who had joined Goldman in 1977 after a thirty-year career at Morgan Guaranty Trust. At first, Weinberg was just going to give the job to Friedman alone, but when Rubin heard about the potential change, he convinced Weinberg that he should be Friedman's partner to make sure a trading mentality was also part of the fixed-income leadership equation. Although Weinberg said he had no intention to retire anytime soon, he figured Friedman and Rubin would have the job for "a couple of years," which would be important to round out their knowledge of the firm's businesses. But Weinberg was not willing to anoint Rubin and Friedman as his successors. "They are very capable, very talented people," Weinberg told the *Times*. "But we have a lot of talented guys around here."

The *Times* article made the point that Smeal had improved the division since he took it over but there was plenty of work still to be done, as Goldman badly lagged Salomon Brothers and other fixed-income power-houses in the often-lucrative issuance of both mortgage-backed securities and high-yield bonds. Others thought Smeal had done a lousy job at making Goldman competitive in fixed income. Friedman recalled "talking to a guy who was a heavy partner at Salomon Brothers" who told him, "I hate competing with you guys in the merger area. I really hate it. You have your act together and you're able to get your firm organized in this area. But I love competing with you in debt capital markets." Friedman said, "And they did, at that time, they beat our brains out." Friedman saw huge potential in Goldman's bond business and knew Smeal was not the right guy to run it. "Our bond business was *really* disturbing," he explained. "It had the wrong strategy."

For an M&A guy like Friedman to go from running investment banking to running fixed income could not have been an easy transition— to say nothing of being highly unusual—and he compensated for it by asking a blitzkrieg of questions until he got the information he felt he needed to make the right decisions. Fortunately, Friedman had Rubin as his partner running the group, and Rubin did understand trading and debt from a market perspective, as opposed to the more theoretical perspective that an M&A banker would have. They were an effective team.

Friedman was taken aback by the shape he found the fixed-income group when he and Rubin arrived. "It was a shock when you got there," he said, "just how far behind the rest of the firm they were." He was especially concerned that there was "no brainpan" to deal with what they both quickly discovered was a major problem right from the start. "The top of that division was an intellectual vacuum," he said. The fixed-income division traded nearly every debt-related security available, including government bonds, high-grade corporate bonds, high-yield bonds, and mortgage-backed securities. "The business was big, with a lot of risk," Rubin explained. Much to their surprise, Rubin and Friedman discovered that Goldman's "traders had large, highly leveraged positions, many of them illiquid, meaning that they couldn't be sold even at generous discounts to the price of the last trade," he continued. "As losses mounted, Steve and I tried to figure out what to do." Not only did Friedman and Rubin—understandably—not know what to do but neither apparently did Goldman's fixed-income traders.

The traders had lost more than $100 million. "Today that wouldn't mean much," Rubin allowed, "but in that world at that time, it was very meaningful." Worse, they couldn't figure out a way to stop the bleeding. "Suddenly, our biggest trading operation had gone sour, and we didn't understand why or what the future might bring," he continued.

Question time. Friedman and Rubin headed to the trading room. "Let's all sit down and try to understand what we're holding," they told the traders. "If we have positions we shouldn't have, let's get rid of them." The problem was that the bonds Goldman was trading had embedded options that the Goldman traders hadn't accounted for in a rapidly changing interest-rate environment. For instance, as interest rates fell during 1985 and 1986, home owners rushed to refinance their mortgages, as would be expected. This caused Goldman's portfolio of mortgage-backed securities, which contained mortgages with higher interest rates, to be paid off early (through the refinancings) and to lose value rather than increase in value as would be expected when interest rates fell, since the value of a bond with a higher interest rate increases when relative interest rates fall. Goldman had a similar problem in its portfolio of corporate bonds. "What happened to us represents a seeming tendency in human nature not to give appropriate weight to what might occur under remote, but potentially very damaging, circumstances," Rubin observed. This tendency was compounded by the fact that traders had an intuitive expectation that bonds could always be traded at or near the price of the last trade, a fine thought when markets are functioning relatively normally. "But when conditions deteriorate severely," Rubin explained, "liquidity diminishes enormously. Traders often can't sell bad positions except at enormous discounts, and sometimes not at all. Then they may be forced to sell good positions to raise money. . . . Unexpected losses can develop rapidly and be huge."

Understandably, the losses in the fixed-income group led to some serious griping around the firm, especially when the firm lost another $200 million in fixed-income trading in February 1986. "They really got clobbered," Friedman explained. "They didn't have sufficient integration with research. And the internal morale was such that when you'd have monthly partners meetings, investment bankers would be saying to traders as they came off the elevator to go into the meeting, 'Well how much money did you guys lose this month?' That's not a great morale thing."

Friedman and Rubin set about changing the gestalt of the fixed-income group by taking a most un-Goldman-like step: they hired a group of senior traders from Salomon Brothers—the fixed-income leader—to perform an extreme makeover. First, Goldman hired Thomas Pura, thirty-two, who chose to go to Harvard instead of signing up with the Kansas City Royals after high school. He regularly participated in Ironman triathlons and brought to the department "a new intensity and a risky style of trading that was bolder and more aggressive than anything Goldman Sachs fixed-income had ever seen," according to Lisa Endlich in *Goldman Sachs: The Culture of Success*. Then Goldman hired David DeLucia, thirty-three, to head up corporate bond trading, sales, and syndication in New York and transferred to London the previous head of the business, J. Nelson Abanto. Finally, Goldman hired Michael Mortara, thirty-eight, to lead Goldman's mortgage-backed securities trading business soon after Salomon fired him and Lew Ranieri, the architect of the securitization business on Wall Street. "Hiring outsiders for senior positions was rare enough at Goldman," Beth Selby wrote in *Institutional Investor* in December 1990. "[B]ut to bring each in as a partner was almost too much for the culture to bear, so the duo"—Friedman and Rubin—"pulled back. The new [Salomon] partners were told that although they were masters of their trading desks, they must staff those businesses from within the firm—no more new blood."

WHILE GOLDMAN'S TRADERS struggled with how to stanch the bleeding, Goldman's M&A group was booming. Its prowess was so great that the firm took the rare step of participating in a long Sunday *New York Times* profile of Geoff Boisi, the thirty-eight-year-old partner who followed Friedman as head of the firm's M&A group and had just been named co-head of investment banking. Such a massive helping of publicity for a young banker was most unusual at any Wall Street firm, virtually unheard of at Goldman Sachs—and usual fatal. Boisi explained that 1985 was his group's "absolute best year ever"—the contrast with the bond traders could not be more stark—and that Goldman had worked with major companies on a string of high-profile deals, including General Foods in its merger with Philip Morris and Procter & Gamble in its purchase of Richardson-Vicks, and the deal by which Macy's again became a private company (and would lead to its bankruptcy a few years later). Of Boisi's additional role, Weinberg told the *Times,* "We are adding to his responsibilities. He is one of the substantial number of very bright individuals at Goldman Sachs. M&A is a very visible activity. He's done an outstanding job. He certainly deserves everything he gets."

Of course, there were the expected nods to teamwork and long hours. Boisi's role in selling General Foods to Philip Morris captured well the life of an M&A banker at Goldman. For months prior to Philip Morris's offer, Goldman had warned General Foods it might be vulnerable to a hostile takeover, given the popularity of its well-known consumer brands. General Foods' management listened to Boisi and put in place a few defense strategies. Through the summer of 1985 rumors swirled that an offer might be made for the company. On September 24, Philip Morris launched a hostile offer of $111 a share in its stock for General Foods, valuing it at $5 billion. Boisi and his team plus another set of advisers at Morgan Stanley canvassed the market to see if a higher bidder could be found, one that would be friendly. By the end of the week, with Hurricane Gloria wracking the East Coast, Philip Morris raised its bid to $120 a share. General Foods capitulated, in part because Goldman's analysis showed that few potential bidders could match Philip Morris's offer. "We worked round the clock," Boisi said. (And again one of its clients was sold.)

As the legal documents were being drafted deep into the night before they were to be signed, Boisi left around 3:00 a.m. to try to make it home to Long Island before the hurricane hit. When the deal was signed he was notified by a conference call, on which everyone cheered. "It's a difficult life," he said. "There have been more times than I care to remember when the phone rings, I just pick up my briefcase and go out to the airport. No clothes. No toothbrush. A couple of days later the clothes arrive. The deal dictates your schedule." All this success, of course, meant that Boisi was becoming increasingly wealthy, a subject he declined to discuss. Instead, he professed his loyalty to Goldman. "Right now, I can't think of anything more exciting than being at Goldman Sachs." Six years later, in 1991, after a power struggle with Rubin and Friedman, he left Goldman.

The *Times* featured Goldman again six months later, in April 1986, in another long Sunday piece that began by explaining the crucial role John Weinberg had played in the November 1985, $6.3 billion merger of General Electric and RCA, the largest non-oil merger ever. GE CEO Jack Welch called Weinberg personally to get him involved and the Goldman team—of course—"worked day and night over the Thanksgiving Day weekend" to get the deal done. Goldman's fee for the deal was more than $7 million, a whopping amount at the time. Still, all those months later, the article revealed that Weinberg was still smarting a little from the fact that the media attention for the deal seemed to go to Felix Rohatyn, at Lazard, which represented RCA, a longtime client. Rohatyn had let the media know he had initiated the deal at a breakfast at his Fifth Avenue apartment with Welch. There was lavish front-page coverage of the deal in both the *Times* and the *Wall Street Journal*, highlighting Rohatyn's role in bringing the two sides together. A week later, *Time* weighed in with a rare business cover story, "Merger Tango," about this deal and others. Rohatyn "always says he does everything," Weinberg said. "A lot of the things I do are unknown—they won't be in my obituary but I won't be here to read it anyway." Indeed, a subsequent *New York Times Magazine* article about the deal—close to seven thousand words long—mentioned Goldman only once and Weinberg not at all. (Rohatyn had nineteen mentions in the article.)

Weinberg's griping about lack of attention for Goldman's role in the RCA deal was not only out of character but was also a bit odd since

Forbes had, in February, just done a short profile of Goldman and Weinberg—including his photograph—and emphasized how obscenely profitable the firm had become. The magazine estimated Goldman had made $500 million in pretax profit in 1985, on revenue of $1.7 billion, a luxurious margin of 29 percent. Merrill Lynch made one-third as much money with four times more revenue. The *Forbes* piece wondered how many of the firm's seventy-nine partners made more than $1 million a year. "We all do," one partner told the magazine. When asked how Goldman had become so profitable, Weinberg replied that teamwork and the compensation system for the firm's 4,600 nonpartners was the key. He said nonpartners in operations or risk management earned as much as did those professionals with glamour jobs in M&A. "That has left [Goldman] largely free of the infighting and backbiting that plague other firms," Weinberg observed. Still, despite the teamwork, there were occasionally some gaffes that, Weinberg said, "irritated" the entire firm. In April, Jim Cramer told a newspaper that he earned enough money that "there isn't anything I see in a store that I can't buy." Far preferable was Friedman's habit of carrying around his paperwork in "a battered L. L. Bean bag" while also owning a large duplex apartment on the East River in Manhattan. There was a long tradition at some Wall Street firms—like Goldman and Lazard—of being scrupulous about keeping the offices modest, lest clients start thinking the fees they were paying were too high. Ostentatious displays of wealth were reserved for the home, or homes.

BOTH ARTICLES, THOUGH, focused especially on the question of whether Goldman had sufficient capital to compete in the rapidly changing markets and to provide liquidity to the growing number of partners who were retiring. Would Goldman go public as many firms had, including Morgan Stanley in March 1986 and Bear Stearns in 1985? Unlikely, was *Forbes*'s verdict, pointing out that the firm had $1.2 billion in capital at the end of 1985. "With $1.2 billion and $750 million in excess, we have all we need to serve our clients," Weinberg said. To the *Times*, he also minimized the possibility that the firm would go public anytime soon. He reiterated that Goldman had all the capital it needed and the partners could plot their "strategies without having to worry about quarterly earnings."

There was a thread of concern—voiced by anonymous others—that Goldman might need additional capital to compete with Merrill Lynch, which had $2.6 billion of capital, and Salomon Brothers, which had $2.3

billion, as the business became more capital intensive. There was also a sense that a downturn in the business was inevitable and that Goldman would need capital to absorb future losses. "We're going to have to manage the downside of the cycle," Rubin told the *Times*. "The 30-year-olds were not on Wall Street during the last downside, even most of the partners weren't partners then."

———

NOT SURPRISINGLY GIVEN Goldman's ability to muddy the PR waters, Weinberg's assurance about the firm's comfortable capital position was an impressive head fake. It turned out that within weeks of the announcement of the GE deal, a partner at McKinsey & Co., the management consultants, had secretly approached Rohatyn and Lazard about the possibility of taking on a new client, Sumitomo Bank, Ltd., the giant Japanese financial institution. A few weeks later, on January 10, three executives from Sumitomo plus the McKinsey partners came to Rohatyn's thirty-second-floor office at One Rockefeller Plaza. The Japanese banker explained their audacious idea of buying a chunk of Goldman Sachs so that Goldman could teach Sumitomo about the investment banking business. They wanted Rohatyn's help to try to make a deal with Goldman. "Implicit was always the idea that they wanted a passive window into the investment banking business," Rohatyn explained. "I told them we had the highest regard for Goldman, that they were one of the best-managed, if not the best-managed, firms in the business." In February, Rohatyn flew to Tokyo to meet with the Sumitomo executives, where the seriousness of Sumitomo's intent was conveyed to the Lazard investment banker.

Ironically, while Rohatyn was in Tokyo getting his marching orders, Goldman's traders were busy losing another $200 million in trades they were having trouble understanding. That was the moment when Rubin and Friedman first broached the idea of an IPO of the firm with the Management Committee. Not only would having more capital help the firm absorb these outsize trading losses—until they could be stanched—but a group of older Goldman partners were looking to take as much as $150 million of their capital out of the firm and then retire. Then there was Goldman's evolving business plan, which required more capital to increase Goldman's principal investments in proprietary trading, private equity, and real estate. Upon hearing Rubin and Friedman's pitch, the Management Committee—comprising partners nearing the end of their reigns—could see the wisdom of cashing out with an IPO. The consensus on the committee was that the firm should go public sooner rather than later. While Weinberg claimed to be largely indifferent to the idea, he endorsed the consensus view and agreed that Rubin and Friedman should present the idea to the annual partnership meeting later that year.

Then in March, Rohatyn called Weinberg out of the blue and broached the idea for the first time of Goldman taking an investment from Sumitomo. Unsure of what to think about such a far-fetched idea—this was well before foreign investment in the United States became commonplace—Weinberg agreed to have the meeting. In an effort to avoid being detected, Koh Komatsu, the president of Sumitomo, and a colleague took a page from a le Carré novel and flew from Osaka to Seattle and then from Seattle to Washington, and then flew up to New York on the shuttle. Wearing dark glasses to avoid being detected, they arrived at 85 Broad Street to see Weinberg. "I had to tell him," Weinberg recalled, "that taking the shuttle from Washington National to LaGuardia was no way to hide. Those planes are full of guys from Wall Street—and reporters!" But what Komatsu proposed that day was as audacious as it was brilliant: for $500 million—not a penny less—Sumitomo would take a 12.5 percent stake in Goldman and agree to have no voting rights and no role in the firm's governance. Sumitomo's offer valued Goldman Sachs at $4 billion, a whopping 4.6 times Goldman's $868 million in equity capital and an equally astronomic 3.3 times Goldman's total capital of $1.2 billion, which included another $333 million of subordinated debt. Goldman's rival, Morgan Stanley, had sold a portion of itself to the public at a valuation below three times book value. There was simply no ignoring an offer this sweet.

Weinberg could barely contain his excitement after Rohatyn and the Sumitomo executives had left his office. He called up his partner Donald Gant, a Harvard Business School graduate and investment banking coverage officer. "You won't believe this, not in a million years," he told Gant. "But I've just had the most amazing visit. Don, this may be nothing, but if it does work out, it could be very, very big. Come over to my office right away so I can fill you in. We've got work to do!" When Gant arrived, Weinberg told him about Rohatyn's visit with the two Japanese bankers, wearing dark glasses. "Don, give Felix Rohatyn a call right away to see how serious this guy is about what he said to me," Weinberg recalled, "that Sumitomo Bank wants to be a partner in Goldman Sachs. See if they're really serious! Who knows? We may soon be Goldman Sake!"

Gant, who knew Rohatyn a little from the deal world, spoke with the Lazard banker and reported back to his boss that Rohatyn and Sumitomo were indeed serious. "We can't just dismiss it," Gant told Weinberg. "They have the money and want to be a silent partner. If we negotiate this the right way, Rohatyn says we can write our own ticket." Weinberg deputized Gant to take the lead in the negotiations. "Knowing the Japanese, it could take a lot of time!" Weinberg said. He knew the Japanese well, having fought them as a marine during World War II and having been in Nagasaki after the bomb had been dropped to help open a prisoner-of-war camp.

Gant and Goldman's chief financial officer, Robert A. Friedman, spent the next few months negotiating the deal with Rohatyn and three of his Lazard partners. "The negotiations were long and difficult," the *Times* reported, as the two sides had to balance the rules about foreign ownership, what commercial banks were allowed to own of investment banks, and Goldman's desire to have the Japanese money without giving up anything close to control or influence. Goldman also knew how powerful another $500 million in equity could be—it was close to 60 percent of Goldman's equity capital, which had been built up over 117 years—especially when it could be leveraged thirty times over. That $500 million could be turned into $15 billion of trading power. In the end, the two sides agreed Sumitomo would pay $500 million to buy a form of debt convertible into 12.5 percent of Goldman's equity over time. Also, either side could terminate the deal after ten years.

At the end of June, Goldman's partners overwhelmingly voted to endorse the deal and it was announced publicly in the first week of August. Although the Federal Reserve still needed to approve the investment, it was big news.

At first, the Federal Reserve did not like the deal, which resulted in a lot of "soul searching," according to the *Times*. "At issue to many Fed officials is whether a foreign banking institution's purchase of a 12.5% nonvoting ownership stake in an American securities firm sets a bad precedent and is, in fact, legal considering the separation of banking and underwriting set forth in the Glass-Steagall Act of 1933," the *Times* reported. "Fed officials seem to worry that control is a subtle influence and that, despite the nonvoting agreement, Sumitomo might end up exerting some influence over Goldman's activities and decisions." The Fed decided to hold a public hearing on October 10. "We want people to discuss not only the specific terms of the Sumitomo-Goldman deal but the broader issues," a Fed official explained. "Is this the end of Glass-Steagall, or is this indeed just a passive investment?"

At a rare public hearing at the Fed, which was attended by more than two hundred people, Michael Bradfield, the general counsel, seemed particularly focused on whether the investment would "lead to

Sumitomo influencing the management decisions of Goldman Sachs" and be a violation both of Glass-Steagall and the Bank Holding Company Act of 1956, which limits to 25 percent the nonvoting stock ownership from another entity. While the worry about Japanese control of an American financial institution seems quaint after that country's epic economic collapse in the 1990s, the concerns about the breaching of Glass-Steagall were prescient—and ironic, considering Robert Rubin's role in repealing the law when he was Clinton's treasury secretary, after which he took a very high-paying job at Citigroup, a chief beneficiary of the law's repeal.

Scott Pardee, a vice chairman of Yamaichi International who had worked at the Federal Reserve Bank of New York for nineteen years, testified that the distinction the Glass-Steagall Act made between commercial banking and investment banking was an important one and worth preserving. "I may be old-fashioned," he said, "but I believe that there are distinctions that can be made between the two kinds of business. I think those distinctions are major. A commercial bank accepts deposits and has a responsibility for the safekeeping of depositors' money. For a bank to use depositors' money to engage in high-risk business raises the stakes for everyone, including the depositors, the bank's competitors, who may feel obliged to follow suit, and the central banks, which must stand ready to perform their lender of last resort function, should the bank fail to maintain adequate capital and sufficient discipline in risk management." While he said he did not think the deal under consideration violated the intent of Glass-Steagall, he added, wisely, his concern that "as the globalization continues . . . you will require more resources and active involvement" from the Federal Reserve.

On November 19, the Fed approved the deal after both Goldman and Sumitomo agreed to make subtle changes to it, including capping the Japanese investment, requiring that Sumitomo raise more capital—highly unusual since Sumitomo, as a Japanese bank, did not fall under the Fed's jurisdiction (despite the fact that Sumitomo owned a small bank in California)—and that Goldman and Sumitomo not move forward with their planned business joint ventures in London and Tokyo. It marked the first time a large foreign bank holding company had taken a significant stake in an American securities firm. "In our view, with these changes the investment is truly passive," Bradfield said. In a statement, the Fed said, "The board was concerned that this combination of significant equity investment and maintenance of extensive business relationships would give the investor both the economic incentive and means to exercise a controlling influence over the management policies" of Goldman. Weinberg seemed happy to make the changes. "This was a passive investment from the first word," he said, "and there was never a desire on Sumitomo's part to get control."

The Fed's approval cleared the way for Goldman to get Sumitomo's money by December 1. "This will give us additional capital to provide clients with a broad range of investment," Weinberg said. But the bigger question floating around the halls of 85 Broad Street was whether the Sumitomo capital was enough. Should Goldman still go public as Rubin and Friedman had proposed earlier in the year?

————

THIS WAS THE question confronting the 104 Goldman partners who had gathered Saturday morning, December 6, in the firm's second-floor meeting room. It had been a surreal few days before the meeting. Not only had Goldman received the Sumitomo millions on December 1—and now had a large Japanese bank as an investor—but that same day, thirty-seven new partners had been named. The nine-member Management Committee had already endorsed the idea of an IPO and in the days leading up to the partners' meeting had been canvassing the rest of the partnership for their support. Fairly uniquely on Wall Street, each partner's vote counted as one, regardless of how many shares he—or she—owned. (The firm's first woman partner, Jeanette W. Loeb, had been selected on December 1.) That meant that the thirty-seven new partners would have just as much say as the Management Committee—but a totally different agenda. As new partners, they had not had the chance to build up their wealth in the firm, and many of them believed it was too soon to go public.

The nine members of the Management Committee sat on the stage at the front of the room facing the ninety-five other partners in the audience. Many members of the committee spoke up in support of the IPO, but everyone paid particular interest when Friedman and Rubin got up together to speak in favor. Weinberg had positioned them, after all, to lead the firm after he retired. They made the case that with even more capital, Goldman could soon be a rival to Salomon Brothers in trading and could also become a leader in proprietary trading (for its own account) as well as in private equity and other forms of principal investing. Then they touched on the issue of partner liability. As a partnership, each of them individually was responsible for absorbing the losses the firm incurred in an amount equal to his entire net worth. This was no small worry, given the recent trading losses and such existential threats as the lawsuits that had hit the firm in the wake of the Penn Central bankruptcy. Who knew what might be lurking out there that could zap Goldman again? Rubin and Friedman argued that the time had come for the IPO for many reasons, with the hope being that if the partners agreed it could be done before the next financial crisis, which Rubin for one suspected was imminent.

Oddly, though, their presentation landed with a thud. "The presentation made to the partners that Saturday has been described as, at best, uninspiring and weak," according to Endlich. "Others have called it haphazard and half-baked, emphasizing that its quality was far below that of presentations the firm routinely gave its clients. Most agree that it was an amateurish effort; what was presented was little more than a concept." Partners were given a document that outlined the new structure whereby they would become "managing directors" whose stock would be worth around three times more than what they paid for it originally. Furthermore, many of the numbers didn't add up, and the investment bankers in the audience were busy trying to reconcile them. Emotions ran high. Chaos reigned. "By afternoon, an impassioned debate had erupted . . . ," Endlich continued. "Partners screamed and cried . . . it was a cathartic experience."

Soon enough, it was clear that the new partners had little interest in going public since they had not yet had a chance to build up enough value in their Goldman stock to benefit sufficiently from an IPO, while the investment banking and M&A partners were indifferent to the idea because their businesses required very little capital to operate and were already world leading and extremely profitable. Many wondered who really owned the firm—the present generation lucky enough to be around to cash out when the firm went public, or the future generations for whom the present generation was just a steward? And why should the current partners get filthy rich as a result of the work done by the thousands of people who came before them in the previous 117 years? Eleven years later, Weinberg reflected back on the 1986 partners' meeting: "I always felt there was a terrific risk, and still do, that when you start going that way you are going to have one group of partners who are going to take what has been worked on for 127 years and get that two-for-one or three-for-one. Any of us who are partners at the time when you do that don't deserve it. We let people in at book value, they should go out at book value."

The partners' meeting lasted through the day and ended inconclusively. That night, the partners reassembled for a black tie party at Sotheby's. "Each partner was engaged in a balancing act," Endlich recounted, "an internal struggle to weigh the different factors that would affect his vote. Personally most partners wished the firm to remain a partnership; yet a judgment needed to be made as to whether the firm required a larger and more stable capital base in the near future. And then there was raw self-interest, a very personal calculation of the optimal way to enhance one's wealth." Regardless, the final decision would be made the next day through a vote of the partners.

But when the partners reconvened at 85 Broad that Sunday morning, it was clear that both of Sidney Weinberg's sons—John, the senior partner, and his brother, Jimmy—were against the idea. John Weinberg had not said much of anything on Saturday—which spoke volumes—but when Jimmy Weinberg got up to speak, his words carried immense weight, if only because of the partners' respect for the Weinberg name. According to Endlich, "Jimmy told the group the proposal made no sense. Goldman Sachs had a heritage, and he was on the side of preserving it. He reminded the partners of their stewardship, of their responsibility to the next generation. He would feel uncomfortable reading about the partners in the newspapers, of having details of their financial situation made available for public consumption. People stared in amazement." And that was that. There was no vote. Jimmy Weinberg "had a real aversion, if not allergic reaction, to anything public," Peter Weinberg explained about his father. "He's really, really focused on that." Goldman would not be going public, at least in 1987. "Guys cried . . . ," one unnamed partner told *Institutional Investor* nine years later. "[John Weinberg] didn't want to ram it through." The time was not right. "We were not psychologically ready to be a public company, with all that entailed," Boisi recalled. "I found it ironical, being an adviser to corporate clients on equity offerings, our own blindness to what the impact was going to be on our own culture." The next day—Monday—John Weinberg circulated a memo throughout the firm, under his signature: "The partnership will continue to review all appropriate financing structures and alternatives which will continue to allow us to be a leader in the global investment banking arena."

CHAPTER 11

BUSTED

Two months later, the question of a public offering for Goldman Sachs anytime soon was moot. On the morning of February 12, around eleven thirty, Thomas Doonan, a United States Marshal and an investigator in the U.S. Attorney's Office for the Southern District of New York, entered the Goldman building at 85 Broad Street in search of a senior partner, Robert Freeman. Freeman, then forty-four years old, was the head of Goldman's hugely important risk arbitrage department on the twenty-ninth floor, having taken over the day-to-day management from Rubin, his friend, boss, and mentor. On that cold February day, Freeman's assistant told her boss that Doonan was waiting for him in his small office, just off the trading floor. When Freeman walked in, Doonan closed the door and pulled down the shades. Doonan, who at first mispronounced Freeman's name, told him he was under arrest for insider trading and a breach of federal securities laws. "I don't know why I did this," Freeman recalled many years later. "Maybe it's my tenacious half, I don't know. I said, 'Well, the least you can do is get the name right.' And the guy came right up to me, put his nose up to me, and then he backed off." They calmed down and took seats.

In shock and disbelief after hearing Doonan's words, Freeman opened the door to his office slightly and asked his secretary, Bernadette Smith, to call Lawrence Pedowitz, a lawyer at Wachtell, Lipton, Rosen & Katz whom Goldman had hired the previous November when Freeman's name first surfaced as someone the government was tracking as a result of the arrests—also for insider trading—of the arbitrageur Ivan Boesky and two Drexel Burnham Lambert executives, Dennis Levine and Martin Siegel. Two months earlier, in September, David S. Brown, a vice president in Goldman's investment banking group, pleaded guilty to two counts of insider trading for selling tips—for thirty thousand dollars—

about two pending mergers to Ira Sokolow, a Shearson Lehman Brothers banker, who passed the tips on to Levine, who made $1.8 million from them.

Now, just as the firm was recovering from the Brown embarrassment, one of its most senior partners was under arrest, also on insider-trading charges. "Bob, you gotta be kidding," Pedowitz said to him. Pedowitz, who had been a criminal prosecutor in the United States Attorney's Office for the Southern District of New York before joining Wachtell, asked Freeman to put Doonan on the phone. "Look, Bob Freeman's a very good guy," Pedowitz told Doonan. "Please don't handcuff him in the office."

Doonan obliged, and a humiliated—but uncuffed—Freeman was led across the trading floor, in front of all his Goldman colleagues, to the elevators and then was taken down to Broad Street. Once outside, he was handcuffed, put in a van, and taken to the federal courthouse in Foley Square to be arraigned. Doonan also took with him a bunch of deal files from the firm. When Freeman got out of the van, Goldman's head of security, Jim Flick—a neighbor of Freeman's from Rye, New York—threw a raincoat over Freeman's wrists, and the assembled press snapped pictures of the Goldman partner heading into the courthouse. He was photographed and fingerprinted. His passport—which had to be retrieved from his home—was confiscated. So frazzled was Freeman that when asked his Social Security number, he could not remember it. "Something was happening to me and I was sort of outside of myself observing," he said. His bail was set at $250,000—he thinks Goldman whisked the money out of his Goldman account—and he was released to a life that would never be the same. "Wall Street went into shock," *Fortune* reported, capturing well the sentiment at the time. "Goldman Sachs has long been perhaps the most respected of the big investment banking houses. If anyone seemed beyond suspicion, it was Goldman, and Freeman was well known on the Street as one of its most highly prized partners. For them to be caught up in this sleazy affair seemed almost beyond belief."

Also arrested that morning a few blocks away from Goldman was Richard B. Wigton, fifty-two, a vice president at Kidder, Peabody and a senior arbitrageur who had worked with Martin Siegel at Kidder before Siegel went to Drexel. The previous evening, another Kidder vice president, Timothy L. Tabor, thirty-three, was arrested at his East Side apartment and then jailed overnight at the Metropolitan Correctional Center. Like Freeman, Wigton and Tabor were charged with insider trading that had produced million of dollars of illegal profits, according to federal prosecutors, led by Rudolph W. Giuliani, the U.S. Attorney for the Southern District of New York. Freeman alone was charged with having profited personally from the insider trading since he—allegedly—had done some of it in his personal Goldman account, which Goldman had allowed, in a long-standing departure from an early rule against partners even taking out loans.

Even though he knew his name had been mentioned in the paper three months before and suspected, as he said, that "one day I might hear from the government," in the hours after his arrest, "I was totally shocked," he said. "It wasn't one hundred percent a surprise that some day, I was going to hear something from the government. But, usually, these things, there's an investigation and they subpoenaed documents, none of that."

When he got the call from Freeman, Pedowitz thought it was a joke. "I thought he was pulling my leg," Pedowitz said. "But he made it clear he was not pulling my leg." After spending three months reviewing the trading records and interviewing Goldman traders and bankers, he was convinced Freeman should not have been mentioned in the same breath as Siegel, Boesky, Levine, and the rest of the motley crew of insider traders. At worst, he thought it might be possible the SEC might bring a civil action against Freeman or Goldman. "The very first insight we had that there was going to be a case as opposed to just the rumor mill generated by the article, was Bob's arrest," he said. "I was totally shocked. I thought it would likely be an SEC case. I had no idea that the U.S. Attorney's Office was involved or that he would be arrested." Pedowitz was aware of Boesky's allegations and had studied Goldman's trading records for the Boesky deals. He knew there was big money involved. "Goldman was super sensitive," he said, "not only to the fact that Boesky might touch them, but also that reputationally, this could affect their investment banking business, which in those days was a huge portion of their revenue too. They really wanted to understand this. The anxiety about Bob was not huge because people basically believed he had done his business appropriately with a huge amount of research."

At a 1:00 p.m. press conference an hour or so after the arrests of Freeman and Wigton, Giuliani said that none of the three men had been given an opportunity to cooperate with the government or even knew that they were specifically being investigated and were arrested so publicly and without warning because he feared they might have fled the country if they had become aware the government was closing in on them. Hence Giuliani's decision to also take their passports from them. "It's not at all unusual for us to arrest people for federal felonies," Giuliani said at the press conference. The three men's appearance before U.S. district court judge John F. Keenan was preliminary and no pleas were made. Indeed, there had been no indictments handed up of the three men because a grand jury inquiry was still under way. Goldman released a statement in Freeman's defense, claiming that Pedowitz's internal investigation showed that "there has been no wrongdoing by the head of our arbitrage department or our firm."

After his arraignment, Freeman went back to Goldman, this time to the thirtieth floor to meet with the Management Committee. Freeman saw Rubin and told him, "It's not true, Bob. It's just not true. I didn't do this. I'm innocent of it." All these years later, Freeman still remembers the moment as "surreal" and "unbelievable" but happening nonetheless. "One minute I am a person with an impeccable reputation and then I become something that was a complete lie," he said in an interview. "All of a sudden, I'm in this—I've often made the analogy to Dorothy— tornado flying in the wind to the yellow brick road. That's what it felt like." Even though Freeman lived on a private road in Rye, television crews, cameramen, photographers, and reporters staked out his home. At one point, his wife and youngest son had to leave for a friend's birthday party. Freeman's wife "did not want to subject" their son to the media scrum, so the Freemans' gardener, who also was a police detective in town, arranged for a police cruiser to come by the house and disperse the news media. "You become a caricature," Freeman said. That night, he was on the national TV news.

In the days following his arrest, Freeman voluntarily took *five* lie detector tests during a two-day period—all paid for by Goldman—and passed them all. He was scared as hell to take them. "Bob Rubin said to me, he said, 'Bob, you're probably the only arbitrageur here on Wall Street who can pass a lie detector test,'" Freeman recalled. Freeman and his lawyers had two objectives for taking the tests. "One was used to show that Siegel was caught in the lies in Doonan's complaint so that the government would go back to Siegel and say, 'Look, you lied. This guy took a lie detector test. What's the story here?' and that they would confront him for the liar that he was," Freeman said. "But, I also believe, and I have no confirmation of this, I also believe that it gave further assurance to Goldman Sachs that in backing me to the hilt, that they were doing the right thing." As for Doonan, the author of the complaint and his arrester, Freeman said, "My impression of him was that he knew nothing. What is still incredible to me is that the arrests were made solely on the uncorroborated allegations by Siegel, an incredible denial of due process. Had the prosecutors done even a superficial prior investigation it would have been overwhelmingly obvious that Siegel was lying. My and Wigton's lie detector tests after the arrests only reinforced that Siegel was lying. Why didn't Giuliani insist that Siegel take a lie detector test?"

———

GIULIANI'S ELIOT NESS moment had begun in earnest two days earlier, on February 10, when Doonan swore out a six-page complaint against Freeman based on information given to Doonan by "a person who is cooperating in this investigation and to whom I shall refer hereinafter as 'CS-1,'" and who quickly was revealed by the news media to be Marty Siegel. According to Doonan's complaint, CS-1—Siegel—had provided Doonan with "very extensive details about an illegal insider trading scheme involving Kidder and Goldman in which CS-1 personally participated with the defendant Robert M. Freeman and other individuals during the period from about June 1984 through about January 1986." Doonan had put his faith in Siegel and the "reliability and trustworthiness" of Siegel's "information" not only "in light of the extensive details that [he] provided" and "in light of [his] admissions of [his] own participation in the above-described scheme" but also because Siegel had "agreed to plead guilty to two felony counts, one pertaining to the" alleged conspiracy with Freeman "and the other . . . related to another scheme involving the misappropriation and stealing of inside information."

In other words, Siegel was a crook and had fingered Freeman, Wigton, and Tabor in exchange for leniency from prosecutors. Specifically, in his complaint, Doonan claimed Freeman and his "co-conspirators" at Kidder had twice used inside information to make illegal profits: In April 1985, Doonan claimed Freeman disclosed to Kidder, Peabody "nonpublic inside information material to the efforts of Unocal Corporation to resist a hostile takeover," information Freeman had supposedly gleaned from his fellow M&A bankers at Goldman who were helping Unocal craft its (ultimately successful) defense to keep from being taken over by corporate raider T. Boone Pickens. According to Doonan, at the time Pickens announced his hostile takeover of Unocal, Kidder's arbitrage department "had purchased a substantial amount of Unocal's stock for its own account" to bet on whether or not the deal would happen. Soon thereafter, Doonan alleged, Freeman called Siegel at Kidder and disclosed "confidential, non-public details" about the defense strategy that Goldman had developed for its client whereby Unocal would buy back some but not all of its common stock and specifically would exclude the stock Pickens had accumulated in Unocal from the buyback. Freeman supposedly shared with Siegel specific details about how the buyback would work.

Armed with the valuable information from Freeman, Siegel, who was not in the office at the time, called Wigton and Tabor and discussed with them "possible ways that they could maximize Kidder's profit on the situation." The three Kidder executives then devised a plan to buy "puts"—the right to sell stock at a specified future date for a specified amount—on Unocal's stock, figuring that if Freeman was right and the company would only be doing a partial tender offer, only a portion of the Unocal stock Kidder owned would be bought out—at a profit—but the remainder of its holdings would trade at a lower price. Buying the puts would protect Kidder—in advance of the offering being made public—when the shares traded down after the tender offer was complete, and Kidder would make a fortune by having agreed in advance to sell its remaining stock at the higher, exercise price of the put options.

The other infraction, Doonan alleged, was that in a telephone call also in April 1985, Siegel had shared with Freeman "material, non-public information" about buyout firm Kohlberg Kravis & Roberts's confidential planned takeover of Storer Communications, a big cable company. At the time, according to Doonan, Siegel had been advising Kohlberg Kravis & Roberts on the Storer deal. In the alleged telephone call, Freeman had told Siegel that he had bought Storer stock for his own personal accounts after rumors started appearing in the press that it might be a takeover candidate. Freeman also allegedly told Siegel he intended to sell call options to hedge his Storer position, since this would allow him to pocket immediately the premium paid by the buyer of the call option. Siegel told Doonan that the information about KKR's Storer deal allowed Freeman to "determine an appropriate price at which to sell such call options" to make sure he made money on them. Siegel also told Doonan that Freeman had told him there was no "conflict of interest" in Freeman trading for his own account "since he was permitted to do so if Goldman had finished taking its position."

Doonan wrote in his complaint that he included "only a small portion of what CS-1" had told him and that Siegel's "reliability and trustworthiness" had "been amply established." Among the more curious aspects of what Doonan revealed in his written statement was not only that Kidder, Peabody had an arbitrage department—something that was not then generally known on Wall Street—but also that Siegel was part of it at the same time that he was Kidder's head of M&A. If true—and it turned out to be true—Doonan's revelation was shocking and unprecedented: no other firm on Wall Street allowed its M&A bankers to also make principal bets on the outcome of deals. In any event, the next day, Siegel pleaded guilty to insider-trading charges. Observed Pedowitz about the charges made by Doonan and the prosecutors, "They screwed up the complaint something fierce."

As the shocking events surrounding Freeman's arrest were percolating around the thirtieth floor at Goldman Sachs, Bob Rubin picked up the phone and called his partner Steve Friedman, who was on the beach in Casey Key on the west coast of Florida. "That triggered a truly dreadful period of stress," Friedman said. After digesting the news and talking the situation over with Rubin, John Weinberg, and Larry Pedowitz at Wachtell, Lipton (who was about to start a ski vacation when the news broke and had to cancel it), the Goldman leadership—chiefly Friedman and Rubin—made two important decisions. First, according to Friedman, "We told the organization that we will come through this, that you all just run your businesses, we don't need a committee of eight thousand people, whatever it was, working on this. We will handle it. Run your businesses, this too will pass."

The second key decision the firm made was to stand behind Freeman with all the firm's resources, both financial and political. "I went to the lawyers," Friedman recalled, "and I said, 'Okay, I'm a big boy. Explain it to me. Give me the word here, worst-case scenario.' And the worst-case scenario really was chilling. I don't know how you would assess it in probabilistic terms or weight it but let me put it this way, it was deeply troubling in terms of the risks, exposures." If Goldman had been criminally indicted along with Freeman, for instance, it would have been the end of the firm, since no company has ever survived a criminal indictment, let alone a private partnership where the partners had ultimate liability. "[B]ut we did not feel that Bob had done anything illegal," Friedman continued. "We're not saying that every judgment call was perfect, but we made the decision that we were not going to be abandoning him. And by the way, this wasn't some tribal loyalty thing that, 'Hey you were wearing our colors, no matter what you did, you're our guy,' because when we thought someone did something wrong, and we felt you've let us down and we're damn upset about that, we'd come down like a hammer." Freeman remained a partner at Goldman Sachs, and Goldman paid for his attorneys—Paul Curran, a former U.S. Attorney for the Southern District of New York and a partner at Kaye Scholer, and Robert Fiske Jr., a partner at Davis Polk & Wardwell. Pedowitz remained Goldman Sachs's lawyer in the matter.

Upon hearing the news of Freeman's arrest, fellow arbitrageur Sandy Lewis called Rubin from overseas, where he was traveling. Rubin had been away from Goldman's arbitrage business for years. "In my daily experience, there was nothing Bob Freeman knew that Bob Rubin did not know better," Lewis said later. "I did not know what they knew. I just knew what they said. Bob Rubin said, the day Bob Freeman was arrested and escorted out, 'There but for the grace of God go I,' " suggesting that any arbitrageur at the time could just as easily have been wrongly accused by the likes of a Marty Siegel. Observed Rubin, "I had enormously strong feeling about Bob, and I never thought Bob should be" arrested on the charges.

Freeman said it was wrong for Lewis to "try to drive a wedge between" him and Rubin. "I did nothing wrong," Freeman said. "Bob Rubin did nothing wrong. People were saying, 'Oh, Bob Rubin—you took the fall for Bob Rubin.' I didn't take the fall for Bob Rubin. None of us did anything wrong. But there are people who want to believe the worst and some Goldman Sachs people, to this day, think that, 'Oh, well, you took the fall for Bob Rubin.' Siegel lied about me to save himself. I did nothing wrong. I know I'm being redundant here. I just want to make the point. I did nothing wrong. Bob Rubin did nothing wrong."

In his November 2003 memoir written with Jacob Weisberg, Rubin devoted one short paragraph to this sordid chapter in Goldman's history and does not even mention Freeman's name, an oversight he blamed on overzealous lawyers who, he claimed, were worried that he might offend Rudy Giuliani, who had gained national prominence as New York City's mayor during the September 11 attacks. (Nowadays, Rubin tells people Freeman deserves a pardon and, at the right time, will do what he can to make that happen.)

On April 9, nearly two months after the original arrests, a federal grand jury in the Southern District of New York finally got around to indicting Freeman, along with Wigton and Tabor, and charged them with four felony counts, including conspiracy to commit securities, mail, and wire fraud and three counts of having committed securities fraud. Crucially, the grand jury did not indict either Goldman or Kidder, despite the two firms allegedly having benefited from the scheme. As did Doonan's complaint, the nine-page indictment focused on the allegations that Freeman and Siegel—this time Siegel was named—conspired together to make illegal profits by sharing confidential, nonpublic information about both Unocal Corporation and Storer Communications. But the indictment abandoned several key accusations that Doonan had made: gone was the idea that Kidder had bought puts in April 1985 (since this had not happened, a check of trading records revealed) and the wrongdoing alleged about Storer was made exceedingly vague. "A number of lawyers involved in the case, criminal law experts and Wall Street executives said they were struck more by what was not in yesterday's indictment than by what was included," the *Times* reported.

———

FREEMAN'S ACCUSER, Marty Siegel, was something of a whiz kid who made his name defending companies from hostile takeovers. He was highly compensated by Kidder, Peabody, but apparently that wasn't enough. He had become friends with the wealthy arbitrageur Ivan Boesky, a relationship that involved Boesky paying Siegel enormous sums for inside information—once, $150,000 paid in $100 bills; another time $400,000—at the same time that Kidder was paying him millions more in salary and bonus.

Boesky had no qualms about paying Siegel, especially since Siegel's information was worth many millions of dollars in profits to him. Boesky's profile continued to rise on Wall Street, along with his wealth. He wrote a book, *Merger Mania,* about doing deals. He started to be written about in the media. A few of the articles about Boesky began to suggest that he seemed to have an unusually close relationship with Siegel and noticed that Boesky was making an awful lot of money on deals where Kidder was an adviser. These innuendos made Siegel extremely concerned, and so, after a $400,000 payment from Boesky for his services in 1984, he decided to stop sharing with him his inside information. Perhaps his transgressions could remain in the past, he hoped. (While miffed at Siegel's decision, Boesky had by then lined up any number of other M&A bankers and lawyers willing to feed him a steady stream of illegal tips about deals.)

But while he eschewed the cloak-and-dagger activity with Boesky, Siegel could not do without the adrenalin rush he derived from illegal behavior. Against his initial instinct, Ralph DeNunzio, a senior partner at Kidder Peabody, decided, in 1984, to set up a secret arbitrage unit inside Kidder. He asked a couple of low-key, somewhat unseasoned Kidder traders—Tabor and Wigton—to be in the group, and he made Siegel their boss and the man in charge of arbitrage at the firm. DeNunzio instructed the group to keep its existence quiet. As if it were not enough of a conflict to have an M&A banker run an arbitrage department, which was to take large positions in the stocks of companies involved in Kidder's M&A deals, Siegel made DeNunzio's bad decision even worse by speaking regularly to other arbitrageurs on Wall Street, including Bob Freeman occasionally, but without sharing that he was arbing deals. The arbs thought Siegel was simply a senior M&A banker and the conversations were just the typical ones arbs had with bankers (as curious as that practice was). In both 1984 and 1985, Kidder's secret arbitrage department made some $7 million, making it one of the most important sources of profit at the firm in those years.

Kidder continued to reward Siegel—to the tune of $2.1 million in 1985—apparently oblivious to its star banker's ongoing misdeeds. For his part, Siegel saw greener pastures. While Kidder and Siegel made a $7 million fee for advising KKR on its acquisition of Beatrice Foods—the deal had been Siegel's idea, which he brought to Henry Kravis at KKR—Drexel had made $50 *million* by financing the acquisition. Siegel began considering a previous offer from CEO Fred Joseph to join Drexel. And, of course, he was feeling—acutely—a need for a clean break from his still-hidden past with Boesky and the Kidder arbitrage department. He thought a move to Drexel, at triple his Kidder pay, would be the answer.

Joseph had first contacted Siegel about coming to Drexel in June 1985. The attraction for both sides was obvious: it was the opportunity to marry Drexel's financing prowess, under the leadership of junk-bond king Michael Milken (whom Tenenbaum had once recruited heavily to come to Goldman), with Siegel's highly regarded M&A skills. The combination would be a powerful one in the marketplace. In February 1986, Siegel said his perfunctory good-byes to Albert Gordon, one of Kidder's founders, and to DeNunzio, and he left Kidder.

After the arrest of Drexel's Dennis Levine on insider-trading charges in May 1986, Siegel considered himself unbelievably lucky that Levine had been the one nabbed by the feds and not him. Still, he was scared. And he suspected time was running out. Finally, with the advent of "Boesky Day" in November 1986—the day Boesky was arrested and pleaded guilty to insider trading—Siegel knew the net would close. The next day, with the help of legal counsel, he arranged to turn himself in to the federal authorities, who already seemed to know all about his illegal dealings with Boesky. With the agreement of the U.S. Attorney's Office in New York, Siegel pleaded guilty to two felony counts—one for securities fraud and one for tax evasion. He agreed with the SEC to give up all of his money—some $9 million—plus another $11 million in stock and guaranteed bonuses he was due, thanks to his Drexel contract. While cooperating with the government, he was permitted to keep his two homes. He quickly sold the properties in Westport (for $3.5 million) and Manhattan (for $1.5 million). He and his wife and their three children moved to the Atlantic coast of Florida and bought a $4 million mansion on the beach, in Ponte Vedra Beach, just south of Jacksonville. He immediately filed a homestead exemption on the property, protecting the house from his creditors in the event of a bankruptcy. In December

1986, he also purchased—for a premium of $2 million—a single-premium life insurance policy from First Colony Life Insurance that allowed him to "borrow" $180,000 a year without diminishing the principal of the policy, nor could his creditors demand that the policy be liquidated for their benefit. In other words, Siegel was allowed to buy a life insurance policy that gave him a 9 percent yield annually on his $2 million investment without having to worry about his creditors.

As part of his deal with the government, Siegel agreed to wear a wire and to work undercover. While he became a pariah on Wall Street, he helped to corroborate many of the events involving Boesky. He also provided the information to Giuliani and Doonan that resulted in the shocking arrests and indictments of Freeman and Siegel's two colleagues in the secret arbitrage department at Kidder. In truth, though, Siegel's specific allegations against Freeman and his two former Kidder colleagues were pure fiction. "The sole basis of the complaint on which Messrs. Freeman, Wigton and Tabor were arrested was totally uncorroborated information supplied by Martin Siegel as part of a plea agreement with the U.S. Attorney's Office," according to a document prepared by Freeman's attorneys in his defense. "Siegel had been implicated by Ivan Boesky in a massive and blatantly criminal insider trading scheme in which Siegel sold clients' secrets to Boesky in exchange for suitcases full of cash. Siegel's tips had generated profits for Boesky in the tens of millions, if not hundreds of millions, of dollars." But by the time anyone bothered to figure that out, Freeman's career was over and Goldman was on the edge of another existential crisis.

───────

ACCORDING TO FREEMAN, one of the cardinal rules of arbitrage at Goldman was that the firm could only invest in announced deals. "We didn't play the rumor stocks," he said. "Every one of them was after announcement. We were the most conservative arbitrageurs in the world. We did it one, because there's the likelihood that if a deal got announced, we might be representing one side. So, it would look bad. Two, there were so many rumors going around, it wasn't a great way to invest. It was good for Boesky, because he was getting inside information, but it wasn't a good business, because stocks, rumors come up, and it was a different rumor every day." Also, Freeman could not invest more than $50 million on Goldman's behalf in any one deal. The whole portfolio of Goldman's arbitrage positions at the time was $600 million. The firm targeted an annualized 25 percent return on its money. The typical arbitrage would be—once a deal was announced—to buy the stock of the company being acquired and sell short the stock of the company doing the buying. Goldman also bought the shares held by institutional investors that wanted to sell their stock in a company being acquired after a deal was announced rather than wait around the three or four months it took for a deal to close. "We were by far the number one player in that business," Freeman said. In a world before the proliferation of hedge funds and private-equity funds, the place the Goldman partners would invest their money would be the firm's arbitrage deals. "This was the proprietary account for the partners," he said. And he, too, could invest his personal money in the same deals the firm was arbing.

As soon as a deal was announced, Freeman said, his desk would open a file about the companies involved and get—and read—the public information filed with the SEC about the companies. Then the calls would start. "We would typically call the companies and/or the investment banking firms representing each side, which they had done since going back to L. Jay and Gus's time," Freeman explained. "Asking the sort of traditional questions: What is the antitrust situation? Is there an antitrust problem? What are the regulatory approvals? What do you think the timing is? Very boilerplate kinds of things."

As a result of various M&A deals over the years, he also spoke with Marty Siegel. But, ironically, he only met him once—when Siegel asked for a tour of the Goldman trading room in 1975—given that Siegel had become the principal accuser against Freeman. And Siegel said later he did not even remember meeting Freeman. Freeman was no wallflower. A graduate of Dartmouth College and Columbia Business School, he was aggressive about pushing other bankers to share information with him about pending deals. Ali Wambold, a banker at Lazard, used to tell the story of how Freeman berated him on the phone in an effort to get information. "I used to say, 'You come in in the morning, you put on your uniform, and you compete and then at the end of the day you assume your more laid back style,' but in the office I was pretty competitive, hard charging," Freeman said. But he generally believed that he was calm under pressure, as was Rubin. "When everyone was running around crazily we tended to be pretty cool under fire," Freeman said. "Everything about his persona was cool, calculating, lawyer-like." They sat next to each other for eighteen years on the trading floor and had a symbiotic relationship; Rubin would focus on the legal aspects of a potential merger—the antitrust risk, for instance—while Freeman would crunch the numbers, even if using a slide rule was not his forte.

IN APRIL 1987, the grand jury handed up the indictments of Freeman, Wigton, and Tabor, with their arraignment scheduled for the following week. Each man's attorney said his client was innocent, would plead not guilty, and would fight the charges in court. If the cases went to trial, they would have been the first ones to do so since whole insider-trading scandal broke with Levine's arrest in May 1986. The other ten Wall Street bankers and lawyers caught up in the insider-trading scandal had pleaded guilty. At the arraignment, Judge Louis Stanton set May 20 as the day the trial was to begin.

But within weeks of the arraignment, Giuliani's office said that it intended to file a new "superseding indictment with broader charges," which would delay the start of the trial. In mid-May, Giuliani's office asked for a two-month delay because "of what it said were difficulties in bringing the new indictment," the *Times* reported. At a hearing before Judge Stanton on May 12, John McEnany, an assistant U.S. Attorney working for Giuliani, conceded that the government had moved too quickly in arresting the three men in February. "Now, we know that the defendants have made much of the argument that they were arrested," he told the judge at the hearing. "With the benefit of hindsight, I would have liked to have factored in another two or three months before commencing this case. We can be faulted with trying to proceed too fast." (Giuliani himself acknowledged the error—on an August 18, 1989, "walking tour" along Forty-second Street. "It was a mistake to move with that case at the time that I did and—to that extent—I should apologize to them," he said.)

McEnany asked the judge to postpone the trial beyond May 20 or else the defense would have "an obvious tactical advantage" and that the "complexity of the purported crimes" required that the prosecutors have more time. He also said the government believed the stocks of nine companies—not two, as originally stated—had been subject to insider trading. But the judge denied Giuliani's request for a delay, citing the requirement of the Sixth Amendment, which provides for speedy and public trials.

The next day, following Stanton's decision not to grant Giuliani a two-month delay in starting the trial, the U.S. Attorney's Office stunned everyone and announced it was *dropping* the original indictment against the three men and would soon be filing a new indictment "containing a substantially greater number of counts," according to Neil Cartusciello, another assistant U.S. Attorney. The four counts in the original indictment were "a mere small fraction of what this case is all about," Cartusciello said. "The tip of the iceberg." He reiterated the idea that nine stocks were involved, not two. "The evidence before the grand jury continues to grow," he said. In an interview with the *Times,* Giuliani tried to spin the decision to drop the indictment as simply part of a growing conspiracy among the traders. "It would have been irresponsible to go to trial on that indictment," he said, "given what we know now." Not surprisingly, the defense attorneys were furious that the trial had been delayed by the government's slick legal maneuvering. The motion was "a cynical and transparent evasion of a defendant's right to a speedy trial . . . ," observed Wigton's attorney, Stanley Arkin. "What they're saying is that they made a grievous mistake in making the arrests. Now we're going to do it another way." He then elaborated: "My client was arrested in February without ever knowing he was under investigation, without ever getting a chance to tell his side of the story to a grand jury, on the say-so of one man, Marty Siegel. He was publicly humiliated. He lost everything he built up over the years, and he wants a speedy trial. Usually, when the government says they're going to drop an indictment, they're saying they made a mistake and they're going to drop the whole thing. Here they're turning the whole thing on its head."

As the defense lawyers were quick to point out, Doonan's complaint—which resulted in the arrests of Freeman, Wigton, and Tabor—had not been vetted by a grand jury. No subpoenas were served prior to the arrests. No documents were sought or produced prior to the arrests, and Giuliani's office made no attempt to contact any of the defendants or their firms prior to the flamboyant arrests. What's more, they said, "[a] subsequent investigation conclusively demonstrated that the complaint was blatantly false." For example, Doonan alleged that, in April 1985, Freeman tipped Siegel about Unocal's defense strategy—against T. Boone Pickens's hostile offer—whereby the company would "announce an 'exclusionary' partial buy-back offer for its own stock," that Siegel called Tabor and Wigton and told them what Freeman had allegedly just told him. Wigton and Tabor then "decided . . . to buy puts."

But, Freeman lawyers contended, "[t]hese allegations about an April 1985 conversation between Siegel and Mr. Freeman were utterly false. The alleged conversation and tip never took place and Kidder did not buy puts in April 1987. On the contrary, Kidder *sold* puts at the time alleged"—a big difference—"[and] Kidder's first purchase of puts did not occur until one month after this alleged inside information about the self-tender had been made public." When asked about this discrepancy, Siegel "sought to minimize the falsehood that caught him in his lie by suggesting that the error was nothing more serious than a clerical error," according to Freeman's attorneys. Siegel said that a federal agent had erroneously transcribed Siegel's version of events, stating the puts were bought in April 1985, instead of May 1985.

Likewise, in Storer, Freeman's trading records—which Giuliani did not subpoena until the day after Freeman's arrest—revealed that Freeman did the exact opposite of what Siegel claimed Freeman did based on the tip Siegel allegedly gave him. Siegel claimed that his tip to Freeman about Storer resulted in Freeman selling Storer calls. Instead of selling Storer calls and stock during April 1985—as Siegel alleged—Freeman and Goldman actually bought Storer stock and calls. The trading evidence showed that Siegel was wrong about the trades that Freeman and Goldman had supposedly made regarding both Unocal and Storer. "Quite simply, Siegel has been caught in two impossible lies," Freeman's attorneys found. "At this point, Siegel should have been exposed for the liar he was. The government, however, in order to justify the histrionic arrests, refused to admit they had been so blatantly conned by Siegel."

"In sum, the complaint was one big lie," Freeman's attorneys claimed. They believed that "the pressure on Siegel was enormous" and "if he 'cooperated' with prosecutors by implicating someone else, he might get a minor jail term and retain some of his assets. If he failed to implicate anyone else, he faced complete and total financial ruin and jail sentences totaling hundreds of years." As a result, Siegel's decision was "easy" even though "it meant that he had to implicate innocent persons." Nevertheless, Giuliani in his "fervor to prove that [his] arrests had not been reckless or irresponsible, refused to abandon Siegel, who was responsible for those false arrests, and expose him for the liar he was."

———

THE EDITORIAL PAGE of the *Wall Street Journal* quickly caught Giuliani's errors. In a May 21 editorial titled "Rudolph the Red-Faced," the editorial writer stated that the dismissal of the indictment "adds to the impression of grandstanding in the frisk-and-cuff arrests of the suspects back in February." With the prosecution said to be working on a new indictment, the *Journal* wrote it has discovered "it can't win on these trades, so a new indictment is going to be about different trades entirely." The *Journal* suggested that "Mr. Giuliani has a pressing need to make up lost face."

What's more, Siegel and Giuliani had accused the three men of having a "virtual conspiracy," since none of them had ever met or even knew one another. "Never well conceived to begin with," Christopher Byron wrote in *New York* magazine, "the case against the trio began to crumble as soon as defense lawyers got a look at its details. Here was a virtual conspiracy of strangers: Tabor didn't know Freeman, and Freeman didn't know Wigton. Moreover, instead of subpoenaing the men's trading accounts to see whether Siegel's assertions were true, the prosecutors had simply arrested the men. When they finally did get around to checking the documents, the information in them proved nothing." And, of course, Freeman had only met Siegel once, and Siegel didn't remember the meeting.

Siegel and Freeman did speak regularly about deals on the phone—the *Journal* would later report that the two men spoke on the phone 240 times during the period of the alleged conspiracy. But Pedowitz—the Wachtell lawyer who represented Goldman—argued that there was nothing untoward in that relationship between one of the Street's leading arbitrageurs and one of the Street's leading M&A bankers, especially since Freeman had no idea—and passed lie detectors tests to prove it—that Kidder had an arbitrage department. "While there was clearly a phone relationship with Siegel," Pedowitz explained, "it was not much different from Bob's many such relationships with arbitrageurs, wealthy investors, buyout firms, corporate officers, investment bankers, and lawyers. The phone at the time was the essential tool for those who made their living trying to gather 'market color' information so that they could trade profitably." The remarkable admission from Pedowitz was not that Siegel and Freeman often spoke on the phone but in how close to the edge arbitrageurs, such as Freeman, needed to be on a daily basis "so that they could trade profitably." It's no wonder, then, that a number of M&A bankers, lawyers, and arbs crossed the line.

As for the near obsession that the arbs had for "making the calls" and trying to glean whatever shreds of information they could in order to gain an information advantage in the marketplace—a practice that certainly nowadays has the whiff of insider information—Pedowitz found the practice "common" among arbs generally and that the arbitrageurs at Goldman felt "free to ask questions about publicly announced deals and would only be supplied with information that the companies felt was in their interest to share and that the companies wanted the arbitrageurs to know." Wachtell allowed that "seeking out information of this sort in this manner seemed consistent with insider trading case law as it existed at that time, and the practice of freely asking questions and fishing for information was common across the industry. During that period, companies would often find it advantageous to communicate information in one-on-one conversations with reporters and market participants." (Now, of course, with the SEC's issuance of Regulation FD, these sidebar conversations are supposedly no longer permitted, and no one market participant can have information unless everyone has it.)

Pedowitz kept Weinberg, Rubin, and Friedman and the rest of the Goldman Management Committee apprised regularly of his findings.

"They knew our view that the firm's trading appeared to be proper," he observed. "They knew also that the arrest complaint was riddled with errors and that the charges in the dismissed indictment seemed extraordinarily contrived. They also learned that the trading records of both Goldman and Kidder undermined the numerous suggestions of tips that were coming from Siegel. They also knew that both Wigton and Tabor were adamant that they, too, had done nothing wrong." As a result, Goldman "fully supported" Freeman throughout the case, paying for his separate legal advice and keeping him as a partner, although he was moved eventually into the firm's merchant banking division and out of arbitrage. In reality, Freeman spent most of his time on his defense and trying to clear his name. "I was, basically, in an icebox up in the merchant banking, which was very small at that point," Freeman said. "I was isolated, almost never talked to people in the trading room because the next day, they might be subpoenaed and be asked, 'What did you and Mr. Freeman discuss?'"

Yet, as convinced as Team Goldman was that Siegel and Giuliani had fingered Freeman irresponsibly and unfairly, the U.S. Attorney's investigation of Freeman continued, even after the abandonment of the original indictment. More than ninety document and witness subpoenas were issued, and more than sixty witnesses were interviewed or appeared before the grand jury during the ongoing investigation. Many Goldman partners and associates recalled being very nervous when asked to appear before the grand jury as witnesses shortly after Freeman was arrested. "I was uneasy . . . ," recalled one former partner. "It was frightening. The thought that they could indict the firm—that would be life-threatening. I never dreamed I'd be going to a grand jury." Bob Rubin and Steve Friedman also appeared in front of the grand jury, as did nearly every senior Goldman partner except for John Weinberg.

At one point, in June and July 1987—after the indictment had been dropped—Wigton waived his Fifth Amendment rights and spent four days being interrogated by Giuliani and his deputies. But the U.S. Attorney's Office "was unable to elicit one bit of evidence against Mr. Freeman or one bit of evidence to corroborate Siegel," according to Freeman's attorneys. After the intense questioning, Wigton took a lie detector test, "which confirmed his denial of all of Siegel's allegations." Later, in 1989, "in an extraordinary move," according to Freeman's attorneys, Giuliani offered Tabor "complete immunity" in "exchange for offering anything that would corroborate Siegel's allegations that he told Mr. Tabor that he was receiving inside information from Mr. Freeman." Giuliani made this offer to Tabor despite the fact that he was "a man [the government] had arrested and indicted in 1987 on sweeping insider trading charges and against whom it conducted a grand jury investigation for two years." Tabor rejected Giuliani's offer, though, because he could not "corroborate Siegel's lies" and "it was impossible for him to implicate Mr. Freeman by telling the truth." Tabor refused to "lie, even if it meant he would gain freedom from further prosecution," is the way Freeman's attorneys put it. The trading records were getting Giuliani nowhere either, and so he subpoenaed Freeman's college records and the records of an architect who built a home for the Freemans in 1984 and 1985 "in his desperation to find any scintilla of criminal activity."

NEVERTHELESS, GIULIANI CONTINUED to pursue Freeman, mostly through strategic leaks to *Wall Street Journal* reporters Daniel Hertzberg and James B. Stewart, both of whom would win Pulitzer Prizes in 1988 for their richly detailed and lyrical accounts of the insider-trading scandals. It would be difficult for readers not to be seduced by the portraits they painted. But Freeman and his attorneys insist—to this day—that the stories the two men were writing were largely inaccurate since they were based upon inaccurate information leaked by the prosecutors. "Trial by press release" was the way Freeman's attorneys described Giuliani's tactic. "Grand jury proceedings are never supposed to be public," Freeman explained, "but it [is] well known that prosecutors leak grand jury material. It became so outrageous early in my case that my lawyers went to Judge Stanton to try to get it stopped. Giuliani, [Charles] Carberry, etc. leaked grand jury information to Stewart and Hertzberg throughout the case. Every bit of Stewart's writings was from direct government leaks."

This seemed to be the case right from the outset. For instance, within days of Freeman's arrest, on February 17, Hertzberg and Stewart wrote a riveting narrative of Marty Siegel's rise and fall, culminating in his guilty plea on two felony counts and his decisions to pay a $9 million fine, to forgo another $11 million in compensation due from Drexel, and to cooperate with Giuliani's investigation. Siegel's downfall was a "dream gone wrong" and his plea was "the biggest coup since the capture of Mr. Boesky." Their *Journal* article also said that "it is known that Mr. Siegel is not the principal witness against Mr. Freeman but his testimony could be valuable corroboration if the government's case against Mr. Freeman goes to trial," although in the end the U.S. Attorney's Office admitted that "Siegel had been the sole witness against Messrs. Freeman, Wigton and Tabor." Dean Rotbart, a former *Journal* columnist and the founder of the *Journalist and Financial Reporting*, criticized as "shocking" Stewart's failure in the Siegel story to disclose "his long-term symbiotic relation-ship" with Siegel, who, according to Freeman's attorneys, Stewart used "as an anonymous source for stories concerning takeover battles and Siegel used Stewart to send the market messages that were beneficial to Siegel and his clients."

A March 6 Stewart article claimed that "[r]ecords seized by the Government from Goldman Sachs & Co. show that Robert M. Freeman, the firm's head of arbitrage, engaged in massive trading in stocks that later became targets of takeover bids" and then described the records in detail. "This established the pattern for the whole case," Freeman explained. "This was an egregious violation of leaking confidential grand jury information to discredit me and give credence to the prosecutors' absurd 'tip of the iceberg' claim." A May 14 article included an interview with Giuliani in which he explained that several witnesses had been granted immunity and were now "providing testimony and records that could lead to more charges against the three men and to the naming of additional defendants." Giuliani also took to the airwaves himself to make his case. On February 22, he appeared on CBS's *Face the Nation.* "You can be sure we would never arrest the head of arbitrage at Goldman Sachs if he was the only witness," Giuliani said of Siegel. On May 17, he appeared on *Business World,* a TV show, and reiterated his "tip of the ice-berg" comment. "Imagine how frightened I was," Freeman said. "He was throwing out all these lies." Freeman remains incredulous about the quality of the *Journal*'s reporting, specifically Stewart's. He cannot under-stand to this day why Stewart and Hertzberg did not pull the 13D disclo-sure forms that investors must file with the SEC when buying public equity securities. "I think he's absolutely dishonest," Freeman said of Stewart. "I think he just published anything that they gave him, never checked out one thing. Never did one ounce of investigation. Most of what we put together, all this stuff we put together, much of it was based on publicly available information. We didn't have subpoena powers in Boesky's stuff. We relied on public information—all the SCA stuff, all the Disney stuff, the Storer stuff about Boesky, the Continental Group stuff, the St. Regis stuff. That was all publicly available. How hard is it to get 13Ds on anybody? Not very hard, is it?"

Of course, even though Freeman's name was on the complaint and the indictment, Goldman Sachs was still very much at risk for the poten-tial criminal behavior of its partner, especially since it was a private part-nership where the liability to individual partners was unlimited. "As a matter of law, the firm was legally responsible for criminal activity," Pedowitz said. "The law is that if you engage in criminal activity as an employee, even if it's in violation of your firm policy, if you are doing it in part for the financial benefit of the firm, that's sufficient to create criminal liability for the firm, for the corporate organization—in this case, a partnership. So the legal responsibility was there almost by definition." Since charging the firm was something the prosecutors could do at their own discretion at any moment, Goldman and its lawyers were walking a fine line, where they were careful not to do anything too rash that might invite prosecutorial ire while at the same time making sure the prosecutors were aware how wrong Goldman thought they were about the facts. "Obviously, we cared deeply about Bob," Pedowitz continued, "and obviously we cared deeply about Goldman Sachs. Our objective was not to sort of punch [Giuliani] back in the eye because the last thing in the world we needed was for them to get angry at Goldman Sachs. If at the end of the day they had a criminal case, I didn't want it being brought against Goldman. It was bad enough that it might be brought against Bob, but the last thing we wanted to have happen is to have all of those people who were working at Goldman Sachs basically see their firm disintegrate."

FREEMAN'S TRAVAILS ONLY worsened. The prosecutors zeroed in on a brief conversation Freeman had had with Siegel, when Freeman was trying to ascertain if KKR's previously announced $6.2 billion acquisition of Beatrice Foods was in trouble. Freeman had earlier spoken with Bernard "Bunny" Lasker, an arbitrageur, close friend of Bob Rubin's, and former chairman of the New York Stock Exchange, who said he had heard rumors the deal was in jeopardy. In January 1986, when Freeman asked Siegel, KKR's M&A banker, about this, Siegel replied, "Your Bunny has a good nose," which went on to become one of the most infamous lines in Wall Street history, and soon enough the crux of Giuliani's crusade against Freeman. While Freeman did sell his and Goldman's Beatrice shares after the conversation with Siegel—thereby saving Goldman (and himself) a large amount of money—he and his colleague in the arbitrage department, Frank Brosens, had received information from other sources, too, indicating the deal was in trouble.

The initial charges against Freeman and the two Kidder arbs referred to trading in Storer and Unocal. Now, on the one-year anniversary of Freeman's arrest, the *Journal* reported that from time to time both Goldman and Freeman personally had allegedly profited from trading in the stocks of companies such as St. Regis Corporation, SCA Services Inc., and Beatrice Foods based on insider information. In the case of St. Regis, the *Journal* article stated that Freeman knew that St. Regis was on the firm's "gray list" of stocks that could not be bought or sold because the firm possessed inside information about the company and what might happen to it. While the claim in the *Wall Street Journal* against Freeman for trading in St. Regis stock and passing information about it to Siegel was a bombshell, and extremely damaging to Freeman's reputation and to Goldman's, it was—unfortunately—not true. St. Regis was *not* on Goldman's gray list and "thus both Goldman Sachs and Mr. Freeman were free to trade the stock" and "both did" without "the benefit of confidential information." Freeman's "individual trading was completely in compliance with Goldman Sachs's internal rules," his lawyers wrote.

Despite these flawed assertions made by Stewart and Hertzberg—and there were still others involving Storer Communications, one of the original stocks mentioned in the complaint and the indictment—what really caught Freeman's attention as he read the *Journal*'s anniversary story in Snowmass, Colorado, was what the reporters wrote about Beatrice Foods in the last eight paragraphs. Nothing about Beatrice had been mentioned in the original complaint or in the indictment. But Freeman had to take seriously what the article was saying about Beatrice, if for no other reason than he figured Stewart and Hertzberg had a direct line to Giuliani's office. Stewart and Hertzberg had portions of the story but not all of it. For instance, they did not know about—or did not put in the paper, anyway—Freeman's conversation with Richard Nye, another arbitrageur, or about his conversation with Bunny Lasker, which was the basis of Siegel's comment and explains why the paper printed the phrase with a lowercase "b" rather than an uppercase "B"; the reporters didn't realize Siegel was talking about Bunny Lasker, not a bunny rabbit. The new allegations in the front-page anniversary article stung both Freeman and Goldman deeply. But Goldman had not lost faith in the plethora of facts that Wachtell, Kaye Scholer, and Davis Polk had been digging up about what Freeman may or may not have done in each of these deals. "We are not going to respond to what are blatantly improper leaks to the press," Fiske and Curran wrote in a statement to the *Journal*.

NEARLY TWO YEARS after he had been arrested, and then handcuffed as he left 85 Broad Street, Freeman was still in prosecutorial limbo, despite Giuliani having said at the time he dropped the original indictment that new charges would be filed against Freeman, Wigton, and Tabor "in record-breaking time." On January 10, 1989, Freeman's purgatory took on a whole new character when Giuliani announced his resignation as U.S. Attorney for the Southern District of New York, effective at month's end, amid speculation that he would try to ride his record of prosecutorial success in to the New York City mayor's office. (Giuliani did end up running for mayor in 1989 but lost to David Dinkins; he did become New York's mayor four years later.) At his final press conference as U.S. Attorney, he was asked about the nearly unprecedented arrests of the three arbitrageurs in February 1987, and he said he wouldn't have approved the arrests of the men "if we had known all the things that we subsequently learned." He declined further comment because, he said, the case was still pending and the investigation continuing. The further prosecution of the case, if any, was left to Benito Romano, a Giuliani colleague and his hand-picked interim successor until September 4, when Otto Obermaier was sworn in to succeed him. Romano, "it was becoming abundantly clear," according to Freeman's attorneys, was "unlikely to further embarrass Giuliani by dropping the investigation against Mr. Freeman."

Indeed, some members of the media were beginning to question not only Giuliani's aggressive behavior that had led to the arrests but also his failure to bring charges against the men after two years of limbo. And now he was leaving his office to run for mayor. Writing in *Manhattan, Inc.*, in April 1988, Edward Jay Epstein suggested that the charges Stewart made in the *Journal* could only have come from prosecutors with access to supposedly secret grand jury proceedings, a violation that Stewart was well aware of because in an earlier book, *The Prosecutors,* he had written that "grand jury proceedings . . . are required by law to be kept secret. . . ." Concluded Epstein, "[T]he public flailing of Freeman [by prosecutors and reporters] breaking their public trust, cheat us all out of our confidence in justice."

Throughout this long slog, the U.S. Attorney's Office kept a federal grand jury impaneled to hear witness testimony, and from time to time bankers and traders from Goldman Sachs, and other firms, were asked to appear before it to testify. During the spring of 1989, Frank Brosens appeared before the grand jury for many hours. As his testimony was nearing its logical conclusion, the prosecutors asked Brosens a general question—something along the lines of "Can you remember any situation in which you heard about a conversation that Bob Freeman had with Marty Siegel in which there was a suggestion that Marty Siegel provided material nonpublic information to Bob Freeman?" At that moment, Brosens said he was "flummoxed" and asked to step outside the grand jury room to talk to his attorney, Robert Morvillo. Ever since the anniversary article appeared more than a year earlier mentioning the bunny quote, Brosens and Morvillo, as well as Pedowitz, figured a question like this was coming. He had no choice but to answer the question honestly;

the failure to mention the bunny conversation could have meant facing charges of having lied to a grand jury. In the brief conversation outside the grand jury room, Morvillo, Pedowitz, and Brosens concluded that although the prosecutors had not asked directly about Goldman's trading in the Beatrice Foods deal, when he returned to the grand jury room, he should share with the jurors the story of Goldman, Freeman, Siegel, and Beatrice, including Siegel's parting comment to Freeman: "Your Bunny has a good nose."

This proved to be *the* pivotal moment in the floundering case against Freeman and, accordingly, one of *the* pivotal moments in Freeman's life. Soon after Brosens testified, the prosecutors began to latch on to the Bunny testimony and to think that the phrase, coupled with Freeman's subsequent trading and profits, would be persuasive evidence against him before a criminal-trial jury. The prosecutors began to conceive of a way to perhaps bring their ongoing embarrassment in the case to a rapid close by using the existence of the Bunny testimony—which of course was not part of the original complaint or indictment and was not even a phrase Siegel remembered uttering—against Freeman.

After two years of behaving like the Keystone Kops, the prosecutors began to wise up. Shortly after Brosens testified, Laurie Cohen, an investigative reporter at the *Wall Street Journal* and a protégée of both Stewart and Hertzberg, wrote a "legal perspective" column below the headline "RICO Law Keeps Insider Trading Case of Goldman Sachs' Freeman in Limbo." Her article, which all but said the government's prosecutors were seriously considering charging Freeman under the RICO statutes, scared Freeman to death. Cohen's article suggested a new indictment against Freeman was imminent and that he would likely be charged under the RICO statutes because one of the alleged charges of insider trading against Freeman supposedly involved a tip Freeman had given Siegel more than five years earlier about Continental Group, Inc. RICO statutes allow prosecutors to stay the statute of limitations as long as other alleged crimes occurred within the five-year period. The RICO statutes also allow prosecutors to ask a judge to freeze a suspect's assets and to seek treble damages in a civil suit.

Once again, Freeman had no advance warning of the article or of the fact that prosecutors were considering using the RICO statutes as part of a new indictment. What made the combination of the Brosens testimony and the Cohen article particularly painful for Freeman was the fact that he and his lawyers had been beginning to think, with Giuliani's departure, that Romano might be willing to drop the case.

Pedowitz said Freeman was faced suddenly with a life-or-death choice. The prosecutors were telling Team Goldman's lawyers, " 'We can resolve the case based on Beatrice or your guy is going to get indicted for RICO,'" Pedowitz said. "'We're going to throw a whole bunch of things up against the wall and see which ones stick.' Bob was faced with an arbitrage for his life, which was, Do I run the risk, do I take this case to trial? And at the end of the day they convict me of a RICO violation and I go to jail for a long, long time and find any personal wealth that I have disappear? Or do I resolve the case based on the thing they think they've got—Beatrice—and have a minor financial settlement that leaves me, and my family, secure for the rest of our lives? It was a heartbreaking choice that he had to make: Do I fight this or do I resolve it?"

But settling—by pleading guilty to a felony—was a major step for Freeman to take, especially since he believed he had done nothing wrong, an idea reinforced by the legal opinions of both his and Goldman's lawyers. What's more, Freeman's guilt or innocence was quickly becoming one of just several considerations for him and his attorneys, and maybe not even the most important one any longer. Even if he was innocent, would he be able to convince a jury of that fact? Freeman's attorneys had commissioned jury research and discovered—not surprisingly—that investment bankers were held in very low esteem. "Investment bankers were about as popular then as they are today," Pedowitz said. "Investment banks were perceived as problems." Then there was simply the complexity of the facts regarding arbitrage in general and the nuances of puts, calls, options, and the like. And the coup de grâce was the daunting statistic that the government, to that point, had won approximately 90 percent of the criminal trials it prosecuted. If Freeman lost at trial, under a RICO statute, the implications for both his freedom and his fortune would be devastating.

On August 17, Freeman pleaded guilty to one count of mail fraud involving Beatrice Foods. "I pleaded guilty not because I believed I was guilty," Freeman explained, "but because I believed I could have been found guilty." He also resigned as a Goldman partner. In his letter of resignation to John Weinberg, Freeman wrote that the decision to plead guilty was "surely the toughest one I ever had to make." In his letter, Freeman said, "[I]t is important" that Weinberg understand why he pleaded guilty. "I want to assure you once again that I never conspired with Martin Siegel to swap inside information for either his or my personal benefit or for the benefit of Goldman Sachs or Kidder Peabody," he wrote.

To continue the litigation, he wrote Weinberg, "would consume another year or more of my life, with even then no guarantees of finality.

This, on top of the strains on me, Margo and our children for the past 30 months, would be just too much to bear. So, I have decided that the best thing to do is to end this matter here and now. I regret that I will no longer be able to work with some of my closest friends. . . . One final note: The loyal and caring support of my partners and colleagues at Goldman Sachs has been a crucial factor in helping me to cope with the events of the past two and one-half years. Margo and I will never forget it, and we will be forever grateful."

Weinberg circulated the letter, which went into great detail about the Beatrice transaction and trades, to enable Goldman's employees to "better understand the facts" that formed the basis of the plea.

On April 17, 1990, federal judge Pierre Leval sentenced Freeman to one year in prison and suspended eight months of the sentence, requiring him to serve four months. He also sentenced Freeman to a further two years of probation and community service of 150 hours a year. He fined Freeman $1 million and gave him a month to come up with the money. He also agreed to Freeman's request to serve the time at Saufley Field, a federal prison in Pensacola, Florida. "The particular crime was a matter of a temptation, an indiscretion, all of which took place so far as I can see in a matter of minutes," Judge Leval said. "It was the crime of trading on inside information." Freeman "made a telephone call which is not proper to make," the judge continued. "He made a telephone call seeking to learn from an inside source whether there was truth to the rumor of the problem [with the Beatrice deal]"—probably no different than thousands of such calls seeking information he and Levy, Tenenbaum, Lenzner, Rubin, Brosens, as well as younger arbs Tom Steyer, Daniel Och, Eddie Lampert, and others likely made at Goldman Sachs—"[a]nd although the answer that he received was couched in veiled language, it constituted illegal transmission of inside information."

Judge Leval figured Freeman had profited by approximately $87,000 as a result of the information and that Goldman had profited by about $460,000, or a total of about $548,000 "of loss avoided by the placement of four orders shortly after the receipt of the tip." The judge noted that in the plea hearing, Freeman told him he knew "full well that he was breaking the law in calling Siegel seeking from him confirmation of the rumors of problems and then making trades on that." As a result, Leval could not fail to impose a prison sentence. (Freeman now says he did not believe that to be true and made that statement under duress, because if he didn't make it, Judge Leval would not accept his guilty plea.) Moreover, the judge observed, "one of the unfortunate consequences of eminent power and wealth is that there are down sides. The defendant was trading for a very wealthy firm, a leader in the market-place, in huge quantities to realize huge profits. I cannot pass a sentence that would give the world a message that when people in those positions violate the law, the court will treat it as trivial whereas when a common thief steals a few dollars' worth, that calls for jail time."

During Rudy Giuliani's aborted 2008 effort to win the Republican Party's presidential nomination, Goldman Sachs was the only large securities firm unwilling to host a fund-raiser for him, despite the firm's well-established pattern of financially supporting powerful politicians. When Giuliani's representative approached Goldman about why that was and to see if Goldman could be persuaded to host such an event, the representative was told "in no uncertain terms" that it would not happen because of what Giuliani had done to "our partner Bob Freeman." He was told, "You do not understand. It is the Goldman Sachs DNA."

CHAPTER 12

MONEY

As if the arbitrage desk didn't already have enough to contend with in the face of the tsunami of publicity that accompanied Freeman's arrest and ongoing ordeal, it suffered serious losses when the stock market crashed on October 19, 1987. The next day, Rubin stopped by the desk—now being run by Frank Brosens, a vice president—and after inquiring about the extent of the losses, which had nearly wiped out everything the group had made year to date, he then sought to reassure the group, Brosens among them. "I understand you guys may have lost a little money yesterday," Rubin joked with them. He reported that the Management Committee had "100 percent confidence in you as a team and in the way you run your business. So, if you want to double up on your business, go right ahead." Brosens took Rubin's comments as permission to be bold, while other firms were licking their wounds and stayed "worried for months and months." Brosens's aggressive stance produced record profits for the arbitrage group in 1987, turning around the losses quickly. "I determined right then that I was going to stay at Goldman Sachs as long as Rubin was there," Brosens said. "His words that day meant the world to me."

According to Steve Friedman, the 1987 stock market crash—when the Dow Jones Industrial Average lost 22.6 percent of its value in one day—did not threaten the firm's survival, but it once again pointed out the flaws in Goldman's plumbing and communication systems. "On the day of the crash, I was walking around the fixed-income floor," Friedman recalled, "and someone came up to me and said, 'Do you realize that the firm sent a rather large check' to the such and such [commodity] exchange in Chicago?" as part of a settlement payment Goldman owed the firm. The idea was that most of the monies paid would come back to Goldman in the next few days—as long as the firm in question did not itself go bankrupt in the interim. Friedman said he hadn't been aware the payment had been made "because it wasn't my world"—the payments part of the business was considered routine—but he determined in the wake of the crash "to make it his world." "We weren't threatened," he said about Goldman's post-crash future. "But if the Chicago exchange had gone down, everyone would have had a hell of a problem."

The stock market plunge also tagged Goldman with an after-tax loss of between $17 million and $20 million as a result of having just launched a large underwriting of the shares of British Petroleum. Following through on an underwriting in the middle of a seismic financial calamity is every investment bank's worst nightmare, since it undoubtedly means that it will have to make good on its commitment to a client to buy stock at a certain price, even though the underlying market for the shares has collapsed. The BP underwriting was just that disaster, writ large. The four U.S. underwriters on the deal—which amounted to the last of the privatization of the British government shares in the company—were Goldman, Morgan Stanley, Salomon Brothers, and Shearson Lehman Brothers, with Goldman being one of two firms selected as global coordinator of the offering. After years of investment in London, BP's selection of Goldman—over its traditional banker, Morgan Stanley—was a coup for sure.

The market crash, though, was making the coup very expensive indeed. The four American firms were staring down a loss of $330 million on the offering, or $82.5 million each, the largest underwriting loss ever. "By a malign coincidence," observed Nigel Lawson, the chancellor of the exchequer, "the world's largest-ever share sale collided with the world's most dramatic stock-market crash." Some at the various underwriting firms, including Goldman, believed that the crash had been an act of God and could provide a much-needed legal escape hatch. But Weinberg would have none of that thinking. As painful as it would be to absorb the loss, he knew Goldman had worked too hard for too long to try to get out of the underwriting using a claim of force majeure. He decided this was the moment to take the pain and prove to the world that Goldman was a firm of honor, a firm that would stand by its commitments. "We bought it and we own it," he told his partners. "If we cut and run away on BP, we won't underwrite a doghouse in London." Traders in the London office gathered around the internal squawk box to listen as Bob Mnuchin, the head of equity, blew out Goldman's position in BP. "It was over very quickly," explained David Schwartz, then a Eurobond trader, in London. "It was painful but over very, very quickly. We traded in and out of the security on the secondary market." And that was that.

On November 20, 1987, a month after the crash, and while the firm was still grappling with the fallout from Freeman's arrest, Weinberg named Rubin and Friedman vice chairmen of Goldman, effectively anointing them as his successors, although Weinberg still refused to say so. "They're both capable guys," Weinberg said, "but I've made no commitment to anybody. I haven't named my heir apparent and I never will until I'm ready." He then added, "I'm going to work till I'm ninety-nine." In the internal memo distributed throughout the firm, Weinberg reiterated his intention "to remain with the firm as chairman, senior partner and chief executive officer for many years" and wrote that his health was "fine." Despite the loss from the BP underwriting, Weinberg said 1987 would be "one of the best years" in the firm's history.

In fact, 1987 did turn out to be the firm's second-best year in its history. "Think about it," David Schwartz said. "The partners can sit around the table. Forty partners sit around a table, and slap high-fives for having come through one of the biggest financial crises the firm had faced. They shut down the trading floor because everything was being processed by paper! They were just completely flooded. They locked the doors. People stayed overnight to process every trade. The firm emerged unscathed and had the second-best year in its history!" As in the more severe crises of 2007 and 2008, Goldman managed to thrive while others on Wall Street went under—and the general public suffered. At the end of 1987, Goldman had 7,500 employees—one-third of whom had MBA degrees—in eighteen offices around the world, six of which were overseas. The firm's capital stood at $2.3 billion, the sixth largest on Wall Street.

The October crash and Freeman's troubles weren't the only issue the firm faced at that time. Within weeks of Freeman's decision to plead guilty to a single charge of mail fraud, Weinberg found himself having to explain to Goldman's employees and to the press the bizarre "psychosexual drama" involving partner Lewis M. Eisenberg, Freeman's Dartmouth classmate and close friend of Henry Kravis. Eisenberg was then the head of Goldman's institutional equity sales division—the block-trading business—and a stone's throw from being on the Management Committee.

The golden future evaporated for Eisenberg, then forty-seven and the married father of three children, in August 1989, when two uniformed policemen entered 85 Broad Street and headed to the twenty-ninth floor, looking for him. (What was it about law enforcement officials and Goldman's twenty-ninth floor?) When they found Eisenberg, they served him with a criminal-harassment complaint filed by his longtime assistant Kathy Abraham, thirty-seven, with whom Eisenberg was having a seven-year consensual affair that had turned nasty—and very public. It quickly became another embarrassing situation for Weinberg, Rubin, and Friedman.

Both Abraham and Eisenberg were placed on administrative leave. By Halloween, though, Goldman had fired Abraham. Then, a few days before Thanksgiving, Weinberg sent around a memo to Goldman's employees saying that Eisenberg had resigned.

The tale was nothing if not sordid, and journalist Dorothy Rabinowitz recounted it in fine detail in a long article in *New York* magazine. According to Rabinowitz, Abraham was a divorced mother with a young daughter. Her family had left Hungary in the 1950s. She attended a yeshiva in Queens, graduated from Queens College, and settled down with her with new husband in Kew Gardens Hills, a neighborhood with a large Orthodox community. She started working at Goldman Sachs in 1976. Her marriage ended five years later. By that time, she was working for Eisenberg. He was from Chicago, where his family owned a seed-processing company. He had graduated from Dartmouth in 1964 and then received his MBA from Cornell, joining Goldman soon thereafter and moving to Rumson, New Jersey. He became a partner in 1978.

After Abraham's divorce, Eisenberg "became an increasingly important source of comfort" to her, according to *New York*. Their affair began one evening after work, when Eisenberg asked Abraham to join him and a few work colleagues for a drink. That same night, they had dinner together and Eisenberg drove her home to Queens. Soon thereafter, Eisenberg reportedly announced to Abraham that he wanted her to be his mistress. "Just like that, 'I want you to be my mistress,'" she told Rabinowitz. Tuesday was their meeting night. He arranged to have a suite for them at the Vista International Hotel, in lower Manhattan. "For a while at the beginning, I really didn't mind too much," she said. "I mean this was an important person to me. I had feelings for him—*of course* I had feelings for him, at first."

But Abraham quickly grew tired of the Tuesday routine (to say nothing of the stress of then having to work for Eisenberg the rest of the week). "If I said I didn't want to meet him, he would become *enraged*," she said. "And life at the office that day would become intolerable." She was rapidly losing her self-esteem and her dignity. "I felt humiliated," she said, "and I *was* humiliated. Going to that hotel, always the *hotel*. And there I would be leaving the office carrying this bag with my overnight things. He would leave for the hotel a half-hour before me. When I got there, I would have to call my mother—this was the night my child stayed with her father—so that my mother wouldn't call and not find me home. So much *lying*." She kept kosher and, not surprisingly, the Vista

International did not have the most robust menu selection for her. She usually would order a bagel with lox and eat it as slowly as possible to delay the inevitable.

After dinner, where Eisenberg would talk about himself, they would head upstairs to watch X-rated videos. "I was so bored I would fall asleep," she said, "and then he would become upset." According to Abraham, Eisenberg preferred to watch as she masturbated. "That's why I stopped using birth-control pills," she said. "Why risk your health when there was no reason for them?" The dismal plot thickened when Eisenberg would often articulate his desire for Abraham to have sex with some of his Goldman partners. Apparently, this was more than just a fantasy. "And he began to nag me about it at work," she said. "One day when he was doing this, I ran out of his office crying, and then he stopped." In April 1989, Eisenberg moved with his family to the Upper East Side and demanded to see her more often, including at her house in Queens. "I know there are women that would have been stronger than me," she said. "But I didn't have the strength. He understood that very well. Those times I would try to tell him that I didn't want to meet him—when he would be in a rage at me at the office—I was the one who always ended up having to apologize to him." She said she wanted to end the affair. "But he wouldn't," she said. "He had an obsession, and I was it."

A more complex and debilitating situation would be hard to fathom, but when, in early 1986, Abraham met Gary Moskowitz at the synagogue in Kew Gardens Hills—and fell in love with him at first sight—things got completely out of control. Like Abraham, Moskowitz was an Orthodox Jew. He was also a New York City police officer, one of the very few religious Jewish officers on the force. After Abraham met Moskowitz, she told Eisenberg the affair was over. Her determination held for two months, until Eisenberg demanded she meet him after a Goldman party at the Plaza Hotel, where he had rented a room. She refused and instead went out with Moskowitz that night. "He was furious," she said.

At the office the next day, Eisenberg told her he had sat in a parked car in front of her house so that he could see who she was coming home with. "That's when the grilling really started," she said. "Then he found out Gary's name and who he was. Lew would call me up on the weekends and ask, 'Are you seeing Gary?' I actually used to make up the names of friends I was supposed to be seeing." On the weekends, Eisenberg would sometimes track her movements. One Monday morning, he asked her how her weekend had been and she lied and said she had visited her mother. "No, you didn't," he said to her. "I saw your car parked in front of Gary's house. The two of you walked out of his apartment at 1:40 in the afternoon." Eisenberg was right; they had come out of Moskowitz's apartment at that time.

During the summer of 1989, Moskowitz figured out who Eisenberg was, called his home, and left a message with his wife. "The call alarmed Eisenberg," Rabinowitz wrote. He arranged to meet with Moskowitz on June 28 at a diner in Flushing. He drove up in a limousine. "In that neighborhood in Queens, we don't see too many stretch limos," Moskowitz said. The conversation did not go well. "He was worried about his family, his job," said Rabinowitz, "but he also kept telling me, 'Kathy and I have a beautiful relationship.' Then he tells me, 'You're just a peon cop—what do you know about anything?' Do you hear that? *A peon cop.*" After this meeting, the situation deteriorated further, with much personal acrimony, implied threats, traps set, and promises made and broken. It was very ugly.

In mid-August 1989, Abraham filed her criminal-harassment complaint against Eisenberg. She charged Eisenberg with threatening "to fire her if she did not submit to his sexual advances" and that he tried to "annoy and alarm" her by "staring at her, walking around her desk, [and] going into her garbage for the past three years." Moskowitz also filed a complaint against Eisenberg, claiming he had harassed him, too. "If you go to the authorities, I will have to protect myself by making charges against you . . . ," Moskowitz claimed Eisenberg told him. "I'm going to have you taken care of . . . even cops have accidents." But Manhattan district attorney Robert Morgenthau declined to prosecute the cases against Eisenberg.

After filing her complaint, though, Abraham went to see Rubin, and according to Rabinowitz, "told him everything." Then, shortly thereafter, Eisenberg went to see Rubin and confessed to him the relationship he was having with Abraham. A day or so later, according to Abraham, Rubin told her Goldman was prepared to offer her a generous settlement. But she said she told Rubin she didn't want the settlement; she wanted the job she had been angling for as a trader-in-training at Goldman that Eisenberg had arranged for her to have.

But just as she was to start her training as a trader, the *Wall Street Letter*, an industry newsletter, got a tip about the police visit to see Eisenberg at Goldman and wrote a story. The next day, the *New York Post's* Page Six gossip column picked up the *Wall Street Letter* story. "Cops have come calling at the grand old Wall Street investment house of Goldman Sachs," Page Six reported. "Office workers at the firm—which saw one of its partners arrested for insider trading in 1987—swiveled their heads recently when uniformed police notified partner Lewis Eisenberg that his former assistant was charging him with sexual harassment." Moskowitz told the paper, "This guy is a sick man. He has an obsession for this girl. I just want him to stay away from Kathy. I don't want him to show up at either of our houses any more or I'm going to have him locked up. He did horrible things. I want him off the streets so he can't hurt any-one else." As to Eisenberg filing a report with the internal affairs department, Moskowitz said, "He's run a vicious campaign to ruin me. He has a lot of money to do what he wants. I'm not going to stand for it. Just because I'm a cop, I'm not a second-class citizen."

The following Monday after the stories appeared, instead of start-ing her new job, Abraham was given administrative leave and told to work out her differences with Eisenberg. On October 31, she was fired. Gold-man wrote in her dismissal letter that her actions had been "hostile" to the firm. Then Eisenberg was gone, too. Moskowitz also became collat-eral damage: he lost his job with the police department. A Goldman spokesman said, "The firm had no reason to suspect there was anything other than a business relationship between Kathy Abraham and Lewis Eisenberg. Ms. Abraham never made any complaint regarding Mr. Eisenberg or any request for a change in her job. In fact, her administra-tive supervisors from time to time offered her a transfer of assignment so as to increase her responsibilities and advance her career, and on each occasion she declined to consider it. We are satisfied that whatever per-sonal relationship she may have had with Mr. Eisenberg had no effect on the terms and conditions of her employment." Novotny tried to dismiss the contretemps with one persistent reporter by explaining, with some obvious condescension, "Lew Eisenberg is a *friend* of mine."

Of the three people caught up in the scandal, Eisenberg—not surprisingly—fared the best. Rabinowitz reported that Eisenberg left Goldman with around $30 million in Goldman stock and investments. He served as chairman of the Port Authority of New York and New Jersey—the same board Gus Levy was on when he suffered his fatal stroke—from 1995 to 2001. In 2001, New York governor George Pataki named Eisenberg to the Lower Manhattan Development Corporation, the chairman of which was John Whitehead. Eisenberg has always been a force in Republican politics and was considered briefly for the job as head of the Republican National Committee. Professionally, after Gold-man, Eisenberg co-founded Granite Capital International Group, a hedge fund, and Granum Communications, an owner of radio stations, eventually bought by KKR. In February 2009, he joined forces with his friend Henry Kravis, at KKR, as a senior adviser to the firm. (Abraham still lives in Queens but could not be reached for a comment. She later recanted her accusations against Eisenberg and said he never harassed her or hurt her in any way. Moskowitz, who would like to return to the New York City police force, teaches martial arts, mostly in Queens. His two-year-long legal effort against Goldman and Eisenberg ended in January 1992, and a police hearing officer said his actions against Eisenberg "bordered on criminal extortions.")

After the Eisenberg scandal made headlines, Weinberg instructed Jonathan Cohen, a longtime "human capital" partner at Goldman, to find out within twenty-four hours if any *other* partners at the firm were carrying on in ways similar to Eisenberg. Cohen sent around a voice mail. "If I hear about it now, you'll get amnesty, but there will be no mercy if I hear about it after today," was the gist of the message. "The phone was ringing off the hook for the next twenty-four hours," said someone familiar with what happened.

———

WHETHER THESE ONGOING public scandals began to take their toll on John Weinberg—in the way that the litigation surrounding Penn Central affected Gus Levy—is hard to know for sure. On the other hand, how could they not? The culture carriers at Goldman prefer to speak about Weinberg's grit and determination, attributes he honed as a marine in combat in Japan during World War II, of his moral rectitude and his unflappability.

But on August 15, 1990, Weinberg announced he was stepping down as Goldman's senior partner, to be replaced by Rubin and Friedman as co-chairmen of the firm beginning in December. He was sixty-five years old and had been running the firm for fourteen years, the last few of which were especially trying. Rubin and Friedman followed the Weinberg-Whitehead model and did not divvy up responsibility by business lines. They made clear that one of them could speak for both of them. "This worked because we shared the same fundamental views about the firm, trusted each other totally, kept in close touch, and were both analytical in our approach to problems," Rubin wrote in his memoir. "When this structure does work—and that is a rarity—the advantages are substantial: there are two senior partners to call on clients and two people who can work together on issues with no hierarchical baggage, and who can reinforce each other in discussions with the rest of the organization. Also, when difficulties arise, having a partner reduces the feeling of loneliness at the top."

On the rare occasions when they did not agree on important matters, their rule was to defer to whichever one of them felt more passionately about the topic at hand. For instance, it turned out that Friedman believed that it was important to differentiate partner compensation by giving more profit points to those partners who had distinguished themselves over the years. Rubin was more of the view that the internal strife caused by the slight favoring of one partner over another would add immeasurably to the social unrest at the firm. He had seen firsthand one partner's fury at another being given one-eighth of a point more of the firm's profits, and he figured life was too short for those kinds of blowups. "Over the years," Rubin wrote, "I had seen partners who earned millions of dollars a year become deeply unhappy over tiny distinctions in partnership shares." Friedman referred to Rubin's preference for relative peace as "solving for maximum social harmony." Since Friedman believed more deeply about the importance of making the distinction between partners, that's what the two men decided to do, although the differences were often more tempered than Friedman would have preferred.

Goldman wasted little time establishing its new leaders' bona fides and authority. In a lengthy December 1990 cover story about them in *Institutional Investor*—"The Steve and Bob Show"—less than a month into their tenure, they let no light between them. "Our minds work in similar ways, and we will tend to see things in relatively similar ways," Friedman said. "[I have] a kind of recipe for co-managements to be successful: If there's no demarcation [of responsibilities], then you'd better agree on things 90 percent of the time. And second, you'd better have a chemistry that enables you to resolve the other 10 percent of the time pretty well. We just found we had that mix." The article made no mention of Freeman or Eisenberg by name—the closest it came to a whiff of the recent scandals was an innocuous reference to "the way" Goldman "handled" the Eisenberg "sexual harassment suit," and that it did "little to dispel Goldman's reputation for insensitivity"—and instead focused on the usual Goldman tropes about ethics and teamwork. "If you say 'I,' you are being abrasive," the article quoted partner Robert Mnuchin, who had just retired after thirty-three years. The article claimed that "[n]owhere else on Wall Street has a firm attempted to institutionalize something as intangible as a corporate ethic. When Whitehead drew up a list of the business principles by which the employees of the firm would abide, he came up with four more than God gave Moses to codify all earthly morality. These principles are still read aloud at Goldman gatherings, and tyros have been known to tack them above their desks, perhaps to inspire them to greater glory." No mention was made of how the business principles dovetailed with the reality of human nature and Goldman's ongoing scandals.

The thrust of the message that the Goldman brass was trying to convey was that much-needed change was coming to the firm. There would soon be a Goldman Frankfurt office—after six months of study—even though John Weinberg would have continued to wait before opening one. When other banks decided to leave Latin America after trouble there, Goldman had moved in, "smell[ing] opportunity." In six months, Goldman had created from scratch a structured-equity-products division. In most un-Goldman-like fashion, Goldman had also gone outside the firm to hire the three Salomon Brothers traders and made them partners in order to "jump-start" Goldman's mortgage-backed securities and junk-bond businesses.

The truth was that Goldman needed to modernize. The firm relied too much on its reputation, but the financial world was evolving toward ever more complexity and speed. In his time, Whitehead had decided that Goldman could no longer be run as a Florentine guild. He had had to figure out how to extend the firm's reach beyond Sidney Weinberg's friends and to learn how to impart the firm's collected wisdom and knowledge more broadly as the firm grew more rapidly. This led him to create the New Business Group and the firm's fourteen principles. These innovations, however, took the firm only so far toward the modernization it desperately needed. To get the firm the rest of the way fell to the next generation of the firm's leaders, Friedman and Rubin.

According to *Institutional Investor*, the firm's new leaders established an "Ad Hoc Profit Maximization Committee," whose members were "intelligent men from Mars," according to Friedman, and the purpose of which was "to bring new perspectives to the firm's various businesses by questioning how things are run . . . without threatening the ethos." Then there was the "bevy" of new consultants who showed up at the firm. Marketing consultant Anthony Buzan—a "creative provocateur," Geoff Boisi said—had been hired to counter the perception that Goldman was a follower, not a leader, when it came to financial innovation. At an investment banking retreat in upstate New York, Buzan tagged along and got the Goldman bankers to engage in a little finger painting while also getting their creative juices flowing. Indeed, Boisi had implemented an annual award for financial creativity—$25,000 plus a slab of Baccarat crystal—that was won in 1989 by a woman banker whose name has been lost to history who created Goldman's business in employee stock-ownership plans (then all the rage on Wall Street in facilitating employee buyouts of companies). In the wake of the Eisenberg debacle, Goldman hired Alterna-Track to devise and implement a system of part-time and flex-time positions for the firm's women who also wanted to start families. "If we can keep high-powered women involved and active at Goldman Sachs, this will be a tremendous competitive advantage for us," Rubin explained. "I think it's terrific." Alterna-Track was started by Karen Cook, who worked at Goldman for twelve years as an equity trader after bulldozing her way into the firm in 1975. By serendipity, Rubin had overheard her insistent—but unsuccessful—efforts to get an interview and decided to interview her on the spot. Two weeks later, she had a job.

They brought in Booz-Allen to review the firm's real estate and its infrastructure, much of which proved to be antiquated. "There was a lot that needed to be fixed there," Friedman said, "and they told us how we could take out a lot of costs and be more efficient. We were just doing some things like some big, bureaucratic company. If someone needed something in terms of telecommunications, there was a book, and if you needed something new and the book said 'Everyone will have the same thing at great expense,' then either you couldn't get it or we'd have to rip out everyone else's and they'll get the same thing. And metaphorically, if you were running an area and you said, 'I need pizza for dinner for my people,' the book in effect said we're going to deliver this in a chauffeured Bentley."

ONE EXAMPLE OF a Goldman practice that could have benefited from some cleaning up occurred on Memorial Day weekend in 1991. That Friday, at the start of the holiday weekend, at a time when most people who could would be thinking about heading out of town, forty investment banking newbies were told to report to a conference room on the twenty-ninth floor, at 5:00 p.m. "No mercy for the yuppies," explained Anthony Scaramucci, one of the forty Goldman associates in the conference room that afternoon. Hour and after hour passed without the partner who had told them all to be there showing up. By 8:30, three of natives were getting restless. "What's up?" one of them said. "Where is this jerk? I have plans in the Hamptons and want to get going." After another half hour, the three rebels left. "They were MBAs from top grad schools," Scaramucci observed. "They were the future Gordon Gekkos."

The rest of the group waited around. At 10:00 p.m., the partner appeared, passed around a sheet of paper, and asked everyone there to sign his or her name on it. With that minor bit of bookkeeping completed—and taking a page from the nineteenth-century French writer, Stendhal, in *Lucien Leuwen*—he said, "So, today's lesson is about waiting patiently for those who are more important than you. Someday you may be in the lobby of a billionaire, and he or she may make you wait. Your job as a representative of Goldman Sachs is to sit there. We are in the client service business. We wait patiently and graciously. Now you may have a fancy degree from a fancy place, but that will never replace having the right attitude. Have both and there is nothing you can't do. Without the right attitude, you are not the right stuff for Goldman Sachs." With that sermon completed, the partner dismissed the class.

The following Tuesday, the three Masters of the Universe who had left early were fired. "It was a lesson I will never forget," Scaramucci explained. "It communicated the culture of the firm without bluster, cheerleading, or empty rhetoric."

Other messages were communicated constantly to the young Goldman employees as well. One of them was how to make money from others' misfortune, as when a Goldman trader boasted to MBAs at Columbia Business School how much money the firm had made from the January 1986 explosion of the *Challenger* space shuttle. Another of them was that Friday is "Goldman Sachs Day." One Goldman trader remembered how strong his boss felt about this and conveyed it to the team on a regular basis. "His view was Friday is the day everybody's been out boozing and kind of writes off as a nonevent and doesn't do anything," he said. "So, if you come in on Friday with your head down, intent on actually doing something, everyone has their guard down and is less competitive and that's when you can make a big difference. So, at the end of every meeting, he'd say, 'Yeah, it's Friday. It's Goldman Sachs Day.' I can see the logic of it from a trading perspective. People are surfing the Internet. They're kind of leaving early. They're off to the Hamptons at two o'clock. Whatever it is, they get out and go on Friday."

Another message was how special they were and how fortunate they were to be working at Goldman. "It's sort of like being around the Sun King kind of thing," remembered one former Goldman senior banker. "It's the center of everything that's going on, the nexus of so much that's going on on Wall Street." What made the firm special, in his mind, and different from other firms on Wall Street was "[t]he people are so bright, so driven, and just unbelievably consistent. At a lot of places, you have ninety-nine-percentile people, but you also have eighty-two-percentile people and seventy-four-percentile people. At Goldman, the bell curve sort of centers around ninety-five and one tail goes to ninety-nine and the other tail goes to ninety-one. The consistency of the people is extraordinary. The recruiting, the talent management and retention is probably one of the great strengths they have. Then, the information flows are extraordinary. The information that courses through that place is like nothing you've ever seen before. Then, thirdly, I think there are relationships that they have with boards, with governments, with key decision makers and what qualifies as being important there versus at other places is just a whole other level of discourse that they're having with their clients. They are able to sort of turn their head away from the immediacy of a trade, or a piece of business that doesn't have all of the things they're looking for and really focus on the biggest, most important deals and stay really disciplined along those lines. They're always whale hunting. They're not out to catch fish every day. They go days without hitting or harpooning a whale while other guys are filling the boat with little bitty fish. But then when they start bringing in the whales, people's heads turn. That's an interesting metaphor. They are definitely whale hunters and they're not really fishermen."

There was also something known around Goldman as "Le Concierge," which can accomplish for Goldman's employees (or clients) pretty much anything they want, including taking shirts to the cleaners or getting hard-to-get restaurant reservations. The service was less a reward per se than recognition by Goldman of how hard the firm expected people to work and that they probably wouldn't have time to take care of basic chores. "You literally did work one hundred and ten hours a week," explained one former banker. "You have to sort of try to do the math as to how that's possible. There was a long period of time for me where if I got four hours of sleep a night, I actually felt well rested. Often, if you had a couple of hours of spare time during the day, people would go down to the nurse's office downstairs and pass out in one of the beds down there for two hours to get some sleep. I met my wife actually at Goldman. I remember her first day at work. She actually did an all-nighter like right out of the gate. So, it was like that. You worked as hard as you sort of humanly could. . . . I'm sure you're making less on an hourly basis as an analyst at Goldman than you would if you worked at McDonald's."

What did Goldman expect in return for providing these concierge services? "You, twenty-four seven," explained another banker. "Conference calls, all day Saturday and Sunday. Voice mail constantly. . . . There were people that just sat in their house for hours and hours and hours and hours over the weekend. A lot of business there gets done over the weekend. That's classic Goldman: all the big decisions are on Sunday and it was always that way. It was always like if anything was a rush job, you always had to do it on Sunday evening. Everything at Goldman was always getting initiated on Sunday: big deals, big capital commitments, big this thing, big that thing. . . . I think that those are the people that are going to be successful at Goldman, the folks that are willing to sort of just sacrifice all. All. Everything. To the greater glory."

Then there were the seemingly inevitable problems that developed between Goldman's male and female employees. In this regard, Goldman was no better or worse than other Wall Street firms, which for many years had a heinous track record of mistreating their women employees. Sometimes the abuse was physical, sexual, and humiliating, as in the case of Lew Eisenberg and Karen Abraham. Sometimes the abuse was subtler and psychological, but no less devastating.

The Eisenberg case may have been more sensational and headline grabbing, but it was hardly an isolated incident. For instance, in 1973, Anne Brown Farrell, a graduate of Trinity College and the Wharton School of Business, joined Goldman as the first woman in its fixed-income group. She worked on the trading floor with "masses of people, no privacy, food all over the place, and at the time . . . *everyone smoked!!!*" she later observed. Once that fall, all the new associates at the firm were invited to the Yale Club for dinner with Gus Levy. When Farrell arrived at the door of the Yale Club, she was not allowed to go inside. She was told, "No women allowed—club policy." Her male colleagues streamed by her to go have dinner with Levy. "No one even looked back," she explained. "For over half an hour, I tried every way I could think of to slip in unnoticed. It was impossible. I didn't know what to do and I was beginning to panic. I had to be at that dinner!"

She eventually slipped twenty dollars to a steward at the club who let her go up the service elevator. "All eyes were on me when I finally entered the dining room," she continued. "I was late, I was young, and I was in trouble." Levy announced to everyone that she was "a disgrace" for showing up late and gave her no chance to explain. Her boss was not happy either. She tried to explain about the club's policy but, she said, her boss didn't care. Fortunately, Levy overheard the conversation. "He was infuriated and demanded to know which idiot had chosen the Yale Club," she explained. "That person turned out to be my boss, but not for long!"

In July 1985, Kristine Utley started working at Goldman Sachs as a sales trainee in the fixed-income department in New York. In February 1986, Goldman transferred her to its Boston office as a sales associate in the money market department. She was the only woman sales associate in the department. For the next twenty months or so, the men in the Boston office made her life hell. According to someone with knowledge of her circumstances, the men in the Boston office "viewed her as a foreign body to be expelled at the earliest possible moment" and "apparently, the story goes, she was invited to a meeting in the conference room where the projector went on and a hardcore porn film was showing just to humiliate her." In the fall of 1987, Paul Gaul, who ran the Boston office, asked Utley to consider a transfer back to New York. She refused to move back to New York as she believed "she was singled out for transfer on the basis of her sex," according to court documents. Goldman then fired her. On December 6, 1987, she filed an eight-count lawsuit against Goldman in Massachusetts, alleging sexual harassment and discrimination and that "she was subjected to a hostile working environment in which women were demeaned." On April 8, 1988, she filed a lawsuit claiming her civil rights had been violated. Goldman tried to get the lawsuit thrown out and to force the matter into arbitration, but an appeals court rejected the firm's argument and said the matter could be tried in court.

She later testified that "office humor was a source of sexual harassment" and that memos at Goldman introducing new women employees "were illustrated with nude *Playboy* pin-ups" and with phrases such as "beer is better than women because a beer always goes down easy." Soon thereafter, Gaul was dismissed from Goldman. Utley received an unspecified settlement from Goldman.

Then there was case of Jacki Hoffman-Zehner, who endured abuse from the rank and file but support from higher-ups. After graduating from the University of British Columbia, Hoffman-Zehner joined Goldman in 1988 as an analyst in the mortgage-backed securities department. By 1991, she was trading fifteen-year pass-through mortgage securities for Goldman's institutional clients. One day that year, Frank Coulson, known as "the Big Guy" because of the size of the trades he did for his clients, asked Hoffman-Zehner to execute a huge trade, worth more than a billion dollars. "Jacki, this is as big as it gets," he told her. She knew it would be the trade of her career and Coulson had given her an important break by asking her to execute it. Time was of the essence and she focused intently on finding the right prices to quote for the client. "Call me when you have the prices, but don't take too long," the Big Guy told her.

There was no time for superfluous razzing from her, perhaps envious, male colleagues. But just as she was focusing on getting the prices for Coulson, one of the other traders on the desk—a mortgage-backed securities trader—wanted Hoffman-Zehner to help him work on a deal. "This guy was a self-described Wall Street Hitter: big paycheck, fast cars, huge apartment, and an ego to match," she observed. "He was extremely talented and very charismatic and loved to be at the center of attention." When she didn't respond by dropping whatever she was doing and helping him, the Hitter took to the internal squawk box and announced: "Excuse me, everyone, but our fifteen-year [mortgage] trader cannot do two things at once, so I cannot work on pricing a CMO"—collateralized mortgage obligation—"for you currently. My opinion is that she might well be in the wrong profession." Other traders started piling on, like lions "circling," she explained.

But she could not afford to be distracted by the juvenile, narcissistic behavior. She continued to figure out the prices to give to Coulson so the trade of her career could be executed successfully. Ten minutes later, she had the prices and had conveyed them to Coulson. Having completed the higher-priority task, she then walked over to her "attacker" to see what he wanted and to be helpful to him, if she could. "He could tell I was upset by his teasing and chose to acknowledge it by laughing at me as if to say, 'What's the matter girl, can't you take it?' " she recalled. She was pissed but tried to remain calm. "You respect me, I respect you," she said. "[T]hat is what we as professionals of this firm are called to do. Don't you ever treat me like that again." Just as she finished her reply, and was walking back to her desk, the Big Guy announced over the intercom: "Jacki, the trade is done." She spent the rest of the day managing the risk related to the trade. "Never before had I felt so completely and professionally exhilarated," she later wrote. "It was the trade of a lifetime, entrusted to me by one of the most talented and respected fixed-income salespeople ever on The Street."

But it had been a trying day. She retreated to the ladies' room—her "office," she called it—went into the last stall, sat on the toilet seat, and cried for ten minutes uninterrupted. "I had to release the stress of executing the largest trade of my career, while at the same moment experiencing undeserved humiliation," she said. "It wasn't until I had patted my last tear dry that the smile crept onto my face." Eight years later, age thirty-two, she was the youngest woman and first woman trader to become a partner.

But despite some notable exceptions, the road is still hard for the women who work at Goldman. In March 2010, Charlotte Hanna, a former Goldman Sachs vice president, sued the firm in federal court in Manhattan, claiming she was fired because she chose to work part-time and then took maternity leave during and after her two pregnancies. She also said that when she returned to work after the birth of her first child, her responsibilities were much diminished, her reporting lines had changed, and even her office had been taken from her. One week before she was to return to Goldman from her second maternity leave, Hanna was told her position had been eliminated. Sadly, Hanna's lawsuit reads like many recently filed gender-related discrimination claims against Wall Street firms. "When Ms. Hanna decided to take the 'off-ramp' provided by the firm to devote time to her children, there was no 'on-ramp' that enabled her to return to full-time employment," her complaint claimed. (Goldman and Hanna settled the suit in November 2010.)

In September 2010, three former women employees of Goldman Sachs—a former vice president, a managing director, and an associate—filed a class-action lawsuit in federal court in the Southern District of New York against the firm claiming that it systematically discriminates against women in both pay and promotions. In the complaint, one of the women—H. Cristina Chen-Oster, who spent eight years at the firm and became a vice president before leaving in March 2005—told the story of how, in the fall of 1997, her department went to Scores, a topless dance club in Manhattan, to celebrate the promotion of a colleague. Afterward, a married male associate insisted on walking Chen-Oster to her boyfriend's apartment building a few blocks away. But, once there, the male associate ended up "pinning her against a wall, kissing and groping her, and attempting to engage in a sexual act with her." She wrote that she did not "invite or welcome the attempt and had to physically defend herself." The next morning, he "apologized profusely" and asked her to keep quiet about the incident. Yet that same morning, the associate told his supervisor about what happened. The supervisor was supposedly his friend and was also Chen-Oster's supervisor.

Eventually, in May 1999—some eighteen months later—Chen-Oster reported the incident to her supervisor. Then, she alleged, her career at Goldman started a slow decline into oblivion. In keeping with an ongoing pattern of behavior, both her account responsibilities and her compensation were reduced over time, especially when compared with those of her male colleagues. In 1999, for instance, the male associate who had accosted her got paid 50 percent more than Chen-Oster, despite the fact the she had been promoted to vice president one year earlier. He did generate more revenue than she did, she conceded, but only because the more lucrative accounts had been taken from her and given to him. In 2000, her supervisor moved her to the opposite end of the convertible-bond trading floor from him—a sure sign of diminished status—and did not allow her to write performance evaluations for some of the people with whom she worked. In 2001, she also told her supervisor that the women on the convertible-bond desk felt that Goldman "did not treat them equally" and "felt uncomfortable with the sexual banter that regularly occurred on the trading floor."

That same year, the man she says attacked her was promoted to managing director, earning millions annually and twice as much as she was paid. In March 2001, her attacker was named sole head of U.S. convertible-bond sales and the next year he was named a partner. In 2002, someone she was working with sent around racially offensive e-mails, including to Chen-Oster, who is of Chinese descent. "Learn Chinese in 5 Minutes," read one. "Our meeting is scheduled for next week. . . . Wai Yu Cum Nao?" and "Great . . . Fu Kin Su Pah." After two maternity leaves, when she returned to Goldman Sachs, she was asked to sit among the administrative staff, even though she was a trading profes-sional. On March 10, 2005, she resigned rather than continue to be humiliated. During her career at Goldman, she was promoted once and her pay increased 27 percent. Her attacker was promoted continuously, became a partner, and saw his pay increase 400 percent.

Shanna Orlich, another plaintiff in the September 2010 class-action lawsuit against Goldman, started working at the firm in the sum-mer of 2006 while studying for her JD/MBA degree at Columbia University. After graduating from Columbia in 2007, she returned to Goldman to work in something called the Capital Structure Franchise Trading Group, which had twelve professionals, two of whom were women. Throughout 2007, Orlich had performed well and her supervisor told her so. She had joined Goldman with the intention of becoming a trader, but when she started, she was told there was no trading position on the CSFT desk available and she would have to be an analyst, work-ing with other traders on the desk. When she asked about the prospect of becoming a trader, she was told that there were no such openings at the time, even though one of her business-school classmates—a man—had started with her and had been given a seat as a high-yield debt trader. By way of explanation for how this might have happened, Orlich described how "Goldman Sachs' managers often challenged this male classmate to do push-up contests on the trading floor." Around the same time, a man who had been just hired from college was given a seat as a trader on the CSFT desk.

In January 2008, Orlich spoke with a senior woman trader about the possibility of being allowed to trade. Soon thereafter, her direct supervisor assigned her to be a junior trader to another male trader on the CSFT desk. By April, though, both the male trader she had been assigned to work with and her direct supervisor had left Goldman. Once again, her trading prospects were dimmed. In July, she spoke to a male managing director and asked about becoming a trader and he told her he did not think she had the "right fit" to be a trader and was surprised she had been hired for that role. When she spoke with a partner on the Goldman senior management team about trying to be a trader, he told her to be "a team player" and stay as an analyst. She was often asked to perform clerical tasks for other traders, such as making photocopies, taking calls from wives, and setting up BlackBerry accounts.

What's more, even though she had played golf since childhood and was on her high school's varsity golf team, she—along with other women traders—was excluded from company outings to country clubs to play golf. At one golf outing, where eighty Goldman professionals attended— only one of whom was a woman—she was told she could not attend because she was "too junior," even though "several male analysts right out of college attended the outing." In November 2008, Goldman terminated her employment.

———

IN GENERAL, GOLDMAN had much work to do when it came to making sure its employees believed they were being given sufficient opportunity to succeed. When Friedman and Rubin took over, the firm hired consultant Reed Whittle to beef up the firm's human resources function and to create a more robust employee evaluation system. When Whittle looked at Goldman's personnel evaluation system, he was appalled. "You're doing everything wrong," he told Friedman. "I don't mean you're doing two things wrong or a lot of things wrong, I mean you're doing *everything* wrong."

"And we probably were," Friedman said. He remembered once when someone came into his office after he had received his annual review and fingered Friedman for writing that he didn't think the person was "very bright." While Friedman wasn't sure that's what he wrote, he found the breach of confidentiality unacceptable. "You have to have a system of confidentiality, you have to have a system of candor, you have to have a system where people say, 'Friedman, this is something you really have an issue with and you have to work on it,' where I don't sit there thinking, 'Who is the Iago who whispered that in my boss's ear?' We were given the personnel reviews clearly without adequate data."

That's when Goldman decided to implement a confidential 360-degree review system and to separate the annual reviews from the award-ing of compensation. "I'm a huge believer in them . . . ," Friedman said of the 360. "If you have a bunch of people giving their views on Bill, you will discover a remarkable degree of consensus about what his strengths are and what his weaknesses are, and if it's done in a standardized manner and it's known that it's taken seriously, then when your boss sits down and says, 'Bill, here's an issue. It's a serious issue we want you to be working on . . . but let me just read you some of the comments.' I never met anyone who . . . could stay in denial when they'd had ten different comments about them pretty much around the same weakness."

Then there were the conversations with hotshots Friedman or Rubin wanted to move overseas. "You say to another partner who's an immensely talented guy, 'We really need you—we are globalizing this firm—and the only way we're going to get to be a global firm is to have some of our real talent go overseas. . . . We are prepared to make you a partner two years ahead of your class if you will go to Asia and we want you to take one for the firm,' " Friedman explained. "And the guy says, he's thought about it and has come back and said, 'I can't do it, my girl-friend, my mother, my dog doesn't travel well,' We're not at all vindictive about it. 'We hear you, you'll be considered together with your class in two years.' But then you go to another guy on your list and you make that offer and he goes. He becomes a partner two years ahead of the class." The message got around, fast, as Voltaire understood when he coined the phrase *"pour encourager les autres."* Then there were the conversations about sexual harassment (which apparently were less effective). "You go to a third guy and you say—and we've been loud and clear about no inti-mate relationships, consensual or otherwise, with people in your chain of command—'You are an intensely able person, you ought to be a partner in this firm, you've broken the ground rules, you ain't gonna be a partner this time. I really want you to stay and we will really, really make sure that this is put behind you, but you're going to pay your debt to society.' Now I promise you that no one is going to tell anyone that so-and-so didn't become a partner because he'd been having an affair with a woman in his department. No one is going to say the other guy didn't become a partner because he wouldn't move overseas, but I can promise you the organiza-tion figures it out very quickly, and the message gets across that when we say, 'There's a one-firm concept,' and a culture we must abide by. We really mean it."

WHATEVER SOCIAL AND behavioral problems the firm seemed to be having as the John Weinberg era faded away, there was no question Goldman Sachs—more than ever—still knew how to make money. *Insti-tutional Investor* estimated the 1990 "honeypot" at "north of $600 mil-lion," and *Forbes* wrote, without caveat, that the firm made $1 billion in net income in 1991. The Ad Hoc Profit Maximization Committee seemed to be working quite well. Goldman was not only the leader in the traditional investment banking businesses of underwriting debt and equity securities and in advising on M&A deals, but it had also started to become a leader in the business of investing its own capital, as a principal in trades and as a major investor in a variety of its own private-equity, bridge loan, and hedge funds. For years, there had been a reluctance under the traditional investment bankers Whitehead and Weinberg to take risks as principals, but there was no holding back now that the transaction-oriented Rubin and Friedman, arbitrageur and M&A banker respectively, were in charge. And besides, many of Goldman's competitors were way ahead of it in taking these risks; Goldman, playing catch-up to some degree, was determined to show the rest of Wall Street how to take these risks, in a prudent fashion (or so it hoped). By the early 1990s, Mark Winkelman had resurrected J. Aron, in part by broadening the commodities it traded, including oil and grain, among others. Winkelman rode his masterful management and turn-around skills to a seat on the Management Committee and as co-head of fixed-income with a successful trader named Jon Corzine. J. Aron had become a big part of Goldman's profit story. After years of acting only as an agent in the buying and selling of interest-rate swaps, Goldman had started acting as a principal in that business, too. "We were in the chicken camp on that," Friedman said, before Goldman found courage. Goldman had also started a $783.5 million distressed investing fund, the Water Street Corporation Recovery Fund—named after a street that runs perpendicular to Broad Street in downtown Manhattan—with $100 million of its partners' money to invest in the discounted debt securities of companies as a way to control them after a restructuring process.

Like other firms, Goldman had started a series of private-equity funds to invest its own capital, and that of third parties, in companies and in real estate that the funds—and Goldman—would control. The first Whitehall real-estate fund—named after another downtown street—was started in 1991 to buy skyscrapers, particularly in Manhattan, and other massive real-estate projects around the globe. Goldman's first private-equity fund, with more than $1 billion in it, began in 1992. Like many of its competitors, Goldman even started to make "bridge loans"—secured and unsecured loans put on Goldman's balance sheet—to companies in the process of buying other companies, enabling them to "bridge" their financing needs. The loans offered Goldman the potential for huge fees—after all, the financing made the deals possible—but also the huge risk that the loans might not be paid back or syndicated to other investors (oops!). By December 1990, a number of these loans that Goldman had made—for the leveraged buyouts of Southland Corp., the owner of 7-Eleven, of National Gypsum, and of R. H. Macy—had come a cropper. And one bridge loan in particular—made by First Boston in March 1989 for an acquisition of the Ohio Mattress Company, owner of the Sealy and

Stearns & Foster mattress brands—became known as "the Burning Bed" deal and almost sank the venerable investment bank after the $457 million loan could not be repaid in the wake of the collapse of the junk-bond financing market. The loan represented 40 percent of First Boston's capital and forced the bank into the arms of Credit Suisse.

Goldman's growing fascination with its principal businesses—whether in trading or investing—was understandable, especially from a good, old-fashioned moneymaking perspective. After all, advising on an M&A deal could take a year, or longer, between germination of an idea and a successful closing. While the fee on a big merger assignment could easily be in the tens of millions of dollars and require little capital to accomplish (bridge loans aside, a product that quickly faded from the scene given the deadly risks), there was also the risk that a deal team could spend huge amounts of time working on a project that might not happen or another company might win the asset, leaving nothing to show for many hours of work. The same could be said, too, for the underwriting of debt or equity securities, which may or may not end up happening, and, worse, tie up the firm's capital, as Goldman knew well from the 1987 BP underwriting. Even a successful underwriting—for instance, Goldman's handling of the Ford IPO—could take years and yield relatively little in fees (but huge bragging rights for sure). A successful trade, though, while also requiring the firm's capital, could be resolved far more quickly than an underwriting or an M&A assignment, usually in days or weeks. If the traders were clever and astute and (mostly) avoided reckless trades, the profit potential could be enormous, as Goldman was discovering.

The market had started to take notice of the changes taking place at Goldman. Under the "reign" of Friedman and Rubin, *Forbes* reported in 1992, "Goldman seems to be putting less emphasis on serving clients and more on dealing for its own account." The magazine noted that while other firms were ahead of Goldman in this activity, "for Goldman it is a landmark departure" and that while "[s]uch is the power of the firm that no one wants to criticize it in public," one former partner said "flatly" that "[t]here has been an enormous change [at Goldman], from worrying about clients to worrying about revenues." (Sensing that the *Forbes* article could be critical of the firm, Goldman executives declined the magazine's requests for interviews.) For instance, for years under Whitehead and Weinberg, Goldman resisted entering the asset management business because those two senior partners did not want to compete with the money managers who bought the stock and bond offerings Goldman underwrote. But, under Friedman and Rubin, Goldman's asset management business had grown considerably, to reach $30 billion in assets under management. "Goldman is only doing what the other firms do," *Forbes* observed. "But that's the point: In the past, Goldman set itself apart." By 1991, Goldman found itself at loggerheads with investment banking clients. Some complained that Goldman's Water Street Corporation Recovery Fund, set up to buy bonds of troubled companies, was working against them. They also accused the fund of basing investments on confidential information they had supplied to Goldman bankers.

RUN BY PARTNERS Mikael Salovaara, Alfred "Fred" Eckert III, and to a lesser extent Kenneth Brody, from the outset the Water Street fund was known for Salovaara's brilliant—but aggressive—tactics and its high returns. In the rough-and-tumble world of investing in the debt of distressed companies or those involved in a restructuring—where successful investors were known as "vultures"—there were many courageous and clever investors. Nevertheless, at thirty-seven years old, Salovaara stood out among them for both his investing savvy and his ability to turn arcane bankruptcy laws and practices to his advantage. But the very skills that made Salovaara an admired investor made him a lousy partner, and Goldman started very quickly to rue its decision to start the Water Street fund, which became an unwanted poster child for conflicts of interest—a supposed outlier for a firm that prided itself on being able to manage its conflicts.

Salovaara's highly profitable investment in the bonds of Tonka Corporation, the toy-truck maker—where the fund made $71 million on an investment of $84 million—was a case in point. Water Street began buying the distressed bonds of Tonka during the summer of 1990, shortly after the fund started, when toy maker Mattel, Inc., made an amorphous public announcement about wanting to make an acquisition. Tonka, although struggling, was an obvious acquisition target for Mattel, so Salovaara made the decision to start loading up on its bonds, which were trading at a discount given the company's financial difficulties. It was a risky bet, to be sure, because if no acquisition emerged, Tonka could be in serious financial trouble.

In late September, John Vogelstein, a principal at buyout firm Warburg Pincus—the largest shareholder in Mattel—called Salovaara and told him Mattel was considering making an offer for Tonka. After the discussion, Water Street bought more Tonka bonds. In the end, Mattel did not make an offer for Tonka, since a third toy maker, Hasbro, made an offer for Tonka instead, and Mattel chose not to compete. Eventually, Hasbro acquired Tonka, but not until Hasbro increased its original offers for the Tonka bonds in order to win Salovaara's support for the deal, leading to huge financial gains for Water Street—and speculation that Water Street had used inside information about a potential deal for Tonka to load up on its bonds. The *Wall Street Journal* reported that Vogelstein and Salovaara had spoken, and then Water Street bought more Tonka bonds. This "led to concerns among some Goldman clients, and was viewed as an embarrassment by some Goldman partners," according to the *New York Times*. But this was a seriously gray area since insider-trading laws apply to trading in stocks, not bonds—although there remains to this day no good reason for a legal distinction to be made, especially since the bond market is exponentially larger than the stock market and inside information just as valuable. The SEC did investigate the matter, though, without making public its findings.

The Water Street fund was also the focus of other charges of conflicts of interest with other Goldman clients, such as the Journal Company, a bankrupt owner of newspapers that Goldman had previously worked with as an investment banker, and USG Corp., a gypsum-board manufacturer working hard to restructure out of bankruptcy, for which Goldman had underwritten securities. Despite Water Street's success, the negative publicity around the appearance of conflicts of interest was more than Goldman bargained for. In early May 1991, the firm announced that Water Street would immediately stop making investments and wind down. "The intensity of the unforeseen reactions was out of the range we had anticipated," a Goldman official told the *Times*, speaking on condition he not be named. "This is a client-driven firm. We are sensitive to the perceptions of people." By July, the three Goldman partners—Salovaara, Eckert, and Brody—announced they were leaving the firm.

Other senior Goldman partners were leaving, too, including Geoff Boisi, the head of investment banking and subject of the slavish profile in the *New York Times*. Friedman had a bruising falling-out with Boisi, his onetime protégé in Goldman's merger department. "No star shone brighter than Boisi's," Lisa Endlich wrote. "He was dyed-in-the-wool Goldman Sachs, a culture carrier of the first order and a formidable money generator. Like most of those who rose to the top of Goldman Sachs' banking hierarchy, Boisi was intensely ambitious, with an understanding wife and family. The claims of the job seemed to have no limit." After graduating from Wharton in 1971, he joined Goldman's M&A department and became a partner in 1978. Two years later, he was head of the merger department. By 1988, he was named head of investment banking and went on the Management Committee. There was little question Boisi's ambitions and talents made him a leading candidate to be part of the succession equation at Goldman Sachs whenever Friedman and Rubin decided to retire. But, in 1990, Boisi unexpectedly—and involuntarily—gave up his job running investment banking to take charge of strategic planning at the firm. With his power and prestige stripped from him, it was just a matter of time before he departed. He was forty-four years old. Neither Boisi nor Friedman will discuss what happened, but the scars in both men remain visible.

————

THE WATER STREET debacle aside, being a principal required capital. Goldman had at its disposal its partners' capital, the profits it retained annually, the $500 million Sumitomo had invested in 1987, and billions of dollars in borrowings. Nothing was more highly prized than equity capital, though, since that money could be leveraged—borrowed against—to create a bigger pile of cash that could be used to invest and to make bets. The downside of equity capital was that it could be expensive financing, in that it usually required parting with an ownership stake in the company. For instance, for its $500 million, Sumitomo owned a 12.5 percent nonvoting stake in Goldman, an investment Sumitomo assumed would increase in value over time as long as Goldman was prudent. Of course, from Goldman's perspective, if the firm did well and its value increased, Sumitomo's equity would likely be worth far more than the $500 million invested—which is exactly what happened—but if the firm did poorly, there was no obligation to pay the money back to the investor. By contrast, debt financing can often be far cheaper than equity financing, since a debt investor expects to receive for his borrowed money the return of the original principal plus a fixed rate of interest. Most companies have a mix of both debt and equity financings.

In 1990, in order to supplement the Sumitomo investment, Goldman obtained another $275 million from a consortium of seven large insurance companies in the United States, United Kingdom, and Japan. Two years later, in April 1992, Goldman turned to a new outside investor—a Hawaiian educational trust, Kamehameha Schools/Bishop Estate—for another $250 million in equity. The trust, known as the Bishop Estate, was established in 1884 after the death of Princess Bernice Pauahi Bishop, a great-granddaughter of King Kamehameha I, who unified the Hawaiian Islands in the early 1800s and kept them independent from European colonizers. At the time of her death, Princess Pauahi owned approximately five hundred thousand acres of prime Hawaiian real estate, among the most valuable oceanfront property anywhere, and this acreage became the chief asset of the Bishop Estate. The chief beneficiary of the trust is the Kamehameha Schools, a private institution for children of Hawaiian ancestry. Although Goldman would not say specifically what percent of the firm the Bishop Estate received for its $250 million, the *New York Times* reported that the money bought between 5 percent of the firm, valuing Goldman at $5 billion, and 6.25 percent, valuing Goldman at $4 billion. Given that the valuation of Goldman was $4 billion for Sumitomo's investment five years earlier, the likelihood was that Goldman was worth $5 billion in 1992 and that the Bishop Estate's investment was closer to a 5 percent stake.

Most Goldman partners credited Jon Corzine, the co-head of fixed-income and CFO, with arranging for this investment, but the lead was really brought in by an obscure fixed-income institutional salesman in the San Francisco office named Fred Steck.

Two years later, after another $250 million cash infusion into Goldman from the Bishop Estate, Steck was up for partner. A bunch of senior Goldman partners were discussing whether Steck had the right stuff. "Fred Steck, you know, I don't really think Fred Steck should be a partner," one of them said. "He doesn't have the capability and he's not broad-based. I'm not sure it's the right thing." But Corzine stood up for Steck. "Shut the fuck up," Corzine said. "He just saved the firm." Steck became a partner.

CHAPTER 13

POWER

One of the people Goldman hired as a consultant during its consultant-hiring spree was Lawrence Summers, a Philadelphia-born Harvard economist whose two uncles—Paul Samuelson and Kenneth Arrow—had both won Nobel Prizes in economics. Summers's parents, Robert and Anita, were also economics professors.

During the summer of 1986, when Rubin and Friedman were still the co-heads of Goldman's fixed-income group, Jacob Goldfield, a precocious and gifted young Goldman trader, suggested to Rubin that he and Summers should meet. Goldfield grew up in the Bronx, where his mother was a clerk in the New York City Health Department and his father had a small store, wholesaling women's clothing. After graduating from high school in the Bronx, Goldfield studied physics at Harvard but also dabbled in graduate-level courses that interested him, including econometrics. At Harvard, Goldfield was famous for being really smart. One day, he and a friend, also a physics major, were studying for the exam in econometrics and decided to go see Summers the day before the exam, since Goldfield's friend knew Summers and figured he could help them understand the difficult subject matter. Summers tried to help the two undergrads but finally gave up. Time was too short and the subject matter too complex. Even Summers hinted he would have trouble getting an A on the exam. In the end, Goldfield took the exam and got the highest grade the professor had ever given on a final. This was sometimes the way things went with Goldfield, whose intuition and different way of thinking generated occasional flashes of brilliance. Since Summers was in the economics department, he ended up hearing about Goldfield's rather astounding achievement on the econometrics final. This led to their having regular discussions and the occasional meal together.

After graduating from Harvard, Goldfield bounced around Europe for a bit and then headed back home to the Bronx, where he lived with his parents. While at home, he took the LSAT and applied to Harvard and Yale law schools. He chose Harvard Law because he believed it to be less intellectual than Yale and therefore more practical and likely to lead to a better career (ironically, the opposite of Rubin's reasoning). After his first year at Harvard Law, he managed to get an interview at Goldman for a summer job, which was not easy, since the firm did not recruit at Harvard Law, even though its two senior partners-to-be—Rubin and Friedman—were both lawyers. Through the Harvard Business School, Goldfield finagled an invite for lunch with a number of Goldman's leaders. He got the summer job in the sales and trading group. Then, so he wouldn't go to another firm, Goldman offered Goldfield a full-time job trading government bond options. He dropped out of Harvard Law School and joined Goldman Sachs.

Goldfield got off to a bit of an odd start. One day filling in for a trader, he lost $140,000 on a trade, some 7 percent of the annual revenues for this government bond option group. This was not auspicious. Then, a week or so later, filling in again—his supervisors were apparently not as horrified by the initial 7 percent loss as Goldfield was—he made $1.1 million on a trade, more than half the group's annual revenues. "For what it was, it was shocking," he said. Although he was not entirely sure how this happened, he would study the data on the hour-long subway rides to his parents' apartment in the Bronx, where he was living at the time. The next year, the revenues in this little group shot up exponentially to around $35 million, from $2 million.

His unprecedented success got him noticed during his first year at the firm. First, Corzine came by his desk and congratulated him. Then, one day, relatively early on in his tenure at the firm, Rubin called him in the Bronx. His mother answered the phone. They developed a close friendship. It turned out Rubin wanted to adopt Goldfield, metaphorically speaking. Rubin's infatuation with Goldfield put him in awkward positions. "He went very far out of his way to include me in meetings where I didn't belong," he said. "There would be meetings to figure out what we should do about some big thing and all the senior people would be involved, and me—that kind of thing." But Rubin took mentoring seriously, especially when he found someone unusually bright or creative. "This was bad because of course it created resentment," Goldfield said, "but obviously interesting."

That's when Goldfield thought about introducing Rubin to Summers. "At some point," Goldfield recalled, "I said to Rubin, 'Oh, I have this smart friend' "—Summers—"I guess I already appreciated that he valued intellect highly." Summers and Goldfield had kept in touch during the five years since he had graduated from Harvard, especially on topics of mutual interest. "We had a lot of energy for very long calls," Goldfield said. Sometime in 1986, the three men had lunch in Rubin's office, off the equity floor. The lunch did not go all that well actually, and Summers figured—incorrectly—that he had heard the last of Rubin. (Summers was not the only smart economist Rubin brought to Goldman. For instance, Goldfield remembered Paul Krugman, from Princeton, also dropping by 85 Broad Street to meet with Goldman partners.)

Over time, Rubin developed a special affinity for Summers. By this point, Summers had served a stint as an economist on Reagan's first Council of Economic Advisers (even though he was a Democrat) and had returned to Harvard as a full professor of economics, one of the youngest ever. These significant accomplishments at an early age once again caught Rubin's attention. "It's easy to see why Bob and Larry developed a close working relationship," Goldfield said. "Bob liked bright people who would challenge him. Larry greatly valued Bob's judgment and appreciated his astonishing ability to form a consensus on difficult decisions." At one point, Summers came to Goldman and gave a lecture about the efficient market hypothesis.

The two men also shared an interest in Democratic Party politics. Although Rubin had been elected the president of his fourth-grade class and had dabbled in a few local New York political campaigns, his interest in national politics advanced after outgoing treasury secretary Henry Fowler joined Goldman in 1969. " 'Joe,' as everyone called Fowler, was a courtly Virginia lawyer whose ancestors had come to America in the seventeenth century," Rubin explained. "Many people at Goldman were not that interested in what Fowler had done in government. But to me, Joe was a fascinating figure—someone who had gone to Washington during the New Deal and served in every Democratic administration thereafter." During one of their many discussions about politics, Rubin mentioned to Fowler that he would like to become more involved. Fowler called Robert Strauss, the irrepressible Akin Gump attorney and legendary behind-the-scenes fixer who had become treasurer of the Democratic National Committee in 1971.

Strauss told Rubin that if he was interested in shaping policy, he had no use for him. But if he wanted to raise money, they should talk. Strauss wanted Rubin's help raising money for Democratic congressional candidates in order for the Democrats to retain control of Congress in the face of what was certainly looking like a Nixon landslide reelection in 1972. Strauss then gave Rubin a valuable piece of advice about politics: *Follow through.* Lots of promises get made in politics, especially when it came to fund-raising, so if you say you are going to help, you'd better help or else don't bother getting involved. "You know, you look good on paper," Strauss told him. "But now that I've met you, I don't think you'll amount to much. So you better work hard." Properly insulted, Rubin took a week off from work and started dialing for Democratic dollars. Not many of his fellow arbitrageurs were interested in supporting Democrats, but he did manage to raise $25,000. "In those days, that wasn't a bad start," Rubin explained.

Rubin was quite taken with Strauss (and vice versa). "Bob has a magnetism that reminds me of Gus and Bunny [Lasker]," Rubin wrote in his memoir. "When he walks into a room, the effect is electric." Strauss gave Rubin some "early political advice" that he remembered: "Let me tell you about Washington, Bob, I could call President Carter once a week and just say anything—even talk about the weather. After that, I could walk around town telling people that I had just been talking to the President today and, while it would mean nothing substantively, it would have meaning in Washington. That's just the way this city works."

As the Carter administration was nearing its end, Rubin got a payoff of sorts in the form of a job offer at the White House to head up the Council on Wage and Price Stability, which was part of the effort to bring inflation under control. Rubin explored the opportunity. "Few notions were more appealing to me than seeing the world from inside the White House," he wrote. He went down to Washington, met with the relevant people, but decided against taking the job. "I was left with the impression that that job wasn't positioned to work, in terms of either staffing and authority within the administration or its conceptual approach," he continued.

In 1982, Strauss asked Rubin to be the chairman of the congressional campaign dinner in Washington. This was code for raising money for the elections. After checking around, Rubin determined that he needed to be able to raise at least $100,000 or he shouldn't agree to take the job. He called a family friend in Florida "who had made a lot of money from my arbitrage advice" and he and his partner agreed to put up $20,000 each. Rubin also agreed to put in $20,000. With $60,000 raised immediately, he told Strauss he'd take on the responsibility. He ended up raising more than $100,000 on his own, and the dinner itself took in more than $1 million, "large numbers by the standards of that era," he explained. Rubin's success finding the "mother's milk" put him on a higher trajectory within the party. Soon, both Walter Mondale and John Glenn, two Democratic senators seeking their party's nomination for president in 1984, came looking for his help.

Rubin decided to support Mondale, whom he met through Jim Johnson, Mondale's campaign manager. He ended up serving as the New York State finance chairman for Mondale. Over time, he participated in policy discussions with Mondale, Johnson, and other top campaign leaders. "Some people like opera," Rubin explained. "Some like basketball. I like policy and politics." His cluttered Goldman office on the trading floor—filled with unopened boxes—also had pictures of him with presidents Carter and Reagan. He knew that someday he wanted to work in the White House, although with Mondale's defeat at the hands of Ronald Reagan he knew that wasn't going to be anytime soon. Afterward, Mondale had nothing but praise for Rubin. "I definitely would have offered him a position in my administration, one that would have been significant and matched his skills and interests," Mondale told *Institutional Investor* in 1990. "Bob is the ablest person I have ever met."

In 1988, Rubin worked on the Dukakis campaign, both as a fundraiser and as a policy adviser. In his memoir, Rubin downplayed his involvement with Dukakis. He wrote that he "met" Dukakis a "few times," raised money for him, and "contributed a bit of advice to his campaign." Rubin was part of a small group of outside advisers to the Dukakis campaign—including Roger Altman and Laura D'Andrea Tyson—whom Dukakis and Gene Sperling, a midlevel economic staffer on the campaign, would speak with fairly regularly. The two economic advisers who were "first among equals," according to Sperling, on the Dukakis campaign were Summers and Robert Reich, Summers's Harvard colleague, although Summers was an economics professor and Reich was a professor at the Kennedy School of Government. Summers, Reich, and the economics staff—including Sperling—would have a conference call every night in 1988 during the presidential campaign. Summers and Reich gave their time freely. "They were hungry to be involved," Sperling said. Sperling described the Dukakis campaign as Summers's "political awakening" and remembered that he started off being incredibly wonkish—pushing to reform copyright laws or the GATT (General Agreement on Tariffs and Trade) treaty—until Dukakis berated him once, "Larry, GATT, schmatt!" and he started to get with the program.

For much of the summer of 1988, Dukakis was way ahead of George H. W. Bush, and the inevitable speculation began about which Dukakis adviser would have what position at the White House or in the cabinet. Many people assumed Summers would be Dukakis's head of the Council of Economic Advisers, the natural post for a leading and influential economist. But by the time September rolled around, Dukakis found himself trailing Bush and then he lost big in November. Dukakis's defeat hit Rubin, and others, hard. "[M]any in the party felt bitterly toward him for the way he handled his candidacy," Rubin wrote, without elaboration. For his part, while disappointed by the Dukakis defeat, Sperling looked back on it and instead recalled that it was that campaign that brought together for the first time the people—Rubin, Summers, Reich, Tyson, Roger Altman, George Stephanopoulos—who would soon become household names. "It's amazing how much goes back to that Dukakis campaign," he said. "It's amazing. I walked out of there after ten months—we had lost—but little did I know that people I'd worked with would all end up being highly consequential."

———

OF COURSE, RUBIN'S entry point into this circle of politics could be boiled down to the fact that he brought in the money. Politicians need cash, and bankers crave power, if only to prove to themselves they have a higher purpose than becoming obscenely wealthy. In 1991, while he was still an economics professor at Harvard, Summers wrote an influential chapter, "Planning for the Next Financial Crisis," that appeared in a book published by the National Bureau of Economic Research. Other chapters in the book were written by economists Hyman Minsky, Paul Volcker, William Poole, and Paul Samuelson, Summers's uncle. "It used to be said that a repeat of the depression of the 1930s was inconceivable now that governments better understood how to manage their economies," Summers wrote. "Yet, both Latin America and Europe have suffered economic downturns during the 1980s on a scale comparable to the 1930s. And, in 1987, the world's stock markets suffered the greatest one-day drop in their history. It is little wonder that the possibility of financial crisis with major economic consequences has again emerged as a major cause for concern."

In this remarkably prescient essay, Summers wrote about the need for a "lender-of-last resort"—the Federal Reserve—to step in during a financial crisis but warned that such non-market-based financial support could lead to "moral hazard" and a too-big-to-fail mentality. "In the presence of a Federal safety net, depositors will not scrutinize the loan portfolios of financial institutions," he wrote. "This will encourage excess risk taking. The problem is magnified because a few aggressive institutions can put pressure on the rest by offering premium interest rates. Safe institutions that do not desire to take unfair advantage of lender-of-last-resort protection then must choose between raising the rates they offer and accepting fewer deposits. Just as bad money drives out good, there is a tendency for bad financial institutions to drive out good ones." In researching the article, Summers spoke with Rubin, at Goldman. "Bob set up for me to talk to some other people at Goldman as I was working on that article . . . ," Summers said, during a 2009 interview in his White House office. "That's the only consulting I did for Goldman." (A year later, Summers's spokesman, Matthew Vogel, wrote that Summers was confused about his intersections with Goldman and Rubin during this period. "I think there's some conflating going on here," he wrote. "The only thing Larry did for Goldman for which he was paid was a seminar he conducted for some of their people on behavioral finance in the late 1980s. The [NBER] paper had nothing to do with it." Goldman would eventually pay Summers $135,000 to speak at the firm in April 2008.)

After Rubin became co-chairman of Goldman, in 1990, Strauss threw a dinner party for Rubin in Washington to celebrate. "Not because of me, but because of him, it was quite an assemblage," Rubin recalled. At the time, Rubin had become increasingly concerned about the growing federal budget deficit and the lack of a bipartisan focus in Washington on figuring out how to close it. He was also concerned about the country's "deep denial" about its social problems—drug use, poverty in the inner cities, continued deterioration of the efficacy of public education—and wondered whether political and financial leaders would have the courage to tackle any of them. These concerns were very much on his mind when he rose to speak at the Strauss dinner. "The gist of it was," he recalled, "that on the one hand, we were the world's largest economy, but on the other we had a set of problems—public education, crime, drugs, the inner cities—and social costs that flow from those problems: the deficit, the savings rate, the comparison between our somewhat failing infrastructure and the more modern infrastructures of Europe. You look at all these together, and it was not a prescription for a healthy future—quite the contrary. It seemed to me, unless we dealt with those problems, we would have a mediocre economy as far in the future as you can see. And I said I was not optimistic personally that we would deal with these problems, because it did not seem to me our political process wanted to do the things that were necessary." The failure to face up to these systemic problems, Rubin concluded, was the "risk of inexorable national decline."

BY 1992—AND twelve years of Republican rule that resulted in many of the problems he had railed against—Rubin was sifting through the various potential Democratic presidential aspirants in order to decide which one to support. He and David Sawyer, a well-regarded political consultant and documentary filmmaker, held a series of small dinners for the candidates along with about a dozen business and media types. Bill Clinton, the governor of Arkansas, was the guest one night in mid-1991. Rubin was blown away. "I've been to many events where a candidate spends much of the time talking," Rubin recalled. "For more than three hours, Clinton engaged in a real dialogue—a serious give-and-take—on the issues important to us." At the end of the dinner, Rubin turned to Lew Kaden, a New York attorney (and later Rubin's colleague at Citigroup), and said, "This guy Clinton is amazing. It's remarkable how well he understands this stuff." By March 1992, the *New York Times* had reported that Rubin was solidly in Clinton's camp. It is the nature of modern politics in America that people who want to be president of the United States must first audition for people like the chairman of Goldman Sachs.

A few months later, in May, Clinton, edging closer and closer to the Democratic nomination for president, invited a group of informal advisers to Little Rock to discuss economic issues. The media had not been alerted to the meeting, and the meeting was not reported at the time. Rubin was invited, along with both Altman and Reich, from the Dukakis campaign, and Rubin's fellow Goldman partners Ken Brody and Barry Wigmore. Although Rubin regarded the meeting as a form of window dressing, Clinton ended up taking off a day from his campaign to evaluate what the group of advisers was thinking. "Doing that showed a remarkable seriousness of purpose for a candidate in the midst of a campaign," Rubin recalled. He remembered the group had "a range of opinions" but agreed on the importance of deficit reduction, greater investment in education and health care, and the wisdom of reducing trade barriers.

Clinton asked the group to draft an economic statement. That task fell to Gene Sperling, who had just joined the Clinton campaign and "instantly became its economic engine." Rubin took a prominent role as a media spokesman for the Clinton campaign on economic issues. Under Sperling's careful tutelage, he learned how "to engage with the media" in a Washington context. Sperling, he explained, told Rubin it was "crucial to get my points across" in answering questions on Clinton's behalf.

On September 19, *Barron's* reported that if Clinton was elected president, he would name Rubin treasury secretary. Goldman said that *Barron's* had not interviewed Rubin for its article and that it was just idle speculation. At the end of October, the *Times* reported that Rubin was in line for a top economic post if Clinton won. Rubin spent election night in Little Rock "celebrating Clinton's victory." A couple of weeks later, Clinton summoned Rubin to Little Rock to meet with him. They spoke together "for a couple of hours," Rubin remembered, but very little of the discussion was about economic policy, which Rubin later told his wife seemed peculiar.

At the meeting, Clinton asked Rubin who should be treasury secretary. Rubin recommended Texas senator Lloyd Bentsen, who was the chairman of the Senate Finance Committee, Mondale's running mate, and "well equipped for the job," Rubin allowed. Of his own qualifications, or lack thereof, Rubin explained that he didn't feel he had "the experience in dealing with Congress, the media, policy or politics to handle the job at that point." He and Clinton also spoke about Clinton's idea to create an economic equivalent of the National Security Council at the White House to coordinate the many agencies and offices that participate in economic policy making in order to distill down the many different viewpoints about which economic paths to take and make useful recommendations to the president.

On November 19, the *Times* reported that Robert Reich, the head of Clinton's economic transition team, had given assignments to frame economic policy to a dozen advisers, leading to further speculation about whom Clinton would choose for his team. Among those asked by Reich to write papers were Summers and Tyson. The paper reported that both Rubin and Altman, a friend of Clinton's from Georgetown University, would be helping Summers, then on leave from Harvard at the World Bank, to craft a paper on tax policy and whether a fiscal stimulus program was needed. Beyond reporting these amorphous assignments, the press seemed at a bit of a loss to figure out who was in line for what job, which is precisely the way Clinton had designed the process. Those brash enough—or foolish enough—to speak with reporters about their visit to Little Rock were immediately eliminated from consideration. Rubin, of course, was keeping very quiet.

Shortly after Rubin's interview with Clinton in Little Rock, Warren Christopher, the head of Clinton's transition team whom he knew from the board of the Carnegie Foundation, called Rubin to talk about a job in the new administration. Christopher didn't mince words. "If you don't become Treasury Secretary," he said to Rubin, "would you be interested in running the National Economic Council at the White House?" Rubin told Christopher he would be interested in the position. Rubin recalled Christopher seemed a little surprised, since a staff job at the White House might be considered a step down for the co-chairman of Goldman. But Rubin preferred not to view it that way but rather as being the person responsible for coordinating economic policy.

A few weeks later, at the beginning of December 1992, Rubin was on a business trip in Frankfurt, Germany. At 2:30 a.m., the phone rang. It was Christopher. He wanted to formally offer Rubin the NEC job. "Without any further deliberation, I said yes," Rubin remembered. "Then I went back to sleep," but not before calling his wife and telling her he had accepted the position. "She was more surprised than Christopher," Rubin allowed. Why someone so devoted to "probabilistic thinking" had accepted a new, untested job as a policy adviser in the White House was a question Rubin would get frequently over the years. The answer, he explained, was that he just really wanted the job and did not let the negatives overwhelm his thinking. "My fascination with Washington and the political process—and my desire to get involved with issues I care about—overrode all other considerations," Rubin wrote later. He had more than enough money, but the lure of power was irresistible.

In early December, Rubin flew to Little Rock to be part of Clinton's first announcement about his top economic appointees. Bentsen would be treasury secretary and Altman would be his deputy. Leon Panetta would be the director of the Office of Management and Budget; Alice Rivlin would be his deputy. Rubin was named director of the new National Economic Council. Before they all went to the press conference, Sperling warmed up the appointees with some questions that he figured the press might ask. "How can a wealthy guy from Wall Street possibly relate to the problems of working Americans?" Sperling asked Rubin. "Aren't you just totally unsuited to understanding the problems of ordinary people?" While Sperling's question was tongue-in-cheek, there was no denying Rubin's accumulated wealth. Goldman had paid him $26.5 million in 1992, and his Goldman stock, although not publicly traded, was said to be worth $150 million. Nevertheless, he was still being described as a frugal ascetic who wore the "same pinstripe suit, white button-down shirt and patterned necktie every day." In answer to Sperling's questions, Rubin "deadpanned," "Well, I think you've got a good point."

At the press conference, Clinton introduced Rubin last. "I have asked Robert Rubin to serve as assistant to the [p]resident for economic policy and to help to coordinate and to direct our new Economic Council," Clinton said. "I've created this new role, similar to that of the national security adviser in the present White House, because the coordination of our nation's economic policy is every bit as essential as the coordination of foreign policy to our long-term national security."

After the Little Rock press conference, Rubin flew back home to New York. There was never any doubt in Friedman's mind that if Clinton got elected, he would ask Rubin to be part of his top team and Rubin would take the job. "It was very clear that he was very, very focused on that," Friedman said. The next morning, before heading down to Washington, Rubin showed up briefly at Goldman Sachs. He and Friedman arranged for the two senior partners to meet for the final time together with the firm's partners in a conference room on the thirtieth floor of 85 Broad Street. This was Rubin's somewhat emotional good-bye.

Looking back, Friedman said he was happy for his longtime partner—"We'd never had an argument that I can recall. We agreed on most things and when we differed, we worked it out," he said—but happiness was not the prevalent emotion that emerged during the impromptu partners' meeting on December 11. After the requisite jokes about how quickly Rubin had become irrelevant to the assembled Goldman partners, Friedman told the group the meeting would be brief because Rubin had to be on his way to Washington. "This has been an exceptional partnership . . . ," Friedman said. "I am going to miss him a great deal."

Rubin seemed disheveled. He said he was "caught up in a mess" but had managed to make a few notes on the flight back from Little Rock about what he wanted to say. "I looked at them this morning and they don't really quite express my feelings," he said. "On the one hand, I think this has the opportunity to be an extraordinary experience," he said. "I mean if I have nothing other than yesterday it would have been an extraordinary experience sitting around with these people that are going to run this bloody place and it's a strange kind of thing. On the other hand, just deciding to do this I have come to realize ever more—I'm not an enormously emotional person ordinarily—how much Goldman Sachs and its people have meant to me and how much a part of my life they've been."

Rubin moved to Washington, living in a suite of rooms at the Jefferson Hotel, near his office at the Treasury. The annual rent on the suite was more than his government salary, much of which he declined to take.

A few days before Clinton's first inauguration, the *New York Times* profiled Rubin. In trying to assess Rubin's tenure at Goldman, the *Times* reporters wrote about how profitable Goldman had become under his aegis, earning $1.1 billion in pretax profit in 1991, more than any other Wall Street firm. The paper noted that he favored "management by cross-examination" and used his "keen wit to poke fun at himself and cut sharply into others and, while a patient listener and open-minded, he nonetheless can be impatient." Friedman agreed with that assessment.

"He is very unaccepting of intellectually weak and flabby arguments," he told the paper. "He will cut right through that." One unnamed Goldman partner, asked to assess Rubin's leadership tenure at the firm, said, "Bob is not a legendary figure, like some people who have run this firm. I don't think he wants to be. But he has been a better leader than some of the legends."

CHAPTER 14

THE COLLEGE OF CARDINALS

J ohn Weinberg was not asked by the *Times* to comment on Rubin's unplanned departure, but he was not happy about it. In fact, he was highly pissed off. He had carefully groomed both Rubin and Friedman to be his successors. Not only had they proved to be seamless in their decision-making and leadership of the firm, their knowledge of and experience in the two sides of the firm's business—investment banking and trading—were perfect complements. While Rubin and Friedman had rotated together as co-heads of Goldman's fixed-income division, there was no question that Rubin's skills were highly focused on trading and principal investing—taking serious risks with the firm's capital—while Friedman's banking skills revolved around providing M&A advice and other client-related services. Some Goldman partners believed Rubin had been taking 80 percent of the responsibility for running the firm, leaving the balance to Friedman. Friedman had only a tangential understanding of how the increasingly important aspect of Goldman's business—risk taking—actually worked. The two men—and his selection of them—represented his legacy. "I don't think John was particularly sympathetic when Bob Rubin exercised his patriotic duty to go to Washington," his nephew Peter Weinberg explained. "Bob was asked to be the co-senior partner of the firm, and that was exactly what he was expected to do. Period." In short order, John Weinberg would also rue the day that Steve Friedman was left to run Goldman Sachs by himself. "The single most serious thing that happened to the firm was when Rubin went to Washington and left Steve in charge," said one former Goldman partner.

———

AT FIRST, the Goldman financial juggernaut roared ahead on all cylinders. Goldman's traders had made a huge bet on something Friedman described as the "European currency mechanism," which was just an elaborate bet—in the days before the euro was created—on the direction a group of European currencies would trade against one another. At that time, the deutsche mark was the strongest European currency and Goldman bet it would continue to remain strong and the other European currencies that were pegged to it—the Italian lira and the French franc—would continue to be weak. "If your trade was to be long the deutsche mark and short the lira you were highly unlikely to lose money because it was highly unlikely that all of the sudden the lira's going to get much stronger against the deutsche mark," Friedman explained. "Much more likely it would get weaker. And I think to some extent the non-German central banks were artificially propping up their currencies to keep them within this band."

Normally, Friedman said, he tended to be cautious—although "you're in a risk business so caution doesn't mean we've got to be in a fetal position," he said—but this was an obvious moneymaking opportunity. "I looked on it as the best trading opportunity I'd ever seen," he said. Many traders were making a similar bet, including hedge-fund manager George Soros, and winning fortunes. "That's the time you break up the furniture and throw it in the fire," Friedman said, recalling how Cornelius Vanderbilt made his fortune by betting on steamships. "Other times you cut back, cut back, cut back. But things were going well for us and we did very, very well in 1992 and 1993." That was an understatement. Goldman made $2.7 billion in pretax profits in 1993—by far the firm's most profitable year ever to that point. Friedman made $46 million, and other members of the Management Committee pocketed at least $25 million each—unheard-of sums of money on Wall Street at that time.

Not surprisingly, the firm's success rekindled the idea among some on the Management Committee that the time had come—again—for Goldman Sachs to go public. Jon Corzine, the co-head of fixed-income (with Mark Winkelman), the firm's former CFO, and a member of the Management Committee, was the leading advocate for beginning the IPO process after the blowout performance in 1993. Corzine raised the matter with Friedman, who was not against the idea. Friedman saw it as "a crucial thing to do for the long term when you're going to be competing on a global basis against people with permanent capital." But, he told Corzine, even though the firm had done spectacularly in 1993, Friedman remained concerned about the reputational fallout from the Freeman and Eisenberg scandals and he worried that despite the success of the European currency trade, he didn't think Goldman had its "trading legs under us very well." That must have come as a bit of a shock to Corzine, who had just presided over the huge trading gains. Friedman was also thinking about retiring at the end of 1993—going out on a high note, so to speak—and there could be no IPO without a leader.

The idea of the IPO got bandied around on the Management Committee at the end of that year, but Friedman rejected it and decided not to retire—"to give it one more year," he explained. He said he wanted to try to complete several strategic imperatives he and Rubin had started, for instance, to continue Goldman's international expansion and to more fully integrate the private-equity business into the firm and to manage the firm through what he thought might be a down year in 1994.

———

FRIEDMAN WAS ALSO deeply worried about another simmering crisis: Goldman's involvement—and potential liability—in helping to prop up the financial house of cards that was the transatlantic publishing empire of onetime British tycoon Robert Maxwell. On November 5, 1991, Maxwell allegedly committed suicide by jumping off his yacht, *Lady Ghislaine*, near the Canary Islands, although many conspiracy theories abound about his demise. In any event, he suffered a heart attack and drowned. The working assumption was that he knew that his financial empire was quickly coming unraveled. His death exposed Maxwell's colossal scheme to defraud his companies' creditors and shareholders. He had been desperately trying to prop up the value of the shares in his companies since he had pledged them as collateral for loans he had taken out. Maxwell had also secretly transferred more than $800 million from his companies' employee pension funds to try to stay one step ahead of his creditors. "The complex ownership and financial structure of his empire and the concealment of the use of the pension funds made it difficult for banks to gain a clear picture," according to a 2001 report of the financial collapse by Britain's Department of Trade and Industry.

Maxwell's complex relationship with Goldman is detailed in the DTI's withering 407-page report—and then some more in a 355-page appendix. It began in August 1986 when Goldman agreed to take a five-year lease on an office building—Stand House—in Central London that Maxwell had bought the previous February for £17 million. After reaching the lease arrangement with Goldman, Maxwell sold the building, in November 1986, to Pergamon Holdings Limited, one of his affiliated companies, for £18 million, a nifty profit, and renamed the building Maxwell House. Goldman set up its U.K. trading operation at Maxwell House. Soon thereafter, Goldman's business dealings with Maxwell increased dramatically.

In June 1987, Goldman underwrote and syndicated a £105 million loan, secured by a group of Maxwell's real-estate assets, including

Maxwell House, the value of which was appraised at double its value seven months earlier. Back in April 1986, Maxwell announced that it was his intention to transform Pergamon Press, a scientific-journal and reference-book publisher that he started in 1951—and would rename Maxwell Communications Corporation—into a global communications and information company with revenues of £3 billion to £5 billion by the end of the 1980s. This was to be no mean feat considering that the company's revenue at the end of December 1985 was £265 million. By September 1986, Goldman had started helping Maxwell expand his empire through a series of block trades that helped Maxwell acquire Philip Hill Investment Trust PLC, which had £331 million of investment assets. "It was the start of a significant relationship," according to the DTI report. "It was an important and profitable piece of business for Goldman Sachs." Some at Goldman, including a few partners in London, questioned the wisdom of doing business with Maxwell, but any concerns were quickly jettisoned in favor of the moneymaking opportunity.

Of course, had Goldman—and Eric Sheinberg, Maxwell's banker at Goldman in London—given serious consideration to a 1971 DTI report about Maxwell's duplicitous nature, the firm might have stayed away from Maxwell completely and avoided the scandal. The DTI's earlier report arose after a deal between Maxwell and Saul Steinberg, the flamboyant New York corporate raider, went sour. According to Roger Cohen, in the *New York Times,* Maxwell was "a Czech-born Jewish immigrant who had changed his name three times and survived humiliation by Britain's clubby City establishment [and] he was incorrigibly suspicious of others."

In June 1969, Steinberg's Leasco agreed to buy Pergamon from Maxwell. But Steinberg quickly came to believe Maxwell had deceived him about the value and substance of Pergamon. The DTI's report seemed to back Steinberg. The agency found Maxwell's "apparent fixation as to his own abilities causes him to ignore the views of others if these are not compatible" and that his shareholders' reports betrayed "a reckless and unjustified optimism" that sometimes led him "to state what he must have known to be untrue." He was found to have inflated the revenue at his encyclopedia business and sold scientific journals to his other private companies to make revenue at Pergamon look higher. "He sold a lot of scientific journals to related private companies and inserted them as profit," Ronald Leach, an accountant who was one of the DTI's investigators on the matter, told the *Times.* "It's an old accountancy trick, but not one to be recommended." The report concluded: "We regret having to conclude that, notwithstanding Mr. Maxwell's acknowledged abilities and energy, he is not in our opinion a person who can be relied on to exercise proper stewardship of a publicly quoted company." Maxwell was soon ousted from Pergamon.

When Eric Sheinberg heard about the DTI's 1971 report on Maxwell, he gave little weight to it, since he knew Saul Steinberg and found him unsavory. Plus there was money to be made from Maxwell. Sheinberg had learned about risk from Gus Levy, who had taught him "never worry about how much money you are going to make on a trade . . . focus instead on how much you are going to lose if you make a mistake." Sheinberg told the DTI team investigating Maxwell again after his death that Maxwell "was thought to be enormously wealthy and apparently dealt with virtually every major UK financial institution." Sheinberg said he thought Maxwell "was controversial." He had heard of the 1971 DTI report about him but "from his knowledge of the other party to the dispute"—Steinberg—"that had given rise to the [report], he was inclined to think that [Maxwell] would have behaved the better." But Owen Stable, a judge and the other author of the 1971 DTI report, told the *Times* in December 1991 that Maxwell simply repeated his bad behavior. "What has happened now amounts to a repeat performance," he said. "I thought back then that he was one of the biggest crooks I'd ever met. He invented deals between his private and public companies. He was incapable of distinguishing between other people's money and his own."

After the DTI report, Maxwell seemed determined to restore his tarnished reputation. In 1974, he bought back Pergamon from Leasco, where it had performed poorly without him. In two years' time, he had restored Pergamon to profitability and then used it as an acquisition vehicle. In 1981, he bought the money-losing British Printing Corporation and made it profitable by busting unions and slashing staff. In 1984, he bought the *Daily Mirror,* fulfilling a lifelong ambition to own a newspaper. The paper was losing money, but he made it profitable by again destroying the union and brutal cost cutting. Soon thereafter, he made the bold prediction that his private company would have billions in revenue "and profits to match." In 1988, for $3.3 billion, he bought Macmillan Inc., a New York book publisher, and Official Airline Guide, using billions of dollars in debt to do so. By the beginning of the 1990s, Maxwell was still short of his goal—his revenue was just shy of $1 billion—but he had divested his printing business as well as Pergamon, his original business, for $446 million.

As a credit crunch took hold worldwide in the early 1990s, the prices Maxwell had paid for many of his assets—especially Macmillan—

looked excessive and the debt burden loomed heavily. "When most of my colleagues looked at Maxwell Communications [in 1991], we felt that the profits were overstated, the debt burden was quite likely to lead to downfall, and we'd become increasingly concerned by the way in which it seemed the share price was rigged," John Kenny, an analyst at Barclays de Zoete Wedd, told the *Times*. "I did not see anyone buying the stock, yet on many occasions it was going up."

Part of the alleged blame for the apparent manipulation of Maxwell's stock rested with Goldman, according to the DTI report and various newspaper accounts, and two put options that Maxwell and his son had sold Goldman on 45.65 million Maxwell Communications shares, representing 7 percent of the shares outstanding, a huge and atypical option. An August 14, 1990, option gave Goldman the right to sell 15.65 million Maxwell Communications shares on November 30, 1990, for 185 pence each, or about $3.60 at that day's exchange rate and 15 pence above the prevailing price of Maxwell's stock. Goldman bought the put to protect the value of the 16.7 million Maxwell shares it already owned and paid a fee to Maxwell for the right to sell shares to him. The option Maxwell granted Goldman expired two days after the end of period during which Maxwell could not buy his company's shares.

During August, September, and October 1990, Goldman accounted for nearly half the trading in Maxwell Communications stock. Goldman exercised the first option the day it was to expire. Maxwell's stock was trading at 155 pence. Since Goldman could sell the Maxwell stock back to Maxwell at 185 pence, the firm locked in a substantial profit—said to be around $4.5 million—on those Maxwell shares. "We did nothing illegal or wrong," a Goldman official told the *Times* in December 1991. According to *The Economist,* in December 1991, "Goldman insists throughout this buying spree it was acting as a conventional market maker. The firm expected to sell the shares to Maxwell, but had no prior agreement to do so. The proof is in the risk it took. At the end of November 1990, Maxwell rebuffed an offer from [Sheinberg] to sell its entire positions," then about 30 million shares. Goldman took a loss of "several million dollars" as a result when it had to mark its holding to the prevailing market price of 140 pence.

On January 4, Maxwell sold Goldman another put option, this time for 30 million Maxwell Communications shares at 152 pence each, two pence above the prevailing price. On February 15, Goldman exercised the option, selling Maxwell the block of stock at three pence above the market price. Goldman made another windfall. In the spring, Goldman started lending Maxwell money—as much as $75 million—secured by

33 million Maxwell Communications shares and then, after it went public in May 1991, 40 million Mirror Group shares, about 10 percent of the company. More than three months late, on August 14, Goldman got around to disclosing to the British authorities that it owned around 7.5 percent of Maxwell Communications, which was a part of its collateral for its loans to Maxwell. Goldman said it "made an honest mistake" in not disclosing the position sooner. "Maxwell's hunger for cash and willingness to sign away the public companies were the first public signs of his mounting panic," *The Economist* observed.

Indeed, this turned out to be typical Maxwell. He had pledged the stock he owned in his public companies as collateral for loans he had received to finance his acquisition spree and his private companies. He also cadged from his employee pension funds. Some have argued that Maxwell granted the unusually large put options to Goldman at 185 pence as a way to keep the value of the stock high since it was being used as collateral for as much as $4.4 billion in debt. If someone—it turned out to be Maxwell, although no one knew that at the time, except for perhaps Goldman—was willing to pay 185 pence for the stock, it must be worth at least that amount. That is why Kenny, the research analyst, concluded the share price had been manipulated. (The DTI concluded pretty much the same thing, too.)

Beginning in August 1991, Goldman became increasingly skeptical of the financial health of Maxwell's empire. On August 2, as Maxwell was contemplating spinning off his businesses in the United States— Macmillan Inc. and Official Airline Guide—and loading them up with some of his debt, Goldman and Merrill Lynch attempted to sell $75 million in Official Airline Guide preferred stock. But the auction failed to find buyers at acceptable rates and signaled that trouble could be afoot. Maxwell denied there were any financial problems at his company and vowed to try to sell the preferred again on September 20. "It will be successful," he said. On August 12, Maxwell telephoned Sheinberg and told him he would not make a $35 million loan payment to Goldman due that day. "Mr. Sheinberg told us that this was the first time Robert Maxwell had reneged on a deal and that it represented the end of their business relationship," according to the DTI report. "From that time on Goldman Sachs' efforts were directed to obtaining repayment of the loans they had made and settlement of the outstanding transactions."

When Goldman and Merrill tried again to sell the preferred, it again failed to find buyers. With the knowledge that Maxwell was having trouble getting new financing, in a replay of Penn Central, Goldman started pressing him to repay its $75 million of loans. On October 22,

Sheinberg met with Maxwell one last time to try to get him to repay the money owed to Goldman, then three months overdue. If Goldman was not repaid immediately, Goldman would sell the Maxwell Communications shares it held as collateral. "If you do that, you'll kill me," Maxwell told Sheinberg. When he did not make the agreed-upon payments, Goldman started selling the Maxwell stock it had as collateral. That day, Goldman sold 9 million shares. In response, Maxwell agreed to make a payment on October 29. When he failed to make that payment, Goldman told him it would sell more collateral. Despite a request by Maxwell's son, Kevin, not to do so, on October 31, Goldman sold another 2.2 million shares. Goldman continued to sell Maxwell shares for the next five days.

On November 4, Eugene Fife, a London partner, called Edward George, deputy governor of the Bank of England, and told him there would be a public announcement that Goldman had been selling the Maxwell Communications shares it held as collateral for the loans Goldman had made to Maxwell. According to George's notes from the conversation, "Gene Fyfe [sic], Chairman of Goldman Sachs, telephoned the Deputy Governor on 4 November to inform him that Goldmans had decided to sell the collateral on two outstanding loans to Robert Maxwell, one for £20 million and one for £30 million. This action had been taken after Goldmans had granted several extensions to the loans. They had now got tired of waiting, particularly given that Maxwell appeared to have sold a number of entities recently, but had not distributed any of the proceeds to Goldmans. The collateral consisted of a block of Mirror Group stock and a block of Maxwell Communications stock. Goldmans intended to sell the Maxwell Communications stock first and to do it as quietly as possible in the hope that there would be no disruption to the market. Maxwell himself was aware of Goldmans' intentions."

On November 5, at 1:05 p.m., Goldman's message about the sale of the Maxwell Communications stock hit the newswire. Within hours, Maxwell was dead. At the time of Maxwell's death, Goldman still owned 24 million shares, which quickly became worthless as Maxwell's scheme unraveled. At the time of Maxwell's death, he still owed Goldman $62 million. According to the DTI report, Maxwell denied having manipulated the price of Maxwell Communications stock by entering into the put agreements with Goldman. "The suggestion that I distorted the shares in MCC is untrue," he said. "I did not support the share price with a view to deceiving or distorting the market and such actions as I have taken have not been designed to preserve my personal wealth at the expense of others."

But the relationship between Maxwell and Goldman was fraught with contradictions and disagreements, including about the nature of the relationship itself. For instance, Kevin Maxwell, one of his father's trusted advisers and executives (who was later accused and acquitted of criminal charges in the matter), told the DTI that during 1990 and 1991, his father and Sheinberg spoke daily whether Maxwell was in "London, New York or on the yacht." His father was "exceptionally vulnerable to any trader who described a strategy that would lead to an increase in the Maxwell Communications Corporation share price" and that "faced with such a strategy Maxwell would always be a purchaser and Mr. Sheinberg exploited that." Kevin Maxwell said that Sheinberg told his father that Goldman would "mop up shares in the market, enforce physical delivery by short sellers and so cause the price to rise." The strategy "would get rid of the bears and, in Mr. Sheinberg's phrase, 'reduce the liquidity of the stock in the market,' thus improving the share price. They agreed on this strategy and, if Robert Maxwell heard there was a bear raid on [Maxwell] shares, he would at once telephone Mr. Sheinberg."

Kevin Maxwell recalled "conversations between Robert Maxwell and Mr. Sheinberg when the talk was of driving the share price up to £4, £5 even £10." Robert Maxwell "believed Mr. Sheinberg when he said he would do this, as he believed Mr. Sheinberg was assisting him as his client," he told the DTI. When Kevin Maxwell questioned this, his father told him he knew nothing and that "the great Mr. Sheinberg knew everything, as was his belief from the many deals done since 1986." Kevin Maxwell did not regard this to be a wrongful manipulation of the market but, rather, using a market maker to counteract those who were manipulating the price of Maxwell shares downward. Kevin Maxwell concluded that "[i]t was plain that Mr. Sheinberg must have come to the view at some time that Robert Maxwell was fixated on the share price and as a result moved from someone carrying out a trade to someone who would scheme against his client. Mr. Sheinberg had lied to Robert Maxwell."

For his part, Sheinberg told the DTI that "there was never any agreement with Robert Maxwell to cause the price to rise," that "he always followed his own trading strategy and never described it to" Maxwell, that "it would have been irrational to commit himself to a fixed trading strategy," that he "may have spoken to Robert Maxwell about the share price going to £4, £5 or even £10, but that was in the context of what might possibly happen if there was a large short position," and that "he did not speak daily with Robert Maxwell."

In other words, there was total disagreement between the two sides. Goldman told the DTI that the firm made approximately £23 million from its dealings with Maxwell. Sheinberg told the DTI that Maxwell was not a "sucker" but rather a "trader's trader," and in DTI's words, "someone who would decide quickly whether or not he wanted to deal and who traded on instinct and impulse."

The fallout from Maxwell's sudden death and the subsequent unraveling of his financial empire cast yet another unwelcome light on Goldman Sachs, leading Friedman to reach the wise decision that 1993 would not be a good time for Goldman to consider an IPO. "I could see the Maxwell thing wasn't resolved," Friedman said. "You could see where it was going. But that took a lot of time, a lot of attention. It was very, very painful." With Maxwell, Goldman had failed to follow, in dramatic fashion, one of the cardinal rules of trading and market making: know your customer. "Of all the reputations smudged by the scandal, that of Goldman Sachs, an American investment bank, was the brightest," *The Economist* reported soon after Maxwell's death.

BEFORE LONG, 1994 would bring a whole new set of problems to 85 Broad Street. As 1993 was drawing to a close, the idea of retiring was on Friedman's mind. Whether he wanted his legacy to be the $2.7 billion in pretax profits or whether he was just exhausted from grappling alone—without his wingman—with the ongoing fallout of Goldman's numerous scandals and the job of running a hugely complex, global enterprise remains unclear. There is no question that being the sole senior partner of Goldman Sachs was taking its toll on Friedman. Where he once could divide up international travel and flag-waving with Rubin, in 1993 Friedman was on his own. There were also questions raised about both his physical and his mental health. People would often come up to him and tell him he didn't look well. He knew he felt tired but began to think there was something more to his chronic fatigue. Occasionally, when he would travel, Friedman would experience heart arrhythmia, where his heartbeat would speed up dramatically and uncontrollably. Understandably, this ailment made him very nervous about flying, something that others noticed.

But Friedman kept forging ahead and, for the longest time, failed to have his ailments checked out medically. He also knew that Sidney Weinberg had died soon after retiring and Gus Levy had died in office, so to speak. "I had no desire to die in the saddle and no desire to get greener and greener in the saddle," he said. "But, also, hey, there's a lot of other stuff out there in the world. And I'd like to have time to think about it and explore it. It'd be kind of sad if you were just doing the same thing over and over."

Whatever the reason—health, fatigue, exasperation, a feeling of accomplishment, or perhaps some revisionist history—Friedman decided at the beginning of January 1994 that he wanted to retire at the end of the year. "I wanted to do it young enough so that I could do something else with my life," he said. "I always thought it would be kind of a sad thing if you had nothing but life inside one firm." He told his wife. He told Robert Rubin, then at the White House, over dinner in Washington. And he told Robert Katz, Goldman's general counsel, who following tradition had come to Goldman from Sullivan & Cromwell and who had helped Friedman put out the Freeman, Eisenberg, and Maxwell fires. The crucial piece of the strategy—much like Whitehead's years earlier—was not to tell anyone about the decision, including the other Goldman partners, lest it risk making Friedman a lame-duck executive. Instead, he would drop amorphous hints here and there that he might be starting to think about moving on.

But from the outset, Friedman's strategy ran into trouble. He had hoped to designate Henry Paulson, a highly respected investment banker from Chicago, as the firm's sole next senior partner. Friedman and Paulson were simpatico—as an M&A banker and client banker would be—and Friedman had a deep regard for how highly Paulson's clients respected him and eagerly sought his counsel. "Hank would be the first guy to tell you that he's not Mr. Smooth," Friedman said. "He just happens to be a terrific talent and I noticed early on that here was a young investment banker and the leading CEOs in Chicago were leaning on him." CEOs would ask to speak with Paulson privately after a meeting and not just rely on him to "deliver the firm" by making sure an M&A team or equity–capital markets team was available. "That's heavy and he had good judgment," Friedman said. "And he was smart and it used to irritate the merger guys because after he'd heard their pitch at board meetings a few times he could do it himself just as well." Starting in 1990, Paulson was one of the three co-heads of investment banking at Goldman, with Willard J. "Mike" Overlock, who had been running the merger department, and Bob Hurst, who had been running the investment banking services group. They were known as the "Three Nots"— "Not Here, Not Smart, and Not Nice." Paulson was "Not Here," in that he lived in Chicago. He also spent huge amounts of his time building up Goldman's presence in Asia, especially in China, where early on he befriended the country's leaders and perceived its potential as a land of business opportunity for clever investment bankers. The "Not Here" name stuck, even though he spent plenty of time in New York, too.

Just as Friedman was deciding to retire at the end of 1993, coincidentally Paulson told Friedman he was thinking of leaving Goldman. They were having a conversation one weekend, and Paulson was at his modest home in Barrington, Illinois, on a plot of land he had bought from his family's nearby farm. "Not because I wanted a promotion," Paulson said, "but I'd had opportunities to do a couple other things. I was questioning whether I might want a different career, as much as I liked Goldman Sachs." He had been approached about being the dean of a few business schools and about being a senior executive at an industrial company. He also thought about indulging his lifelong passion for conservation, bird-watching, and fishing. He also dreamed of writing novels. "I'd have liked to be another Faulkner, of course," he said. Knowing Paulson's potential departure might foil his own plans and be a major loss to the firm, given his moneymaking skills, Friedman invited Paulson and his wife, Wendy, to have dinner with him and his wife, Barbara, in New York. At the dinner, Friedman dropped a few not-so-subtle clues. "I might not be here forever," Friedman told Paulson. "I'm looking to you for the future." But Paulson missed the message, especially since Rubin and Friedman had only started running the firm at the end of 1990. "So, you've just got to understand from my perspective I thought, well, that just meant he wasn't going to go out with his boots on like Gus Levy," he said. In any event, Friedman could not sell the idea of Paulson to Katz, who didn't think Paulson had enough political support on the Management Committee at that time to be the sole leader of the firm.

So Friedman took a new tack: he started to urge pairs of partners to work together on various projects to see if any two of them could gel the way he and Rubin had. He pushed Paulson together with Corzine to work on various projects, and he pushed Winkelman to work with Roy Zuckerberg, the head of equities. This felt a bit awkward to Paulson. "I would come to New York, work, and then get out of New York," he said. "I didn't go out to dinner with other people on the Management Committee. I didn't socialize. I didn't politic." Friedman kept urging Paulson to be more sociable. "He started saying to me, 'Well, I'd like you to get to know Jon Corzine better,'" Paulson recalled. "'I'd like you to know Jon Corzine. Spend time with Jon Corzine.' And I was little thick. And then finally he said, 'You like Asia. He likes Asia. Why don't you two take a trip together through Asia?'" Paulson and Corzine traveled to Asia together to wave the Goldman flag. Paulson went alone; Corzine traveled with an entourage.

Paulson missed this message, too. "We were both interested in Asia," he said of his trips with Corzine, "and with his understanding of the trading and the sales side, I took it as the two of us going around and sending the right signal to people there. Not that 'We should be cooperating better or working better together when we made these business decisions in Asia.' It hadn't occurred to me that we were going to be joined in some way to help run the firm."

———

BUT MUCH OF this social calculus quickly got pushed to the back burner as the firm's traders started to stumble—badly—racking up huge losses during 1994 of as much as $100 million, or more, a month. "I don't like the feel of this," Friedman remembered thinking. "Our trading is not right and they think they're better than they are. They did real well in 1992 and 1993 but I think they were shooting fish in a barrel." Especially on the heels of the huge profits the year before, these ongoing losses rattled the firm and raised the question for the first time about how the loss of Rubin was affecting Goldman. "They were a great pair," one partner said of Rubin and Friedman. "They trusted each other, liked each other, collaborated. They complemented each other. Bob understood the sales and trading much better than Steve. It didn't seem that disruptive when Bob left, because the firm went on to have these fabulous years. But the thing that disrupted the transition was when we had the significant trading losses." By the early 1990s, Goldman "hardly lived up to its century-old image as a staid investment bank making money through old-line relationships," Steven Drobny observed in *Inside the House of Money,* his 2006 book about how hedge-fund traders make money. "Rather, it turned into one of the biggest proprietary risk-takers among investment banks, with its traders making huge bets with the firm capital in global fixed-income, foreign exchange, commodities and derivatives."

What tripped up Goldman's traders was a massive wrong-way bet on interest rates. "Credit spreads just blew out," Paulson explained. Recalled another Goldman partner, "In December 1993, the Fed raised interest rates, and it just completely fucked up the firm's trading position. And the firm didn't really know what the risks were." Goldman's biggest losses were in the fixed-income arbitrage "book" of Michael O'Brien, who was running trading in London. He was heading up a firm of proprietary traders composed, in large part, of people who came from J. Aron. Christian Siva-Jothy worked for O'Brien as a proprietary trader in London at the time, having joined Goldman from Citibank in March 1992. He found the trading culture at Goldman diametrically opposed to that of Citibank. During his first week at Goldman, he placed a $50 million bet involving deutsche marks and Swiss francs. It was Siva-Jothy's largest trade ever. That first week, O'Brien came by and asked him how things were going. "I'm short 50 mark Swiss," he told O'Brien.

"I like a guy who averages into his positions," O'Brien deadpanned before turning and walking off.

"It was a bit of a free for all at [Goldman] in the early 1990s," Siva-Jothy explained, "but the opportunities were there. There were no limit structures per se, no value-at-risk system. It was just kind of get on and do it and hope for the best." He described the attitude at the time among Goldman's proprietary traders as "suck it and see," which translated into English roughly as "if you want to try a big position, try it" and "make mistakes but learn from them." He recalled a moment during Goldman's 1993 bonanza when one trader went on the internal squawk box and said, "Buy Bunds," a reference to German federal government bonds. When a broker wanted to know how many Bunds he should be buying, the reply came: "I said buy Bunds. I'll tell you when to stop."

Another time, Goldman's chief economist in London, Gavyn Davies, came by the proprietary trading desk to offer his macroeconomic view of the world. One trader cut Davies off and "with his boots up on the desk," told him, "With all due respect, Gavyn, I do my own research. I was in quite a few bars in Spain last weekend and let me tell you something—they were empty." He followed this bit of trenchant analysis with another: "I've got another rule that I live by: 'If you can't drink the water, sell the currency.'"

Siva-Jothy said he found the Goldman approach "incredibly powerful" and a "wonderful environment in which to work" but also "it was to have its downside as we discovered in 1994." Siva-Jothy realized that at some point in 1993, it seemed like every trader at Goldman in London had become a proprietary trader. "There were 500-plus prop traders at Goldman Sachs then and they all had the same position," he said. He made "well over $100 million" in profits that year "and I was a bit full of myself."

The dynamic began to change in December 1993. Siva-Jothy had made a massive bet that the British pound would rise against the yen. "It was over £1 billion, which was the biggest position I'd ever run," he said. The bet paid off in December and January as the pound rose in value. He was up about $30 million on the trade. "People were starting to say, 'Christian is going to do it again,'" he recalled. He was so confident, he even added to his position by selling puts.

In February, disaster struck. Not only were the monthly British inflation numbers terrible but also President Clinton had blasted the Japanese on their trading policies, threatening tariffs and quotas. "Sterling went into a free fall," he observed. "It was classic—the market found me." During the course of fifteen trading days in February, the pound lost

10 percent of its value against the yen. "I was selling out of the position as fast as I could but I was selling just to stand still because I was short these puts," he said. "It was a disaster. Markets have a great way of taking it out of you." At one point during the trade's collapse, Siva-Jothy remembered being overcome by a desire to stand up and walk out. But he stayed and took the pain. By the time the final accounting was in, Siva-Jothy had lost somewhere between $100 million and $200 million—and he was just one trader making one bet.

Another trader, Lawrence Becerra, had joined Goldman in London in 1992 as a senior proprietary trader. "Becerra was probably the trader with the highest appetite for risk of all of those people," remembered David Schwartz. Becerra had put on a large trade involving the Italian Treasury market. "They kept on piling on the position," Schwartz said, "and it kept on going against him. And the culture at the time—and this was throughout the trading culture—was that you don't tell a trader what to do. And O'Brien obviously understood that they were losing money and losing a lot of it, but Becerra believed in the trade and, I guess, Mike did as well. But the trade just never worked out. Eventually, they had to cut it, and in cutting it, they lost even more money."

Before long, the losses in London had spiraled so far out of control, Corzine and Winkelman flew to London to see if anything could be salvaged from the trading positions. Winkelman met with Siva-Jothy. "Christian, sit down, what's this all about?" Winkelman asked him.

"I've lost [more than $100 million]," he said. "I've liquidated everything. What do you want me to do?"

"If you hadn't liquidated and come in here, you wouldn't be working at Goldman Sachs anymore," Winkelman told him. "What I want you to do now is go out and make it back, with lower risk limits." Siva-Jothy was surprised—and impressed—that he hadn't been fired. (He actually was promoted to run the entire revamped proprietary trading desk in Europe.) He then established a new trade betting that fixed-income securities would fall in value. When the Fed started tightening the money supply and interest rates rose, bond prices fell, and his short bet began paying off. He made back about 35 percent of what he had lost.

Back in New York, though, the losses were still resonating. "When the market went against us, the lesson I took away was the lack of discipline in that department," Paulson said. "And a real lack of rigor. And there was an arrogance: 'We know that the market's going to be like this . . . and we like it better every month. Because we just think the markets are going to come back.' Of course, Goldman Sachs wasn't a hedge fund. And we just couldn't afford to do that. There wasn't the level of scrutiny we should have had at the Management Committee level."

One of the problems, it turned out, was that Corzine was wearing two hats at once. He was both co-CFO and co-head of fixed-income. "He wasn't independent," explained one partner, from the investment banking side of Goldman. "You just really need independent control functions and it just is critical that you have that to run any kind of trading business. You need to have people on the control side and the compliance side to independently mark the books, to go head to head with the traders, to have a totally independent career track. And you need to look at everything in terms of the size. You know Bob Rubin always talked about small but deep holes. You can't afford to lose a lot of money even if the odds are very low. You just have to protect yourself."

One of the ways Friedman sought to protect the firm from the growing monthly losses was by cutting expenses, which on Wall Street means cutting people, since by far the largest single cost at a Wall Street firm was—and is—compensation. But Friedman was hesitant to unilaterally make the decision to cut people as the year unfolded, in part because he had already decided to retire and didn't think it would be fair to his partners to saddle them with the lower growth prospects that having fewer traders might cause. He also knew that it was possible that the trading environment could improve suddenly, and without traders in the seats, money could be left on the table. He put the question of cutting people to a vote, but he and the financial types were the only ones who thought the firm should do it. As the losses continued, Friedman broached the subject again, and again he got shot down. "I was always very, very careful with my management clout," he said. "When you are the senior partner at Goldman Sachs, you have more power than you needed. Your job was to make sure that people felt included and free and empowered and obliged to tell you stuff you didn't want to hear. I would always lean over backward to get people involved in the decisions."

But by the summer, as the trading losses mounted, Friedman was increasingly frazzled. Bob Hurst remembered seeing Friedman in Jackson Hole, Wyoming, where they both have homes, and thinking that the senior partner was hurting. " 'Your job's impossible,' " Hurst remembered telling Friedman. " 'I have no interest in it.' I said it from a perspective of I thought he had a couple of years to go and not that he was quitting that fall." Another partner put it more bluntly: "Steve hated his job as CEO. He hated it because he felt he had lost control of his life."

Hurst remembered hearing about a telephone call between Friedman and Corzine where Corzine told Friedman that another $50 million had been lost in London that week. Friedman was trying to get Corzine to cut back the trading positions. "He just won't do it," Friedman told Hurst. "He says it's a great trade." Part of the problem for Friedman was that, without Rubin, he was not expert enough in fixed-income to know for sure whether to overrule Corzine. The other part of the problem was that 1992 and 1993 had been such amazingly profitable years in fixed-income that Corzine would have been difficult to overrule under any circumstances.

While Friedman couldn't stop the trade, he did start insisting that personnel cuts be made. "But people weren't as worried as I was," he said. Friedman started to micromanage. "I spent a lot of time with the traders," he said. "I was not really happy with how a lot of that was going. We were in an industry-wide bear market and our traders were out of sync. I really made them contract a lot of their positions. I'd see guys who hadn't made any money in their positions for whatever the hell it was, nine out of ten months. . . . So, we reduced our positions sharply and maintained a lot of liquidity. I did feel our traders had been much too confident about their abilities."

As the year dragged on, the pain across the Goldman partnership became more acute. "Every month, Corzine and Winkelman would stand up and say, 'I'm sorry, guys, we've lost another hundred and fifty million bucks,'" remembered one partner from the banking side of Goldman. "My capital account in 1993 was like seven million dollars, something like that. And it went down to four million dollars. Every month, it went down three hundred thousand, four hundred thousand dollars. And you're just saying like, 'What the fuck? This is unbelievable.' It was pretty out of control, but no one knew. People were just completely off the reservation." There was also a growing concern among the partners that because their liability was not limited, their entire net worth was on the line as the losses mounted. Some partners were beginning to think that everything they had built up for so long at Goldman might be at serious risk of being lost, since their capital remained at the firm and their annual cash compensation was limited to an 8 percent dividend on their capital account. "Partners are seen outside as mega-rich, but that is not the case at all," Mike O'Brien told *The Independent*, a U.K. newspaper, in September 1992. "Their capital stays with the firm. My C-registration Ford Granada is testament to that." (On the other hand, one of O'Brien's London partners, David Morrison, drove a Ferrari around town.) For the banking partner who started 1994 with a $7 million capital account and ended with a $4 million capital account, after absorbing the trading losses, his cash compensation for the year decreased to $320,000, from $560,000. Suddenly, some serious sand had been tossed into the gravy train's engine.

Toward the end of the August, while his concern for both his own and the firm's health continued to increase, Friedman's hints about his future were becoming less opaque. "We had a really bad dynamic in the firm," Corzine recalled. "It was made all the worse almost every other day by something coming out about Maxwell. Pretty tense period of time." Finally, a decision was made to cut the losses on the bad trades. "It didn't matter how intelligent the trades were . . . ," Corzine said, but a change had to be made. "I didn't think it was existential. But you *have* to stay calm or you can't make good decisions. Otherwise, you end up making an emotional decision as opposed to a calculated, probability-based decision."

Corzine also remembered a conversation he had with Friedman in the late summer that left him "with the idea" that the senior partner was getting ready to retire. "We had an indirect conversation that led me to believe my promotion was what would take place," Corzine said. He could tell something was not right with Friedman. "He did not feel well," he continued. "You could see it on his face as we were trying to get our world squared. As for Steve, it wasn't obvious that it was only a health issue that was troubling him. This was another one of those times when people who run firms that take on risk—they may earn a lot of money, but they earn their keep." Other partners were aware of Friedman's health problems, too. "He had things where his heart, when he traveled—it's just the rigors of the job—and his heartbeat would speed way up," one of them said. "And it scared him."

––––––

THROUGHOUT 1994, Friedman and Katz had had a number of dinners to discuss how the succession plan at the firm would unfold. They intentionally chose to meet in offbeat neighborhoods around New York where they assumed few Goldman partners would be hanging out. At the first dinner, they chose an Italian restaurant on West Seventeenth Street, far from the usual haunts of the Upper East Side, but were interrupted by a partner who was dining there.

By discussing repeatedly how the announcement should be made and how the new senior partner should be selected, Friedman and Katz were hoping to avoid the internecine political warfare that generally accompanies Wall Street succession. "I wanted to avoid anything that was political, and I wanted to give myself and other management committee members the opportunity to continue to evaluate how different people worked together," Friedman explained in October 1994. "We had seen numerous firms in which the succession dragged on and had been the subject of rumors and, thus, divisions, or where they had a long, drawn-out transition with too many hands on the steering wheel. We were convinced our firm could avoid that."

Friedman had wanted to "drop his bombshell" in August, but after more conversations with Katz and Rubin, he decided that the Management Committee's schedules would be easier to coordinate after Labor Day, when everyone was back in New York after the summer holidays. On Tuesday, September 6, the calls went out to the Management Committee to make sure they were in New York the next day. "I had no special call from him," Paulson said. "No warning. We were told we were supposed to be there. He wanted us all there." Usually, Paulson would join the Management Committee meetings from Chicago by videoconference and would often forget that he was on camera and start reading the newspaper. Someone in New York would step out of the meeting and call him and tell him, "Don't forget you're on the screen. Stop picking your nose."

This time, Paulson flew to New York. "I knew something was up," he said. "It was right after Labor Day." For Bob Hurst, who is Jewish, attending the special Wednesday meeting meant not observing the second day of Rosh Hashanah as he usually did. But Bob Katz insisted he be there. When Hurst asked Katz what the meeting was about, he told him, "I can't tell you." When everyone on the Management Committee had assembled, Friedman told his most senior partners that within the next week, he planned to retire and to name his successor, or successors. "It was an enormous shock," Hurst said. Another partner told Friedman to stop joking around. "I'm not kidding," Friedman said. Paulson, for one, could not believe what he was hearing. Had Friedman lost his mind? Right afterward, he went to see Friedman, alone. "You can't leave right in the middle of all this," Paulson said he told him. "You've got to stay for a transition." Without going into too much detail, that's when Friedman told Paulson about his heart ailment. Paulson was shocked but didn't say much. "Steve looked younger than I did," recalled one Management Committee member when Friedman later told him, too, about his health issues. "He was vigorous. I had no idea until he told me about the problem. And so it just came as a shock. . . . The pressure was immense. I think people that criticize him and come down hard on him for it—John Weinberg and others did—never knew what he was going through, never walked in his shoes." Barbara Friedman was especially concerned that he had informed his partners that his decision was definitive and final. He assured her that he had been crystal clear.

Suddenly, despite the best efforts of Friedman and Katz to plan out the succession, the power vacuum at the top of Goldman Sachs was palpable for the first time. Other leadership changes at the firm may have been equally sudden—for instance, after Levy's death or Catchings's decapitation—but the successors had been carefully groomed or were obvious. Not in 1994. An immediate power struggle ensued, unlike any other in the firm's long history. What made the dynamic even more intense was Friedman's directive to the group that he intended to announce the new leadership team at the regularly scheduled monthly partners' meeting the following Monday, five days later. The decision had to be made by Sunday night. "There were guys who had the bit in their mouth and really wanted to run Goldman," said a member of the Management Committee.

Although there were twelve members of the Management Committee at that time, there were only a handful of likely contenders to lead the firm. Paulson had emerged as a favorite of Friedman's and a proven rainmaker, but his support was limited to the investment bankers. Paulson's co-heads of investment banking—Hurst and Overlock—were possible, too, but considered more long shots. (Hurst especially became a long shot after he inadvertently confessed to Friedman in Wyoming that he didn't want the job.) There was also Roy Zuckerberg, the oldest member of the Management Committee, but although he wanted the job, few saw him as anything more than a self-promoter and an interim solution at best. Corzine and Winkelman, the two co-heads of fixed-income, were both serious contenders for the top job, despite presiding over the huge losses the firm was—still—experiencing in 1994. Winkelman, known by some at the firm as the "Grim Reaper" for personnel cuts he had made at J. Aron, was very highly regarded not only for the turnaround he had engineered at J. Aron but also for the success the firm had in fixed-income in 1992 and 1993. He had been appointed co-head of fixed-income, in part, to tame some of Corzine's more reckless trading instincts. "Mark had turned out to be enormously talented," Rubin recalled, "and, although I was responsible for [J. Aron], Mark was the one who really went around and figured out how to reposition the company, so it became an immensely profitable activity."

Not surprisingly, the combination of Friedman's announcement and his stated goal of having a new leader, or leaders, anointed quickly set off a fierce round of jockeying for power. Immediate comparisons were made between Goldman's Management Committee and the Vatican. People were looking for puffs of smoke everywhere. Friedman, then fifty-six years old, admitted as much. "Our management committee is like a college of cardinals," he said. "They're very talented people, and in the college of cardinals, a substantial number of them have a reasonable, legitimate belief that they should be elevated. I'd be wary of a firm that didn't have a large number of people with the self-confidence to think of themselves as capable of taking the top job. I think that's an absolute sign of strength."

Paulson was Friedman's preferred choice to lead the firm in the wake of his abdication. "You've got to recognize I was in Chicago," Paulson said; "people didn't know me very well. I didn't look like an investment banker, didn't dress like an investment banker, didn't talk like an investment banker, was rough around the edges and had a *lot* I had to learn. I questioned, frankly, that maybe I wasn't ready, but I was sure a lot readier to run the firm after being in New York and in the trenches there for a few years than I was stepping right in from Chicago." To a number of the Goldman intelligentsia, the choice of Paulson seemed implausible at best. He was a relatively unknown coverage banker from Chicago with a certain bull-in-the-china-shop demeanor and had very little understanding or knowledge of the trading side of the business. But he was a major producer of business. "Hank had the nerves of a bandit," Rob Kaplan, a former senior investment banker at the firm, remembered from the days when they worked together on Inland Steel and Outboard Marine.

Paulson had always cultivated Friedman. The two men were friends, having found common ground as athletes. Indeed, at an offsite in Westchester County a few years after Paulson had joined Goldman, Friedman, the national wrestling champion at Cornell, challenged Paulson, a former All-American lineman at Dartmouth, to a wrestling match. Paulson had done some intramural wrestling at Dartmouth but hadn't wrestled since he was eighteen. Still, he took one look at Friedman, who was smaller and lighter, and felt a bit sorry for him. Friedman, meanwhile, had kept fit working out with the Cornell wrestling team at the Downtown Athletic Club. "So I took him down, very quickly, with the fireman's carry," Paulson said. "The next thing I knew I was on my back. I'd never been pinned before. So I got angry. I thought, 'This little guy, I don't care if he *is* my boss, I'm going to pick him up and I'm going to hurt him.' I went back at him about five or six times. And I got pinned five or six times. The next morning when I was trying to get out of bed, it took all my pride and everything else to pretend like nothing had happened and to get out of bed and get dressed and get out there." Fortunately, his suit covered up his myriad of bruises and scrapes from the matches.

(Friedman also used to challenge Jide Zeitlin, another partner, who was a wrestler at Amherst, to impromptu wrestling matches.)

To check himself about Paulson, Friedman flew down to Washington and met Rubin at the White House—Rubin had not yet ascended to treasury secretary—to discuss the leadership matter with him. Rubin agreed that Paulson was the right person to lead the firm. After that meeting, Friedman approached Paulson. "He immediately made the pitch to me in the first meeting," Paulson recalled. "He hoped that I'd be one of the people that came and ran the firm." But he could hardly respond. "I was so taken aback and shocked by the whole thing that I just couldn't get my mind around it," he said. "I said good-bye to him and literally left. Didn't talk to anybody else. I got in a plane and flew back to Chicago." He called Wendy from the car and told her what had happened. "In the worst way she didn't want me to do it," he said. "I told her I thought it was very unlikely that I would. And that I thought there would be other people chosen." But, false modesty aside, Paulson did want the job as much as anyone else.

Friedman told the Management Committee he wanted to hear everyone's views about who the next leaders of the firm should be. He told them he wanted to meet, alone, with each member of the committee and go through the usual "crossruffing" of having them share with him what the best leadership structure should be along with whom they wanted to lead the firm. He asked them to write down their thoughts as well and encouraged them to meet together. They were stunned, and angry. "It took a number of the Management Committee partners by complete surprise," one senior Goldman executive explained. "I know that they were very angry. They expressed that anger to me. I was sort of surprised how angry they were. They felt that 1994 was not a great year for the firm and they felt that the firm was in real trouble. They needed stable leadership through the crisis, and they weren't getting it from him. They felt that he had left at the most inopportune moment."

Over the next two days, Friedman met with all but two members of the Management Committee in person; those two he spoke with by phone. He opted for this tight time frame as a way to avoid leaks—he figured the matter could be kept a secret for a week, at best—and to minimize the politicking. "I wanted to see as pure a decision as we could make it," he said. At one point, someone overheard David Silfen, a member of the Management Committee, say to Hurst, "I knew this was gonna be a bad year, Bob, but honestly, I had no idea how bad it would get."

While there is little question that, at the time, nearly every person on the Management Committee fantasized about running Goldman

Sachs—including Hurst—Hurst could see relatively quickly which way the tea leaves were trending. "Corzine was a given," he said. "There was no issue, I don't think, about Corzine. Corzine had wanted it. He was very aggressive about wanting it. He was our chief financial officer and he was co-head of the biggest division"—some at Goldman saw this dual role that Corzine had played as a major negative. "Fixed-income had to be represented in the equation. Jon was very personable and he was a man of the people. . . . Then the question was, what's the permutation? Is it co-heads? Is it one and two?"

What emerged was a surprising consensus that some combination of Corzine and Paulson should lead the firm. Indeed, a preponderance of the committee thought Corzine could lead the firm alone, although that view was tempered—insistently by the investment bankers—by the feeling that Corzine needed Paulson as a decisive number two. "There was no one or virtually no one other than Corzine or Paulson who would have had any votes for the job from someone other than themselves or from someone other than their best crony," Friedman said. "What you could safely say is, there would have been no broad support for anyone other than those two, and Corzine was accepted by most people as a part of the solution. Remarkably though, even by people who felt that way, it was, 'But you have to have someone strong paired with him.' I recollect no one other than Corzine being comfortable with Corzine alone. And most people thought Hank was the strongest one to be partnered with him."

By the weekend, when Paulson returned to New York, it was clear that some combination of Corzine and Paulson would be leading Goldman Sachs. The only open question was whether the two men could figure out an acceptable arrangement between themselves. Before Paulson left on Wednesday, in shock, for Chicago, sensing in what direction the decision would go, Friedman had urged Paulson to call Corzine and talk about working together. Paulson placed the call, but Corzine didn't return it. When they spoke a day or so later, Paulson recalled, "It was pretty clear to me that he wanted to do it by himself." This didn't feel right to Paulson. "I was really quite unsettled by the whole thing," he recalled. "Steve leaving so suddenly and the need to select new leaders in a week affected me." Before he flew back to New York, he told his wife, "I don't think you need to worry. I'm not sure I want to do this. I believe others will be chosen." He felt sure things wouldn't work out for him.

On Saturday, Friedman met with Corzine and Katz at his large Beekman Place apartment overlooking the East River. That was where Corzine announced definitively that he wanted to run the firm as CEO—even though the title made no sense in a partnership—and would accept

Paulson as his chief operating officer. "They nurtured me all along," Corzine said. "They put me in the CFO's position. They took me out of the trading room and had me talking to banks and other stakeholders. I began to recognize that they were thinking of me in bigger terms. It's a little bit like running for political office. You think, 'Maybe I have a chance to win the primary, maybe I have a chance to win the election.' But nothing in life is certain."

At Friedman's urging, Paulson had breakfast with Corzine. Paulson was staying at the Pierre, on Fifth Avenue, and they had breakfast there together on Sunday morning. "When you spend time with Jon you'll see he's a very charming guy, incredibly charming," one Goldman partner said. "But he's very indirect." At the breakfast, Corzine told Paulson, "I'll be the best partner you ever worked with." He also told Paulson he wanted to be the CEO and he wanted Paulson to be the COO. "I remember being willing—not because I was so eager to run the firm— but because that was what I'd always seen," Paulson said. "There had always been co-heads. We'd had John and John and Steve and Bob. We didn't have CEOs and COOs. There was no CEO. We were a partnership. The senior partners were our bosses but everyone on the Management Committee had a vote, so no one could really dictate."

After breakfast at the Pierre, the two Goldman partners headed to Central Park, where they continued their discussion while walking around. "After their walk Paulson was not quite sure what Corzine was saying" about how their power-sharing agreement would work. Paulson remembered. "He kept saying to me, 'You're not going to believe what a good partner I am or how well we will work together.' I remember thinking to myself, 'I'm not sure this is going to work. Am I going to do well at it? Am I going to like it? Are we going to work well together? And I certainly don't want to be a senior partner that quits. So I want this to work.' " From Central Park, they took a cab to Beekman Place. Paulson got out and went to speak with Friedman. Corzine went off with Bob Katz, his close ally.

When Paulson got up to apartment, Friedman asked him if he and Corzine had had a conversation. Paulson said they had spoken. "Well, he told you he wants to be senior partner and have you be COO?" Friedman asked.

"Well, he didn't say it quite that way," Paulson told Friedman. "I wasn't quite sure what he was saying."

"Well, that's what it is," Friedman told him. "And I think you should do this." Friedman later commented, "We came to believe their chemistry would be very good, and we had a good sense of optimism about it. They wanted to work together."

That afternoon, the Management Committee reconvened at the U.N. Plaza–Park Hyatt Hotel. Friedman officially nominated the two men, who then spoke briefly to their partners and answered questions. While the committee discussed the nominations, Paulson and Corzine left the room and went to watch the men's U.S. Open tennis final on television. Soon enough, the committee unanimously approved the new management team, with Corzine as CEO and Paulson as COO. After a quick champagne toast, the Management Committee turned its attention to the biannual process by which new partners would be named. Friedman called Whitehead and told him the news and then, that night, went to Scarsdale and had dinner with John Weinberg, the firm's senior chairman, and told him about his decision. "I really thank you for your sensitivity," Friedman said Weinberg told him, "and I understand and I appreciate this—your coming—and I understand." But Weinberg was not the least bit pleased that his careful succession plan had come totally unwound.

A number of Paulson's banking partners—for instance, Bob Hurst, Mike Overlock, and Gene Fife—on the Management Committee questioned his decision to be Corzine's deputy. They thought Paulson should have insisted on being a co-senior partner with Corzine in order to ensure that the firm's investment-banking partners felt sufficiently empowered. They thought Paulson should use the leverage they felt he had. "I remember afterwards members of the Management Committee saying to me, 'You shouldn't accept this position,'" Paulson said. But he told his colleagues, "Well, I feel comfortable with this to the extent I can feel comfortable. I feel uncomfortable with the arrangement generally. But this is either going to work between Jon and me or it's not going to work. And if it's not going to work, it's not going to make any difference if we're co-heads or whether we've got this other arrangement."

Paulson admitted that his argument to his fellow banking partners at the time was most likely a justification for not getting the support he needed from the Management Committee to become the co–senior partner. "On the other hand, you just need to realize how fast this whole thing came upon me," he said. "And what a huge thing it was. To move to New York, to be doing this job, to be tied as a co-head to someone I did not know." Corzine was likable enough and friendly—a politician even then—but the two men could not have been more different. Paulson remained hesitant. "I was not of the view that 'I am ready to run this firm, that I'm capable of running all aspects of it, I want to run it all, and, by God, I'm determined and I'm going to fight to do it,'" he said. "That was not my mind-set."

The next afternoon, on Monday, Friedman, Paulson, and Corzine told the 150 partners worldwide about the management change. One New York–based banking partner was in San Francisco that day and remembered being dumbfounded by the announcement. "I was listening to the call," he said, "and Steve Friedman gets on the phone. He goes, 'I'm not feeling well, and I'm gonna retire.' I'm thinking, 'Well, what the fuck?' We thought the firm was going under. . . . First of all, who were the senior partners of the firm? John Weinberg, Bob Rubin, Steve Friedman, Jon Corzine, Hank Paulson. Five CEOs in ten years. I mean, I can't even name a company, let alone a decent one, that's had five CEOs in ten years. In 1994, literally, people thought the firm was going bankrupt."

On September 13, Goldman announced that Friedman would retire in November and that Corzine, forty-seven, would succeed him as senior partner and chairman of the Management Committee—the CEO, in Corzine's mind—and Paulson, forty-eight, would "assume the No. 2 job," according to the *Times*, as vice chairman and chief operating officer. Friedman would join Weinberg as "senior chairman" of Goldman and move to the firm's office at the Seagram Building on Park Avenue. The news raised inevitable questions as to why Friedman had decided to leave. Was it his health, had he been toppled in a coup, or did he not have the right stuff to manage Goldman through the very difficult year? "When the job is done with maximum intensity, it can be more than a little tiring," Friedman wrote in a memo to the firm. But in an interview with the *Times*, he focused on other things. "How come I'm doing this?" he asked rhetorically. "Take a look at this view"—and then he pulled out a large photograph of the snow-covered mountains surrounding his home in Jackson Hole, Wyoming. "Now take a look at that view"—pointing out his office window at 85 Broad Street to a jumble of office towers and a sliver of a water view. "Which is better?" As for the rumors about his health, he denied them. "My health is great and that's how I want to keep it," he said. "Only on Wall Street do people think it bizarre that I don't want to spend half of my day on the telephone and the other half on an airplane." He said he ran up to six miles every day.

Coincidentally, Paulson also had his own health problems in 1994, although nobody inside Goldman Sachs was aware of them. Some people at his church on Central Park West who had heard Paulson discuss these health scares there recalled him describing them as being cancer, but he denied having said that was the disease, although he cannot be sure what it was. "As a Christian Scientist, I don't go to doctors and get diagnoses," he said. "I don't believe I was dealing with cancer. I sure didn't feel well for a period of time in early 1994, and in the summer of 1994, I remember working from home and doing a lot of praying for a couple months where I felt no energy at all. I didn't feel well until the problem was met. I have relied on prayer for health care all my life." He believes he has had many physical healings.

As for the idea that a cabal of unhappy partners had led an insurrection in part because of his "aloof" behavior, Friedman replied, "I'm not going to tell you that all hundred and fifty partners are happy. I've been described as aloof before. But we have had the most collegial Management Committee in my experience here. And it bothers me when someone outside of the firm says there's a mess here because there isn't." Corzine, too, denied the firm was having problems. "I wouldn't be jumping into a mess, willingly or unwillingly," he told the *Times*. Guy Moszkowski, then an analyst at Sanford C. Bernstein who covered the financial industry, observed that, in 1994, much of Wall Street was "going through the same thing. A top person leaving a firm is not going to leave because of the current environment." The *Times* noted that Corzine was "seen as more open and personable" than Friedman and that he was "popular with clients" and might be "better able to rally the sometimes contentious egos in an organization at which hundreds in the firm are millionaires." Paulson would likely be "simpatico" with Corzine, the paper reported, since he was an investment banker and could complement Corzine's trading skills. "They spoke warmly of working as a team," the paper said. Their fitness was also noted: Corzine was into longdistance running (as well as chess) and Paulson jogged at least three miles a day. Left unmentioned was the fact that Corzine had high blood pressure (and that once someone scared "the bejeezus out of him" by telling him about a correlation between deep lines in his earlobes—which he has—and heart attacks). No mention was made, of course, of Paulson's cancer scare. Friedman, Corzine, and Paulson also all wore similar Timex Ironman digital watches; Paulson's was a gift from Friedman. Corzine also sought to assuage Winkelman's hard feelings. "My relationship with Mark has been one of the great experiences of my life," he told *Institutional Investor*. "We sat in the same office; we shared high points and low points. I think he's one of the brightest, ablest people I've ever been around. Goldman Sachs is a hell of a lot better off with Mark helping build our future."

———

IN CHOOSING CORZINE and Paulson to lead the firm, Goldman's politburo could not have found two more different people. Corzine was born and raised on a family farm in Willey Station, Illinois—population forty. Corzine's family lived in the shadow of the Great Depression.

Using borrowed money, his grandfather had been a very successful farmer in the 1920s, owning 2,500 acres and a bank. He was a state assemblyman and a leader in the state Republican Party.

But during that financial crisis, his grandfather's family lost everything, an experience that understandably had a lasting effect on Corzine's father. "My father never had a credit card, was afraid of *any* kind of financial risk because he saw what happened to his father," Corzine said. His father, then sixteen years old, went to work in a coal mine. After serving in World War II and fighting in the Battle of the Bulge, his father rented about 120 acres of farmland from his aunt—he was a "tenant farmer," Corzine said. His father sold insurance at night to supplement the family's modest income. His mother taught elementary school for thirty years.

Corzine went to the Taylorville public schools. His focus in high school was sports—basketball and football—and trying to get the occasional date. "It was a very happy time of life to be honest," he said. He was a six-foot two-inch guard on the high-school team, where basketball was a form of religion. He was the captain. He was also the starting quarterback of the high-school football team for three years. Playing sports in high school taught him the clichéd lessons about how to get through life. "You've got to work for everything you do," he said. "And when you get beat, you've got to get up. You've got to work together, particularly if you're not the smartest or you're not the biggest or you're not a Michael Jordan. It was a great life lesson."

He had his first job when he was thirteen, selling hot dogs during the summer at the county fair. A few years later, in addition to athletics and schoolwork, he ran a dance hall at the fairgrounds. Then for a couple of summers he worked on a construction site, helping to build a nuclear power plant.

After graduating from high school in 1965, Corzine went to the University of Illinois at Urbana-Champaign, forty-five miles away. "I used to say the biggest change that ever happened in my life wasn't coming from Chicago to New York, or Columbus to New York, but was going from Taylorville to the University of Illinois, which had about fifty thousand kids," Corzine said. In addition to being inexpensive—a couple of hundred dollars per semester—his high-school sweetheart, Joanne Dougherty, was also going to Illinois. At Illinois, he majored in economics.

After he and Joanne married and graduated from college in 1969, they packed up their belongings into a U-Haul and drove to California, where Corzine had been accepted into the PhD program in economics at UCLA. He attended four weeks of classes and then got the inevitable: a letter from the Taylorville draft board ordering him into the armed forces. "If you came from a place like Christian County, which is where I was from, you might as well just drive on down to the induction center," he said. He decided to enlist in the marines and served his basic training in San Diego. His drill sergeant nicknamed him "the Professor." "I was the only college graduate in my platoon . . . ," he said. "I remember getting the shit kicked out of me regularly."

From boot camp, Corzine spent some time at Camp Pendleton, in California, learning how to shoot a mortar, but he was never called on to serve in Vietnam. By this time, Joanne was pregnant, and the Corzines moved back to Taylorville, where Joanne got a job teaching school. Corzine tried to find work, without luck, and eventually he moved to Chicago. He sent around his résumé to all the banks and finally got hired, in 1970, to work in the back office at Continental Illinois National Bank and Trust advising smaller community banks in Illinois, Wisconsin, and Michigan about their investment portfolios. He traveled three days a week. At night, he studied for his MBA at the University of Chicago, part of which was paid for by the bank. Corzine remembered taking a night course with Fischer Black, then a professor at the University of Chicago. "I swear I don't know what the course was about to this day," he said. "It was all equations, all the time, and he gave me a C plus. He was very kind. That was the moral equivalent of flunking." (Black later won the Nobel Prize in economics and became a Goldman Sachs partner, thanks in part to Corzine.)

After three years traipsing around the Midwest for Continental Illinois while simultaneously studying at the University of Chicago and raising a baby daughter, he decided to quit the bank to be a full-time MBA student. To pay for the final year at Chicago, he borrowed from his credit card—just what his father would never do. "That's true of all this baby boom generation," he said. "They learned to borrow early and big."

By the time Corzine graduated from the University of Chicago, in 1973, he wanted to work on Wall Street. Both Merrill and Salomon rejected him. Fortunately, his former boss at Continental Illinois had moved to Bank One in Columbus, Ohio, and hired Corzine to help him manage the bank's bond portfolio, deciding what municipal and Treasury securities to buy and sell.

An institutional bond salesman at Goldman, in Chicago, used to call on Corzine at Bank One to sell the bank government bonds. They spoke on the phone most days and eventually the Goldman salesman decided to ask Corzine if he wanted to interview for a job at Goldman. The firm had just started building up its fixed-income group after years of neglect, and a Chicago MBA seemed to be a valuable credential, along with his experience at Bank One. Corzine suffered the usual endurance test of twenty interviews, culminating in meeting George Ross, who was head of Goldman's Philadelphia office but was then running fixed-income. Corzine had never met anyone at Goldman in New York before he showed up there in 1975 for his first day of work. "First time I ever came to New York was the first day I walked in the front door at Goldman Sachs," he said. "Never been to New York before. I walked in with a sport coat. I looked like a country hick."

He was hired as a trainee on the government bond desk. He had been making about $15,000 per year at Bank One. Goldman offered him $50,000. But Corzine had big debts to pay off—he had a home mortgage by then plus the school loans—and he and his wife had had a second child. He took the job at Goldman, but for nine months his wife and the two children stayed behind in Columbus, where Joanne was teaching school. His job was to deliver trading confirms, get coffee, and answer the phones before the second ring. "Oftentimes, it was a hooker or a bookie," one member of that desk said. But Corzine was basically clueless about how to trade or about what made a good trader. Eventually, though, he started to fill in for traders on vacation and began to trade U.S. Treasury bonds and bills.

Corzine got one break after his boss, Don Sheehan, left for the night at five o'clock and asked him to check up on the Treasury bonds he had been buying during the day. Corzine realized that Sheehan had bought up bunches of Treasury bonds that had attached warrants—the right but not the obligation to buy more bonds at a set price. Sheehan had loaded up on them without being properly hedged. "I was sort of 'holy sheep shit,'" Corzine said. "We have this great miscalculation. We were supposed to sell bonds at the same time we were buying warrants, and our team forgot to sell the bonds." Corzine stayed with the clerks until four o'clock in the morning to figure out the magnitude of the problem. "We found out we were long—ten times over our limits—and it turned out to be a great trade," he said. "But we had to call the Federal Reserve because we were over our regulatory limits." This was how Corzine met Gus Levy, who called him on the phone and let loose. "He was madder than hell," Corzine said. "That's all I remember. . . . We worked our way out of that trade and made more money than the desk had made in the previous couple of years. It was $10 million or something. It was a meaningful amount that should have never occurred, so nobody got any credit for making the money because it could have been a big mistake." But Corzine learned a lot from Sheehan. "He knew how to maneuver in a market better than anyone I have ever seen," he said. He also liked that the government bond desk seemed to be filled with Irish Catholics. "An Irish crowd in a Jewish firm," he said.

A bigger break came after about eighteen months, when a group of government bond traders at Goldman, led by Sheehan, walked out and joined E. F. Hutton. It took Goldman months to hire new traders to replace those who had left suddenly. During that time, Corzine was pressed into service. "I got to trade everything for about three months before the firm could go reload . . . ," he said. "I made more money . . . than the desk had made in the previous couple of years. Pure luck, I'm sure, but it caught people's attention." Corzine quickly came under the wing of partners Eric Schoenberg and Victor Chang. When Frank Smeal was hired from JPMorgan to rebuild Goldman's fixed-income business, Smeal took a shine to Corzine as well. "If you were successful at Goldman Sachs people paid attention to you," he said. "If you worked harder than most folks they paid attention to you." One year he got paid a bonus of $150,000, more money than he could imagine. He called his father and told him the news. "You ought to come home," he told his son. After taking over the running of the government bond desk in 1979, Corzine became a partner the next year. He had made the run in four and a half years, a major accomplishment under any circumstances. He was thirty-three.

Mark Winkelman came to Goldman in 1978 after a four-year stint as a senior investment officer at the World Bank. At first, Corzine and Winkelman did not get along. "He and I went head to head for a long time because we both saw the same opportunities," Corzine said. But after Goldman bought J. Aron, in 1981, Rubin figured out how solve two problems at once when he separated the two men and sent Winkelman to run J. Aron, while Corzine remained on the bond desk. "Then we both began to understand that a lot of the stuff Aron was doing there and a lot of stuff we were doing in fixed-income was really the same thing," Corzine said. Around 1986, Goldman decided to merge J. Aron and Goldman's fixed-income businesses to create a super group called "FICC," short for "Fixed-Income, Currencies and Commodities." Winkelman and Corzine were working together again. (Some Goldman partners said Corzine needed—and benefited from—Winkelman's intelligence and oversight.) This time, the two men made the partnership work. "We translated that into a very effective partnership on many things . . . ," Corzine said. "He is a really, *really* smart guy—as opposed to me—he could do the math as well as anybody, anywhere, anytime, and he was disciplined." (Other partners said the relationship between Corzine and Winkelman was strained, at best, right from the start.)

Part of the reason that Weinberg, Rubin, and Friedman thought Corzine could use a little more oversight had to do with an incident that occurred during 1986 and involved a large and risky trade that the firm had concocted and that was not going well. It turned out that Goldman had bought, in quantity, Treasury securities with a coupon of 8.75 percent and shorted Treasury securities with a coupon of 9.25 percent. The trade went in the opposite direction of what the Goldman traders hoped, and soon the firm faced hundreds of millions of dollars in potential losses. Corzine, who had been managing the department, had to jump back into front-line action. "I went back on the desk for seven months," he explained. "*Every* desk—the corporate desk, the muni desk, the J. Aron people—*all* had this same trade on." Goldman had expected the Japanese and the few hedge funds that owned the securities to roll them over, but that did not happen. "A huge, huge short squeeze developed over about six months," Corzine said. "I think it was the biggest loss that I had ever been responsible for on a mark-to-market basis." Although a member of the Management Committee, he had to report to the committee every other day about what was transpiring with the trade. Finally, after about five months of worry, the bet began to reverse and the bonds behaved as the traders had expected.

Corzine had turned a $150 million potential loss into a $10 million gain. "That's the last time I was a day-to-day trader," he said. One of the traders came away impressed by Corzine's guts. "He went around, he took everyone's position, and he just traded it himself," he said. "Good or not, it was very leaderly, and it worked out well enough. He was leaderly, strong. He was there late at night, because Japan was a major player in this, so he traded Japanese hours." Quite understandably, though, the firm's investment bankers didn't appreciate how risky the trade turned out to be and questioned how Corzine could have allowed such a potential loss to metastasize. The 1986 near miss was the obvious precursor to what would happen again, in spades, in 1994, but Corzine believed his ability to navigate the 1986 crisis successfully put him on a trajectory that eight years later would lead to his becoming the firm's senior partner.

ASIDE FROM THE fact that they both grew up on farms in Illinois and both were non-Jews in a predominantly Jewish firm, Hank Paulson's upbringing and career had little in common with Jon Corzine's. Paulson's grandfather on his father's side, Henry Paulson, owned a fine-watch wholesaler. Eventually the company became the largest watch whole-

saler and watch repair operation in the Midwest and "supported a prosperous lifestyle," including a home in Evanston, Illinois, and "a modest"
winter home in Palm Beach, Florida.

Paulson's father, also named Henry Paulson, loved farming, and
after graduating from Principia College, a small Christian Science
school—a "Christian Science family" is how Paulson described it—in
southern Illinois, convinced his father to buy some farmland in Stuart,
Florida, north of Palm Beach, where the Paulsons moved after World
War II and started a ranch to raise Brahman bulls. Henry Paulson—the
third, known as Hank—was born in Palm Beach on March 24, 1946.
That same year, Paulson's grandfather's business started to fail, and his
father was forced to sell the Florida ranch and move back to Chicago to
take over the watch business, which eventually went bankrupt. The family lived in a small apartment in a garage in Winnetka, Illinois, before
moving to a seventy-five-acre farm in Barrington, Illinois, about forty
miles west of downtown Chicago.

Much of Hank Paulson's early life revolved around the Barrington
farm. "We always had horses, hogs, cows, sheep and chickens, not to
mention my pet raccoon and crow," Paulson wrote in his 2009 memoir.
"I spent a lot of time doing chores—milking cows, mucking out stalls,
bailing hay. We churned butter for cream, drank milk from our cows. We
put up food for the winter, butchering the chicken, hogs and sheep.
Mom froze vegetables from the garden."

Paulson's father had a "fierce work ethic," Paulson explained, and
the message came early that Hank was expected to rise early and not
linger in the shower for more than a few minutes. "You got up, you
worked, you were useful," Paulson wrote.

Before he started seventh grade, his parents concluded the family
was "land rich but cash poor" and decided to sell the seventy-five-acre
farm and buy a smaller, fifteen-acre property farther away from Chicago.
Paulson described himself as a typical public school kid. "I was an Eagle
Scout as early as you possibly could be an Eagle Scout," he said. "I was a
good student. I was a good football player. I was a good wrestler. I had a
gold-star mentality." On his high-school football team, Paulson played on
both sides of the line, playing every minute of every game. "I was a very
good football player," he said.

Bob Blackman, the football coach at Dartmouth College, recruited
Paulson heavily for Dartmouth. At Dartmouth, Paulson majored in
English and started every game he could as the right tackle from sophomore year on. At six-feet two-inches tall, he wasn't that big—two hundred pounds—but he played against defensive linemen who weighed fifty

or sixty pounds more. Working on the farm and taking wilderness vacations had given Paulson the strength of a stevedore. In 1965, he was honorable mention All-American.

The Paulsons were Christian Scientists, and Hank Paulson regularly attended the Christian Science church. In his memoir, Paulson was matter-of-fact about his religious beliefs. "Christian Science has always been a big influence on me," he wrote. "It is a religion based on a loving God, not a fearsome one. An authentic confidence comes out of this." He also tried to debunk the myth that Christian Scientists are not permitted to rely on modern medicine and doctors to heal ailments. "There is, in fact, no prohibition against medical treatment," he wrote. "But I am comfortable relying on prayer because it has proven to be consistently effective for physical healing, for dealing with challenges in my career, and for spiritual growth."

His senior year, he was offered the Reynolds Scholarship to study English at Oxford but chose instead to apply to Harvard Business School, which was unusual for an English major without any business experience.

Like Corzine, Paulson was very concerned about being drafted into the Vietnam War after he graduated Phi Beta Kappa in 1968. He had joined the Naval ROTC program at Dartmouth and spent the summer after graduating from Dartmouth before going to Harvard at an ROTC program at Purdue University, in West Lafayette, Indiana. "It was a strange place for the Naval ROTC surrounded by cornfields with no water in sight," he wrote. But there was a public swimming pool that he and a girlfriend—it was a summer romance—decided to hang out at during one of the last nights of the ROTC program. She was a lifeguard at the pool. Since it was after hours, the fence around the pool was closed and locked, but Paulson and the girl decided to scale the fence and hang out in the pool anyway. Paulson was jumping up and down on the diving board when the police came. Since Paulson does not drink, he was not drunk, which was a point in his favor.

The policeman was new to the West Lafayette force and had let someone out of jail the day before who had vandalized the pool area. He was not in a good mood when he saw Paulson on the pool's diving board. "He took us down to the station, fingerprinted and mugged us, and charged us with misdemeanor trespassing," Paulson recalled. They also towed his car, illegally. The next day, Paulson explained what had happened to his ROTC captain. "He checked out my story and found out it was true and there was no damage done," he said. "The charges were dropped."

During his final semester at Dartmouth, Paulson had met Wendy

Judge, a junior at Wellesley, on a blind date. That fall, Paulson started at Harvard Business School. He also began dating Wendy in earnest. "I did well enough there without studying too hard, and I spent much of my time at Wellesley," he wrote. Like Paulson, she was a Phi Beta Kappa English major who loved the outdoors and wore secondhand clothes. She was president of her senior class at the same time that Hillary Rodham, her classmate, was the president of the student body. After she graduated from Wellesley, she was going to spend the summer teaching sailing and swimming in Quantico, Virginia. Paulson, now "very much in love," wanted to be near her for the summer between his first and second years at Harvard Business School. He had been slated to spend the summer at sea with the navy, an adventure inconsistent with the desire to be with his girlfriend.

Instead, he picked up the phone and cold-called the office of the secretary of the navy, John Chafee, to see what he could finagle. He ended up being redirected to speak to Stansfield Turner, a navy captain (and later the director of the CIA under Jimmy Carter). Out of the blue, Paulson proposed to Captain Turner that he undertake a study of the ROTC program on Ivy League college campuses—this was during the summer of 1969, mind you, a time when students were torching ROTC offices throughout the country. Turner agreed, and Paulson spent the summer in a cubicle at the Pentagon. "My motive was to be next to Wendy, and so I wrote this report and I made a number of contacts," he said. He also proposed to Wendy that summer. They were married eight weeks later.

After graduating from Harvard Business School in 1970, the Paulsons moved to Washington. Paulson headed back to the Pentagon to work for the Analysis Group, a small, elite cadre of bright young men working on special projects for Robert Moot, the assistant secretary of defense, comptroller. "The Analysis Group at the Pentagon was like a little investment bank," Paulson said. "We had projects where we worked with various senior people in the Pentagon."

While Paulson was happy working at the Pentagon, he really wanted to work at the White House, an idea that Treasury Secretary John Connally had planted in his head. When a colleague left the Analysis Group to go to the White House, Paulson had his connection to get some interviews in order to make the move. In April 1972, Paulson went to work at the White House for Lewis Engman, who was John Ehrlichman's liaison with the Treasury Department. Working as a staff assistant on the Domestic Policy Council, he focused on tax policy, minority and small-business issues, and the minimum wage. The Watergate break-in occurred in June 1972, and Paulson, like others, didn't pay the incident much attention. After the November election—where Nixon was reelected in a landslide—Engman left the White House to run the Federal Trade Commission, and Paulson replaced him as the White House liaison to the Treasury Department, then run by George Shultz (later Reagan's secretary of state). Paulson recognized what a unique opportunity he had at such a young age. It was a "huge promotion," Paulson said.

Early on during Paulson's White House tenure, Ehrlichman told him it was "important not only to do the right things, but also to be perceived to be doing them right." In January 1973, Paulson recalled speaking with Ehrlichman after stories had begun to appear in the press about H. R. Haldeman's role in Watergate. The next day stories appeared about Ehrlichman's role, too. "By February, Ehrlichman and Haldeman were out . . . ," he said. "That was very disillusioning because I saw Ehrlichman as a real force for good in that White House—really focused on policy, a moderating influence. . . . But it's never really interesting why bad people do bad things, or why good people do good things; it's really interesting to understand why good people do bad things." Neither Paulson nor his direct boss was involved in any of the shenanigans. "The White House had a lot of power in those days before Watergate busted things open," he said. "When a tax memo would come to the White House, I'd be the one that wrote the cover memo and went in to see the president and got back to the Treasury." By December 1973, though, Paulson realized that the end was near for Nixon, and he decided to leave.

Despite suffering tremendous disillusionment as a result of the Watergate scandal, Paulson counted his time at the White House as an important and formative experience. He learned that he liked working on more than one project at a time. He also learned not to be intimidated and to be comfortable around powerful people. "I was never going to be awed by authority just because someone had a big title or a big position and they told you what to do," he said. "It also helped me a lot in my early investment banking days since—when I was quite young— the fact that I had worked with the president and with senior cabinet officers gave me great self-confidence. I wasn't afraid to go directly to the CEO."

By the middle of 1973, Paulson had started interviewing for his next position. His eclectic background and his desire to work with CEOs made Wall Street—and investment banking, in particular—a perfect career path. He thought that Goldman or Salomon Brothers would be best for him because they each had large, respected Chicago offices, led by individuals—James Gorter, at Goldman, and J. Ira Harris, at Salomon—

who also had seats on their respective firms' management committees. Both firms wanted Paulson, and neither firm was the industry leader it would soon become.

When Paulson started to meet the Goldman brain trust, the rapport was instant. "Not only did I love Jim Gorter," Paulson said. "But I also met Whitehead, Weinberg, Rubin and Friedman and a whole bunch of other people and I just said to myself, 'I don't care where they rank in the league tables, these are really smart, good people and I want to work with them.'"

In January 1974, Paulson joined Goldman in Chicago as an investment banking associate, covering big industrial companies in the Midwest. It was a tough year financially at Goldman, given the Penn Central litigations. In this difficult financial environment, the Paulsons' frugality served them well. They bought five acres of land from Paulson's parents on the Barrington property where he grew up and built a "rustic" glass-and-steel house on a hill overlooking a prairie. He called the property "Merimar Farm" and cut the path for the driveway, constructed the retaining walls, and split boulders that were used in the stone fireplace.

At first, Paulson worked closely with Gorter on his existing client relationships, such as Amoco and Walgreens. Then he was given his own list of companies, where Goldman Sachs had been stymied for years, including Caterpillar, Kellogg, Inland Steel, and Archer Daniels Midland. Gorter told him to relax and not to worry about winning business from these companies in the short term. "If you do a good job," Gorter told him, "I'll be able to see it and see you're making progress, and then ultimately if you do the right thing, the revenues will follow."

The early years at Goldman were tough for Paulson. "Everything else I'd done," he said, "if you were bright and worked hard, you were assured of success, but here you needed to win people's trust." But then he started getting a few breaks. First, the general increase in M&A deals—driven by hostile takeovers—made it more natural for bankers to talk to the CEOs of companies about how to prevent a corporate raider from making a move. This played to Paulson's confidence in dealing with powerful people. His unique, somewhat disheveled style played well. He also defined his role as a coverage banker "expansively," he said—another trick he learned in government—and he figured he would have a better relationship with a CFO if he had an excellent relationship with a CEO (even though this risked offending the CFO).

Like that of a character from a David Mamet play, Paulson's objective in a meeting with a CEO was to make sure he got another meeting. "Every time I see that person they've got to learn something, they've got to find it useful, and they've got to say, 'I want to see this young guy again,' " Paulson said. "I didn't try to be their buddy, didn't try to be their equal." He talked to the executives about the performance of their stock, or about M&A deals in their industry—subjects he knew they would be interested in. Over time, he came to realize CEOs were lonely and didn't often have people to bounce ideas off. He would be their sounding board. "I would give them advice on a range of subjects some of which had nothing to do with traditional investment banking . . . ," he said, "such as weaknesses in their company, or I didn't think this particular CFO was strong and there might be someone at another company that was stronger, or whatever. Or about the composition of their boards. I was candid sometimes to the point of bluntness. That was my trademark." For a young banker, without much experience, Paulson had an unusual store of chutzpah. Sometimes clients would tell him to give them a breather, and not call so often. But he could hardly control himself.

Before long, Paulson began generating one major piece of business after another: a Eurobond issue for McGraw-Edison, creating a joint venture in Japan with Inland Steel, and selling a bunch of small businesses for Sara Lee. His success with many of these companies stemmed, in part, from the fact that he was not Jewish. There was no secret at that time that some executives at many large corporations in the Midwest were anti-Semitic and did not want to do business with a Jewish firm. "That was not lost on me . . . ," Paulson said. "In the late 1970s, you'd have a lot easier time doing business if your name were Morgan Stanley . . . I just literally never gave it a thought. To me, the firm was a meritocracy." Paulson spent his time focusing on winning business away from competitors. He loved being the underdog and fighting for greater and greater market share. "We loved to compete against Morgan Stanley," he said.

With Paulson's rainmaker banking skills increasingly obvious, he was named a Goldman partner in 1982. By then, although Bob Hurst might have disagreed, Paulson thought of himself as one of the firm's top bankers. "I tried to be the best new business producer at the firm," he said. When Paulson had his conversation with George Doty about how much capital he would have to invest in the firm upon joining the partnership, he told Doty that he had only been able to finish two-thirds of his Barrington home and that he and his wife were sleeping in an open loft above the dining room, next to the children's rooms. "We were going to put this addition on to the house," Paulson told Doty, "but I'm not going to put the addition on now so I have 'this much' to put in the firm." But Doty took pity on Paulson and told him to build the addition to the house and put a smaller amount of capital into the firm. "I even forgot what it was, but it was a relatively small amount of capital I put in," he said. "Being a partner was extraordinarily important until I became one and then afterwards it was something I never really thought about much again." Even though Paulson became increasingly wealthy, his material interests remained minimal, especially for a Goldman partner. Wendy wanted her husband to be happy but otherwise, he said, "she could care less," about the money. "We lived out in a rural area where people didn't know what Goldman Sachs was," he said, "and they certainly didn't know what a Goldman Sachs partner was."

The word around Goldman was that *nobody* worked harder than Paulson. "I worked hard," he said. But in addition to both his legendary work ethic and his revenue-generating ability, part of Paulson's appeal to people like Whitehead, Gorter, Rubin, and Friedman was his combination of frugality and family values. Paulson didn't drink or smoke or chase women. There was a sense that Paulson would never put himself in the position that Lew Eisenberg had. Nor was he likely to spend his growing wealth conspicuously. "Johnny Weinberg used to say—and I think this was very insightful—'As people progress some of them grow and others swell,'" Gorter said. "And when you can sense that people are swelling, you want to get the hell out of there because they're losing their initiative and they're not going to do the job. Hank never swelled. He always grew."

To be sure, Paulson was no Boy Scout. He made plenty of enemies at Goldman. His brash, take-charge mentality offended some of his partners who thought he spoke too quickly or made decisions too impulsively. "He's an action-oriented person, and one of his great skills was identifying smart people and absorbing good ideas that they had, and then pulling the trigger," was how one of Paulson's rivals at Goldman described him, choosing every word very carefully. Paulson had heard the criticisms and didn't deny that he has his flaws.

But none of these imperfections seemed to hamper his career. After Paulson made partner in 1982, Gorter asked him to run Goldman's Midwest investment banking operations. By then Gorter had been on the Management Committee for years, was a real power at Goldman, and could not have been a better rabbi for Paulson. For his part, Paulson said he hadn't given much thought to being in management. But he took on the responsibility and found that the regional banking effort needed to be rebuilt. He hired a bunch of new bankers and then trained them. From there, Gorter and Friedman decided Paulson should be more involved in thinking about Goldman's long-term strategy and asked him to join two committees devoted to that topic.

Working on the firm's overall strategy not only gave Paulson input into decisions about how best to deploy the firm's limited resources and how best to expand internationally—exposing him to the leaders of Japan and China, among others—but also gave him ongoing access to Friedman, an opportunity Paulson did not fritter away. "Even though I was in Chicago, Steve and Bob made me feel relevant," he said. "They always seemed very interested in what I had to say about strategy and my views on how we should be working with clients, and I had *very* strong views about the role that Investment Banking Services"—or IBS, the evolution of Whitehead's New Business effort—"should play and how we should work with clients." But Paulson claimed that as much as he enjoyed the management responsibilities, he never aspired to a leadership position at Goldman. "It never had occurred to me that I would someday run Goldman Sachs or that I would want to run Goldman Sachs or that I'd want to run a big group of people or that I would want to ever go to New York," he said. "What I aspired to do was to be an outstanding investment banker in the Midwest."

With Gorter's retirement in 1988, Paulson became head of the Chicago office. At the end of 1990, Friedman asked Paulson to co-head investment banking with Hurst and Overlock. At first, the arrangement was a bit awkward, but the three men got along reasonably well and were able to divide up the managerial responsibilities. They also continued to work with clients, an arrangement that made Paulson comfortable. He also took on responsibility for Asia, which for Paulson was a revelation, since most of his international experience centered on canoeing trips in Canada. "I got Asia by default," he said. "No one wanted to go to Asia. We had almost no business there. I remember Bob Hurst telling me, 'You should go to Asia because Chicago's closer.'"

Paulson said he became "fascinated" by Asia and determined to build up the firm's presence there. One way to do that—as he and Rubin had done in Mexico with Goldman's assignment to privatize Telmex, the telephone company—was to work hard to win the assignment to privatize formerly state-owned enterprises. Paulson believed this represented a "branding opportunity" for Goldman in these foreign countries. He convinced Goldman's partners to invest $1 million in STAR TV, the largest satellite-TV provider in Asia, owned by Hong Kong billionaire Li Ka-shing. He convinced Tung Chee Hwa, a shipping executive who became the first chief executive of Hong Kong in 1997, to take him to China, in 1992, to meet Jiang Zemin, just before he became China's president. "I was very impressed with President Jiang Zemin and what he knew about the U.S.," Paulson said. "And what he knew about markets." Paulson and

J. Michael Evans worked together intently to win for Goldman the assignment to underwrite the IPO of China Mobile. "I still remember the legendary Chinese premier Zhu Rongji, whom I greatly admired, looking at Mike Evans and saying, 'Mr. Evans, if I had ten people like you I'd restructure all of our state-owned enterprises. And if I had 100, I'd turn around this country,' " Paulson recalled.

There was no question that by the fall of 1994—and his walk in Central Park with Corzine—Paulson was a premier investment banker. The question on the table, though, was could he figure out a way to work with Corzine in a subservient position to lead Goldman Sachs out of its funk?

IMMEDIATELY AFTER FRIEDMAN'S announcement that he would resign came the stories that Goldman would experience an unprecedented "wave of retirements" of limited partners that could "suck about $400 million of partners' capital out of Goldman" in the next five years, reducing the firm's $5 billion capital account. Friedman then admitted the firm was in discussions with private investors to replace the capital that its limited partners—including Friedman, who reportedly had $100 million tied up in the firm—might take out after they left. But there was no pressure on Goldman to raise new money, Friedman insisted. "We have never been in a stronger capital position," he said. "Each time we raised money we didn't have a pressing need for it." Two months later, on November 29, Goldman announced that it had raised another $250 million in equity capital from the Hawaiians, at the Bishop Estate, for between another 4 percent and 5 percent of the firm, which valued it at between $5 billion and $6.25 billion, a higher valuation than two years earlier. The new investment increased the total ownership by outsiders in Goldman to 20.5 percent, from 16.5 percent.

With his decision to take the number-two job at Goldman made and announced, Paulson had some serious explaining to do to Wendy. He had left Chicago a few days earlier, telling her his view that he was unlikely to become a leader of the firm. Indeed, such was his mind-set going into the weekend that he did not bring enough clothes with him for an extended stay in New York. Someone went to Brooks Brothers and bought him a bunch of shirts and ties. Wendy sent him some suits. He moved into the Pierre for months. "I didn't go home," Paulson said. "I just stayed in New York." He called her on Sunday night before the public announcement. She was in a state of shock. "Wendy, I have to do this," he told her. He just needed to help the firm get "through the crisis and then I can reassess." He told her he needed to help the firm in its time of acute need. With Corzine's appointment as the firm's new leader, he felt his presence was essential to make sure the firm's strategic direction stayed on track and to make sure that any personnel cuts were not made irrationally. "The investment bankers were so disillusioned with what was going on," he said. "We had a disproportionate number of investment banking partners relative to the profit, and they were very concerned about the trading losses." He told his wife, "I'll be able to play a key role in getting them to stay. I just have to stay and work here and get this done." Wendy Paulson was not happy with the turn of events. "Wendy has always been very supportive of me," Paulson said, "and she basically said, 'This is terrible, but I'm going to come to New York and find an apartment for us.'" (In February, they moved into a modest apartment in a building above the movie theater at Sixty-seventh and Broadway, around the corner from the Second Church of Christ, Scientist, at 77 Central Park West, which the Paulsons attended regularly. Later, they bought two apartments in the building, for $2.88 million, and combined them; they sold the combined apartment in 2006 for just under $8 million.)

Even though Friedman wasn't due to retire until the end of November, he quickly vacated 85 Broad Street and moved to Midtown, where he joined John Weinberg. He also had his health checked. "I frequently felt crummy," Friedman said. "I couldn't tell you how frequently I got these episodes"—the arrhythmia—"because I wasn't smart enough to know I was having them. I just thought I was suffering from jet lag." He visited with doctors at Mount Sinai Hospital, New York Hospital, and the Cleveland Clinic. His condition was not a rarity. "What they worry about is not how fast your heart is going," he said. "When they diagnosed me, it was going 150 beats a minute. They worry about the irregularity. Can a clot form and, you know, get a stroke? It never occurred to me— and, hey, I'm a jock—it never occurred to me to take my pulse." After receiving the diagnosis, the doctors gave him blood-thinning medication.

Years later, at the end of 2002, Friedman would join the parade of Goldman partners working for the federal government. Joshua Bolten, a former Goldman partner who was then the White House chief of staff, wanted to recruit Friedman to replace Lawrence Lindsey as an assistant to President Bush for economic policy and the head of the National Economic Council, the same job that Clinton had created for Rubin a decade earlier. (Bush had fired Lindsey abruptly after he bucked the party line about the potential true cost of the Iraq War, suggesting it could be—correctly—as much as $200 billion or more.) One night, after dinner, Friedman was reading something and suddenly had another heart "incident." Next thing he knew, he had spent nine hours on a gurney at New York Hospital "having stuff dripped into his veins." When he got back home, he decided to call Bolten at the White House and tell him he could not take the job. He was too concerned about his heart and the stress that being at the White House would put on him. "My wife is standing there and she was doing high-fives," Friedman recalled.

About five minutes later, the phone rang. Barbara went looking for her husband. "It's the White House calling," she told him. "I think it's the president." Friedman got on the phone with Bush. His wife could only hear his side of the conversation—a lot of "Yes, sir" this and "Yes, sir" that. Recalled Friedman: "He said, 'Look, you go talk to your doctors. We really want you here. You take your time. You talk to the doctors. And if they say you can do it, do it.' His father, Bush 41, had this and has this. He said—and this is the clincher—he said, 'You know, my old man fought a war with this. You can be an economic adviser.'" After agreeing to take the proper medication, the doctors cleared Friedman to take the job, and he did. "And by God, I went two years in Washington without an episode," he said.

CHAPTER 15

$10 BILLION OR BUST

From the outset, Corzine and Paulson had to figure out
ways to apply tourniquets to the blood rushing out of the
Goldman Sachs corpus. The trading losses continued in
September, October, and November. "Big losses, hun-
dreds of millions [of dollars] in a big part of the firm," one partner said.
Some partners attributed the ongoing losses to Winkelman shutting
down after he realized he was not going to be running Goldman Sachs.
"Mark Winkelman was literally dysfunctional because he wasn't running
the firm," explained another partner. "I don't know if it was a nervous
breakdown or whatever. You just have to talk to him and have him tell
you what he went through." (Winkelman declined repeated requests to
be interviewed.) The problem with Winkelman was compounded by the
fact that he was still head of fixed-income and Corzine, his former partner in running fixed-income, did not want to micromanage Winkelman
after he became the head of the firm. "For a long time he just sort of sat
in his office," one partner said of Corzine. "He would sit in his office
breaking out in tears at various times while the firm was losing all this
money."

Goldman's ongoing losses, of course, ate into the firm's finite capital, and since the firm was highly leveraged—at that time nearly 50 to 1,
meaning that roughly $100 billion of assets were being supported by
roughly $2 billion in partners' capital—the risk of financial disaster
started looming larger and larger. "There's two sets of issues," Paulson
said, speaking about the firm's problems in 1994. "There's leverage and
the lack of permanent capital. Then there's liquidity. Now when banks
and investment banks die they die quickly because of liquidity problems." In 1994, liquidity was not a problem for Goldman, but there were
factors that could make it one in a hurry.

One ongoing threat to the firm's liquidity at that time was the partners themselves. If they decided to leave, they could take out their accu-

mulated capital—albeit over time—and deplete the firm's finite overall capital. As the losses in 1994 mounted, many partners became increasingly nervous that the firm was at risk. They personally might lose the wealth they had accumulated at the firm, wealth that remained out of their grasp while they remained general partners. The abrupt departure of a large group of partners—all demanding their capital at the same time—could have resulted in a run on Goldman Sachs. "Jon and I made a huge effort to persuade partners to sign up," Paulson said. "To stay and not leave. . . . We had some people who got very scared and left."

A lot actually. Some forty partners left Goldman at the end of 1994, the first time anything like that many partners had voted with their feet. "People resigned out of fear," one partner said. "That should tell you something." A number of the departures were very upsetting and cut through the muscle of the firm into the bone. Howard Silverstein, the partner in charge of Goldman's Financial Institutions Group, left. "He was perceived as being an expert," one partner on the Management Committee said. "And all he did was just do a simple calculation if this continues. You know: wiped out." The departure that really shocked people was that of Charles "Chuck" Davis, who was running Goldman's banking coverage group. "I almost slugged him," another member of the Management Committee said when he heard Davis was leaving. Frank Brosens also took this opportunity to leave Goldman. More than balancing out the departures, however, was the naming of fifty-eight new partners, the largest group of new partners in the firm's history. (The class of 1994 included such future Goldman leaders as Gary Cohn, Michael Evans, Christopher Cole, Byron Trott, and Esta Stecher, as well as Eric Mindich, who at twenty-seven was the youngest Goldman partner ever.) Although Paulson was plenty worried by the financial losses and the unprecedented departures, he said he never believed Goldman was "going to fail" in 1994. "I always believed that we would get enough people to sign up" to stay as partners, he said.

The key to getting enough partners to stay was Paulson's tough decision to cut around 25 percent of the firm's costs. "We just cut to the bone," Paulson said. "If you have to do something like that it's just brutal. We found fat that we took out. That's what it took to get a lot of the partners to stay." Paulson cut people, travel expenses, allowances for overseas living, and many of Goldman's vaunted perks. He even cut back on the use of a corporate jet and recalled grueling overseas trips flying around Europe and Asia on commercial flights, waving the Goldman flag with clients and nearly falling asleep in the meetings. Something like one hundred bankers and traders were dismissed. "Due to the prolonged, industry-wide turndown, some belt-tightening has been necessary," Goldman said in a November 14 statement. "Each business unit and office has been doing their own reassessment, and several have made small, selective staff reductions where appropriate; others are still in the midst of the review process."

Another way Corzine got people to stay who might otherwise have left was by promising them the firm would soon go public and they would be rich. "His idea being to have people think it was lucrative to stay," according to one partner who stayed.

———

BUT GOLDMAN'S PROBLEMS at that time weren't only ones of cost and bad bets. A culture of undisciplined risk taking had built up over many years. "A lot of these practices were set up when [Rubin] was there," one top partner said. "Okay? The lack of a risk committee, trusting individual partners, model-based analytics—that by God you can be smart and figure it all out—and letting traders become too important and being afraid to confront them if they've been big moneymakers. All that sort of stuff built up." One change Paulson and Corzine made quickly was to take the dysfunctional Winkelman out of his seat and give the job of heading fixed-income to Michael Mortara, the Salomon Brothers recruit. "He stood up and said to all the partners, 'There's a new sheriff in town and the risk taking, particularly in our London office, was going to be curbed,'" Paulson recalled. "He spoke with great credibility." They also quickly established a formal risk committee and made the auditing, risk, legal, and accounting functions at Goldman Sachs as important and respected a career path as being an M&A banker or a derivatives trader. "Out of that 1994 period came a lot of the processes and procedures we put in place, the infrastructure, the people to manage risk," Paulson said. Added another partner: "Any great crisis can bring people together or push them apart."

One banker in the Financial Institutions Group who worked for Howie Silverstein was selected to be a Goldman partner in October 1994 and a month later signed the partnership papers. He was "excited over the moon," he said. Friedman told him (before he abdicated) what his compensation would be, something like $750,000. "It wasn't two hours later that my boss"—Silverstein—"came in and said. 'It's half of that.' I then went in to see him about an hour later and said, 'I'm leaving for the day. So if you want to cut my compensation again I'm not here.'" Next thing he knew, Silverstein had quit. "Obviously, the firm's having a tough time," he explained, "so you sort of say to yourself, 'Well, what's up with that? Aren't these the guys that I've been slaving with—not for, with? I mean really working hard with for a long time, and they're quitting? I don't get that. How can you leave? I mean, just how does that square? When it gets tough, you're supposed to get tougher.'" One day, in November, Winkelman left the firm. "Winkelman, who has been a key figure in recent years, was angered after losing out in the contest to succeed Mr. Friedman," the *Times* reported.

————

GOLDMAN SEEMED TO be coming unglued. Weinberg's succession plan had come off the rails. Partners were leaving in bunches. Those who stayed had their compensation slashed. Ditto the new partners. The firm was losing lots of money each month; it was in danger of failing to meet its capital requirements with the SEC. Indeed, given how the year unfolded financially, some senior Goldman partners questioned why Friedman had not made his announcement to leave earlier in 1994—say in March—and then use the next six months to run an orderly succession process with less pressure, or put in place the next leaders under him and then leave after six months.

Friedman has heard the criticism. "If I had known how the last quarter was going to be," he said, "I wouldn't have retired. But by that time, it was done. I hadn't known, and what could I do about it? I never thought the situation was remotely as troubling as people seemed to feel. I'd lived through these goddamn crises. I'd lived through the 1987 market break, the Freeman thing, and the Maxwell thing. And I'm not the world's bravest person. I knew what really upset me. The Freeman thing did and the Maxwell thing; 1987 did. This didn't. I thought, 'My god, if you can't stand the heat—I mean, you're way ahead on profits if you aggregate the last few years.' The positions were always liquid and . . . we always had the option of just taking the positions down to almost nothing. You then reduce overhead" and return to profitability. (The firm supposedly ended up making around $500 million pretax in 1994, well below the $2.7 billion it made the year before. Others dispute that the firm made money in 1994. They say the firm was able to make it look like it broke even in 1994 by reversing capital accruals that had been built up to cover calamities such as the losses in 1994. "It was a loss of hundreds of millions of dollars," one person said.)

What worried Friedman were not the monthly trading losses, which could be quantified and unwound. Rather, with the rise of derivatives and other asynchronous bets, he worried more about a catastrophic blowout, especially since the firm was private and had finite capital. "Part of what irritated me," he said about the events of 1994, "was I was one of the people who came to feel in the 1980s that Goldman Sachs needed to go public, not because of any offensive reason—though an offensive reason was part of it—but I thought for defensive reasons. In a difficult world, where you're competing with giants who might increasingly use risk as a competitive measure, I felt we needed permanent capital. Today from the vantage point of the Goldman Sachs board, it's obvious that there would be no room for a global private partnership."

Corzine, for one, said he sympathized with and understood what Friedman was going through, especially after Rubin had abandoned him with a crisis in the part of the business he understood the least well. "Until you've actually traded and had to deal with one of those Come-to-Jesus moments," he said, "with a bad position and you have to make the decisions about whether to eliminate it, hold it, reduce it—those kind of existential moments involving the people you work with and your firm—those are the kinds of things that really get your attention. I think this is the first time that Steve had taken that burden on primarily himself, and rightly or wrongly between the interaction of that incredibly high pressured market situation and the Maxwell situation, I think he was thinking along existential terms. He was also very frustrated because he had believed long ago—1986—that the place should have had permanence of capital and he was probably more aware, based on his conversations with bankers in particular, that people were not going to stick around at the end of 1994 and that you would have probably had a pretty heavy turnover of partners and their capital."

Aside from why Friedman had seemingly botched his departure, the other lingering question that remained among many of the Goldman partners was how Corzine could have emerged as the firm's leader when he was leading the very division—fixed-income—that had lost hundreds of millions of dollars in 1994. "He's the only one who understood how to get out of it," explained a fixed-income trader. "You have to have someone who knew how to get out of it."

Paulson tried to explain how this could have happened. "Fixed-income trading had grown to be a big part of the firm and its profits," he said, "so effectively there wasn't a choice. There had to be someone from the fixed-income side overseeing that business because that's where the problems were." Added another partner, about Corzine, "He is charming. He's got a *really* nice style. He comes in an attractive package, so although he has got a huge ego and huge ambition—which far exceeds his ability in both those things—he comes across in a laid-back, low-key, disarming style. And yet, I have asked myself—all of us have asked ourselves—how could this have happened?" The "only way to explain it," he continued, was that even though fixed-income "while he"—Corzine— "was running it" had "almost taken the firm down," Goldman's fixed-income business had grown so big and complex—and so profitable, at least in 1993—that there almost had to be someone with a deep understanding of the subject at the top of Goldman. The only other viable choice to do that, aside from Corzine, was Winkelman. But "despite great respect, I think, every one of us had, to a man, for Mark Winkelman, none of us wanted him to run the firm or to work for him," this partner continued, "because Mark didn't see shades of gray, he saw things as black and white."

By contrast, some people at Goldman used to refer to Corzine as "Fuzzy," not only because of his beard but also because he was "a fuzzy thinker," one partner said. "He wasn't crisp and wasn't black and white. He fuzzed things when he communicated."

With Winkelman not a viable option, Goldman was hostage to Corzine. "There was this big beast," one partner said, "that was a huge profit driver, and a huge risk, and you had to keep the traders there, you had to figure out how to solve some of the problems. So there's no way Steve could have left and said, 'Here's the idea: let's have Mark and Jon leave—because I doubt whether Jon would have stayed without being head of the firm—so let's take those two guys out and let's have some investment bankers run the firm or let's pick someone who is not even on the management committee to be co-head of the firm.' There effectively wasn't a choice." Despite this impeccable logic, the fact remained that Goldman had selected as its new leader the very person who had just presided over a complete meltdown in Goldman's fixed-income business and who, as a result, never fully had the trust and faith of the firm's investment bankers. "*That* is one good question," one Goldman trading partner said. "At a normal place, it would be discordant. You couldn't imagine it. And I guess at this place, somehow you could, because maybe the place really did sort of get into this long-term thinking that Rubin always used to talk about."

––––––

BUT THE FIRM did not dwell for long on its misfortunes. For starters, there were fifty-eight new partners to indoctrinate into the Goldman Way. "There's no difference between us and every other investment bank out there—except your hard work, your management, and the people you hire," Mark Winkelman told Gary Cohn before Winkelman left Goldman. "Think about it. We work in the same buildings. We have the same computers. We fly on the same planes. We sleep in the same hotels. We even have the same clients." Cohn told *Fortune,* ten years later, he "thinks about this ten times a day." This idea of Goldman's exceptionalism was one of the firm's oft-repeated mantras.

Despite the 1994 losses and the management chaos, Goldman continued to emphasize the opportunities ahead and the rarefied air its partners breathed. "We were ready to drink the Kool-Aid," one member of the 1994 partner class told the *Financial Times*. On November 4, 1994, the Kool-Aid was flowing at the new partner orientation at Doral Arrowwood, the Rye Brook, New York, conference center favored by Goldman.

Mark Schwartz, a graduate of Harvard College, Harvard Business School, and the John F. Kennedy School of Government at Harvard, was a Goldman "culture carrier"—as they were known at 85 Broad Street—one of the few partners sufficiently steeped in Goldman folklore and mythology that he was selected to speak to the incoming partners. "We're going through a very rough period right now and we're all going to be tested," he told the new partners. "But remember this—we have three things that make us the best firm on Wall Street, three things that our competitors want: our people, our clients and our reputation. These three things are our most valuable assets. How we manage these assets will determine how successful we are in the future. And how we manage our people through this period now will be our greatest challenge in the last twenty years."

Schwartz's Arrowwood presentation focused on three precepts: how to manage "your" people, how to manage "your" business, and "how to behave." "None of this is profound," he said. "All of it is common sense. If we do these things we'll be fine; otherwise we'll be in trouble." The key to managing, he said, was to "find the right people" by interviewing and recruiting. "Don't delegate away this responsibility," he said. "Hiring the right people is the most important contribution you can make. Hire people better than yourself. Don't self-select. We've made this mistake for years. There's richness in diversity yet we've been risk averse in hiring. We go to the same schools and select the same people year after year."

Schwartz then turned to the subject of communication. Goldman, he said, had "moved from a senior partner whose favorite word was 'eleemosynary' to one whose favorite word is 'shithead.'" Schwartz told the new partners that sometimes it was just as important to be spending time with colleagues in the firm as it was to be spending time with clients soliciting business.

He then conveyed to them another one of Goldman's secrets: the ability to know when to copy the innovations of others and when to be an innovation leader. "Sometimes it's great to be a genuine innovator but often it's desirable to simply copy or market other people's ideas," he said. "We've been pretty successful at picking up a pioneer's market share without having to pay a pioneer's research and development costs. We were late in mortgages, swaps, junk bonds and emerging markets in the last ten years, but we watched others make mistakes and we recovered very quickly." He noted that Goldman remained behind other firms in asset management and was still debating how deeply to be involved in Asian markets. "But on balance, I still think it's usually wise to wait on markets and products and aggressively copy or tweak others' successes."

On the flip side, Schwartz explained, was unprofitable innovation. He said in 1994, Goldman created a new tax-deductible preferred stock security—called MIPS. The firm marketed and sold it extensively, building a 90 percent market share in the product. "The only problem is that we've lost money doing all this business," he said. "We've been very creative, we've marketed the idea very successfully, and solved some important capital structure problems for many important clients. But we haven't made much money, given this very substantial effort."

Schwartz finished his lecture by daring to tell his audience "how to behave." He knew this would be risky. "I probably have no right and no authority to tell you how to act but this comes from the heart and I wish Jon and Hank would say it to the rest of our partners," he said. "First, be inspirational. Be a leader. Set high standards for yourself and your group. And keep raising the bar. Push people as far as possible, to be the best in this business." He urged the new partners to "be outspoken, independent, irreverent. Challenge the way we think and act. But be prepared for lots of resistance. People like the status quo and prefer incremental change." He noted that shaking up the status quo at Goldman was especially important in 1994. "The biggest benefit from this very difficult year is that we are being forced to change our management structure, our organization, and we're reexamining each client relationship and every line of business. Re-engineering *is* the buzzword and I hope we have the courage to radically restructure the way we approach certain businesses. To be visionary, but also pragmatic."

He also recommended they take chances and in true corporate fashion equated firing people with bravery. "Be creative and take risk," he said. "Take risk in your own careers, take risk in shrinking and growing businesses, take risk in moving people around, take risk in making decisions. At difficult times like this, you have to demonstrate the ability to make hard, tough decisions—streamlining businesses, curtailing growth, laying off people. Making tough decisions will actually make us more credible in our business units. Lean organizations need strong values and ironically if you make tough decisions and communicate them, your groups will appreciate you for your candor, fairness, facing reality and being decisive. You'll earn loyalty and respect from your group and you'll boost the productivity of your business."

Finally, after reminding the new partners that "*we* own this business," he exhorted them to act like partners. One could almost hear the voice of Vince Lombardi. "We are partners—emotionally, psychologically and financially. There can be no borders between us, no secrets. Treat one another differently from this day forward. Do not be quiet, anonymous or part of a silent majority of partners. Be active, involved, outspoken. Exert leadership. When you're down, pick yourselves up. Most people don't. That's the reason many people fail. Many people get knocked down and lack energy and willpower to get back up. . . . If you think you already exhibit most of these qualities, that's wonderful. This firm needs an infusion of active, motivated, inspired people like you. We need it now more than ever. We're vulnerable right now—but we're also capable of greatness and excellence. Don't let another day go by without believing that. As Robin Williams said in *Dead Poets Society*—*Carpe Diem*, Seize the Day. Be very proud to be a Goldman Sachs partner, get very intense and seize the day."

One Goldman managing director, who endured his share of these types of meetings, likened working for Goldman to playing for the New York Yankees. "Why do people go to the New York Yankees, right?" he wondered. "You get paid a lot of money. They want to win World Series rings. They want to be viewed in posterity as the greatest in the position of all time and in the Hall of Fame. The best path to fame, recognition, and excellence is through the Yankees. I think it's an interesting analogy to draw at Goldman because they sort of give you that feel that 'hey, I'm going to be viewed differently now.'" Indeed one year, he remembered, after winning a World Series with the Yankees, Joe Torre, then the Yankees' manager, showed up to give a speech and said, "What can I tell you, this audience, about teamwork that you don't already know? I could learn a lot from you."

––––––

RIGHT FROM THE start, there was bad blood between Corzine and Paulson, and not because one was a trader and the other was a banker—the usual reason given for tensions in full-service Wall Street firms. Rather, the antipathy between the two men was almost a chemical, visceral one. To a certain degree, any hope Paulson had for a true partnership with Corzine was dashed from the outset when Corzine made clear that he wanted to be the firm's sole senior partner.

Despite this, Corzine and Paulson worked "relatively well together" at first, Paulson said. The magnitude of the trading losses continued to grow during the last three months of the year. Corzine focused on solving that situation after it was determined that the firm should cut its losses and move on, while Paulson had to oversee the process of cutting costs by 25 percent, which on Wall Street meant cutting people. "When you're boiling in oil, in the middle of a crisis, the challenges are all so consuming, there is no time for anything else," Paulson said. "I certainly wasn't focused on issues or problems with Jon." Paulson and Corzine focused together on the Herculean task of getting partners to stay while at the same time figuring out what to pay people. "Partners were looking over their shoulders at each other, wondering who was going to jump ship next," one vice president remembered. "There was an air of barely controlled panic as you watched people watching each other trying to decide as decision time approached."

Paulson and Corzine actually complemented each other in their ability to focus on different groups of partners who needed convincing to stay. For instance, Paulson was especially focused on keeping John Thornton at Goldman. Thornton, an M&A banker based in London, had been responsible for building up the firm's M&A and banking business in Europe. He was threatening to go to Lazard, where he was hoping to be in line to succeed Felix Rohatyn as the firm's chief rainmaker. But after Rohatyn disabused him of the notion that he would be running Lazard anytime soon, Thornton decided to stay at Goldman.

But just as Thornton decided to stay, the firm suffered a big blow when Kevin Conway, a well-regarded thirty-six-year-old vice president in the M&A group, turned down his offer of a Goldman partnership to take a job, instead, as a partner at Clayton, Dubilier & Rice, a successful private-equity firm. Making matters worse, Goldman had announced Conway as a partner in October, only to have him reject the offer weeks later. Conway's rejection of one of the most sought-after prizes on Wall Street was very big news.

Although Paulson and Corzine handled the partner departures as well as could be expected—and seemed to work well enough together doing so—there were small signs of the trouble brewing between them. For instance, Paulson remembered flying around the world that fall—by commercial jet, of course—and going from world capital to world capital visiting with Goldman's professionals, and with clients and foreign leaders as time permitted. It was grueling. "I went through Europe to India and had one night in a hotel in Delhi and then we left Mumbai at like eleven o'clock at night and I was in a coach seat on a plane," Paulson recalled. "And went from there to Singapore and had meetings there and almost fell asleep at the dinner table with clients." While Paulson was on this whirlwind trip, Corzine had drafted a letter to the firm's shareholders—mostly the firm's partners, of course—from Corzine alone, in which he made some gratuitous comments about Paulson. Paulson thought the letter should be from both men. "The deal with the titles was one thing," Paulson said. "But we were going to do this together and as partners." Paulson confronted Corzine about the shareholder letter and Corzine conceded the point. The letter was sent from both men. "I think at the outset we worked as well together as you could have two very different people with different styles work together," Paulson said.

———

ONCE THE TURMOIL caused by partners leaving—and those staying being upset by their low pay—calmed down, Corzine saw one of his first responsibilities as the firm's leader as needing to resolve the outstanding Maxwell litigation against the firm. On May 2, 1994, two pension funds representing Maxwell's employees—who were facing a loss of £400 million as a result of the Maxwell scandals—filed suits against Goldman in New York State court claiming that Goldman had sold 25 million Maxwell Communications Corporation shares in April 1991 owned by the pension funds, and instead of returning the proceeds of the sale— about $94 million—to the pension funds, Goldman had transferred the money to two Swiss companies controlled by Maxwell himself. The complaints claimed that Goldman and Eric Sheinberg, the London partner who was Maxwell's banker, sold the 25 million Maxwell shares "despite their knowledge" that the pension funds would not get the proceeds and that Goldman had followed the instructions of Kevin Maxwell "without asking reasonable questions about the knowledge which the pension-fund trustee had of the transaction or taking reasonable steps to insure that the trustee was fully informed and approved such an extraordinary transaction." For its part, Goldman called the suits "invalid, misdirected and [representing] an expensive and time-consuming distraction" and said it was merely acting as an agent on behalf of its client, Kevin Maxwell. The lawsuits sought a return of the $94 million, plus damages.

Exacerbating the two pension-fund lawsuits against the firm were other potential claims from banks and other creditors seeking a piece of Goldman's hide, especially since the firm had made $2.7 billion in 1993. Quietly, Goldman's limited partners had asked Jim Gorter and H. Fred Krimendahl, another former partner, to research Goldman's behavior in the Maxwell matter and the charges being lodged against the firm. Gorter and Krimendahl came back with startling news: to wit, "if we were the plaintiffs we would not settle." Gorter told Charles Ellis, "With Robert

Maxwell, supervision was lax. We didn't have the necessary checks and balances. A trading relationship that started out okay got bigger and bigger and became so different in composition that it was not okay. In the end, it cost us a lot of money."

Goldman was headed for more trouble, and Corzine knew he had to get the Maxwell matter behind him. Goldman tried to get the judge in the pension suits to dismiss the cases but, instead, she ordered them to proceed and claimed that Goldman had "virtually ignored all the allegations at the heart of the plaintiffs' case" when it filed its motion to dismiss. With the litigation hanging over the firm, Corzine decided to pay $254 million to settle the two pension cases plus the remaining potential claims against the firm. (He thought the actual cost to Goldman was closer to $400 million, once the cost of unrecovered loans, lost business, and fines was included.) According to the *New York Times,* the amount Goldman paid was more than twice what the market had expected. Worse, the paper reported, the cost of the settlement would be borne by those people who had been partners in 1989, 1990, and 1991—with 80 percent of the settlement cost paid by the 1991 partners. "Assigning the costs caused a rift at Goldman because 84 of the 164 partners who were asked to pay are limited partners and have no day-to-day responsibility for managing the firm," the paper reported. "These partners wanted active colleagues, called general partners, to share the burden." In a memo to the partners, the Management Committee wrote that the settlement "should meet the appropriate expectations that anyone who has been a general partner should have developed regarding how a matter such as this would be handled if it ever arose."

Less well known was the fact that if Gene Fife, the partner negotiating on behalf of Goldman with Sir John Cuckney, the government-appointed arbitrator, had been unable to reach a settlement, Goldman would have been charged criminally. "Gene, I think you might be interested in this document," Cuckney told Fife after they reached an agreement. "Had we been unable to agree to terms as we have just done, it had already been decided that our negotiations would have been terminated completely and Goldman Sachs would have been formally charged this day." Corzine knew in his gut the time had come to get the matter behind the firm. "I have one of these theories, you turn up a rock at almost any place, any time, particularly where there's trouble, there's gonna be more trouble," he said. "That's how I felt about Maxwell. . . . I figured we were going to take a lot of flak for settling, but we were going to take a lot more flak every day and every month if we didn't. For the life of me, I still don't know for sure what happened. But it was one of these episodes that felt to me like it could go very negative for the firm."

———

IN ADDITION TO believing that he had to get the Maxwell lawsuits resolved, Corzine also wanted to expunge the fog of pessimism that seemed to have curled into every corner of the firm in 1994. "There was a psychology that needed to be broken about whether we could be successful at Goldman Sachs," Corzine explained. "The 'culture of excellence' had come unwound and deeply bruised. And there were a bunch of pessimists who were willing to accept that, and I just wanted to challenge that psychology."

At the annual partner offsite, at Arrowwood in January 1995, he put up a slide that caused audible gasps in the room. "I'm not really good at the vision thing," Corzine told his partners, "but I'm gonna do the vision thing." Coming off one of the worst years in the firm's history, Corzine challenged the partners to generate $10 billion in pretax profits in the five years between 1995 and 1999, or $2 billion pretax per year. "There were a lot of people who were mumbling and grumbling; I could tell the minute the slide went up," he said. "Some people thought it was ridiculous, some thought that I had undermined myself by doing that."

Corzine said he didn't mind the cynicism because he *wanted* to challenge the status quo at Goldman. He said that was "the art of leadership" and it was unacceptable to "sit around accepting that just because the immediate past was what it was, that's what the future held." He said it was "essential to change the attitude" at the firm "about whether we could be successful" again "and I absolutely believed that we could be successful again."

The financial markets, though, were still concerned about Goldman's financial health. As a follow-up to the $250 million in equity it had raised from the Bishop Estate in November 1994, in March 1995 Goldman "quietly raised" another $272 million in the private debt markets, according to the *Wall Street Journal*. "The latest capital drive is remarkable because it shows that while Goldman may be the top-rated brokerage firm by the credit agencies, institutional investors aren't quite as sanguine about the firm's credit prospects," the *Journal* reported. The paper reported that Goldman had to pay an interest rate of close to 9.5 percent to attract investors for a ten-year security, significantly above the 8.846 percent rate that Lehman Brothers had to pay two weeks earlier to sell its own ten-year bonds.

A month later, two of the *Journal*'s investigative reporters, Alix

Freedman and Laurie Cohen, wrote a 4,200-word front-page story about how the Bishop Estate was able to maintain its tax-exempt charitable status at the same time that it had an increasing array of profitable investments—for instance, its investment in Goldman Sachs—that it was permitted to shield from income taxes after winning one private favorable tax ruling after another from the IRS. Freedman and Cohen revealed that Bob Rubin, who had by then replaced Lloyd Bentsen as treasury secretary, had sought out the Bishop Estate with an unusual request in December 1992, when he was leaving Goldman—along with a reported $26 million pay package—to take the reins at the National Economic Council. Most of Rubin's net worth was tied up in his partnership interest in Goldman, of course, and he was anxious to preserve the wealth he had meticulously built during his Goldman tenure. While it was not clear what the origin of the idea was, just after the Bishop Estate finished its first investment in Goldman and just as Rubin was leaving Goldman, the firm placed a call to the Bishop Estate, which agreed to guarantee—for a $1 million fee—the value of Rubin's stake in Goldman, in the unlikely event that Goldman ever went bankrupt. "Bishop will get to pocket about $1 million in fees from Mr. Rubin and to enjoy the satisfactions, however intangible, of having a lasting relationship with the man who now, it turns out, oversees the IRS," the *Journal* reported. Rubin also faced criticism for using the Treasury's $20 billion discretionary fund to help bail out Mexico, which suffered a financial crisis shortly after devaluing the peso in December 1994. One of the main beneficiaries of the Mexican bailout was Goldman Sachs, which was one of the chief underwriters of Mexico's sovereign debt and would surely have faced billions of dollars in lawsuits had the rescue financing not been put in place, which helped restore confidence in the Mexican economy and kept its bonds from defaulting.

Freedman and Cohen were granted a rare audience with two of the Bishop Estate trustees, Henry Peters and Richard "Dickie" Wong. During the interview, Peters and Wong "broke out of their reserve to lavish praise" on Goldman: the firm was an "astronomical opportunity" and a "long-term play" for the foundation because it was the "crème de la crème" of Wall Street. Soon enough, Freedman and Cohen elicited from Peters and Wong that what the Bishop Estate wanted from its $500 million investment in Goldman was a massive payday, the kind a Goldman IPO could provide. "Without being asked, Mr. Peters raises the topic of Goldman's 'IPO potential,'" the *Journal* reported, "then coyly says he won't comment. But in the next breath, Mr. Peters blurts out: 'Heck, I see an opportunity.'"

A COMBINATION OF a general improvement in market conditions in the middle of the decade—coming out of the credit crunch of the late 1980s and early 1990s—plus the power of Corzine's positive thinking began to have its intended effect on the type A personalities at Goldman Sachs. "He had enormous energy, unbounded energy," one partner said, "and he was, in that sense, an energizing element in the firm. From where I sat in 1995, he looked like a good thing." Corzine seemed to motivate people at Goldman. "Jon is inspirational," David Schwartz said. "He would come to London three or four times a year. We'd all go into the conference room, and we would leave feeling so great about being a part of Goldman Sachs. . . . Corzine was able to convey the culture in a really profound way."

Another cultural change that Paulson and Corzine instituted after they took over and that seemed to ignite the troops was the new system of risk controls, accountability, internal police, and open lines of communication. Around that time, Goldman partner Robert Litterman, a former professor at MIT who had joined Goldman in 1985, created the "value-at-risk" model, which attempts to quantify how much Goldman could lose trading on any given day. (Many Wall Street firms still use a version of Litterman's model, including Goldman, although the model's ability to gauge genuine risk remains controversial.) Goldman created a risk committee that met regularly. The firm empowered internal accountants and risk assessors and gave them the authority to challenge traders on a regular basis about what they were doing. A chief risk officer position was created. Goldman completely transformed the way risk was assessed, calculated, and communicated on Wall Street—although no other firm on Wall Street took the matter nearly as seriously as did Goldman, in part because the firm had survived so many near-death experiences and in part because, unlike nearly every other large firm on Wall Street, the firm's partners had their own money at risk on a daily basis. (In November 1996, the firm would become a limited liability partnership in order to further limit some of downside risks partners faced.)

One of the people who became a partner during the 1994 turmoil was Armen Avanessians, a 1981 graduate of MIT with a master-of-science degree from Columbia University. Before joining Goldman in 1985 as a foreign exchange strategist, he was an engineer at Bell Laboratories, in New Jersey, where he worked in the common subsystems laboratories. Avenessians, more than perhaps anyone else at Goldman, was responsible for creating the internal, proprietary computer system that gave the firm an enormous competitive advantage in the assessment and monitoring of risk. Together with Mike Dunbo—who is now in charge of technology at Bank of America's Global Markets Group—Avenessians created at Goldman what is called "SecDB," short for "Securities Database," an internal, homegrown computer system that tracks all the trades that Goldman makes and their prices, and closely monitors on a regular basis the risk that the firm faces as a result. "It meant that you didn't have the corporate bond guys in New York doing something different than the corporate bond guys in London," according to someone familiar with SecDB. As important, SecDB put sophisticated real-time securities pricing information in the hands of both the bankers and the traders, allowing bankers to have conversations with their clients about how a security might be priced in the market without having to consult with traders, which was often the path that bankers at other firms were required to follow. "You can have sophisticated bankers thinking about the same problems, but with exactly the same tools that the guys on the desk are using that were trading the billions of dollars," this person continued. "You had a holistic view of how you looked at things. It's been broadened out over fifteen or twenty years. It's taken a long time, but it's grown so that there's a real uniformity to the way the risk is viewed."

These changes began to pay off, and the firm became immensely profitable. By the second half of 1995, Goldman had turned its business around. In the last six months of the year, the firm earned $750 million, pretax, and its annual run rate for pretax profitability had improved to $1.5 billion. Corzine was becoming increasingly confident that his $10 billion pretax goal was within reach. The old culture had been a trading free-for-all, where, according to one partner, "if you were trading Treasuries and you liked oil, you just put a bet on for oil. And if you were trading equities and you wanted to buy corn, you just put on a corn bet. There weren't a lot of limits. People were just doing things all over the place." It now changed to a far more disciplined machine where risks were closely monitored. "What came out of the 1994 debacle was best practices in terms of risk management," Paulson said. "The quality of the people, and the processes that were put in place—anything from the liquidity management to the way we evaluated risk and really the independence of that function—changed the direction of the firm." When the firm "post-mortemed" 1994, Corzine said, the Goldman leaders had to parse between a "failure of strategy" and "a failure of execution." They agreed that the strategy had been correct but the execution had been flawed, at least that year.

The top executives at Goldman Sachs became risk managers as much as anything else. "I didn't say, 'I'm a banker, I don't understand this stuff,' " Paulson recalled. "I was at every risk committee meeting. I was doing everything I could to understand the firm's risk. I did that right up until I left the firm." In September 1995, Corzine explained to *Institutional Investor* that he had "rededicated the firm to client service" and the "days of Goldman being a hedge fund in disguise are over." But he was careful to say that did not mean Goldman would simply return to being a low-margin broker between buyer and seller. "You can't achieve the kinds of returns we want by just buying on the bid and selling on the offer," he said. "Reading flows and taking positions is still a very attractive revenue producer for Goldman Sachs in the fixed-income and foreign exchange areas." Corzine conceded that Goldman had been hurt by the departure of the forty or so partners who left at the end of 1994. To help compensate for the loss of talent, Corzine moved John Thain, the CFO, to London to co-head Europe with John Thornton, the M&A banker, to help "clean up the fixed-income mess."

By the annual partners' meeting at Arrowwood in mid-January 1996, the firm was hitting on all cylinders. In the weeks leading up to the offsite, the papers were filled with speculation about whether *this* time— after five rejections in the previous twenty-five years—the Goldman partners would decide to go public. Corzine himself fueled the speculation by saying an IPO was being considered. "If you did not have this discussion there would be a big debate about why we aren't talking about this," he said. "In the long run, Goldman's capital structure is expensive and vulnerable," one rival Wall Street CEO said at the time. "It's not as strong as a public company's would be. It's untenable." He said, "If earnings are high, the capital structure is not a problem. . . . But if earnings are not great, they are vulnerable, and if they lose money there will be a crisis."

The other looming question, though, about the potential Goldman IPO was a simple one of greed and mathematics. Since Goldman named new partners every two years, the fact was that 98 of the firm's 174 partners, or 53 percent, had been partners only since the end of 1992. With 1994 being such a bad year, the majority of the firm's partners had not had the chance to build up sufficiently large capital accounts to make it seem worthwhile to them to push for the IPO. They had not had "a shot at the golden carrot" yet, as one competitor put it. It seemed like déjà vu all over again. For Corzine, with a reported 1.5 percent stake in Goldman's profits—the largest individual stake at the firm—the rewards were obvious, but he was just one vote. Corzine knew he had to tread carefully. "Now would be a good time to go public," one newspaper observed on the eve of the meeting, "but it doesn't need to. . . . Should the older partners risk alienating the younger ones by pushing for a flotation which would allow them to take their cash out?" Added another observer as the meeting opened, "If Goldman's partners are salivating a little today, it will not be over the pheasant on the dinner menu. But not everyone will be so enthralled. Partners only recently instated will have accumulated much smaller stakes, perhaps of only $1 million, and will favour waiting for them to grow larger before the bank is sold. They want the jackpot, too."

———

WITH THIS BACKDROP, Corzine and Paulson assembled the Goldman partnership at the Arrowwood meeting. "A year and a couple of months does make a significant difference," Corzine said in his remarks. "We—all of us—have turned the tide for this great organization." Goldman had earned $1.4 billion pretax in 1995 (and its run rate during the last six months of the year was $1.75 billion) and therefore to meet Corzine's goal, the firm needed to earn an average of $2.2 billion during the next four years. Up went his $10 billion chart again. "A year ago," he said, "the chart behind me was categorized as, at best, improbable and, at worst, simply Pollyannaish." Not anymore. "It's a big objective," Corzine told his partners. "But it is clearly doable."

Corzine articulated three goals and aspirations for the firm, the likes of which no other Wall Street firm had ever attempted, at least with anything resembling a straight face. First, Goldman needed to be "the world's recognized best at providing a broad range of financial services" in the judgment of "our clients, outside regulators and creditors and, most importantly, in the eyes of our partners and people." Second, Goldman needed to "constantly maintain and enhance our culture of excellence." He noted, of course, the importance of "teamwork and mutual support." The firm was committed to focusing on the long term and to a "merit-based reward system," where "what you do" determined "your career path" not "who you know."

Then, having fed the crowd boilerplate rhetoric, Corzine got to the heart of what Wall Street firms were really about: Goldman Sachs existed to "provide superior wealth creation for the owners and the best people" at the firm. The firm's "financial objective," he said, "was to achieve meaningful absolute profits" that would generate after-tax return on equity—net income divided by the firm's capital—of "at least 20%." Then Corzine mentioned in passing the subject that had been on his mind for years: whether Goldman would remain a private firm in the future or would go public. It was just a quick mention, but it offered a glimpse of what he planned to talk about the next morning and indicated that it was a matter of some ongoing importance to Corzine, especially since the whole idea had been dismissed summarily a year earlier. "We are going to move to a [return-on-equity] orientation regardless of our future capital structure," he said. "In a private firm, ROE is a means for capital allocations, and in a public firm ROE is what drives multiples and therefore shareholder wealth." He emphasized that focusing on ROE was a significant change for the firm and "will stimulate changes through time in how we run our business" and cautioned his partners that "we must get the benefits" of focusing on ROE "without its potential for seeding divisiveness" by favoring certain businesses over others, depending on their relative profitability.

He spoke about the need for Goldman to develop further its "proprietary businesses," those where the firm took risks as principals—whether in trading or in private equity or in hedge funds—and wanted to have "a unique blend of client and proprietary businesses" because Goldman was "uniquely positioned" to do it. Corzine's vision was for Goldman's "proprietary activities" to "tie to and support our client focus. And they can." His logic was simple. "It is certain that we will know markets better and can give better advice by being a participant rather than an observer," he said. "It is certain that many of our clients expect and welcome the firm's use of its capital to facilitate meeting their objectives." Corzine wanted Goldman to be "a recognized leader in financial and quantitative research," in the "development and use of technology," and in "innovating products and in solving financial problems." When conflicts arose—as they inevitably would between acting as an agent and acting as a principal—Corzine argued that the conflicts could be managed if the right "checks and balances" were in place. "That is execution," he said.

The "biggest challenge" of leadership, he said, was "getting the right balance between the energy of the enterprise and the hustle of 174 partners, especially in the context of a firm with the potency and reach of Goldman Sachs." Then he explained how he intended to keep the balance. "Risk control is fundamental," he said. "Legal, credit, market, operational, reputational, expense, and liquidity provision must have first-order priority. A breakdown here can be fatal." Next, "performance accountability must be accepted" and focus on total profits, profit margins, and return on equity. But was this relentless focus on profit a recipe for dispensing with the system of "checks and balances" that was in place to prevent conflicts between client needs and Goldman's own trading accounts? This question would come back to haunt Goldman with a vengeance in 2010.

To Corzine, the lessons of 1994 were clear. "Permanency of capital was essential," he said. "You could not have everybody's life at risk because people have different risk tolerances and can take their capital out at a moment's notice. I didn't have religious fervor [about an IPO] in 1986, but I was supportive. I had religious fervor after 1994 because you can't have a two-hundred-and-fifty-billion-dollar balance sheet stretched around the world, operating twenty-four hours a day built on capital that could walk out the door and have no real transparency whatsoever about what you're doing." What he could also have mentioned—but didn't—was that Goldman's balance sheet was increasingly leveraged, risky, and costly, chock-full of capital invested from Sumitomo and the Bishop Estate (which were taking away a combined 25 percent of the firm's profits annually) and with capital borrowed from institutional investors at rates of interest averaging around 10 percent.

By 1996, the firm was the only major Wall Street securities firm that still operated as a private partnership, and there was no longer any doubt that the firm needed more capital to compete and also needed a new corporate structure to shield the partners from potential catastrophic liabilities.

Before turning the podium over to Paulson, Corzine broached the delicate subject of the Goldman IPO. "We are the strongest and best firm in our business," Corzine said. "The question for us is how to assure that Goldman Sachs continues to optimize its strengths. In that regard, we must ask now—when our health is strong—the question of where our future weaknesses might arise. The experiences of 1994 and the events of the last decade raise long-term questions with respect to our jugular vein—our capital structure." During the next day, the conversation would be about Goldman's capital structure and whether to keep things the same, "create an enhanced partnership," or go public, via an initial public offering of stock.

Corzine knew the issue was contentious. He had quickly lost support for an IPO the year before—the firm was in no shape for it then, of course—and in the interim year, he had been lobbying his partners relentlessly in order to build support for the idea. By then, the tension was well known between those who wanted to keep Goldman private and those who believed the firm needed ready access to capital to compete. Left unarticulated was that every Goldman partner present on the day of the IPO, as well as every limited partner (albeit to a lesser degree), would become mind-bogglingly rich as a result. "Goldman Sachs had been a partnership for well over one hundred years," Paulson said, "and so for one generation to reap the rewards, and sell it, so that no other generation could do what the one generation had done, when you do it you'd better do it in a first-rate way, and it better be driven by strategic reasons, not by one group wanting to harvest the rewards that were built for those who went before them and take the opportunity away from those that came after them. You had to have a good strategic reason for doing it."

That fact cast a pall over the group. "The important thing is to keep an open, dispassionate mind," Corzine said. For Corzine, the matter came down to one question: "What's in the best interest of the firm and its people—all 8,200?" He said, "The question should not and cannot be what's in your own self-interest."

For his part, Paulson barely mentioned the possibility of the IPO, thinking that it would be the main subject for the following day. Instead, he spoke about the need for "paced expansion" and to continue the firm's growth outside the United States in a more judicious manner while not neglecting its backyard. He also mentioned a number of opportunities the firm was seeing in trading—high-yield debt, syndicated bank loans, foreign exchange—and described two strategic initiatives the firm would focus on in the coming year: growing Goldman's asset management business and building up its electronic distribution system.

Finally, Paulson spoke about the problem of managing the firm's increasing number of conflicts, as Corzine had, but with considerably more concern. "In order to realize our strategic objective of creating a unique blend of client and proprietary businesses," he said, "we must develop a sophisticated management approach for 'relationship' conflicts as well as legal conflicts." This had not been going too well in recent years. In 1996, he said, Goldman needed "to do a much better job of managing conflicts" internally and in how "we articulate our business principles, policies and procedures." He wondered, rhetorically, why the firm was experiencing increasing problems with conflicts and then answered that the reasons were the firm's "growing principal investing business," its "growing market share and increasing global reach," and the efforts by competitors to "use conflicts as a ploy to take business from us or tarnish our reputation directly with clients or indirectly through the media." He also thought it was partly because clients "seem to be more sensitive about their competitors" and had been demanding "exclusive relationships" with their bankers. But, he said, the problems stemmed, too, from "our own inability to understand, articulate and manage these issues as well as we should." He said the firm owed its clients "full disclosure" about conflicts, "100% dedication to achieving their interest," and "professional execution." One thing "we don't owe them," he said, was the "pledge to never work with anyone else who may have a competing economic interest." The key to success, he concluded, was "keeping our momentum, our hustle, and executing with intensity."

―――

PAULSON WAS RIGHT to be worried about the firm's increasing problem with conflicts of interest. Goldman had been confronting the issue of conflicts for years, ever since Levy set up the risk arbitrage department in the 1950s. Time and time again the firm had to decide whether to arb a merger or advise on a merger. Sometimes the decision would be complicated by timing, as in the case of KKR's interest in Beatrice Foods. In that case, Goldman had been hired to work with Beatrice's management to take the company private and, at that moment, Bob Freeman put Beatrice on the gray list, which theoretically prevented Goldman from trading its securities. But after that management-led buyout failed, Beatrice came off the gray list and Freeman started trading the Beatrice stock (much to his own personal misfortune, it turned out). But in the late 1980s and 1990s, as Goldman's principal business exploded—among them private equity, hedge funds, and the Special Situations Group, or SSG, a little-known fund of partners' money run by Mark McGoldrick—the potential for conflicts exploded, too. Increasingly, the joke around Goldman was, "If you have a conflict, we have an interest." The updated version of Goldman's conflict with KKR over Beatrice came in May 1995 when KKR hired Goldman to represent it in the purchase of Westin Hotels & Resorts from Aoki, a strapped Japanese company that needed to sell. Peter Weinberg, the grandson of Sidney Weinberg, was KKR's banker at Goldman at the time. This was his first assignment working for KKR since he had joined Goldman from Morgan Stanley, and he had never met Henry Kravis before. The two firms signed an engagement letter for the Westin deal and Weinberg went to see Kravis. As he was walking in to the KKR offices, Goldman put out a press release that its private-equity arm had joined with two other investors to buy Westin. "You got to be kidding me!" Kravis said to Weinberg. Indeed, "the stress between KKR as a principal and Goldman Sachs as a principal was always enormous," according to someone familiar with their relationship.

There were also many examples of unethical behavior. For instance, in 1995, government regulators forced ITT Corporation to divest its financial services business, known as ITT Financial Corporation. There were several different pieces to the business, and Goldman, along with Lazard Frères & Co., was hired to sell it all off. A big chunk, known as ITT Commercial Finance, was sold to Deutsche Bank's U.S. subsidiary in December 1994. Six months later, in June 1995, ITT announced it had sold the rest of the division off in various pieces to buyers it did not identify. According to a former Goldman executive, one of the pieces of ITT Financial was a portfolio of "really weird" consumer loans that the Goldman banking team studied and decided might be an interesting acquisition for Goldman's partners themselves, perhaps through SSG, the secret fund of partners' money. Once the decision was made that Goldman wanted to buy the loan portfolio, word was that Goldman then slow-rolled the sale process, minimized its efforts to find a buyer, and eventually reported back to the ITT executives involved that no buyer could be found for the portfolio. That was the bad news. The good news was that the Goldman partners' fund had agreed to buy the portfolio at a price at least $100 million below what the loans were worth. According to the former Goldman executive, when this was reported to the client, the ITT executive went ballistic—because there was the sense that Goldman had not been forthright in its marketing effort. But, instead of contrition, the Goldman banker involved expressed his own fury. "He screamed to the [ITT executive] that he had been busting his ass for nearly a year trying to sell the assets and if he heard one more word along those lines he was going to talk to Jon Corzine, who would talk to Rand Araskog [the ITT CEO]," the former Goldman executive said. "And that was the end of that. When he got off the phone, everyone was giving each other high-fives because they knew they had just made $100 million. That was not an uncommon M.O. at Goldman." So much for checks and balances.

Paulson said he understood clearly that as the firm ratcheted up its principal activity, the likelihood of conflicts of interest would rise exponentially. He said some people urged him to wall off the principal investing businesses completely from the banking and trading businesses. "You could have someone up in the Arctic Circle and if he's doing the Water Street activities, clients are going to be angry at you," he said. "You had to do it with great transparency and with just a high level of integrity, and for people to know what it is you're doing." As the firm got bigger and bigger and more deeply involved in trading and principal activities, the task got even harder. "There's more room to do something that's unethical," one senior-level partner said. "In other words, when you're doing things in securities areas—not that the traders or salesmen are less ethical than bankers—but the markets give you an opportunity every second of the day to misbehave. You just have to look for behaviors. You have to look for people who are listening into conversations they shouldn't be listening in on. You need to force traders to go on vacation so you can monitor their books. You've got to rotate people all the time. You've got to have fresh eyes. You've just got to look for people that are acting differently.

And then when you see something that's not right, you've got to take action." As always, the defense against conflicts of interest on Wall Street seems to boil down to the old adage "Trust me, I'm honest."

———

THE FRIDAY SESSION at Arrowwood was plenty intense, and while the vast majority of the partners went off to dinner and to the bar to unwind, Corzine convened the newly reconstituted six-member Executive Committee to discuss further the prospect of the Goldman IPO. He was still intending to make his case for it, explicitly, the next morning. He wanted to know he had the support of the senior managers of the firm before proceeding. "I got a little more preachy about it," Corzine recalled, "and that undoubtedly didn't set well with guys who said, 'Well, we don't need all this trading,' and so that created a [negative] dynamic [about an IPO] even when we were becoming increasingly successful." Corzine was right. The support was not there: Paulson, Hurst, and Thain were against the IPO, and Eric Dobkin, who had been asked to do the financial analysis about the IPO, believed Goldman would trade at a discount to Morgan Stanley because its earnings were so volatile and so heavily dependent on trading. By the time Corzine arrived at Arrowwood's bar at 2:00 a.m., after a long battle inside the Executive Committee, he got an earful from a number of his inebriated partners: Drop the plan for the IPO.

After a few hours of sleep, Corzine succumbed to the inevitable, yet again. Although no vote was taken (again), he quickly ditched the printed agenda for Saturday—which had him arguing for the IPO—and scratched out a new speech. As the Saturday session opened, the opponents of the IPO had mobilized and one after another gave brief speeches in opposition. After an hour, Corzine proclaimed: "There will be no IPO. The IPO is off the table. It's over." With the IPO once again rejected, the Arrowwood retreat ended early on Saturday afternoon. But the issue was hardly resolved. "He isn't going to jam it down the partners' throats," one partner said of Corzine. "Like anyone in that kind of position, he wants to keep his job. But he won't give up on the idea."

CHAPTER 16

THE GLORIOUS REVOLUTION

While the passion inside Goldman about the IPO had—once again—been doused, the rancor between Corzine and Paulson was heating up. The first bone of contention between the two alpha males was, of course, size. "Everything to him, if it was a position, if it was a hundred, he liked it better at two hundred and he liked three hundred better than two hundred," explained one partner who knew Corzine well. From the outset, Corzine also seemed infatuated with making Goldman Sachs a bigger firm, through acquisition. During 1995, he spoke with Deryck Maughan, the CEO of Salomon Brothers, about a merger. He spoke with Sanford "Sandy" Weill, the CEO of Travelers Insurance (which owned Smith Barney) about a merger. He spoke with Douglas A. "Sandy" Warner, the CEO of J.P. Morgan & Co., about merging their two firms. He had these exploratory, preliminary conversations quietly and on his own and then asked Paulson to go meet with these executives further to see if any of the deals made sense. Paulson said he basically thought one potential deal was more ridiculous than the next.

Paulson's first shock came in early 1995 when Corzine told him about his interest in buying Salomon Brothers. The news "just hit me like cold water in the face," Paulson said, but he resolved to do what Corzine asked him to do—meet with Maughan and discuss the idea—and then to use the experience to try to educate Corzine about why putting the two firms together was not such a great idea. One senior Goldman partner remembered thinking about why Corzine seemed to be so keen on a Salomon deal. "He was a government bond trader," he said. "We hit Salomon Brothers at about the knees. And so he sort of looked up to them. They were the heroes for what he did." Paulson did the analysis for a potential merger with Salomon and talked with Maughan. Salomon had barely survived a scandal involving trading in Treasury securities, after investor Warren Buffett came to its rescue. But by 1995, Buffett had had enough of the business and wanted to sell Salomon and recoup his investment. But to Paulson the deal made no economic sense. "Their trading businesses overlapped with our trading businesses," he said, without passing judgment on Salomon Brothers. "So do you want to be twice as big in the government bond business? This is not two plus two equals four. It's two plus two equals three." Then there was the fact that the firms had duplicative offices around the globe, which would have to be closed and scores of people dismissed. "It just was so obvious that it was absurd on the face," one person said.

But Corzine was insistent. He kept calling Paulson and urging him to take the idea seriously and to figure out, possibly with Maughan, how it might be made to work. Paulson would have none of it and could not understand why Corzine was having such trouble understanding how little sense the combination made. Then Corzine would sic J. Christopher Flowers, the head of the Financial Institutions Group, or FIG as it was known, on Paulson to try to make the case again. Of course, Paulson's relationship with Corzine would have been much simpler and easier if he had said, "You're right, Jon, let's go buy Salomon Brothers." But Paulson couldn't do that, even though his life would have been better had he simply acceded to the CEO's wishes. He just did not think the deal made any sense for Goldman Sachs. Corzine had to tell Maughan the discussions were off. Then Corzine insisted Paulson go talk to Sandy Warner, at JPMorgan, who had an idea that Goldman and JPMorgan should be merged with Warner as the leader of the combined firm, or as the co-COO with Paulson. That discussion went away faster than did the one about merging with Salomon Brothers. JPMorgan had lost some of its "pizzazz," Paulson said, and the idea of working *for* that management was a nonstarter. "Those guys thought they should run the organization, and none of us wanted to pursue that," he said.

But the combination that made the least sense to Paulson—although it seemed to make great sense to Corzine—was the one between Goldman and Sandy Weill's Travelers. Nevertheless, Corzine begged Paulson to go meet with Weill and hear his reasoning. "I remember Sandy Weill saying to me his first choice was to buy Goldman Sachs because he needed international presence and his second choice was to buy JPMorgan," Paulson recalled. "I said, 'Sandy, what if neither one of those are available? Why don't you buy Salomon? They're available.' Just to test him. And he told me all the reasons why he wouldn't buy Salomon." (In recounting the story, Paulson laughed uproariously because in September 1997, Travelers bought Salomon Brothers for $9 billion.)

In many ways, Weill reminded Paulson of Corzine. "If it's available, buy it" seemed to be their basic business philosophies. But Weill had a far deeper bench when it came to integrating acquisitions than did Corzine at Goldman Sachs, which had bought exactly one company— J. Aron—and wrecked it long before figuring out a way to make it pay off. Paulson could not make sense of the Travelers deal, either. "At least I couldn't figure it out," he said. "I wouldn't have known how to make the combination successful, *particularly* when there was, in my judgment, no strategic rationale. Size is the enemy of excellence in investment banking, especially when you are trying to put together two different cultures." Besides, he had had a tough enough time cutting people at Goldman in the wake of the 1994 losses; the thought of having to rationalize two overlapping businesses was not an assignment he relished in the slightest.

For his part, Corzine said the discussions with Salomon Brothers, JPMorgan, and Travelers were not in 1995, but were actually in 1996 and after. (A later *Wall Street Journal* article did peg the Salomon discussion to 1995.) He said he agreed to have the meetings—a dinner with Sandy Warner here, or a "delegation" sent to meet with Sandy Weill there—because the bankers in his FIG, chiefly Flowers, thought the meetings were good ideas. Corzine believed the discussions were just casual encounters between CEOs of financial services companies and not particularly serious, nor were they intended to be. Throughout these discussions, he said he remained convinced that Goldman's valuation would be higher if it conducted its own IPO rather than if it merged with an existing public company.

Corzine also mentioned a dinner held between Goldman and AIG—six people on each side of the table—to explore a possible combination, with Corzine and Maurice R. "Hank" Greenberg, the strong-willed leader of AIG, leading the way. (For his part, even though some people think he arranged for the meeting, Paulson said he had no recollection of any discussion with AIG; Greenberg said AIG wanted to invest in Goldman, especially if Sumitomo and the Bishop Estate were investors—he was a close friend of John Weinberg—but could not recall a discussion about a combination of AIG and Goldman.) "It was very, very exploratory," Corzine said. "It wasn't like we were committing to anything. But the question was, was there something to be done between these two firms? There were some people advocating a combination between investment banking and insurance." Corzine said that while Greenberg was a "good leader and a good person," he was also "an intimidating guy" and so he was always skeptical of the potential deal. "Wasn't exactly like

I'm gonna sign up to be number two here," he said. More important, few at Goldman liked the idea of a deal with AIG. "A lot of us on the trading side," he said, "looked at that and said, 'You've gotta be kidding.' First of all, we're going to get swallowed up in a bureaucracy, and second of all we don't understand Financial Products at all"—a reference to AIG Financial Products, the London-based group that decided to sell billions of dollars of insurance against the potential default of various financial securities. (Later on, of course, Goldman's involvement with AIG would have major consequences in the financial crisis of 2008.)

As irritating as these merger overtures were to Paulson, it wasn't only the megamerger conversations that got him miffed about Corzine. There were also the failed efforts to acquire two money managers: Miller, Anderson & Sherrerd, with $29 billion under management, which Morgan Stanley ultimately bought; and RCM Management, with $22 billion under management, which sold to Dresdner Bank. Corzine also wanted to open new offices around the world. "Jon wanted to do business in every country, everywhere, and wanted to be big," one partner said. "He was like the guy going through a cafeteria and he wanted to take everything and put it on his tray. That concerned people." In 1995, Goldman opened offices in Shanghai and in Mexico City and created joint ventures in India and Indonesia. Paulson thought Corzine was moving too quickly to open offices and seemed never to have met a location he didn't like. Lloyd Blankfein used to joke that "he was going to go away someday and wake up and find out we were opening up an office in Guatemala."

For Paulson, the irony of working with Corzine was that while he was a much beloved figure around the firm, he was not an easy person with whom to work. Others noted that while Paulson often seemed not to be listening—his kinetic energy often had him bouncing around in the middle of a conversation—he was considered a very good listener, while Corzine looked like he was listening carefully to people but was often not paying attention. (His beard and cardigan sweaters made him look avuncular.) "He loved the firm," one former partner said about Corzine. "He was committed to the firm. He worked incredibly hard. That was the biggest part of his life. But he had a real hard time compromising, and that was a strange thing. To work jointly with someone, to work well with them, you have to be able to say, 'Okay, on matters of ethics or principle or conscience, I hold my ground,' but if there is something that the other guy feels very strongly about and it's not irrational or stupid on the face then you go that way.' The key is to figure out what are the really big issues, and to Jon every issue was a big issue. He just saw it that way."

Corzine also seemed to make loyalty to him the litmus test for everything. "When you'd say, 'Here are the three reasons why this doesn't make sense,' he would never say, 'Well, I disagree with you for this reason' and debate you," said one member of the senior management of the firm. "He just would say, 'Gee, I really think this makes sense,' and 'Gosh, I'd like you to support me on this. I just know this would be good.' He'd put his arm around people and a lot of them would agree with Jon. But there were plenty of people at Goldman Sachs that didn't want to do that. . . . It's always been, at Goldman Sachs, more about a bigger group of partners than just the leaders at the time."

In August 1997, the *Wall Street Journal* got hold of the fact that Goldman had considered buying Salomon Brothers two years earlier, and the idea was born that the firm was seriously considering a merger as a way to go public rather than doing an IPO. It was as if the firm's thinking from two years earlier had found its way into the paper on a time-released basis. The Salomon talks—between Corzine, Maughan, and Robert Denham, Salomon's chairman—"were merely exploratory," the paper reported, and didn't amount to much, especially after Goldman reportedly insisted on running the combined firm but showed "that taking itself public may not be the only route open to Goldman should it decide that it wants to become a public company." The paper also reported that AIG had considered taking a 25 percent stake in Goldman after the 1994 debacle. At the time of the *Journal*'s article, mergers were rampant on Wall Street, as was speculation about what deals were next. In May, Morgan Stanley merged with Dean Witter, in a surprising bid to diversify its institutional franchise into the retail market. Then there were a series of three smaller Glass-Steagall-busting deals between commercial banks and investment banks that had people scratching their heads: Bankers Trust Company bought Alex. Brown Inc.; BankAmerica Corp. bought Robertson Stephens & Co.; and NationsBank Corp. bought Montgomery Securities. (Glass-Steagall's repeal—long de facto—became de jure in November 1999, thanks in large part to Bob Rubin.)

The article speculated on the reasons why a merger with an existing public company would appeal to Goldman's younger partners—particularly the fact that no so-called IPO discount of between 10 percent and 15 percent would be required to attract investors—but the whole idea that a company with as formidable a brand as Goldman Sachs would go public through a "back-door IPO" seemed far-fetched.

Indeed, quite the opposite seemed true: the firm performed so well in 1996 and 1997 that a Goldman IPO looked increasingly inevitable at some point during 1998, when the partners would reconvene for their biannual meeting. Whatever else could be said about Corzine and his management style, there was no denying that he got the Goldman workforce out of its funk and focused intently on profits. In 1996, on revenue of $6.1 billion, the firm earned $2.6 billion in pretax profits, an unheard-of margin of 43 percent. In 1997, on $7.4 billion in revenue, Goldman earned $3 billion in pretax profit, a 41 percent margin. With regard to ROE, the performance measure Corzine had instituted in 1996, the firm's performance was off the charts: 51 percent in 1996 and 53 percent in 1997. In the wake of the 1994 disaster, Corzine and Paulson had turned Goldman Sachs into a profit machine.

But Paulson was not happy. He had been paid millions of dollars in compensation for years. He owned 4.1 million Goldman shares worth hundreds of millions of dollars and was on the brink of realizing much of that wealth, assuming Goldman moved forward with an IPO in 1998 as expected. Instead, he was burned out. He had been traveling through Asia for much of the year, while at the same time overseeing the firm's banking, private-equity, and asset management businesses. He could not get along with Corzine. "The differences between Corzine and me became huge," he said. "I was tired of bumping my head against a wall." He believed Corzine surrounded himself with his cronies, who told him what he wanted to hear, and was irritated by an increasing number of Corzine's decisions that he thought were wrong. For instance, one particularly galling situation occurred when Paulson fired a partner in Chicago who got caught having an affair with a twenty-one-year-old secretary. Corzine reversed the decision and reinstated the partner in New York. Or he would hear from his friends that Corzine was going around behind Paulson's back and trying to undercut him with other partners.

Before the Christmas break, Paulson went to see Corzine and told him he was thinking of leaving. "I said to him I didn't think it was healthy for both of us to be here," he said, "and that I was willing to leave. We just needed to negotiate who was going to be paired with him to run the firm because I wasn't comfortable having him run the firm unchecked." He wanted to negotiate with Corzine a bigger management role for both John Thain and John Thornton, who were quickly emerging as the leaders of the next generation at the firm. Corzine ignored him. "He didn't really respond," Paulson said. Corzine's nonresponse was increasingly typical of him, some of his partners had noticed, with growing frustration, when he seemed to be giving them "the limp leg." The "Fuzzy" nickname was heard with greater frequency within the halls of power at the firm. Paulson used the Christmas vacation to think about how to respond to Corzine's indifference. He and his family went to the Yucatán Peninsula for a little kayaking, birding, and fishing. Wendy counseled him not to be rash and to think through his decision. "You're miserable now," she told him. "I want you to be happy. But just make sure you're going to be happier if you leave."

———

PAULSON DECIDED TO keep fighting and went back into battle in 1998. Within weeks, though, Corzine made a major political misstep— or at least that's how it was perceived—and handed Paulson the opening he had long been seeking that would give him the upper hand at the firm.

Chris Flowers, the highly respected FIG banker, was one of Corzine's closest allies at the firm. Flowers was classic Goldman. Born in California, he had moved to Weston, Massachusetts, a suburb of Boston, at age six, when his father retired from the navy and took a job as an administrator at Harvard Business School. In high school, Flowers was a math whiz and a chess champion.

He then enrolled at Harvard, where he majored in applied mathematics. He said, "I found people at Harvard who made me look like a moron at math." Flowers knew he wanted to go into business. He got a summer job at Goldman Sachs after his sophomore year, and after graduating from Harvard a semester early, Flowers joined Goldman full-time in March 1979, working as an analyst for Steve Friedman in M&A. "The first thing I learned at Goldman was how to work hard," he explained. That first year he worked "three hundred and sixty-five days straight," and Goldman paid him $16,000. He says he also learned how to "sell," the mundane but crucial aspect of investment banking that requires bankers to persuade clients to hire you and your firm rather than someone else and his firm. Flowers bloomed at Goldman. He was invited into Goldman's nascent Financial Institutions Group as the M&A guy and quickly shone. By 1988, he'd been named a partner at the tender age of thirty-one, the youngest at the time to attain that distinction.

Corzine seemed utterly captivated by Flowers. They had worked together for ten years on different assignments, and Flowers impressed Corzine with his understanding of both strategy and capital markets. "He was our franchise with financial institutions and he was extraordinary," Corzine said. "I don't think anybody would dispute that he was number one or two in the world at giving advice to financial institutions." Flowers went out of his way to introduce Corzine to the other leaders in the financial industry. "Some of the original introductions were actually from Chris," Corzine said.

One of those introductions was to Frank Cahouet, the CEO of Mellon Bank. Mellon and Cahouet had been a longtime client of Goldman and Flowers. For instance, in April 1997, Mellon hired Goldman to sell its corporate trust business. Then, in October 1997, Mellon hired Goldman to represent the bank in an unfriendly $18 billion bid to acquire CoreStates Financial, another Pennsylvania bank (Goldman's principles about not representing hostile bidders having once again fallen by the wayside apparently). When CoreStates rejected Mellon's offer, Mellon dropped its bid. Early in 1988, Flowers arranged for a meeting between Corzine and Cahouet. To Corzine, the potential combination of Goldman and Mellon made tremendous sense. Mellon had no investment banking business (so no overlap) and a huge asset management business (one of the key areas in which Goldman was looking to grow) plus a commercial banking business that would allow Goldman access to a steady form of cheap financing from customer deposits. Mellon also had a nascent prime brokerage business, which provided brokerage services to hedge funds and other large institutional investors, another area that Goldman was also looking to build. In many ways, a combination with Mellon made tremendous sense for Goldman—at least on paper. "It was one meeting," Corzine said. "I was more enthusiastic about that, though, than any of the others. If we had been able to get through the 'King of the Hill' stuff, maybe it could have gotten done. But that wasn't happening with Frank and so it really wasn't going anywhere. I think it got deeply exaggerated by some of the folks who wanted to use it as another excuse to say I didn't know what I was doing." Corzine told Paulson about the meeting, told him it was "very preliminary" but that it "made a lot of sense" and that he thought he and Cahouet would be co-CEOs and Paulson would have the "much bigger role" of being head of the combined firms' commercial and investment banking businesses.

From Paulson's perspective, Corzine's "one meeting" with Cahouet was actually something more. Paulson worried that perhaps Corzine had already started negotiations to put the two firms together. Then, "after he was pretty far along he said something to me," Paulson said, "and then he said he wanted Chris Flowers to talk with me about it." Flowers, whom Paulson described as "incredibly commercial, really bright, and quite straightforward," had an amazing message for Paulson. "Chris had explained to me that my stock would be worth $850 million after we got done [with the merger]," he recalled. "I remember they thought that would really do the trick." After his meeting with Flowers about the deal, Paulson said he spoke with Corzine and raised some objections—particularly that he thought Corzine might be getting ahead of himself—and that if he was going to have another meeting with Cahouet, Paulson wanted to be there.

But Corzine told him he was just getting to know Cahouet and wanted to do the next meeting by himself. He told Paulson he wasn't going to get into any details, he was just going to listen and take notes. Paulson wasn't happy about Corzine's decision, but Corzine was the CEO. What could he do? After Corzine had the second meeting with Cahouet, Paulson asked him how it went and what had transpired. "Well," Corzine told him, "I just listened. I didn't get any details." Then Paulson called Flowers—"a heat-seeking missile looking for the money," he said—and asked him to come by and see him that day, which happened to be a Sunday. Flowers told Paulson that Corzine had made a merger proposal to Cahouet, including specifics on the economics of the deal, the exchange ratio, and who would be leading which business units. "I got angry," Paulson said.

At the Management Committee meeting the next morning, Paulson asked Corzine to describe what had happened between him and Cahouet and the possibility of a merger between Goldman and Mellon. Corzine didn't respond. "He gave a limp leg and basically said nothing," one partner at the meeting recalled. Incredulous, Paulson then asked Flowers to come to the meeting and give the Management Committee a briefing. Flowers came in and gave all the details of the discussion, just as he had done the day before with Paulson. "Jon's so mad and angry, he ran out of the management committee and into his office," another participant in the meeting said. Corzine's allies on the Management Committee then got angry with Paulson. "One person said, 'You guys shouldn't have done that. You've embarrassed him and now what if he quits or something?'" But the majority of the Management Committee was so irate at Corzine for discussing a merger with Mellon without its knowledge or consent—and then not coming clean about it—that they decided to prevent him from engaging in any future strategic discussions at all. The committee gave that responsibility to Paulson exclusively. Not a word of this decision leaked beyond the Management Committee itself. The discussions with Cahouet and Mellon were terminated immediately.

———

PAULSON PUT TOGETHER a strategic-planning committee—including on it Lloyd Blankfein, the head of FICC, Goldman's immensely profitable business focused on fixed-income, interest rates, and currencies; Steven Einhorn, the head of research; Christopher Cole, another prominent FIG banker; and Peter Weinberg, one of the three heads of investment banking—to begin to explore what the future of the banking industry would look like and whether (again) the firm should go public or should consider a merger. "We concluded we needed a lot of capital," Paulson said. The committee was divided about whether an IPO was the right answer or whether a strategic merger would get the firm to the place it needed to be. For his part, Paulson was again becoming increasingly irritated. First, Flowers was going around and showing various senior partners how much his or her Goldman stock would be worth in an IPO, behavior Paulson thought especially uncouth. Flowers's attempts to appeal to employees' greed infuriated Paulson to the point where he resolved that Flowers's days at the firm were numbered. Second, in the wake of the Mellon breach, Paulson was now openly feuding with Corzine. Their arrangement made him uncomfortable under any circumstance, but on the eve of what certainly was looking like a serious vote of the partnership in mid-June about the idea of an IPO, it was terribly unseemly for the two senior partners running the firm to be clashing.

Paulson made the decision to leave Goldman if Corzine remained the firm's CEO. He told his allies on the Executive Committee what he had decided. There was little doubt that Paulson was willing to follow through on his threat, but he must have known that his preferred outcome would be the one the committee would insist upon instead: to wit, there was no way the firm could afford to lose Paulson on the eve of the firm's long-awaited IPO. Not only could he not leave, the committee—or at least the three of the four members on it (Hurst, Thornton, and Thain) not abstaining (as Paulson and Corzine might be inclined to do)—demanded that Paulson take the reins of the firm with Corzine. Thain, a onetime close ally of Corzine's and one of the executors of his estate, was asked to speak with Corzine about the committee's decision.

Thain's message was clear and delivered to Corzine as a fait accompli: he had to agree immediately to become co-chairman and co-chief executive with Paulson. The other members of the committee were so concerned about Corzine's freelancing and that Paulson might follow through on his latest threat to leave that they gave Corzine little choice. They also knew that with the stock market booming, especially for financial stocks in the wake of the blockbuster merger between Travelers and Citibank to form Citigroup (the merger that effectively ended Glass-Steagall), the time was fast approaching when the Goldman partnership would have little choice but to vote to go public. They knew they would need a CEO to lead them and decided Paulson would be the man to do it, not Corzine.

Sometime around Memorial Day 1998, Paulson and Corzine met to discuss the Executive Committee's decision. Corzine tried to talk Paulson out of it, or to at least convince him to wait until the full partnership had voted on the IPO at the upcoming mid-June retreat. But Paulson told him no, he would not wait. Corzine had to agree to the new arrangement immediately. The message delivered to Corzine was crystalline: "There's a hard way and there's an easier way." Corzine took the news hard. Those walking by his office that day recalled hearing him get physically sick. But Corzine came around to the new reality. At a dinner with several other executives at the Park Avenue Café, at one point Corzine and Paulson stood up, and Corzine announced that he had decided to make Paulson his partner running the firm. The two men then hugged, sending the eyes rolling of the other men who witnessed the brief—and highly unlikely—bromance.

On June 1—the Monday after the Memorial Day weekend—Goldman announced that Paulson had been promoted to run the firm with Corzine and that the two nineteen-member operating and partnership committees had recommended that the full partnership vote on the IPO proposal at the June 12 partners' meeting. In the coverage of the two blockbuster announcements, the media understandably focused more intently on the news of the IPO. Paulson's promotion was mentioned in passing, along the lines that it was in keeping with Goldman's tradition of having two senior partners running the firm. No mention was made of the feud between Paulson and Corzine or the events that had precipitated the leadership change. "While Goldman has discussed proposals for its public sale seven times over the past 27 years, the recommendation by the two committees . . . is significant because it indicates there is broad support for a public sale," Dow Jones reported.

The firm's bankers working on the IPO—led by Flowers—had valued Goldman at $30 billion, according to the news service, at the high end of comparable estimates. Flowers based his valuation off the firm's 1997 pretax profit of $3 billion and a first-quarter 1998 pretax profit of $1.02 billion. The media speculated that four members of the firm's six-man Executive Committee—Corzine, Paulson, Hurst, and Zuckerberg—favored the IPO, while Thain and Thornton appeared less enthusiastic.

There was also plenty of speculation about whether the $30 billion was correct, what percentage of the firm would be sold—generally thought to be between 10 percent and 15 percent—and how the proceeds of the offering would be divided up. There was also speculation about whether Goldman would trade at a premium to Morgan Stanley, which traded at four times book value, and Merrill Lynch, which traded at 3.5 times book value. With Goldman's equity at roughly $6.3 billion, these were not idle questions, especially since the firm had had an excellent second quarter and seemed to be on track for $4 billion of pretax profits, its best year ever. Regardless of what the multiple of book value would be—4 times, or even higher—the current general partners stood to make a killing, with estimates ranging from $100 million for junior partners to more than $200 million each for Corzine, Paulson, and Roy Zuckerberg, then the longest-serving partner. Also realizing massive windfalls would be both Sumitomo, which by then had $736 million of invested capital, and the Bishop Estate, which had $658 million of invested capital. An unanswered question in the early stages of the discussion was how to treat Goldman's limited partners—those former partners who had helped create the firm's success but who were no longer part of the day-to-day business. "At a multiple of two times book, I would think everyone would be very happy," one limited partner told the *Times*. "At three times book, I think everyone would be positively delirious." He had no comment, apparently, about how everyone would feel at a 4 times book valuation.

After a weekend meeting of the partners at Arrowwood—a far less contentious meeting than in years past—Goldman announced that a "majority of its partners" approved of pursuing an IPO and that the firm's Executive Committee had "unanimously" agreed to recommend that course of action to the full partnership—implying that any opposition to the idea by Thain and Thornton had melted away. "The partnership is determined to match the firm's capital structure to its mission of being the preeminent, independent investment bank in the world," Corzine and Paulson said in a grandiose statement. "As a public company, Goldman Sachs will have the financial strength and strategic flexibility to continue to serve our clients effectively as well as respond thoughtfully to the business and competitive environment over the long term. This action will also meet a fundamental objective of the partners—to share ownership, benefits and responsibilities more broadly among all of the firm's employees."

Paulson and Corzine wrote that the decision to pursue an IPO came after "lengthy, open and intensive dialogue in the best tradition of Goldman Sachs. Our culture of collaboration and teamwork, which has been inextricably linked to the firm's success, will continue to flourish in the new structure, reinforced by the manner in which we implement our plan." They wrote that Goldman was "confident" and has never "been stronger in terms of the depth and breadth of our client relationships, the quality of our people and the market positions of our key businesses, many of which enjoy dominant leadership positions." While immodest, it was difficult to argue with what Goldman was claiming: it *was* the predominant, preeminent, and most envied, feared, and revered investment bank in the world. But deciding to go public—while plenty momentous—was the not the same as pulling off a successful IPO, and the firm's ability to do that in increasingly choppy markets remained to be seen.

Corzine had managed to get 74.7 percent of the partners to vote for the IPO. "I went from being the object of intense criticism at all times to having restored the belief that I knew what I was doing, that Corzine was not only going to survive but thrive," he said. "I went from being a man who could not only make money to also someone who could get something done that nobody else could get done."

Of course, the events of the weekend weren't nearly as smooth as the public announcement would have people believe. For instance, like a congressman who knows that what he really wants to happen will happen no matter what he says in public, Paulson actually got up and spoke *against* the IPO. "I believed we were going to need to go public to get permanent capital," Paulson said. "But when we all got together to vote I spoke against doing a public offering because I had a lot of experience—unlike some other people on the Management Committee—working with public companies, working to take companies public, understanding what an important change it is, how flawlessly you need to execute, and I felt with the management situation as unsettled as it was with Jon and me, with all the issues we had, and with all the issues that Goldman Sachs had had, and with Jon making this all about money and sending Chris Flowers around to meet with everyone and explain to them this is exactly what you'll get if we go public, that it was the wrong time and the wrong way to get into this." Others were offended by Flowers's raw display of greed, even as they were seduced by the numbers. Many partners were "troubled by even secretly being greedy, culturally," one of them said. Based on what other people said publicly, too, Paulson would have guessed Goldman would have remained private. "Some people were made to feel that if they voted for the IPO, they were voting against the history, the heritage, the culture," Paulson said. "They were voting to take the dollars rather than looking at it strategically." In the end, though, the vote was overwhelmingly in favor of the IPO.

What had bought Paulson's support was Corzine's agreement to make Paulson the co-chairman and co–chief executive officer. From that moment on, Corzine and Paulson's mission was to sell, and that's what they were busy doing. Goldman was nothing if not a massive selling machine. In an interview with the *Times,* on June 15, the two men made clear how little they expected Goldman would change in light of the decision to give up the firm's privacy. They explained that Goldman would not become a "financial conglomerate," it would not merge with a "Main

Street" broker, and it would not entertain merger proposals from a commercial bank. Nor was the IPO about making Goldman's partners even richer than they already were. "Contrary to what you might read, we are not doing this because of the money," Corzine said. "This is not about money or cashing out." Instead, Corzine emphasized that Goldman intended to use the IPO—and the capital generated from it—to become an even fiercer competitor. "We intend to be the pre-eminent, independent global investment bank," he said. "We are going to be damn tough, and we will have the capital to compete."

He also seemed to have found religion on the subject of mergers. That idea was off the table, he said, although Goldman might consider a few smaller acquisitions, especially among asset managers, where Goldman was still trying to grow the $160 billion it had under management. "We will have some new strategic opportunities, and we will go into acquisition mode," he said. "I am not talking about mergers, but acquisitions." As an example, Corzine could have mentioned Goldman's May 1997, roughly $100 million acquisition of Commodities Corporation, a $2 billion managed futures, commodities, and currencies hedge fund based in Princeton, New Jersey, that counted among its founders Paul Samuelson, Larry Summers's uncle.

———

INTERNECINE WARFARE ASIDE, in the aftermath of the IPO announcement, Goldman Sachs seemed to be floating on a cloud: the partners were united behind a task (underwriting an IPO) for which they were the world's experts and behind a cause (themselves) that provided them with all the incentive they could ever need to execute flawlessly. The valuation being bandied about for the firm seemed to grow daily— $30 billion, $35 billion, even $40 billion didn't seem far-fetched. After all, if Morgan Stanley was worth 4 times book, then Goldman Sachs— universally acclaimed as the world's best investment bank—should be worth even more. The Goldman IPO was very big news, and Wall Street seemed obsessed by it. True, the occasional analyst did wonder why the public should buy if Goldman Sachs was selling—"These guys are very smart, the best on Wall Street, and they are saying it is time to sell shares," one analyst observed. "Is this the top? If anybody knows, they would"—but most people on Wall Street seemed to be caught up in the euphoria over the Goldman IPO.

———

WHAT A SHAME, then, that a little crisis—in the form of the blowup of the hedge fund Long-Term Capital Management, or LTCM as it was known—would come along at just this moment to spoil Goldman's coming-out party. LTCM was the brainchild of John Meriwether, a famed Salomon Brothers bond trader and one of Corzine's trading heroes. Meriwether started LTCM in 1994. Corzine had considered having Goldman make an investment in LTCM and even considered buying the firm itself. But, in the end, Goldman decided to be one of LTCM's many trading partners on Wall Street.

As has been well documented in Roger Lowenstein's best seller, *When Genius Failed,* LTCM combined all of Meriwether's supposed trading expertise with the technical expertise of Nobel Prize–winning economists Robert Merton and Myron Scholes and with the regulatory expertise of David Mullins, the vice chairman of the Federal Reserve Board, who resigned his position to join LTCM. It was a partnership designed to maximize the seduction of potential investors.

Needless to say, LTCM was the envy of Wall Street—in the days before hedge funds were a dime a dozen—and firms rushed to do business with it, including Goldman. LTCM's computer-driven investment strategy was to make so-called convergence trades, involving securities that were mispriced relative to each other, taking long positions on the inexpensive side of a trade and a short position on the expensive side of a trade. For the first two years, the strategy worked splendidly. Investor returns were around 40 percent during that period, and the assets under management swelled to $7 billion. The original partners and investors were getting richer and richer.

In September 1997, even though LTCM had earned $300 million in one of its best months ever, "the firm's prospects were steadily dimming," according to Lowenstein, because it was having trouble finding profitable trades in the shifting markets. On September 22, Meriwether wrote to investors that the fund "had excess capital" and intended to return to investors all the profits made on the money invested in 1994 and all the money invested in the fund after that date. This amounted to a return of about half the fund's $7 billion in capital. The LTCM partners and employees kept all of their money in the fund. Investors saw this not as a lucky windfall—an idea hard to imagine today—but rather as if they were being deprived of water in Death Valley. They clamored to stay fully invested in LTCM, since the geniuses who had founded the firm were minting money. But the firm turned most of them down.

In 1997, LTCM earned a respectable 17 percent return for its investors, after fees. The performance was the worst of the firm's short life but hardly fatal. As promised, LTCM returned to its investors $1.82 for every dollar they'd invested, although their original investment stayed in the fund. Meriwether's concern about the markets and LTCM's prospects proved prescient as 1998 unfolded. On August 17, Russia announced a devaluation of the ruble and a moratorium on the payment of $13.5 billion of its Treasury debt. The devaluation and the moratorium caught many investors off guard, not only at LTCM but at Goldman Sachs, too.

This opened up another fissure in the relationship between Paulson and Corzine, who had been on their best behavior in the weeks following the June IPO announcement. But the events in Russia were reminding Paulson an awful lot of 1994, and he was nervous. Not surprisingly, Corzine—the trader—wanted Goldman's traders to ride out their positions. Paulson—the banker—was highly skeptical of that strategy. "Maybe if we hold on to some of these positions as you suggest, Jon, our losses will be less, but we're not a hedge fund," Paulson remembered telling Corzine. "We're Goldman Sachs. And I want to get out of these positions and take our losses." At this particular moment, Paulson had the upper hand at the firm, having just won the backing of the majority of the Executive Committee to promote him to co-CEO. He also figured that after taking the losses, the firm's ROE for the year would still be in the very respectable range of 18 percent. Corzine told Paulson to his face that he agreed with the decision to cut and run but the message getting out around the firm was a different one. "Paulson and Corzine would communicate to the traders," one partner recalled, "and Paulson would be communicating one thing and Corzine would be talking to them behind his back and maybe he was just fuzzy in what he said, but they sure weren't hearing the same things from Corzine they were hearing from Paulson." This made Paulson crazy.

On August 21, the full import of Russia's decision hit world markets, and a massive flight began immediately out of risky investments, such as the debt and equity of emerging markets, into the supposedly less risky Treasury securities of the United States and Germany. "Minute by minute, Long-Term was losing millions," Lowenstein wrote. That Friday, LTCM lost $553 million in a single day, or 15 percent of its capital. At the start of the year, LTCM had had $4.67 billion in capital, but after the losses suffered on August 21, the firm's capital had been reduced to $2.9 billion. When Meriwether got the word of the massive trading losses, he was in China. He took the next flight back to New York. Before he did, though, he called Corzine at home. "We've had a serious markdown," Meriwether told Corzine, "but everything is fine with us." But, according to Lowenstein, "everything was not fine." That weekend, the LTCM partners gathered in Greenwich, Connecticut, and realized quickly that the firm needed a savior. A quick call was placed to Warren

Buffett to see if he would buy LTCM's $5 billion portfolio of merger arbitrage positions. Buffett declined.

After Corzine got the call from Meriwether, he called back and warned him, "We aren't getting adequate feedback. It could hurt your credit standing." Corzine—and the rest of the market—wanted to know more about LTCM's positions and the extent of its problems. If it wanted to raise new capital, LTCM had little choice but to begin to reveal its positions, a disclosure that allowed its trading partners—including Goldman—to begin to dump similar trades, exacerbating LTCM's downfall. On August 27, the *Times* wrote that the "market turmoil is being compared to the most painful financial disasters in memory."

On Monday, August 24, while Meriwether and LTCM were dialing for dollars, Goldman filed its "long-anticipated" S-1 registration statement with the SEC. As was typical for such preliminary filings, much financial information was left out, including what the implied valuation of the firm would be based on, the number of shares sold, and the price they would be sold at. What was shared, for the first time, was how obscenely profitable the firm had been since 1993. In the five and a half years between the end of 1992 and the first six months of 1998, Goldman had made pretax profits of $12.2 billion, an astounding figure by any measure, especially when 1994 was included—as predicted, the S-1 showed $508 million of pretax earnings that year (1994), but that was before paying out distributions to partners, making the year a loss. Essentially, because of the partnership accounting, much of the $12.2 billion had been paid out to the Goldman partners or retained in their capital accounts at the firm. The S-1 filing confirmed what many had long suspected anyway: Goldman Sachs was a gold mine. Corzine had been right to exhort the Goldman alpha males to overcome the events of 1994 and rededicate themselves to the firm. "He was really endlessly optimistic," one partner said, "and it turned out to be true. Despite all the bad things that have happened, he was right."

Also remarkable was the S-1's revelations about the growth in Goldman's principal lines of business. For instance, since 1982, the volume of worldwide M&A deals had grown at a compounded annual rate of 25 percent, worldwide equity issuance had increased at an annualized rate of 19 percent, and worldwide debt issuance had increased at an annualized rate of 25 percent. Worldwide equity market capitalization had increased at an annualized rate of 15 percent.

Not surprisingly, the S-1 began with Whitehead's fourteen business principles. Number one, right at the top, was "Our clients' interests always come first. Our experience shows that if we serve our clients well, our own success will follow." But, even inside Goldman Sachs, fewer and fewer people were able to take this seriously. Indeed, several Goldman traders remembered what partner Peter Briger used to say about this commandment: "Yeah, and when we do, make no mistake about it, it's a business decision." Nevertheless, Whitehead's business principles made good reading, as did the reason Goldman gave for wanting to do the IPO in the first place. "As a public company, we will have greater financial strength, greater strategic flexibility and broader alignment of employee interests with the interests of our shareholders," the firm wrote. "From a financial perspective, public ownership will give us a more stable capital base, broaden our sources of capital and lower our funding costs. From a strategic perspective, while we expect most of our growth will continue to be organic, public ownership will give us a currency with which we may choose to pursue strategic acquisitions. From an employee perspective, public ownership will help us meet a fundamental objective—to share ownership broadly among the Firm's employees."

The S-1 also contained a long list of "risk factors" that most investors ignored, including what would become a very relevant warning about how dependent Goldman—like the rest of Wall Street's securities firms—was on short-term funding in the public debt markets. "The Firm depends on the issuance of commercial paper and promissory notes as a principal source of unsecured short-term funding for its operations," according to the S-1. "As of May 1998, the Firm had approximately $16.7 billion of outstanding commercial paper and promissory notes with a weighted average maturity of approximately 100 days. The Firm's liquidity depends to an important degree on its ability to refinance these borrowings on a continuous basis. Investors who hold the Firm's outstanding commercial paper and promissory notes have no obligation to purchase new instruments when the outstanding instruments mature."

Within weeks of Goldman's S-1 filing, liquidity in the debt markets was drying up. "The end of August is always a slow time in markets," Lowenstein wrote, "but this August, trading in bond markets all but vanished. The market for new bond issues simply dried up. Scheduled new offerings were abruptly withdrawn, which was just as well, because there was no one to buy them."

Despite the increasing shakiness in the markets, Goldman held firm to its IPO schedule. On September 8, in an internal conference call, Paulson said Goldman would continue forward with its plan for the IPO. "Nothing that's happening in the markets today, last week, tomorrow or next week should substantially change that objective or our positive outlook we have for our firm in the next five to ten years," he said. "The IPO process is still on track." That same day, Goldman announced that Flowers was "retiring" from Goldman at the end of the year, the consequence of his souring relationship with Paulson and his thwarted attempt to be appointed one of the three co-heads of investment banking and to the firm's Management Committee. Paulson asked him to postpone his leaving for a year until the IPO had been resolved because he was afraid that Flowers's departure at that moment would send the wrong message to the market. But the pissed-off Flowers ignored the request. "Twenty years is a long time to be in one place," Flowers told the *Times* the next day. Years later, though, he said his unequivocal support of Corzine cost him as Paulson became more ascendant at the firm. "It was a very bitter disagreement between these guys," he said, "and I was an important part of the Corzine faction. . . . But the politics of it had been very bitter and divisive and ugly and I felt that I personally was as far as I was going to get at Goldman. The future was not bright for me there." (The Flowers-Paulson feud continued for years, including when Flowers was getting ready to do an IPO, in February 2004, of Shinsei Bank, the renamed Japanese bank he and investor Timothy Collins bought—and turned around—after Flowers left Goldman. Flowers refused to let Goldman into the IPO, even though Goldman had the best research in the area. When it came time for the secondary sale of shares, a bit later, Goldman again wanted an underwriting role. At first, Flowers said no but then agreed that if Paulson came to his house on a Saturday and begged, Flowers would consider it. Paulson showed up and on bended knee asked Flowers for the order. But Flowers still said no. The Shinsei deal made Flowers and Collins billionaires.)

By mid-September word of LTCM's losses had leaked into the market, and the laws of self-fulfilling prophecies took over. Late in the day on September 10, the assets that LTCM had "in the box" at Bear Stearns, its clearing agent, fell below $500 million for the first time, triggering a provision in the agreement LTCM had with Bear. Warren Spector, the co-president and co-COO of Bear Stearns, called Meriwether and told him Bear would send a team to LTCM's offices in Greenwich that Sunday to examine the books and make a decision about whether to stop clearing for the firm, which would put LTCM out of business. Out of desperation, Meriwether called Corzine, who was in Venice celebrating his anniversary, and told him LTCM needed $2 billion or else it would go out of business. Meriwether also went to see James E. Cayne, Bear's CEO. "I asked if he had any assets at all, and he said, 'I've got a $500 million line [of credit] at Chase,'" Cayne recalled. "I said, 'Well, take it down.' He said, 'It expires in ten days and they know we're not going to be able to pay it back.' I said, 'I know, but you can take it down.' He said, 'How do you know that?' I said, 'I don't know that. Go talk to a lawyer. But to me, if you've got a line take it down and let them go whistle or do something, but that's salvation." Soon enough, LTCM had taken Cayne's advice.

Before deciding whether to draw down his line of credit, Meriwether turned again to Corzine. Without Paulson's knowledge, Corzine offered to have Goldman invest $1 billion of its own and its clients' money into LTCM in exchange for a 50 percent stake in the LTCM management company, unfettered access to LTCM's trading positions, and a right to limit its trading. Corzine also pledged to help Meriwether raise the other $1 billion he thought LTCM needed. "Merely informing the world that Goldman was in Long-Term's corner might stop the bleeding," Lowenstein wrote. "Meriwether could not say no."

The agreement between Goldman and LTCM allowed a SWAT team of traders, led by Jacob Goldfield—Rubin's protégé—and lawyers from Sullivan & Cromwell to comb through every crevice of LTCM during the week of September 14, with LTCM's permission, of course. According to Lowenstein, citing "witnesses," Goldfield "appeared to be downloading Long-Term's [trading] positions, which the fund had so zealously guarded, from Long-Term's own computers, directly into an oversized laptop"—a fact that Goldman later denied. In an interview, Goldfield said he did nothing wrong, inappropriate, or unauthorized. "If it were true," he wrote in an e-mail, referring to Lowenstein's claim, "the most interesting story would be my hacking skills given that this was highly confidential data and I was in plain sight." He was just doing necessary due diligence, with LTCM's approval, so Goldman could evaluate the potential investment in LTCM. Goldfield shared a spreadsheet that LTCM gave him about its trading positions. LTCM also faxed Goldfield its counterparty positions to help him do the analysis. "The biggest revelation to us," Goldfield wrote, "when we saw LTCM was how low tech they were. Goldman Sachs was much more sophisticated than they and I had thought it was quite the opposite."

Meanwhile, Goldman's traders in New York sold some of the very same positions. "At the end of one day, when the fund's positions were worth a good deal less, some Goldman traders in Long-Term's offices sauntered up to the trading desk and offered to buy them," Lowenstein wrote. "Brazenly playing both sides of the street, Goldman represented investment banking at its mercenary ugliest." Meriwether complained "bitterly" to the New York Federal Reserve Bank about Goldman's alleged "front-running," or trading against LTCM based on the knowledge it had gleaned from looking at its confidential books, but "Goldman was hardly alone," Lowenstein wrote and then quoted a Goldman trader in London. "If you think a gorilla has to sell, then you sure want to sell first," the trader said. "We are very clear where the line is; that's not illegal." (The idea of not crossing a line about "front-running" was confirmed in an interview by Eliot Spitzer, the former New York State attorney general who had studied the allegation against Goldman and certainly would have prosecuted the firm had he found the evidence.) Lowenstein noted that the previous "stewards" of Goldman—he must have been referring back to Sidney Weinberg—had disdained proprietary trading because the temptation to trade on "customer flow" would be too great. "But by 1998," he wrote, "Goldman was known as an aggressive, bare-knuckled trader that had long since abandoned any pretense of being a gentleman banker." Corzine later told Lowenstein that Goldman's traders "did things in markets that might have ended up hurting LTCM. We had to protect our own positions. That part I'm not apologetic for." He said, though, that Goldman did not take the information it had gathered about LTCM in Greenwich and trade on it.

As Goldman tried to round up the usual suspects who might be able to invest $1 billion in a sinking ship, it quickly found that LTCM had already made those same calls. On September 17, the LTCM partners went to see Corzine and Thain—though plenty pissed at Goldman for what they believed was trading on its inside information—and told them that Goldman was "our last chance." The outlook was bleak for LTCM. Later that same day, even though his hedge fund was largely unregulated, Meriwether had let the New York Federal Reserve know what was going on, specifically William McDonough, its president, and Peter Fisher, his deputy. LTCM's equity was down to $1.5 billion, a 60 percent decline in a month.

With Flowers gone, Peter Kraus, another senior banker in the Financial Institutions Group, was leading Goldman's efforts to try to find another investor for LTCM. As one potential candidate after another dropped away, Kraus kept talking to Buffett. Buffett hated the structure of LTCM and wanted none of its overhead or its resident geniuses. He might, though, be interested in the LTCM's severely depressed trading positions, he told Kraus. Out of this idea, Kraus and Buffett hatched the idea that Berkshire Hathaway, Buffett's company, Goldman Sachs, and AIG could put together a consortium bid for LTCM's assets. While at a Beethoven concert in Newark that Friday night, Kraus got up and called Buffett in Omaha. "He and Buffett penciled out some numbers for a deal," Lowenstein wrote. Shortly thereafter, Buffett took one of his jets to

Seattle to meet Bill Gates to start a long-planned two-week vacation in some of the remotest parts of Alaska. "Now the dream was alive that Buffett would rescue Long-Term—as he had, coincidentally, Salomon seven years earlier," Lowenstein wrote.

On Saturday, Corzine called Buffett and found him, with a shaky cell phone connection, in "the depths of an Alaskan fjord." They spoke briefly, although the connection kept fading in and out. "He was doing this float-around," Corzine told Lowenstein. "You'd lose contact and couldn't speak for two to three hours." But the message got through: "Buffett was willing to let Goldman handle the details, but under no circumstances did he want his investment to be managed by LTCM or to have anything to do with John Meriwether," Lowenstein wrote. "Then the connection blacked out." They spoke again on Saturday, and Buffett was still somewhat uncertain about a deal. Later that night, Corzine called Fisher and told him that a private rescue seemed unlikely. Fisher broached the idea of getting a group of the biggest banks together at the New York Fed and seeing if they could save LTCM. Corzine told Fisher that idea made some sense.

LTCM was in a death spiral, losing money hand over fist. The potential new investors, including Goldman and Buffett, wary to begin with, became increasingly spooked. McDonough and Fisher, meanwhile, after examining LTCM's trading positions, became increasingly concerned about the interconnectedness of all of LTCM's trades with the leading firms on Wall Street. Not only had Wall Street invested in LTCM but many of the firms had also piggybacked on LTCM's trades. They were also counterparties with one another. The Fed was not concerned about the potential losses that investors would suffer—they were big boys—but was worried about a failure of the system. "[I]f Long-Term failed, and if its creditors forced a hasty and disorderly liquidation, [McDonough] feared that it would harm the entire financial system, not just some of its big participants," Lowenstein wrote. "McDonough evoked a parallel fear—that losses in so many markets and to so many players would spark a vicious circle of liquidations, extreme fluctuations in interest rates, and then further losses: 'Markets would . . . probably cease to function for a period of one or more days and maybe longer.'"

But the fat lady had not yet sung. While the heads of many of the world's largest banks were cooling their heels at the New York Fed, Corzine and Thain had pulled McDonough aside and told him that Buffett was ready to bid after all. To verify the accuracy of what the Goldman team had told him, McDonough called Buffett—now at a ranch in Montana—and learned that he was ready to send in his bid, which theoretically anyway would relieve the consortium of banks that had gathered from having to put together a rescue. McDonough had no choice but to let the Buffett proposal play out. He told the waiting bankers there would be a pause in the action. "In the main room, the CEOs rose with a look of disgust," Lowenstein wrote. "They were furious at Goldman for dealing behind their backs." Buffett then called Meriwether and told him an offer for LTCM was on the way; Kraus was busy working on it. When the offer came to Meriwether an hour or so later, he was incredulous: Berkshire, Goldman, and AIG had offered to buy LTCM for $250 million, and then would inject another $3.75 billion into the firm to allow for something like normal trading to continue. Of the $3.75 billion, Berkshire was putting up $3 billion. What had been worth $4.7 billion at the beginning of the year was now worth $250 million. The LTCM partners would lose their jobs and be wiped out. Buffett gave Meriwether less than an hour to decide. He then became unreachable.

The offer letter was technically and legally flawed—for inexplicable reasons—and with Buffett unavailable, Meriwether, who disliked the deal anyway, let the offer lapse. He decided to take his chances with McDonough, the Fed, and the bank consortium. The time had come to act. Based on a proposal made by Herbert Allison, then president of Merrill Lynch, the sixteen banks that were LTCM's largest counterparties would contribute $250 million each—a total of $4 billion—to LTCM in exchange for the vast amount of the firm's equity that had been owned by the original partners. LTCM's investors would be wiped out, but Allison hoped his plan would allow for an orderly liquidation of the firm's positions and prevent a systemic crash. By this time, Paulson was more than a little fed up with Corzine's antics with LTCM—first wanting to buy the hedge fund outright and then making a bungled show of trying to make a last-minute investment in LTCM—and started to lash out. He insisted that Thain trail Corzine at every turn. "It was really a matter of trust and confidence and making sure someone understood the numbers," Paulson said. "And that we were doing this in a disciplined way, where the firm's reputation wasn't going to get hurt. Because this was a mess. Goldman Sachs was trying to do several different things at once, and I didn't even know about some of them."

On the evening of September 22, Fisher and McDonough asked the heads of the sixteen banks to come to the New York Fed building on Liberty Street to discuss a Fed-orchestrated bailout of LTCM. Fisher permitted each bank to bring two representatives. Corzine came with Thain. Throughout parts of that meeting and during meetings on subsequent days, Paulson was on the phone with Thain, and he was increasingly angry that Goldman would have to pony up, first $250 million, and then $300 million (chiefly because Bear Stearns had declined to participate at all). With the basic agreement finally in place, the lawyers drafted up the paperwork over the next five days, trying to herd the cats toward a final agreement.

Many compromises were made along the way and much pain was taken by the consortium of banks. By agreeing to invest close to $4 billion in the LTCM carcass, they were saving themselves at the expense— of course—of the LTCM partners, who certainly deserved to take it on the chin. Early Sunday evening, September 27, while Corzine was returning to Manhattan from his 6,200-square-foot "majestic beach-front home" in Sagaponack (sold in 2010 for $43.5 million to hedge-fund manager and Goldman alum David Tepper), Bob Katz, Goldman's general counsel, informed the assembled lawyers that Goldman would drop out of the deal if any of the nearly $4 billion being put into LTCM went out the door to Chase, which was planning to take back the $500 million that LTCM drew down from its revolving line of credit as disaster struck, per Jimmy Cayne's suggestion. "The point was to rescue Long-Term, not to rescue Chase," Lowenstein wrote, and the other bankers, who felt the way Goldman did, were only too "happy to let Goldman play the heavy."

Chase thought Goldman was bluffing. Thomas Russo, the Lehman general counsel, did, too, and told Katz so. Without the payment, Chase said it would walk. With the payment, Goldman said it would walk. "There was no deal," Katz said later. When Corzine called in to the meeting while on the road back from beach, he reiterated Goldman's position. "Jon," exclaimed the Chase banker, "there is no polite way to say this: Goldman can go fuck themselves." Corzine held firm. The deal was dead, at least for Sunday night. Herb Allison at Merrill was caught in the middle. He knew that if Goldman walked, the whole deal would fall apart. "One always has to indulge the bad boys at Goldman," Lowenstein wrote. Later Sunday night, Chase caved in and allowed the newly recapitalized LTCM to keep the $500 million in the fund and to not pay the money out to the bank syndicate. Goldman was back on board. "None of us liked having to step up," Paulson said. "But it was really the only thing to do. When John Thain recommended that we do it and that we put together a structure where we had a fighting chance of avoiding very big losses, I signed off on it."

Thain said the decision to put $300 million into the LTCM rescue was very controversial inside Goldman, and the controversy was exacerbated by the fact that Jimmy Cayne and Bear Stearns decided not to contribute. "I don't think there was ever any real question of whether we were going to do it," he said, "but it was controversial and people were very concerned but there's a little bit of being a good citizen. When the head of the New York Fed says, 'Look, we have this problem, and I need you guys to help,' we were helping fix a problem that was going to be a problem for the system as a whole. Even though it was controversial, there was never really any doubt that we were going to do that. Bear Stearns and Jimmy Cayne, in particular, basically told the system 'Screw off.' That's never a very good thing to do because sometime you may need help, and when you refuse to be a good citizen and help somebody else, then people remember that." Of course, Goldman's subsequent role in exacerbating Bear Stearns's spectacular demise in March 2008 has been much debated, with some linking it to lingering anger over Cayne's decision not to participate in the bailout of LTCM.

The consortium of banks working together—albeit warily—had put their collective finger in the dike and prevented the collapse of the financial system. Alan Greenspan, the chairman of the Federal Reserve at the time, defended the Fed-orchestrated bailout. "Had the failure of LTCM triggered the seizing up of the markets," he told the House Banking Committee on October 1, "substantial damage could have been inflicted on many market participants and could have potentially impaired the economies of many nations, including our own." When Representative Barney Frank, of Massachusetts, criticized Greenspan for having the Fed organize the bailout that left "some of the richest people in the country better off than if you didn't intervene," Greenspan countered, "No Federal Reserve funds were put at risk, no promises were made by the Federal Reserve and no individual firms were pressured to participate," a curious reinterpretation of the facts.

There was no getting around the damage that the combination of the Russian and LTCM crises had inflicted on the markets, especially on the stocks of financial companies. The next afternoon, after the market closed on September 29, Goldman announced it was withdrawing its IPO and cited the "unsettled conditions" in the markets as the reason. Shares of many financial services companies had fallen as much as 50 percent since August. "You just have to look at how financial institutions are faring," Corzine told the *Times*. "Those valuations are really dramatically lower." Added Paulson about pulling the IPO, "This was not a close decision. This was a clear decision. I would conjecture that there would be very few people, if any, at Goldman Sachs who would question this decision." Whereas during the summer, Goldman's value was in the $30 billion range, the events of the previous weeks had reduced that to closer to $15 billion, and accordingly the amount of proceeds Goldman would get from the IPO would be reduced to $1.5 billion from $3 billion. In a "transatlantic rallying call" the next day, Corzine and Paulson told the firm not to fret about the withdrawn IPO. "Our watchword is steady as you go, full steam ahead," Corzine said. "We have important work to do." He added that "market dislocations have often provided opportunities for the firm in the past. Great institutions can distinguish themselves in difficult times." Regarding the LTCM crisis, Paulson told the firm that it was an "earthquake without historical precedent" and the "subterranean shifts are still playing themselves out." Corzine said of LTCM that Goldman was a "leader in seeking to dampen the systemic risk." As phone handsets were "clumsily put down," according to one account, Corzine left the firm with the exhortation: "Let us go forward!"

Nineteen ninety-eight being an even-numbered year, Goldman would normally have been in the process of picking a new partner class to be announced at the end of its fiscal year, in November. But as part of the decision to pursue the IPO, the firm had decided not to make any new partners in 1998, in order not to change the pool of partners who would partake in the IPO bonanza, a honeypot worth between $50 million and $125 million (or more) per partner, depending on their seniority and influence at the firm. Now, with the IPO withdrawn, Goldman announced on October 21 the names of fifty-seven new partners (among them Christian Siva-Jothy, the London trader who cost Goldman millions in losses in 1994)—putting them in line to become nearly instant multimillionaires the minute the decision was made to move forward again with the IPO. Goldman also announced the decision to force the retirement of between twenty and twenty-five existing partners—who would "become limited" in Goldman's argot—a decision that would correspondingly cost those partners millions. "I am sure that with the prospect of an I.P.O. just around the corner, there are some in that batch of retired partners who are not happy about it," one retired partner told the *Times*. "But I am sure there are others who just thought this was the time. You can't wait forever, and being a Goldman partner is an extremely demanding job."

Unbeknownst to most people, the decision to "withdraw" the IPO, as opposed to "delaying" the IPO, was another clever piece of Goldman Sachs alchemy. This was the brainchild of Bob Hurst—"He emerged as the real hero," Paulson said—who asked the lawyers if there would be any tax consequences of reconstituting the partnership by retiring a bunch of older partners and adding a new generation of younger partners. Being able to do this was very important to Paulson philosophically because he wanted to be "forward looking" by giving more of the IPO bonanza to the future generation of Goldman partners than to the past generation of Goldman partners. After examining the issue, the lawyers told Goldman that by "withdrawing" the IPO, the Goldman partnership could be "reconstituted" without tax consequences. Even though the process of pushing a bunch of partners into limited status with the IPO so close was exceedingly painful, Paulson said, it was the best thing for Goldman Sachs. "Politically, it was probably a mistake," he said, "because I had to talk with some people who were some very good friends of mine—really good friends—and we treated them fair economically, but retired them before we went public. I thought that the more money the more senior people had, the worse it was going to be. I wanted to put shares in the hands of the future. The idea of making fifty-seven new partners that would have some stock and we would bind them to us seemed important."

Among those that Paulson shoved out the door in October 1998 was Executive Committee member Roy Zuckerberg—a Corzine ally— and, at sixty-two, then the longest-serving Goldman partner. He was also the firm's largest individual shareholder, and becoming "limited" would cost him millions. No matter, he had to go. It was yet another fateful decision. Zuckerberg put the best face on it he could. "I decided the best thing for me in this case was to move on," he told the *Times*. "I have been here 31 years. The business has become extraordinarily intense as it has become more globalized. I was faced with a decision whether to sign an agreement to stay on for another two years and decided not to." He said he planned to serve one year as chairman of the Securities Industry and Financial Markets Association, a key Wall Street industry group, and spend time at his recently purchased $7.1 million house on eleven acres in East Hampton, with an eight-acre agricultural reserve suitable for farming and horses. "Now I have more time and can enjoy it more," Zuckerberg said. Michael Corleone had nothing on Hank Paulson.

The firm had also—relatively quietly, amid the IPO commotion— taken the unprecedented step of further bolstering its world's-best M&A department by hoovering up the top M&A bankers at its major competitors. Turned out it wasn't too difficult: Who could possibly resist the allure of being named a Goldman partner before its game-changing IPO? In short order, Goldman hired Ken Wilson, then a senior partner at Lazard, to work in FIG; Gordon Dyal, the head of M&A at Morgan Stanley; and Michael Carr, the head of M&A at Salomon Brothers. It was an M&A street sweep of unprecedented proportions and one only Goldman Sachs at the height of its powers could have had any hope of accomplishing. (To complete the sweep, in March 2000, Goldman also hired Jack Levy, the head of M&A at Merrill Lynch.) Not even when Goldman was desperately trying to build up its fixed-income business in the 1980s—and hired a group of traders from Salomon Brothers—had the firm done anything so audacious. Such was Goldman Sachs's power at the end of the second millennium.

———

IN THE WAKE of the LTCM crisis and the $300 million contribution to solve it, the pulled IPO and the contentious decision to force the retirement of a group of older partners, the relationship between Corzine and Paulson had reached a breaking point. Adding to the growing rift, Goldman had nearly $1 billion in trading losses in the second half of 1998. (The firm's pretax income for the year was $2.9 billion, some $100 million below 1997.) What would soon be known around 85 Broad Street as "the Glorious Revolution" was imminent. Unlike the civil war that broke out between the traders and bankers at Lehman Brothers that ended up tearing that firm apart in the 1980s, the war between the states at Goldman was less turf driven than personality driven. Paulson and Corzine simply did not get along, and the events of the second half of 1998 had merely shown others that the rift could no longer be covered up. Unfortunately for Corzine, he had shown himself to be the more strategically reckless of the two men and had lost his political support.

On November 8, seemingly out of nowhere, the *Sunday Times,* in London, ran a 375-word story under the headline "Goldman's Corzine Urged to Resign." (An earlier version of the story appeared on October 28 but then seemed to disappear.) According to the paper, "a leadership crisis is developing at Goldman Sachs in the wake of its aborted attempt at a stock-market flotation this autumn. The situation has become so extreme that Jon Corzine, chairman, is facing calls to resign." Citing "senior figures within the firm," the article said, "Goldman was badly in need of leadership and clarity on its future" and that since the IPO had been withdrawn, "the firm has seemed unable to recover its former confidence and recriminations have been rife." The *Sunday Times* floated the notion that Thornton and Thain—both working in London (with one of them likely being the unnamed source for the story)—who were "the most public in opposing" the IPO, might be the next logical leaders of the firm. In any event, the story was an extremely rare breach of Goldman's Victorian decorum. "For almost a year they ate, slept and drank the IPO," explained one partner. "Suddenly they understood that it could not go ahead and were plunged into coping with issues like LTCM. It is not surprising that against that background you don't have total clarity in the direction of the firm." The paper even added the gratuitous thought that the firm's preoccupation with the IPO had hurt the quality of its work—the "quality of Goldman's work is not what it used to be."

According to Charles Ellis, Corzine was in London when the story first appeared on October 28. (Goldman naturally denied the accuracy of the paper's report.) He had breakfast with a fellow partner and the story became the topic of conversation. When Corzine said he was not sure what he was going to do about it, his partner blew up. "You should be sure, Jon," he reportedly said. "Since you're wearing a business suit, I assume you have another meeting scheduled this morning, so here's what you should do: Cancel any other meetings you've booked. Go directly to Heathrow and fly back to the States. Before you take off, call Roy Zuckerberg and Bob Hurst and tell them to meet you at your house in New Jersey today and make it absolutely clear to everyone that before the executive committee meets Monday morning, both Thain and Thornton are out—fired for playing politics and doing it in public so that it hurts the firm. . . . If you do this immediately, everyone will understand and will back you. And if you don't, you'll be in real trouble, because in six months *they* will force *you* out." Corzine replied, according to Ellis, "I couldn't do that. It would hurt the firm." And he didn't.

There was no question Paulson had had it with Corzine. He could no longer envision the possibility of working with him as the co-CEO of a public Goldman Sachs. If the firm was to remain private, they could have divvied up responsibilities along business and strategic lines, but as a public company with public shareholders, that would simply not be possible. Even though the IPO had been withdrawn, there was no question that when markets improved—and when the firm's leadership conundrum had been resolved—a new S-1 would be filed. Paulson simply could not wait any longer. While Corzine was skiing in Telluride, Colorado, he demanded clarity from his fellow senior partners.

Before Christmas vacation, Paulson told them they had to choose between him and Corzine to lead the firm. But there was no real suspense. Once upon a time in the modern era of Goldman Sachs, the firm's bylaws required a vote of 80 percent of the full partnership to remove any partner from the firm. But sometime in the 1990s (no one was precisely sure when), one partner who was fired refused to leave. In order get him out, the partners agreed to change the partnership agreement to make it possible for a vote of 80 percent of the Management Committee (or the Executive Committee, as Corzine had renamed it) to be what was needed to get rid of a partner, including the senior partner of the firm. With Zuckerberg gone from the Executive Committee and no one yet selected to replace him, the fait was accompli: Hurst, Thornton, and Thain (and Paulson, obviously) were resolved that the time had come for Corzine to go. The 80 percent was in hand. Had the vote been put to the full partnership, Corzine's personal popularity would have likely carried the day—a point Paulson conceded. "He was more popular among the partners than I was," Paulson said. "He was better known than I was."

On January 12, the time had come to implement the palace coup. It was decided that the cerebral Thain, a onetime protégé of Corzine's, should be the one to deliver the bad news (again) to the former government bond trader. As part of the coup, Thornton and Thain were named co–chief operating officers under Paulson. It was perfectly Shakespearean. But Thain was extremely nervous about confronting Corzine with this decision and supposedly mumbled the words to him that he would have to go and the decision had been made. Corzine got pissed at him, forcing Paulson to double back and deliver the news to Corzine himself: Corzine needed to immediately give up the title of co-CEO but could remain at the firm as co-chairman with Paulson until the completion of the IPO, whenever that would be. After that, he needed to leave. "And that's how it all worked," explained the senior Goldman partner, matter-of-factly.

Corzine took the news hard, very hard. "He tends to be very emotional," one partner remembered being told about Corzine's reaction. "There were elephant tears and vomiting and things like that. But he got the message. He was very unhappy, but he took it like a man."

Looking back, Corzine said he was blindsided by the turn of events, which seems somewhat hard to believe for a man with his political gifts. "I couldn't quite understand why there so much dissidence but there was," he said. "But most of it at the end of the day was about whether we went public, how we went public, and the timing of that issue. The tension just constantly festered underneath the surface, with the known characters on one side" and Corzine on the other.

Corzine said that perhaps he was too trusting of Thain—the quickly jettisoned former executor of his estate—and failed to conceive of the fact that he could turn on him. "I was devastated," he said. He said he is still not sure why Thain changed his mind. "Maybe somebody whispered very sweet nothings in his ear," Corzine said. "I don't know. Maybe he was just convinced of the alternative strategy. I, frankly, never thought John Thain would ever turn, and by my calculation that gave me enough to protect myself." One former Goldman partner said the coup came about because of raw, alpha-male Darwinian behavior. "It was just pure ambition between these guys about who was going to run the place," he said. "And I thought the behavior, particularly of Thain, was just reprehensible. You know, Thain would just be one more guy if Corzine had not lifted him up and made him the important guy he is and he just absolutely stabbed the guy in the back. It was absolutely pathetic and it was just all about who was going to run the place and ambition and all that shit. Thain wanted to take over after Paulson." For his part, Thain said, "Corzine and Paulson fought constantly and completely inappropriately and couldn't get along, and they got to the point where they made us choose between the two of them." His said his decision to support Paulson over Corzine was an exceedingly difficult one and ended his relationship with Corzine. "It was very hard for me because I was much closer to Corzine," he said. "I had worked for him. I was closer to him personally. I liked him a lot as a person, but I had to pick who I thought would be the better long-term leader of the company, so that was a very hard decision to make."

There are those who believe that Thain and Thornton were willing to make a deal with Corzine that would have saved Corzine his job: if Corzine had been willing to name Thain and Thornton the heirs apparent, they would have voted with him against Paulson and Hurst. But Corzine couldn't make that deal. He didn't feel the two men were ready, plus neither of them understood the trading side of the business as well as he figured they should. Besides, there was Lloyd Blankfein coming up fast in the leadership ranks of the firm. Whatever the reason, Corzine did not make the deal with Thain and Thornton and it cost him his job. "I may not be the smartest guy in the world," he said. "But I'm certainly not the dumbest but I'm not the smartest. I knew you needed different perspectives in the management. The irony of all of this was I accelerated Thornton onto the management committee among his peers and obviously Thain before that. Their actions caused me great emotional frustration."

"This Time, Shared Reins Didn't Work at Goldman" read the headline in the New York Times the next day. The dissolution of the working partnership between Paulson and Corzine came as a "surprise" to many and was laid at the doorstep of the fact that, in the end, the two men didn't like each other very much. "The biggest single factor here is that the two guys really did not get along with each other," explained one partner. "Hank and Jon are not friends." The Times observed that "the failure of Mr. Corzine and Mr. Paulson to bond together and become a close team" became "a liability," especially with the news earlier in the week that Paulson thought the Goldman IPO would happen in 1999 and "Goldman's top executives felt that they could not risk management instability while they were trying to sell the firm to the public."

Observed the *Financial News* astutely, "The news that Jon Corzine had been abruptly pushed aside came as no surprise to experienced Goldman Sachs watchers. Never the most friendly of firms, the recent in-fighting at Goldman has reached new levels of ferocity. There are two principal reasons for the dissension. First, the failed IPO last summer. You would have to be a Goldman manager to understand the humiliation of having to withdraw the issue. Wall Street folklore says that Goldman Sachs never makes mistakes. Second, Goldman has suddenly realised that it is no longer the best investment bank in the world. This indignity is almost as embarrassing as fluffing the IPO. Goldman was always a cut above the rest, but now the firm is being run ragged by Morgan Stanley Dean Witter. With so much egg on their faces either Corzine or Hank Paulson had to go and it was no secret in London that outspoken investment banking superstar John Thornton was orchestrating a 'night of the long knives.' In the end, Corzine was made to walk the plank."

The *Economist* observed, "The danger is that the brusque treatment of Mr. Corzine, and a perception that Goldman's investment banking side has scored a victory over its trading arm, will unleash further conflict. That could make for a bumpy road to the IPO, and, by damaging Goldman's traditionally cohesive culture, reduce its chances of a successful long-term future." A few weeks later, with the likelihood of reviving the IPO clearer as markets bounced back from the collapse of LTCM, the magazine made another astute observation that "Goldman cultivates an image of dedicated teamwork, austere workaholism and intellectual prowess—as if to make clear that it is somehow different from the sordid run of other greedy bankers. So the firm understandably bristles at the public perception that partners are salivating for their multi-million dollar pay-offs. Instead, the decision to go public is couched in strategic terms."

Some would say the brusque treatment of Corzine by his partners continued until the day he left the firm in May 1999. But no matter. The long march to the IPO had finally come to its end with the revival of the markets. With little fanfare or dispute, on March 3, the Management Committee endorsed the plan for another run at an IPO. On March 8, the firm's 221 partners approved the plan, the same day that Corzine announced his "retirement" from Goldman. "The completion of the public offering will mark a logical and appropriate point for me to move on in my career and life," he said. "As of the closing of the offering, I will stand down from my remaining duties at the firm." Goldman filed its new S-1 IPO prospectus with the SEC on March 16. Corzine was mentioned only in passing. He was included as a director and co-chairman of the firm "but will resign both positions immediately prior to the date of the" IPO, the document added, helpfully. He no doubt left with a fine consolation prize of more than 4 million Goldman shares, but it must have stung nonetheless to be so summarily excluded from the transaction he had worked tirelessly to make happen.

———

IN THE FIRST few months after the coup, Corzine worked together with John Meriwether to try to buy LTCM back from the consortium of banks that owned it. But that had more or less fallen through—despite their putting together a syndicate willing to invest $2 billion—when Frank Lautenberg, the U.S. senator from New Jersey, announced in February 2000 that he was not going to seek reelection. Corzine decided he had heard his calling. Using some $62 million of his Goldman fortune (estimated to be more than $500 million), he ran for the Senate as a Democrat and defeated Republican Bob Franks. Corzine won with 50.1 percent of the vote. In 2005, after the resignation of then-governor James "Jim" McGreevey, Corzine decided to run for the governor's office. This time, he spent more than $40 million and defeated Doug Forester. Corzine won 53.5 percent of the vote. In November 2009, he lost his bid for reelection. Four months later, his friend Chris Flowers selected Corzine to be chairman and CEO of MF Global Holdings Ltd., the world's largest independent futures broker, of which Flowers was one of the largest shareholders.

CHAPTER 17

It's Too Much Fun Being CEO of Goldman Sachs

I n the aftermath of Paulson's coup and the revival of the markets, no obstacles to the long-awaited Goldman IPO remained. On April 12, 1999, with investor demand surging, Goldman announced that it had raised the estimated range of its IPO to between $45 and $55 per share, from $40 to $50 per share. Of the 60 million shares being offered for sale in the IPO, both Sumitomo and the Bishop Estate were selling 9 million each, with Goldman selling the balance of 42 million shares. On the evening of May 3, Goldman priced its IPO at $53 per share and increased the offering to 69 million shares to reflect demand of some 10 times more than the supply. During the day on May 4, the stock traded as high as $76 per share and was the day's highest-volume issue—with more than 20 million shares traded. It finished the day at $70 per share, up an impressive 32 percent on the first day of trading—a huge success by any measure. Goldman's equity value at the end of the day was $33.3 billion, based on 475 million shares outstanding (and exclusive of another 75 million unvested shares set aside for employee stock and option awards). Goldman sold 51 million shares in the offering, raising $2.7 billion for the firm's capital account. "We have secured permanent capital to grow," Paulson crowed in a statement that day. "We have shared ownership broadly among our employees now and through future compensation, and have gained the flexibility to use publicly traded securities to finance strategic acquisitions." At the start of trading that day on the New York Stock Exchange, Paulson rang the opening bell. At the end of the day, his 4.1 million Goldman shares were worth $287 million.

LOST IN MUCH of the commotion about Paulson's palace coup were the roles played in it by the *new* Two Johns—Thain and Thornton—whom Paulson appointed as the firm's co–chief operating officers underneath him, a clear signal they were his likely successors. The possibility of this happening must have seemed tantalizingly close to Thain and Thornton at the time, because Paulson had made it clear that he did not intend to stay as Goldman's CEO for very long. While Thain was the man who had betrayed his mentor by casting the deciding fourth vote to eliminate Corzine from the firm, Thornton had played a more subtle game during the drama, leaving few of his fingerprints on Corzine's cadaver. But many people at Goldman had the impression he had masterminded the whole operation.

Although sprung from vastly different backgrounds, the two men were similarly brilliant, cerebral, and political. Thain, known around Wall Street as "I Robot" for his chiseled good looks and athletic build that closely resembled the futuristic robot in the 2004 movie of the same name, joined Goldman from Harvard Business School in 1979. The *I, Robot* comparison of course merely reinforced the idea of Goldman being a bunch of remote-controlled automatons working as part of the Borg. Born in 1955, Thain grew up fifty miles north of Chicago, in Antioch, Illinois, when the surrounding area "was still all cornfields," he said. Thain's father, Allan, was a local doctor. John Thain was pretty much the smartest kid in town. He was the valedictorian of the class of 1972 at Antioch Community High School and was also captain of the school's wrestling team. Thain decided to attend MIT to study electrical engineering instead of Stanford University because he had "heard more about it." He had never been to either coast of the United States before he got off the plane in Boston to matriculate at MIT.

After graduating from MIT—where he met his wife—he enrolled immediately at Harvard Business School. From Harvard, Thain was off to Goldman Sachs, after triumphing during the lengthy and rigorous interview process. He was one of six hires that year into the firm's Corporate Finance Department, where his job was to work with corporate clients to help them raise debt or equity capital or to advise them on mergers and acquisitions. "They were smart," he said of the people he met at Goldman. "They were energetic. I just thought it would be a fun place to work."

For nearly six years, he executed financing or M&A deals for his clients. Then, after he was promoted to vice president, the firm asked him to move over to the fixed-income department, specifically to the mortgage area, to help build up the firm's fledgling effort. This was a bit unusual, even by Goldman's standards, because he had no previous training in the complicated world of issuing and trading mortgage-backed securities. He worked with Mike Mortara, who had just been hired from Salomon Brothers. "I knew nothing about trading," he said. "I knew nothing about mortgages. Goldman has a tendency to just take smart people and put them in new jobs and challenge them and say, 'You'll figure it out.' " Thain became a partner in 1988.

After his stint in mortgages, Goldman asked him to be the firm's treasurer, another unusual request. From there, he was named CFO, a position he held during the firm's meltdown in 1994. "I started in investment banking, went to fixed-income, and then went to what was called operations technology and finance," he said.

If Thain was Goldman's Mr. Inside, Thornton was Goldman's Mr. Outside—at least in and around London, where he lived for many years, and in the other financial capitals of Europe, where he was well known. He grew up in Bronxville, just north of Manhattan, the son of two successful attorneys. He spent his summers in East Hampton, playing tennis and hanging out at the beach. When he was young, his brother died of leukemia. His godparents died young, too. The deaths "had a profound effect on me," he told the *Sunday Times,* in May 1999. "The deaths made me determined to live life intensely and use my talents to the full, preferably for the benefit of other people. I learnt early on that life is not a dress rehearsal." He left Bronxville to attend the prestigious Hotchkiss School, in Lakeville, Connecticut. He was the quintessential preppy, with a mop of long, floppy hair and horn-rim glasses. He was the editor of the school newspaper, the captain of the tennis and basketball teams, and a fan of Buffalo Springfield. Not surprisingly, he was voted "most likely to succeed."

After graduation from Hotchkiss in 1972, Thornton was off to Harvard, where he studied American political history. While he was at Harvard, Thornton worked in the Senate office of Ted Kennedy, with whom he played tennis. From there he spent two years studying law at St. John's College, Oxford, ending up with a bachelor's and master's degree in jurisprudence, but then he abandoned his plan to become a lawyer. Instead, he switched course and enrolled at the Yale School of Organization and Management. He joined Goldman in 1979 in its nascent M&A department, working for Friedman and Boisi. In 1985, they asked Thornton to move to London to set up Goldman's M&A presence in Europe at a time when American firms were beginning their assault on the clubby and dominant world of British merchant banks. That Friedman and Boisi asked Thornton was a sign of his increasing importance at the firm, and also a litmus test for his future suitability at the top ranks of Goldman. (Some said he had also ruffled too many feathers in New York and needed a change of scenery.) He could have said no, of course, and stayed in his cushy Manhattan lair, but in the world of Goldman alpha males, there was now no greater badge of honor than a willingness to pick up and move, as requested, and take one for the team. In 1988, he was rewarded for his service—and his many accomplishments—by being named a Goldman partner.

By the early 1990s, Thornton "had turned the British banking establishment on its head as he imported hard-nosed U.S. investment banking techniques into what had been a staid and very well-behaved M&A environment," according to one profile of him (of which there were many, often without the appearance of his cooperation). "Camping out in restaurants, relentless calls to potential clients—he would do whatever it took to bring a reluctant city establishment over to his side." Thornton's personal ambitions rankled many of his colleagues, who discerned that his penchant for publicity was not particularly in keeping with Goldman's fourteen principles. Descriptions of Thornton included: "He was constantly turning up at meetings to which he was not invited," "He tended to monopolise information, to control clients personally," "It was received wisdom in the firm that the guy was incredibly ambitious, that at some point he would get there," and "He was always regarded as a bit of a maverick."

He was also a fierce competitor, both in the rough-and-tumble world of M&A and on the tennis court. Famously, he was said to have compiled a list of the one hundred most important people in Europe and was determined to make them—all—Goldman clients. He was referred to as a "tycoon groupie" and counted among his friends Rupert Murdoch, Richard Branson, Harvey Weinstein, Li Ka-shing, William Ford Jr. (a friend from Hotchkiss; Thornton is a member of the Ford board of directors), Sir John Browne (whom the Thorntons entertained regularly at Saturday night salons), and Ed Victor, the literary agent. The best man at his wedding was John Eastman, the noted attorney and brother of the late Linda McCartney, Paul's wife. He used to rent a villa in Tuscany with Bill Bradley, the basketball star and former New Jersey senator.

Thornton hated to lose and once reportedly announced at a new-business pitch, "If we do not get this mandate I will personally slit the throats of all my team and drink their blood." Goldman got the assignment. Once he had a mandate, he was equally determined that his client would win, at nearly any cost. When Storehouse PLC was looking to fend off the raider Asher Edelman, Thornton hired the private investigator Terry Lenzner—brother of former Goldman arbitrageur Bob Lenzner and a famed former civil rights lawyer. Lenzner "uncovered enough dirt to persuade some of" Edelman's financial backers to drop the deal. Another time, on a different deal, Lenzner's team was caught going through garbage bags in an effort to thwart a hostile takeover of Racal, the defense electronics firm, causing "obvious embarrassment" to Goldman. Thornton's greatest M&A triumph seems to have been his ruthless 1991 defense of ICI, the chemicals company, from the clutches of Lord Hanson and his Hanson Trust PLC. "He undertook a vicious, no-holds-barred demolition job in the Press and in the City on the predator, exposing Hanson Trust to allegations of rampant tax avoidance and excessive executive indulgence," according to *The Independent*. "Hanson's City reputation never recovered from the assault."

In 1996—after Thornton had threatened to leave Goldman for Lazard a year earlier—Paulson and Corzine named him chairman of Goldman Sachs Asia, to re-create in Asia the success he had in Europe. In 1998, thanks in large part to Thornton, Goldman was selected to lead the $18 billion IPO of Japan's DOCOMO, the cellular phone giant.

Not surprisingly, along with business prowess, Thornton had a knack for making enemies. Lord James Hanson accused Thornton of using "dirty tricks" to discredit him. Lord Timothy Bell, a former adviser to Margaret Thatcher and then an adviser to Goldman, said of Thornton, "He is someone you want to have on your side, not someone else's." In one profile of him, one anonymous banker urged the writer to "let him have it with both barrels" and then concluded, "he is a terrible man." Added a former colleague, "He has a huge number of enemies . . . he knocks people about."

Invariably, the profiles of Thornton—once they get done describing his ruthlessness in a business setting—get around to talking about his picture-perfect personal life. "John Thornton has one big flaw—he is just too perfect," began one profile of him in the *Sunday Times,* in May 1999. (His friend, Rupert Murdoch, owned the London paper.) "If you called central casting and asked for a Wall Street banker, they would send Thornton. . . . Bankers are often dull, pompous or both. Thornton is neither and he and his wife Margaret"—a Tennessee Williams scholar—"are seen as great catches on the London social scene. He is 45, rich (the float values him at £121 million), successful and happily married. No wonder some people hate him." (And no wonder, at one point, Paulson told Thornton to crank down the publicity machine. Thornton declined repeated requests to be interviewed for this book.)

But these profiles ignored the claim that he likes to throw around his wealth and his power. His affinity for high-priced real estate is legendary. In 2008, he paid $81.5 million—the asking price—for businessman Sidney Kimmel's 32,000-square-foot oceanfront mansion on South Ocean Boulevard, in Palm Beach, Florida. Real-estate taxes alone on the house were $517,775 in 2007. In 2001, he paid $18 million for the 118-acre Dunwalke estate in Bedminster, New Jersey. Both the Palm Beach and

Bedminster homes were record prices in their locales at the time Thornton bought them. He also owned a home in the tony Belgravia section of London. He and his wife bought and restored a $1.3 million antebellum mansion in Charleston, South Carolina, where she was born. At Hotchkiss, where Thornton is chairman of the school's board of trustees (and where three of his four children went—or are going—to school), he has bought up a number of homes around the lake on which the school sits, much to the consternation of his neighbors, who are worried about what he might do. He also used his influence at the school to replace a tennis coach with a coach being used by his son—who was excluded from the tennis team by the original coach and then was included when the new coach was installed. "He is a real dick," one "rival" banker told the *New York Observer* in a 2001 profile of Thornton. "How do you think he got where he is now?"

Along with Thain, Thornton was one of the leaders of the opposition effort inside Goldman to the IPO in 1998, whether he was standing on principle—as it was often portrayed—or because Corzine was leading the firm was not entirely clear. When Corzine succeeded in getting the IPO approved by the Goldman partnership in June 1998, many observers thought Thornton's days at the firm were numbered. "Mr. Thornton always denied that he was opposed to the float," *The Independent* observed, "but if there was a focal point for opposition, he was it." After the partners approved the IPO, Thornton "seemed sidelined," the paper wrote. "If his opposition had been a bid for Mr. Corzine's job, he appeared to have misjudged it."

Thornton's fortunes changed, of course, when he teamed up with Thain, Paulson, and Hurst a few months later to oust Corzine in the wake of the withdrawn IPO. Suddenly, Thornton was on board for the IPO, now that Paulson was the CEO. As co–chief operating officer in the new Paulson regime, Thornton moved back to New York—somewhat reluctantly—and holed up in the Carlyle, a hotel, on Madison Avenue. The plan was for Thain and Thornton to sit tight, wait for Paulson to retire, and then be crowned as the new leaders of the firm. Paulson told them he only wanted to stay around for two years. "John Thornton and I had the expectation that he was going to stay for two years and then he would leave and we would be elevated," Thain explained. For some reason, Thornton rarely went into the office at 85 Broad Street, preferring to stay at the Carlyle when he was not on an airplane.

A number of factors quickly made the situation untenable for Thornton and Thain. First, where the power at the private firm had resided in the one-man, one-vote Management Committee (or briefly, the Executive

Committee) with the senior partner as leader but not the ultimate authority, now, as a public company, the power at the public Goldman resided with the chairman and CEO—Paulson—and with the company's board of directors, which was basically in Paulson's pocket. In addition to Paulson, Thornton, Thain, Hurst, and John Weinberg (as a courtesy), the first Goldman board had Paulson's friend John Bryan, CEO of Sara Lee; Thornton's friend Sir John Browne, the CEO of BP Amoco PLC; James Johnson, the former CEO of Fannie Mae and a Rubin friend; and Ruth Simmons, the president of Smith College. Second, as co–chief operating officers, Thain and Thornton had people reporting to them but no direct management responsibility themselves for particular business lines, such as investment banking, FICC, or asset management. Such a job would have been fine if they were elevated to be co-CEOs in 2001, as was the original plan. They then could have been simply CEOs-in-waiting and learned the ropes. But the logic of their appointment began to dissolve in the wake of the third factor affecting them, which was that Paulson decided he liked the job of being Goldman's CEO and did not want to relinquish it. He liked making decisions and wasn't that keen on consulting with the two men. "The two of them sat there," one partner said, "and Paulson wasn't about to sit there and collaboratively say, 'Let's take a vote and make the decisions.'" Paulson had yet another troubling situation brewing, and he knew it.

———

BUT FIRST THERE was money to be made. In 1999, its first year as a public company, Goldman rang the cash register. Thanks to the growing Internet bubble, revenue skyrocketed to $13.3 billion, from $8.5 billion the year before. Pretax income, which now included the cost of compensation—in years past, pretax income did not include partners' distributions—also soared to around $4.2 billion (excluding a onetime $2.2 billion gift to employees), from $2.9 billion in 1998.

Paulson was euphoric. "Our performance far exceeded the financial goals we set for ourselves in the lead-up to our initial public offering," he wrote to his new shareholders. "We told potential investors that we saw numerous opportunities to grow the firm's businesses, but emphasized that we work in an industry that does not produce predictable earnings on a quarter-to-quarter basis. Recognizing this reality, we set financial targets of an annual return on equity of more than 20 percent and 12 to 15 percent earnings growth over the cycle. In 1999, on a pro forma basis, we had a 31 percent return on equity, and our net earnings rose by more than 100 percent." As for the future, he wrote, "As we begin the new century, we know that our success will depend on how well we respond to change and manage the firm's rapid growth. That requires a willingness to abandon old practices and discover new and innovative ways of conducting business. Everything is subject to change—everything but the values we live by and stand for: teamwork, putting clients' interests first, integrity, entrepreneurship and excellence. These values sustained the firm and set us apart during the 20th century. They must never change, but much else will. We can afford nothing less if we are to become a nimble, highly focused, technology-centered, 21st century business and remain the world's premier investment bank and securities firm." Paulson was paid $25 million for the year, and his nearly 4 million shares of stock were worth $571 million; Thain and Thornton were each paid $21.5 million, and their stock was worth $552 million and $447 million, respectively.

In 2000, there was more of the same, only more of it. Net revenues grew again, to $16.6 billion, and pretax income was $5 billion, up 20 percent. Part of Paulson's success as a banker and as a CEO was his ability to lead by example. Nobody worked harder, of course, but nobody was better at "asking for the order," getting close to CEOs, or encouraging the sharing of vital information about clients or markets or trades around the firm. The impact of Paulson's high level of engagement on the rest of Goldman cannot be underestimated. In an era before e-mail, Paulson was a relentless user of voice mail and would spend hours a day leaving messages, forwarding messages, and copying others on messages. This also sent a powerful—message—to the organization. Paulson constantly bombarded his partners: "Here's what I just heard. Boom." He was a "great networker of information," explained one partner. "A great communicator, ironically. Not in a Ronald Reagan sense, but in an 'I hear it, I get it out' sense. That's how he made his career in banking, too, was as a user of information, calling CEOs and saying, 'What are you doing? This is what I heard.' " Everyone at Goldman would have hundreds of voice mails to deal with every night that would require hours of attention. Spouses would be left speechless. One partner said his wife would look at him every night and think, "Nuts. Nuts. Nuts."

During 2000, Goldman made—by far—its largest acquisition, spending $6.65 billion in cash and stock to acquire Spear, Leeds & Kellogg, a leading specialist firm, the acquisition of which made Goldman the largest market maker on both the New York Stock Exchange and American Stock Exchange, and the second-largest clearing firm on the NASDAQ. "We have no doubt that as the [New York Stock] Exchange changes, as there is more done electronically, I'm sure like a lot of functions the specialist function will evolve," Paulson said. "But we have no doubt we're going to need those skills. We think the winning combination for the future is going to be strong people skills and strong technology." The market liked the deal, and after it was announced, Goldman's stock closed up $8 per share, to around $132, near its fifty-two-week high. Analysts liked the deal, too. "It basically allows them to internally cross more of their NASDAQ volume," Guy Moszkowski, at Merrill Lynch, said. "It takes the number of stocks that they can make markets in on the NASDAQ up over 6,000 from 300 or so stocks they do now." But, in time, as the specialist system on Wall Street slowly dissolved in favor of electronic trading, the Spear, Leeds deal would prove to be a poor one—not that it would particularly matter, given how much money Goldman was making in its core businesses.

Although profits were higher at Goldman in 2000, the troika at the top of the firm was paid less—$19 million for Paulson and $16 million each for Thain and Thornton—and by the time Paulson wrote his annual letter for 2000, in early 2001, the market had begun to crack. The bursting of the Internet bubble on March 10, 2000, when the NASDAQ peaked intraday at 5,132, had a grave impact on Wall Street. Tens of thousands of investment bankers lost their jobs, and the compensation for those who remained was much diminished. "The markets of the last months of 2000 and the first part of 2001 produced a much less favorable business environment than earlier in 2000, and reminds us that our greatest challenge remains in managing growth," Paulson wrote. "We will be disciplined in our approach, but we will continue to build for the future."

UNLIKE MANY OF its Wall Street peers—Merrill Lynch, Morgan Stanley, and Lehman Brothers—Goldman suffered no fatalities on September 11. Its headquarters, at 85 Broad Street, while near the New York Stock Exchange and about a quarter mile from Ground Zero, was unscathed except for being covered in white dust. But the calamity that day opened a few fissures among the top executives of the firm. On the day of the attack, Paulson was in China, Thornton was in Washington, and Thain was in New York. It turned out that Paulson got back to New York before Thornton did, which did not sit well with the CEO. Why Thornton remained in Washington, instead of rushing back to 85 Broad Street, has never been made clear. But Thornton's immobility left his partners dumbfounded. Some say he didn't show up at Goldman for months after September 11. "It was pretty clear from a leadership standpoint that that was a moment in time—the CEO is in China—let's go," explained one Goldman partner. "Thain's here, command central. He's in Washington—just drive here, whatever. Even if you've already been told you're out, a natural leader would have come back to New York. When people saw that, I think that was sort of . . . let's just say he didn't last that long after that. . . . People reacted different to nine-eleven. Maybe he just didn't get it. But if you have ambition to run a firm, what are you doing? In a crisis like that? Come on." Many partners lost complete confidence in Thornton at that moment. "There are a lot of people that think Thornton was an empty suit," said one. "A lot of people. I thought Thornton was strategically very smart. And he always wanted to have an angle in front of a client: 'What's the edge? What are we saying? Let's not just go in there and say nothing.' But then as a leader, and a manager, he wouldn't be in the top twenty-five. Which is sort of sad, because he had it. He could have done it. He was right there." Soon thereafter, Paulson confided to some partners, "I'm going to push Thornton out."

IN THE MONTHS before and after the September 11 attacks, Paulson was faced with a number of embarrassing situations, some of his own making, some not. For instance, there was the unfortunate story of Kevin Ingram, the onetime head of adjustable-rate mortgage, or ARMs, trading at Goldman. He was one of five children, raised by a single mother "on the gritty streets" of North Philadelphia, according to one story about him. But he rose above these difficult circumstances and graduated from MIT with a degree in chemical engineering. From MIT, he was off to graduate school at Stanford, also in engineering, when he heard that Wall Street was increasingly interested in such skills. He switched immediately to the MBA program at Stanford. Ingram was a highflier at Goldman and was friendly with both Rubin and Corzine. Not only was Ingram a proven moneymaker at the firm year after year, but he was also black, which put his career potential on an even higher trajectory, especially since Goldman had few, if any, black partners at the time. Rubin, especially, took a shine to Ingram. "Kevin is very smart and had a very scientific approach to trading," a Wall Street colleague told the *Times,* in October 2001. "His engineering background meant he could understand complex mortgage-backed securities and structured transactions in a market-efficient way. And he had loads of support on Wall Street. He had the varsity of the varsity behind him." He also lived well: he had a yellow Ferrari, a silver Porsche, a Bentley, a Lexus, a Range Rover, and a forty-four-foot yacht.

In 1996, Ingram got passed over for partner at Goldman, losing out to Steve Mnuchin, the son of the longtime Goldman partner Robert Mnuchin. "He was livid," remembered a former colleague. "He was much smarter than Steven, had accomplished a lot more, but his dad wasn't Robert Mnuchin. And he left." In short order, Deutsche Bank hired Ingram to lead its global asset-backed trading desk. (Sadly, years later, Ingram would engage in a tawdry money-laundering scheme and would go to prison.)

As blame began to be apportioned in the fallout from the collapse of the Internet bubble, Goldman came in for more than its fair share of criticism. For instance, in early October 2002, the House Financial Services Committee, under the leadership of Representative Michael Oxley, a Republican from Ohio, issued a report accusing Goldman of distributing chunks of shares in so-called hot IPOs—including Goldman's own IPO—to twenty-one CEOs of big companies with which Goldman did significant amounts of investment banking and trading business. After receiving the shares of the much-sought-after IPOs, the CEOs often sold them quickly into the market—in a process known as "spinning"—at prices substantially higher than what they paid for the shares, often netting huge profits. Some observers quickly took to likening what Goldman did in facilitating spinning for favored clients to bribery. According to Representative Oxley, Margaret "Meg" Whitman, then the billionaire CEO of eBay and a Goldman director, and Jerry Yang, one of founders of Yahoo!, each received shares in more than one hundred hot IPOs managed by Goldman and then flipped the shares for a fast profit. EBay had paid Goldman $8 million in investment banking fees since 1996.

According to Representative Oxley's report, Goldman's generosity seemed to be reciprocated in spades. For instance, Goldman served up shares in more than twenty-five IPOs to Edward Lenk, the former CEO of eToys, which paid Goldman $5 million in fees. Martin Peretz, former director of TheStreet.com Inc., received more than twenty-five IPOs, and his company paid Goldman $2 million in fees. Goldman allocated shares in more than fifty IPOs to iVillage co-founder Nancy Evans; iVillage paid Goldman $2 million in fees. Then there were the IPOs Goldman allocated to executives of companies that ended up at the center of the meltdown, including Enron, WorldCom, Global Crossing, and Tyco. Three of these four were Goldman clients—Tyco, which had paid Goldman $57 million in fees since 1996; Global Crossing, which had paid Goldman $45 million in fees; and WorldCom, which had paid Goldman $19 million in fees. Representative Oxley also found that Goldman's own IPO, which rose in price dramatically on the first day of trading, was a way for Goldman to reward favored clients and investors. For instance, Michael Eisner, CEO of Walt Disney Co., received thirty thousand Goldman shares at the IPO price. Disney had paid Goldman $51 million in investment banking fees since 1996. William Clay ("Bill") Ford Jr., a director of Ford Motor Company and Thornton's friend from Hotchkiss, received four hundred thousand shares of Goldman's IPO; Ford had paid Goldman $87 million in banking fees since 1996. "There is no equity in the equity markets," Representative Oxley proclaimed in releasing his report.

Naturally, Goldman found Representative Oxley's report to be outrageous. Lucas van Praag, Goldman's spokesman, said that Goldman had simply made IPO stock available to its high-net-worth clients—of which there were seventeen thousand with investable funds of more than $25 million—and the CEOs Oxley singled out just happened to be among them. In addition, the information he was basing his claim on had been given to Congress by Goldman. "Their conclusion is not based on anything in fact," he said. "We provided the information they asked for and they never asked us a single question about anything we gave them." Asked about Ford, in particular, van Praag said, "We chose to give [Goldman] shares to people who we thought would be useful to our business and would be long-term holders. Bill Ford was one of them. He bought a lot of shares and still owns every one of them." But Goldman's logic— giving valuable IPO shares to people "useful to our business"—was hardly exculpatory.

When Paulson heard about Oxley's report and his interpretation of the information Goldman had shared, he was apoplectic. He said he was "absolutely stunned" and "furious." He called Oxley four times in the next two days, and when they finally connected, Paulson told him that while the information he relied on for his conclusions was accurate, his interpretation of those facts was "meaningless and insulting." When Eliot Spitzer, then New York State's attorney general, heard about the spinning scandal, he wanted to put an end to it immediately (although his fellow Wall Street regulators Mary Schapiro and Robert Glauber were not supportive of him). "If an investment bank wants to curry favor with a company, and give that company a discount on a fee to get it to do business, great, wonderful," he said in an interview. "If an investment bank wants to give the company a hot stock allocation and it goes into the corporate treasury, that's great. That's a business transaction. But if the investment bank gives it to the CEO, that's—not to mince words—that's bribery, because it's a corporate asset, not the individual's asset. It's no different than a contractor giving somebody money under the table to get the bid. So the ban was premised on the notion that the CEOs had a fiduciary duty to the company and that when they took those shares into their own personal account, they're violating their obligation to the company."

Then, in November 2002, came word that the SEC had sent Goldman a Wells notice of its intention to bring civil charges for a practice known as "laddering," whereby Goldman was supposedly allocating the shares of hot IPOs to investors that it knew would buy more of the stock in the aftermarket at higher prices, thus ensuring the (then) much-coveted first-day trading "pop," or rapid increase in the stock's price. The investors' reward was to get greater and greater allocations of other hot IPOs in the future that would also likely accelerate in price. The investor would also get the reward of buying the IPO low and selling it high. Spitzer might have referred to this practice as "bribery" as well. Goldman was outraged by the SEC's investigation. "We categorically deny any allegations of wrongdoing and believe there is no basis for the SEC to take such a position," Goldman said in a statement.

Goldman's view that the SEC's charge was fiction was severely challenged by Nicholas Maier, who worked for Jim Cramer at the hedge fund he set up after leaving Goldman. Maier joined Cramer's hedge fund in January 1994 and, for the next five years, his job, in part, was to make sure Cramer's hedge fund got serious allocations of the hot IPOs, many of which came from Goldman. To do that, he claimed in a May 2005 deposition in Brattleboro, Vermont, he would do everything he could to convince brokers at Goldman and other Wall Street firms that Cramer was a long-term investor and wouldn't flip the stock for a quick profit. But that was a fiction. "Our company was very, very rarely in for the long haul," Maier testified. "And with IPOs, I would say the average turnover was within a few hours of the opening. I mean, there were occasions where we held on to it. But overall it was, as my boss [Jim Cramer] said, you know, 'If someone comes up and gives you twenty bucks, put it in your pocket and walk away.'"

Then he explained how laddering worked at Goldman and how he and Cramer would play along to get the IPO allocations that they coveted—and the free profits that came with them. During the process of allocating the stock of a hot Internet company, the demand from institutional investors, including hedge funds, would be so strong that Goldman would create a checklist of behavior that would be required for a fund to get an allocation. These would include attending the "road show," where the company would present its story to investors; calling the research analyst at the Wall Street firm that was covering the company "and act[ing] as if he really loved the stock"; putting in an order for 10 percent of the stock, knowing that such an amount would never be granted; and paying millions in trading commissions to the Wall Street firm in a given year, which he testified was the "most important" factor "and why the little guy can never expect to get in on hot IPOs." And then came the whole process known as the "aftermarket order."

Maier explained how in order for Cramer to get the IPO allocation, Goldman would demand that Cramer buy stock in the aftermarket at set prices. "If you really are very interested and deserve your five thousand shares in the IPO price[d] at twenty dollars," he testified his broker at Goldman told him, "you should promise to buy fifty thousand more shares wherever the thing opens, be it fifty dollars or five hundred dollars. Take a typical 'hot' deal. I get five thousand shares of an IPO price[d] at twenty dollars that we think is going to open at fifty. I want it so much that I agree to buy another fifty thousand at any price. I therefore wholeheartedly agree with the investment bank that the IPO is a legitimate and valuable company. Nearly all of the major investment banks made us commit to aftermarket orders, and they kept score. The investment bankers went to their brokerage house's trading desk to make sure that if Cramer and Company committed to buying in the aftermarket, Cramer and Company bought in the aftermarket. This was their way of making sure hot deals stayed hot. If we didn't buy in the aftermarket, we wouldn't get any shares in the next IPO."

In a July 2002 article in the *Washington Times,* Maier was quoted as saying about Goldman and laddering: "Goldman from what I witnessed, they were the worst perpetrator. They totally fueled the [market] bubble. And it's specifically that kind of behavior that has caused the market crash. They built these stocks upon an illegal foundation[, then] manipulated [the stock] up, and ultimately, it really was the small person who ended up buying in" and losing money. He added, "Goldman created the convincing appearance of a winner, and the trick worked so well that they seduced further interest from other speculators hoping to participate in the gold rush. The general public had no idea that these stocks were actually brought into the world at unnaturally high levels through illegal manipulation."

In his Brattleboro deposition, Maier made clear that Cramer told him how to deal with Goldman on these matters. "They are going to tell you what to do, and you are going to do it," he said Cramer told him when he started on the job. "And all I care about is that. If there is a deal that opens up, I want to be there. You play the game they tell you to play so that we can make as much money as possible." He acknowledged that since these Internet companies by and large had no earnings and barely any revenue, doing a fundamental analysis of their value was not only not possible, it was beside the point. "It was too much of an intangible," he said. "We chose what was not an intangible, which was that, by playing this game and having somebody walk up to me, like Goldman Sachs, and put half a million bucks in my pocket for a couple of lunches, a couple of phone calls, and a little playing around in the trading, that was tangible. That was, you know, easy money, and we would take it." He recalled this happening in at least two Goldman underwritten hot IPOs, for Amazon and for Exodus Communications.

Much the same version of Maier's assertions in his Brattleboro deposition were contained in his March 2002 book, *Trading with the Enemy,* about his time on Wall Street working for Cramer. Cramer was not pleased by Maier's account of what occurred at his hedge fund and threatened to sue Maier for libel but never did.

In January 2005, Goldman paid $40 million to settle a civil suit with the SEC related to its penchant for laddering investors in the hot IPOs it underwrote. One of the many examples the SEC cited in its complaint involved Goldman's handling of investors in the IPO of WebEx, an Internet video-conferencing company that Goldman took public in July 2000. On July 27, the institutional sales rep for an investor told the Goldman "deal captain" about his client's willingness to buy WebEx shares in the aftermarket: "They'll take the full amount and will hold it for at least 30 days unless you say longer BUT this is a relatively new relationship with a lot of business to do and I'd like to avoid hurting them too much if this one is in serious trouble." The deal captain responded, "We're looking for something longer term. No lack of demand. Want to wait for the next one?" The salesman responded, "They'll hold it for at least 90 days and they'll buy 3 for 1 up to $17" in the aftermarket. The next day, when WebEx started trading, the deal captain wrote to the salesman about when it would be good for his client to buy in the aftermarket: "first trade would be great." The salesman replied that his client had complied: "Just sent it in—they got 10 so they're buying 30 with a 17 top. These guys ALWAYS do what they say—if they got 100 they would be buying 300."

But the spinning and laddering, while seemingly illegal and unethical, were a mere sideshow to the massive deception that Goldman—and nearly every other major underwriter of Internet stocks during the 1990s—participated in by rewarding with big bonuses their supposedly independent research analysts for writing favorable reports about the stocks of the Internet companies the Wall Street firms were taking public. Even though many research analysts did not believe what they were writing about these stocks, the pressure on them from their own firms' investment bankers to write favorably was intense because the fees that the bankers could reap by underwriting and trading the hot IPOs were irresistible. Big fees meant big bonuses in an era where bankers were rewarded with huge bonuses based on how much revenue they generated rather than how much profit the firm overall generated.

Spitzer and the SEC led the charge against Wall Street in the Internet research scandal and successfully got the firms to collectively cough up fines totaling $1.4 billion. Goldman was far from the most egregious violator of the compact that allegedly existed between underwriters and investors—that title belonged to Salomon Brothers, which forked over $400 million—but Spitzer got Goldman to pay $110 million. Even from the evidence in a smattering of e-mails, it was clear that Goldman was helping to rig the game just like everyone else. "Certain research analysts at Goldman Sachs were subjected to investment banking influences and conflicts of interest between supporting the investment banking business at Goldman Sachs and publishing objective research," the SEC wrote in its complaint against the firm. "The firm had knowledge of these investment banking influences and conflicts of interest yet failed to establish and maintain adequate policies, systems, and procedures that were reasonably designed to detect and prevent those influences and manage the conflicts."

The documents and e-mails the SEC and Spitzer provided in the settlement documents make clear that a number of Goldman's research analysts felt pressured by bankers to write favorably about their clients in order to help the bankers generate revenue from them. One analyst, asked what his three most important goals were for 2000, wrote: "1. Get more investment banking revenue. 2. Get more investment banking revenue. 3. Get more investment banking revenue." In another analyst's year-end review, some of his colleagues criticized his close ties to the bankers. "He has been in the incredibly awkward position of having the investment bankers have a stronghold over his written work—STOR [StorageNetworks], LDCL [Loudcloud] to name a few embarrassments," observed one colleague. Another one added, "One gets the sense that he's been held captive to the agenda of others within the Firm and that, were he allowed to exercise an independent investment thesis, he would have had a decidedly different take of this group's prospects."

Not surprisingly in this environment, bankers would bring research analysts along on IPO new business presentations, with the promise that the analyst would cover the company—favorably—after the IPO, which of course Goldman should lead. In an April 2000 e-mail, a Goldman investment banker wrote to the Goldman research analyst covering Loudcloud: "For next Wednesday's meeting, we have a challenge before us. We have been guided today by Loudcloud that we must show total focus and commitment from a RESEARCH perspective. [Loudcloud representative] strongly suggested that you guys come prepared to SELL. . . . HERE IS THE SUGGESTION: CAN YOU GUYS PREPARE A BRIEF (3–4 PG) RESEARCH REPORT ON LOUDCLOUD FOR THE MEETING. This is effectively our pitch. . . . This way we can say we are so excited about the story that we have already begun writing the report." (The emphasis was in the original e-mail.) In response, the analyst wrote: "I want to make this thing the best. WE WILL WIN THIS MANDATE."

As the Internet bubble was reaching its zenith, Goldman displayed an increasing inability to deal effectively with its conflicts of interest, erring time and time again in favor of potential investment banking revenue at the expense of institutional and retail investors who might well have preferred to know the truth. In January 2001, the management of WebEx, the videoconferencing company that Goldman had taken public six months earlier, tried to use its muscle—effectively, it turned out—to influence a research report that the Goldman analysts covering the firm were working on. "As discussed," he wrote, "I want NO mention of any funding issues in this written report. I told you if people called and asked you why your plan shows a need for modest funding, you can verbally tell them that management believes they have adequate funding and it is probably because management has a less conservative plan than you do."

The Goldman analyst responded, "The webx [sic] funding issues is a key area of investor concern, as such will remove any mention from the top section of the note, but will address it in a manner this [sic] is consistent with your recommendation for verbal responses to client inquiries in a later section. To exclude it completely detracts from the intention of the note, which is to address key investor concerns upfront and then give them a reason to buy the stock." He attached a copy of the revised report to his e-mail. The WebEx executive replied: "Thank you. This is much better. The other note said the company has a funding problem, but we think it isn't very big. This says that the company believes it has enough funds, but there could be a problem; and if there is it will be minor. Thanks again for the change." Goldman issued the revised report on January 22, 2001.

———

TOWARD THE END of January 2003, Paulson was speaking to investors about the firm at a Salomon Smith Barney conference and did himself no favors. Goldman had been reducing staff during this period, so nerves were understandably raw around the firm. During the question-and-answer period, a question arose along the lines of, "Hank, you've been cutting, and you've been cutting, and you've been cutting staff in this terrible environment. At a certain point, you have to start cutting muscle. Have you hit that point yet?" In his answer, Paulson implied that between 80 and 85 percent of Goldman Sachs's employees were irrelevant to the company's success—a message that flew in the face of the company's professed antisuperstar ethos. "I don't want to sound heartless," he said, "but in almost every one of our businesses, there are 15–20 percent of the people who really add 80 percent of the value. I think we can cut a fair amount and not get into muscle and still be very well-positioned for the upturn." Understandably, Paulson's comments did not go over well at the firm. "News of that comment spread through the firm like wildfire," remembered David Schwartz. "It was afternoon London time, but before I went home, I knew about it. I think in New York, there were buttons that were made up the next morning: 'Are you one of the 80 percent or the 20 percent?' It was instantaneous flow of information around the whole fucking firm. I gather that Paulson's phone did not stop ringing that afternoon."

Paulson quickly realized he had to put out the fire he started. In a voice mail message to the firm's twenty thousand employees, Paulson acknowledged that his remarks were "insensitive" and "glib." He apologized. "The eighty-twenty rule is totally at odds with the way I think about the people here," he said, adding he would also apologize in person at a series of upcoming town hall meetings. According to one report, "He reaffirmed the importance of teamwork over individual glory and acknowledged that he was embarrassed by his choice of words." Schwartz recalled that "it wasn't more than forty-eight hours and Paulson apologized to the entire firm for his comments. He said they were 'ill-considered' and they did not reflect what he really believes. He apologized to everyone and asked for forgiveness. It was abject apology. There was no ducking or diving." Schwartz thought the incident, while appalling, revealed Goldman at its best. "The ability to process the information almost instantaneously through the whole organization and to come up with the right solution to the problem equally instantaneously in a way that, I think, very few other CEOs would have done was very impressive," he said. "Other CEOs would say, 'It's really true. People should just get over it.' Not Hank. Hank is a stand-up guy."

Paulson was a natural at certain aspects of being Goldman's CEO. He was a guy who liked being in charge. With his bald pate, imposing build, and military demeanor—he seemed so authoritative—he was the type of man who could get other people to take the hill on his orders. He was very decisive when a decision needed to be made, even if he lacked the requisite expertise or knowledge to make it. In those instances, he was clever enough to gather around him the people with the knowledge, hear their thoughts, and then move forward. He loved being the CEO of Goldman Sachs, in part because it meant he could get to see pretty much anyone on earth he wanted to see. When he was Goldman's CEO, the premier of China consulted with him about setting up executive training programs throughout China and about establishing a business school at the premier's alma mater, which the top seven Chinese leaders attended. He talked to the Chinese leaders about privatizations and about how to deal with the ratings agencies. Angela Merkel, the chancellor of Germany, would visit with Paulson and talk for hours about world events and economics. Before her first meeting with President Bush in January 2006, she consulted with Paulson. When she got out of the meeting, she called Paulson and debriefed him from her car. He also occasionally worked on big deals as he had for years as a banker. For instance, he got personally involved in Procter & Gamble's January 2005 $57 billion acquisition of Gillette, which Goldman advised. At one point, when the deal seemed like it might fall apart, Paulson helped bring the two sides back to the negotiating table. Indeed, by his own admission, he was having such fun being Goldman's CEO—and he was so good at it, he said— that he decided he would not follow through on the promise he had made to Thornton and Thain to relinquish the position after two years. (In Paulson's telling, the board would not let him leave even if he'd wanted to.) He would not have relinquished it easily under any circumstances, but after September 11 and after Goldman got ensnared in one Internet bubble scandal after another, he also came to the conclusion that neither Thornton nor Thain was up to the task of being the next CEO of Goldman Sachs.

In Paulson's version of events—a rare and not wholly convincing attempt at spin—he blames himself for putting both Thornton and Thain in roles at the top of the firm in which they could not succeed, especially when he—and the Goldman board—decided he needed to remain as Goldman's CEO beyond the originally conceived time period. What started as a reward for their loyalty in supporting Paulson in his single-minded desire to overthrow Corzine ended in Paulson having to engineer their exits from the firm. "I'm the guy who was working with clients in Chicago, running the investment banking and private equity," Paulson said. "I had a fondness for smart people, and they were both very smart. Thain was just good at thinking through risk, at protecting the firm and making sure we had excess liquidity and also worked extremely hard. Let me just tell you something. In terms of the commitments to committees— the capital committee and the risk committee—John Thain ferreted out more things that didn't smell right and didn't look right. In terms of protecting the integrity of the firm, he was great there. I just thought these were two really young, outstanding guys. They had experience all over the world.

John Thornton was instrumental in building our international M&A business. John Thain started out in banking and in the trading division and knew the trading side of the business well, and then really understood the infrastructure of the firm. And the business being as dangerous as it was, having someone with his expertise there as a co-president of the firm, and then having a brilliant, global investment banker matched with him, it looked like good fit."

But, once again, a presumed succession plan had failed. This was not Paulson's favorite subject and one he discussed only with great reluctance. "I really liked both guys," he said. "They are very talented. They were close to me. They were helpful and it was an impossible situation for them in many ways because their titles were co-presidents and co–chief operating officer. And neither one of them was an operating officer and neither of them wanted to be an operating officer. Neither one of them had ever run a business. They thought that I'd be leaving in a year or two, so they thought of themselves as heirs apparent. We signed every memo 'Hank, John and John.'"

But increasingly over time, the other executives at Goldman grew resentful and referred to them as the "owner's sons." Resentment continued to build not only after the Internet IPO scandals but also after Goldman's dot-com initiatives—such as investments in Wit Capital and a number of electronic trading platforms, including Primex Trading, a joint venture among several Wall Street firms and Bernie Madoff's securities firm—soured and as it became clear that the Spear, Leeds acquisition was basically a bust. "In doing things like that they were hopeful when we were executing," said one Paulson loyalist about Thornton and Thain, "but when we were dealing with a mess they weren't around."

As it became clear that Paulson was sticking around, he encouraged both men to use one of Goldman's supply of "management coaches," who could help them think through how to adapt to the new situation, and to begin to take on more and more operating responsibilities, to help relieve some of the burden on Paulson. According to the Paulson loyalist, Thornton's coach and his "well-meaning friends" had a simple message for Paulson: "You know something? He can't survive in this spot. If you don't want him to be CEO then he'll have to leave. But otherwise he's just in an untenable position."

But Thornton had few fans at Goldman outside those who knew him well in London or in the M&A department. For some people, he was a "patron saint," Paulson said. Others, though, saw Thornton as "arrogant," according to a number of Goldman partners, and a glaring symbol of the Goldman meritocracy gone haywire—someone who was rewarded with a position far beyond what his considerable accomplishments merited. "The organization overall didn't like John because it didn't know him," explained one partner.

To help pick up the operating slack, in March 2002, Paulson named Robert Steel, Lloyd Blankfein, and Robert Kaplan as vice chairmen of the firm, a move many saw as setting up a new group of potential leaders in competition to one day succeed Paulson, since he had pretty much decided that neither Thain nor Thornton would work. The topic of succession planning had been an acute one at the board level, and the appointment of the new vice chairmen was one result of those discussions. Kaplan, one of the former co-heads of investment banking, would oversee both investment banking and asset management. Steel and Blankfein would oversee the firm's huge—and hugely important—FICC businesses. (Meanwhile, Bob Hurst, previously the firm's sole vice chairman, was on his way out of Goldman by the beginning of 2002, as he was spending at least half of his time leading the 9/11 United Services Group, an umbrella charity for victims of the September 11 attack.)

Blankfein's career trajectory angled further upward during the course of 2002 as the performance of the FICC group—his baby—put up impressive numbers, making close to $1 billion in a difficult financial market. (Investment banking's pretax profits, meanwhile, plunged to $376 million in 2002, from $1.7 billion in 2000.) Paulson rewarded Blankfein at the end of 2002 by paying him $16.1 million (nearly 50 percent more than both Thornton and Thain)—making him the highest-paid individual at the firm—and then nominating him for a one-year term on the Goldman board of directors. No doubt, the combined effect of Blankfein's promotion, compensation, and nomination did not sit well with the highly ambitious Thornton and Thain.

Thornton was the first victim of Paulson's revised thinking. By March 2003—at least eighteen months after he had probably made the decision that Thornton would not get the top job—Paulson decided Thornton had to leave Goldman, and quickly. He had hoped Thornton would step up and help the firm deal with the Internet scandals, but instead he seemed to disappear, spending more and more time at the Carlyle or in Washington, where he had become chairman of the Brookings Institution. He had hoped Thornton would take on more day-to-day operating responsibility for one or more business lines—such as investment banking—and relieve Paulson of having those daily interactions, but he did not. On March 24, Goldman announced Thornton was retiring from Goldman as of July 1, and would also leave the Goldman board of directors. Although he received no severance, he would not be leaving empty-handed. He was paid $11.2 million in 2002. His Goldman shares were then worth around $230 million. He was named a senior adviser to the firm and agreed to be available to "work closely" with Paulson and Thain "on certain strategic matters" involving Goldman and its clients. He was also going to spend more time at Brookings, and—thanks to Paulson and his connections—was named a full professor at Tsinghua University, in Beijing, described alternatively as the "MIT of China" and "China's foremost institution of higher learning." (Among Tsinghua's graduates are Zhu Rongji, China's former prime minister; Hu Jintao, China's president; and Wu Bangguo, the chairman of National People's Congress.) For reasons not entirely clear as to why this honor was bestowed upon him—he spoke no Chinese—Thornton was the first non-Chinese to be named a full professor at the university and was named the first director of the university's newly established (thanks to Paulson) Program for Global Leadership. Goldman also announced that Thornton would serve as a special adviser on China to Richard Levin, Yale's president.

All things considered, Thornton's forced retirement came with a number of nifty consolation prizes. Paulson even managed some happy talk on the firing. "John will be greatly missed," Paulson said at the time. "He exemplifies the best of our firm: a tireless devotion to client service, to excellence, and to the development of our people. From the beginning of his career, John recognized the importance of the international business and has been a driving force behind our development into a global firm. We are grateful for his dedication and service over the past 22 years, and we are pleased that he will continue to be available to us as an advisor."

The truth of what happened to Thornton—like many things at Goldman Sachs—was not quite the official version. One popular scenario had Thornton getting tired of waiting for Paulson to abdicate the Goldman throne, telling him he wanted the top job and asking Paulson to leave immediately. Offended by the raw power play, in this version of events, Paulson supposedly told Thornton that he was fired and sent him—immediately—to find the elevators and to leave the building. Another had it that Paulson just got fed up, once and for all, with Thornton's elusiveness and failure to dig into the leadership role he had been given. Paulson denied that anything remotely like either scenario happened, especially since Thornton was a brilliant tactician and would never have initiated a coup without having already lined up the support needed to succeed. But there is no denying that something occurred to damage irrevocably their relationship between February 27, 2003—the date Goldman filed its proxy statement where the firm recommended Thornton be elected to a new three-year term as a director—and March 24, when his unexpected departure was announced. In an interview that day, Thornton told the *Wall Street Journal* that he left because "it was clear to me that Hank is staying around for a while. When I was younger, I said I wanted to get out of the business at 40, but now I am nearly 50 and ready for a change. It is time to do something different and touch people's lives in a different way."

A number of people close to Paulson confided that Paulson fired Thornton deliberately. "Thornton left because Hank pushed him out," explained one former senior Goldman partner. "The reason he pushed him out was Thornton was a very political guy. He had enormous talent, by the way. But something weird happened after nine-eleven where nobody could find him for weeks and months. Thornton always acted like he was a secret agent. Nobody ever knew where he was. And Hank finally concluded that he was a sinister force. So Hank created this opportunity in China and he pushed him out."

What must have seemed like fabulous news to Thain in his quest to replace Paulson—his main rival's departure—rapidly became more muddled. "At first, he thought he was a shoe-in," a top Goldman executive said of Thain's thinking after Thornton's ouster. "John A. Thain is not a flashy banker or a man with a thousand relationships," the *New York Times* reported the next day. "But this understated, austere man who knows the firm's inner workings might be the right man for the times at Goldman Sachs. With the abrupt departure of John L. Thornton, Mr. Thain becomes the sole president of the firm and the presumptive heir apparent to Henry M. Paulson Jr. As such, he represents the rapid rise of the numbers guy on Wall Street. . . . Glossed over was the broad gulf in the operating styles of the two ambitious executives. Mr. Thain, who has a degree in electrical engineering from the Massachusetts Institute of Technology, is a clinical, dispassionate man with a military bearing, say those who know him. He has a keen eye for the firm's bottom line, keeps meetings short and spends less time traveling the world than most bankers at his level."

Soon after Thornton's departure, Paulson began to rain on Thain's parade. He suggested to Thain that Blankfein, the rising star, be named his co-president, replacing Thornton. Thain would have none of that suggestion. "He thought it was unfair and uncalled for, for me to suggest that Lloyd move up and share a title with him," Paulson said. Paulson tried to reason with Thain. "I explained that he was doing an outstanding job working with his part of Goldman Sachs," he said. "But that what Lloyd was doing he was doing well with the FICC organization. I thought that they could work together as co-heads and I thought that they complemented each other very, very well and it was a very big job"—being sole president of Goldman—"and I thought that they could very well both move up and succeed me. And I think the board thought we should have more than one candidate."

Either the two of them would succeed him as CEO or they would compete against each other and one would emerge as the obvious choice. "I actually thought when I paired Lloyd with John," Paulson said, "we'd see how they both would develop and one or the other or both of them would be my successor. John didn't want any part of that. He wanted to be CEO, and he left to go be one." Under those circumstances, Paulson likely would not have been too pleased with Thain's subsequent decisions to go skiing for two weeks at Christmas and then for another two or three weeks in the spring. He might have hoped the two men would compete head-to-head to allow the board to determine who his successor would be, but the fight seemed to go out of Thain after Blankfein's appointment.

In any event, Thain kept rebuffing Paulson's suggestion, telling him he wouldn't agree to it. "There's no pretense to Hank," Thain said. "Hank says what he means. He means what he says. He's not in any way a guy who veils his feelings or his thoughts. He certainly was good at maneuvering around and he had the power and authority and he used it."

The other influencing factor was that the two men did not get along. Like Paulson and Corzine before them, the *gemütlich* and brilliant Blankfein could not have been more different than the diffident and cerebral Thain. "He seems much more self-deprecating than Hank," one Goldman executive said about Blankfein, "but it's not true." Their growing rivalry could not have been helped by a November 2003 article in the *New York Times* about the scandal that had erupted two months earlier involving the outrageous compensation package—said to be close to $140 million—that Richard Grasso received as the president of the New York Stock Exchange and that resulted in his firing. The *Times* article linked the rise of the tech-savvy Blankfein at Goldman with the demise of Grasso, who rose to power at the exchange by defending the status quo of floor brokers and specialist firms. Blankfein's ability to produce increasing amounts of profit from trading for Goldman—like Gus Levy before him—made him too important to the firm to ignore and "has allowed him to consolidate his power," the paper reported. First came his appointment as a vice chairman, then came the board seat. In September 2003, Blankfein appointed Gary Cohn, one of his longtime deputies, as head of the firm's equities division. "Executives say Mr. Blankfein is now the most likely candidate to succeed Mr. Paulson," the *Times* said. "But Mr. Paulson, at 57, shows no sign of retiring soon."

By then, Thain had secretly started discussing with John Reed, the interim CEO of the New York Stock Exchange and the former Citigroup co-CEO, the idea of succeeding him (and Grasso) as CEO of the NYSE, while Reed would stay on as the NYSE chairman. Reed and Thain seemed cut from the same cloth and knew each other well from the MIT board of trustees. "Both are known as cool and professorial with a deep affinity for exploring how technology and finance intersect," the *Times* reported. Thain's name was reportedly at the top of the search committee's list of possible permanent replacements for Grasso. On December 18, Thain's decision to leave Goldman to become CEO of the NYSE was made official. He would start at the NYSE in January 2004. "I grew up in a small town in the Midwest," he told the *Times*. "I never heard of Goldman Sachs growing up, and I never viewed myself as the president of Goldman Sachs or the C.E.O. of the New York Stock Exchange." While he fulfilled one ambition—to become a CEO—it came at a substantial cut in compensation to $4 million a year, from the $20 million he received from Goldman in 2003, although he retained his Goldman stock worth at the time around $300 million. (For some reason, nobody seemed to object to the obvious conflict that Thain retained a large financial stake in Goldman at the same time that he was running the NYSE.)

Given Blankfein's ascendancy and Paulson's lingering, Thain said the opportunity was too good for him to resist. "There were a lot of public policy reasons to do it," he said in an interview. "The exchange was in a lot of trouble. The combination of the opportunity to be the CEO, the opportunity to really make a difference to help a part of the U.S. financial system that needed a lot of help, and the fact that Hank wasn't leaving led me to decide to run the New York Stock Exchange."

Thain told Paulson he was leaving Goldman two days before the public announcement. Paulson was "stunned," Thain said in a later deposition, and "didn't say anything for several hours." Some accounts of that conversation had Paulson raising his voice in anger at Thain's decision and its timing. But Paulson said he did not raise his voice, although he said he was not pleased to hear the news from Thain. He said he told Thain he thought taking the job was a mistake and tried to talk him out of it (although some people think Paulson orchestrated Thain's appointment much as he had orchestrated Thornton's nine months earlier). "I told him I thought the NYSE was a very difficult business to manage," Paulson said. "I thought the way the world was going he was putting himself into an impossible situation. I was wrong. He said I showed no signs of leaving, no signs of anointing him as my successor. He wanted to go and learn something else and when he left I think it was a bigger issue than just not getting my job."

On the same day that Thain announced publicly he was leaving Goldman, the firm announced that Blankfein would become the firm's sole president and chief operating officer. Goldman also announced that Steel would be leaving to teach at the Kennedy School of Government, at Harvard. "These were not easy decisions for me personally," Paulson said. "But I just felt an enormous responsibility as CEO of a public company. And I wanted to be in the position where I wouldn't have to do the job forever." He harked back to the lunch conversation he had with Steve Friedman as he was thinking about what to do with Thornton and Thain. Friedman had rejoined the Goldman board of directors in 2005 after his two-year stint as one of Bush's top economic advisers. At the lunch, Friedman asked him if he controlled Goldman Sachs on his own and his entire net worth was tied up in it, whom would he have run the place in his stead? "Without skipping a beat I said, 'Lloyd,'" Paulson recalled.

As long as Paulson retired at some point, Blankfein's path to the top job was clear. "But if Mr. Blankfein hopes to succeed Mr. Paulson, he may have to be more patient than Mr. Thain was," the *Times* reported. "As long as Mr. Paulson is chairman and chief executive—and he could hold those jobs for five years or more—no drastic changes are expected at Goldman Sachs. Mr. Paulson has overseen the firm's strong recovery this year and, by all accounts, has the full support of its directors." Indeed, the paper quoted Jim Johnson, the head of Goldman's Compensation Committee, saying he hoped Paulson would be staying around for a long time. "The board has the view that Hank Paulson is doing a fabulous job," Johnson said. "We think he is one of the most outstanding C.E.O.s in the world."

IN CASE ANYONE was worried that Hank Paulson, investment banker extraordinaire, would cut back on the risks that a newly—and successfully—publicly traded Goldman Sachs would be taking, they need not have bothered. Paulson embraced risk taking with alacrity, in nearly every part of Goldman's business. "We managed the transition from a partnership to a public firm seamlessly without losing a beat," he said. "We didn't lose people. We went from being the medium-sized firm to being a large firm and we kept the best attributes of the culture. We went from being a firm where we were behind Morgan Stanley and right there with Merrill Lynch to being a firm that was clearly the global leader." By the time Blankfein was named Paulson's heir apparent, Goldman's transformation to a risk-taking juggernaut was obvious, both anecdotally and in its financial performance. "When people think about Goldman Sachs, they think about a first-class investment banking franchise," Henry McVey, an analyst at Morgan Stanley, told the *Times* at the time of Thain's departure. "Blankfein's appointment reminds investors and clients that some of the company's heritage is in capital markets and trading." He said replacing Thain with Blankfein was a "subtle shift" rather than a change of great import because "the trading and risk-taking are already substantial." For 2003, Goldman earned net income of $3 billion, up from $2.11 billion in 2002. Like Thain, Paulson and Blankfein were each paid $20 million in 2003.

But one Goldman banker said that the rise of Blankfein also led to the explicit—no longer just implicit—suggestion that clients could be exploited for Goldman's benefit. "There was this huge change that came with Lloyd where he wanted to 'monetize client relationships,' " this banker said. "I think it was a euphemism for sort of harnessing the relationship banking side of the house to generate investment opportunities for both the various internal funds and the other businesses Goldman was in. So you got into a situation where there was—rather than it just being sort of a happenstance or just sort of a something like it fell out of a client situation—it became a method, became programmatic where we would push a client to pursue IPOs, or you were supposed to push secondary offerings. Or if you got an advisory assignment, you were then supposed to say, 'Oh, by the way, we can put money into a PIPE"—a private investment in a public company—"or to see if one of the Goldman private-equity funds can get involved. Does he want to sell himself or be taken private by our private-investing group? It changed the emphasis a bit at the margin. It created more 'relationship tension' for bankers to manage." Conflicts? "No, 'relationship tension' was the preferred descriptive," he said.

As never before, Goldman Sachs was a beehive of global activity, across virtually every imaginable product line in finance, with the sole exception of taking deposits directly from consumers (although like many Wall Street firms, Goldman did have a small commercial bank in Utah). Goldman was now many different things to many different people. As a result, the firm's exposure to conflicts of interest had never been greater, although its confidence that it could manage the increasing number and complexity of its conflicts had not diminished one whit. "Business conflicts continue to be a particularly important area of focus for us," Paulson and Blankfein wrote in the firm's early 2005 annual letter to shareholders. "How we identify, disclose and manage real and apparent conflicts will be critical to the long-term success of our business. We operate with the knowledge that what many may have considered acceptable industry practice yesterday will be the target of intense scrutiny tomorrow. We must conduct ourselves accordingly and ensure that we have thoroughly and thoughtfully analyzed all of our business priorities. At the same time, it is naïve to think we can operate without conflicts. They are embedded in our role as a valued intermediary—between providers and users of capital and those who want to shed risk versus those who are willing to assume it."

To try to manage the conflicts, Paulson made numerous efforts to try to indoctrinate the firm's leaders in the ways of good behavior. He instituted a firmwide program called "Compliance and Reputational Judgment" training to "reinforce our compliance culture," Paulson wrote. In 2005, he began the "Chairman's Forum," where Paulson met with more than twenty small groups of managing directors to discuss "at length business practices, reputational judgment and compliance leadership." He explained, "We will emphasize to all our [managing directors] that our highest priority is to enhance our reputation for integrity in every aspect of our business."

Paulson also wanted to institutionalize the best aspects of the firm's culture—if he could—and so he created, in 2000, a leadership institute, named "Pine Street" (after the location of the firm's first headquarters) and modeled after GE's highly respected John F. Welch Leadership Center at Crotonville, New York. Paulson even recruited an executive who started Crotonville, Steven Kerr, to run Pine Street and to serve as Goldman's chief learning officer. "Pine Street is dedicated to strengthening the culture of the firm, enhancing the success of Goldman Sachs and its clients, and developing world-class leadership and management talent," according to Goldman's website. "Distinguished businesspeople, noted academicians and the firm's own leaders serve as faculty. Pine Street combines formal classroom experiences with extensive mentoring and coaching to establish a common language and skill set of leadership throughout the firm." Observed one Goldman banker, simply, about the Goldman culture: "It was the firm, firm, firm, firm, firm, the firm, it's the firm."

According to one of the Goldman executives who worked at Pine Street, Paulson was very concerned that when the firm went public something special about Goldman would be lost. "You have a company that is going public," remembered this person, "and their whole culture is about apprenticeship and leaders teaching leaders. Then, suddenly it's going to change. How could the company then, after going public, justify that decision and say, 'We're still all about an apprenticeship. We're still all about leaders teaching leaders. We're all about a culture. How can we make sure that culture remains a competitive advantage at Goldman Sachs? How do we make sure we don't lose our secret sauce?'" John Rogers, Goldman's consigliere, explained how important culture was—

and is—to Goldman Sachs's continued survival, echoing one of the firm's common refrains. "Our bankers travel on the same planes as our competitors," he said. "We stay in the same hotels. In a lot of cases we have the same clients as our competition. So when it comes down to it, it is a combination of execution and culture that makes the difference between us and other firms. Behavior is shaped by it. People who think culture is just a bunch of bacteria in yogurt set a tone that strips values from a company. That's why our culture is necessary—it's the glue that binds us together. We hold on to the values, symbols and rituals that have guided us for years, and anything new that we add to the culture always supports what already exists."

Pine Street was an idea born of paranoia, Blankfein said, since Goldman Sachs was "an interesting blend of confidence and commitment to excellence, and an inbred insecurity that drives people to keep working and producing long after they need to. We cringe at the prospect of not being liked by a client. People who go on to other commercial pursuits frequently self-identify as a former Goldman Sachs employee, long after they have left the firm. Alumni take a lot of pride in having worked here."

The future leaders of the firm were selected to attend, making the experience "aspirational," the former employee explained. The rewards for those selected became clear, too, as they seemed to be promoted more rapidly than their peers. "Pine Street was presented to me from the start as a way to make senior people here feel special, to connect them to one another—as some group of them will continue to rise and lead parts of the firm, as well as lead practical projects within their business," explained one Goldman banker. "When I realized it had the full sponsorship of the executive office, that gave credibility to the program for me."

The genius of Pine Street was that about half of the programs were geared to Goldman's clients, not just its future leaders. The firm's coverage bankers would offer their clients the opportunity to attend a very special seminar or lecture or discussion and then be able to spend "quality time" together, away from the typical boring banker flip-book pitch. "We would create these small, intimate, world-class programs where, as a relationship manager—as a banker, all you want to do is spend time with your client and learn what's going on in their organization—these programs were the ultimate way for that sort of information to be exchanged," according to one Goldman banker. "They're coming because during the breaks or during the actual sessions, when you break out with your client and discuss with them the changes they're facing and their challenges that they're facing in the organization, you probably learn more during that day than you do taking your client to dinner or to a Rangers game." In November 2006, Harvard Business School professor Boris Groysberg published a thirty-eight-page laudatory "A" case about Pine Street, how it got started, and what, ideally, it would accomplish. As a follow-up to that case, Groysberg also drafted a "B" case about how effective Pine Street turned out to be in practice. He checked quotes with various people but then never published the B case. Goldman decided the A case should be the only document published about Pine Street.

Just in case the managing directors did not get the message about the importance of maintaining the culture, the firm also had a "reputational risk" department in the basement of 85 Broad Street, staffed by an Orwellian mix of former CIA operatives and private investigators. Its purpose was "to protect the reputation of Goldman Sachs," explained one Goldman executive. What this meant was once a potential new hire survived the firm's arduous interview process but before an official offer of employment was made, the candidate had to be investigated thoroughly by the reputational risk department. "They turn your life inside out," one Goldman banker recalled. "I mean they check everything. They call your high school."

Explained one Goldman trader, "After I went through the processes of being offered the job by businesspeople, then you have to run through the legal and background checks, where they basically ream, steam, and dry clean you. They look into every aspect of your life. It was just a license to ask anybody anything. They tell you if you lie about any of this, we rescind our job offer. I was always sort of convinced that they did that to build a dossier on you, so if you ever gave them a problem, they could use it against you." He remembered once when a former head of Goldman Sachs Asset Management, who had been fired, wanted to trade with Goldman at his new firm and the Goldman legal department told him he had to first submit the idea to reputational risk to have them clear the firm's association with its former partner. "This guy there explained to me—it was this big guy who looked like an ex-cop—that their job was to look into everybody and everything and to watch out for the interest of the partners," the former Goldman executive recalled. "I was told a story that there had been a partner who had a problem with an extramarital affair and the reputational risk department handled it. The stuff I took away from it was, that this is basically an internal police force that would also take care of any issues outside the firm that were threatening the firm. Almost like a mob kind of feeling. There was an aura about it that was pretty scary."

Even though the trader had been gone from Goldman for more than a decade, the firm's power and its tentacles still frightened him. "Not that they would come to my house and beat me up or something or kill my children," he said. "But certainly they would drag you through court or do something to screw up your life. If you did anything to hurt that firm in any way, all bets were off, because God knows I saw what they did to their customers. That was bad enough—they'd steal from them, rape them, anything they could do."

———

A NUMBER OF Goldman's clients had noticed the way the firm was treating them and they were not happy about it. This was not necessarily a new or recent development but rather one with a lineage that went far back into the firm's history. For instance, the Chicago investor Samuel Zell—who had a serious run-in with Goldman in the late 1980s about the sale of Rockefeller Center, which he lost in a heated battle to Goldman and the developer Jerry Speyer—remembered that Rubin and Friedman came to see him in his Chicago office in the hope of getting Zell to do more business with Goldman Sachs. "I am happy to do business with you," Zell told the men, "just tell me whether you are my agent or my competitor. I am happy with either one, just not both." Although Rubin and Friedman assured Zell that Goldman had "Chinese walls" to prevent any confusion, the truth was that Goldman was constantly blurring the lines and more and more clients were getting angry. Despite their anger, many clients seemed reluctant to do anything that would end up alienating the firm, since it was generally acknowledged that Goldman had the best deal flow and had access to the best investment opportunities. Pissing off Goldman Sachs—it turned out—would be bad for business.

Despite Blankfein's concern that Goldman did not want its clients upset with the firm, sometimes the firm left its clients little choice. For instance, in February 1999, somewhat out of the blue, Société Générale, the big French bank, announced a preliminary agreement to acquire Banque Paribas, another important French bank with a big investment banking business. The deal was large—more than $17 billion—and took people by surprise because it had basically been negotiated between the two leaders of the banks, Daniel Bouton, at SocGen, and André Lévy-Lang, at Paribas. Once the two banks had figured out what the chairmen had done, there was a push made after the fact to hire legal and M&A advisers to make sure everything was buttoned up properly. Naturally, every Wall Street firm wanted to be part of the deal, including Goldman, which at the time had been working on three separate projects for Soc-Gen: a review of its investment banking business with a look at potential acquisition targets, a review of its investment management business, and a global review for the bank's top management of strategic initiatives, complete "with all the inside information you could imagine," said a knowledgeable SocGen insider. "They were in our pants in a big way."

Goldman was as surprised as anyone by the news of the Soc-Gen/Paribas merger and, understandably, wanted to be hired as an M&A adviser. Goldman's message to the bank was simple: "If you won't hire us then somebody else will." (This was not an unusual veiled threat on Wall Street.) In the end, SocGen hired Morgan Stanley for M&A advice and Sullivan & Cromwell for legal advice. Goldman, miffed, rounded up a new client—Banque Nationale de Paris, or BNP as it was known—and began working hard to disrupt the SocGen/Paribas deal. The battle raged for the next year, with BNP at one point launching hostile takeover bids against both Paribas and SocGen. (So much for the policy against launching a hostile bid, although in fairness this was *two* hostile bids.) In May 2000, BNP emerged the victor with an agreement to acquire Paribas, while SocGen was able to remain independent.

Goldman's behavior left some executives at SocGen stunned. "It was extraordinary to me that armed with all of this inside information that they actually had the chutzpah to come out and make a competing bid at the same time that they had access to all this information about our strategy," explained one insider. "And they did it in the usual way, by saying that they had a separate team and 'Chinese walls' and all sorts of things. I was so livid about that I pushed hard for a lawsuit against them based on the conflict. It seemed to me, and others, that we had the better of that argument. But even if we didn't, the fact was throwing that kind of dirt in their face where it belonged was something that I wanted to do because I knew that we had a good chance of getting a preliminary injunction. But even if we didn't get that far, we would do a lot of damage to just slow them down and to be able to take discovery of how they were using this information and how the Chinese walls were working, because it was just so outrageous to me. It was about as outrageous as anything I've seen, frankly, in the business."

While the idea of bringing a lawsuit against Goldman was raised—Sullivan & Cromwell obviously recused itself since Goldman was a major client—in the end Bouton, the SocGen chairman, decided not to sue Goldman. "Goldman has always been aggressive about its own interest when it comes to a big fee particularly, and against its client's interest in situations like that," said the insider. "And that was the clearest one that I'm aware of. And pretty high stakes, obviously pretty visible and you can imagine how much fun it would have been to file an action in New York federal court and watch what happened next. Because in a battle like that, any commencement of a litigation would have put a chill through their whole operation internally. It would have given us the right to take discovery on whether the Chinese wall was a legally sufficient defense."

Even other financiers who partnered with Goldman to buy companies were often left dazed by the firm's behavior. "They're kind of hugely mediocre," said one private-equity executive who has partnered with Goldman on deals. "They do things exactly the way most firms do—they say one thing and they do another. They talk about hard work, discipline, and commitment and then they always do what's in their own financial interest to do. Like a law firm or bank that pitches a business, gets the business, and then does the bait and switch. It's not in their DNA—we're only talking their private-equity investments—it's not in their DNA to be engaged. Their financial engineers are crude. They're quick. They're slam-bam-thank-you-ma'am, but they like to present it as a committed relationship. It's only—and all—about the money and maintaining the veneer."

Goldman's behavior was not unusual, he said. Indeed, it was quite common and he liked that the firm had a relentless desire to win. What made it unusual was that the Goldman team liked to act as though it had higher standards of ethics and behavior. He marveled at how Team Goldman continued to believe passionately in the myths created about the firm. "They have been inculcated to portray themselves as differentiated for a long time," he said. "It's partially because they haven't torn down their icons. They've been very clever about that. You talk about John Weinberg. John Weinberg has not been torn down. Even with the kinds of bruises he's been taking, Rubin, by and large, has not been torn down, certainly not by the firm. Sidney Weinberg is still the great Sidney Weinberg! Gus Levy is still the great Gus Levy! They have what the Yankees have, which is the monument park in center field and they celebrate it and they're, to some degree, hated for it but they still get to put on the pinstripes and intimidate other people just by showing up."

A former banker himself, he could not get over how well the Goldman professionals stay on message. "They're a little bit more comfortable lying to your face than other firms," he continued. "Goldman will tell the story and actually never blink at you. Everyone else is going, 'We always put our clients first,' and it's a little bit like one of those TV things where you look behind you and go, 'Bullshit, we do.' Goldman actually will say—hand-over-heart, guys—'This is what we're about. This is our culture. It's about client service. Our culture is about always doing what's right in the long-term interest.' And other firms will kind of go, 'Okay, now that I've given my stupid speech, let me tell you the truth.' Goldman, there's again, that discipline."

———

SOMETIMES THIS SO-CALLED "discipline" shows up when Goldman is asked to advise a big, publicly traded company on an assignment and then takes its sweet time about going through the internal "conflicts" check before deciding to take it, or not. Most firms would respond in a time-sensitive situation in twenty-four hours, max, but Goldman has been known to take as long as a week, while it decided where its highest expected value might be. Should it work for the company that asked first? Or, using the knowledge it gained from the conversation, should Goldman find another party to work for that might pay a higher fee or have a higher likelihood of succeeding in the situation. Often, clients enable Goldman to string them along in this way, in part because of the respect many of them have for the firm. "The clients give them more rope than most of us would have any instinct to ask for," explained one gray-haired competitor.

As far as the public was concerned, no deal crystallized the evolution of Goldman's approach to conflicts—and its perceived ability to "manage" them—than the high-profile, $3.2 billion April 2005 merger between the New York Stock Exchange and Archipelago Holdings, the company that owned the Archipelago Exchange, the first "totally open" fully electronic equity-trading exchange. For students of Wall Street conflicts, the merger had everything: Goldman advised both the NYSE, code-named "Navy," and Archipelago, code-named "Army," on the deal, the rare and proverbial Holy Grail of M&A assignments. John Thain, the NYSE's CEO, had, of course, spent his whole prior career at Goldman, rising to the position of president and second-in-command to Paulson. He did not recuse himself during the deal even though he owned hundreds of millions of dollars' worth of Goldman stock. For its trouble, Goldman was paid a $3.5 million fee by Archipelago. The NYSE also paid Goldman $3.5 million. Goldman also owned—in various pockets around the firm—7.3 million shares of Archipelago, or 15.5 percent of the company, and was the second-largest shareholder after General Atlantic, another private-equity firm, which owned 22 percent of Archipelago. Goldman was one of the lead underwriters of the Archipelago 2004 IPO. On the day the NYSE-Archipelago merger closed, in March 2006, Goldman's stock in the combined, publicly traded NYSE was worth close to $500 million. Goldman also owned 21 seats on the NYSE—out of a total 1,366 seats—worth around $4 million each. Goldman ended up with a 5.7 percent stake in the combined company.

The deal caused a firestorm of criticism about the many hats Goldman wore during the merger. "Wall Street has been buzzing with criticism of Goldman Sachs's role in the transaction," the *Wall Street Journal* reported. "Some wonder whether Goldman Sachs deprived NYSE seat owners—and Archipelago shareholders—of the best possible deal, while making a deal that benefits the firm. Former NYSE director Kenneth Langone, who is trying to mount a possible bid for the NYSE, has pointed to what he describes as Goldman Sachs's 'unseemly' role in arguing that the deal undervalues the Big Board." But Goldman, as usual, would have none of the criticism. "Managing conflicts effectively is fundamental to the business of investment banking," said Goldman spokesman Lucas van Praag.

The criticism forced Archipelago to take the unusual step of releasing Goldman's April 15, 2005, engagement letter, which showed that not only did both sides acknowledge Goldman's many conflicts but also deliberately limited Goldman's role to setting up meetings and doing some financial analyses. "We will assist the company"—Archipelago— "and the New York Stock Exchange in connection with a potential transaction which assistance may include facilitating discussions between the company and the New York Stock Exchange with respect to a transaction," according to the fee letter. "As part of our services, we will perform certain valuation analyses, including with respect to any pro forma combined company resulting from a transaction. Notwithstanding the foregoing, we will not (i) negotiate on your behalf the financial aspects of a transaction with the New York Stock Exchange or (ii) render a fairness opinion in connection with a transaction." Anticipating the negative reaction to Goldman's dual roles, the two sides had agreed to hire both Lazard and Citigroup to provide fairness opinions about the deal.

The engagement letter also explicitly prevented either side from suing Goldman about the conflicts. Archipelago "understands and acknowledges that we are rendering services simultaneously to the company and to the New York Stock Exchange in connection with a transaction," Goldman's letter said. "The company understands and acknowledges that potential conflicts of interest, or a perception thereof, may arise as a result of our rendering services to both the company and to the New York Stock Exchange."

Looking back, Thain defended his decision to have Goldman serve on both sides of the deal. "We needed someone to help us put the deal together," he said. "We didn't need two people to help us put the deal together because having two firms kind of vying for who's a better negotiator didn't really make sense. We did bring in a third party at another firm"—Lazard—"to bless it. But I think it was mostly just sour grapes on the part of other people, and in terms of getting the deal done in an expeditious way, it made a lot of sense. Now was it worth making everybody mad? Probably not, but from the point of view of getting the deal done it made a lot of sense." He praised Goldman's bankers for having expertise in the "space" and for knowing the people on both sides of the deal.

Thain also defended the deal as the best way for the NYSE to survive. "We kept it from becoming irrelevant," he said. "We modernized its business model. We diversified its product. When I got there it was private, not for profit, only traded New York Stock Exchange listed stocks, and was losing market share rapidly. We changed its governance structure. We changed its corporate structure. We diversified it product-wise, and in the end we globalized it, so it traded New York listed stocks, over-the-counter NASDAQ stocks, options, futures, and derivatives, and bonds. We moved from only New York stocks to pretty much the full range. When I started you could've bought a seat on the exchange for a million dollars. There were one thousand three hundred and sixty-six seats. That means the whole market value of the New York Stock Exchange was one point four billion dollars. When I left, the market value of the combined company after the Euronext deal was about twenty billion dollars."

For his part, Paulson defended the legality of the assignment, given the various disclosures that occurred about the firm's conflicts. But he did question the wisdom of the assignment from a public-relations perspective. "The New York Stock Exchange isn't just another company," he said. "Okay? It's a national treasure. It's not just another company and what happened was when the editors from the press found out it was a public-relations problem." He remembered telling the Goldman board, "There's not an ethical breach. This is legal. It's ethical. The deal probably wouldn't have gotten done but for this confidential [arrangement] where you needed people that really understood it and both sides very much wanted Goldman Sachs and Goldman Sachs was a partial owner of Archipelago and that didn't bother the New York Stock Exchange or their board, or John Reed or John Thain."

A few weeks after this conversation about the NYSE/Archipelago merger, Paulson called back. He had given the situation more thought and felt uncomfortable enough about the role Goldman had played to want to clarify his thinking about it. He remembered that Peter Kraus, the Goldman banker on the deal, had come to see him to both warn him that the firm could catch some flak for its dual roles and to take a "victory lap" for what would normally be considered a marquee transaction. He started processing what Kraus had told him: that Goldman would be a big owner of the combined company and that Thain had been a former Goldman president and that his key lieutenant, Duncan Niederauer, had also been a Goldman partner. (Niederauer is now the CEO of the NYSE.) "I questioned whether we should represent both sides because I thought we will take some bad publicity and some flak," Paulson said he told Kraus. "There's nothing unethical or wrong about it but I think some flak's coming. I'm making a decision right now we're not going to represent both sides. Just for that reason and the New York Stock Exchange and John Thain is more sophisticated so we'll represent Archipelago and you call John Thain and tell him that."

Kraus called Thain as instructed but Thain was not happy. "Peter showed up [in his office] and said John was angry, John was very insistent," Paulson recalled. Kraus had brought a group of bankers with him to Paulson's office to discuss the pros and cons of representing both sides. They collectively decided to move forward representing both sides. "Over history there'd been plenty of mergers of equals or mergers that had been done that way," Paulson said, correctly. "They're not the most common but they have been done that way."

He continued, "This wasn't that we did something wrong, something unethical. This was Goldman Sachs getting a deal done, after which everyone said, 'Boy, this is a superb deal. This makes great sense. It's brilliant.' This was Goldman Sachs understanding the market, understanding how you would put these two companies together, how you would manage the technology integration and those kinds of questions. Again this was not Goldman Sachs trying to push itself on clients to haul in fees. This was Goldman Sachs acceding to the wishes of the clients and to the boards. This was really a conflict that was seen by the press and by other bankers and by the public because it was just a bridge too far to explain it. And what I missed was, as I said, this was the New York Stock Exchange and every single major investment banker said, you know, 'I've got a vested interest in this. I care about this.' This is a public institution in many ways and it just came across as arrogant and as fairly simple for overreaching. But it wasn't any conflict where we were screwing a client or doing something that was against the client's interest. This was Goldman Sachs coming up with an idea, executing a brilliant transaction, and doing it ethically but missing the forest for the trees and appearing arrogant and looking like we were trying to be all things to all people."

———

IN APRIL 2006, the august *Economist* put Goldman Sachs on its cover, in an effort to describe the firm's "magical hold at the summit of its industry." Goldman, of course, had long been the envy of every other firm on Wall Street, not only because of all the money it made year after year for its partners (and everyone else who worked there) but also because regardless of what questionable things the firm did—and there were plenty—its reputation for excellence and professionalism never seemed to suffer. Other firms could become embroiled in scandals, and clients would flee like cockroaches when the lights go on. But at Goldman Sachs, the firm seemed to have a permanent Teflon veneer. If no one ever got fired for hiring IBM—as the old corporate adage went—the very same comment could be said of Goldman, and often was. This simple fact created much jealousy of Goldman from the rest of Wall Street. A common refrain—among bankers anyway—was that for all their vaunted reputations, when it came to the nitty-gritty of an M&A deal, the Goldman guys were just not that *good*. Where was the special insight or kernel of advice that set them apart from all the other French-cuff and Hermès-tie-wearing bankers?

But there were—are—important *cultural* differences behind Goldman's extraordinary ongoing success that set the firm apart from its peers. *The Economist*'s April 2006 cover story about Goldman tried to capture some of these unique aspects of the firm's culture. "The secret of Goldman's success is the stuff of constant speculation, above all among the investment bank's competitors, none of which has come close to matching its sustained record of superior performance," the magazine observed. "Back before Goldman went public in 1999, the firm was looked upon with a certain awe—a secretive, private partnership, the last truly large such entity in American finance, that consistently minted money without having to disclose anything. In 2006, despite public filings that are so large they can be more easily measured in weight than in pages, Goldman Sachs remains just what it was in 1999, only more so: it is a hugely profitable enterprise—return on equity during the first quarter of this year approached 40%, notwithstanding a compensation scheme for employees that would make the old partners jealous—and it remains something of an enigma. Over time, that enigmatic quality has only increased, defying predictions that the greater transparency supposed to accompany going public would reveal to the world Goldman's secret formula. In part, this is deliberate. Its primary source of profit has shifted from banking to trading, and the firm is intentionally quite vague about how, and precisely where, those trades are made or, equally relevant, from whom the profits are coming. One line in its accounts, 'fixed income, currency and commodities' (referred to as FICC) accounts for a huge chunk of revenues and this is because . . . well, no one outside Goldman knows exactly why."

The magazine touched on Goldman's Svengali-like ability to massage its public image. "Whether Goldman was, in fact, really different in its approach to vice, or virtue, than any other Wall Street firm is the cause of some debate, but beginning in the 1960s the bank graduated from the second-tier to pre-eminence at least in part because it was perceived by its clients as the one to trust," the article continued. "Symbolically, for years it advised on few hostile takeover bids. This role has, theoretically at least, become increasingly tenuous as Goldman has moved from being mostly an agent (as an underwriter) to a principal, as a trader and direct investor. Inevitably, in setting a price either for a security or a company that it might buy or sell, Goldman is no longer looking after only its client's interest. Indeed it has become harder to distinguish between who is a Goldman client and who is a Goldman competitor." After citing a few examples of where Goldman's conflicts have gotten it into a public-relations fix, the magazine concluded, "Mostly, though, Goldman's formidable reputation works in its favour."

There was also mention made of the stealthy and secretive process by which Goldman weeded out older partners, clearing room at the top for the next generation. The magazine suggested this delicate surgery was Paulson's purview. "Often enough, someone important is quietly asked to leave," *The Economist* reported. (According to Goldman lore, Paulson had such a hair trigger that he fired one partner, even though his colleagues decided to rethink the initial decision. But it was too late.) "This is one of Mr. Paulson's most critical roles. He apparently does it well enough that word rarely leaks out in the firm. Sometimes even the person being dismissed is unaware they are being forced out—there is a brief discussion about a more interesting future. Typically, senior Goldman employees are on several charitable boards and, invariably, there is a lot of personal wealth to be invested, given away, or, after a lifetime in an office, spent on something grand. Goldman, says Mr. Paulson, is a hard place to be hired, a hard place to be promoted and a hard place to stay. And if you want an explanation of how Goldman endures, that, perhaps, is the best explanation of all."

———

BY THE TIME the *Economist* article appeared, Paulson was deep into highly secretive negotiations with the president of the United States, George W. Bush, and with Josh Bolten, Bush's chief of staff and a former colleague of Paulson's, about becoming the seventy-fourth treasury secretary of the United States. Paulson told virtually no one at Goldman Sachs that Bolten had approached him about taking the Treasury job to succeed John Snow. He shared the news with John Rogers, Paulson's chief of staff at Goldman and a longtime power behind the throne at the firm, but he did not share the news even with Ken Wilson, Paulson's partner and close friend at Goldman who would soon enough join Paulson at Treasury as an unpaid adviser. "The idea of being Treasury secretary in the abstract appealed," Paulson told *Vanity Fair* reporter Todd Purdum, "but my initial inclination was that it wasn't right for me to take that step." Purdum reported that Paulson clicked through the issues in his mind that he cared most about—"reforming Social Security and Medicare, overhauling the tax code, rethinking trade and investment policy"—and concluded that given the president's lame-duck status and abysmal political standing, his chances of accomplishing his agenda were minimal. ("He would be right about that," Purdum wrote.) Paulson recommended someone else for the job.

But Bolten kept after his former boss. He "offered something almost unheard of for the Bush team," Purdum continued, "a private meeting with the president even before Paulson decided whether he wanted the job." Not surprisingly, Paulson agreed to meet with Bush but not before thinking to himself, "Wait a minute—what am I smoking? . . . You know, how could I possibly presume to take the president's time" but then not take the job being proffered? "Part of the reason I hadn't then taken this on was I said [to myself], 'How many Cabinet secretaries had I seen come to Washington and leave in recent times with a better reputation than they came with?'"

Paulson's rhetorical question, of course, had the obvious answer of "very few," with the notable recent exception of Robert Rubin, who had indeed proved himself to be a much admired treasury secretary—though many grumble that he helped created the conditions that led to the Great Recession by supporting deregulation of the financial industry from whence he came and then took for himself a $115 million serving of pie from Citigroup while urging the traders there to ratchet up the risks they were taking. Paulson decided not to meet with Bush, after all. But a month or so later, he changed his mind—"There are no dress rehearsals in life," a friend told him—and decided to meet with Bush and accept his offer to take the job. Bush, as part of the bargain to lure the CEO of Goldman Sachs to Washington, ceded an unprecedented amount of power to Paulson to run the economy and Treasury as he saw fit. This was probably the equivalent of giving him the sleeves off his vest, considering how little Bush really knew about business and the functioning of the capital markets—despite being a graduate of Harvard Business School, a member of Ken Wilson's class—and how little political clout he had in the final quarter of his difficult presidency.

Bush announced Paulson's nomination on a beautiful, sunny late

May 2006 day in the Rose Garden. The ceremony lasted eleven minutes. Paulson would take "this new post at a hopeful time for American businesses and workers," Bush said. "The American economy is powerful, productive and prosperous, and I look forward to working with Hank Paulson to keep it that way. As Treasury Secretary, Hank will be my principal advisor on the broad range of domestic and international economic issues that affect the well-being of all Americans. Hank shares my philosophy that the economy prospers when we trust the American people to save, spend and invest their money as they see fit." Bush—with no inkling of how ironic the statement would become—also said Paulson, an active Republican, knew a little something about fiscal restraint and intended to show some. "Hank also understands that the government should spend the taxpayers' money wisely or not at all," Bush said. "He will work closely with Congress to help restrain the spending appetite of the federal government and keep us on track to meet our goal of cutting the deficit in half by 2009."

Paulson told Purdum that after he changed his mind and decided to move to Washington and take the new job, he called Blankfein, then Goldman's president and chief operating officer and Paulson's obvious successor, and told him the news. "I think I surprised and delighted him," Paulson said, adding that Blankfein, who has a highly evolved sense of humor, "thought it was great for the country—and for *him*."

At Paulson's confirmation hearing, on June 27, the most pressing questions the Senate Finance Committee—and in particular its chairman, Iowa senator Charles Grassley—had for him pertained to getting a copy of a settlement agreement between the IRS, which is housed in the Treasury, and the Nature Conservancy, a nonprofit organization to which Paulson had donated tens of millions of dollars. (His family foundation has set aside $100 million for donations to conservation causes.) Senator Grassley was concerned that "too many" people who worked at tax-exempt organizations take advantage of them for their own personal benefit. "As you have seen first-hand with the Nature Conservancy, with the best of intentions, things can run afoul," Senator Grassley said, a reference to accusations that the Nature Conservancy had violated the IRS rules regarding the donation of conservation easements. He then asked Paulson about his specific concern. "Despite repeated requests by our committee, we still have not received a copy of Nature Conservancy's closing agreement with the IRS based on the IRS audit of the Nature Conservancy," Senator Grassley said. "It is important for the public to understand, what was the resolution of matters raised by the press and the Finance Committee in the review of the Nature Conservancy." Paulson answered the senator that he was not the CEO of the organization, merely its chairman of the board—the current CEO of the organization, Mark Tercek, is a former Goldman managing director installed there by Paulson in July 2008—but said that he preferred that the document Senator Grassley was seeking come from the IRS itself, "so it would be kept in confidence," rather than come from the Nature Conservancy.

That was about as tough as things got for Paulson. Piped in Senator Trent Lott, "I am excited that you have agreed to take this assignment. It is a very critical one. You know what the issues and the problems are that we face, but your background, your experience in administrations over the years, your experience at Goldman Sachs, your education: you have everything we need in this very important position, so I congratulate you on your nomination and certainly will vote for your confirmation."

On June 30, just after the Senate unanimously confirmed his appointment as the nation's seventy-fourth treasury secretary, Paulson filed a shelf registration to sell 3.23 million of his Goldman shares—worth around $500 million. He retained, for the moment anyway, another $75 million in restricted shares and close to seven hundred thousand vested stock options. Under the government's conflict-of-interest rules, Paulson had no choice but to sell his Goldman stock, but to make up for the hardship of the forced sale—again thanks to the government's rules that only an investment banker could truly love—he was spared having to pay immediately capital gains taxes on the sale of his low-basis Goldman stock. Under the rules, Paulson could defer his capital gains—while locking in a high price for the Goldman stock—and then reinvest the proceeds into Treasury securities or an approved mutual fund. If and when he sold the Treasuries or the mutual funds, the capital gains tax would have to be paid. *The Economist* estimated the exemption saved Paulson around $200 million at that moment. Paulson received one other unusual benefit upon leaving Goldman midyear: a bonus of $18.7 million and total compensation for the six months of work in 2006 of $19.2 million. No doubt his accumulated wealth helped him absorb the $32.65 million cost of the 7,500 acres he and his wife bought on the über-exclusive Little St. Simons Island, off the coast of Georgia (the only way to get there is by boat), as well as the cost of his $4.3 million Washington home.

———

BLANKFEIN'S PATH TO the pinnacle of finance nearly rivals for degree of difficulty that of his legendary predecessor Sidney Weinberg, who was one of eleven children of a Brooklyn bootlegger and started working at Goldman Sachs as a gofer shining spittoons, in 1907, a few years removed from elementary school. Blankfein moved with his family from the South Bronx—where he was born—to 295 Cozine Avenue, in the East New York section of Brooklyn, "in search of a better life," he explained. He was three years old.

The family lived in the Linden Houses, a complex of nineteen buildings completed in 1957 that contained 1,590 apartments and was—at the time—a predominantly white, Jewish, public housing project. After losing his job driving a bakery truck, Blankfein's father, Seymour, took a job sorting mail at night at the post office—"which in our neck of the woods was considered to be a very good job, because you couldn't lose it," Blankfein said. The late shift paid 10 percent more than the day shift. "For the last few years of his life I'm sure he was doing something that a machine would have done better and more efficiently," he said. Blankfein's mother worked as a receptionist at a burglar-alarm company—"one of the few growth industries in my neighborhood." Blankfein shared a bedroom with his grandmother; his divorced older sister and her son were in the next bedroom.

Richard Kalb, who grew up with Blankfein and has remained friendly with him, said his father worked at the post office, too. "But Lloyd always teased me that my dad was a manager and his was a worker," he said. Kalb and Blankfein went together to the local public school and to Hebrew school at B'nai Israel, near the Linden Houses. They were both part of a program in junior high school that allowed them to complete three years of school in two years by skipping eighth grade. In junior high school Blankfein was "voted most likely to succeed," Kalb said.

They were both bar mitzvahed the same year. Blankfein celebrated his at the Astorian Manor—"the finest in catering," it boasted in neon lettering on its façade—in Queens, with a band, dancing, and a smorgasbord. "He was brilliant as a twelve-year-old boy," Rabbi Abner German said about Blankfein. "He was a great planner." To earn some spending money while attending Thomas Jefferson High School in his Brooklyn neighborhood, Blankfein worked as a lifeguard and got himself into better shape, after years of struggling with his weight. He would also regularly hawk hot dogs and soda at Yankee Stadium, in the Bronx. Blankfein would ask Kalb to go work with him, but Kalb would always decline. "And of course I work for the government now"—at the Department of Homeland Security—"and he's the CEO of Goldman Sachs," he said.

While Kalb and Blankfein were in high school, in the early 1970s, the neighborhood started to deteriorate economically. Two gangs, the Black Panthers—not the better-known political organization of the same name—and the Young Lords, seemed to hold sway at the school. Blankfein would take the bus there in the morning but "if there was a big fuss in front of the building or there was a lot going on or there were policemen, you stayed on the bus and you took it around again and just went home," he said. He adapted to his surroundings and learned to be "careful" but was not isolated. "Even in the projects, there were kids around all the time," he said, and pickup games were easy to come by. "[T]he problem with trying to play football is you ended up with sixteen people on each side," he said. He was a diligent student and, according to Kalb, the teachers loved him. "He was very personable, very witty, and very smart," he said. "So he could interact with them on their level much better than I think most of the rest of us could."

For his part, Blankfein said he did well in school not because he was "some roaring genius" but because he wanted to succeed, whereas most of his classmates couldn't have cared less. "It was easy to distinguish yourself but the motivation to distinguish yourself was a lot harder to come by," he said. He could have graduated at fifteen but stayed for another year. He was the school's valedictorian, class of 1971. "You survive at either one of two things," Robert Steel, one of Blankfein's former partners at Goldman, remembered Blankfein told him about Jefferson High; "you were either a great athlete or funny and entertaining, and I decided to go with funny and entertaining." Harvard recruited at Thomas Jefferson High School, spotted Blankfein, accepted him, and offered up a combination of financial aid and scholarships to make it possible for him to attend. The first time he had ever seen someone wear a tie and jacket—without matching suit pants—was when he went to the Harvard Club, in Manhattan, for his Harvard interview.

At Harvard, he found himself surrounded by a bouillabaisse of legacy students, rich kids, and prepsters, many of whom seemed to know which final clubs to join and how to make the connections that might last a lifetime. Not Blankfein. He was a scholarship student, had to work in the cafeteria, and was shunned by the social clubs. "I was as provincial as you could be, albeit from Brooklyn, the province of Brooklyn," he said. He remembered that when he read *The Catcher in the Rye,* he didn't realize Holden Caulfield was in high school because he kept referring to his "prep" school. "I always thought that a prep school was what some people went to *after* high school to prepare themselves for college," he said.

Blankfein was young and knew it. He settled into a group of friends who shared his modest upbringing. (To this day, many of Blankfein's closest friends come from his youth.) He seemed oblivious to the social jockeying swirling around him. "I wasn't defensive about the fact that I was working," he said. "I always felt that it was the legacy kids that had to justify themselves." David Drizzle, the son of a brick-factory worker in Atlanta, was Blankfein's roommate in Winthrop House, at Harvard. He is now chief counsel at the Federal Aviation Administration. "We were completely unprepared for the world that we entered into," he said of the two of them. "It wasn't the money, because at that time in our society, the flaunting of wealth was pretty much looked down on. But there was a worldliness that most of the students had that he and I were just completely lacking. And so we were socially at sea when we arrived there, and I think that's one of the things that drew us together." Added another friend from Harvard, Roy Geronemus, a dermatologist and the director of the Laser & Skin Surgery Center of New York, "Many of the people who now would beg for an audience with him would have nothing to do with him [then]."

Since Blankfein had been on his high-school swim team, he thought he'd give Harvard's a try. He said he had no idea the top prospects had been in contact with the coach—who had been the coach of the 1972 Olympic swim team—for years. "There were Olympic swimmers and Olympic medalists on the Harvard team," he said. "These guys all looked like a different species." In his tryout, he swam a long-distance event. "I'm not built for speed, if you haven't noticed, but I'm built for endurance," he said. The guy he started swimming with in the race was out of the pool and dressed before Blankfein finished. "I got out of the pool, I toweled myself off, I put my jeans right on over the thing, and I walked to the boathouse," he said. He thought he'd give crew a try, only to meet another crop of perfect physical specimens. But he made a go of it, and he and Drizzle were on freshman crew together.

He may have been equally clueless about his schoolwork. He was a government major but did not do a thesis, as did many others. "To the extent I bloomed, I'm a late bloomer," Blankfein said. Drizzle said that he and Blankfein used to procrastinate by watching *Star Trek* every night and having long dinners before tackling the books. "As exam period approached," Drizzle remembered, "a terror would set in that would focus our attention, and we would basically work all night continuously for several nights and swear that we would do a better job the next semester and then would repeat the same experiential procrastination." What classmates seemed to recall most often about Blankfein were his sense of humor and his memory. "He's able to spot irony in ways that I don't know anyone else who can do it," Drizzle said. He also could sing, from memory, nearly every sitcom theme song known to man in the 1970s.

Blankfein remembered how—when he was in grade school—someone once referred to him as being a "Philadelphia lawyer" and "it kind of always stuck with me," he said, and just naturally gravitated to thinking he was going to be a lawyer. He applied to Harvard Law School and was accepted, although he chalked it up to a predilection for accepting students at the law school from Harvard undergrad. "I don't know that if they had taken half as many that I would have been in there," he said. Drizzle said that at Harvard Law, Blankfein buckled down academically, and he "became more studious," but not in a way that would land him on the law review or result in any other scholastic honor. Blankfein conceded that while at Harvard, "at some point, I can't say that I had a disadvantaged background. After a while, I kind of evolved into having an advantaged background."

In 1978, Blankfein graduated from Harvard Law School and took a job as an associate at Donovan, Leisure, a small "old-line" law firm founded in 1929, by William J. "Wild Bill" Donovan, who later formed the Office of Strategic Services during World War II and was known as the father of the CIA. (He was the fellow who authorized Sidney Weinberg's espionage work in the Soviet Union during World War II.) Donovan, Leisure was so traditional that "tea ladies" served tea and cookies every afternoon on pushcarts. During his four-year stint at Donovan, Leisure, he represented the film industry in a tax dispute with the IRS and spent his time shuttling between Los Angeles and New York. But he was not particularly devoted to the law. In 1980, as part of his Harvard reunion, Blankfein wrote that in his "spare time," he worked "as a tax lawyer, the only career for a real man of action." In 2000, he described his responsibilities at Donovan, Leisure as being "to keep certain large corporations from paying their fair share of taxes."

He also developed some pretty bad personal habits. Once upon a time, he smoked two to three packs of cigarettes a day. His parents both smoked, and he had started when he was a teenager. But the habit got out of control during law school. "If you have the kind of obsessive personality that I have, you put out a cigarette and you light another cigarette," he said. He was overweight. He said his weight "had gone way, way higher, steadily, ten pounds a year for five or ten" years after getting out of college. He had a beard to compensate for the hair disappearing from the top of his head. "My beard turned white and I looked at myself and I thought I was my grandfather," he said. He often dressed ridiculously or ostentatiously.

He also developed a love for recreational gambling in Las Vegas. While working as a lawyer in Hollywood, he and a fellow associate, Greg Ho, sometimes jumped in a rental car on Friday nights and headed to the beach or the mountains or Sin City for a weekend of blackjack or craps. On one such gambling outing, they left behind a memo for their bosses: "If we don't show up Monday, it's because we hit the jackpot," it read.

By 1981, Blankfein was on partner track at Donovan but then had what he called a "prelife crisis" and decided to "abandon law" and make the switch, if he could, to investment banking, which seemed more "interesting" than the law. He applied for jobs at Morgan Stanley, Dean Witter, and Goldman Sachs. He got no offers. "It wasn't a nutty thing," he said, "because here I was a lawyer but I wasn't even doing finance. I was doing kind of tax and tax litigation on the big corporate level." Soon thereafter, a headhunter called and asked him if he would be interested in working at an obscure commodities trading firm, J. Aron & Company, which Goldman had purchased in November 1981. "I didn't know what it was," Blankfein said. "There was no reason for them to hire me." When Blankfein told his then fiancée, Laura Jacobs, that he was leaving law to go to J. Aron, she cried, thinking the comfortable life she was counting on would now be jeopardized. (In an ironic twist, Donovan, Leisure closed its doors a decade ago.) At the end of 1982, Blankfein went to work on the gold bullion sales desk at J. Aron "to trade commodities," he once wrote.

At that time, J. Aron was a serious stepchild at Goldman. For years, J. Aron had made healthy profits, but in the first year of Goldman's stewardship, the firm had lost money. The J. Aron employees were forced to ride in a separate elevator in Goldman's 85 Broad Street headquarters. At one point, Blankfein joined a group of J. Aron employees in wearing red suspenders to make fun of their white-shoe brethren. "We were street fighters," Dennis Suskind, a former J. Aron partner, told *Fortune* in 2008. "We didn't wear suspenders." Blankfein was basically clueless about what J. Aron actually did and what he was supposed to do there. "I had trouble with the language, with the speed and the pacing," he said. "I remember an early review where somebody wanted to know why I never spoke—which if you know me it's not my biggest problem today—I think I was sort of in shell shock, just because it was a trading floor environment. I'd come from a law firm, [with] secretaries outside [the offices]. It was a bit of a different culture."

But soon enough, both Blankfein and Goldman started getting serious about J. Aron, especially after Goldman put Mark Winkelman in charge. He fired underperformers and, at the direction of Robert Rubin, then co-head of Goldman's fixed-income division, set ambitious new revenue and profitability targets for J. Aron. At first, Winkelman was incredulous that J. Aron could earn even $10 million per year, but that modest target was quickly surpassed; in a few years, the business was producing more than $1 billion in profit per year, a meaningful chunk of Goldman's overall bottom line. Winkelman took note of Blankfein's raw intelligence. "He was clearly bright and energetic, even dynamic and passionate," Winkelman told Charles Ellis.

As a salesman, Lloyd Blankfein was a major part of J. Aron's success. Early on, he reportedly designed a lucrative $100 million trade—then the largest of its kind Goldman had ever handled—for an Islamic client to get around the religion's rules against receiving interest payments. He became fiercely defensive of Goldman's mantra of always putting its clients' interests before its own. Winkelman once recalled how he was impressed watching Blankfein grab a phone out of the hands of a fellow trader when that trader was about to berate a client in the aftermath of a money-losing trade. Blankfein figured that irritating the client was not part of Goldman's other mantra to be "long-term greedy." In 1984, Winkelman put Blankfein in charge of six foreign exchange salesmen and then in charge of foreign exchange trading. Rubin advised Winkelman against making that move. "That's probably not the right thing to do," Rubin told him. "We've never seen it work to put salespeople in charge of trading in other areas of the firm. Are you pretty sure of your analysis?" Winkelman did it anyway. Blankfein said he looked up to Winkelman. "He was very supportive of me and I was very appreciative of him," he said.

Blankfein's career took off as a manager of traders. He seemed to have a sixth sense about when to push them to take more risk and when to take their collective feet off the accelerator. "It's not about hanging onto a predisposition," Blankfein told *Fortune*. "The best traders are not right more than they are wrong. They are quick adjusters. They are better at getting right when they are wrong." Blankfein, too, was becoming a quick adjuster, not only to the ways of J. Aron but also in his savvy about what it takes to get to the top of a complex firm such as Goldman Sachs. Even though he was not a trader per se—he said he finds it amusing that people often think he was—he did manage a small trading account with results that could be monitored, "in order to gain credibility with traders," recalled Jacob Goldfield, a former partner of Blankfein's. "It's not like he turned on a button and magically was a brilliant trader, and then got credibility," he said. "He was taking a risk that he could lose credibility, although maybe he realized that even if he lost money he would get credibility because the credibility of being right isn't so important. The credibility of knowing what a trader experiences when they lose might even be more valuable, so maybe he figured out that either way it was good to show that he was learning."

In 1988, along with Bob Steel and some other future Goldman leaders—former co-presidents John Thornton and John Thain, billionaire investor J. Christopher Flowers, hedge-fund manager Frank Brosens, and Gary Gensler, now head of the Commodity Futures Trading

Commission—Blankfein was one of thirty-six men (not a single woman) named general partners. His elbows could sometimes be very sharp. "[He had] plenty of energy for the turf battles, and yet he was very good substantively," recalled Goldfield. "One imagines that usually if you're not good substantively, you've got a lot of energy for turf battles but he was both, which is interesting." He said Blankfein would sometimes send his loyal soldiers to fight his turf battles rather than fight them himself, and this could be especially unpleasant and was seen as cowardly.

Goldfield also recalled that Blankfein was endowed with an unusual combination of humility and self-awareness, two traits not normally associated with hugely successful Wall Street executives. He remembered speaking once with Blankfein about whether other women ever tempted him. "He said, 'I'm tempted, I understand [the temptation], and I wouldn't want to blow this up'"—his marriage—"'so it's a tradeoff.'" When they spoke about the possibility of Blankfein dying young, as his parents had, Blankfein "lamented this possibility because he would fail to see the outcome of the experiment that raising his children is," he recalled.

Blankfein decided to get to work on both his body and his career. He lost weight on the Atkins diet, started using an elliptical exercise machine, started playing "low quality" squash and golf, and made sure to go swimming whenever he got the chance. "One day I just decided that I'm just losing control," he said. "I'm just losing it here and so then I got [my weight] down." He started dressing more like a banker and less like a renegade. At his wife's continuous urging, he also stopped smoking. "That would have been very, very bad if I hadn't stopped, and the person who got me to stop was Laura," he said.

In 1994, in the wake of Winkelman's departure from Goldman after being passed over for the top job in favor of Corzine, Blankfein was selected to run J. Aron. In 1995, he chided his fellow partners for being too risk averse. He left a conference room where they were meeting to discuss placing a multimillion-dollar bet with the firm's money that the dollar would rise against the yen. His stunt worked. Blankfein's bet paid off and he impressed his partners as a prudent risk taker. In 1997, Goldman appointed Blankfein co-head of a merged business unit of J. Aron and the firm's existing fixed-income business, together known as FICC. He ran the division from London in 1998 and 1999. Goldman went public in 1999, which caused enough internal combustion that a number of potential rivals to Blankfein left the firm. Simply put, at the right moment, he was in charge of Goldman's profit engine and propelled the firm to greater and greater heights and himself to the top job.

Curiously, he cannot pinpoint the moment when his career path switched to a higher trajectory, or when, as he said, he had his "Rosebud moment from the time they took the sled away from me in the snow." He said the key to his success at Goldman simply was his ability to adapt to new situations, new circumstances, and new people but not in a Zelig-type invisible way but rather in a forceful, quasi-diplomatic way. "I always had a lot of confidence in my ability to gauge a situation and people and try to understand them and what they were saying and what their context was," he said. "I never was really burdened by too much conviction about what I was thinking. . . . I can shed my own prejudices very quickly and be open-minded. . . . I assume that if something worked some way for a generation, I don't think it just randomly got that way and stuck. I think there's a basis for it. Now the context may have shifted and they may be wrong now and you may have to change it, but I don't assume everybody's a dope."

He also had a talent for making money—"commerciality" was the word he coined—and in as Darwinian and profit-driven an environment as Wall Street, and at Goldman in particular, this quality did not go unnoticed at the top levels of the firm. Blankfein preferred not to dwell, though, on his ability to make money, although a number of his former partners believe he was obsessed about his own compensation and making as much money as he possibly could—partly haunted by the memory of his parents' financial struggles.

He certainly lived well. In 2008, he paid $26 million in cash for a duplex apartment, facing Central Park, in Robert A. M. Stern's tony building at 15 Central Park West, which is partially owned by a Goldman Sachs investment fund. "Wall Street's new power address," the *Times* called the Stern building. He bought the new apartment before selling his old five-bedroom duplex at 941 Park Avenue, which eventually he did for $12.15 million in August 2010, according to public records. He also agreed to spend $41 million in 2007 on Old Trees, a thirteen-bedroom "cottage" in Southampton, New York, on the Atlantic Ocean. But after word of the deal was leaked to the press, Blankfein backed out—it was too much of a public display of conspicuous consumption. He and his family decided to keep their existing home in Sagaponack, which he had listed for sale in 2007 at just under $14 million. The Blankfeins received some unwanted publicity in the summer of 2009, when the day after Blankfein left a voice mail message for Goldman's employees urging them "to avoid making big-ticket, high-profile purchases," his wife and the wife of another senior Goldman executive were described in the *New York Post* as being disruptive and "causing a huge scene" at a big-ticket charity shopping event in the Hamptons.

By then, Blankfein had impressed Goldman's board of directors, and especially Paulson, with his tenacity, his ambition, and his hands-on management of the business. "Hank became increasingly concerned about whether Thornton or Thain"—the co-presidents of Goldman before Blankfein—"would assume responsibility for the business units and show they could run things," said one former Goldman partner. "Lloyd showed a willingness to assume responsibility." Paulson and Blankfein became an effective team, with Paulson globe-trotting and hobnobbing with clients and Blankfein assuming more and more operational control of the firm. Year after year, the firm was making billions in profits. "Lloyd made everything run," said this former partner.

In an interview in his heavily book-filled office at the Johns Hopkins School of Advanced International Studies, in Washington, where he worked after his stint as treasury secretary, Paulson discussed the reasons he chose Blankfein to succeed him. "What I'd come to see in him—which I admired greatly—was he ate, slept, drank the business and the markets," the former treasury secretary said. "He loved them. He was innately quick and very intelligent. But that can be overestimated because there are plenty of really, really bright guys that aren't good guys or get you in trouble or don't have good judgment. The thing that hit me about him was sort of a positive insecurity. There was no sense of entitlement. There was no arrogance to Lloyd. He was always conscious of his weaknesses and wanted to get better. So you look at certain people when they've been around for fifteen or twenty years and get to a level of seniority, their weaknesses become exaggerated either because they become ingrained or because they're just more exposed at a more senior level, and so people need to compensate for their weaknesses. Good leaders need the self-awareness to recognize their weaknesses and the ability to grow. And I watched Lloyd just get better and better."

He recalled once again how after the Goldman IPO—and when Paulson was the firm's undisputed leader—the hypothetical question that former senior partner Steve Friedman asked him about the future leadership of the firm. "He said, 'If you owned Goldman Sachs lock, stock, and barrel, if it wasn't a public company, you just owned it, who would you have running it if you had all your money in it?' and I said, 'Well, this is not the only test, Steve, if you had all your money in it.' He said, 'Yeah, but if you did?'" At this particular moment in the firm's history Thornton and Thain were the firm's two co-presidents and heirs apparent. Blankfein was below them in the hierarchy and not well known outside the firm. Once Paulson understood fully Friedman's question, he replied, "I wouldn't even think about it—it would be Lloyd Blankfein."

CHAPTER 18

ALCHEMY

I t is exceedingly difficult to get a job at Goldman Sachs. The interviewing process can be a brutal endurance test, often spanning many months and as many as thirty individual interviews. Part of the challenge for the best and the brightest the world over who aspire to work at the firm is to withstand the lengthy, seemingly random process in the first place, while keeping their ambitions and ego in check. Goldman likes team players, literally—with many of those offered jobs having played competitive sports in high school and college—or people who are perceived to be able to subordinate their individual ambitions for the betterment of the firm as a whole. It is no place for prima donnas, or so they would have one believe. But it is a firm stuffed to the gills with high-achieving alpha males, or "aleph males," as one former Goldman professional described them, a reference to the firm's Jewish heritage. "It was—of course—a very, very intense place," he said, comparing it to other Wall Street firms he had worked at previously. "You got the feeling that every high-school valedictorian was there. In whatever role, you had someone who had been the star elsewhere. They were trying their very hardest to prove how well they could perform, whether they were a lower-level person or an upper-level person. There was a real sort of humming feeling of people striving. Then, there's also an incredible stress put on doing everything with group consensus. And it takes a good deal of getting used to because one of the reasons I think that Goldman is so good is because it's like this giant hive mind where you have all these smart people and they're also all talking to each other. Everyone is very quickly focusing on the same issue and getting the best result they can think of all together and then they go on to the next issue and the next issue. So it's the advantages of having a lot of smart people focus on something without the usual disadvantage of it getting bogged down. In order to function well there, you have to put a lot of attention on posting people on what's going on and getting people to sign off. And it's just a very different style of working. It was very, very different. And so it's very, very intense."

Unlike at most other Wall Street firms, pedigree seems to be of little moment at Goldman Sachs. While it is certainly true that the firm has its pick—year after year—of the smartest graduates of the nation's best colleges and universities as well as of its top graduate schools, the firm's hiring process seems to revolve largely around merit. Whereas other firms—such as Lazard or Morgan Stanley—prized the hiring of scions of the rich and famous politicians or CEOs and sought them out, Goldman seems to be swayed less by what your last name is and more by how bright you are. Goldman's obsession with finding the smartest people in any room became such that even Bill Gates noticed. He once remarked that Microsoft's biggest competitor was not another software company but rather Goldman Sachs. "It's all about IQ," Gates said. "You win with IQ. Our only competition for IQ is the top investment banks."

Fortunately for Goldman, the firm hired, nurtured, and promoted Josh Birnbaum, whose insights and business acumen played a huge role in Goldman's astonishing Houdini act during the cataclysmic market collapse that began in 2007. Raised for a time in Paris with his two sisters, he eventually moved with his family to Oakland, California, where his father wrote software for a computer company. Birnbaum attended the Head-Royce School, a private day school in Oakland, from which he graduated in 1990. His interest in finance was encouraged by an uncle—whom he greatly admired—and who one day showed his nephew the *Wall Street Journal*'s options table. His fascination with options and how much money potentially could be made from them grew out of that moment. He was twelve years old. He had his own trading account at Charles Schwab, and although he said he does not know "what the audited returns" in it were, he was "very focused on finance from a young age."

To further pursue that interest after high school, Birnbaum headed to the University of Pennsylvania's Wharton School, where he majored in finance, as did most of his classmates, and dreamed of getting a job on Wall Street. After his sophomore year at Wharton, he wanted to get an internship in finance but knew that since he was only in his second year, his appeal to Wall Street would be limited because it would be two years before he was able to start working full-time. But Birnbaum was crafty; he had sufficient credits under his belt to claim to be a junior. So he headed to the school's placement office and started scanning into a computer the piles of business cards that Wall Street executives had left there during the job interview process. He then sent out hundreds of letters trying to convey the idea each time that he had always wanted to work at that particular firm.

He received many responses, but the two that were the most intriguing were from J.P. Morgan and Goldman Sachs. The Goldman letter came from the mortgage department, which at the time was run by Mike Mortara, the transfer from Salomon Brothers. Mortara had worked with the legendary Lew Ranieri—the godfather of the securitization business on Wall Street, where mortgages and other cash-flow streams, such as credit-card receivables and auto-loan receivables, are packaged up into securities and sold off to investors. Birnbaum's first interview at Goldman was with Gary Gensler, who was then a partner and a trader in the mortgage department, trading collateralized mortgage obligations, which were known around Wall Street as CMOs. According to an internal Goldman "mortgage primer" document, CMOs "are created by pooling" various kinds of home or commercial mortgages "and splitting their cashflows into a number of tranches."

Birnbaum wanted to be a summer CMO analyst. He even knew what CMOs *were*, even though he was barely nineteen years old. He got the job at Goldman, in part because of his palpable intelligence and in part because he looked like a textbook Goldman employee: he was handsome and athletic, favoring tightly fitting spread-collar shirts.

In the early 1990s, there were often debates among the best and brightest young finance students about whether it was better—more lucrative, that is—to be a banker or to be a trader. This had been a perennial question on Wall Street for at least a generation. Some years the bankers would be the Kings of Wall Street, garnering the highest compensation, the most prestige, and the magazine covers; other years, the traders would be the Big Swinging Dicks, as they were known, and bring home the fattest paychecks. But Birnbaum had no such conflicts about whether he wanted to be a banker or a trader. "Trading appealed to me always just because it was more mathematics," he said. "I was always a math guy."

During the summer of 1992, as Wall Street was slowly emerging from a deep credit crunch brought on by the aftermath of the crash of 1987, investment banks were competing fiercely to underwrite CMOs, even though there was not a lot of money in doing so. Mortara and Goldman were busy fighting it out with Kidder, Peabody, and its star trader, Michael Vranos. In 1993, Kidder paid Vranos $15 million—a huge amount at the time (and still, frankly)—and he was often referred to as "the most powerful man on Wall Street," since Kidder underwrote twice the volume of CMOs as its nearest competitor. "There was a big land grab for league tables," Birnbaum explained, referring to the way Wall Street keeps score of how much business it does in a particular product area.

Birnbaum sat on the CMO trading desk during his summer internship and worked on structuring the debt securities. What made his experience so unusual was that it wasn't about networking or booze cruises or rotating from one product area to another during the course of the summer. "This was a trial-by-fire, put-your-butt-in-a-seat, we-really-need-you-to-structure-stuff-right-now kind of thing," he said. "There's no orientation, there's none of that crap. It was just a phenomenal experience for me to be able to do something real in a very hot area at the time." Goldman asked him to return the following summer. Once again, he structured CMOs. "It was still a great time to do it in 1993," he said. "There was a steep yield curve"—meaning the cost of debt was higher the longer someone could take to pay it back—"so intellectually it was an interesting thing." He had straight As when he graduated from the Wharton undergraduate program in December 1993—a semester early—and because of that, and having Goldman Sachs on his résumé for two summers, he had any number of job offers to choose from. But he decided to return to Goldman, as do the vast majority of people who work there during the summers before they graduate. "I had a lot of goodwill built up already," he said, "and it was a great firm. I was interested in the products. I liked the people. In terms of really seriously considering other things, I didn't."

He continued doing what he had done the previous summers, structuring CMOs. For the uninitiated (which would be almost everyone before the financial crisis of 2007), Birnbaum's job was to buy mortgages from mortgage originators—at the time, other Wall Street dealers or mortgage bankers, such as Countrywide and New Century Financial Corporation. The originators would, in turn, ask Fannie Mae or Freddie Mac—the two quasi-government mortgage agencies—to "wrap" the mortgages. Meaning Fannie and Freddie would—for a fee—guarantee the timely payment of the principal and interest on the mortgages. In those days, the mortgages were sold in small lots, so it was the job of Birnbaum and his colleagues to buy up a bunch of the mortgages so they could be packaged together into securities and sold off to investors. It was the Wall Street version of a factory floor. "The traders who were trading mortgages would sit on a row," Birnbaum explained, "and then a row behind that would be the mortgage banking sales force, and they would sit there on two phones and they would say, 'Countrywide has two million Fannie Mae six percents for sale, what do you bid?' And then the guy would yell out, 'I'll bid ninety-nine and seven-eighths!' and nothing was electronic back then, so there was a lot of yelling and it was kind of an

exciting environment to work in, especially as a young and impressionable kid." While Birnbaum would sit nearby calculating internal rates of
return on his Lotus 1-2-3 software, there was a "constant flow of this
kind of chatter," he said. At that time there was a huge wave of mortgage
refinancing.

The art of the deal was to figure out ways to structure the CMO securities to appeal to different types of investors. CMOs "are able to satisfy
disparate investors' needs for cash flows with varying levels of average lives,
coupons, and stability profiles," according to Goldman's marketing material. "The primary purpose of this structure is to create [mortgage-backed
securities] with varying average lives and to redistribute prepayment risk."
For instance, the steady stream of mortgage payments appealed to commercial banks as short-term investments as did the price of the securities
relative to more expensive—but less risky—U.S. Treasury securities. The
problem for banks was that if borrowers started to refinance their
mortgages—which usually happened when interest rates fell—what they
thought would be a long-term, fixed-rate asset would suddenly be gone.
People like Josh Birnbaum were in business to chop up these streams of
mortgage payments into different cash payments—tranches, they were
called on Wall Street—so that investors who wanted a fixed-rate, long-
term return could get that and those willing to take more risk (of, say, a refinancing) could get paid a higher interest rate to take that risk. "The whole
concept behind the CMO was to be able to give the more risk-adverse
investors a portion, which is going to be less risky, or [have] less variability
in terms of the cash flow," Birnbaum explained, "and then, if you will, subordinated investors—or what they called 'support tranches'—would bear
more variability. . . . The CMO would do that."

There was also an element of salesmanship to the business. "What's
the art of arbitrage?" Birnbaum continued. "There was some combination
of math skills and sales skills and trading skills. You were generally never
selling the whole thing. So the art was a combination of those things. You
know you needed to sell your sales force in order for them to sell their
clients. But you also needed to be able to know how to price risk because
you were taking risk for the firm, you were putting stuff on the firm's balance sheet, and you needed to understand the math of these structures
because they were complicated. How to optimize how much of a structure would be safe versus less safe was not something that most people
kind of do in their head. Typically the senior guys on those desks were
really good math guys."

What started out as a simple idea—say, prioritizing cash flows to
certain types of investors—had become quite complicated by the time

Birnbaum made his way to Goldman's mortgage desk. "These CMOs were being divided into—in some cases—more than one hundred different classes, and you weren't just playing games with them," he said. "Let's say that it's trading at one hundred and five cents. But you have a buyer who doesn't want to pay more than one hundred cents. So you could actually take that tranche or that collateral and you could divide it into two pieces: one that's got a coupon that's lower that trades at one hundred and one that's got a *really* high coupon, in some cases only a coupon that you would sell to a more speculative investor. Or you might have an investor that says, 'I don't want any fixed-rate risk—I'm a floating-rate investor, I want floaters,' so you create a floater. What is the opposite of a floater? Inverse floater. So you have this whole conservation of cash flows and kind of giving people what they want." The idea was not dissimilar to buying all the disparate ingredients to make cakes in a bakery and then selling the finished cakes for more than the cost of the ingredients.

This bit of Wall Street alchemy represented a serious evolution of the way mortgages were previously bought and sold. Once upon a time, a local banker would provide a mortgage to his neighbor so that he could buy his own home and have a small slice of the American Dream. Before making the loan, the banker would know all about the fellow—his reputation, his standing in the community, his income, his net worth, and his prospects for repaying the borrowed money. That mortgage would then sit on the local bank's balance sheet for thirty years, unless paid off sooner, and the bank's profits—*its* ability to make money from money— would be determined in large part by how good a credit risk the borrower turned out to be. If he paid the interest and principal on the mortgage on time, it was a good bet the loan would be profitable for the bank. Knowing your customer was good business.

That tried-and-true formula began to change in 1977 when the Brooklyn-born Lew Ranieri came up with the clever idea that everyone would be better off—the borrower, the bank, and of course Salomon Brothers, his employer—if there were a way to buy up the mortgages from the local banks, put them all together, thereby spreading the risk presented by any one borrower across a broad portfolio of borrowers, and sell pieces of the resulting securities backed by these mortgages to investors the world over, offering varying rates of interest depending on an investor's risk appetite. Ranieri, who started at Salomon in the mail room, assembled a team of PhDs to package, slice, and sell the mortgages after he realized mortgages were "just math" and streams of cash flows that investors might want to buy. This powerful idea—dubbed "securitization"—was one of those once-in-a-generation innovations that revolutionized finance. Ranieri's idea caught on and, so the theory goes, helped reduce the cost of mortgages for borrowers all over the country, since the market for the mortgages was far more liquid than when they simply sat on a bank's balance sheet tying up capital for thirty years.

Ranieri brought a similar magician's skill to the streams of payments for car and credit-card receivables, which were also securitized and sold off to investors worldwide. Salomon Brothers—and Ranieri—made a fortune from implementing Ranieri's insight. In 2004, *BusinessWeek* dubbed Ranieri "one of the greatest innovators of the past 75 years." But what Ranieri and his innovation really did was change forever the *ethic* of Wall Street from one where a buyer knew a seller, and vice versa, to one where the decision to buy something was separated from traditional market forces. No longer was a buyer making an affirmative decision to buy something from a seller he knew; now he was buying a slice of a package of stuff wrapped in a pretty bow that had the appearance of being worth what was advertised, but wasn't really. "When securitization arrived," explained Salim "Sandy" Lewis, a onetime Wall Street arbitrageur, "the 'I buy' moment in mortgage making evaporated. Accountability vacated. Fees replaced liability, as liability was sent offshore, on advice of compliant, crooked counsel. This is enabling. All of them did it."

Of course, as with any innovation on Wall Street—the introduction of junk bonds in the 1980s (courtesy of Michael Milken, at Drexel Burnham Lambert), the bridge loan in the 1980s (courtesy of the late Bruce Wasserstein, then at First Boston), or the Internet IPO in the late 1990s based on nothing more than the number of claimed "eyeballs" on a fledgling website (courtesy of Frank Quattrone, then at Morgan Stanley)—it was just a matter of a short amount of time before the new idea was replicated, and often improved upon, by the competition, especially when there was money—always lots of money—to be made. Warren Buffett has referred to this phenomenon as the "three I's of new markets": the Innovators, the Imitators, and the Idiots, who end up taking a fine idea and pushing it to the brink of lunacy. "People don't get smarter about things that get as basic as greed," Buffett once said. "You can't stand to see your neighbor getting rich. You know you're smarter than he is, but he's doing all these [crazy] things, and he's getting rich . . . so pretty soon you start doing it."

Such was the life cycle of Ranieri's brainchild—the mortgage-backed security. Over time, Ranieri's lieutenants—including Mortara—were hired away by other firms and began to build important mortgage businesses at Salomon's competitors, like Goldman Sachs and Merrill Lynch.

For all the envy it inspired and the prestige it radiated among its Wall Street peers, when it came to financial innovation Goldman Sachs was more akin to Microsoft than to Apple—as Mark Schwartz had pointed out in his speech to the incoming Goldman partners at Arrowwood—in the sense that product innovations were never particularly its greatest strength. But the firm was sufficiently astute to recognize the innovations of others and their moneymaking potential and was able to quickly deconstruct their technology and copy it.

Mortara, one of the original innovators of securitization, helped Goldman catch up with its peers at Salomon Brothers and Kidder, Peabody in the world of selling and trading mortgage-backed securities. "He was the most dynamic guy I've ever worked for, without a doubt," Birnbaum explained. "He was very respected. He carried around— playfully—a baseball bat, and he'd sit there in meetings with his little bat. He definitely toed the line from where you're supposed to be feared versus loved." In 1992 and 1993, during his summer internships at Goldman, the CMO market was hot and Goldman was turning out the securities "like it was a fortune cookie factory," Birnbaum said.

But by 1994, his first year as a full-time Goldman employee and one of Goldman's periodic *anni horribiles,* the market for CMOs slumped dramatically, and the pace of work on the mortgage desk slowed considerably. "Doing a CMO was a much riskier endeavor, or was perceived to be a much riskier endeavor, so you weren't allowed to print a CMO deal in the mortgage department unless Michael approved it, and that was a big departure," Birnbaum said. He had spent much of the year redesigning Goldman's financial model for structuring mortgage-backed securities to make it more automated and more proprietary, a source of pride and competitive advantage at the firm. He also helped to create and to automate a database of all the mortgage-related deals priced in the secondary market so that the trading desk would have the best possible information. Most nights, he worked until eleven o'clock. "But there was almost no issuance [as 1994 progressed], so we were like, 'Oh, God, I created this great package and I'm not even sure when we're going to do more CMOs.'"

At this moment of frustration, Birnbaum asked to move over to the trading desk—from the structuring desk—to get more action. Goldman accommodated him. "They were willing to try to make me happy and keep me intrigued, and that was a great move for me," he said. Working with the more senior traders, he started buying and selling balloon mortgages, fifteen-year mortgages, and thirty-year mortgages. He made markets for Goldman's clients. He made proprietary trades for Goldman itself. He traded with other big institutions as well as with Fannie Mae and Freddie Mac, which had started buying mortgages for their own portfolios. He also began exercising that part of his brain intrigued by options and option trading and somehow came to focus on buying and selling options on mortgages and asking the more senior traders on the desk such esoteric existential questions as, "If you own a call option on a mortgage and a mortgage itself is short a call option, what do you end up owning?" (His boss replied that the answer was "complicated" and "not worth going into." In other words, he had no idea what the answer was.)

Birnbaum immersed himself in trading mortgages. "I traded pretty much every seat in that business," he said. "It gave me a ton of exposure with accounts and sales forces around the world, with flow trading. It's a unique skill set all its own. I remember one of the guys on the desk early in my career said of trading, 'The best analogy I can make is to quote from Chuck Yeager: the more sorties you do, the better you are, and you can't underestimate the value of experience.' Well, the more trades you've done, the more times you've been put in the line of fire, you're just going to be that much better than the new guy that comes in." Birnbaum also began to get exposure to the most senior executives of the firm, especially to Jon Corzine. Corzine would come around and chat with the mortgage traders, including Birnbaum, on a regular basis. "He'd just reach out and chat with the mortgage traders for long periods of time," he said of Corzine, "and I thought that was pretty cool that the head of the firm thought our area was that important."

Goldman soon promoted Birnbaum to a full-fledged associate after the end of his two-year post-college stint as an analyst. In 1998, Birnbaum became "intrigued," as he said, with the growing intersection between the mortgage market and what was known as the "swaps market," which traditionally had been for those investors who had a fixed-rate debt instrument and for whatever reasons wanted a floating-rate debt instrument. In the swaps market—for a fee—an investor could swap the fixed for the floating and everybody would be happy. "But you could kind of swap anything," he explained. "One guy wants one thing, another guy wants another thing." In mortgages, the perennial issue had always been what the prepayment rate on mortgages would turn out to be as people inevitably sought to refinance their home loans. "So there was an idea: 'Hey, why don't we create some swaps that are based on the realized prepayment experience of a certain type of mortgage?' And that was the first time that the swaps concept was applied to mortgages, and ultimately, fast-forward the clock all the way to the CDS [credit-default swaps] market, that was based on credit and that was what ultimately brought down

AIG and other places like that. But the first time that swaps appeared in mortgages was based on betting on prepayments. I thought that was a very interesting business."

At first, Birnbaum did deals between those counterparties who were willing to bet prepayments would be low and those willing to bet prepayments would be high. That was a nice business. But things got much more interesting and lucrative when Birnbaum started to come up with some innovative, interesting new structures. One of these he dubbed a "synthetic CMO," based upon certain investors wanting one part of a CMO but not another. Some investors found some parts of the CMO cheaper than other parts based upon the collateral associated with it. Birnbaum exploited these differences. "Our concept was why don't we isolate a portion of the CMO deal that we view as being expensive and why don't we just facilitate the underwriting to that and take that risk instead of selling all the parts," he said. Whatever Birnbaum had come up with precisely, Goldman made a lot of money from it, and Birnbaum's career began to take off.

He was soon promoted to be head of Goldman's swaps business; as that did increasingly well, he was promoted further to be head of Goldman's mortgage derivatives business. Four years into his tenure at Goldman, he was promoted to vice president, like every other person who had been at the firm for four years. "The VP designation is typically robotic," he said. "You don't get it earlier if you're killing it or later if you're underperforming. You just get it kind of in four years." Goldman was trying—it seemed to him—to distinguish his pay from that of his peer group. "They were doing their job and paid me just enough to keep me around," he said.

In 2001, he came up with another new innovation: something he called "CMM," for constant maturity mortgage, a kind of interest-rate product tied to mortgage rates, instead of LIBOR (for London Interbank Offered Rate). A CMM was "an attempt to simplify the trading of mortgage price risk by transforming the most liquid portion of the mortgage market into a rate-based market" and can "be used to hedge for mortgage products that are sensitive to changes in mortgage rates." Regardless of whether mere mortals understood the new product (or not), Birnbaum's point about it was "that it was another innovation that did well and made good money doing it," of around $100 million a year or so. At one point, in July 2002, Birnbaum, along with Goldman colleague Ashwin Rao, published "A Simple Algorithm to Compute Short-Dated CMM Forwards," which of course was anything but simple. Still, the short paper, filled with such complex ideas as "$P_C(x) = P_C(E[x]) + Dur_C(E[x]) * \Delta x + 1/2 * Conv_C(E[x]) * (\Delta x)^2$," or, roughly translated, as Birnbaum's calculation that mortgages prices were "purely quadratic functions of the level of swap rates," must have impressed Goldman's clients.

In the thirteen years Birnbaum had been at Goldman, much had changed at the firm and on Wall Street. Inside 85 Broad Street the firm had been transformed from one where investment bankers held sway to one where traders, and trading, were the dominant force in the building. The 1999 IPO accelerated this trend because the money raised gave the firm even more capital with which to trade. What's more, it was other people's money with the extra benefit that the rewards—in the billions of dollars annually—for taking risks with it went mostly to the Goldman employees and the losses, should anything go wrong, belonged to the firm's shareholders and creditors.

During Birnbaum's career at Goldman, Wall Street had changed in other ways as well. Whereas in 1992, LBO firms, or leveraged-buyout firms, were few and far between—once you got beyond the well-known firms such as KKR and Forstmann Little—by 2005, buyouts firms, now known as private-equity firms, were everywhere. Goldman, which had a $1 billion fund in 1992, was on its fifth fund by 2005, with $8.5 billion to invest. (Goldman is now on its sixth fund, with $20.3 billion to invest.) This was just one of many such funds at Goldman, which also included a technology fund, an infrastructure fund, a loan fund, a real-estate fund, a mezzanine fund, and a little-known fund of partners' money, which for instance had made an absolute killing (that few people knew about) investing in Jinro Ltd., a Korean liquor manufacturer that had been in receivership. "They got *enormous* in this thing and it made multiple, multiple, multiples!" recalled one impressed hedge-fund manager.

More important, from Birnbaum's perspective, were the surprising number of former Goldman bankers and traders who had left the firm to start their own hedge funds and were making tens of millions of dollars in annual compensation—in some cases, hundreds of millions of dollars and even billions of dollars in compensation. Among them were people such as Thomas Steyer, Daniel Och, Richard Perry, Jonathan Savitz, Eric Mindich, Edward Mule, David Tepper, David Einhorn, Edward Lampert, and Mark McGoldrick (who used to be in charge of Goldman's Special Situations Group). Birnbaum, though a few years younger than most of these men, became increasingly tempted by the idea of the mountains of money he thought he could make on his own or working as a principal at another hedge fund.

Goldman certainly recognized Birnbaum's talent and was doing what it could to keep him at the firm. "I was still there," he said. "I was still listening. They weren't saying the wrong things. But it was more driven by just an intellectual desire to try to maximize my potential." One of the more intriguing opportunities that Birnbaum spied in the market by the end of 2005 was the increasing use of credit-default swaps, or CDS—a form of insurance that could be bought on whether a debt would in fact be paid—in the mortgage or any other debt market. Increasingly, insurance companies, such as AIG, or other Wall Street firms were willing to sell protection on whether the mortgages that went into mortgage-backed securities would in fact be paid. To get the insurance, buyers had to pay premiums to the issuers, as they did to obtain any other form of insurance. Instead of buying life insurance, or fire insurance on your house, or auto insurance on your car, buying a credit-default swap allowed investors to make bets on whether people ended up paying their mortgages.

There were a number of reasons that the markets for mortgages and for credit-default swaps started to intersect in the summer of 2005. First, there was the sheer magnitude of the market for mortgage-backed securities. By the first quarter of 2004, the market for mortgage-backed securities was $6.9 trillion, some 40 percent larger than the market for U.S. corporate debt, which was $5 trillion, and the market for U.S. Treasury debt, which was $4.9 trillion. The mortgage market had more than doubled in ten years. As a result, on a sheer volume basis alone there would likely be increased demand for protection against default, especially since some prognosticators, such as David Rosenberg, the chief North American economist at Merrill Lynch, had started publishing research, in August 2004, questioning whether the real-estate market was heading for trouble. Under the headline "If Not a Bubble Then an Oversized Sud," Rosenberg wrote, "We assess the likelihood that the housing sector has entered into a 'bubble' phase. There are numerous shades of gray, but when we examine the classic characteristics of a 'bubble' (extended valuation, over-ownership, excessive leverage, a surge in supply, complacency (denial?), and speculative behavior), it seems to fit the bill. At the very least, housing is overextended, and even the Fed has acknowledged as much. The next question is what pricks the 'bubble' if in fact there is one?"

In February 2005, Paul Volcker, the former Federal Reserve chairman, picked up that thread in a speech at Stanford University, where he indicated he was increasingly worried about the bubble he thought might be forming in the real-estate market. "There has been a lot of good news in the past couple of years," he said that day, but "I have to tell you my old central banking blood still flows. Under the placid surface, at least the way I see it, there are really disturbing trends: huge imbalances, disequilibria, risks—call them what you will. Altogether the circumstances seem to me as dangerous and intractable as any I can remember, and I can remember quite a lot. What really concerns me is that there seems to be so little willingness or capacity to do much about it." Volcker's observations came some four months after Alan Greenspan, the Federal Reserve chairman at the time, gave a speech in Washington where he allowed that although "pockets of severe stress within the household sector . . . remain a concern," the likelihood of "housing price bubbles" appeared small. By January 2006, even Goldman itself was claiming that "the oft predicted, overly anticipated subprime blow up MAY occur" in 2006 but then dampened that by suggesting that "a blow up" was less likely than a "fizzle out." Still Goldman's economists believed U.S. housing prices to be "overvalued by 15%+."

The other reason for the increasing use of CDS in the mortgage market by the end of 2005 was more technical. In June 2005, the Wall Street firms got together and "standardized" the CDS contracts that were used to insure the risks in the mortgage market.

The combination of the standard contract for credit insurance, plus the explosion of mortgage issuance—especially to borrowers of lower and lower credit quality—and the outlines of concern as a result, led to a noticeable increase in the purchase of CDS on mortgages. "Particularly in the fall of 2005, you really had some of the early hedge-fund trades, significant hedge-fund trades . . . but this was when [hedge-fund manager] John Paulson first crept up and started doing some trades," Birnbaum recalled. According to Goldman, there were $150 billion of credit-default swaps outstanding on "structured product" at the end of 2005, up exponentially from $2 billion the year before. The use of CDS to protect against mortgage-securities' defaults "[g]rew faster than even we predicted," Goldman wrote in its marketing documents.

At the same time, Birnbaum had also noticed that the cost of the premiums to buy the insurance on the mortgage payments had spiked upward, tripled in price really, from costing 1 percent of the aggregate amount being insured to 3 percent of the aggregate amount being insured. Like any market, the cost of the insurance is driven by supply and demand—the greater the demand to insure a certain debt, the greater the likelihood of a higher cost associated with it. In this market at that time, since it was so thinly traded, a sudden increase in demand can have a particularly noticeable effect on the price of the insurance. "It was just like this huge, 'What the heck's going on?' " he said. "The Street got blindsided." Birnbaum was not trading the CDS on mortgages at that time, but he was fairly sure that John Paulson—and perhaps another hedge-fund manager—was starting to build his portfolio of CDS. They were buying credit protection against the default of individual tranches of mortgage-backed securities. "All I know is there was a very thin market, so probably this much inquiry for protection would probably create a huge change," he said. Curious about this new dynamic in this obscure market, Birnbaum decided to buy some credit-default swaps on his trading desk—just to dabble in the market, really—and then sold them relatively quickly, making enough money to impress his colleagues. "Oh, nice job doing that," one of them told him, although it was just one trade. "It was an alert to a lot of folks who had never looked at this market that 'hey, there's something interesting going on here,' " he said.

At the same time that a standardized CDS contract for mortgages came into being and John Paulson was starting to buy increasing amounts of CDS against mortgages, Wall Street also got together and created an index composed of securities backed by home loans issued to borrowers with weak credit that, for the first time, allowed investors to bet on the performance of the subprime mortgage market. This new index—the ABX.HE, or ABX for short—was the brainchild of people like Rajiv Kamilla, at Goldman Sachs, then in his early thirties and a former nuclear physicist. The idea, Birnbaum said, was to create "an index that was a portfolio that everyone could agree upon that was representative of the subprime market, and then instead of trading each single name, you would trade this portfolio and it could be more liquid and maybe you could trade it as a hedge instrument, maybe as a speculative instrument."

An obscure partnership—with the odd name of CDS IndexCo LLC—owned by sixteen investment banks, including Goldman, created the index in January 2006 and for the first time, investors had a way to bet on the performance of the subprime mortgage market. (Brad Levy, a Goldman partner, served as CDS Index's chairman). Another firm—Markit.com, based in London, and of which Goldman also owned a piece—collected and published on a daily basis the data from Wall Street firms related to the securities in the ABX index, effectively administering the index. (Markit.com was, in 2009, the subject of an investigation by the Justice Department, which, according to *Forbes*, "wants to know if the firms"—like Goldman and JPMorgan—"benefited from the way prices of credit indexes were posted on Markit.com. These prices, taken from the average of quotes from the dealers themselves, could only be accessed in the afternoon via the site. Otherwise, the buying and selling of credit derivatives has been completely invisible to the investing public.")

Before the creation of the ABX index in January 2006, if the mortgage-backed securities market sold off, no one really knew for sure by how much. But with the creation of the ABX, there was now a published index that people could observe and, more important, could short to hedge whatever risks they perceived existed in the mortgage market.

The more he heard about the ABX, the more interested Birnbaum became in the possibility of trading it. This, he thought, might be his next opportunity and a way for him to stay at Goldman. (In a January 2006 presentation to a mortgage client, Goldman's bankers described the January 19 launch of the ABX index as "THE market event" of the first half of the year.) When his managers at Goldman, Mike Swenson and Dan Sparks, agreed to let Birnbaum trade the index, he decided he would stay and do it. "The thinking was that I had all that flow experience," he said, "but I also knew the guts of the mortgage cash flows very well. This was something where knowing both would be really useful to you." Birnbaum recalled that Swenson, known around the office as "Swenny," was particularly supportive of the idea. A former hockey player at Williams College with four children, a preppy demeanor, and a wry sense of humor, Swenson had been at Goldman since 2000. "He's one of these guys who has a great nose for kind of knowing when people are going to be good at something," Birnbaum said. Birnbaum gave Swenson "a lot of credit" for bringing to that desk "the right guys" with "complementary skills" and "not worrying about turf wars or ego or politics." The idea was to put the best team together, one that would outsmart and outhustle the competition.

In early January 2006, Birnbaum moved to the desk where the ABX index would be traded. It was about four or five rows of desks away from where he had been sitting. The move was a little unusual, but all parties to it embraced the idea as a good one. The first ABX trade occurred on January 19. "At the time nobody had any sense that ABX or the credit-default swap market and mortgages would be anything close to what it ultimately was," he said. "But it was still a very interesting product. . . . I think that Goldman—and myself personally—we had a very bullish view on what the index would do in terms of trading flows and just what the business prospects were in terms of having an index trading business, more so than I think any other bank."

That first day, Birnbaum did some thirty different trades involving the ABX index and made $1 million in profit. The next closest bank trading the index had made five trades. "We approached it as a great opportunity," he said. "We were a liquidity provider from day one and printing a lot of trades. Other banks had more trepidation: 'What is this index? How does this affect our business? How does this affect what was traditionally a long-only asset-backed business?' We were, like, this is a new regime. This is going to be a two-way business in mortgage credit from now on, and there's a potential flow product with a lot of interest from lots of different kinds of market participants. From day one that thesis was corroborated by virtue of the net we made"—the $1 million—"and the number of trades we did first versus our competitors. So out of the gate we were really, really happy." At first, Birnbaum traded the index on behalf of his clients and made money buying and selling as in any "flow product," he explained. At that moment, neither he nor the firm had any "conviction" about the direction the mortgage market would move in, and so he and his colleagues were just content to make markets for clients and take what amounted to a fee. "We hadn't necessarily formed a view one way or the other," he said. "We were trading the market more agnostically on behalf of our clients at that point on day one. The view at that point was simply this is a great business opportunity. The view wasn't, 'We're going to buy it and we're going to sell it and we're going to take a huge position.' It was, 'This is a great opportunity to have this product to trade at this time.'"

————

AT THE SAME time that Birnbaum and his colleagues (among them Deeb Salem and Jeremy Primer, in addition to Swenny) on the structured products desk at Goldman were gearing up to trade the ABX index and wondering about if, and when, to get some "conviction" on the direction the mortgage market might take during the next six months or so, other parts of the firm—then composed of 22,500 people—were continuing to go about their business. One such group was still busy aggregating mortgages from mortgage originators, such as Countrywide or New Century, and getting ready to package the mortgages up and sell them to hungry investors in the form of mortgage-backed securities.

One of those mortgage-backed securities—awkwardly named GSAMP Trust 2006-S2—was a nearly $700 million deal underwritten and sold by Goldman Sachs to investors at the peak of the market in the spring of 2006. It provides an exquisite example of its ill-conceived genre, right down to the fact that there was no way to ever figure out, in all of its prospectus's life-sustaining two hundred or so pages, how much money Goldman made from it. Considering that Goldman exists to "make money with money," according to David Viniar, the firm's longtime chief financial officer, this fundamental bit of opacity would be troubling if it weren't so essential to the firm's success.

Like insects preserved in amber, among the many hidden secrets the GSAMP Trust 2006-S2 document reveals is a world of rampant greed and risk taking run amok, encased in a nearly incomprehensible language that only a securities lawyer could truly love. It was designed to befuddle all but the most sophisticated investor. Here, in March 2006, as signs of an impending financial crisis were beginning to be revealed, Goldman Sachs—while taking very little risk itself—had put the considerable cachet and imprimatur of its storied 137-year history on the line in order to offer investors the opportunity to buy pieces of a pool of 12,460 *second* mortgages on homes from one end of the country to the other.

And what a collection of borrowers and properties it was. Not only did another creditor have the *first* mortgage on the homes—meaning a priority claim on all payments related to it—but also some 29 percent in number and 43 percent in value of the mortgages had been made to home owners in California. Some 6.5 percent of the mortgages came from Florida, and some 5.6 percent of the mortgages came from New York. The California borrowers had an average credit rating score of 672—out of a possible score of 850—and owed an average of $87,915 on their second mortgage. Only 32 percent of these mortgages resulted from "full-doc" loans, meaning loans that had been made based upon a comprehensive understanding of borrowers' financial capability to repay them; the remaining 68 percent were based on a far more flimsy underwriting, a combination of unverified facts and circumstances about the borrowers. Not surprisingly, given the risk involved, the average interest rate charged on the California second mortgages was a healthy 10.269 percent.

What's more, 99.82 percent of the mortgages in the pool of California residences had a loan-to-value ratio in excess of 80 percent. These homes were leveraged to the max, and the slightest drop in the value of the home would immediately impair the underlying second mortgage and thus the value of the mortgage-backed securities that Goldman was underwriting. Fortunately, thanks to required disclosures, Goldman was willing to concede this point in the prospectus. "Mortgage loans with higher original combined loan-to-value ratios may present a greater risk of loss than mortgage loans with original combined loan-to-value ratios of 80 percent or below," the lawyers wrote on Goldman's behalf in the prospectus.

The prospectus contained plenty of other warnings, too. For instance, right up front Goldman announced the sobering risk that the underwriting standards on the underlying mortgages were probably lousy. The "assets of the trust" backing the securities being sold "may include residential mortgage loans that were made, in part, to borrowers who, for one reason or another, are not able, or do not wish, to obtain financing from traditional sources," the prospectus read. "These mortgage loans may be considered to be of a riskier nature than mortgage loans made by traditional sources of financing, so that the holders of the securities may be deemed to be at greater risk of loss than if the mortgage loans were made to other types of borrowers."

In typical Wall Street fashion, Goldman had not made any of these home loans itself. It had no idea who the borrowers were or whether they could repay the mortgages. Goldman knew something about their credit scores but that was about it. It was counting on both the perceived power of the ongoing housing bubble to keep housing values inflated and a diversified portfolio to spread the risk across the pool of geographically diverse mortgages in order to minimize the risk of any one individual borrower or group of borrowers. Of course, Goldman had no intention of keeping the mortgages itself but rather bought them for the sole purpose of packaging them together and selling them off to investors for a fee determined by the difference between the price it paid for them and the price it sold them for. In other words, pretty standard Wall Street practice.

By the spring of 2006, Goldman was considered a respectable underwriter of mortgage-backed securities, ranking twelfth worldwide in 2005 in the underwriting of so-called structured finance deals—those for asset-backed securities, residential and commercial mortgage-backed securities, and collateralized debt obligations—worth $102.8 billion. By 2006, Goldman had moved up to tenth in the league tables—underwriting 204 deals globally, worth $130.7 billion—but still was far behind Lehman Brothers, Deutsche Bank, Citigroup, Merrill Lynch, and Bear Stearns. These other firms were coining money underwriting mortgage-backed securities and became so concerned about having access to a steady flow of mortgages to package up and sell that they all bought mortgage origination firms—Bear bought EMC Mortgage; Merrill bought First Franklin Financial Corp. from National City Bank in December 2006—at the top of the market—for $1.7 billion. Goldman was content being in the middle of the pack when it came to this activity, and the firm never bought a mortgage origination company, despite having numerous opportunities to do so. "Exactly what we didn't want to do," explained Viniar. That being said, Goldman did buy, for $14 million, Senderra Funding, a small South Carolina–based subprime lender, in February 2007; and, for $1.34 billion—a tidy sum—Litton Loan Servicing, a mortgage servicing business, in December 2007; and Money Partners LP, a British mortgage lender, soon thereafter.

But aside from that particular corporate bias—against buying a significant mortgage origination business and toward servicing those mortgages—Goldman was no different in its approach to the business than other Wall Street firms. According to a lawsuit filed in September

2009 by aggrieved investors in GSAMP Trust 2006-S2, "[W]ith the advent and proliferation of securitizations, the traditional model gave way to the 'originate to distribute' model, in which banks essentially sell the mortgages and transfer credit risk to investors through mortgage-backed securities. Securitization meant that those originating mortgages were no longer required to hold them to maturity. By selling the mortgages to investors, the originators obtained funds, enabling them to issue more loans and generate transaction fees. This increased the originators' focus on processing mortgage transactions rather than ensuring their credit quality. Wall Street banks, including Goldman Sachs, entered into the high-margin business of packaging mortgages and selling them to investors as MBS, including mortgage pass-through certificates. As is now evident, far too much of the lending during that time was neither responsible, prudent, nor in accordance with stated underwriting practices."

———

FOR GSAMP TRUST 2006-S2, as it had many times before and would many times after, Goldman bought the mortgages it wanted to securitize and sell off from third-party mortgage originators. In this case, Goldman bought all of the mortgages from NC Capital, an affiliate of New Century Financial Corporation. In other underwritings, Goldman had also bought mortgages from—to name a few—Fremont Investment & Loan, an indirect subsidiary of Fremont General Corporation; Long Beach Mortgage Company; Argent Mortgage Company; Countrywide Financial; First National Bank of Nevada; and GreenPoint Mortgage Funding, Inc. By buying the mortgages from others, Goldman effectively abdicated any role in the underwriting process of the mortgages, relying instead on the judgment of others, again a fairly typical practice on Wall Street, especially late in the cycle as underwriting standards deteriorated and greed prevailed.

New Century, formed in 1995 by three entrepreneurs, ended its first full year in business, in 1996, with 300 employees and a "loan production" volume of $350 million. In 1997, the company went public. By 2003, the company employed 3,700 people and had originated some $27 billion in mortgage loans since its inception. By 2005, New Century employed 7,200 full-time employees and had originated some 310,389 mortgages with a face value of $56.1 billion.

Many pages in Goldman's GSAMP Trust 2006-S2 prospectus were given over to explaining New Century's underwriting standards as a way, presumably, to give comfort to investors about the company's rigor (and to try to be absolved of blame if things went sour). According to Goldman, New Century's underwriting standards "are primarily intended to assess the borrower's ability to repay the related mortgage loan, to assess the value of the mortgaged property and to evaluate the adequacy of the property as collateral for the mortgage loan. All of the mortgage loans were also underwritten with a view toward the resale of the mortgage loans in the secondary mortgage market. While New Century's primary consideration in underwriting a mortgage loan is the value of the mortgaged property, New Century also considers, among other things, a mortgagor's credit history, repayment ability and debt-service-to-income ratio, as well as the type and use of the mortgaged property."

The underwriting standards of the issuers of the mortgages—such as they were—was the first line of defense against borrowers' failure to make their mortgage payments. The next level of supposed protection for investors in these mortgage-backed securities came from the ratings agencies—primarily Standard & Poor's and Moody's—which were required to rate the securities being issued and in return received fees from the underwriters such as Goldman Sachs and Lehman Brothers. The ratings agencies were careful to caveat their ratings with the idea that investors were aware that their ratings were just opinions about the likelihood that the principal and interest on the mortgages would be paid, not any kind of guarantee that they would be paid. "Ratings on mortgage-backed securities address the likelihood of receipt by security holders of all distributions on the underlying mortgage loans or other assets," the Goldman prospectus said. "These ratings address the structural, legal and issuer-related aspects associated with such securities, the nature of the underlying mortgage loans or other assets and the credit quality of the guarantor, if any." But among the many voices raised during the crisis was that of Jules Kroll, the founder of the eponymous financial investigation firm. He told *The New Yorker,* in October 2009, that the ratings agencies' arguments were deeply flawed. "Credit ratings turned out to be a false god," he said, while also acknowledging that he planned to start a competing service. "People relied on those ratings. Now they're saying, 'Oh, we gave it a high rating but we were just expressing an opinion.' And that's bullshit. These structured instruments—why shouldn't we be able to rely on these ratings, as investors?"

In this particular case, there were ten tranches of securities offered for sale—A1 to A3 (the senior tranches) and then M1 to M7 (the subordinated tranches)—each with different risk profiles and thus a different interest rate. (Often, Wall Street firms were forced to keep for themselves the even *riskier* tranches of these securities because they were so difficult to sell.) All three A classes were rated AAA by both S&P and Moody's, meaning the likelihood of default was supposed to be minimal. Only six companies in the

United States were rated AAA—Johnson & Johnson, ExxonMobil, Berk-shire Hathaway, Automatic Data Processing, Microsoft, and Pfizer—in 2009. The fact that both credit-rating agencies had bestowed AAA ratings on $505.6 million—or 72.4 percent—out of the total $698.4 million of the mortgage-backed securities Goldman was selling in April 2006 no doubt conveyed a level of security to investors that probably never existed, espe-cially since investors did not do their own detailed due diligence on the underlying mortgages but rather instead just relied upon the Goldman imprimatur and that of the ratings agencies to make their investment deci-sions. (Goldman's similar behavior vis-à-vis the ratings agencies leading up to the Penn Central bankruptcy springs to mind; it's déjà vu all over again, as Yogi Berra would say.)

By spring 2006, investors were probably not aware of the growing internal doubts of analysts at both S&P and Moody's about the mortgage-backed securities they were rating. For instance, at a weeklong housing conference, held on Amelia Island, Florida, in April 2005, two S&P credit analysts noted that the housing market seemed to be getting a lit-tle frothy and that the financial risks to the industry were ratcheting up as housing prices skyrocketed and lending standards deteriorated. "Despite these risks," explained Ernestine Warner, a director in S&P's residential mortgage-backed securities surveillance business, "there isn't any performance information available on any of these products just yet because they are still very new to the market. Due to the time lag associ-ated with delinquencies and losses in RMBS"—residential mortgage-backed securities—"pools, and the nature of these risks, it will be several years before the product performance is tested." The Amelia Island con-ference followed Paul Volcker's speech at Stanford University, where he had observed that the growing risks in the housing market left him think-ing that "we are skating on increasingly thin ice."

In a January 19, 2006, paper S&P stated its belief "that there are increasing risks that may contribute to deteriorating credit quality in U.S. RMBS transactions; it is probable that these risks will be triggered in 2006." Four months later, in April 2006—just after Goldman brought GSAMP Trust 2006-S2 to market—S&P announced it was updating its "mortgage analytic model," and then on June 1, 2006, the firm put out a research note that said that based on a study of the results from the new model, the "propensity of low FICO borrowers to default was higher than we previously believed"—not exactly a shocking conclusion, but one that at least acknowledged a deteriorating credit and housing environment, not that many people had noticed.

As delinquencies and defaults on both subprime and so-called Alt-A mortgages—made to those people with better credit than subprime—ticked up heading into the fourth quarter of 2006, S&P's own structured finance specialists began to worry. "Ratings agencies continue to create [an] even bigger monster—the CDO Market," E. Christopher Meyer, an associate director in the Global CDO Group at the firm, wrote in an e-mail to a colleague on the evening of December 15. "Let's hope we are all wealthy and retired by the time this house of cards falters." He then used an emoticon signifying a wink and a smile. Meyers's colleague, Nicole Billick, responded to Meyer's e-mail, in part, by writing that if he was right, then this "is a bigger nightmare that I do not want to think about right now."

As S&P kept slapping investment-grade ratings on soon-to-be-shaky new issues, Raymond McDaniel Jr., the CEO of Moody's, S&P's major competitor, held a series of town hall–style meetings for Moody's professionals. At one, McDaniel told his managing directors about his perception of the growing problems in the mortgage market: "The purpose of this town hall is so that we can speak as candidly as possible about what is going on in the subprime market. What happened was it was a slippery slope. What happened in 2004 and 2005 with respect to subordinated tranches is that our competition, Fitch and S&P, went nuts. Everything was investment grade. It didn't really matter. We tried to alert the market. I said we're not rating it. This stuff isn't investment grade. No one cared, because the machine just kept going."

At S&P, meanwhile, the inmates seemed to be running the asylum, according to one text-message exchange between two analysts, Rahul Dilip Shah and Shannon Mooney, on April 5, 2007. "Btw, that deal is ridiculous," Shah wrote to Mooney about some mortgage securities they were rating.

"I know, right . . . model def[initely] does not capture half the risk," she replied.

"We should not be rating it," he answered.

"We rate every deal," Mooney replied. "It could be structured by cows and we would rate it."

Answered Shah, "[B]ut there's a lot of risk associated with it. I personally don't feel comfy signing off as a committee member."

In a little-known lecture, in October 2008 at Harvard University, Lew Ranieri said he began to realize "in late 2005" that the markets for mortgage-backed securities had entered the "insanity" phase when homes were no longer being viewed as shelter but rather as a "new form of ATM machine" where home owners were borrowing larger and larger sums against their homes, all the while hoping their value would continue to increase. Ranieri reminded his Harvard audience—at the Graduate School of Design, no less—that not only could housing prices fall occasionally but also that interest rates had a habit of increasing after a period of historic lows. This double whammy is precisely what happened, of course, and it helped to precipitate the crisis. Ranieri, who had once aspired to be an Italian chef but was asthmatic and could not breathe in a smoky kitchen, said of his financial baby that he had "wanted to make a lasagna but ended up with a bouillabaisse."

IN THE MONTHS following Goldman's March 2006 sale of the GSAMP securities, a U.S. affiliate of Deutsche Bank, the large German bank—in its role as the trustee of the trust that held the mortgages—issued monthly reports about the performance of the underlying mortgages, essentially a running catalog of the interest and principal payments and whether or not they were being paid on time, if at all. At first, not surprisingly, all went mostly well. In April 2006, 282 of the second mortgages were prepaid voluntarily, leaving a pool of 12,176 mortgages with an outstanding loan amount of $721.9 million. There were no foreclosures by that date, but there was one troubling sign: after just one month, 362 of the mortgages were already delinquent on their payments by at least thirty-one days.

And then the deterioration began to accelerate. By the end of October 2006, some 799 of the mortgages, or 7.62 percent of the total number, valued at $50.8 million, or 8.3 percent of the total value, were at least thirty-one days delinquent in their payments. By the end of December 2006, 927 mortgages—worth $59.1 million, 10.2 percent of the total— were at least thirty-one days delinquent in their payments. Another 26 homes had been foreclosed upon and another 75 of the borrowers were in bankruptcy proceedings. Some seven months after the mortgages were packaged up by Goldman and sold into the marketplace, 1,029, or 11.2 percent, of the loans were either delinquent, foreclosed upon, or subject to bankruptcy proceedings. The graph of the number of mortgages three months or more behind in their payments looked like a hockey stick and represented 10.3 percent of the total number of loans. By May 2009, according to the lawsuit filed by an investor in GSAMP Trust 2006-S2 against Goldman Sachs (and others), some 12.25 percent of the underlying mortgages in the trust were delinquent. (A subsequent Goldman offering, GSAMP Trust 2006-S3, which followed S2 by only a couple of weeks, had an even worse performance, with some 18 percent of its mortgages in trouble after around nine months, even though the ratings agencies had rated some 73 percent AAA.) Within weeks of the December update, Deutsche Bank had filed a notice "of suspension of duty to file reports" and that was the end of the monthly reports.

By December 2006, not only had Goldman sold the GSAMP securities—and probably made around $10 million, and likely more, for its trouble (after selling the cakes in the bakery for more than the cost of the ingredients)—but the firm had also made a fundamental decision about the dangers that appeared to be lurking in the mortgage securities market: the time had come for Goldman to get out of the mortgage market.

CHAPTER 19

GETTING CLOSER TO HOME

By the middle of 2006, Josh Birnbaum, and his colleagues Swenny and Deeb Salem, had been buying and selling the ABX index for some six months, mostly just on behalf of the firm's clients. Birnbaum described this as, "A client says, 'Where do you bid the index?' and you give him the price. If he says, 'Where are you going to sell the index?' you give a price. Just try to buy as many at lower prices as the ones you sell. In other words, a classic Wall Street market-making model." (Whatever they were doing seemed to be working. Birnbaum's desk would make $288 million in the first quarter of 2007, compared with $163 million for the *full year* in 2006.)

By around June 2006, Birnbaum started to notice a rise in the number of borrowers becoming delinquent in their mortgages, thanks to the monthly reports filed publicly by the trustees of the mortgage-backed securities such as GSAMP-S2. "There were some early cracks in the subprime market," he said. "In terms of the early cracks, the way people were looking at stuff back then wasn't in terms of losses but it was just the borrowers going delinquent." Prior to that, he said, "many people had qualms and concerns about what was going on in mortgages—and specifically in mortgage credit—but they were more theoretical concerns than corroborated concerns." Among the concerns being voiced were that borrowers were taking out mortgages they knew they were unlikely to repay, that they didn't "have any skin in the game," or that their down payments and FICO scores were too low.

Hedge-fund manager John Paulson was one of the first to start trading the ABX index aggressively in early 2006, consistent with his utterly bearish macro bet on the U.S. housing market. At first, he did the bulk of his trading through Deutsche Bank. "He was a bit of an enigma to many people at that time," Birnbaum said, "because he wasn't anything close to the John Paulson we all know today." In February or March, Paulson contacted Birnbaum's desk at Goldman to inquire about trading the index with Goldman as well. "It was one of these things where we get the call on the desk," Birnbaum recalled, "and it's Paulson. [People were wondering,] 'Who is that? Who is this guy? What's he doing?' Most people had never met him before. Even the senior guys in the bank. We didn't know what he was up to."

At first, Birnbaum did the ABX index trades for Paulson without giving him too much thought one way or the other. But as the year progressed, Birnbaum started to wonder what the guy was up to and how serious he was planning to be in going short the mortgage market. He asked for a meeting with the Paulson team. He wanted to get to know his client. "It was some combination of a diligence meeting and a kind of 'testing-the-guy' meeting," a Goldman executive said. "There was a concern at Goldman to some extent that 'did this guy know what he was doing?' There was almost a kind of a suitability aspect to the meeting because at the time you're talking about a very different viewpoint about housing and about these indices that are new and that when we look back, it's a completely different situation. But then we had a suitability issue that we were checking out because he was doing this trade bigger than a lot of folks." At that time, Paulson was asking Goldman to undertake individual trades of several hundred million dollars at a time. "Which is very significant in the context of—particularly looking back—of what each one of these trades meant in terms of economic value at risk," he said. In other words, the trades that Paulson started to do with Birnbaum were the very ones that ended up paying off fabulously well for him and his firm, making him a multibillionaire in the process. Goldman needed to make sure Paulson was legit—could satisfy the men in the basement office—before deciding to do serious business with him.

At the meeting, Birnbaum decided to judge Paulson's suitability by asking probing questions of Paulson and his team about how much conviction they had about this bet. There was an element of Kabuki theater to the meeting, what with all the alpha-male head fakes. "Part of it was just testing his thesis as to whether or not he knew what he was doing," Birnbaum said, "and part of this was, frankly, the guy was doing big trades and as a market maker you need to figure out how big is this guy gonna be? And he's not going to tell you to your face how big he's gonna be. He's not gonna tell you, 'Oh yeah, I had three more trades to do and they're gonna be this big,' because then we might price the market a certain way. He's gonna try to hold his cards here"—holding his hand close to his chest—"and not reflect what the size of his program is. But as best I could, I was trying to ascertain what's the size of his program, what's the strength of his thesis? In doing this, we almost try to play devil's advocate."

Birnbaum was trying to ascertain whether Paulson was going to continue to make trading bets of hundreds of millions of dollars or whether he would be increasing his bets into the billions of dollars, making him potentially a very large and important client. "We were in completely new territory at the time of this product," he said, "and were just trying to understand his assumptions and poke holes in his assumptions and see how his answers stacked up." This was a bit of high-stakes psychological warfare. "You can always tell if you poke holes in someone's assumptions and you see a lot of self-doubt in them. If their assumptions don't hold up so well, you might have a better sense of what their program is going to look like. On the other hand, if you poke holes in their assumptions and they're coming back with vehement arguments, you get a different view of what their program is going to look like. A lot of it was just how strongly do these guys really feel when you test them? When you test their thesis that this is going to be the trade of the century . . . how well does their argument hold up?"

Trading the ABX index or buying huge amounts of credit-default swaps was not for the faint of heart. It was financial gambling of an unprecedented nature. "It's not like trading IBM," Birnbaum said. "These are much riskier transactions. Consider them huge block trading transactions where there's an element of luck. There's an element of really needing to understand what are the next three chess moves that your counterparty is intending to do because that's really going to affect how you price the next trade. It's just a very different dynamic, and that was even then. Looking back now—where you can see how much the price ended up moving on these things—it's unprecedented to trade that kind of risk with that frequency on Wall Street."

Birnbaum said he thought his intense probing rattled some of the younger professionals on Paulson's team and got them to question the wisdom of their thinking. "You've got a guy who is the main trader . . . at Goldman Sachs—good firm, reputation and all that—who is sitting there asking probing questions and raising doubt, with the intention of testing their nerve," he said. "For certain members of their team—and I'm not saying for John [Paulson]—but certain members of their team probably found themselves questioning their assumptions based on the level at which I was asking these questions." According to *The Greatest Trade Ever*, Gregory Zuckerman's bestselling account of how Paulson made his billions, Birnbaum kept calling Brad Rosenberg, Paulson's trader, to find out how much protection Paulson intended to buy. "When Paulson and [Paolo] Pellegrini"—Paulson's partner in conceptualizing the bet against the mortgage market—"got wind of Birnbaum's inquiries, they told Rosenberg to keep him in the dark. They worried that Birnbaum might raise his prices on the CDS insurance if he knew more buying was on the way."

According to Zuckerman, Birnbaum persisted with Rosenberg and insisted on having a meeting. "If you want to keep selling, I'll keep buying," Birnbaum reportedly told Rosenberg, Paulson, and Pellegrini. "We have a few clients who will take the other side of your trades. And I'll join them." Not only was Birnbaum trying to discourage these guys from continuing to make the bearish bets, but he was also "trying to tell Paulson he was making a big mistake." Rosenberg, in particular, seemed rattled after the meeting with Birnbaum, according to Zuckerman, and walked into Paulson's office and asked the boss if they should tone things down. "Keep buying, Brad," Paulson reportedly told Rosenberg. (John Paulson declined repeated requests to be interviewed.) With Paulson's backing, Rosenberg called Birnbaum when the Goldman trader got back to his desk and told him he wanted to continue the bets against the ABX. "Really?" Birnbaum supposedly said.

The description of the meeting in Zuckerman's book was too "heroic," Birnbaum recalled. "It makes it look like the whole world was against John Paulson—including Goldman Sachs—but that they persevered and they were right," he said. "What drama! What better bank to personify the world being against Paulson than Goldman, right?" Zuckerman's account of the meeting *was* accurate in one sense, he said, in that he, Birnbaum, was trying to intimidate the Paulson team. "Being cynics, they weren't sure if I was just trying to catch them off their game or maybe was trying to get them to do something different than what they were doing in order to benefit Goldman," he said.

Birnbaum said he learned a lot from the meeting. In particular, he said, he came out of it convinced "these guys were here to stay in terms of being active and buying protection on subprime. We dealt with them differently after that." Goldman ramped up the amount of capital it made available to Paulson & Co. for its huge bets against the ABX index. As important, though, was Birnbaum's decision after that meeting with Paulson to give deeper thought to Paulson's trade and its implications. Should Goldman follow suit? Should Birnbaum and his colleagues on the structured products desk get some conviction with regard to what might be happening in the mortgage markets and make a directional bet with Goldman's capital? Was Paulson . . . right? Birnbaum's meeting with Paulson—regardless of which version of it is most accurate—turned out to be momentous, if for no other reason than Goldman soon enough thereafter began mimicking Paulson's bet. "Not necessarily right at that time, but shortly thereafter in 2006, we were changing our views from being more agnostic to be directionally short," is the way Birnbaum described this moment.

With Goldman changing its "view" from being agnostic on the mortgage market to betting aggressively against it, the relationship between Goldman and Paulson became somewhat more adversarial and competitive. Virtually overnight, Paulson & Co. went from being a good client of Goldman Sachs to becoming a competitor of Goldman Sachs. Much to the consternation of many of its clients, it was a dynamic that had occurred often at the firm, especially since Goldman went public in 1999, as it had seriously bulked up its proprietary trading, its hedge-fund business, and its private-equity business and found itself competing with some clients in those businesses. "Obviously if I am looking to short the market, if you're John Paulson and you're looking to short the market and you call me up, it's not my favorite phone call anymore," Birnbaum explained. "We'll make a market for you, but we may not be the best price anymore to sell you protection, whereas three or six months earlier you might have been the best price. So there was a change." But this being Goldman Sachs and Wall Street, Paulson and Goldman would soon enough find other ways to work together, even as they were competing on the purchase of credit-default swaps on the mortgage market or on shorting the ABX index.

By the beginning of the third quarter of 2006, Birnbaum and his colleagues had decided to get short, real short, and in a big way. Birnbaum is not able to pinpoint the exact moment he made the decision or whether there was one particular reason for his change of heart. It was more a combination of factors. First was the increasing rate of delinquencies in one mortgage-backed security after another. The problems in the GSAMP 2006 deal and its increasing delinquencies were typical of the kind of negative statistics that were catching Birnbaum's eye. "Whereas the view on the market before that for the Volckers and the Meredith Whitneys and these people was more of a visionary thing: 'Where this *could* happen . . .' When you actually saw it happening, in the form of delinquencies on some of the more recent subprime vintages—they were showing acceleration of delinquencies that were at a rate where they were at least as bad as the prior bad vintages of 2000, 2001, and in fact they were proving to even be worse as each month went by. The fundamentals were just not improving. The housing market was starting to lose steam."

Birnbaum also had at his disposal a proprietary computer model, designed and built by his colleague Jeremy Primer, that allowed him and his team to analyze detailed scenarios of how bad things could get for mortgage securities if the assumptions on defaults were increased beyond the conventional wisdom. "Pretty complicated stuff to figure out what a CDO is worth," Birnbaum said. "In common sense, we know it's not worth one hundred [cents on the dollar], right? But what is it really worth? Is it worth seventy or fifty or whatever?" That's where Primer and his modeling expertise proved an invaluable competitive advantage. Primer was just your typical Goldman professional. Primer grew up in Maplewood, New Jersey, the son of two English professors at Rutgers University. Naturally, Primer became a math whiz. When he was sixteen, in 1981, he won a gold medal for the USA International Mathematical Olympiad team. A typical problem he had to answer was: Three congruent circles have a common point O and lie inside a given triangle. Each circle touches a pair of sides of the triangle. Prove that the incenter and the circumcenter of the triangle, and the point O are collinear. Primer thought the test was embarrassingly easy. "It was a joke," he told *Time* after the test. He graduated magna cum laude from Princeton, was elected to Phi Beta Kappa, and then went on to get a master's degree in mathematics from Harvard.

He joined Goldman in 1993 as part of the prepayment modeling group in the mortgage derivatives business. By 2000, he had become head of mortgage modeling and was a prepayment strategist. Primer's model could analyze all the underlying mortgages and value the cash flows, as well as what would happen if interest rates changed, if prepayments were made, or if the mortgages were refinanced. The model could also spit out a valuation if defaults suddenly spiked upward.

Primer's proprietary model was telling Birnbaum that it would not take much to wipe out the value of tranches of a mortgage-backed security that had previously looked very safe, at least in the estimation of the credit-rating agencies that had been paid (by Wall Street) to rate them investment grade. For instance, suppose an investor owned the BBB-rated slice of GSAMP-S2, meaning there were investors supposedly taking more risk that were below the BBB slice in the structure and investors taking less risk in the structure because, as holders of the AAA-rated slice, they had the first claim on incoming cash-flow payments. In a typical mortgage-backed security, 8 percent of it was below BBB rated, 2 percent was BBB rated, and the rest, or 90 percent, was rated higher than BBB. What Birnbaum and Primer figured out was that it would not take a particularly significant increase in mortgage defaults for the investors in the BBB slice of the security to not get paid, even though BBB was an investment-grade rating. "As long as losses are below eight percent, your bond's money good," Birnbaum explained, meaning it would be worth 100 cents on the dollar. "You're fine. If losses are nine percent then you're losing half on your two percent tranche. If losses are ten percent then you're losing all of it. So merely by having losses go from eight percent to ten percent you're going from money good to wiped out. The problem I had with this was that we were basically completely out of sample when it came to predicting where losses would be on these mortgages, particularly if home prices went down. We had no data on it. Okay? So any model that was pretending to know what was going to happen was just completely putting its finger in the air with an arbitrary estimate."

He figured out that very small differences in the losses on the underlying mortgages could lead to a very large difference in the amount of losses investors suffered on the BBB tranche of the security, which was where a lot of the bets were being placed. "Just putting those two facts together, it doesn't take a genius to know that if you start to see any level of distress in the underlying mortgages the market is going to have to apply an uncertainty risk premium to what future losses are," he said, "and in light of that uncertainty risk premium, that could lead to vastly different views of the tranche's value." Birnbaum concluded that as losses in the BBB tranche increased, the typical distressed investor—who might be interested in buying a corporate bond as its value slipped—would not be a buyer because the risk that he could then be wiped out was too high. "It's going to be lights-out," he said. By tweaking the various assumptions based on events that seemed increasingly likely, Primer's models were showing a marked decrease in the value of mortgage-related securities. "His models said even if you don't believe housing prices are going to go down, even if we apply low-probability scenarios about it going negative . . . there's no way this stuff can be worth anywhere near one hundred [cents on the dollar]." And yet, that's exactly where many of these bonds were trading. Primer's models had them pegged at anywhere between 30 cents and 70 cents, valuations that screamed out for a short bet.

AN E-MAIL EXCHANGE among various members of Goldman's mortgage securities group on October 19, 2006, illustrated the inevitability of the conclusion Birnbaum and Primer were in the process of reaching about the growing risks in the market. A Goldman mortgage-backed securities sales executive, Mitchell Resnick, had been running into some resistance from investors increasingly worried about the risks of being long the new crop of residential mortgage-backed securities (RMBS) then coming to market. "Do we have anything talking about how great the BBB sector of the RMBS is at this point in time?" he wrote Jonathan

Egol, a trader on the structured products desk. "A common response I am hearing on [two deals Goldman was then marketing] is a concern about the housing market and BBB in particular. We need to arm sales with a bit more—do we have anything?"

The response came from David Rosenblum, another mortgage-trading professional. "So amazing you should ask," he wrote. "[W]e had this convo for an hour last night—[Alan] [B]razil and [Michael] [M]arschoun and [P]rimer—THIS IS WHAT WE'RE TALKING ABOUT! Can you come to the rescue here?" Five days later, another mortgage trader, Geoffrey Williams, wrote to Egol, in another indication of emerging trouble. "Thinking we need to better leverage syndicate to move open risk from our bespoke trades given that most of them did not go through the initial syndication process," he wrote. "[G]uessing sales people view the syndicate axe"—being "axed" in a security was Goldman-speak for wanting to sell it, fast—"e-mail we have used in the past as a way to distribute junk that nobody was dumb enough to take first time around." Egol responded, "LDL," for "let's discuss live," a way for the Goldman traders to avoid writing something in an e-mail that might prove embarrassing later.

The other dynamic in the securitization market that appealed to Birnbaum—and gave him additional confidence that the short side of the bet could be a big winner—stemmed from the nature of creating a collateralized debt obligation in the first place. To do so, Wall Street firms needed the raw material—mortgages and other debt securities—to stuff into a CDO before turning it into a security that could be sold to investors. (Gotta break a few eggs to make an omelet.) For instance, in the case of GSAMP-S2, Goldman had to buy the mortgages from New Century first—since Goldman itself did not originate mortgages. Once Goldman had enough mortgages to bundle them up into a security, the security would get made, and then sold. Often it would take six months or so for enough mortgages to be purchased to be able to make the security. During this period, investment banks, such as Goldman, would keep the mortgages in "warehouses" and collect interest and principal payments from borrowers during the time before the mortgages were made into securities and sold to investors (who then became the beneficiaries of the payments, as long as they were being made). In the meantime, "I have a positive carry trade because these are bonds that I'm earning interest on at a higher rate than where I'm financing them," Birnbaum said, "and as long as the world doesn't blow up it's nice extra P&L"—profit—"for the deal. So the Street loved it, senior managers loved it. So they kept these warehouses out there for long periods of time."

What Birnbaum realized as he was readying his big bet against mortgages was that as the mortgages in the warehouses started to lose value, the executives at the Wall Street firms would want to get rid of them as fast as they could, making for a classic supply-and-demand imbalance that would vastly favor the buyer of such an asset over the seller. What was once an asset that provided extra vig in the deal would quickly turn into a liability for firms with big warehouse exposure as they tried to unload the toxic waste. What's more, many of these warehouses were not even on the balance sheets of the Wall Street firms. It was another lightbulb moment for Birnbaum. "What that means is that you had a huge amount of off-balance-sheet, unquantified risk at the banks," he said, "and that when, or if, the shit hits the fan and the liabilities of the CDOs—meaning the bonds that the CDO was going to be created from and then sold to investors—you wouldn't be able to sell those bonds anymore if the market blew up. Then the banks would be hung with all this extra stuff in their warehouses, which wasn't being quantified anyway and they would wake up and be like, 'Oh shit, what are we going to do with these warehouses?' " That's when Birnbaum figured the selling pressure would be at its most intense. He figured these banks would conclude, "We're going to have to liquidate these warehouses, and then they're all going to be going through the door—a small door at that point—at the same time."

Compounding the problem would be the fact that buyers would be few and far between, exacerbating the selling pressure. "You would have a massively unraveling event, and a lot of negative momentum," Birnbaum said. It would be like the final scene in the 1983 movie *Trading Places,* when Dan Aykroyd and Eddie Murphy turn the tables on their nemeses the Duke brothers, forcing them into liquidation. The way Birnbaum figured it, Goldman would be plenty happy to buy when others were selling, since by going short it would already have sold the security at a higher price. By buying it back at the lower price, the difference— sell high, buy low—would be pure profit. On Wall Street, this was known as "covering your short" and was a way to make a killing. "That last point was something which was very powerful, because it's great to say that you're going to put on a directional trade or any kind of trade and then you're going to be right, but if you can't monetize that trade, then there's no exit strategy," he said. "Not only was this a way that the market would go down, but it was also the exit strategy because as the CDO managers are liquidating their warehouses, on the way down, you're sitting there going, 'Do I want to buy any debt from them or not?' But at least you have a supply that you can use to cover your shorts. So this was a very important realization and part of the strategy."

BUT BIRNBAUM AND his colleagues couldn't just start placing the bet the mortgage market would collapse until they had begun to reduce their previous bets that it would remain robust. "We had pockets of our business that were long the market," he said. "You can't get short until you're at zero. So, the first order of business was taking the pockets of our business that were long the market and getting them closer to home, meaning getting them closer to flat."

At the same time, the risk-management apparatchiks at the firm were closely monitoring what Birnbaum and company were doing. "Whether you're long or short, generally the message from risk management is 'Take less risk,'" he said. "They would love you to make infinite profits on zero risk." One of those apparatchiks—unnamed, of course—defended the practice of working hard to minimize risk as being in the best interests of Goldman Sachs and as part of what makes the firm successful. "I call it both seamless horizontal and vertical communication," he said, "and not just on the business side, but on the control side as well. We have a lot of checks and balances in place in both the business side and the control side and information sharing. This commitment at Goldman to a rigorous daily mark-to-market, constantly kind of re-assessing and checking and really listening to the market. Contrary to popular belief, we're certainly not smarter than the market. We're a participant in the market. But having the commitment to daily mark-to-market and having the communication both laterally and up and down makes a huge difference. Having been at Deutsche Bank and Morgan Stanley, I can just say here that the way that information flows to people that need that information and the collegial atmosphere in terms of the sharing of that information—you know, businesses aren't siloed, risk isn't siloed here—and that's a big difference from what I've seen at other places."

On October 26, 2006, in a move to reduce the firm's exposure to the mortgage market, Michael "Swenny" Swenson decided to sell $1 billion worth of the ABX index and to buy another $1 billion of protection, using credit-default swaps on BBB-mortgage securities. "This is estimated to reduce the scenario risk by approx. $90mm," according to an e-mail circulated in the group. This lowered exposure would no doubt be welcomed news to David Viniar when Birnbaum and his team met with him to analyze Birnbaum's risk positions. The message from Viniar throughout 2006 was always the same: take less risk, and make more money doing it.

ONE OF THE most important responsibilities Viniar had as Goldman's CFO was to monitor closely the amount of risk the firm was taking on any given day. He looked at the income statements—known as "P&L"s, for "profit and loss"—of Goldman's roughly forty-five business lines every day. He also made a particular habit of speaking directly to the firm's risk managers and its head traders to gauge the extent of the dollars they had on the line at any given moment. Not only did Viniar make this part of his daily routine, but so did both Lloyd Blankfein and Gary Cohn, Goldman's president. "I can give you one hundred different risk-management rules," Viniar said, "but that's a good early warning sign—just 'How are they doing?' " These open lines of communication from the bottom of the firm (the traders) to the top of the firm (its CEO, president, and CFO) made Goldman pretty unique on Wall Street.

Like the rest of Wall Street in December 2006, Goldman Sachs was mostly "long" mortgages, meaning that the firm's traders thought their value would increase over time and so had invested some of the firm's more than $70 billion in capital in that idea. "The world was good, right?" Viniar said. "You are long everything because everything went up in value. We're not very long, but we're long. . . . The other thing we do is mark all of our positions to market every day. We're really diligent about that."

At one point during mid-December 2006, Viniar began to observe a trading anomaly. "I get the P&L every day, and for something like ten days in a row the mortgage desk lost money," he explained. "They didn't lose a lot, but they lost money ten days in a row." Not a lot of money by Goldman's standards—somewhere in the $5 million to $30 million range—but a pattern of daily losses that was troubling to Viniar.

Viniar had also been hearing on a regular basis from Daniel Sparks, the Goldman partner who headed up the four-hundred-person mortgage-trading department. Sparks had just been named head of the group in December 2006 and had a seat on the firm's powerful—and powerfully important—risk-management committee, which met weekly to assess and discuss the firm's financial risks. He often spoke directly to Viniar and to Cohn and Blankfein about what was happening in the mortgage department. "Subprime market getting hit hard," he wrote to Thomas Montag, William McMahon, and Richard Ruzika, three of his senior colleagues in the fixed-income division at Goldman, on December 5. "[H]edge funds hitting street. . . . At this point we are down $20mm today." Then, in a plug for Birnbaum's emerging strategy to get shorter more quickly, he added, "Structured exits are the way to reduce risk. Our prior structured trade closes today. We are focusing on ways to do it again much faster."

Sometimes these discussions were very frank and direct about the risks the firm was taking in this area. "One of my jobs at the time was to make sure Gary [Cohn] and David and Lloyd knew what was going on," Sparks said. "They don't like surprises, so they need to know in real time if there's good or bad things happening. They were the kind of guys that I think were good enough managers so if you tell them that, then they can deal with it." Sparks was becoming increasingly nervous about Goldman's mortgage portfolio. He was worried that loans Goldman had made to mortgage originators, like New Century (which owed Goldman millions), were not being repaid on a timely basis. He was also worried about the warehoused mortgages Goldman had bought that had not yet been turned into securities and that borrowers were increasingly defaulting on. The mortgage originators had an obligation to buy back from Goldman the mortgages that were not performing; this was not happening either. "We were seeing signs in the department level that were concerning," Sparks said. "The firm had exposure. . . . David asked me to put together basically a review of all of the different risks that we had in the department and there were a lot of risks." Birnbaum credited Sparks with realizing that the mortgage originators—particularly New Century—were not paying their debts as they became due and decided to cut off their access to credit from Goldman. "That was kind of a first sign," Sparks said, "but it also potentially meant that a lot of other bad things could be happening, too."

After hearing repeatedly from Sparks about his growing concerns, Viniar called a meeting, for December 14, of the five people running the firm's FICC group—fixed-income, currencies, and commodities—and the various controllers, auditors, and risk managers who work with them in those divisions. In sum, about twenty people had collected around Viniar in his thirtieth-floor conference room at 85 Broad Street for one of the most momentous meetings in Wall Street history.

The mortgage traders came to the meeting with a two-inch-thick report detailing all the firm's mortgage-related trading and credit positions. Viniar said the firm had not made big bets one way or the other, but rather had a series of bets that tilted toward prices going up or down. At that moment, Goldman's bias was toward betting the value of the trades and the underlying mortgages would increase. But even so, there were disputes about the value of the mortgage securities with some of Goldman's trading partners.

The meeting dragged on for close to three hours. Each position was reviewed and then reviewed again. The firm had lost money ten days in a row because, Viniar said, it was betting mortgage-based securities would rise, when "the market was going down." They talked about the big bet that John Paulson—the hedge-fund manager—had made that the mortgage market would collapse. As the meeting was winding up, Viniar concluded by saying, "It feels like it's going to get worse before it gets better." Looking back on the meeting, he commented, "Nobody there knew how bad it was going to get. We didn't have a clue that things were going to go crashing down." There was as close to complete consensus in the room about Viniar's conclusion as was possible. "A pretty good consensus developed that we needed to reduce our risk," said someone who was at the meeting.

Kevin Gasvoda, a managing director who attended the Viniar meeting, wasted little time in directing the troops to begin aggressively unloading Goldman's long mortgage positions, even if it meant selling into a market without many buyers and taking losses. The new mantra was being broadcast. "Although liquidity will be light the next few weeks[,] pl[ea]s[e] refocus on retained new issue bond positions and move them out," he wrote. "There will be big opportunities the next several months and we don't want to be hamstrung based on old inventory. Refocus efforts and move stuff out even if you have to take a small loss. Talk to me if you have concerns or questions but we need to be turning risk over aggressively to stay well positioned."

According to Sparks's summary of the meeting—contained in an e-mail to Montag and Ruzika written the same day—the group reviewed six areas of risk related to subprime mortgages, including the ABX index, credit-default swaps, and CDO warehouses. According to Sparks, there were seven "follow-ups" from the meeting, number one being "[r]educe exposure, sell more ABX index outright." Other conclusions were to "distribute as much as possible on bonds created from new loan securitizations and clean previous positions"—in other words, get rid of Goldman's long mortgage positions as quickly as possible. The group also agreed to "[s]tay focused on the credit of the [mortgage] originators"—such as New Century—"we buy loans from and lend to" because they were likely to fail. In sum, the idea was to "[b]e ready for the good opportunities that are coming (keep powder dry and look around the market hard)." After the meeting, at 1:00 a.m., Montag forwarded Sparks's e-mail to Viniar and asked him, "Is this a fair summary?," prompting Viniar to respond that morning that it was. "Dan and team did a very good job going through the risks," Viniar wrote. "On ABX, the position is reasonably sensible but just too big. Might have to spend a little to size it appropriately.

On everything else, my basic message was let's be aggressive distributing things"—selling off the long positions—"because there will be very good opportunities as the markets goes into what is likely to be even greater distress and we want to be in a position to take advantage of them."

So Viniar and his colleagues quickly decided to reduce Goldman's risk in this area to as close to zero as possible. "The words we used were, 'Let's get closer to home,'" Viniar said. He figured the mortgage market would continue to fall—again he did not realize how far and how fast—but by reducing the firm's exposure in December 2006 and in subsequent months, Goldman would be in position to buy when others were forced to sell and would benefit.

The next day, Birnbaum wrote to a colleague, "[W]e've had good traction moving risk through our franchise on a variety of fronts." But not always fast enough for the team. For instance, on December 15, Swenson reported that Salomon Brothers sold to Goldman, for 65 cents on the dollar, an undisclosed amount of a GSAMP security that Goldman had sold earlier in the year at 100 cents on the dollar. It was not clear from the Swenson e-mail whether Goldman believed the GSAMP deal made sense at 65 cents or whether Goldman felt it had to make a market for a counterparty. In any event, Deeb Salem, Birnbaum's colleague, replied about the trade, "This is worth 10"—meaning the GSAMP bonds were worth 10 cents on the dollar, not 65 cents. "It stinks. . . . I don't want it in our book." Swenson replied, "It is not that bad." But Salem would have none of his colleague's modest optimism. "[Credit-default swap market] thinks that deal is one of the worst of the year . . . hopefully they r wrong."

Sparks began implementing the new orders almost immediately. On December 17—a Sunday—he reported to Viniar, Montag, Ruzika, and McMahon, and copied Gary Cohn, that "[w]e made progress last week" in reducing the firm's long exposures to the mortgage market—on BBB-rated securities—"but still more work to do." In the three days at the end of that week, Sparks reported to his bosses that his group had reduced the firm's long exposure by $1.5 billion in BBB- and BBB-minus-rated securities that had been originated in 2005 and 2006, but to reduce the long exposure to flat, Goldman still needed "to lay off about another $1 billion notional." He worried, though, about how much more he could sell in the last two weeks of the year because of the "ability/motivation for certain hedge funds to shove market either way with respect to year-end performance measures" and because of the "noise" in the mortgage origination market. "[M]ore will go down (when not if)," he wrote. "Trading desk is looking to buy puts"—make bets the companies will fail—"on a few [mortgage] originators."

On December 20, Stacy Bash-Polley, a partner and the co-head of fixed-income sales, noted that Goldman had been successful in finding buyers for the super-senior and equity tranches of CDOs, but the mezzanine tranches remained a challenge. She suggested the mezzanine tranches be packaged up and sold as part of other CDOs. "We have been thinking collectively as a group about how to help move some of the risk," she wrote in an e-mail released in January 2011 by the Financial Crisis Inquiry Commission. "While we have made great progress moving the tail risks—[super-senior] and equity—we think it is critical to focus on the mezz risk that has been built up over the past few months. . . . Given some of the feedback we have received so far [from investors,] it seems that cdo's maybe the best target for moving some of this risk but clearly in limited size (and timing right now not ideal)."

Goldman reduced its exposure to mortgages "early," Viniar said, "before most people had a view that the world was getting worse." One of the ways Goldman was able to "get closer to home" and reduce its exposure to the mortgage market was to sell the mortgages it owned, for whatever price they could garner in the deteriorating market. But that strategy could get the firm only so far, since too much selling would force the price of the securities lower and lower and defeat the purpose of trying to get out at a decent price. And some buyers were starting to balk. For instance, back in October 2006, in an e-mail correspondence between two Goldman executives about trying to sell off pieces of one CDO, Tetsuya Ishikawa wrote his colleague Darryl Herrick that another colleague thought one Goldman client was "too smart to buy this kind of junk" and then had gone radio silent. "Very interesting," Herrick replied. At the end of December 2006, one Goldman vice president tried to steer his colleague away from trying to sell the increasingly squirrelly securities to sophisticated investors, who he figured should know better. It was just the fact that "[t]his list [of potential buyers] might be a little skewed towards sophisticated hedge funds with which we should not expect to make too much money since (a) most of the time they will be on the same side of the trade as we will, and (b) they know exactly how things work and will not let us work for too much $$$, vs. buy-and-hold rating-based buyers who we should be focused on a lot more to make incremental $$$ next year."

Another way for Goldman to protect itself was to buy credit-default swaps—insurance policies that paid off when the debt of other companies lost value—on the debt of individual companies as well as on individual mortgage-backed securities, such as GSAMP Trust 2006-S2. A third way for Goldman to hedge its exposure to the mortgage market was for Goldman's traders to short the ABX index—the very trade that Birn-baum was now advocating in the wake of his meeting with Paulson.

Sparks then "backed them up during heated debates about how much money the firm should risk" betting against the subprime market. There was always some understandable tension about how much of the firm's capital to risk on any given day, in any given opportunity. The structured products group not only made markets in securities for Gold-man's clients but it also had the authority to "trade Goldman's own capi-tal to make a profit" if and when "it spots opportunity," according to the *Wall Street Journal.* Even harder to do, with all these high-powered traders, was to take risk *away* from them by not permitting them to make the bets they were all geared up to make.

Following the December 2006 meeting in Viniar's thirtieth-floor conference room, Goldman decided in earnest that "getting closer to home" meant finding a way to hedge the firm's long exposure to the sub-prime market as a result of its ongoing underwriting of mortgage-backed securities. In manufacturing and selling these securities, of course, the goal was always to hold on its own balance sheet as few of the securities as possible. But as the market began to crack at the end of 2006 and the beginning of 2007, Goldman—like other Wall Street firms—ended up getting stuck with more and more of the riskiest tranches of the securi-ties. It turned out, according to one Goldman partner, that across Wall Street the quantitative analytics behind the risks of the mortgage-backed securities were deeply flawed. That instead of relying upon what the mathematical whiz kids assumed was the proper assumptions for risks and defaults, a more direct approach was needed. "What you really needed was very hands-on people saying if this happens, this is what our risk is," the partner said, instead of just relying on a computer approxima-tion of what the consequences of too much risk might be.

Unlike other firms, though, Goldman had the collective where-withal to do what it could to hedge its exposure. That meant shorting the ABX index at a time when doing so was a relatively inexpensive proposi-tion, since much of the rest of the world still wanted to be *long* mortgage securities. The short trade was therefore unpopular and inexpensive. But the market was not robust and so it took time—some two months—for Goldman to accumulate enough credit-default swaps and other hedges to be confident that its long exposure would be covered. "There was increasing strain in pricing for a lot of stuff," Birnbaum recalled, "and we had not fully articulated our short strategy at that point because the tim-ing was such that we had certain businesses that were exposed to mort-gage credit. We were taking the risk down in those businesses in the second half of 2006 and when we really had an opportunity to flip the switch and get short that happened in December and January." Birnbaum attributed Viniar's willingness to make this decision—in effect supporting the arguments being made by him and Swenny—to the virtues of Goldman's culture, which encouraged prudent risk taking and giving voice to contrarian points of view. "One of the reasons that Goldman was able to navigate this crisis so well was it had a senior management, and Viniar being one of them, that was very receptive to the views and the desires of their traders," he explained. "And it's not to say there weren't other smart traders on Wall Street who may have held similar views, but they simply were not given the rein to trade the way we were. . . . In a dynamic where these are smart guys, you give them an idea . . . and they're going to be responsive to that. The bank was simply able to switch directions or put on significant trades in a short period of time that other banks, I don't think, would give traders the rein to do."

––––––

BUT THERE WERE moments of intense fear and nervousness at Goldman as the firm wrote down the value of its mortgage-related products and took its losses at a time when other Wall Street firms were still coining profits in the product. Goldman also angered clients by shutting down entire lines of business—such as providing financing to mortgage originators. "I had senior guys come to me and say, 'What are you doing? The guys at Merrill Lynch hedged out all their risk,'" Sparks recalled. "It was a very tough time here. We were taking these losses. We were doing what we felt was right. We kind of thought of ourselves as doing the right thing but we didn't know for sure. We took losses. We shut deals down, angered clients, and then we cut our positions down."

The pressure on Sparks and his team ratcheted up. For six months straight, he was the only guy on the risk committee at Goldman who was talking about the dangers lurking in the mortgage department. "It was *tough,* okay?" he said. "And I mean *tough.* Everybody communicates well, but the rigor that Goldman Sachs puts on people is *unbelievable.* Especially when there's a problem, a problem meaning a concern or issue. I went up there to the thirtieth floor and said, 'Hey, look, I've got a problem'—I probably said this to them like five times—'We have a problem. Here it is. Here's what's going on. Here's what I don't understand. Here's what I'm worried about.' As soon as you do that, to their credit they get the risk controllers and all kinds of people involved— people that may not understand exactly what you do—but I mean they're all over it. That's the right way, I think, in that business you need to be, but it was hard. There's always a peanut gallery of people who don't have all the facts but want to just be compensated. I was really proud of my team for the way they dealt with what I thought was a really challenging situation; people generally didn't lose their cool. They were all trying to do the right thing. And the firm just came in and did what it's supposed to do. It was a very confusing time for everybody because I was talking about how concerned I was about things and it wasn't showing up in any other market. Some people just thought I was wrong. Or maybe what was happening in my world was just kind of a—maybe I was too conservative or it was just an outlier. It was a very hard time because nobody knew what the right answer was."

———

BIRNBAUM BEGAN PUTTING on "the big short"—as Viniar would later refer to Birnbaum's bet in a July 2007 e-mail to Gary Cohn—in December 2006 and January 2007. His group's long positions had, by that time, been sufficiently neutralized that the bet began to make financial sense. "If you want to talk about historic moments," Birnbaum said, "this is when stuff really was historic and I think changed the direction for the bank, forever." What made the bet so heroic—and risky—was that the rest of the market, Paulson and a few others aside, still had not come around to this way of thinking and were only too happy to bet against Goldman. "You had a two-month period when you had a big difference of opinion out there in the investment community as to what was happening in the mortgage credit market," he said. "On the one hand, you had prices that were coming down, like the ABX index, which always had been kind of [traded] right around one hundred and was starting to trade into the low nineties. You had a CDO-manager community that was looking at the index, and discounting it as being just a technical vehicle that hedge funds are trading and it was depressed based on technical arguments, but the names that they were putting into their deals were good names and in fact this weakness in the mortgage credit market was a buying opportunity."

In fact, the CDO managers—those bankers still putting together CDOs and selling them off to investors—thought they had their own major opportunity on their hands. "What the CDO community was doing in December and January is they were buying a lot of risk," Birnbaum said. "What they viewed as a great buying opportunity because in [the first quarter of 2007] they were going to turn around and sell liabilities on these deals at yesterday's spreads in their mind and they were going to make a huge profit." In other words, other Wall Street dealers were betting the market for these mortgage securities would soon recover and the value of the CDOs they were manufacturing would recover their previous pricing and they would lock in a big profit. Birnbaum was, of course, betting the opposite would happen, and in a big way.

Those bankers looking to construct and sell new CDOs during these two months were busy collecting some $20 billion of collateral—other debt securities, including mortgages—to put into their CDOs. On Wall Street, this practice was known as "ramping," and the $20 billion was a very large amount relative to other periods of time, suggesting that many on Wall Street believed the market for these CDOs was soon to recover and they wanted to have the product on hand to sell. Birnbaum bet against them. "During that period of time we were attempting to buy protection"—taking a short position—"on as much subprime as we possibly could within the context of reasonableness," he said. "So we were always looking to be the best bid for protection during that period of time and we purchased approximately *half* of the available amount that was out for bid. That meant that Goldman effectively was able to buy protection on approximately ten billion dollars in subprime during that two-month time frame. It's a huge, huge number." Being able to buy so much credit protection during these two months allowed Goldman "to flip the risk," Birnbaum said, and to become "significantly short" the market by the end of January 2007. "It's hard for me to imagine any bank having that kind of market share—north of fifty percent—for a twenty-billion-dollar buying program," he said. "It's a short period of time."

A natural question for Birnbaum and his colleagues at Goldman was how much impact did John Paulson and his huge bet against the mortgage market—a trade Goldman was intimately familiar with by the end of 2006—have on Goldman's decision to also short the mortgage market? According to Birnbaum, not much. "I think he influenced us more from the perspective of here's a gorilla who's trading in our market." Birnbaum said he thought Paulson might have had more influence on his thinking had he had some involvement with mortgage securities before he had become a hedge-fund manager, rather than a mediocre M&A banker at Bear Stearns. But, he conceded, the fact that Paulson was an outsider and had very little direct experience in mortgages turned out to be the key to his extraordinary success. "The beauty of what he did though—and that really no other real mortgage guys did with very few exceptions—was that he wasn't colored by all sorts of preconceptions of the past in terms of analyzing the mortgage market," Birnbaum said. "So he was able to just look at it with a totally clean slate and say, 'This doesn't add up.'"

CHAPTER 20

THE FABULOUS FAB

O ne of Fabrice Tourre's responsibilities at Goldman was to create and sell what were known as "synthetic CDOs," or collateralized debt obligations that contained no mortgages or other debt obligations at all but rather just the *risk* associated with them. This was kind of a mind-blowing concept. Tourre, a twenty-eight-year-old vice president in Birnbaum's group in 2007, had been a straight-A student at the Lycée Henri-IV, one of France's most prestigious schools, housed in a sixth-century abbey in Paris, and then studied math at the École Centrale Paris, one of the top French universities, before getting a master's in management science and engineering from Stanford University. Tourre and Goldman would construct these securities, for a fee, at the request of those clients looking to assume the risk that the underlying debts would get paid and for other clients looking to bet that the underlying debts would not get paid. These were the very securities that Tourre referred to as "monstrosities" and that he hoped might "make capital markets more efficient" in one of his now-infamous e-mails.

The supposed genius of the synthetic CDO was that instead of having to accumulate mortgages in a warehouse until you had enough to build and then sell a CDO, Goldman could create the CDO virtually overnight using credit-default swaps, those insurance contracts offering a holder protection on whether a debt security would fail or not. It would be as if you could buy and sell the *idea* of selling cakes without actually having to buy the ingredients for the cakes, make them, and then sell them.

Warren Buffett might consider this one of the eureka moments in the creation of financial weapons of mass destruction, as he referred to derivatives and credit-default swaps. "This was the trade, basically," Sparks said. "CDOs were writing protection on CDS and doing synthetic CDOs. Most of the guys that bought the protection were hedge funds and then we, or others, might be in the middle of that trade. Now there was a period of time where hedge funds bought protection on individual RMBS deals from the Street, and then the Street bought protection from CDOs, and everybody knew what trade they were doing. The CDO buyers knew they were getting long credit risk and the hedge funds knew they were getting short credit risk and the Street was doing their job as a trader. . . . It seems crazy—based on what's happened—but, for a period of time, it was very important to a lot of your clients to be able to give them risk and buy protection from them."

To Birnbaum and Tourre, it was more like genius, providing Goldman with yet another product to sell. In a December 10 e-mail to David Lehman, one of the co-heads of Birnbaum's group, Tourre wrote that he believed "managed synthetic CDOs," where Goldman would find investors for a fee, was an "opportunity" for 2007, along with the idea of renting the firm's synthetic CDO platform—known as ABACUS—to "counterparties focused on putting on macro short [trades] in the sector." There seemed to be nobody at Goldman, or at the other firms on Wall Street, questioning whether this was the kind of business the firm should be doing or wondering how far things had strayed beyond Goldman's traditional role of raising capital for clients and of providing M&A advice. Some even saw an ironic benefit in the synthetic CDO, in that the risk that borrowers might fail to pay their mortgages could be taken without actually having to create any more risky mortgages. "It was a totally fundamental change in the nature of collateralizing a CDO deal," Birnbaum said. "All you had to do was go out to Wall Street and say, 'Where do you bid protection on the following names?' And then based on that and writing those trades you now had synthetic collateral—like that!—to put into your CDO deal. . . . It just took a lot less time to amass a critical mass of collateral. When the collateral was securities, you can only buy the securities one by one and they tend to be small or notional. . . . If you're putting a synthetic in or creating a synthetic out of thin air, you just have to have a counterparty who is really willing to facilitate that trade."

It turned out that John Paulson was one such useful counterparty willing and eager to facilitate such a trade, and in December 2006 Paulson asked Goldman to work with his firm in creating a $2 billion synthetic CDO—to be known as ABACUS 2007-AC1—where he would be willing to buy the protection on a bunch of mortgage securities (i.e., bet that they would fail) while other sophisticated investors would take the opposite position. This was just another one of the many bets Paulson was making that the mortgage market would collapse, although by that time very few, if any, of them had paid off for the hedge-fund manager.

Goldman put Tourre in charge of creating, marketing, and selling the deal. This in itself was bit odd in that a trader—rather than a banker—structured and sold a deal that had more of the look and feel of a private placement rather than a pure trade (Goldman in fact did put an end to that practice in early 2011). The Paulson team had identified more than one hundred BBB-rated residential mortgage-backed securities that it thought could run into trouble, and they wanted the ABACUS deal to reference—or provide insurance on—these troubled bonds. During the last few weeks of December, Tourre and his team concentrated on finding a "portfolio manager" to select the securities to be referenced, and this led to some internal debate about which firm would want to be involved with Paulson. For instance, on December 18, Tourre suggested a firm but then thought better of it. "They will never agree to the type of names [P]aulson want[s] to use," Tourre wrote to his colleagues. "I don't think [redacted] will be willing to put [redacted's] name at risk for small economics on a weak quality portfolio whose bonds are distributed globally." Geoffrey Williams, who was helping Tourre with the deal, responded, "The way I look at it, the easiest managers to work with should be used for our own axes"—being those securities Goldman itself or other people would like to sell quickly, hopefully at acceptable prices. "Managers that are a bit more difficult should be used for trades like Paulson given how axed"—or anxious to do a trade—"Paulson seems to be (i.e. I'm betting they can give on certain terms and overall portfolio increase)."

Through the back and forth with Paulson and Paulson's deputy Paolo Pellegrini, a former Lazard M&A banker turned hedge-fund analyst, in the creation of the Paulson ABACUS deal, the Paulson team also revealed its growing concern for the financial viability of Wall Street itself. This proved to be a bit of a revelation to the Goldman team. In an e-mail sent late on the afternoon of January 6, Tourre reported to Sparks, Swenson, and Lehman that there was "one issue" outstanding for Paulson about the potential transaction. "[I]t is related to the fact that Paulson is concerned about Goldman's counterparty risk in this illiquid CDO transaction, even with the existing CSA"—a "credit support agreement" that provides for collateral payments between counterparties—"that is binding Goldman and Paulson," Tourre wrote. Incredibly, Paulson was so worried about taking the risk of having Goldman as a counterparty that he demanded a structure that would insulate him from Goldman's own credit risk. "As an FYI," Tourre wrote, "for single name CDS trades that Paulson is executing with dealers such as Goldman [and two unnamed others], they are buying large amounts of corporate CDS protection (on the broker dealer reference entities)"—or insurance in case say Bear

Stearns, Lehman Brothers, or Goldman were to default on their debt—
"to hedge their counterparty credit risk!!!"

This was quite a revelation in that Paulson—in early 2007—was
worrying that Wall Street firms might get into financial trouble and he
wanted to be insulated from it. "I cannot believe it!!!" Swenson replied to
this news. "Absolutely amazing." An hour later, Tourre elaborated with
more news, this time about the risks Paulson perceived about doing business with Bear Stearns, where Paulson once worked. "The meeting itself
was surreal," he continued. "Am hearing that Paulson bought $2bn of
[redacted] CDS protection, sucking all the liquidity on that name in the
corporate CDS market. Also, on the side, [redacted] mentioned to me
that he had heard from many different sources that one reason the ABX
market was trading down so much in December was related to
[redacted] building a sizable short and buying large amounts of ABX protection from the market." The mystery firm—on which firm Paulson had
been buying insurance—would be revealed by Swenny two minutes
later. "I wonder who gave [B]ear the liquidity," he wondered. In other
words, Swenson wanted to know who had sold the CDS to Paulson on
the Bear Stearns debt.

There was no answer—at least on e-mail—from Tourre, but
chances are good that Paulson made an additional bundle betting his
old firm would collapse. At the end of December 2006, the cost of buying insurance against a default on Bear Stearns debt was 0.18 cents per
dollar of protection. Since Paulson had bought $2 billion worth of pro-
tection, his cost would have been $3.6 million. During the week before
JPMorgan Chase bought Bear Stearns, on March 16, 2008, and saved
its debt from defaulting, the cost of buying that insurance had skyrocketed to 7.5 cents per dollar of protection. Assuming Paulson sold his
protection before JPMorgan bought Bear—and rendered that protection worthless since the risk of default had evaporated with the
merger agreement—Paulson would have pocketed tens of millions.
Within months, Goldman had mimicked Paulson's bet that Bear Stearns
would collapse.

———

TOURRE HAD FOUND a firm—ACA Management, LLC—and a
senior managing director there, Laura Schwartz, to help to choose the
securities that would serve as the reference bonds for ABACUS, to vet
Paulson's proposal, and to act as the portfolio selection agent for the deal.
By this time ACA had already managed twenty-two CDOs representing
some $15.7 billion of assets. The ABACUS deal was to be the twenty-
third CDO sponsored by ACA and the fifth "synthetic" using residential

mortgage-backed securities. ACA's main business had been insuring municipal bonds, but after Bear Stearns Merchant Banking invested $115 million in the company, in September 2004, for a 28 percent stake, ACA replaced its longtime management and began to get involved in the far more risky business of CDO asset management, including taking principal positions in CDO deals by insuring their risk. (In the end, this proved disastrous, and by April 2008, ACA would go out of business, although what's left of ACA is pursuing litigation against Goldman for this ABACUS deal.)

On January 8, 2007, Tourre had a meeting at Paulson's office with teams from both Paulson and ACA to construct the ABACUS deal. The next day, Goldman forwarded to ACA a list of the 123 2006-vintage mortgage securities Paulson wanted to bet against. That same day, ACA performed an "overlap analysis" and determined it had already purchased 62 of the 123 securities on Paulson's list. Tourre informed ACA that he "was very excited by the initial portfolio feedback" because it looked like the deal could come together. Goldman was to make a $15 million fee for constructing ABACUS. On January 10, Tourre sent ACA an e-mail confirming ACA's role in the deal that Paulson would "sponsor," and where the "starting portfolio would be ideally" Paulson's list "but there is flexibility around the names." Four days later, Schwartz was concerned that she had somehow offended Tourre during a phone call and that ACA might lose the business. She wrote in an e-mail that she hoped she "didn't come across too antagonistic" but that the "structure looks difficult from a debt investor perspective." She wrote that she could understand "Paulson's equity perspective but for us to put our name on something, we have to be sure it enhances our reputation." One of Tourre's Goldman colleagues replied, "Absolutely not—[F]abrice and the team hold you in the highest regard and would very much like to have you involved in this transaction, but only if you are comfortable with it." On January 18, Tourre confirmed to his colleagues that "ACA is going to be ok acting as portfolio selection agent for Paulson, in exchange for a portfolio advisory fee of at least $1mm per year."

On January 22, ACA sent to Tourre a list of 86 "sub-prime mortgage positions that we would recommend taking exposure to synthetically," 55 of which were on Paulson's original list of 123 names. Three days later, Goldman sent Schwartz a draft of an engagement letter for the deal. She then replied she had a few questions, about ACA's potential fees for the deal and a preferred legal counsel ACA would like to use. She also seemed worried still that ACA might lose the deal. "[D]o you believe that we have this deal?" she asked. "[D]o we need to do the work on the engagement letter before we know if we have the deal?" Thirty minutes later, Tourre responded that "Paolo at Paulson is out of the office until Wednesday of next week"—he was skiing with his family in Jackson Hole, Wyoming. "We are trying to get his feedback on the target portfolio you have in mind, as well as on the compensation structure we have been discussing with you. Subject to Paolo being comfortable with those 2 aspects, it sounds like we will be in a position to engage you on this transaction."

By a strange coincidence, Schwartz also happened to be in Jackson Hole and ran into Pellegrini. They agreed to meet for a drink on the afternoon of January 27 to discuss the proposed portfolio to be included in the ABACUS deal. They met at the bar, both with their laptops. "[H]e may [be] as much of a nerd as I am since he brought a laptop to the bar," Schwartz wrote. "[A]nd he also seemed to have a worksheet from DB [Deutsche Bank] and another manager." They talked about what collateral the ABACUS deal should reference and Schwartz noted that Pellegrini seemed to have plenty of data about each mortgage-backed security that might be referenced in the deal. He wanted to know why so many securities needed to be part of the deal. "I said Goldman needed 100 [individual securities] to help sell the debt," she later reported to Tourre. "We left it that we would both work on our respective engagement letters this week," she wrote. "I certainly got the impression that he wanted to go forward on this with us." Tourre responded, "[T]his is confirming my initial impression that Paolo wanted to proceed with you subject to agreement on portfolio and compensation structure." They agreed to meet on February 5 to work more on the deal.

A few days before the Jackson Hole rendezvous, on January 18, Gillian Tett, a columnist for the *Financial Times,* wrote a column featuring a number of foreboding messages she had received about how the real-estate debt bubble might end poorly. "Hi Gillian," Tett quoted one correspondent. "I have been working in the leveraged credit and distressed debt sector for 20 years . . . and I have never seen anything quite like what is currently going on. Market participants have lost all memory of what risk is and are behaving as if the so-called wall of liquidity will last indefinitely and that volatility is a thing of the past. I don't think there has ever been a time in history when such a large proportion of the riskiest credit assets have been owned by such financially weak institutions . . . with very limited capacity to withstand adverse credit events and market downturns. I am not sure what is worse, talking to market players who generally believe that 'this time it's different,' or to more seasoned players who . . . privately acknowledge that there is a bubble waiting to burst but . . . hope problems will not arise until after the next bonus round." Tett also recounted how she had spoken to an analyst at JPMorgan who made the case for the "CDO boom" and how "there is a very strong case to be made that the CDO market has played a major role in driving down economic and market volatility over the past 10 years." Tett concluded with the prescient thought that "if there is any moral from my inbox, it is how much unease is bubbling, largely unseen, in today's Brave New financial world."

Tett's column made the rounds in Birnbaum's structured finance group at Goldman. On January 23, Tourre forwarded it to Marine Serres, his "gorgeous and super-smart" French girlfriend living in London, and suggested she read it because it was "very insightful." Tourre rambled on to Serres, in an odd mixture of worry, self-deprecating humor, and love note. She was also working at Goldman at the time, as an associate in the structured products sales department. "More and more leverage in the system," he wrote to her, and then went on briefly in French, which has been translated as "the entire system is about to crumble at any moment. . . . The only potential survivor, the fabulous Fab." Tourre then switched back to writing in English, following the "fabulous Fab" comment with "as Mitch would kindly call me, even though there is nothing fabulous abt me, just kindness, altruism and deep love" for Serres. (Mitch Resnick was a Goldman mortgage-backed securities salesman.) He wrote to her that he was "standing in the middle of all these complex, highly levered, exotic trades he created without necessarily understanding all the implications of those monstruosities [sic]!!! Anyway, not feeling too guilty about this, the real purpose of my job is to make capital markets more efficient and ultimately provide the US consumer with more efficient ways to leverage and finance himself, so there is a humble, noble and ethical reason for my job . . . amazing how good I am at convincing myself!!! Sweetheart, I am now going to try to get away from ABX and other ethical questions, and immediately plunge into *Freakonomics,*" the best-selling book she had recommended to him. ("I love when you advise me on books I should be reading," he continued before waxing poetic about his love for her.)

Tourre seemed to be increasingly stressed by the ABACUS assignment. On January 29, he started a long e-mail chain, in French, to Fatiha Boukhtouche, a postdoctoral fellow at Columbia University, where she was researching the causes of autism. Boukhtouche and Tourre appeared to be friends with benefits, despite Tourre's pledge of love a few days earlier to Serres, then far off in London. "Yep, work is still as laborious, it's bizarre I have the sensation of coming each day to work and re-living the same agony—a little like a bad dream that repeats itself," he wrote to

Boukhtouche. "In sum, I'm trading a product which a month ago was worth $100 and which today is only worth $93 and which on average is losing 25 cents a day. . . . That doesn't seem like a lot but when you take into account that we buy and sell these things that have nominal amounts that are worth billions, well it adds up to a lot of money.

"When I think," he continued, "that I had some input into the creation of this product (which by the way is a product of pure intellectual masturbation, the type of thing which you invent telling yourself: 'Well, what if we created a "thing," which has no purpose, which is absolutely conceptual and highly theoretical and which nobody knows how to price?') [I]t sickens the heart to see it shot down in mid-flight . . . it's a little like Frankenstein turning against his own inventor ;) Anyway I don't want to bore you with my stories, I'm going to look in the yellow pages for the phone number of the ABX market and I'll send it to you, because I believe that a soft and sensual feminine intervention is necessary for Fab's survival[.] Kisses Fab)." Her response, filled with more "bizzzzzzzzzoux" (kisses), was to wonder how she could help him in a way that was "soft and sensual."

Despite his concern that Frankenstein might be turning on him, he continued to market his monstrous creations. That same day, he shared with his Goldman colleagues that he had received a new-business inquiry from GSC—a firm that had passed on the ABACUS deal before ACA took it, "given their negative views on most of the credits that Paulson had selected," Tourre wrote—wanting "to see from us a trade" using the same structure as the ABACUS deal but with a different portfolio of securities. "This is a trade we would show to IKB"—a large German bank that couldn't seem to get enough of the long side of these trades—"for the reverse inquiry program we have been working with them on." In response to a question from a colleague, Tourre explained a "few nice things about this idea," which he summarized by saying, "In a nutshell, we have a lot of flexibility from a risk management standpoint, while committing to take little risk"—a thought that may best summarize one of the more important of Goldman's business aspirations after nearly 140 years of existence. The digital conversation was clearly not sitting well with Jonathan Egol. "Where are you going with this?" he asked. To which Tourre replied, in Goldman fashion, "LDL."

On January 31, as the two of them were planning on a weekend dinner date, Tourre wrote to Boukhtouche, "[W]ell I don't know what you've done to the ABX markets, but you must have some sort of influence since today was a relatively calm day." He then launched into a mini-tirade on the frustrations of life at Goldman Sachs. "[N]evertheless

I am still stuck at work at 10 pm," he continued, "but it's been six years since I've been functioning on this @!$#@!$@$# schedule, so who cares!!! On top of which I have to 'mentor' others, in view of the fact that I am now considered a 'dinosaur.' In this business (at my firm the average longevity of an employee is about 2–3 years!!!) people ask me about career advice. I feel like I'm losing my mind and I'm only 28!!! OK, I've decided two more years of work and I'm retiring ;)." That same day Goldman priced another CDO deal—Camber 7—and made a profit of $10 million. After taking an overnight flight to London, Dan Sparks relayed the good news to his boss, Tom Montag. "Need you to send message to [two members of the deal team] telling them what a great job they did," Sparks wrote. "They structured like mad and travelled [*sic*] the world, and worked their tails off to make some lemonade from some big old lemons."

Also on January 31, the ABACUS deal team at Goldman gave Schwartz, at ACA, an update. They suggested removing two names from the hundred-name portfolio because they were "both on negative credit watch by Moody's" and in their place Goldman wrote that Paulson wanted to include two GSAMP deals. "We will continue our discussions with Paolo to confirm his agreement with the proposed transaction as structured and look forward to discussing the transaction and the draft Engagement Letter."

On February 2, Tourre and ACA met again with Paulson at his offices to discuss the portfolio to be included in ABACUS. "I am at this [ACA] [P]aulson meeting, this is surreal," Tourre wrote to a Goldman colleague, without elaborating. Later that day, ACA e-mailed a list of eighty-two mortgage-backed securities that Paulson and ACA agreed should be in ABACUS, plus a list of another twenty-one "replacement" bonds, and then sought Paulson's approval. "Let me know if these work for you," ACA wrote. Three days later, Paulson finalized the list of ninety-two bonds, with Tourre's agreement, and sent an e-mail of them to ACA. That same day, ACA gave preliminary approval to the portfolio to be included in ABACUS. On February 8, Tourre wrote to Sparks that he was finishing up the engagement letters for the ABACUS deal that "will help Paulson short senior tranches off a reference portfolio of . . . subprime RMBS risk selected by ACA." Tourre wanted to know if the trade needed the approval of the "Mortgage Capital Committee," an internal Goldman group set up to approve such things, even though he thought there would be "no commitment for us to take down any risk." Responded David Rosenblum: "Still reputation risk, so I suggest yes to MCC." On February 20, Tourre updated his Goldman colleagues with the latest ABACUS thinking and said that he thought Goldman's fee would likely be increased to $19 million, from $15 million. David Lehman responded to Tourre, "As u know, I am for doing this deal for them/with them, let's just make sure we are charging enough for it given our axe as principal in this type of risk." Lehman was concerned that Goldman get paid enough on the deal since it also wanted to sell similar securities to get short and that as an underwriter on the ABACUS deal might end up being long some of the mortgage-related risk when overall it wanted to be short. (Which is exactly what happened—Goldman did get stuck owning some of the long side of the deal when it could not sell the whole thing.) He encouraged Tourre to meet with Birnbaum and Swenson "live" as a "gut check and walk them through it."

Tourre responded that he thought the team "will be on board with this" but conceded he needed to speak with Birnbaum. "It is really Josh I need to walk carefully through my thinking," he wrote Lehman on February 21. "Sparks is really relying on us at this point. He is mostly focused on covering our single-names/idiosyncratic short trades to get better observability [sic]"—a reference to the ongoing efforts to establish "the big short." Lehman responded, again, that it was important to "[w]alk Josh through the $, if that makes sense let's go." Lehman also said he needed reminding about whose idea ABACUS was in the first place. "My idea to broker the short," Tourre replied. "Paulson's idea to work with a manager. My idea to discuss this with ACA." Finally, on February 26, after further discussion, Paulson and ACA reached agreement on the ninety bonds that would make up the reference portfolio for ABACUS. That same day, Goldman and ACA prepared a sixty-five-page "flip book," or PowerPoint presentation, that would be used to market ABACUS to investors who might be willing to take the long side of the trade while Paulson took the short side.

———

As the ABX index fell in the first few months of 2007, Goldman's mortgage department minted money, some "several hundred million dollars," according to the *Wall Street Journal*. But there were limits to how far Goldman wanted to push this bet, especially since the whole world seemed to be on the other side of it against the firm and a few other bold hedge-fund managers. There was also the matter of the losses Goldman would have to take as it lowered the value of its long positions on its books. Goldman knew the pain of the losses would hit well before the profits from the shorts could be realized. On February 2, Sparks wrote to Viniar, Ruzika, and Montag, "Gasvoda alerted me last night that we will take a write-down to some retained [long] positions next week as the loan performance data from a few second lien sub-prime deals just came in (comes in monthly) and it is horrible. The team is still working through the numbers, but the amount will likely be in the $20mm loss zone." He informed his bosses that the team was also working on trying to return the souring mortgage loans to their originators, such as New Century, Washington Mutual, and Fremont, as was permitted by contract. That was becoming more difficult as these companies started to run into greater financial difficulties. "[T]here seem to be issues potentially including some fraud at origination," Sparks wrote, "but resolution will take months and be contentious." He concluded that his "[f]ocus is cleaning out rated bond positions and the put back process. Sorry for more bad news." Montag wondered about Sparks's "fraud at initiation" comment and Sparks replied, "We'll be sorting through all the potential breaches of reps and warranties, and fraud at origination (appraisal, income, occupancy) would be a likely one. Fraud is usually borrower, appraiser or broker fraud—not necessarily fraud by the seller of the loans to us. But generally for reps & warranties the loan seller is responsible if fraud happened. The put backs will be a battle."

On February 8, Sparks provided his bosses with another update and this time also posted Gary Cohn and Jon Winkelried, the Goldman co-presidents. Essentially, there was more bad news. "Subprime environment—bad and getting worse," he wrote. "Every day is a major fight for some aspect of the business (think whack-a-mole). Trading position has basically squared"—news that the long risk had been finally mitigated—"plan to play from short side. Loan business is long by nature and goal is to mitigate. Credit issues are worsening on deals and pain is broad (including investors in certain GS-issued deals)"—oops! "Distressed opportunities will be real, but we aren't close to that time yet." He also addressed a question from Winkelried about whether Goldman was establishing the new trading prices or "chasing them down," meaning following the leads of other traders. "We have been chasing them down based on loan performance data as it comes out," he continued. At the end of the same day, Cohn asked Sparks for an update. After reviewing the situation throughout the day with the traders and the controllers, Sparks wrote to Cohn—soon after 11:00 p.m.—that the two constituents agreed Goldman's loss on the securities should be reflected at $28.4 million, higher than the original thought that it would be a $22 million loss.

Just before midnight, Tourre e-mailed Serres in London. He sent to her an internal analysis by a vice president in mortgage credit trading about the increasingly gloomy outlook for subprime mortgage-backed securities. "There has been an increase in early delinquencies and defaults in the Subprime market, most notably those deals backed by . . . collateral originated in mid-to-late 2005 and 2006," it read. "We have seen this trend in our 2006 Subprime . . . deals," including GSAMP S2. The analysis went on in that depressing vain for several more pages. "You should take a look at this," Tourre wrote to his girlfriend.

The next day, the push to sell Goldman's long positions in mortgage securities continued. A list of around thirty of the long positions Goldman owned and wanted to sell fast was circulated. "Below are our updated RMBS axes," the memo stated, using the argot of traders looking to unload positions. "The focus continues to be on moving credit positions. Again, these are priority positions that should be a focus for everyone before quarter-end. . . . Let all of the respective desks know how we can be helpful in moving these bonds." At the end of the day, Walter Scott informed the mortgage group that "this week, a total of [$]169+mm in axe positions were sold" but that "obviously we need to continue to push credit positions across subprime and second liens. We are working with both the desks and the strats to do so." Kevin Gasvoda replied, "Great job syndicate and sales, appreciate the focus."

A few hours later, just before midnight, Gasvoda sent Montag a detailed accounting of the financial risks in Goldman's mortgage portfolio. He explained that the firm had taken around $70 million of write-downs on the overall mortgage portfolio in the first five weeks of 2007, with another $70 million more likely to come. He said the losses had all been in those securities in HPA—home price appreciation—sensitive sectors. "They've crumbled under HPA slowdown as these are the most levered borrowers." Gasvoda told Montag that to "mitigate" these losses, Goldman had stopped buying subprime second liens in the summer of 2006 and instead focused on prime mortgages and what were known as Alt-A mortgages, those between subprime and prime. Goldman had also focused on selling new mortgage-backed securities "at any clearing levels," or whatever price the market would bear, to get rid of them and had given traders, such as Birnbaum, the authority to sell any remaining "retained bonds."

Three days later, on Sunday, Montag passed Gasvoda's analysis on to Winkelried and Blankfein. "Very good writeup of our positions in each sector[,] hedges we have on and potential for further write-down over next six months," he wrote. Fourteen minutes later, Blankfein responded, wanting to know the "short summary of our risk" and what "further writedowns" would be. Montag replied with a summary of Gasvoda's analysis, although it was not that easy to follow. "If things got no worse," he concluded, "the desk—perhaps in wishful mode—feels they have gains we haven't shown. [T]hey did make [$]21[mm] on Friday outside of write down." Blankfein replied in short order, "Tom, you refer to losses stemming from residual positions in old deals. Could/should we have cleaned up these books before, and are we doing enough right now to sell off cats and dogs in other books throughout the division[?]" This question got Montag thinking. "Should we have done before?" he replied, rhetorically. "Most likely." He then explained the steps the firm had taken but added that he thought the cleanup had been ongoing "for years" and took credit himself for moving "residuals out of origination and into traders" for them to sell.

But there were plenty of crosscurrents buffeting the mortgage market in February 2007 and plenty of people who disagreed with Goldman's decision to get short the mortgage market. For instance, the next day—February 12—Gyan Sinha, a senior managing director at Bear Stearns in charge of the firm's market research regarding asset-backed securities and collateralized debt obligations, held a conference call for some nine hundred investors where he spelled out his beliefs about the market's reaction to the news that New Century, the mortgage lender, was having financial trouble. To that point, Sinha had been very well respected and had even testified in front of Congress about the subprime mortgage market. "It's time to buy the [ABX] index," he said, adding that based on his modeling, "the market has overreacted" and predictions of rising problems in the mortgage market should be taken "with a large grain of salt." Many investors shared Sinha's view.

Two days later, on Valentine's Day, New Century announced that a wave of shareholder lawsuits had been filed against it and that after two weeks of tough negotiations, Goldman Sachs had agreed to a three-month extension of a line of credit to the company that had been set to expire the next day. Goldman had extracted its pound of flesh by insisting on the ability to get out of the agreement "at the first hint of trouble." At 6:33 that morning, Sparks, who had long been worried about this kind of problem, wrote himself an e-mail, titled "Risk," to help keep track of the increasingly volatile events. "Bad week in subprime," he wrote. He noted that "originators"—such as New Century—"are really in a bad spot. Thinly capitalized, highly levered, dealing with significant loan put-backs . . . now having trouble selling loans above par when it cost them 2 points to produce. Will have to . . . really tighten credit standards which will cut volume significantly." He wondered what the next area of "contagion" might be and answered himself that it would be CDOs, "which have been the buyer of most single name mezz[anine] subprime risk for the past year." He noted that Goldman was doing four things to reduce its risk: finding warehouse "risk partners," giving the secondary trading desk at Goldman—essentially Birnbaum and company—the ultimate authority "so all risk housed and managed by traders," buying protection on CDOs, and "executing deals."

None of this was communicated to Goldman's clients, of course.

Later that morning, Sparks summarized Goldman's "risk reduction program" for his bosses, including Montag, Viniar, Ruzika, and Gary Cohn. He copied Winkelried on the memo. The strategy consisted, he wrote, of selling the ABX index, of buying CDS on individual tranches of mortgage-backed securities, buying CDS—some $3 billion worth—on the "super-senior portions of BBB/BBB- index" and which seemed to be significantly in the money. "This is good for us position-wise," he wrote, "[but] bad for accounts who wrote that protection [to us] (M[organ] S[tanley] Prop[rietary trading desk], Peleton [a hedge fund], ACA, Harvard) but could hurt our CDO pipeline position as CDOs will be harder to do." Cohn sent Montag's e-mail on to Blankfein, without comment.

ON FEBRUARY 17, the *Wall Street Journal* interviewed Lew Ranieri and reported that the "rumpled 60-year-old says he is worried about the proliferation of risky mortgages and convoluted ways of financing them. Too many investors don't understand the dangers. . . . The problem, he says, is that in the past few years the business has changed so much that if the U.S. housing market takes another lurch downward, no one will know where all the bodies are buried. 'I don't know how to understand the ripple effects throughout the system today,' he said during a recent seminar." The growing problem was that 40 percent of the subprime borrowers in 2006 were not required to produce pay stubs or other proof of their net worth, according to Credit Suisse Group, and lenders were relying more and more on computer models to estimate the value of homes. "We're not really sure what the guy's income is and . . . we're not sure what the home is worth," Ranieri said. "So you can understand why some of us become a little nervous." He worried further that with so many mortgages being packaged by Wall Street into CDOs and sold in slices to investors all over the world, U.S. home mortgage risks were being spread to a "much less sophisticated community." The *Journal* made it clear that "Mr. Ranieri isn't predicting Armageddon. Some of the riskier new types of mortgages probably will perform 'horribly' in terms of defaults, leading to losses for some investors. But, he says, the 'vast majority' of mortgages outstanding are based on sounder lending principles and should be fine."

Most Wall Street investors and executives were not sure just what to do. Were the cracks in the mortgage market, as reflected in the decline of the ABX, a buying opportunity, as Bear's Sinha suggested? Or were the cracks the first small fissures in what soon would be a spectacular collapse of the market for mortgages and mortgage-backed securities? Major proponents of the glass-is-half-full thinking were the two Bear Stearns hedge-fund managers, Ralph Cioffi and Matthew Tannin. Apparently unbeknownst to many of their investors who thought Cioffi and Tannin had invested in less risky securities, the two Bear Stearns hedge funds—which together had around $1.5 billion of investor money riding—were heavily invested in mortgage-backed securities, including the synthetic CDOs Goldman had been selling. Like their Bear colleague Sinha, Cioffi and Tannin were generally of the view that the dip in the ABX index was a buying opportunity.

On February 21, Tannin sent an e-mail to his colleagues at Bear in which he sounded quite happy about all the doom and gloom over subprime mortgages in the marketplace. He cited such a negative report from a rival hedge-fund manager and said, "This piece is mostly unhelpful and more than a bit misleading. Scare mongering. I used to fly into a rage when I would read this stuff but now it makes me happy. We need some caution and naysayers in our market—it keeps spreads wider. So I'm glad this has been printed." A week later, Cioffi wrote to the team that he was thinking of "very selectively buying at these levels" since that "in and of itself would stabilize the markets." Tannin responded that he thought it would be a good idea. "Fear + illiquidity + a CDO ready and waiting = a good trade." That same day, Ben Bernanke, the chairman of the Federal Reserve, testified on Capitol Hill that he did not believe a "housing downturn" was a "broad financial concern or a major factor in assessing the state of the economy."

Meanwhile, at Goldman, Sparks reported to his bosses that Goldman's negative bets were continuing to pay off. He wrote to them, in an e-mail, that the firm was up $69 million on the day because the "market sold off significantly." He also shared with them that Goldman had covered its short positions—at a profit—on more than $400 million of bets on single tranches of mortgage securities. "Still significant work to do," he wrote. Within a minute, Winkelried wrote to Sparks from his BlackBerry, "Another downdraft?" To which Sparks responded, "Very large—it's getting messy." Winkelried then asked for some details, if possible, because "I've been on the road in euirope [sic] all week with clients so out of touch with it." Later that night, Sparks responded to Winkelried that there was "[b]ad news everywhere" including that NovaStar, a subprime mortgage originator, announced bad earnings and lost one-third of its market value in one day and that Wells Fargo had fired more than three hundred people from its subprime mortgage origination business. But, he was happy to report, Goldman was "net short, but mostly in single name CDS and some tranched index vs the s[a]me index longs. We are working to cover more, but liquidity makes it tough. Volatility is causing our VAR [value at risk] numbers to grow dramatically," which soon enough would make Goldman's top brass concerned about the level of the firm's capital being committed to these trades.

Not surprisingly, in the midst of all of this intellectual and financial jousting in the market, Goldman's senior executives occasionally wavered from the clear message that Viniar delivered in December 2006. At one point before the magnitude of the problem became crystalline, Viniar thought that Goldman had become too bearish and insisted that the firm's traders reverse course somewhat. One of those moments was in and around February 21, when the directive came from Viniar to close out some of Birnbaum's shorts. Sparks's e-mail that day was meant to be an update on the process following Viniar's new orders. This was plenty controversial on Birnbaum's desk, since he thought he was just beginning to mint money. To close out the positions meant leaving potentially billions in profits on the table, or worse, putting them in the hands of hedge funds, like Philip Falcone's Harbinger Capital Partners, that could cash in on Birnbaum's ideas. But Viniar insisted that the group was taking too much risk. Jonathan Egol, a trader on the structured products desk, identified four trades that the desk could do if "we want to close down shorts." On February 22, Sparks took Egol's list to Birnbaum, Swenny, and David Lehman, another trader, and wrote a cover message to them, urging that some of their short trades be unwound. "We need to buy back $1 billion single names and $2 billion of the stuff below—today," he wrote. "I know that sounds huge, but you can do it—spend bid/offer, pay through the market, whatever to get it done." Then he tried to buck up the traders, who he knew would be disappointed with this directive from on high. "It is a great time to do it," he continued. "Bad news on HPA"—home price appreciation—"[mortgage] originators pulling out, recent upticks in unemployment, originator pain. . . . This is a time to just do it, show respect for risk, and show the ability to listen and execute firm directives. You called the trade right, now monetize a lot of it. You guys are doing very well."

Birnbaum was not pleased. He knew his bets would be proved right—and be worth many billions of dollars—and yet the corporate drones were clipping his wings. "There was a certain amount of tension regarding just how short should our group be," he said. "Because we're the only ones who were taking short risk at the firm level. Just how short should we be? If you were evaluating us as a stand-alone, then we were pretty darn short. If you were evaluating us in the context of some of these other positions, there were some of us who felt that we weren't short enough, and that the quantification of those other desks wasn't being done enough. And the quantification of our desk was done ad infinitum." If he had his own hedge fund, like John Paulson or Kyle Bass, his potential payday would be nearly unfathomable. According to the *Wall Street Journal,* he "briefly lost his cool and slammed down a phone receiver . . . when a more senior bond trader insisted on unwinding some of his trades to cut risk." He referred to the audit gnomes from Goldman's controller's office as the "VAR police" because they were constantly pestering him about the level of risk he was taking. "The sexiest job within accounting at Goldman Sachs was to be focused on the structured products group," he said. "Because the P&L swings were huge. For the most part they were positive swings. . . . It was the Super Bowl if you were in accounting."

Birnbaum saw tremendous irony in the way the "VAR police" reacted to the money Goldman was making from his short bets. The mortgage market would move down, Birnbaum's bets would be more valuable, and Goldman would make more money. But that also meant the market had become more volatile, which is one of the significant variables in the VAR computer model. Birnbaum's desk would make $1 billion in a given month in 2007 and still own the same positions it owned the previous month but then be told the risk had increased. "You had the same position deemed to be twice as risky after you made a billion dollars in one month," he said. "And then someone will come knocking on your door and say, 'Oh, you know, you're taking massive amounts of risk. You need to cut your risk profile.'"

Josh Birnbaum did not appreciate being singled out. He urged the risk managers to instead take a more unified approach and look at the VAR across the spectrum of Goldman's bets, long and short, not just his moneymaking shorts. Alternatively, if his ability to make the short bet would be limited from time to time and compared with what was happening with the long bets, let him manage the long bets and then hold him accountable for those, too. "It'd be one thing if they said, 'We're holistically looking at this. We realize that you're massively short. These guys are long. And we're where we want to be.' Instead it was, 'Don't worry about those other businesses. That's our problem. You're massively short. Your VAR is on fire. Cut your risk,'" said one person with knowledge of this dispute.

So that is what Birnbaum and his team did, much to their chagrin. On February 25—a Sunday—Sparks e-mailed Montag with a progress report on the trading desk's efforts to reduce their risk. He informed Montag that the desk had covered $2.2 billion in short positions obtained by buying credit-default swaps but also had sold short $400 million worth of the BBB-ABX index. "Desk is net short," he wrote, "but less than before. Shorts are in senior tranches of indexes sold and in single names. Plan is to continue to trade from the short side, cover more single names and sell BBB-index outright." Sparks also let Montag know that some $530 million worth of mortgages and mortgage securities that Goldman had been storing in inventory to create new CDOs had been liquidated, and that another $820 million warehouse had begun liquidating. He wrote that after this wave of liquidations, Goldman still had in its pipeline to be sold $2 billion worth of "high-grade deals" and another $2 billion of BB-rated, "CDOs squared," or CDOs composed of other CDOs, a real dog's breakfast of risk. "How big and how dangerous" were the CDO squareds? Montag wanted to know. "Roughly [$]2 bb, and they are deals to worry about," Sparks wrote. One Goldman CDO deal—set to be priced on February 26—was instead liquidated per Sparks's order. "Thought we'd announce deal tomorrow," one Goldman banker wrote to a colleague on February 25, "but if we're just going to liquidate that doesn't really make sense."

On February 27, Sparks again turned up the heat on Birnbaum, Swenson, and company to reduce the desk's risks. He explained that his business's VAR was up due to volatility in the market but that the "[b]usiness [is] working to reduce exposures" and that "a lot of shorts already covered," including $4 billion in shorts on single-name mortgage-backed securities. "[The] [b]usiness [is] continuing to clear out loans," he informed his colleagues.

On the other hand, the origination business was still booming, including the pricing of the firm's largest-ever commercial mortgage-backed security deal that week. "The deal was oversubscribed," Sparks said. He also mentioned an $11 billion commercial real-estate loan. "The deal was very well subscribed," he said. Sparks did not mention to his colleagues that the $2 billion ABACUS deal was still moving forward, but that same day an internal memo was circulated outlining the deal's "marketing points." Among them, "Goldman's market-leading ABACUS program currently has $5.1 billion in outstanding [bonds] with strong secondary trading desk support." The memo said the ABACUS deal would be priced and sold the week of March 5.

On Saturday, March 3, Sparks wrote himself another e-mail summarizing "[t]hings we need to do," including focusing on Goldman's loan exposures to mortgage originators having trouble and speaking to "sales and clients about our deals." Many months into "the big short," this still had not been done, despite Whitehead's famous first principle. He wondered if the "junior people [are] OK" given all the turmoil in the markets. For his traders, he wanted to make sure they knew not to "add risk," to "trade everything from short to flat," to "get out of everything," and to "discuss liquidity of hedges." One consequence of Sparks's ruminations was to consider seriously terminating the ABACUS deal, then on the verge of being priced and sold. Per Sparks's instruction, on Sunday, Jonathan Egol e-mailed much of the mortgage-trading group: "Given risk priorities, subprime news and market conditions, we need to discuss sidelining this deal in favor of prioritizing [another deal] in the short term." To those people getting ready to syndicate ABACUS, he wrote, "[L]et's discuss the right way to communicate this internally and externally" and to Tourre, whom he called "Fabs," he wrote, "[L]et's focus Paulson on trades we can print now that fit." Tourre was none too pleased that his hard work was about to be rendered worthless. "Maybe we could have discussed live first before sending this out," he wrote Egol, with thinly veiled anger. But Egol was not sympathetic. "This is per [S]parks' instructions," he shot back.

Tourre quickly became despondent at this news, as became clear in an e-mail correspondence he had with Serres on March 7. "[T]he summary of the US subprime market business situation is that it is not too brilliant . . . ," he wrote to her. "According to Sparks, that business is totally dead, and the poor little subprime borrowers will not last so long!!! All this is giving me ideas for my medium term future, insomuch as I do not intend to wait for the complete explosion of the industry and the beginning of distressed trading, I think there might be more interesting things to do in Europe." Tourre told his girlfriend that he had been speaking with Michael Nartey, a managing director in London, "who naturally confirmed that 'he would love if I were in London, which would greatly facilitate communication with New York and would push the European sales force to concentrate on the risks of structured finance.'" He told her he was heading to London in April to "get a better sense for the opportunity but I am getting more and more convinced." He signed off with his usual affection and added, "I don't want to give you false hopes but I have a good feeling" about the new job happening.

At this prospect—that Tourre might soon move back to London—Serres was nearly euphoric. "Oh sweetheart, by just implying that you have a good feeling about coming over here, I'M JUST THE HAPPIEST

WOMAN ON EARTH!!!!" She explained how she had had an intense physical workout that morning. "But reading your e-mail, knowing that I can hope to in a day not too far off, wake up in your arms every morning, see the love of the whole world in your eyes and reciprocate it hundred-fold, every day . . . It's a last generation dose of amphetamines! I ADORE YOU FAB. Can't wait to whisper sweet words in your ears in a few hours." To which he responded, "And right now, I'd love nothing more than just curl in your arms, feel the warmth of your skin and just stay there smiling for hours (with occasional—frequent tender kisses) . . . Wake up slowly my love." Tourre had more good news, too: the ABACUS deal had stayed on track.

CHAPTER 21

SELLING TO
WIDOWS AND ORPHANS

There was no question that Goldman's top executives were monitoring closely what Sparks was doing to reduce the firm's mortgage exposure. In a March 5 e-mail circulated to the firm's top brass—including Blankfein, Cohn, Winkelried, Viniar, John Rogers, and J. Michael Evans, a vice chairman of the firm who also ran Goldman's business in Asia—various world market indices had shown some improvement, a fact noted by Evans when he sent the news around. "Feels better," Cohn replied to Evans. "But anything with a + would feel better." "Agreed," Evans wrote, "and the bigger the plus the better." But, Cohn pointed out, that might not necessarily be true. "A big plus would hurt the Mortgage business but [a trader] thinks he has a big trade lined up for the morning to get us out of a bunch of our short risk."

Early in the morning on March 8—12:50 a.m.—Sparks sent the senior executives of Goldman, aside from Blankfein, an e-mail summarizing the firm's mortgage risk. He explained that the firm still had significant exposure on the long side of the mortgage market, including more than $4 billion in CDOs on the books that the firm was trying to get out of—"We have various risk-sharing arrangements, but deal unwinds are very painful," he wrote—some $4.3 billion of Alt-A home mortgages waiting to be turned into securities, plus $1.3 billion in subprime mortgages and $700 million in second mortgages. "This market is also very difficult to execute in," he explained. There was also another $1.65 billion in other mortgage-related securities. "If the credit environment significantly worsens, these positions will be hurt by losses, further lack of liquidity and lower prices," he continued. Then, there was the ongoing process of covering Birnbaum's short bets. "We have longs against them, but we are still net short," he wrote. There was $4 billion worth of shorts on "single name subprime" and another $9 billion in shorts betting against the ABX index. The shorts, he wrote, "have provided significant protection so far, and should be helpful . . . in very bad times." But, he added, addressing the concerns of the firm's senior executives, "there is real risk that in medium-[term] moves, we get hurt in all three parts of the business—the long CDOs, the other mortgage-related securities and on the short positions. Therefore, we are trying to close everything down, but stay on the short side. But it takes time as liquidity is tough. And we will likely do some other things like buying puts on companies with exposures to mortgages."

This last bit—about betting companies with mortgage exposure would collapse—was an interesting new development and the first concession from Goldman that it was hedging itself and would soon be betting that other companies—even some of its competitors—would fail. At that time, Goldman had purchased $60 million, notionally, of equity put options "on subprime lenders" as "risk mitigant to overall subprime business." Betting against Goldman's competitors would follow soon enough.

—————

DESPITE GOLDMAN'S thirtieth-floor decision to do everything it could as a firm to hedge its billions of dollars of exposure—and hence risk—to the mortgage market in December 2006, the firm kept right on packaging up, underwriting, and selling mortgage-related securities of all stripes and sizes: subprime mortgages, Alt-A mortgages, home-equity loans, as well as more complicated CDOs and synthetic CDOs. This activity continued throughout the first half of 2007 until the collapse of the Bear Stearns hedge funds in the early summer of 2007 made that activity nearly impossible. Goldman continued to generate fees underwriting and selling mortgage-related securities at the same time the firm had made the corporate decision to hedge its bets and "get closer to home." According to a presentation made to the Goldman board of directors in September 2007, Goldman had underwritten $4.4 billion of subprime mortgage-related securities to date, seventh in the league tables, just ahead of Bear Stearns. In CDOs, Goldman put together twelve deals in 2007, totaling $8.4 billion, fourth overall but light-years behind Merrill Lynch, which underwrote $72.5 billion of CDOs in 2007. This certainly appeared to be a clear conflict of interest—betting against the mortgage market as principal at the same time as the firm continued to underwrite mortgage securities as agent.

For his part, Sparks said there was no "bright line" demarcating the decisions to "get closer to home," as Viniar said, and the one to keep packaging up the mortgages Goldman had already bought and selling them as mortgage-backed securities as if nothing had changed. "I don't think it was ever that cut-and-dried," he said. "[T]he firm was willing to sell the mortgage securities cheaply and there were still a lot of investors who wanted to buy them. That was part of the plan, and I don't think anybody thought the world was coming to an end. The firm was just trying to cut its risk." Indeed, at that time, Goldman still had plenty of people at the firm whose sole job was to buy mortgages, package them up, and sell them into the market. "That's kind of what the business was," he said, adding that to get rid of the mortgages that had been warehoused, Goldman sold the mortgage securities cheaply to investors who wanted to buy them at the prices being offered, and that Goldman ended up keeping the riskiest tranches that could not be sold. "We lost a ton of money on those deals," he said. "Like we lost a *lot*. A lot of guys [at other firms] decided not to sell because they didn't want to take the losses. We said, 'Okay, we're going to sell and we're going to take the loss.' " By taking these losses, Goldman's mortgage desk lost money in the second quarter of 2007—"the only mortgage department on the Street that lost money" in the second quarter, he said—but positioned itself well for the coming calamity. When the news about the losses in the mortgage department in the second quarter was shared at the quarterly internal "town hall" meeting, one trader in the group said he felt like a failure. "I felt like I was the worst trader on the Street, the worst businessman on the Street from a risk-management perspective," he said. "The reality was we were just doing what we thought was right."

As 2007 unfolded, the investors who bought the mortgage securities Goldman underwrote were suffering. In December 2007, the Massachusetts attorney general began an investigation into whether Goldman's participation in the underwriting of mortgage-backed securities had facilitated the origination and sale of "unfair"—as defined by Massachusetts law—residential mortgages to some seven hundred or so Massachusetts borrowers. The state attorney general wanted to know, among other things, "whether securitizers may have failed to make available to potential investors certain information concerning allegedly unfair or problem loans, including information obtained during loan diligence and the pre-securitization process, as well as information concerning their practices in making repurchase claims relating to loans both in and out of securitizations."

Without admitting to anything, Goldman settled the matter, in May 2009, with the Commonwealth of Massachusetts for what amounted to chump change. First, the firm agreed to pay $10 million to the state. Second, Goldman agreed to make modifications to various Massachusetts mortgages that it still had on its books or, if they had been packaged up and sold off, to facilitate changes to those mortgages through Litton, its servicing arm, or through other mortgage loan servicing companies. The cost to Goldman Sachs of changes to these various mortgages has been estimated to be $50 million. In sum, Goldman coughed up a mere $60 million, far less than 1 percent of its 2009 pretax earnings of $19.9 billion, to settle the Massachusetts dispute. "Since I became Attorney General, our office has sought accountability at all levels of the subprime lending crisis," explained Massachusetts attorney general Martha Coakley. "We are pleased that Goldman cooperated during this investigation and that it has committed to working with our office to help Massachusetts borrowers who are struggling with unsustainable subprime loans."

The investors in GSAMP Trust 2006-S2 fared worse—for the time being anyway—than those aggrieved Massachusetts investors. New Century, the originator of the mortgages packaged into GSAMP 2006-S2, filed for bankruptcy protection in April 2007. In September 2009, the Public Employees Retirement System of Mississippi, which provides current and future benefits to some three hundred thousand Mississippians and was an investor in the GSAMP securities, filed a complaint against Goldman and its affiliates, plus Goldman's Dan Sparks and Jonathan Egol individually, as well as the three most prominent ratings agencies (S&P, Moody's, and Fitch). It claimed that Goldman's prospectus "contained untrue statements of material fact, omitted facts required to be stated therein or omitted to state material facts necessary to make the statements therein not misleading" and alleged that Goldman's prospectus failed to share with investors that New Century had not followed its own underwriting standards, that appraisals on the properties being mortgaged overstated the properties' values, and that the ratings on the securities were flawed and based on outdated and irrelevant models. As a result, the complaint alleged, the securities Goldman offered to investors were "far riskier than represented" and were not "equivalent to other investments with the same credit ratings."

The Mississippi complaint referred often to a 581-page report written by a Washington lawyer appointed to figure out what went wrong at New Century. That report cited "serious loan quality issues" at New Century as early as 2004 and the "failure of New Century's senior management and board of directors" to do anything about it until it was "too late to prevent the consequences of longstanding loan quality problems in an adversely changing market." The report also discussed New Century's "brazen obsession" with increasing mortgage originations and concluded that the company "engaged in a number of significant improper and imprudent practices." Three causes of action were alleged against Goldman and a jury trial requested.

The last word from Goldman—at least as filed publicly with the SEC—about the GSAMP Trust 2006-S2 underwriting came on October 11, 2007. That day, Goldman filed with the SEC a final supplement to the original March 28, 2006, prospectus. The document was filled with the gory details of the practices that led to New Century's Chapter 11 bankruptcy filing and how that filing would likely affect New Century's ability—as Goldman had warranted to investors of the securities would happen—"to repurchase or substitute mortgage loans as to which a material breach of representation and warranty exists or to purchase mortgage loans as to which an early payment default has occurred." Oddly left out of the narrative leading up to New Century's bankruptcy filing was how on Valentine's Day 2007, a wave of shareholder lawsuits had been filed against it and that Goldman had negotiated for itself a safety valve with New Century.

The filing did contain information about how—by October 2007—the three major ratings agencies had downgraded scores of previously AAA-rated mortgaged-backed securities, including some of those that were packaged and sold as 2006-S2. But the supplement failed to make clear that nearly all of the original securities that Goldman offered for sale had been downgraded. Of course, there was little investors could do with the information that their securities had been downgraded—in many cases to junk status—except to take their hits and sell the securities at a steep losses, assuming buyers could be found at all. Of course by the fall of 2007—some three months after the liquidation of the two Bear Stearns hedge funds—there would be no practical way to avoid discussing in such a document the ongoing meltdown in the mortgage securities market.

Goldman and its lawyers had the decency to try to confront the calamity head-on, only to produce statements of masterful legal understatement. "In recent years, borrowers have increasingly financed their homes with new mortgage loan products, which in many cases have allowed them to purchase homes that they might otherwise have been unable to afford," Goldman wrote, trying at first to put a positive spin on the growing disaster. "Recently, the subprime mortgage loan market has experienced increasing levels of delinquencies, defaults and losses, and we cannot assure you that this will not continue. In addition, in recent months housing prices and appraisal values in many states have declined

or stopped appreciating, after extended periods of significant appreciation. A continued decline or an extended flattening of those values may
result in additional increases in delinquencies, defaults and losses on residential mortgage loans generally, particularly with respect to second
homes and investor properties and with respect to any residential mortgage loans whose aggregate loan amounts (including any subordinate
liens) are close to or greater than the related property values."

According to Matt Taibbi, a contributing editor at *Rolling Stone,* in
his famous anti–Goldman Sachs screed in the magazine in July 2009, "In
other words, the mortgages it was selling were for chumps. The real
money was in betting against those same mortgages." In the *Rolling Stone*
article, Taibbi asked an unnamed hedge-fund manager about Goldman's
seemingly duplicitous behavior and was told, "That's how audacious
these assholes are. At least with other banks, you could say that they
were just dumb—they believed what they were selling, and it blew them
up. Goldman knew what it was doing." Incredulous, Taibbi pressed on,
wondering how the firm could get away with playing on both sides of the
ball with impunity. Wasn't that securities fraud, he wondered? "It's
exactly securities fraud," the hedge-fund manager said. "It's the heart of
securities fraud." That remained to be seen, of course, but many people
sensed intuitively that there seemed to be something immoral about the
behavior. Observed Sylvain R. Raynes, an expert in structured finance at
R & R Consulting in New York and a former Goldman employee, "The
simultaneous selling of securities to customers and shorting them
because they believed they were going to default is the most cynical use
of credit information that I have ever seen. When you buy protection
against an event that you have a hand in causing, you are buying fire
insurance on someone else's house and then committing arson."

———

ONE OF THE problems created by Goldman continuing to package
mortgages and to sell them as securities in the market at the same time that
Birnbaum and Swenson were implementing "the big short" was that sometimes Goldman's message to the marketplace got muddled. Dealing with
the conflicting messages coming out of Goldman about its feeling about
the mortgage market also got dumped in Sparks's lap. This was very hard
work. "We started marking our clients" in the first half of 2007 "where we
thought the market was," Sparks said. "The rest of the Street said that
we were totally wrong. Our clients complained vigorously to everybody.
We had major issues because we did what we felt was right. . . . We
said, 'We think this bond is worth eighty.' Another broker/dealer said it was

'worth ninety-nine,' and the clients would be very unhappy with us. But we said, 'OK, well, we'll sell you some at eighty then.'" Sometimes this strategy worked; sometimes it didn't.

The market was rife with confusion. "Seems to me," Harvey Schwartz, the head of Goldman's capital markets business, wrote to Sparks on March 8, "one of our biggest issues is how we communicate our views of the market—consistently with what the desk wants to execute. Dan—realize the desk is swamped—but clearly marketing and sales leadership [can't] operate in a vaccum [sic]—so need someone that will represent trading in driving our communication broadly with marketing[.] [H]ow should we approach . . . as this has been difficult in the past when markets were calmer and less demanding of the [desk's] attention[?] If best talked offline . . . no worry."

Sparks plunged right in, though, in an e-mailed reply to Schwartz and others. Perhaps because he was responding to the partner running the firm's underwriting business, Sparks put the highest priority on continuing to package up and sell Goldman's warehoused mortgages, if for no other reason than to get them off Goldman's books, and fast. "Our current largest needs are to execute and sell our new issues—CDOs and RMBS—and to sell our other cash trading positions," he wrote. "There is the perception out there—I heard it twice today from issuers/managers—that we are having trouble moving cash securities, that it is causing our view of the markets to be overly negative, and that the result is worse execution for them. I tend to think we are just realistic and others are hoping the market is better than it really is, but we have significant positions that we need to move, and I think our offerings should look cheap"—be priced to move—"relative to where it sounds like competitors are. I can't overstate the importance to the business of selling these positions and new issues."

Goldman also used its many tentacles to look for financial opportunities among the increasingly distressed carcasses of the companies that once originated the mortgages that Goldman was so busy packaging up and selling as securities. In addition to New Century, among those that ran into trouble by March 2007—in part because of Goldman's decision to pull back their financing—were Accredited Home Lenders, Inc., and Fremont General, both of which soon enough joined New Century in filing for bankruptcy protection. On March 9, Sparks wrote to his bosses, including Cohn, Winkelried, and Viniar, about what the firm was doing to take advantage of the distress of these mortgage originators. With Accredited, Goldman was working with Cerberus, the hedge fund, as well as Goldman's own private-equity arm plus banking and the mortgage group to consider an investment to help the company stave off a covenant default. With Fremont, Sparks noted that famed bank investor and billionaire Gerald Ford—not to be confused with the former U.S. president—was looking to make an investment in the company. "We will try to tag along and are trying to get Cerberus included," he wrote. With New Century, Sparks wrote that "Cerberus is looking at something and may include us, but we don't think there is much there" and besides, "they are in the worst shape." Goldman was also an unsecured creditor to New Century and was thinking about buying assets from the company as a way to offset what it owed Goldman. Cohn passed the e-mail on to Blankfein.

There was little question, though, that Birnbaum's strategy of shorting the mortgage market was resulting in growing profits for Goldman Sachs, a point underscored by Sheara Fredman, a Goldman vice president, in a March 9 memo to Viniar in preparation for Goldman's first-quarter earnings conference call. In the first quarter, the mortgage group made $266 million in revenues—"a record quarter for the business," Fredman wrote—thanks in large part to Birnbaum's "synthetic short positions." His trading gains had been offset by losses on the long side of the mortgage portfolio, "most notably in our warehousing of financial assets to be securitized in connections with CDOs." In a presentation about Goldman's mortgage business being prepared for the March 2007 meeting of the Goldman board of directors, Sparks thought it important to add some information about the "various things we have done" in the quarter to implement "the big short": on Sparks's list was an alphabet soup consisting of "getting short CDS on RMBS and CDOs, getting short the super-senior BBB- and BBB index, and getting short AAA index as overall protection." Then referring to the new strategy of buying puts on failing mortgage originators, he added, "The puts have also been good." The board presentation also ended up including the idea that Goldman had started the quarter with a notional long of $6 billion on the ABX index but had ended the quarter net short a notional amount of $10 billion.

To the "Firmwide Risk Committee," at its March meeting, Sparks made clear why Birnbaum had been given the green light to execute "the big short." He said it was "Game Over" and "an accelerating meltdown" for subprime lenders, such as New Century and Fremont General. What's more, he told his colleagues—in March 2007—"[T]he Street is highly vulnerable, [with] potentially large [mortgage] exposures at Merrill and Lehman." He said Goldman's mortgage group was "currently closing down every subprime exposure possible" and the "current strategies"

were to "liquidate positions" or "put back inventory" to the mortgage originators. He also suggested that there was a problem brewing in commercial real estate because of "subprime woes." He closed with the thought
that hedge funds were making money but that "it was difficult to tell how
much others are losing because many CDOs with subprime assets are
not" marked to market.

THE PROBLEMS AT New Century and Fremont quickly began to ripple through the market. On March 12, as previously instructed, the
ABACUS deal team, including Egol and Tourre, presented ABACUS to
Goldman's "Mortgage Capital Committee" to get its approval. According
to the memo about the deal, Goldman stood to make between $15 million
and $20 million for acting as an intermediary between Paulson and ACA.
There appeared to be little discussion of the reputational risk the firm
might suffer as a result of the deal, which had been the reason Tourre had
been instructed to get the committee's approval even though Goldman
did not appear, at first, to be committing any capital. Indeed, according to
Egol and Tourre, ABACUS had it all. "This transaction is a new and innovative transaction for Goldman Sachs and the CDO Market," they wrote.
After noting the deal's highly technical "firsts," they continued, "This
transaction addresses the objectives of multiple clients of the firm: it
helps ACA increase [its] assets under management and [its] fee income;
it enables Paulson to execute a macro hedge on the RMBS market; it
offers to CDO investors an attractive product relative to other structured
credit products available in the market. Our ability to structure and execute complicated transactions to meet multiple clients needs and objectives is key for our franchise." The committee approved the deal.

That afternoon, Jörg Zimmerman, a vice president at IKB Credit
Asset Management, a big German bank in Düsseldorf that was taking the
long side of the ABACUS deal, wrote to Michael Nartey, the Goldman
banker in London, with copies to Tourre and Egol, that IKB wanted to
remove both the Fremont and New Century bonds from the reference
list for the ABACUS deal, no doubt because of the two companies' ongoing financial difficulties. Zimmerman wrote that he wanted to go back
to IKB's "advisory comitee [sic]" and "would need consent on" removing
these securities from the ABACUS deal. This was not such great news.
"Paulson will likely not agree to this unless we tell them nobody will buy
these bonds if we don't make that change," Tourre wrote to Egol, who
wrote back wanting to know what "we say to Joerg [sic]?" "As discussed
with Nartey," Tourre replied, "we are taking his feedback into account
and once we have gotten more feedback from accounts across the cap

structure we will decide what the best cours[e] of action is." Tourre's head fake was typical of bankers looking to make it seem there was competition for a deal when clearly there was not. Indeed, IKB may have been one of the few investors the world over willing to take the long side of such a trade with so many red flags emerging about the problems in the mortgage market. (There is no additional documentation about whether Goldman agreed to take out the New Century and Fremont mortgages, but the final ABACUS deal did include mortgages serviced by both companies in the reference portfolio; Zimmerman did not respond to a request for an interview.)

New Century's problems were also giving pause to Rabobank, a big Dutch bank, which was considering investing in Anderson Mezzanine Funding, another Goldman-architected $305 million CDO also coming to market in March. Unlike the ABACUS deal, in the Anderson deal, Goldman was underwriting the equity portion and expected to keep half of it as a principal investment. This prompted Olivia Ha, a 1998 Harvard graduate and Goldman vice president, to e-mail the Anderson deal team at Goldman with a question about how it got comfortable with the New Century collateral since Ha's client at Rabobank, Wendy Rosenfeld, had expressed her concerns about it. "[H]ow did you get comfortable with all the [N]ew [C]entury collateral in particular the [N]ew [C]entury serviced deals[,] considering you are holding the equity and their servicing may not be around[?] [I]s that concerning to you at all?" Rosenfeld needed "more comfort" because she was "getting credit resistance on the [N]ew [C]entury concentration." Eventually, several members of the Anderson deal team at Goldman got on the phone with Wendy to "allay her [N]ew [C]entury concerns. . . . This will be our opportunity to help arm her with ammo for her credit [committee] who is getting jittery on the [N]ew [C]entury exposure/servicing concentration."

The call between Goldman and Rosenfeld did not go as Goldman had hoped. She ended up passing. "At this point in time we are not going to be able to participate in Anderson," she wrote to Ha on March 13. "There are many concerns regarding the percent of NC"—New Century— "originated and serviced collateral." A few days later, several other potential Anderson investors dropped out, also because of "New [C]entury issues." Smith Breeden Associates, a global asset management company, dropped out as well over concerns the deal would get downgraded and because there would not be sufficient cash flow to cover the interest payments. Scott Wisenbaker, the Goldman banker on the deal, agreed to speak with Smith Breeden to "make sure they understand the deal correctly, but regardless, it looks like they are lower probability to be involved."

This was not the answer Peter Ostrem, a more senior Goldman banker and the head of the CDO group, was looking to hear. "Yeah?" he fired back to Wisenbaker. "So—fix the miscommunication so the probability goes up."

Nerves seemed to be getting frayed throughout Goldman. There was growing pressure to deal with what appeared to be the increasing likelihood of a financial crisis brought on by the problems in the mortgage market. On March 14, the firm sent around an internal economic research report that contained an interesting nugget that caught the attention of the firm's senior executives and got them even more worried than they already were. "New data from the Mortgage Bankers Association show that mortgage credit quality problems go well beyond the subprime sector," according to the report. "This can be seen from the fact that delinquencies on prime adjustable-rate mortgages are rising quickly—much more quickly, in fact, than those of subprime fixed-rate loans." When Winkelried read this he grew concerned. "[D]elinquencies in PRIME adjustables with teaser rates growing fast," he wrote to Blankfein, Cohn, and Viniar, plus Ruzika and Sparks, the two guys running the mortgage group. "[I] think this may be a big problem and a lot worse than currently thought. [I] think lending standards are highly variable among originators and [W]all [S]treet focus (servicers and dealers) on quality control has been lost for a while. [D]an, are we doing things to prepare for bleed into prime space?"

Sparks responded quickly. "Trying to be smaller and buying puts on companies with exposure to overall mortgage market," he wrote to the same august group. "We are also short a bunch of sub-prime AAA index." Goldman's schizophrenic behavior continued, though. The same day that Sparks was writing to Winkelried, Cohn, and Blankfein about being short the ABX index and buying puts on companies with exposure to the mortgage market, he also sent Montag an e-mail titled "Cactus Delivers," about Mehra Cactus Raazi, a Goldman bond salesman and former *Rolling Stone* ad salesman, urging Montag to congratulate Raazi on selling off a $1.2 billion short position the firm had in A-rated mortgage securities to Stanfield Capital Partners, a New York–based CDO manager. "He did a great job filling our ax," Sparks wrote to Montag, who then sent the whole e-mail chain on to Blankfein with a note: "Covered another [$]1.2 billion in shorts in mortgages[,] almost flat"—a reference to being neither too short nor too long the mortgage market—"now need to reduce risk." On March 20, after Blankfein received the daily firmwide "net revenues" estimate that showed the firm had generated $111 million in revenues that day—and $37 million in pretax earnings—but had lost

$21.4 million in mortgages, he sent an e-mail to Cohn. "Anything note-worthy about the losses in mortgages?" he wanted to know. Cohn replied, "No[.] [M]arket rallied a bit[.] [S]till short."

The next day, this little executive-level colloquy trickled down-stream.

"Did Josh get out of index trade?" Montag asked Sparks and Bill McMahon, a reference to Birnbaum's short position on the ABX that had started to—briefly—move against him. "I had him liquidate S&P's"—a bet made on the S&P 500 stock index—"and cut equity put position in half yesterday." He then explained what the group was focused on, strategically, which no doubt pleased the VAR police but was equally disheartening to Birnbaum. "Overall as a business, we are selling our longs and covering our shorts," Sparks wrote, "which is what this quarter is really about, as well as protecting ourselves on counter-party risk, planning for the new resi[dential mortgage] world, and trying to be opportunistic. We have shorts that we need to provide overall pro-tection in case we get further move downs—and those shorts have been hurting us."

Sparks's logic may have been flawless, but Montag had little patience, it seemed, for a bet that might pay off down the road but that was moving against the firm in the short term, especially after Blankfein had made his inquiries. "Liquidity is better," Montag conceded, "but actual performance can be much worse obviously." Then he took a swipe at Birnbaum: "Unfortunately[,] the trader [J]osh has not demonstrated a track record of controlling his position. . . . Instead of these lousy hedges he should just be selling his position." Sparks tried to defend Birnbaum. "He has had a very good run in this activity," he wrote to Montag and promised that before long Birnbaum would "lay out [a] plan" for how to proceed and get Montag to sign off on it.

On March 26, Goldman management gave the Goldman board of directors a presentation on the subprime mortgage market. The twenty-four-page document contained a page titled "The Subprime Meltdown," which traced the collapse of New Century's stock and the financial car-nage among the subprime mortgage originators, including the fifteen companies that had already been liquidated or filed for bankruptcy. The presentation also described Goldman's dual, schizophrenic role in the market: one as a buyer, packager, and seller of mortgages and mortgage-related securities to investors for a fee—Goldman "exits loan purchases by structuring and underwriting securitization and distributing securities back by mortgage loans on a principal basis and for clients," the presentation explained—the other as a trader of mortgages and derivatives related to mortgages "to hedge our long credit exposure" in a bet that the mortgage market would collapse. It was quite a pas de deux.

Goldman's management also created a timeline of the firm's reactions to worsening market conditions in the subprime mortgage sector. For instance, in the second half of 2006 and the first quarter of 2007, Goldman "reduces CDO [origination] activity" and "residual assets marked down to reflect market deterioration." Then, the board was told, "GS reverses long market position through purchase of single name CDS"—credit-default swaps—"and reductions of ABX." The gross revenues of Goldman's mortgage business reflected the changing dynamics as well. In 2005, the firm made $885 million in revenues on the mortgage desk, mostly from the origination of residential and commercial real-estate securities. In 2006, Goldman underwrote $29.3 billion of subprime mortgage securities, a ranking of sixth overall, and underwrote close to $16 billion in collateralized debt obligations, ranking fifth. That year, the mortgage-related revenues increased 16 percent with the origination business staying essentially flat, but with Birnbaum's group generating $401 million in revenue, up 64 percent from the $245 million generated the year before. That revenue generation accelerated in the first four and a half months of fiscal 2007, where Birnbaum's group had produced $201 million in revenue, already half of what had been generated for all of 2006. Meanwhile, the residential mortgage security origination business had fallen off the cliff by the first part of 2007, with a $19 million loss in gross revenue. The Goldman board also was shown that the firm was long some $12.9 billion in various mortgage securities, which was offset by a $7.2 billion short bet against the ABX and another $5.5 billion negative bet against mortgages, obtained through the purchase of credit-default swaps. Goldman's net exposure as of March 15, 2007, was some $200 million on the long side, or virtually flat. In March 2007, after Goldman's first-quarter performance was released, Viniar said, "Subprime is under stress, it appears to have been overheated. It's pretty clear there will be a shakeout. It will be a reasonably sized, but smaller market than it has been over the last several months." As to the firm's ongoing role in the mortgage market, he said, "When we extend credit we tend to have security and other terms that will protect us. We do what we can to mitigate our losses, we do what we can to protect ourselves."

Incredibly, many others—among them Ben Bernanke, the Fed chairman, and Henry Paulson, the treasury secretary—were missing the problems that Goldman Sachs and John Paulson were seeing in the mortgage market. "The impact on the broader economy and financial markets of the problems in the subprime market seems likely to be contained," Bernanke testified before the Joint Economic Committee of Congress on March 28. That same day, Paulson told a House Appropriations subcommittee: "From the standpoint of the overall economy, my bottom line is we're watching it closely but it appears to be contained."

Bear Stearns was also projecting a very different outlook on the opportunities in the mortgage market than was Goldman. In a March 29 "Investor Day" presentation, Jeffrey Mayer and Thomas Marano, two of the most senior executives in Bear's fixed-income group, were trumpeting the fact that the firm's "leading mortgage franchise continues to grow." The hits just kept on coming: net revenues had doubled since 2002 to $4.2 billion in 2006; Bear was the "top ranked" underwriter of mortgage-backed securities and asset-backed securities; the firm had expanded its mortgage origination capabilities by purchasing Encore Credit Corporation—a "sub-prime wholesale originator"—to complement Bear Stearns Residential Mortgage Corporation and EMC Mortgage Corporation; and Bear ranked fifth in the underwriting of CDOs, with a volume of $23 billion in 2006, with "volume nearly doubling from last year." The men also boasted of being "well-positioned to handle disruption in the sub-prime market."

Soon after Goldman's March 2007 board of directors meeting, the Goldman mortgage group began closing one challenging CDO underwriting assignment after another, including those for Timberwolf, Anderson Mezzanine, and—soon enough, on April 26—ABACUS, which had been such a roller-coaster ride for Fabrice Tourre. One way the Timberwolf deal got done, according to an internal Goldman memorandum, was because the two hedge-fund managers at Bear Stearns Asset Management, Cioffi and Tannin, bought $400 million worth of the $600 million security—by far the largest chunk—at prices that ranged from just below par (99.7 percent of par) to par.

On Wall Street, Cioffi and Tannin were well-known buyers of squirrelly securities such as CDOs, CDOs of CDOs (known as CDO squareds), and synthetic CDOs. Indeed, in October 2006, Goldman had created a $900 million synthetic CDO squared known as ABACUS 2006 HGS1—a different ABACUS deal than the famous one Tourre worked on—expressly for the two Bear Stearns hedge-fund managers. The security referenced a mix of credit-default swaps on A-rated bonds and synthetic asset-backed securities, "the sweet spot right now" in the market at that time, one trader told *Derivatives Week* in December 2006. Cioffi and Tannin made the Timberwolf deal on March 27, 2007, thanks to the salesmanship of Andrew Davilman, then a Goldman vice president. Some six months later—after the value of Timberwolf had collapsed to around 15 cents on the dollar, Goldman trader Matthew Bieber referred to March 27 as "a day that will live in infamy." Meanwhile one of the Bear Stearns hedge-fund investors, who lost all that he had invested, observed, tongue firmly implanted in his cheek: "Nice trade, Ralph." (According to Michael Lewis, writing in *The Big Short,* at the same time that Davilman was selling Cioffi most of Timberwolf at par, he was buying insurance from AIG, in the form of credit-default swaps, on behalf of Goldman, as principal, betting that similar CDO securities—although apparently not Timberwolf itself, according to a November 2007 AIG memorandum—would collapse.) Indeed, in Sparks's March 9 memo— the one where he wrote that the "#1 priority" was to sell "new issues"— he specifically cited Davilman for making a "major contribution" in helping sell the trading "desk's priorities." A few days after Cioffi bought the senior tranches of Timberwolf, Mehra Cactus Raazi was able to sell $16 million of a lower-rated tranche of the same deal. "Great job Cactus Raazi trading us out of our entire Timberwolf single-A position," an internal memo fairly screamed.

Meanwhile, Tourre was still pounding the pavement trying to sell the ABACUS deal. On March 30, he reported to Sparks that he had been visiting with "selected accounts" during the previous few weeks, many of whom had passed on investing in Timberwolf and Anderson. But there were $200 million of orders—from IKB (apparently having overcome its concern about New Century mortgages being included) and from ACA, the portfolio selection agent. The plan was, he explained, to close the sales of those tranches at the end of the following week and then to try to move the lower-rated tranches shortly thereafter. He urged his colleagues to "steer" accounts "towards available tranches" of ABACUS "since we make $$$ proportionately" when the tranches are sold off.

On April 3, he sought trade approval to sell Paulson & Co. credit protection on $192 million worth of the ABACUS deal, allowing Goldman to book a $4.4 million fee for providing the insurance. He asked Goldman's credit group to make sure it was OK with the traders. By April 11, though, perhaps because of some push back from the credit group, Tourre was also worried about making sure Goldman maximized its ability to profit from its trading relationship with Paulson & Co., especially after ABACUS closed. He wrote to Cactus Raazi that he needed to ask the Goldman credit department to perform an "updated review" of Paulson "to enable us to put more trades on with these guys" since "it appears" that since the beginning of 2007, Paulson had shorted, through

Goldman, $2 billion notional amount of residential mortgage-backed securities, "which is utilizing most of the credit capacity we have for Paulson." Tourre explained to Raazi that "[w]e need to be sensitive of the profitability of these trades vs. the profitability of ABACUS—we should prioritize the higher profit margin business with Paulson." By the next day, it seemed, Tourre had received credit's approval to do the trades with Paulson, and Raazi booked the trades, much to his dismay— apparently—because he suspected Goldman would get stuck on the losing side. "[S]eems we might have to book these pigs," Raazi wrote to Daniel Chan, his Goldman colleague.

On May 8, Tourre updated Sparks on the ongoing ABACUS saga, which he referred to as the "short we are brokering for Paulson." He explained that the "supersenior tranche" of the deal would "most likely" be executed with ACA, through another bank—ABN AMRO, a large Dutch bank—as "intermediation counterparty." Goldman was to "buy protection" on $1 billion of the security and then Paulson was to short a big chunk of it. (How do they think up these things?) But Tourre was worried that Paulson may have changed his mind about doing the deal as originally conceived. There were now two options for Goldman: one would be a "risk-free" deal where Goldman would make $14 million; the other would make Goldman $18 million but expose the firm to $100 million of risk being long a portion of the deal, although Tourre wrote that he felt confident that risk could be sold at a profit. A week later, with the ABX index rallying, Tourre reported that there was a "90% chance" that ACA and ABN AMRO would go through with the deal, but that he was increasingly concerned that Paulson "is starting to get 'cold feet'" on going through with his side of the trade because of the ABX rally. Tourre wanted Sparks's permission for Goldman to "take down," or assume the short side of the trade, instead of Paulson, "in order to avoid loosing [sic]" the ACA/ABN AMRO order.

Two weeks later, Tourre provided the group another update. Paulson had now agreed to his side of the trade—for $1 billion—and ACA/ABN AMRO had agreed to buy $909 million, leaving Goldman with $91 million it was unable to place, although "we are showing this tranche to a few accounts," he wrote. Finally, the next day, the deal was really done, along the lines Tourre had described the day before. Melanie Herald-Granoff, a Goldman vice president in the mortgage-trading group, wrote to Tourre and David Gerst, in the structured products trading group: "Fabrice & David—Thank you for your tireless work and perseverance on this trade!! Great job." By June 5, Gerst was offering up Goldman's $91 million residual—that piece that neither Paulson nor

ACA purchased—to Bear Stearns Asset Management, or BSAM, at par, or 100 cents on the dollar, with a coupon of LIBOR plus 0.75 percent. With plenty of its own problems by then, BSAM declined Goldman's kind offer, leaving Goldman itself on the hook for this piece of the ABACUS deal. After some six months of hard work on the ABACUS deal, Tourre headed to Belgium and then London, in part to visit his girlfriend. "Just made it to the country of your favorite clients [Belgians]," Tourre wrote to Serres on June 13. "I've managed to sell a few [ABACUS] bonds to widows and orphans that I ran into at the airport, apparently these Belgians adore synthetic abs [CDO] squared!! Am in great shape, ready to hold you in my arms tonite."

———

AT AROUND THIS time—with Birnbaum's short bets paying off big—the decision was made to allow his desk to get control of the firm's growing inventory of those parts of CDOs it could not sell to investors, known as residuals. He and Swenson began to give serious thought to the price it would take to move these residuals off Goldman's books and into the hands of other investors. Driven in large part by a combination of what the traders were seeing in the market and Jeremy Primer's models, which kept spitting out lower and lower valuations for the residuals, Birnbaum began to think that the time had come to seriously write down the value of the firm's CDOs, in order to move them out the door. "Part of it was just a general discipline where we had legacy positions that—frankly—we did not like," Birnbaum explained. "This is part of the growing purview that our desk had in terms of all the legacy positions. Looking around, we were like, 'We got to get rid of this shit.' And when you think it's worth par, selling it into a ninety-five bid feels pretty bad. But when you think it's worth seventy, selling it into a ninety-five bid sounds pretty darn good even if you're taking a five-point loss, right? So, the first thing was just to get the culture of Goldman around that concept. The same percolation upward that was occurring with these short trades was also happening with this valuation question on CDOs."

This was easier said than done. One Goldman trader remembered a number of critical and contentious meetings at Goldman where different constituents around the firm would submit, in writing, their thoughts about the valuation of the residuals. "I remember looking at one of these sheets," he said. "There were *huge* differences of opinion on this issue. They were very vehement. There are a lot of senior guys at the firm who have since changed their story very much—and were like, 'Oh, there's no fucking way that stuff's worth that. You guys are crazy.' Some of the more negative people in our group who were more bearish would really be pushing the short trades in general. Some of the senior people thought we were a little nuts"—here he did not want to say which senior Goldman executives felt this way. "Ultimately you had the research guys saying, 'This stuff's worth below fifty,' when it was marked at one hundred." The debate led to a grand compromise. "Fuck it, mark it at seventy," the Goldman trader said, recalling how the decision got made.

By April, Birnbaum had won the internal debate. Not only did Sparks agree with Birnbaum, he became increasingly concerned about the rapidly declining value of Goldman's $10 billion mortgage-backed securities portfolio, as more and more home buyers began to default on their home mortgages and the market for the securities tied to them began to cool. He took the laboring oar in convincing the senior Goldman executives that the time had come to move. "We've got a big problem," Sparks told Viniar and Cohn. The decision was made to sell as much of Goldman's $10 billion portfolio as rapidly as possible, even if the markdowns required to do so were drastic. In the first few weeks of April, the e-mails were flying fast and furious with the mandate to sell the firm's new "axes," composed of the residual CDO inventory.

On April 5, Thomas Cornacchia, head of Goldman's mortgage sales group, sent around a list of thirty positions, totaling $450 million, that Goldman wanted to sell immediately. "Get this done please," he ordered, and then added a little bit of competitive verve: "Who is the better salesperson??" Within the hour, Mehra Cactus Raazi, Goldman salesperson extraordinaire, had sent the list to Brad Rosenberg, at Paulson & Co., and urged him to take a look. "These are all dirty '06 originations that we are going to trade as a block," he wrote. "You are not the only client seeing this[,] so time will be of the essence. Save the price discussion for later— at the moment you might want to figure out whether this portfolio suits your objectives." Later that day, another internal list of "axes" got circulated. "Over the past few weeks[,] we've continued to move several CDO and subprime positions," Anthony Kim, another mortgage trader, wrote to the senior members of the mortgage group. He then summarized for them that $859.4 million worth of the stuff had sold from Goldman's inventory. In a separate e-mail, a congratulatory note went around to the group thanking Robert Gaddi, another trader, for doing a "great job" for "moving us out of [$]6mm of our BBB-, Fremont, subprime risk" along with the request to "continue to focus" on the additional long list of bonds. On April 11, another list circulated. "Please continue to focus on the axes below—they remain a high priority for the desk," the note read. The list came with a further admonition to the sales force: "We are very axed to move" several tranches of the still unsold Timberwolf CDO. The message included the news that the desk was having trouble selling the deal at prices anything like what it had been selling the securities for, and that no longer mattered. "We need levels from accounts that will move this risk," the message said. "We are planning to pay in the context of $20/bond," meaning Goldman was willing to sell the bonds at a sufficient discount to get them sold.

By April 19, Sparks was geared up to deal. Attaching the list of the securities Goldman was anxious to sell, he wrote to V. Bunty Bohra, on the structured products syndicate desk, "Why don't we go one at a time with some ginormous credits—for example, let's double the current offering of credit for [T]imberwolf" to make it look more attractive to a buyer. Minutes later, Bohra responded, "We have done that with [T]imberwolf already. Don't want to roll out any other focus axes until we get some traction there but at the same time, don't want to stop showing the inventory." Birnbaum recalled how the frustrations with trying to sell the residual inventory at gradual markdowns reverberated through the firm, until it dawned on people that more drastic steps were needed.

The difficulty Goldman faced in April trying to sell its "axes" into a market that no longer wanted to buy what it was trying to sell, came to a head in mid-May. "Sparks and the [mortgage] group are in the process of considering making significant downward adjustments to the marks on their mortgage portfolio, especially CDOs and CDO squared," Craig Broderick, Goldman's global head of risk management, wrote to his team in his famous May 11 e-mail. "This will potentially have a big P&L impact on us, but also to our clients due to the marks and associated margin calls on repos, derivatives, and other products. We need to survey our clients and take a shot at determining the most vulnerable clients, knock-on implications, etc. This is getting lots of 30th floor attention right now." Recalled Birnbaum: "So we marked the positions. And started telling the world."

CHAPTER 22

MELTDOWN

O f all of the momentous decisions that Goldman—nearly uniquely among Wall Street investment banks—had been making to curb drastically its exposure to what the firm was increasingly convinced would be a near-complete collapse of the mortgage market, the decision to mark down significantly its own residual mortgage-related portfolio in the spring of 2007 would reverberate the most profoundly through the metaphorical canyons of Wall Street, touching off one conflagration after another for the next eighteen months until Wall Street itself nearly collapsed in September and October 2008.

The firm knew its marks would shock its clients and counterparties, and it braced itself for some anger, since the Goldman marks would sooner or later have to be matched by others with similar securities in their portfolios. Birnbaum was not a salesman, so he was not on the front line of the calls made to clients, but he was aware of their being made. They were the marks heard 'round the world. "Definitely some people were shocked," Birnbaum said. "Some people [started saying,] 'Conspiracy theory, Goldman Sachs: Oh, you guys are short. You're just trying to drive the market down.' The reality was, though, that at that point in time it wasn't completely known in the market that we were short. Up until probably March I'd say the consensus on Wall Street was that Goldman Sachs was long. We did a fantastic job of not letting the Street know which way we were going."

The impact was felt almost immediately. Nowhere did Goldman's seismic change of heart about the value of its mortgage-backed securities portfolio have a bigger impact than on the fate of the two Bear Stearns hedge funds run by Cioffi and Tannin. For forty straight months, the funds had made money for investors. The unblemished record of the two Bear Stearns hedge funds began to get sullied in February 2007, when the newer of the two funds—the Enhanced Leverage Fund—recorded its first monthly loss of 0.08 percent, the first time either fund had lost money since Cioffi started the first Bear hedge fund in 2003. In March, Bear's High-Grade Fund lost 3.71 percent for the month, and the Enhanced Leverage Fund lost 5.41 percent. In April, the bottom fell out of the two funds, in large part because of Goldman's new thinking.

Once upon a time, the problems of one discrete set of investment decisions would have had little bearing, if any, on what happened elsewhere. But somewhere along the line, financial services firms became connected to one another in much the same way roped-up mountaineers are connected on an alpine ascent. If one hiker falls into a crevasse, it can very quickly lead to every hiker being dragged down right behind him, unless immediate and significant remedial steps can be implemented. It turned out that by the spring of 2007, Wall Street and Wall Street hedge funds were every bit as intertwined as mountain climbers on the face of K2.

The way hedge funds—such as those run by Cioffi and Tannin— are required by the Securities and Exchange Commission to value the securities they own is plenty arcane. But it is based on the idea of taking an average of the prices other Wall Street firms and other traders are finding in the market for similar securities, most of which were thinly traded from one firm to another and were rarely traded by retail investors or on exchanges, as with stocks. With these illiquid securities, hedge-fund managers had to wait until the end of each month to get the marks from other brokers and dealers, then average them, and then report the "net asset value," or NAV as it is known on Wall Street, to investors.

For the first forty months of Cioffi's tenure as a hedge-fund manager at Bear Stearns, the marks and the funds' NAVs went up. "Clearly as this market started to get a little bit dicier, in 2007, it was harder to get marks in shops," explained one Bear executive. "People didn't want to value things. They were worried about their own valuations. But we were showing valuations that went from one hundred cents on the dollar down to like ninety-eight. They were going down. But they were going a little bit down." The losses, though, were magnified by the amount of leverage sitting on those assets.

"Going into the month of May, when we were waiting for our April marks, there were no cash trades that you could look at," the Bear Stearns executive explained. "That said to us, 'Wow, this market was falling like a rock.' But when we were waiting for the April marks, [Cioffi and Tannin] were like, 'No, let's see where they come out. We think they're going to be down. But we don't think they're going to be down outrageously.' And sure enough, we get in all these marks. And the marks are ninety-nine, ninety-eight, ninety-seven. They're still in that same ballpark. It was enough to have a second bad month. It was like down six percent but not disastrous. Not good, but not disastrous." Cioffi published the NAV for the Enhanced Leverage Fund for April at minus 6.5 percent.

A week later, "knowing full well we've published our NAV," according to this executive, Goldman Sachs sent, by e-mail, its April marks on the securities to Cioffi. "Now there's a funny little procedure that the SEC imposes on you, which is that even if you get a late mark, you have to consider it," he said. "Suddenly we get these marks. Except these marks are not marks from ninety-eight to ninety-seven. They go from ninety-eight to fifty and sixty. Okay? You get it? They give us these fifty and sixty prices. What we got from the other counterparties is ninety-eight. The SEC rules say that when you do this, you either have to average them—but they're meant to be averaging ninety-sevens and ninety-eights, not fifties and ninety-eights—or you can go and ask if those are the correct marks. But you can't ask the low mark. You've got to go back and ask the high mark. Everybody knows the procedure. So we got to go ask the high mark. We ask the ninety-eight guy—another major Wall Street firm—and you know what he says? Remember, he knows he's high now. He goes, 'You're right. We were wrong. It's ninety-five.' In other words, he gave himself a margin of error, and he said, 'I'm going to drop it severely.' He looked at it with great intensity and said ninety-five. Now, we got nothing we can do but take the fifty and the ninety-five and average them. We have to repost our NAV. And now we go from minus 6 to minus 19"—minus 18.97 to be exact—"and that is game fucking over. By the way, the firm"—Goldman Sachs—"that sent us the fifty made a shit pot full of money in 2007 shorting the fucking market."

The effect of the new marks from Goldman Sachs on Cioffi's hedge funds was immediate and devastating. "Let me see if I can make this clear for you," the Bear executive continued. "Minus six percent announced this week. Oops—minus nineteen percent announced next week. Number one, nineteen percent is a pretty damn big number. So we announce minus nineteen percent. So what happens? Two fundamental things. One, this thing is in free fall—nineteen percent down. Number two, these guys are fucking idiots—six percent one week, nineteen percent the next week. How could that be?" Harder to understand, he said, was that Goldman's marks had been at 98 percent the month before. "Ninety-eight to fifty?" he asked, incredulous. "They were at ninety-eight the month before. There were no cash trades to imply anything like that. Nothing. There was nothing. And you know what? The way the procedure works, all we could [do] was go, 'But, but, but, but, but . . .' " After the decision to send out the revised, significantly lower NAV, Cioffi e-mailed John Geissinger, one of his Bear Stearns colleagues: "There is no market. Don't know what more to say about it at this time[.] [I]ts [*sic*] all academic anyway[.] 19% is doomsday, –18% does not matter one way or another John. We can keep it at 65. Or 50 or 0." The marks had had their devastating impact. "Bear is the canary in the mine shaft at this time," Bill Jamison, of Federated Investors (one of Bear Stearns's largest short-term lenders), wrote in a June 21 e-mail.

In an interview, Gary Cohn, Goldman's president, said the market changed dramatically through the course of the year and Goldman simply reacted to it. "We respect the markets," he said, "and we marked our books where we thought we could transact because some of this stuff wasn't transacting. Or where we actually had transacted. We were not misleading ourselves or our investors. We got blamed for this, by the way. We were not misleading people that bought securities with us at ninety-eight on the first of the month, and we didn't feel like, 'Oh, my God, we sold these to investors at ninety-eight. How can we mark them any lower than ninety-three?' We sold stuff at ninety-eight and marked it at fifty-five a month later. People didn't like that. Our clients didn't like that. They were pissed."

Some Goldman clients, though, turned to Goldman to help them buy insurance on CDOs they were worried about. For instance, on May 25, Avanish Bhavsar, vice president in the convertible bond group, wrote to Deeb Salem that the firm had a new client looking to buy credit-default swaps on CDOs sold in late 2006 and early 2007 as well as wanting to buy residential mortgage-backed securities from the second half of 2006. "They are axed to buy protection," he wrote. After some back-and-forth about what securities Goldman could offer "protection on," Swenson wrote to Salem that Goldman should start taking advantage of the market's reaction by offering "senior protection" to the "[S]treet on tier one stuff to cause maximum pain." Two days later, the same client wanted to buy more protection, and Swenson again believed Goldman was in a position to make some money by taking advantage of the increasing fear. "We should start killing the [senior] shorts in the [S]treet," he wrote to Salem on May 29. "Let's pick some high quality stuff that guys are hoping is wider today and offer protection tight—this will have people totally demoralized."

In his 2007 end-of-year self-evaluation, Salem wrote about how Goldman took advantage of the fear in the market. "In May, while we . . . remained as negative as ever on the fundamentals in sub-prime, the market was trading VERY SHORT, and was susceptible to a squeeze. We began to encourage this squeeze, with plans of getting very short again, after the short squeeze caused capitulation of these shorts. The strategy seemed do-able and brilliant, but once the negative fundamental news kept coming in at a tremendous rate, we stopped waiting for the shorts to capitulate, and instead just reinitiated shorts ourselves immediately."

Others in the market just seemed confused about pricing in general. For instance, at one point, Goldman offered to sell the securities to KKR Financial Holdings, a specialty finance company affiliated with KKR, the buyout firm. Cohn called up Nino Fanlo, one of the founders of KKR Financial Holdings, and offered to sell him Goldman's entire $10 billion portfolio at around 55 cents on the dollar, well below what the securities seemed to be trading for in the market. Fanlo called Cohn back and told him, "You're way off market. Everyone else is at eighty or eighty-five." If that was the case, Cohn told Fanlo, then KKR could have the windfall of buying the securities at 55 cents and selling them at 80 cents. Twenty-five cents' profit on $10 billion face amount of securities was a cool $2.5 billion. "You can sell them to every one of those dealers," Cohn told him. "Sell eighty, sell seventy-seven, sell seventy-six, sell seventy-five. Sell them all the way down to sixty. And I'll sell them to you at my mark, at fifty-five." Cohn said he was anxious to get the securities out of Goldman's inventory. "So if you can do that," he said he told Fanlo, "you can make yourself five billion dollars"—actually half that—"right now." Cohn had been trying to sell the securities at 55 cents on the dollar for a period of time and people would just hang up on him. A few days later, Fanlo called Cohn back. "He came back and said, 'I think your mark might be right,' " Cohn said. "And that mark went down to thirty."

At the time, one Goldman executive explained, dealers and counterparties across Wall Street were being similarly disingenuous—claiming the market still valued these squirrelly securities near par (100 cents) but refusing to buy any of them at Goldman's highly discounted marks. "This is something that I think is missed," he said, "and we're vilified when I think we certainly shouldn't be because our prices were indicative of where we were willing to deal. . . . If it's an opportunity and we're pricing it at sixty and someone else is at eighty, they can buy it at sixty from us. But the reality is everyone was kind of—I'm not gonna say living a lie—but they were in dreamland, to a certain extent, and they weren't willing to own up to it." He recalled a conversation that transpired between Goldman and AIG about the value of one security that AIG had insured and Goldman felt had declined in value and was seeking more collateral from AIG as compensation. "There was a back and forth exchange with some of the AIG employees that was on a taped phone conversation," he recalled. "The conversation was something like: 'Where do you think the market could be?' and he was like, 'I don't know, ninety? Could be eighty. I don't know.' And then there's a part where he says, 'I could probably buy some here, but then any accountant in the world would make me mark it down.' The answer is absolutely true. And so what do some of these shops do? They don't trade, so they don't have to take the markdown. We don't do that at Goldman Sachs."

———

ON NOVEMBER 1, 2010—nearly two and a half years later—Janet Broeckel, a Goldman managing director and associate general counsel, wrote to her counterpart at the Financial Crisis Inquiry Commission, the supposedly bipartisan commission looking into the causes of the financial crisis that began in 2007, to refute the suggestion that Goldman's decision in 2007 to lower its marks exacerbated the problems at the two Bear Stearns hedge funds. In Broeckel's letter, she challenged "the assertions" that Goldman's lower marks "were in some way responsible for the ultimate failure of the BSAM funds" by causing one of the funds to lower its NAV by 12.5 percentage points. "Rather," she wrote, "the revision in the Fund's NAV, and the ultimate failure of the BSAM funds, was attributable to the market-wide decline in prices of mortgage-backed securities during this period, and the highly leveraged Fund's concentrated holdings in those types of assets." She wrote that by providing the "new information" at the request of the FCIC, the commission "will conclude that Goldman Sachs' April 2007 month-end marks could not have caused the revision of the Fund's NAV or the ultimate failure of the BSAM funds."

The gist of Broeckel and Goldman's argument to the FCIC was that the hedge funds were already "in distress" by March 2007; that revisions to its marks in April could have, at most, caused a maximum of $26.3 million of downward revisions—and likely less—and, in any event, "could not have resulted in a 12.5 [percentage point] reduction in the NAV"; that BSAM did not, anyway, "mark its positions consistent with Goldman Sachs' marks"; and that in a June 7, 2007, conference call with Goldman, Cioffi told Goldman's employees that "three undisclosed dealers (not including Goldman Sachs) had significantly re-marked their April 2007 month-end marks"—marked "some positions down big," Cioffi supposedly told Goldman—"and that this caused the BSAM funds to restate their April NAV."

Curiously, the three firms aren't named, and there remains no credible evidence that any other firm on Wall Street was even remotely as aggressive—or accurate, by the way—during this time period as was Goldman with the marking of its CDO portfolio, which makes Goldman's denials all the more perplexing. Under normal circumstances, Goldman would be crowing about its mark-to-market prowess and how it—alone—was being honest about the value of its portfolio (as can be seen in any number of its contemporaneous e-mails), but the postcrash politics of the situation forced Goldman to try to argue against its own considerable skills in favor of deflecting blame.

Another of Goldman's arguments was that it "had no incentive" to cause the failure of the funds because Goldman was a short-term lender to them. At the end of April 2007, Broeckel wrote, Goldman had extended to the funds $453 million in "repo loans," secured by the funds' mortgage-backed securities and so "simply put, it was against the financial interest of Goldman Sachs to cause the failure of the Fund and it did not do so." She noted that had the fund not been able to repay its repo loans, Goldman would have seized the collateral—the mortgage-backed securities—and then sold it into the market and likely "would have suffered significant losses as the securities declined in value throughout the time period." What Broeckel did not mention was that not only was this fact irrelevant, since Goldman was a secured lender, but that the funds *did* default on their repo loans, that Goldman *did* seize the collateral and threatened to sell it into the market, and that Bear Stearns then came to the rescue of the repo lenders, including Goldman and many others, by taking them out at 100 cents on the dollar—a decision that ultimately led to the collapse of Bear Stearns in March 2008.

Broeckel's letter did not mention—or include—Craig Broderick's fateful May 11 e-mail about Goldman's decision to lower its marks and convey that information to the market. Instead, the Goldman documents purport to show that Goldman's marks barely changed at all during March, April, and May 2007 on the squirrelly securities that the Bear hedge funds had in their portfolios, despite what was going on at Goldman. For instance, an ABACUS 2006 HGS1 tranche that was valued at 65 cents in March was valued at 65 cents in May. Another tranche of the same security that was valued at 55 cents in April was valued at 55 cents in May. It's as if the firm would rather appear to be just like every other firm rather than take a victory lap for seeing—and acting upon—what others didn't and couldn't.

The actual timing itself—clearly it was May—was moot because the moment the bid-asked spread on these securities widened to the point where there needed to be such an extensive debate about their value was the beginning of the end for Bear Stearns. For its part, the Financial Crisis Inquiry Commission concluded: "Broderick was right about the impact of Goldman's marks on clients and counterparties." The FCIC's report continued, contrary to what Broeckel, the Goldman attorney, hoped: "As the crisis unfolded, Goldman marked mortgage-related securities at prices that were significantly lower than those of other companies. Goldman knew that those lower marks might hurt those other companies—including some clients—because they could require marking down those assets and similar assets. In addition, Goldman's marks would get picked up by competitors in dealer surveys. As a result, Goldman's marks could contribute to other companies recording 'mark-to-market' losses: that is, the reported value of their assets could fall and their earnings would decline."

———

AFTER ITS SPIKE downward in February 2007 to around 60, the ABX index recovered back to the high 70s by mid-April 2007, before plunging again. The cost for Goldman to continue to hedge its risk against the collapse of the subprime index increased along with the general worry in the market. But Goldman gave Swenson and Birnbaum approval to keep hedging against the mortgage market, despite the rising cost of the insurance. On the morning of April 5, Deeb Salem wrote to Swenson with the idea of selling $200 million of protection against the ABX index. Seven minutes later, Sweeny replied to Salem: "Make that $500mm." A week or so later, though, the market had moved again against Birnbaum's short positions on the ABX index and showed a loss.

Birnbaum and his colleagues kept riding this roller coaster for the next few months. Some days the shorts looked brilliant. Some days the shorts inflicted serious pain. Some days the message was ambiguous. For instance, on May 17, after some bad news about the performance of one CDO that Goldman had some long positions in, Deeb Salem wrote to Swenson that the "bad news" was the firm lost $2.5 million on the write-down of the long positions but the "good news" was that the firm had bought insurance on one of the same securities. "[W]e make $5mm," Salem wrote.

Birnbaum knew he would be proven right if he was just permitted to stick with the trade. He also knew he was right about the falling value of the residual CDO positions the firm was desperately trying to sell. And this meant more screaming from counterparties on the other side of these marks. "Every month brought more and more markdowns," he explained. "But the original motivation for all this was very simple. It was: We owned some of this stuff, and there's a discipline—if you mark the stuff at seventy you're going to be much more likely to accept selling it at ninety-five than if you don't. And we're like, 'Get this shit out of here because this stuff is worth nothing. And there's going to be a window of opportunity to sell this stuff. Take the window. Take your losses and move on.' " This was the message that Birnbaum, Swenson, Salem, and Primer kept pounding away at with the senior executives at Goldman. Sometimes being right, though, does not matter. "From where I was sitting I just saw this thing as sort of like a comedic stalemate where the market was in denial for a long time about things still being worth par," Birnbaum said. "We felt that it was worth a lot less. Somebody was gonna have to blink."

––––––

THAT MOMENT CAME at the beginning of June when the two Bear Stearns hedge funds were forced to revise their monthly performance numbers downward in the wake of the delivery of Goldman's new marks. A June 7 letter to investors not only announced April's 18.97 percent decline in the Enhanced Leverage Fund—just three weeks after a May 15 letter said the loss was 6.5 percent—but also announced the news that redemptions, of some $250 million on a $642 million fund, would be suspended because the "investment manager believes the company will not have sufficient liquid assets to pay investors." On a conference call with investors the next day to discuss the fund's poor performance, Cioffi and Tannin refused to answer investors' questions. "They didn't want to say anything," one investor said. Inevitably, the increasingly angry investors in the fund put the word out about what was happening. On June 12, buried deep in the paper, the *Wall Street Journal* reported that the Enhanced Leverage Fund had fallen 23 percent in the first four months of the year and that redemptions from the fund had been blocked. "While the fund is down significantly, it is hard to tell what the actual losses will be because a few good trades could bring it back into the clear," the *Journal* wrote. "Still, given the fund's heavy exposure to this deteriorating corner of the mortgage market, in which many people are struggling to pay down their home loans, the news isn't good." The paper suggested that while the fund's losses would be a "blow" to Cioffi and Tannin, the "paper losses will have a limited impact on Bear" because the firm only had $45 million invested in the fund.

Ironically, that same day, BSAM was offering for sale $3.86 billion of the highest-rated mortgage-related securities in Cioffi's hedge funds as a way to raise cash. That sale did not go well. A week later, Cioffi and BSAM ended up negotiating a number of bilateral agreements with the hedge funds' lenders, including Goldman Sachs, whereby Goldman would take back its collateral and then attempt to sell it in the market. As part of the deal Bear Stearns reached with many of the lenders, Goldman would be made whole with either cash or securities. Among the collateral that Goldman took back was $300 million of the $400 million Timberwolf securities Cioffi had bought in March from Goldman at par. In an internal June 22 memorandum, Goldman's mortgage trading desk spread the news that it now had to sell a $200 million slug of Timberwolf, at 98.5 cents on the dollar, and a $100 million slug at 95 cents on the dollar. Goldman was eager to sell the Timberwolf securities and advertised them as "Senior CDO axes" and as a "Super AAA Offering." The trading desk described the Timberwolf securities as being senior in the capital structure to between 40 percent and 50 percent of other "Aaa/AAA bonds." After receiving the memo, Montag wrote to Sparks asking for a "complete rundown of everything we bought from [BSAM] and what[']s left?" Sparks offered to get Montag "a complete summary with details" but confirmed that the "main thing left is [$]300mm [T]imberwolfs" as well as "some small [RMBS]"—residential mortgage-backed securities— "positions." Everything else had been sold. Within minutes, Montag replied, "[B]oy that [T]imberwo[l]f was one shitty deal"—giving Senator Levin the cudgel he used to bash Goldman for eleven hours at the end of April 2010. A week later, the Timberwolf securities still had not sold.

The two Bear Stearns hedge funds were officially liquidated on July 30. Investors in the funds lost around $1.5 billion. Since Bear had become the short-term lender to the funds on June 22—replacing Goldman, among others—when the funds were liquidated, Bear Stearns seized $1.3 billion of underlying collateral, which it eventually wrote down in the fourth quarter of 2007, leading to the first quarterly loss in the firm's eighty-five-year history. Bear Stearns collapsed in March 2008 and was scooped up by JPMorgan Chase for $10 a share, after having reached an all-time high of $172.69 in January 2007. To get the JPMorgan deal with Bear done, American taxpayers agreed to absorb losses on $29 billion of "toxic securities" that JPMorgan did not want. As of September 30, 2010, those securities were worth $27 billion, according to the New York Fed.

———

FOR BIRNBAUM, THE trouble at the Bear Stearns hedge funds was a sweet symphony. "Once the Cioffi news came there was really a couple of us on the desk who were like, 'Okay, that's the Come-to-Jesus moment. It's gonna be a big mark-to-market event here. We're gonna go for it again—meaning short the market again.' We had covered a lot of our shorts because the VAR police found us—they caught up to us and we did that in March. We covered, meaning we effectively gave a lot of our positions to hedge-fund managers, gave them our shorts, and they benefited. Many homes in Italy were purchased off of those shorts." Despite being forced to sell off its profitable short bets in March, Birnbaum's desk still killed it during the second quarter of 2007. According to internal Goldman documents, his group made $457 million in profit for the quarter, up from $288 million in profit in the first quarter. Indeed, the structured products trading group seemed to be carrying the overall mortgage department, which managed to lose $174 million in the second quarter—despite Birnbaum's profitable contribution—in large part due to the write-downs on Goldman's long positions in mortgages in order to sell them off into the market.

In early July, in part because the group's VAR had been reduced dramatically in the second quarter, Birnbaum moved quickly to bet the ABX would fall in the wake of the Cioffi hedge-fund debacle. He did not have to seek the approval of the senior executives to make the bet. "We're given a set of quantitative parameters, a box in which we're supposed to play from a risk standpoint," he explained. "And as long as we stay within those parameters, you can do what you want. We were well within our box. So we started shorting the market again." He sold the ABX index like crazy. And by July 12, the bet was already paying off, a fact that can be seen even though an e-mail started by Birnbaum that day has been heavily redacted by the U.S. Senate subcommittee that released it. He sent around the results of the trading of the ABX index to [redacted] at noon that day. Five minutes later, he got a reply: "That's the way to make my markets, [J]oshua, that's my boy!" Birnbaum responded: "Seen massive flows recently. Many accounts 'throwing in the towel.' Anybody who tried to call the bottom left in bodybags." Then came the reply: "We hit a bilsky"—a billion dollars—"in PNL today. . . . I'm not [J]ohn [P]aulson though," causing Birnbaum to reply: "He's definitely the man in this space, up [$]2–3 bil[lion] on this trade. We were giving him a run for his money for a while but now are a definitive #2."

By July 20, the profits Birnbaum was racking up caught the attention of Blankfein. He asked Viniar and Cohn to explain why the numbers were so big. After some back and forth in a fairly incomprehensible internal jargon about hedges here and there, Cohn explained to Blankfein that basically the firm had a "net short" on the mortgage market that was paying off. "Bet all the dads at camp are talking about the same stuff," Blankfein responded to Cohn. On July 24, the daily P&L showed Birnbaum's secondary trading group up $72 million for the day, and overall the firm had made $9 million in pretax earnings. Blankfein e-mailed Viniar and

Cohn. "I've seen worse," he wrote, with some understatement. Viniar replied, "Mergers, overnight [A]sia and especially short mortgages saved the day."

The next day was even better. Birnbaum's trading bet was up $373 million. Goldman then used the cover of Birnbaum's extraordinary profits to write down further the value of the CDOs the firm retained, and could not sell, as well as other mortgage-related residuals. Together, the write-offs in these long positions cost the firm $322 million, but because of Birnbaum's short position, the mortgage group was still able to show a profit for the day of $48.7 million. "Tells you what might be happening to people who don't have the big short," Viniar wrote to Cohn that day. On July 26, Montag wrote to Blankfein and Cohn that "mortgages goi[n]g to show up [$]135 [million] or so today it seems." Blankfein responded: "Is that right?" And then Montag increased the estimate to $170 million "hopefully." Blankfein wondered, "I assume we are properly marking down our longs?" To which Montag responded that the firm had "marked things down [$]100 [million] yesterday. Could have done [$]15 [million] or more today but don't know." He added the thought that there was "not a lot left" to mark down. No doubt pleased with the firm's good fortune, Blankfein replied, "If the shorts went up today, shouldn't the longs have dropped (unless they're already at zero . . . [?])."

Birnbaum understood why the firm would net its mortgage losses against his gains, but it still rankled. "The firm was a great beneficiary of the idea that 'it's very easy to have a clear head and to look at something in an unbiased way when marking things correctly isn't going to hurt you,'" he said. "Right? Because our desk was as short as it was and we were making money on the way down, we effectively had all this dry powder in terms of P&L to play with." Another trader echoed this sentiment: "If we're making $50 million in one day on our desk, it was not unusual to say, 'Okay, we got $50 million to play with. These CDOs, let's mark them down further.' And it would drive us crazy because, you know, we'd be high-fiving, going, 'We made 100 million bucks today.' I mean it was unheard of in one day to make $100 million. And then when the P&Ls would actually go through, you'd be like, 'Oh, the department's up $20 million.'"

This set Goldman apart in the market and caused a fair amount of resentment at other firms that resisted marking their books to the real market, because doing so would mean having to absorb some serious losses. "Other firms didn't have that luxury," Birnbaum explained. "Everybody else couldn't afford to mark this stuff 'cause they had so much of this shit, they couldn't mark it. . . . They were in denial. If they took the full extent of our marks, these guys would have failed earlier.

Everyone was trying to buy time. Just what any trader who's losing money would try to do."

Another part of Birnbaum's hedging strategy had nothing to do with mortgages, or the ABX index, or credit-default swaps. Rather, it was a simple bet that the equity of the firms most heavily involved in the mortgage sector would fall. He made these bets by buying put options, whereby he paid a premium to a third party who was willing to take the opposite side of the trade. Birnbaum was betting the stocks would fall in price by a given date, and the seller of the put option was betting the opposite—that the price of the stocks would go up. According to a July 24 e-mail from Birnbaum, his put options had made a profit of $49 million since he had bought them. Among those companies whose stock he bet would fall were Bear Stearns, Moody's, Washington Mutual, Capital One Financial, and National City.

It is not clear from the note when Birnbaum started buying the puts, but it is clear that he began sometime before June 21, since that was the date, he wrote, that his group "paused" in "our equities trading while we worked with management and market risk to come up with quantitative limits for these positions." He wrote that he thought "we are getting close" to an agreement on the limits but in the meantime he wanted approval "to opportunistically buy puts" on those companies with exposure to the mortgage market. He cited specifically thirteen companies he wanted to buy puts for, including Bear Stearns, Lehman Brothers, Merrill Lynch, Morgan Stanley, and Countrywide. Donald Mullen, then head of Goldman's U.S. credit sales and trading, having joined Goldman from Bear Stearns in 2001, wrote to Sparks the day after receiving Birnbaum's memo with a sharp rebuke: "He is too large [redacted]. Bruce [Petersen, another Goldman managing director] is going to discuss w[ith] him today."

ON AUGUST 9, evidence of the international spread of America's subprime crisis showed up in Paris when BNP Paribas, France's largest bank, blocked withdrawals from three investment funds, which had about $2 billion in assets on August 7, because the bank could no longer "fairly" value them due to a "complete evaporation of liquidity in certain market segments of the U.S. securitization market." BNP's action followed an August 3 announcement by Union Investment Management, Germany's third-largest mutual fund manager, that it had stopped permitting withdrawals from one of its funds after investors pulled out 10 percent of the fund's assets. Also on August 9, the European Central Bank injected £95 billion into the overnight lending market "in an unprecedented response to a sudden demand for cash from banks roiled by the subprime crisis," Bloomberg reported, and more than the central bank had lent after the September 11 attacks.

Hank Paulson, who had been treasury secretary for a year, had been worried about just such a "crisis in the financial markets" since he took his post. He kept his weekly breakfast appointment that day with Ben Bernanke, the chairman of the Federal Reserve, and managed to gobble up his usual bowl of oatmeal, orange juice, ice water, and Diet Coke. "Ben shared my concerns with the developments in Europe," Paulson wrote later in his memoir, *On the Brink.*

When he got back to his office he spoke with Wall Street CEOs, including Blankfein, Richard Fuld at Lehman, Stephen Schwarzman at Blackstone Group, and Stanley O'Neal at Merrill Lynch. "All these CEOs were on edge," Paulson wrote. O'Neal, for one, remembered that call with Paulson. "If you had called me a couple of days ago I would have been more sanguine," he told Paulson. "I'm not anymore." Paulson asked why. "Because you had overnight secured lending fail between rated banks," he told Paulson. "There's something more going on, and it means there are potential risks [to the system, beyond] what we think we see on the surface." O'Neal also knew that Merrill had tens of billions of dollars of CDOs marked at or near par, a ticking time bomb.

On August 17, the Federal Reserve began to take its first steps to try to stanch the bleeding. The central bank cut interest rates by 50 basis points in recognition that "financial market conditions have deteriorated, and tighter credit conditions and increased uncertainty have the potential to restrain economic growth going forward." The Fed pledged to "act as needed to mitigate the adverse effects on the economy arising from the disruptions in financial markets." The Fed also announced that banks could borrow from the discount window "for as long as 30 days, renewable by the borrower," in order for banks to have "greater assurance about the cost and availability of funding." The new plan would remain in effect "until the Federal Reserve determines that market liquidity has improved materially." The two-pronged approach of lowering interest rates and effectively substituting the Fed's balance sheet for the balance sheets of the country's financial institutions, whether troubled or not, arose from a Fed offsite in Jackson Hole, Wyoming, during the third week of August 2007. New York Fed president Tim Geithner dubbed this new approach to the growing crisis "the Bernanke Doctrine."

As the contagion of the emerging credit crisis began being felt across the globe in the late summer of 2007, Goldman continued to rake in the profits from Birnbaum's hedges. "Department-wide P&L for the week was $375mm," Sparks wrote to Montag on July 29, and then added that the trading "P&L on the week was $234mm, with CMBS, CDOs and RMBS/ABX shorts all contributing." Two days later, Montag updated Blankfein—in a mostly incomprehensible e-mail—on the profits and the market, as well as the firm's ongoing efforts to cover short positions and reduce the VAR associated with Birnbaum's hedging. In a presentation that Sparks prepared for Montag to give to Goldman's Management Committee on August 6, Swenson and Birnbaum reported that it was "a phenomenal week for covering our Index shorts" with one desk buying "$3.3 [billion] of ABX index across various vintages and ratings over the past week," with $1.5 billion being used to "cover shorts."

By the following week, though, the VAR police were back on the prowl. One of them pointed out in a widely circulated internal e-mail that Birnbaum's trading group's VAR seemed to be around $100 million, well above its $35 million limit. "[A]re you getting any more heat to cut/cover risk?" Birnbaum wrote to Deeb Salem, on August 9. Birnbaum wrote that he had asked about the VAR police only because he saw the "note about mortgages dropping back down to a permanent limit of [$]35mm (which we are way over). [T]his would mark a change of their recent policy to just keep increasing ou[r] limit. [M]akes me a little nervous that we may be told to do something stupid." Salem quickly understood Birnbaum's point. "[I] do think that is a real concern," he replied. "[H]ow quickly can you work with [the VAR police] to get them to revise our VAR to a more realistic number?" Birnbaum replied that he had a meeting with them on Tuesday, where apparently he was able to get the VAR limit of $110 million extended until August 21. But, on August 13, when VAR for trading overall had increased to $159 million, from $150 million, Viniar was explicit. "No comment necessary," he wrote. "Get it down." Gary Cohn echoed Viniar's comment two days later, after the trading VAR had increased to $165 million. "There is no room for debate," he wrote. "We must get down now."

The concern about the rising VAR on the mortgage trading desk revealed a larger debate then percolating around Goldman: how to take advantage of the misery being felt by other firms as the mortgage markets started to collapse. The problem was that Birnbaum and company continued to see huge profit opportunities to buy when others were forced sellers, but this required putting more capital at risk, which increased the VAR and upset the police, as well as David Viniar and Gary Cohn. There may have been no room for debate, according to Cohn, but the debate was raging all the same.

Sparks took a stab at trying to explain the opportunity up the chain of command. "Mortgage CDO market has continued to be hammered with combination of the large downward move in subprime RMBS, rating agencies action, and no liquidity," he wrote to Montag, Viniar, Cohn, and others. He then gave them the example of how Goldman's own Timberwolf deal, which had been marked at 80 cents on the dollar at the end of May, was then—on August 14—marked at around 20 cents on the dollar. "[I]t's not just liquidity," he wrote, "there are fundamental cash-flow issues." He then explained that the "best opportunity to make a bunch of money" in the near term was to buy the AAA ABX index as well as other residential mortgage-backed securities. He wrote that he thought that the market seemed to be overreacting and that the mortgage desk had been covering its shorts—at a big profit—but "we will likely come to you soon and say we'd like to get long billions" while also staying short the riskier part of the mortgage market. Cohn responded to Sparks that he wanted him to "talk to me before you go long," suggesting that the decision would not be reached simply.

By August 20, Sparks had begun to further flesh out the trade. In an e-mail to Cohn, Winkelried, Viniar, Montag, and Mullen, titled "Big Opportunity," he reviewed for his bosses the ongoing market meltdown. "We are seeing large liquidations," he wrote, brought on by a need for liquidity and that was "fear and technically driven." He mentioned that CIT—the large commercial lender—had called and wanted Goldman to buy $10 billion worth of its loans. "We think it is now time to start using balance sheet," he continued, "and it is a unique opportunity with real upside . . . there's the opportunity for us to make 5–10+ points if we have a longer term hold." Winkelried responded to Sparks, in part, "Clearly [an] opportunity."

The next day, Birnbaum wrote to many of the same executives with his version of what Sparks had described the day before: "The mortgage department thinks there is currently an extraordinary opportunity for those with dry powder to add AAA subprime risk in either cash or synthetic form," he continued. He suggested that the trade would reduce the mortgage department's VAR by $75 million and that the arbitrage opportunity implied by the trade could result in big profits. He thought there would be plenty of distressed sellers to provide the supply and that he intended to "share this trade quietly with selected risk partners."

The proposal was a bold one, and the profit potential huge if Birnbaum and company were correct. But there also seemed to be some concern at the firm's highest levels that the group's recent success had made them a bit cocky. "It would help to manage these guys if u would not answer these guys and keep bouncing them back to Tom [Montag] and I," Mullen wrote to Winkelried and Cohn. Cohn responded, "Got that and am not answering" but then had to admit the trade had merit. "I do like the idea but you call," he replied to Mullen. Montag then weighed in. "Just to be clear," he wrote, "[t]his is buy and hold not buy and sell strategy," suggesting that the firm's capital would be committed for some time. Cohn got that. In the end, Sparks and Birnbaum got the green light to "opportunistically . . . buy assets" at the same time that the mortgage trading group was "significant[ly] covering [its] short positions," according to a presentation given to the Goldman board of directors in September 2007.

By the end of August (and Goldman's third quarter), there was no denying the Birnbaum juggernaut. His structured products trading group was carrying the mortgage business at the firm and keeping it profitable at a time when Goldman's main competitors on Wall Street were struggling mightily. According to a September 17 presentation delivered to the Goldman board of directors, during the firm's third quarter, the mortgage origination machine at the firm lost some $200 million—mostly from writing down the value of soured loans—while Birnbaum and company racked up revenue, which was close to pure profit, of $731 million. Indeed, of the $735 million of gross revenues made by Goldman's mortgage business in the third quarter of 2007, $731 million, or 99.5 percent, came from Birnbaum's desk. What's more, of the $1.017 billion of gross revenues the mortgage business generated through the first nine months of 2007, $955 million—or close to Birnbaum's "bilsky"—came from his desk.

Through all the turmoil, Goldman was minting money. In the third quarter of 2007, Goldman's revenues were $12.3 billion—its second-highest quarter of revenue ever—and its net income was $2.9 billion. Goldman's return on equity was 31.6 percent, nearly unheard of for a public company. On the earnings call, Viniar spoke specifically about the firm's performance in mortgages. "The mortgage sector continues to be challenged and there was a broad decline in the value of mortgage inventory during the third quarter," he said. "As a result, we took significant markdowns on our long inventory positions during the quarter, as we had in the previous two quarters. Although we took these marks, our risk bias in that market was to be short and that net short position was profitable. I would also note that you've heard me express our generally negative views on the outlook for mortgages since the beginning of the year, so you could correctly assume that we've been very aggressive in reducing our long mortgage exposure and conservatively marking down our long mortgage positions."

Peter Eavis, a writer at *Fortune,* was the first to pick up on what he called Goldman's "stunning strategy" of making a "huge, shrewd bet" while "the credit markets went sour" and "seems to have won big." Eavis was not sure how Goldman pulled it off, but he observed cannily on September 20 that "[a]s the credit markets fell apart over the summer, causing the prices of hundreds of billions of mortgage-backed bonds to plunge, Goldman Sachs had already positioned itself so that it would profit massively from a decline in those securities." He noted that Goldman's third-quarter earnings "were far above expectations" with the "chief contributor to earnings blowout" being "trades that made money from price drops in mortgage-backed securities." When he tried to figure out how much Goldman had made from the bearish bets—he did not know who at Goldman had been responsible for them—he observed that Viniar, on the third-quarter conference call, "declined to give a number for the amount of money Goldman made on its mortgage short."

Not surprisingly, Eavis had not known—could not have known—that Birnbaum and company had been shorting the mortgage market for the previous nine or so months. What he did figure out, correctly, was that a decision would take time to make and to implement. "Amassing a large bearish position in mortgages would have required planning and direction from a senior level," he wrote. "On the conference call, Viniar said the bet was executed across the whole mortgage business, implying that it wasn't the work of one swashbuckling trader or trading desk. Of course, the prescience of the short sale would seem to confirm the view that Goldman is the nimblest, and perhaps smartest, brokerage on Wall Street." He noted that Bear Stearns's "mortgage business suffered considerably in the quarter" and Morgan Stanley "wasn't as well hedged to bond losses" (in fact, according to Michael Lewis's *The Big Short*, Morgan Stanley would go on to lose $9 billion betting incorrectly on the outcome of the mortgage meltdown).

Lucas van Praag, Goldman's longtime head of public relations, sent the *Fortune* article around to the firm's top executives. Winkelried, for one, did not appreciate it. "Once again[,] they completely miss the franchise strength and attribute it all to positions and bets," he wrote to the executive team. Blankfein elaborated on Winkelried's observation. "Also, the short position wasn't a bet," he wrote. "It was a hedge. I.e., the avoidance of a bet. Which is why for a part it subtracted from VAR, not added to VAR." (This was a very subtle argument, making a fine distinction—and Blankfein kept making it over and over again, even though few people could follow his logic. The fact of the matter was that Goldman had bet—correctly—that the mortgage market would collapse.) In an e-mail a few minutes later sent from his BlackBerry, Peter Kraus, a longtime

Goldman partner and then the co-head of the firm's investment management division, provided Blankfein a particularly unique—perhaps even myopic—insight. He explained that since the third-quarter earnings announcement he had met with more than ten prospective and current clients. "The institutions don't and I wouldn't expect them to, make any comments like [']ur good at making money for urself but not us,[']" he wrote to Blankfein. "The individuals do sometimes, but while it requires the utmost humility from us in response[,] I feel very strongly it binds clients even closer to the firm, because the alternative of [']take ur money to a firm who is an under performer and not the best,['] just isn't reasonable. Clients ultimately believe association with the best is good for them in the long run." Needless to say, Blankfein did not respond to Kraus.

––––––

On October 11, Moody's—one of the three large bond-rating agencies—downgraded $32 billion of publicly traded mortgage debt that had been originally issued in 2006, the second large and sweeping ratings downgrade by Moody's in six weeks. Swenson shared the news with Montag and Mullen. "This will eventually filter into downgrades in CDOs," he wrote, adding that one of the ABX indexes sold off "by a point" after the news, meaning more profits for Goldman. "ABS [asset-backed securities] Desk P and L will be up between [$]30 and [$]35mm today," he added. Mullen responded, "Nice day." There was also a discussion of other, more technical consequences of the Moody's downgrade that Swenson thought would result in interest payments on some of the bonds "being shut off," or not being paid, which would lower dramatically the value of the securities and mean big profits for anyone—like Goldman—betting they would lose value. "Sounds like we will make some serious money," Mullen responded. Concluded Swenson, "Yes we are well positioned." Actually, the profit news that day was even better than Swenson had originally thought. Instead of the mortgage trading desk making between $30 million and $35 million as a result of the Moody's downgrades, the desk actually ended up making $110 million, $65 million of which came from "yesterday's downgrades which lead to the selloff in aa[-rated bonds] through bbb[minus-rated bonds] today," Swenson wrote to Mullen, taking the proverbial "victory lap" that Wall Streeters are so well trained to do, even at Goldman Sachs, the champion of teamwork. "Great Day!" Mullen replied.

Inevitably, though, since trading is a zero-sum game where for every winner there is a loser, at the same time that Goldman was raking in profits, some of its clients, or "counterparties" as they were known on the trading desks, were bound to be suffering. Worse, apparently, some of

Goldman's European salespeople, who had helped to sell the firm's "axes" earlier in the year, did not feel they were getting the recognition they deserved for pushing the deals out the door. Yusuf Aliredha, Goldman's London-based co-head of European fixed-income sales, wrote to Sparks on October 17: "Dan, Real bad feeling across European sales about some of the trades we did with clients. The damage this has done to our franchise is very significant. Aggregate loss for our clients on just these 5 trades alone is 1bln+. In addition team feels that recognition (sales credits and otherwise) they received for getting this business done was not consistent at all with money it ended making/saving the firm."

Aliredha then described five 2007 CDO deals that Goldman had created and then sold to investors that now had come back to haunt the firm, at least if unhappy clients were any gauge. One of the five was the ABACUS deal, completed just a few months earlier by Fabrice Tourre and Jonathan Egol. Aliredha seemed concerned that ABN AMRO, the big Dutch bank that had shared with ACA around $1 billion of mortgage-related risk on the deal, was not happy. "At the time this was the biggest axe for Egol & Fabrice as the portfolio was predominantly subprime BBB names picked by ACA," he wrote to Sparks. "ABN was the only intermediary who was willing to take ACA exposure. . . . Not sure what the total amount of collateral that's been called so far, but it must be at least $200–300MM on this trade alone." In other words, Goldman was cleaning up and its clients—sophisticated investors to be sure—got killed.

––––––

IN AN OCTOBER 29 internal presentation to the Goldman tax department titled "Contagion and Crowded Trades," Craig Broderick, the firm's chief risk officer, explained how the firm had navigated the rough waters in the credit markets and had reached port safely. He started by commenting that the "overall market events since Jan[uary] of this year—but largely concentrated over the summer period—are as dramatic and interesting as any I've seen in 25+ years in the business. I use the word 'interesting' only because we're past the worst of it at least as far as our own exposure goes[,] [but it was] pretty scary for a while."

He acknowledged that the firm's willingness to mark down its long positions "gave rise to all sorts of stories about how we are marking our books" and to questions about the "significant differences in marks vs. competitors" and that "there are a lot of disputes with clients," but he viewed Goldman's mark-to-market prowess as a singular accomplishment. "Best success here was on our marks and our collateral calls," he continued. "First mover advantage, most realistic marks, competitors unwilling to mark fully given implications for their own trading positions." The next day, Blankfein asked Viniar and Cohn how the "review of the mortgage and [CDO] books" went. Viniar responded, "Extremely well. You will be very pleased."

It was increasingly easy to see why. According to an internal Goldman document about the quarterly performance of the mortgage group, Birnbaum was still printing money, although the pace at which he was doing it had—understandably—slowed in the fourth quarter. Nevertheless, the profit numbers were astounding, especially compared to the financial bloodbath occurring across the rest of Wall Street. Through October 26, Birnbaum's group had made $3.7 billion in profit, more than offsetting losses of around $2.4 billion in the rest of the mortgage business.

———

PICKING UP ON the idea *Fortune* had explored a few months earlier, the *New York Times* explored the idea of how Goldman had done it. "For more than three months, as turmoil in the credit market has swept wildly through Wall Street, one mighty investment bank after another has been brought to its knees, leveled by multibillion-dollar blows to their bottom lines," observed reporters Jenny Anderson and Landon Thomas Jr. "And then there is Goldman Sachs. Rarely on Wall Street, where money travels in herds, has one firm gotten it so right when nearly everyone else was getting it so wrong. So far, three banking chief executives have been forced to resign after the debacle and the pay for nearly all the survivors is expected to be cut deeply." Meanwhile, Blankfein—the *Times* predicted—would easily top the $54 million in compensation he had made in 2006 and likely would receive as much as $75 million. (In the event, it was closer to $70 million.)

The paper then explained how the "notoriously nervous" Viniar called for a "mortgage risk" meeting in his "meticulous" thirtieth-floor conference room in December 2006. "After reviewing the full portfolio with other executives, his message was clear: the bank should reduce its stockpile of mortgages and mortgage-related securities and buy expensive insurance as protection against further losses," the *Times* continued. "With its mix of swagger and contrary thinking, it was just the kind of bet that has long defined Goldman's hard-nosed, go-it-alone style." When the mortgage market crashed in July, Goldman had already off-loaded much of its mortgage-related risks, the paper continued, quoting Guy Moszkowski, an analyst at Merrill Lynch who covered the investment banks. "If you look at their profitability through a period of intense credit and mortgage market turmoil," Moszkowski said, "you'd have to give them an A-plus." Anderson and Thomas then reported: "This contrast in performance has been hard for competitors to swallow. The bank that seems to have a hand in so many deals and products and regions made more money in the boom and, at least so far, has managed to keep making money through the bust. . . . Goldman's secret sauce, say executives, analysts and historians, is high-octane business acumen, tempered with paranoia and institutionally encouraged—though not always observed—humility."

The article also made the important points that Goldman's "flat hierarchy" encouraged "executives to challenge one another" so that "good ideas can get to the top," and that the firm's risk department had as much status, authority—and compensation—at the firm as did the rainmakers, a claim no other Wall Street firm could make. "At Goldman, the controller's office—the group responsible for valuing the firm's huge positions—has 1,100 people, including 20 Ph.D.'s," the *Times* continued. "If there is a dispute, the controller is always deemed right unless the trading desk can make a convincing case for an alternate valuation. 'The risk controllers are taken very seriously,' Mr. Moszkowski said. 'They have a level of authority and power that is, on balance, equivalent to the people running the cash registers. It's not as clear that that happens everywhere.' "

Anderson and Thomas went so far as to compare Goldman Sachs at the end of 2007 to the power and influence that J. P. Morgan & Co. had between 1895 and 1930. "But, like Morgan, they could be victimized by their own success," Charles Geisst, a Wall Street historian at Manhattan College, told the paper. "Mr. Blankfein of Goldman seems aware of all this," the article concluded. "When asked at a conference how he hoped to take advantage of his competitors' weakened position, he said Goldman was focused on making fewer mistakes. But he wryly observed that the firm would surely take it on the chin at some point, too. 'Everybody,' he said, 'gets their turn.' "

Not surprisingly, Lucas van Praag had spent a considerable amount of time "working with" the *Times* reporters to make sure Goldman's perspectives were incorporated into their front-page article as much as possible. This was hardly surprising, of course, as nearly every piece of responsible journalism involves such give-and-take. The Sunday afternoon before the story was to run, van Praag briefed Blankfein, in writing, about what was coming, providing a rare glimpse into how Wall Street executives try to manage the journalists who cover them. For starters, van Praag explained that "we spent a lot of time on culture as a differentiator" with Anderson and that "she was receptive." But, alas, he also reported, "Tomorrow's story will, of course, have 'balance' ([i.e.,] stuff we don't like). In this instance, we have spent much time discussing conflicts, and I think we've made some progress as she a[c]knowledges that most of her sources on the subject are financial sponsors which fact, unless edited out, is included and gives context." (The story did mention that some private-equity firms worry that Goldman's huge private-equity fund had become an unwelcome competitor.)

Van Praag also warned Blankfein of an emerging conspiracy theory about the firm, which the *Times* article might broach. "The article references the extraordinary influence GS alums have—the most topical being John Thain," the former Goldman president and co–chief operating officer and former CEO of the New York Stock Exchange who had, the previous week, agreed to become CEO of Merrill Lynch in the wake of the firing of Stan O'Neal a few weeks earlier. "[B]ut [Bob] Rubin, Hank [Paulson], Duncan [Niederauer, who replaced Thain as CEO of the NYSE] et al[.] are all in the mix too. She hasn't gone as far as suggesting that there is a credible conspiracy theory (unlike her former colleague at the *NY Post*). She does, however, make the point that it feels like GS is running everything."

The twin ideas that Goldman was "running everything" and that there was a "credible conspiracy theory" involving the firm would, soon enough, be major public-relations nightmares for the firm but, at that moment anyway, Blankfein was far more concerned about the promulgation of the idea that somehow the firm had avoided the mortgage meltdown and made a bunch of money. "Of course we didn't dodge the mortgage mess," Blankfein wrote to van Praag. "We lost money, then made more than we lost because of shorts"—so the firm *did* make money, and what he had previously called a "hedge" he was now referring to as a "short." In any event, his next thought made the most sense. "Also, it's not over, so who knows how it will turn out ultimately," he concluded. Unable to resist adding his two cents, Gary Cohn, who had been copied on the correspondence, chimed into the discussion with the thought that Goldman was "just smaller in the toxic products."

But, increasingly, investors and the media wanted to know how Goldman had bested the competition, succeeding wildly where others had failed. To try to answer this question, and in preparation for Goldman's fourth-quarter earnings release—scheduled for December 18—Viniar prepared a one-page PowerPoint slide titled "How Did GS Avoid the Mortgage Crisis?" and subtitled "Our Response." As had Broderick before him, Viniar touched on familiar themes, reinforcing a number of Goldman verities. "We were actively managing our mortgage exposure throughout 2006, and towards the end of the year we became increasingly concerned about the sub-prime market," he wrote. "As a result we took a number of actions at that time and into early 2007 to reduce our risk. In the first quarter of 2007 we stopped our residential mortgage warehousing efforts, shut down our CDO warehouses, aggressively reduced our inventory positions, reduced counterparty exposure and increased our protection for disaster scenarios."

He then launched into a particularly lucid analysis of how being honest with itself about the value of the mortgage securities on its books had made all the difference. No other Wall Street CFO could have made a similar claim. "Key to our ability to do this was our extremely robust mark to market philosophy," he continued. "You simply cannot manage risk effectively if you don't know what positions are worth. An accurate daily marking process makes difficult decisions considerably easier, as you tangibly feel the cost of inaction every day as the market declines. We have extensive price discovery and valuation resources and don't subscribe to the notion that there are instruments that can't be valued. So, we knew the value of what we had and managed our risk accordingly. . . . Given the complexity and diversity of risks in our business, we believe that it is critical to provide our teams with the confidence and support necessary to identify and escalate issues as soon as possible and to prioritize the interest of the entire firm over any individual objectives. In addition, we think it is important for senior leadership to be actively engaged in the business flows and decision-making process, in times of calm as well as crisis."

CHAPTER 23

GOLDMAN GETS PAID

N ot only Bear Stearns but also AIG, the international insurance behemoth, began to feel the effects of the aggressive way Goldman was marking its trading books. Which is not to say Goldman's marks were wrong— quite the opposite actually—but only that they were not without serious financial and social consequences for others at ground zero of capitalism. In the aftermath of the global financial collapse, one of the reasons given for the historic decisions to rescue Bear Stearns and AIG was because of how "interconnected" these institutions were to one another, according to Robert Steel, the former Goldman partner who had joined Paulson at Treasury as undersecretary for domestic finance. Goldman's marks were one of the ways firms became linked to one another. The consequences for the two Bear Stearns hedge funds—which likely would have collapsed anyway—were devastating and were exacerbated by Goldman's marks; at AIG, the Goldman marks were equally momentous, especially since never before had the government saved an investment bank or an insurance company from bankruptcy.

If nothing else, Hank Greenberg, the longtime chairman and CEO of AIG, was a smart and ruthless businessman. He diversified AIG beyond simply writing fire and casualty insurance to become the world's largest underwriter of commercial and industrial insurance. He was also an innovator. He created insurance for directors and officers of corporations to try to protect them against their own blunders. He created environmental protection insurance and coverage for those threatened by kidnapping. AIG "built a team of skilled underwriters who were capable of assessing and pricing risk," he often proclaimed. Greenberg also knew that AIG's AAA credit rating gave the company a valuable and differentiated advantage in the marketplace by allowing it to borrow money cheaply and then to invest it at higher rates of return, and to make money on the spread. If this kind of thing could be done outside the ken of often onerous state regulations that blanket the insurance industry, even better.

To that end, in 1987, Greenberg created AIG Financial Products, known as AIGFP, by hiring a group of traders from the investment bank Drexel Burnham Lambert, led by Howard Sosin, who supposedly had a "better model" for trading and valuing interest-rate swaps and for generally taking and managing the risk that other financial firms wanted to sell. The market for derivatives was in its infancy, but growing, and Greenberg determined that AIG could be at its forefront. According to Greenberg, the overriding strategy at AIGFP was for the business to lay off most of the risks it was taking on behalf of its clients so that AIG was not exposed financially in the event of huge market-moving events that could not be modeled or anticipated. Under Greenberg's watchful eye, he says, the formula worked famously: from 1987 to 2004, AIGFP contributed "over $5 billion to AIG's pre-tax income" and helped the company's market capitalization increase to $181 billion, from $11 billion.

The business Sosin and his team created was nothing more than a hedge fund inside an insurance behemoth with the added benefit that their access to capital was seemingly unlimited and costless and instead of getting the typical "two and twenty" hedge-fund deal, AIGFP's traders got to keep between 30 percent and 35 percent of the profits they generated. This sweet arrangement allowed many of the four hundred or so people who worked at AIGFP to become very proficient about taking risks with other people's money and to get rich.

Things at AIGFP were humming along so well that when Sosin and Greenberg had a falling-out, in 1993, and Sosin quit—taking a reported $182 million in severance with him—the business didn't miss a beat under his successor, Thomas Savage, a mathematician who encouraged his traders to challenge him about the efficacy of the risks the group was taking. Savage retired in 2001 and was replaced by Joseph Cassano. Cassano had been the back-office operations guy at both Drexel and AIGFP before becoming the CFO and then getting the top job. By then, AIGFP had started insuring—innocently enough, it seemed—the risk that corporations might default on the debt they had issued. By selling something that became known as "credit-default swaps" to nervous investors, AIG agreed to pay off the defaulted debt at 100 cents on the dollar. AIG got the premiums; investors got peace of mind. This was the kind of financial innovation Greenberg fancied, especially since AIG's AAA credit rating made its cost of borrowing so low, a real competitive advantage. The biggest part—some $400 billion—of the AIGFP insurance book was written on behalf of European banks looking to take risk off their books as a way of avoiding the need to raise additional capital to appease the European regulators. "This is a great irony," explained a former AIG executive. "The European banks went out and were able to buy credit-default insurance on their assets so that they didn't have to keep as much capital on their balance sheet. So here was an insurance company in the United States with essentially no liquidity, no equity and no reserves providing equity relief for European insurance companies. Talk about the house of cards."

As the writer Michael Lewis explored so elegantly in his August 2009 profile of AIGFP in *Vanity Fair,* Cassano was not a particularly benevolent leader. "AIGFP became a dictatorship," one London trader told Lewis. "Joe would bully people around. He'd humiliate them and try to make it up to them by giving them huge amounts of money." Needless to say, the camaraderie and openness of the Savage era was lost quickly in the savage Cassano regime. "Even by the standards of Wall Street villains, whose character flaws wind up being exaggerated to fit the crime, Cassano was a cartoon despot," Lewis wrote. But none of that mattered particularly at AIG as long as Greenberg was running the show, since Greenberg was every bit Cassano's match in ruthlessness, but a better and more astute businessman.

The dominoes started falling differently than Greenberg planned on Valentine's Day 2005, five days after AIG announced its 2004 earnings of $11.04 billion, a stunning 19.1 percent increase from the year before. That was when AIG revealed it had received subpoenas on February 9 from both New York attorney general Eliot Spitzer and the SEC related to their amorphous-sounding investigations about AIG's accounting for various "non-traditional insurance products" and "assumed reinsurance transactions." AIG said it would cooperate "in responding to the subpoenas." A month later, on March 14, AIG announced that Greenberg would step down as CEO to become nonexecutive chairman of the board of directors and would be replaced by Martin Sullivan, who since 2002 had been AIG's vice chairman and co–chief operating officer and a member of the company's board. The company's spin was that it had "implemented its management succession plan" by picking Sullivan, and since Greenberg was then seventy-nine years old the claim seemed plausible.

But, in reality, Spitzer and the SEC were using the threat of a criminal indictment—which no financial company had ever survived—to put pressure on the board to dispense with Greenberg. It turned out that the regulators were investigating the accounting for two $250 million reinsurance transactions between an AIG subsidiary and General Re Corporation, the reinsurance behemoth and subsidiary of Berkshire Hathaway, in December 2000 and March 2001. "The entire AIG–Gen Re transaction was a fraud," Spitzer later wrote in his civil fraud complaint against AIG, Greenberg, and another AIG executive. "It was explicitly designed by Greenberg from the beginning to create no risk for either party—AIG never even created an underwriting file in connection with the deal."

Spitzer filed a civil complaint in New York State Supreme Court on May 25, 2005—and later dropped it in its entirety. In March 2006, AIG paid $800 million to settle with the SEC and restated its shareholders' equity by $2.26 billion for 2004. AIG also paid in excess of $800 million to New York State to settle charges against the company.

Between the firing of Greenberg, the Spitzer investigation, and the potential accounting restatements, Standard & Poor's, one of the three major ratings agencies, decided on March 30 that it would shoot first and ask questions later. Late that afternoon, S&P lowered AIG's coveted AAA debt rating to AA+, for both its long-term counterparty credit and its senior debt. In making the downgrade from AAA—which was one of AIG's most coveted assets—Grace Osborne, the S&P credit analyst, cited the delayed filing of AIG's annual financial statement, known as a 10-K, with the SEC, and the uncovering of a "number of questionable transactions that span more than five years" that could result in a decrease of $1.7 billion to AIG's reported shareholders' equity. Without mentioning the downgrade, Martin Sullivan, the new CEO, wrote a letter to shareholders on April 4 where he acknowledged the various inquiries and how committed AIG was to cooperating with the company's regulators to resolve any problems or concerns.

Curiously, nowhere in Sullivan's letter, S&P's downgrade analysis, AIG's announcements about Greenberg's departure, or any of the various regulatory or internal investigations into AIG was the name "AIG Financial Products" even mentioned. Indeed, it is probably a safe bet that as of April 2005 very few people outside of 70 Pine Street, AIG's world headquarters in downtown Manhattan, or much beyond AIGFP's Wilton, Connecticut, and London, England, offices had even heard of AIGFP, or of its CEO Joseph A. Cassano, or even how it made increasingly large amounts of money for its parent, AIG. Needless to say, there was little, if any, disclosure to investors of the unprecedented risks Cassano was taking on either.

According to Greenberg, Sullivan's oversight of AIGFP and Cassano dissipated in the wake of Greenberg's firing. "[R]eports indicate that the risk controls my team and I put in place were weakened or eliminated after my retirement," Greenberg wrote in his October 2008 congressional testimony. "For example, it is my understanding that the weekly meetings we used to conduct to review all AIG's investments and risks were eliminated. These meetings kept the CEO abreast of AIGFP's credit exposure." Not only did Cassano appear to be free of management scrutiny but, more important, it would turn out, the loss of AIG's coveted AAA credit rating meant that the counterparties who had paid the premiums to and bought the credit protection from AIG could demand that AIG post collateral—in cash or securities—should the value of the debt being insured fall. This made sense, of course, in that an insured would want to know that its insurance company was good for the money. The posting of collateral in an escrow account makes the insured feel better but requires the insurer to have the cash around to put into escrow. It also required that the insured and insurer agree on how much collateral should be posted to make up for the loss of value in the securities being insured.

At this moment, Greenberg said, Sullivan should have pretty much shut down the credit-default swap operation at AIGFP: "When the AAA credit rating disappeared in spring 2005, it would have been logical for AIG's new management to have exited or reduced its business of writing credit-default swaps," he explained. With little effort, Greenberg ticked off in rapid fire the litany of mistakes then made by Sullivan, Cassano, and company: Rather than curtailing the selling of credit-default swaps, AIGFP ratcheted up exponentially its issuance of them, and no longer just on corporate debt but on a whole new explosion of risk that Wall Street was madly underwriting through the issuance of increasingly risky mortgage-backed securities tied to so-called subprime and Alt-A mortgages. Then there were the credit-default swaps written on collateralized debt obligations, or CDOs, with huge exposures to subprime mortgages. And then there were the swaps sold to hedge the risk of CDOs of CDOs and of synthetic CDOs, where just the risk was bought and sold and there was no underlying security. AIGFP also wrote insurance for something called "multi-sector" CDOs, a collection of more than one hundred bonds ranging from those backed by residential mortgages to those backed by credit-card and auto-loan receivables.

As of December 31, 2007, AIGFP had a portfolio of credit-default swaps totaling $527 billion, of which $78 billion were written on multi-sector CDOs, most of which had some exposure to subprime mortgages. Indeed, it has become widely accepted that without Joe Cassano and AIGFP around to insure the risk that Wall Street was taking in underwriting all these increasingly risky securities, the debt bubble might have deflated rather than exploding as it did in 2007 and 2008. In its defense—which shows up among other places in an August 2009 court filing by law firm Weil, Gotshal & Manges in a shareholder lawsuit—AIG argued first that it only wrote credit-default swaps on the "super senior" portion of the multi-sector CDOs, meaning, incredibly, that AIGFP believed it had very little real exposure "[b]ecause the super senior tranche has priority of payment ahead of even the AAA tranches, [and so] is regarded as having a better-than-AAA rating." Additionally, AIG and Weil, Gotshal & Manges argued that in December 2005 AIGFP stopped writing new credit-default swaps on multi-sector CDOs that included subprime mortgages because "of concerns over deteriorating underwriting standards for subprime mortgages," although AIGFP continued to insure the risks in both "prime" and "Alt-A" mortgages. Weil, Gotshal continued, "As a result, AIGFP's exposure to multi-sector CDOs with more risky subprime mortgages and mortgage-backed bonds originating in 2006 and 2007 was limited, a fact which later provided additional comfort that losses suffered by other market participants would not spread to AIG."

While that last bit of legal spin is certainly debatable, what soon became crystalline—and a major problem for AIG—was that as the value of the toxic securities it *had* insured before 2006 fell and with the loss of its AAA corporate credit rating, AIG's counterparties ratcheted up their demands for collateral from AIG.

At the forefront of these increasingly strident collateral demands was none other than Goldman Sachs. Goldman had insured around $75 billion of these securities through AIGFP, and during the course of 2007, the displeasure with Goldman Sachs was becoming increasingly well known inside AIG. Goldman's lower marks forced AIG to grapple—albeit with great reluctance—with its portfolio of insurance tied to the securities that Goldman kept insisting were worth less and less. "When the credit market seized up," Sullivan testified before Congress, "like many other financial institutions, we were forced to mark our swap positions at fire sale prices as if we owned the underlying bonds even though we believed that our swap positions had value if held to maturity."

———

ON JULY 10, the major credit-rating agencies—that for years were part of the problem through their chronic failure to exercise any independent judgment about the credit ratings they had slapped on a slew of mortgage-backed securities—began to get some religion (long after the fact) and downgraded hundreds and hundreds of residential mortgage-backed securities. The downgrades set off a chain reaction of worry, especially among some of the executives at AIGFP. The next day, in a telephone conversation with his colleague Alan Frost—a transcript of which was released by the Financial Crisis Inquiry Commission, or FCIC—Andrew Forster, the head of credit trading at AIGFP, expressed his dismay at the downgrades. "[E]very fucking . . . rating agency we've spoken to . . . [came] out with more downgrades," he told Frost. "About a month ago I was like, suicidal. . . . The problem that we're going to face is that we're going to have just enormous downgrades on the stuff that we've got. . . . Everyone tells me that it's trading and it's two points lower and all the rest of it and how come you can't mark your book. So it's definitely going to give it renewed focus. I mean we can't . . . we have to mark it. It's, it's, uh, we're [unintelligible] fucked basically."

By late July 2007, in the wake of the downgrades and as a result of the trading it was seeing in the market, Goldman began putting pressure on AIG to pony up more collateral to cover the declining value of the mortgage securities AIG had insured. On July 26, Andrew Davilman, at Goldman, wrote Frost an e-mail telling him Goldman was making its first collateral call. Frost was on vacation. "Sorry to bother you on vacation," Davilman wrote. "Margin call coming your way. Want to give you a heads up."

"On what?" Frost wrote back, eighteen minutes later.

"[$]20bb of supersenior," Davilman replied, just over a minute later. Frost never replied to Davilman's e-mail. Instead, AIGFP decided that Forster, not Frost, would deal with Goldman's requests for collateral payments.

Goldman's marks—and the subsequent collateral call to AIGFP based on them—were, understandably, not welcome news at AIGFP. But the marks were also the subject of some controversy within Goldman itself. "The $2bn margin call is driven by a massive remarking by Goldman Sachs of the underlying [mortgage] securities (down from –6 pts to –20 to –25 pts in some cases), *ahead* of all other dealers in the [S]treet," Goldman's Nicholas Friedman wrote in an internal e-mail the day before the AIGFP collateral call. Ram Sundaram, a Goldman managing director in proprietary trading, was also concerned about the Goldman marks. "After spending the past two days chasing dealers and internal desks for fresh marks," he wrote some colleagues on July 26 at 11:09 p.m., "the result has been the need to call a significant amount of collateral from various counterparties. This is particularly concerning in that these stale marks were also being sent to clients by GS for their own valuation purposes (for example—[W]est [C]oast bonds were quoted at 99 yesterday by the GS trading desk and after we demanded a current bid they were bid at 77.5 today). The extent of the collateral calls being generated overnight is embarrassing for the firm ($1.9Bn from AIG-FP alone)." He urged caution and offered to make sure clients and others understood Goldman's valuation methodology. At the same time, AIOI Insurance, a Goldman client in Tokyo, let the Goldman traders know how upset the company was about Goldman's marks and the margin call that resulted. According to Shigeru Akamatsu, a Goldman vice president, "Suzuki-san," at AIOI, believed Goldman's marks were "more than twice as bad as others," that the margin call was "totally unaccepted," and "warned that he will strongly protest against us."

Goldman's opening salvo against AIG had been fired. The next day, Goldman asked AIGFP for $1.81 billion in collateral; Goldman also purchased $100 million of insurance—by buying CDS—against the possibility that AIG would default on its obligations. (Eventually Goldman's CDS purchase against an AIG default would reach a peak of $3.2 billion.) On July 30, an AIG trader told Forster that "[AIG] would be in fine shape if Goldman wasn't hanging its head out there." The July 27 margin call was "something that hit out of the blue, and it's a fucking number that's well bigger than we ever planned for," Forster said later. He said the marks were all over the place and "could be anything from 80 to sort of, you know, 95" because of infrequent trading. He called Goldman's marks "ridiculous."

When Cassano first heard about Goldman's collateral call, he was blown away and thought that it came "out of the blue," he said in a five-hour June 2010 interview with the FCIC. "What in the world had changed between yesterday and today?" he said he wondered, to prompt the "whopper of a [collateral] call" from Goldman. Goldman's marks were consistently lower than those of other Wall Street dealers—as Goldman itself admitted—and Cassano was incredulous about their accuracy. "I didn't believe the numbers," he said. "These aren't real numbers. The markets had seized up." According to the January 2011 FCIC report, AIG's models meanwhile showed "there would be no defaults on any of the bond payments that AIG's swaps insured." But, according to the report, "[t]he Goldman executives considered [the AIG] models irrelevant, because the contracts required collateral to be posted if market value declined."

Needless to say, the vast discrepancy in the way the two firms looked at the valuation of these securities did not make the negotiations between them any easier. Nor did it help that by the summer of 2007, Goldman would clearly benefit from a decline in the value of the mortgage securities—and had every incentive to convince the market the value had fallen—while AIGFP had an even bigger incentive to claim the value of the securities in the market had held up just fine. This was a zero sum game between the two financial powerhouses.

The Goldman and AIGFP executives debated the matter in early August. In an August 2 e-mail, Thomas Athan, another AIGFP executive, wrote to Andrew Forster about a particularly difficult conversation he had had that day with Sundaram, the senior Goldman mortgage executive. "Tough conf call with Goldman," Athan wrote to Forster. "They are not budging and are acting irrational. They insist on 'actionable firm bids and firm offers' to come up with a 'mid market quotation' " as a way to determine how much collateral AIG needed to post.

Athan did not want to put the details of his call with Sundaram in the e-mail but informed Forster that this needed to be escalated within AIGFP and then he needed to get back to Goldman by noon the next day. "I feel we need Joe to understand the situation 100% and let him decide how he wants to proceed," Athan wrote. "I played almost every card I had, legal wording, market practice, intent of the language, meaning of the CSA"—a reference to the Credit Support Annex, which is a codicil to the ISDA Master Agreement that governs collateral calls in CDS transactions—"and also stressed the potential damage to the relationship and GS said that this has gone to the 'highest levels' at GS and they feel that the CSA has to work or they cannot do synthetic trades anymore across the firm in these types of instruments. They called this a 'test case' many times on the call. It seems Ram has put himself in a bind that the firm is watching him here to see how he works this out and anything other than getting collateral close to liquidation levels will be considered a failure. Someone (like Joe) might need to convince a senior person that there is an alternative way to look at this situation." Athan suggested they all circle up and have a "halo"—a reference to a real-time Hewlett-Packard collaboration and meeting system—the next morning. "BTW," Athan signed off, "[t]his isn't what I signed up [for]. Where are the big trades, high fives and celebratory closing dinners you promised?"

For the next two weeks, AIGFP and Goldman disputed Goldman's marks and its collateral call. It "was unusual to have disputes" with Goldman, Cassano said. "Goldman Sachs is a business partner of ours and an important relationship."

On August 9, Cassano told AIG's investors on a conference call about AIGFP's portfolio of credit-default swaps. "It is hard for us, and without being flippant, to even see a scenario, within any kind of realm of reason, that would see us losing one dollar in any of those transactions. . . . [W]e see no issues at all emerging. We see no dollar of loss associated with any of that business." In reaction to Cassano's bold assertion, on August 13, the *Wall Street Journal* reported in a front-page headline that "AIG Might Be Deceiving Itself on Derivative Risks." According to writer David Reilly, "AIG might not want to whistle too loudly as it strolls past the subprime graveyard." But Cassano pooh-poohed the story. "Hopefully people just ignore it," he e-mailed Forster. "It is a real non-story."

Of course, it wasn't. Instead, the questions intensified about whether AIGFP had the cash to meet mounting collateral calls from counterparties. The ratings agencies wanted to know, as did AIG's outside auditors at PricewaterhouseCoopers and AIG's internal auditors at 70 Pine. One of them, Elias Habayeb, the CFO of AIG's financial services group who reported to AIG's CFO, was particularly nettlesome to Cassano. For months, he had been pushing Cassano for more information about the value of the swaps AIGFP had written and about the collateral availability. "There must be something in the air or the coffee at 70 Pine," Cassano complained in an e-mail to Habayeb on August 31 about the numerous inquiries he was suddenly getting from headquarters. He then went on to detail AIGFP's sources of liquidity and urged Habayeb not to bother Forster and others with further questions. "We have taken many steps to insure our liquidity during this market disruption," he wrote. "In many ways for us this is old hat stuff as we went through a similar shut off of the capital markets in 2005 during the compan[y's] restatement horrors. We have been very careful about husbanding our liquidity resources and I am comfortable that we will be able to see this crisis through and come out the other side being opportunistic value buyers. If you have any other questions please direct them to me. As you can imagine Andy and his team have a big task on their hands keeping tabs on the markets, husbanding liquidity and managing their business. At times like this we all want them exclusively focused on their jobs. Cash is King." (Despite his concerns, Habayeb had been AIG's chief spokesman to the *Journal*'s August 13 story and had said everything was just fine.)

There were also concerns raised about AIGFP's ability to provide the necessary collateral from inside AIGFP itself. Joseph W. St. Denis, AIGFP's vice president for accounting policy from June 2006 and a former assistant chief accountant at the SEC's division of enforcement, got worried when he came back from vacation in early September 2007 and heard about "a multi-billion-dollar margin call on certain" super-senior credit-default swaps that AIG had written. "I was gravely concerned about this, as the mantra at AIGFP had always been (in my experience) that there could never be losses on the" super-senior credit-default swaps. He later told the FCIC that when he first heard about Goldman's collateral call, he was so upset that he "had to sit down." He worried that

AIGFP could be in "potentially material liability position" as a result of the increasing collateral demands. Before the month was out, after several profanity-laced tirades delivered by Cassano to St. Denis, Cassano told him, "I have deliberately excluded you from the valuation of the Super Seniors because I was concerned that you would pollute the process" by questioning too closely the accounting for the swaps. (Cassano denied to the FCIC having said this to St. Denis.) When St. Denis resigned on October 1, he told AIGFP's general counsel that he "had lost faith in the senior-most management of AIGFP and could not accept the risk to AIG and myself of being isolated from corporate accounting policy personnel, especially given the situation with the" super-senior credit-default swaps.

Much to Cassano's further consternation, Goldman wasn't going away, either. "For 14 months [from July 2007], Goldman pressed its case," the FCIC reported, "and sent AIG a formal demand letter [for collateral] every single business day. It would pursue AIG relentlessly with demands for collateral based on marks that were initially well below those of other firms—while AIG and its management struggled to come to grips with the burgeoning crisis." Not surprisingly, Goldman was becoming increasingly frustrated by AIG's failure to own up to its agreements to make good on the insurance it had issued on the mortgage securities. "We couldn't get AIG to give us their line by line prices [on the securities]," one Goldman trader recalled. "We couldn't get them to commit to getting on the phone within a reasonable period of time even to discuss it." Despite the tough early August conversation between Sundaram and Forster, Goldman reduced the collateral call to $1.6 billion, then to $1.2 billion and then to $600 million. "That told me something was up with their numbers," Cassano said. "This market is so difficult, the markets are roiling to say the least. Even Goldman Sachs—a pretty good outfit—was having a hard time getting the numbers themselves." Before Cassano left for a late August cycling vacation in Germany and Austria, he suggested paying Goldman a "good faith" $300 million deposit. Goldman countered with a demand for a $450 million deposit, which Cassano agreed to provide on August 10. In a side letter that same day, AIGFP and Goldman further stipulated that the $450 million did not resolve the collateral dispute between the two firms. "The idea was to get everyone to chill out," Frost wrote to Forster, explaining why AIGFP had decided to give the money to Goldman. "[B]ut we were to start thinking about how to deal with this on a more permanent basis." Soon thereafter, Cassano was off on his bicycling vacation.

On August 15, Alan Frost went to 85 Broad Street to meet with

Goldman executives "to show good faith," he wrote Andrew Forster the next day, and "at least start the dialog." He reported that the conversation "was fine. Everybody wants this to go away, but the primary focus is to think if we can establish a better way of dealing with it if we need to again." Frost was especially concerned with trying to figure out how the two firms would come to an agreement about the underlying value of the securities that AIGFP had insured. The obvious gulf between the two firms was causing much consternation.

Before he left on vacation, Cassano had spoken by telephone to Michael "Woody" Sherwood, a co-CEO of Goldman Sachs International, and other Goldman executives seemed to think the two men had agreed that the matter of valuation would be best resolved by going to the market and getting a bid on $10 million worth of mortgage-backed securities. Frost was concerned that this might not have been what Cassano agreed to with Sherwood, especially since "[w]e run the risk that the market interprets it more [a]long the lines of the way Goldman thinks than the way we think." He was also nervous that Goldman was not "happy about the notion of zero progress until labor day"—"one of the reasons I went in for a face to face," he wrote—but that he "made it unambiguously clear" to Goldman "that I was not going to disturb him"—Cassano—"on his holiday for this." Concluded Frost: "[W]e should be thinking of how we are going to deal with this, because, trust me, this is not the last margin call that we are going to debate."

In response, Forster wrote to Frost that although he had "no colour" on the conversation between Cassano and Sherwood and that the "whole idea was to leave it for a few weeks" until after Labor Day. "I have heard several rumours now that [GS] is aggressively marking down asset types that they don't own so as to cause maximum pain to their competitors. It may be rubbish but it's the sort of thing [GS] would do."

Things quieted down in the markets and between Goldman and AIGFP until September 11 when Goldman asked for another $1.5 billion in collateral based on its marks. By then, AIGFP executives had also become convinced that Goldman's marks were influencing the marks—and resulting collateral calls—of other banks. Cassano was telling his colleagues that one collateral call, by French bank Société Générale, "had been spurred by Goldman." In his subsequent testimony before the FCIC, Cassano said that Sherwood had told him—in their August 2007 conversation—that Goldman's marks may have been too low initially "but that the market's starting to come our way." Still, Cassano said Sherwood told him, Goldman "didn't cover [them]selves in glory during this period."

Regardless, Goldman ratcheted up the amount of insurance it bought against the possibility that AIG itself would not make good on what it owed Goldman. On September 13, Goldman bought another $700 million in CDS protection against AIG, bringing the amount of its insurance against the company at that time to $1.449 billion.

On November 1, Cassano wrote to Habayeb that it was clear that AIGFP and Goldman "have a bona fide dispute" and added, "It is not unusual even in the best of times with normal liquidity to dispute the calls." He noted further that the only other collateral call AIGFP had received had been from Société Générale, the large French bank, "which was spurred by GS calling them. In that case, we also disputed the call and have not heard from SocGen again on that specific call."

On November 2, Cassano said Sherwood gave him a "heads-up" that Goldman was increasing its collateral call again, to $2.8 billion, in addition to the $450 million it already had. "We're not going to pay that amount," Cassano said he told Sherwood. "Yea, I didn't think you would," Cassano said Sherwood replied. On November 9, Forster e-mailed Cassano with comparisons between Goldman's marks and Merrill Lynch's marks on the same securities: Where Merrill's marks on a given security were at 95 cents on the dollar, Goldman's were at between 60 cents and 80 cents. By November 14, both Société Générale and Merrill Lynch had asked AIGFP to post collateral to them as well, in the amounts of $1.7 billion and $610 million, respectively, based largely on the Goldman precedent, according to the FCIC.

By the end of November 2007, Forster had cataloged the extent of its collateral disputes with nine banks and Wall Street firms in an eight-page memorandum. He wrote that because of the "extreme illiquidity" in the market—acknowledged by all the counterparties—the discussions had been "friendly" rather than "disputed," although that thought seems inconsistent with the ongoing confrontation with Goldman. "All of the dealers feel that as the market is under extreme stress that prices should perhaps be lower but none have any real idea as to how to best calculate the price or if indeed that statement is true," Forster wrote. "The market is so illiquid that there are no willing takers of risk currently so valuations are simply best guesses and there is no two-way market in any sense of the term."

Despite the caveat, Forster's analysis of the trades AIGFP had with each firm was quite specific, as were the values of the securities involved. With Merrill Lynch, he noted, AIGFP had close to $10 billion in exposure, in twenty different trades. He noted there was an "8% price threshold"— meaning the price would need to fall to 92 cents on the dollar—"before any posting [of collateral] is required" based on the underlying bond price, not the value of the credit-default swap. As of the end of November, Merrill was asking for $610 million in collateral, but, Forster pointed out, "[W]e are disputing the call with them and they agree prices are too illiquid to be reliable."

With $23 billion of exposure, Goldman was the Big Kahuna for AIGFP. Goldman was the AIG counterparty on fifty-one different positions, in thirty-three trades. Goldman had also negotiated more favorable terms than its competitors, whereby AIGFP had to start posting collateral mostly when the value of the underlying securities fell to 96 cents on the dollar. "They have made collateral calls totaling $3 bn on 38 positions covering 23 different transactions," Forster wrote. He then listed the thirty-eight positions and Goldman's discounted prices for them. There was no mention with Goldman, as there had been with Merrill, of any disagreement or potential dispute resolution. Forster did take note of the price discrepancy of one CDO—Independence V—that Merrill had underwritten in 2004. As of November 2007, Merrill valued Independence V at 90 cents on the dollar, while Goldman valued it at 67.5 cents on the dollar. Cassano sent Forster's analysis to William Dooley, the head of the AIG division under which AIGFP operated, with the note that despite the disputes, the dealers were working with AIGFP in a "positive framework toward seeking resolution."

According to Greenberg, "Goldman had the lowest marks on the Street by everything I hear. There was no exchange. Where was the price discovery? It was all in the eye of the beholder." AIG board members and executives also viewed Goldman's collateral requests with a high degree of skepticism. Some thought it was nothing more than a way for Goldman to get "a free loan from AIG," according to one AIG executive. Goldman would announce that it had marked its AIG swap book down by, say, $5 billion and then insist, "Send us a check for $5 billion." Cassano and Sullivan would explain to the AIG board that Goldman was the only counterparty to be so aggressive about collateral demands. "Goldman's just taking advantage of the company," the two men told the board. Explained one former AIG board member about Goldman: "They were the first demanding collateral and their mark[downs] were always much greater than everybody else's. . . . Goldman was right on top of it. You have to give them credit for that."

In short order, Cassano's house of cards collapsed. On November 7, 2007, AIG announced third-quarter net income of a little more than $3 billion but revealed, deep in the announcement, that AIGFP had suffered a "$352 million unrealized market valuation loss" on its super-senior swap portfolio and that October's loss alone on that portfolio could be another $550 million pretax. The next day, Cassano told investors there was "opacity in the market" and that valuations for the securities underlying the swaps were all over the place, ranging from 55 cents on the dollar (likely from Goldman) to as high as 95 cents on the dollar. If all the valuations were like Goldman's and the collateral calls started pouring in, AIG's write-downs on the swaps would be far greater than the $550 million. But "rest assured," Cassano said, "we have plenty of resources and more than enough resources to meet any of the collateral calls that might come in." On November 23, Goldman demanded another $3 billion in cash collateral from AIGFP; AIG "protested," according to the FCIC, but paid $1.55 billion, bringing the total collateral payments to Goldman to $2 billion. Cassano told the FCIC he decided to make the payment because his boss wanted "to avoid airing dirty laundry" in the market about the disputes. A week later, based on AIGFP's own calculations and other market input, Cassano phoned Sherwood and demanded the money back from Goldman. In an e-mail summarizing his conversation with Sherwood, he wrote that Sherwood had called him back from "his sick bed" and took the request "in stoic fashion with little push back. He certainly sounded discourage[d]. He did ask, 'Well, where do we go from here?' I said, 'I think you need to pay me back my cash.' He said, 'We need to understand your numbers.' I said, 'Sure, we can do that.' He then said, 'Ugh,' and said, 'I guess we will be speaking more next week.' We hung up on good terms." But Goldman did not pay the money back to AIGFP and, in fact, increased its collateral demands further.

Toward the end of November, AIG announced it would convene a conference call for investors on December 5 to review the AIGFP portfolio and its view of the risk in it. On November 29, the top executives at both AIG and AIGFP met with Pricewaterhouse, AIG's auditors, to discuss the ongoing collateral disputes with Goldman. At one point during the meeting, Cassano told Sullivan the AIGFP did not have "the data to dispute Goldman's marks" but that the disagreement with Goldman had the potential to reduce AIG's earnings "by $5 billion" in the first quarter of 2008. "Oh, my God!" Cassano said Sullivan exclaimed. "That could wipe out the quarter . . . I am going to have a heart attack!" (Sullivan later told the FCIC he didn't recall that part of the meeting.) Timothy Ryan, a PricewaterhouseCoopers partner, told Sullivan at the meeting that in "light of AIG's plans to hold the investor conference on December 5" that Pricewaterhouse believed there was a growing possibility of a "material weakness" in AIGFP's credit-default swap portfolio that could result in potentially huge future losses. Such a warning needed to be disclosed to investors, according to SEC rules, but AIG did not disclose the warning for months. In the days leading up to the December 5 call, Cassano was scurrying about in preparation for it and wondering whether he could or should open up the AIGFP black box to investors. "As you know the exposure we have within these transactions is a mark to market, potential replacement cost," he wrote in a November 28 e-mail to his colleague Robert Lewis. "[A]ll the entities that we have swaps with are highly rated (triple A primarily) and in an event of default or nonpayment we generally become pari passu with the bond holders. Once again an extremely remote risk with little real exposure. No other company of our ilk[—] dealers, bank[s] etc[.—]have gone into explaining these exposures in any detail[.] [T]his is just normal course business with highly rated counterparts. Attempting to explain this segment of the business briefly I worry will only add to the confusion of the audience as they will conflate this exposure with the super senior exposures they have such difficulty coming to grips with. [F]urther this will open a new area where we can spend a lot of time drilling down but will have a bit of a turbulent time as we attempt to get the message clarified."

On December 5, still in denial, Martin Sullivan and Joseph Cassano gave an Oscar-worthy performance on the investor conference call related to AIGFP's credit-default swap portfolio—and made no mention of Pricewaterhouse's comment. "AIG has accurately identified all areas of exposure to the U.S. residential-housing market," Sullivan said that day. "We are confident in our markets and the reasonableness of our valuation methods." Added Cassano, in yet another moment of profane understatement: "It is very difficult to see how there can be any losses in these portfolios." Cassano made no mention of the disputes AIGFP was having with Goldman, and presumably some of the other counterparties, about the posting of collateral. "We have, from time to time, gotten collateral calls from people," Cassano said at the meeting, according to the transcript. "Then we say to them, 'Well, we don't agree with your numbers.' And they go, 'Oh.' And they go away."

A week later, after a collateral call that came from Calyon, the big French bank, Tom Athan wrote to a colleague, "We are in uncharted waters for our firm. I realize that. I've been on [Wall Street] for 17 years, mostly in new derivatives businesses so I know how it goes. We'll all get better together. Takes time unfortunately."

On December 14, Forster again tried to get AIGFP's money back from Goldman. He wrote Neil Wright, at Goldman Sachs International, that "Given the significant amount of collateral in dispute that is held by Goldman, we expect either that you now return to us the amount of the collateral that we have called for, or that you continue next week to engage actively and constructively with us in discussions with us toward resolving the dispute. It would not be appropriate to delay the discussions at this stage." But the discussions were delayed further by the holidays. Before Christmas, Cassano wrote both Sherwood and Viniar, Goldman's CFO, that he appreciated getting Goldman's pricing information from the firm on the various securities but even on a preliminary look he could tell the Goldman prices were too low, compared to the rest of the Street. "[I]t's already evident that your exposure calculations are significantly higher than is warranted by third party indications that you yourself have provided to us," Cassano wrote, adding, "You currently hold $2 billion of collateral for these positions, which is demonstrably in excess of what is contractually required." He told the Goldman executives he wanted to resolve the matter early in January.

Cassano was also continuing to feel pressure from Tim Ryan, at Pricewaterhouse, who wanted to get to the bottom of why Goldman's marks were consistently lower than those of other dealers. Cassano told the FCIC that Ryan was "like a dog with a bone" and that he could never figure out why Ryan "held Goldman in such high esteem." On December 18, Ryan visited Cassano in his London office. According to Cassano, Ryan told him that he wanted to go see Goldman himself to discuss the marks so that he could figure out how Goldman derived them. Cassano was incredulous. Not only was Pricewaterhouse also Goldman's auditor—a potential conflict of interest—but also Cassano could not imagine his auditor going to see Goldman and essentially announcing that he did believe his client's marks and wanting to see how Goldman had figured things out. "You will undermine my negotiations with them," Cassano said he told Ryan. "You can't do that." Cassano said he suggested that Ryan simply talk to the Pricewaterhouse partner on the Goldman audit account to get the comfort he was seeking. But Ryan was insistent that he wanted to talk to Goldman directly. When Cassano asked him why, Ryan said simply, it's "good audit procedure." In the end, Cassano succeeded in keeping Ryan away from Goldman.

By early 2008, AIGFP executives were busy scrambling to make sure they had a response to Pricewaterhouse's growing concerns. At the January 15, 2008, Audit Committee meeting, there was much discussion about whether proper controls existed to monitor independently the valuation of the AIGFP portfolio. According to minutes from the meeting: "Mr. Habayeb believes that he is limited in his ability to influence changes, and the super senior valuation process is not going as smoothly as it could. Mr. Ryan said that the control functions are not included in the ongoing process and lose the ability to participate in discussions of the issues. He added that roles and responsibilities need to be clarified, and pointed out that collateral issues could have been escalated to the AIG level earlier in the process."

The next day, Cassano again wrote Sherwood and Viniar. "We believe that your current exposure calculations are too high," he wrote, not surprisingly.

On February 4, at a meeting between the Pricewaterhouse auditors and AIG executives, including Cassano, PWC again broached the idea that there could be a "material weakness" at AIGFP. Cassano told the FCIC that Sullivan and the other senior AIG executives were "gob-smacked and stunned" by the news, although this was clearly not the first time the matter had been discussed. On February 6, the "case" Tim Ryan had made to the Audit Committee about the potential for a "material weakness" at AIG caused Cassano to inform his AIGFP colleagues of a potential problem. "[T]he [AIG] team is now trying to determine whether they have been officially served the notice such [that] they need to file an 8K," Cassano wrote to the AIGFP team, referring to a document filed with the SEC that releases important corporate news publicly in between quarterly filings. He wrote, "Apparently a material weakness finding creates a need for an immediate 8K," seemingly oblivious to the fact that the original warning had come on November 29. He then went on to write about other concerns with the monitoring. "Quite a mess," Cassano concluded. Five days later, AIG announced that as of December 31, 2007, Pricewaterhouse believed AIG "had a material weakness in its internal control over financial reporting and oversight relating to the fair value valuation of the AIGFP super senior credit-default swap portfolio." That announcement, naturally, increased the pressure from counterparties and justified, according to Cassano, "new calls from our counterpart[ie]s stating that they can no longer accept our pricing methodology," which had "weakened our negotiation position as to collateral calls."

On February 28, AIG released its full-year 2007 financial results and announced that those numbers included a charge of $11.47 billion related to unrealized losses from the AIGFP swap portfolio. On March 1, Sullivan announced Cassano's departure from the firm "with our concurrence." In the preceding eight years, Cassano had received more than $280 million, according to Representative Henry Waxman, and was allowed to keep "up to $34 million in unvested bonuses" after his departure. He remained a consultant to AIG for six months thereafter, at a cost of $1 million per month.

On August 18, a week or so after AIG announced more bad earnings, Goldman's well-regarded research analyst on AIG, Thomas Chol-noky, issued a report with the advice "Don't Buy AIG," citing the risks to shareholders from "likely" further rating agency downgrades and capital-raising activities that would dilute shareholders. Among the reasons Cholnoky cited for his report was the potential for an increase in collat-eral calls. He made no mention of the fact that Goldman itself was lead-ing this charge and had been for about a year. (In an interview, he said he did not know about Goldman's ongoing collateral calls to AIG.)

The final nail in AIG's coffin came from another questionable deci-sion made under Sullivan's leadership: taking the cash generated when institutional investors, seeking to sell securities short, borrowed stock from AIG's massive $800 billion investment portfolio and invested it in what turned out to be high-risk mortgage securities. "There's no sense lending [the securities] to [other dealers] unless you're going to take the cash and invest it someplace and earn a spread," explained one AIG for-mer executive. "That's what a AAA rating is for."

But what should have been invested in liquid, low-risk securities like Treasury bonds went instead into the illiquid mortgage market. At one point, AIG had converted some $60 billion of the cash it had received from other dealers into mortgage-related securities. "It scared the shit out of me," said one AIG executive. "My first reaction was, 'What happens if all those guys come back and say, "We want our money back. Here's your damn securities, give us our cash back." ' All the cash had been put into securities that are now twenty-five, thirty percent under-water. If they were government securities, we could turn around, sell them tomorrow, and give them their money back. Well, we had securities that you couldn't sell to anybody." By the late summer and early fall of 2008, borrowed stock was flooding back to AIG and investors were ask-ing for their cash back, further exacerbating AIG's cash crunch. Buried on the last page of Cholnoky's August 2008 report was his concern about AIG's securities lending business. "[D]ue to AIG's aggressive investment strategy into riskier classes, the current market value of the assets stood at $59.5 billion as compared with liabilities of $75.1 billion," he wrote, noting that AIG had agreed to post collateral to make up for these losses.

CHOLNOKY'S REPORT BROKE the camel's back once and for all. On September 16, 2008, the federal government poured $85 billion of tax-payer money into AIG to keep it from falling into bankruptcy as Lehman Brothers had only hours earlier, and in effect took over the company. AIG eventually turned around and paid out $62.1 billion to sixteen coun-terparties to fulfill its collateral obligations related to credit-default swaps

AIGFP had sold. Second on the list, according to TARP special inspector general Neil Barofsky's November 17, 2009, report about AIG's counterparties, was Goldman Sachs, which received $14 billion, or everything AIG owed it at 100 cents on the dollar (Société Générale, a French bank, came in first with $16.5 billion, some of which was then paid over to Goldman, according to the *New York Times*.) There has never been a good explanation of why the money was paid out or why the Fed paid the counterparties 100 cents on the dollar when they surely would have received much less, if anything, had AIG filed for bankruptcy. Indeed, the Federal Reserve Bank of New York unsuccessfully tried to negotiate discounts, known as haircuts, with the counterparties. "Seven of the eight counterparties told [the New York Fed] that they would not voluntarily agree to a haircut," Barofsky wrote in his November 2009 report. "The eighth counterparty, UBS, said it would accept a haircut of 2 percent as long as other counterparties also granted a similar concession to [the New York Fed]." For his part, Cassano told the FCIC that taxpayers would have been far better off if the counterparties had not been paid off at all and if the Fed just held on to the original credit-default swaps. "What I look to is the performance," Cassano testified in 2010, "and to see if anything has been pierced. Now we've gone through obviously one of the worst financial crises in anybody's lifetime. And as we move through this and we come through the financial crisis, the only thing I can do is look at the existing portfolio and say that it is performing through this crisis, and it is meeting the standards that we set. And I think our reviews were rigorous. I think the portfolios are withstanding the test of time in extremely difficult circumstances."

Furthermore, according to a September 2009 report from the U.S. Government Accountability Office, "AIG's securities lending program continued to be one of the greatest ongoing demands on its liquidity" even after the September 16 bailout. As a result, the Fed created a vehicle dubbed Maiden Lane II and funded it with $24 billion to purchase from AIG the most troubled residential mortgage-backed securities it had bought with the cash received from the securities lending program. As of June 2010, AIG owed $16 billion on this credit facility, which Cassano at least took as a sign that AIGFP's underwriting standards had held up. Not everyone, though, agreed with Cassano's self-congratulatory stance. "Of all the events and all of the things we've done in the last eighteen months, the single one that makes me the angriest, that gives me the most angst, is the intervention with AIG," Bernanke said in March 2010 on the television program *60 Minutes*. "Here was a company that made all kinds of unconscionable bets. Then, when those bets went wrong . . .

we had a situation where the failure of that company would have brought down the financial system."

———

ACCORDING TO ONE internal Goldman report, Birnbaum's desk made $947 million in the fourth quarter and $3.738 billion for the fiscal year 2007. Birnbaum said his trading made Goldman $4 billion in profit it otherwise would not have had. And had the VAR police been less demanding, he said he believes he could have made two to three times more profit, or $8 billion to $12 billion instead of $4 billion. "More Paulson-like," he said. "He didn't cut back. He went for it." Birnbaum said the losses Goldman suffered in 2007 from writing down its long mortgage positions was more than $1 billion, but significantly less than the $4 billion his desk made. "The net result for the mortgage department in 2007 was a record year," he said. "Think about that statement: making a record amount of money in a year when everyone else was losing their shirts." The firm could also boast of its trading and risk-management prowess—which it certainly did—and then was able, in September 2008, to attract a $5 billion preferred stock investment from Warren Buffett.

Months later—as the spotlight began to focus on Goldman in the wake of the AIG counterparty payments—the senior brass at Goldman preferred to spin Birnbaum's success differently. Viniar said the decisions to occasionally reduce Birnbaum's short positions in 2007 cost the firm only around $200 million, not the billions of dollars in lost profits suggested by Birnbaum. But he did concede, "They were one hundred percent right. I was one hundred percent wrong." The Goldman perspective was, essentially, that the firm provided Birnbaum the capital he used to execute "the big short" and that he was good at executing the directive. But the opportunity Birnbaum seized at Goldman existed, in large part, because of the emphasis the firm placed on marking to market and because of the existence of Goldman's long positions in mortgage-related securities the firm wanted either to sell or hedge. Without that preexisting condition, Birnbaum would not have found a receptive audience at the executive levels of the firm.

Several Goldman executives don't buy that argument. "When you kind of look back, both at the end of the year and at the end of this cycle and how things can be characterized, the PR's completely different than the reality at the time," one of them said. "The PR now is Goldman was hedging customer positions: we had longs here and shorts here and it was a holistic analysis." He said what really happened was that the top Goldman brass finally figured out the risks inherent in the firm's long positions "after us pounding on them" and convincing them that loans sitting in the CDO warehouse, for instance, had every bit as much risk as CDOs being traded in the market. He said his trading group was "frustrated" because "we felt like we don't want to have a situation at the end of the year where they pat us on the back and go, 'Boy, the department did great. You guys made $4 billion minus everything that was lost over here.' We're like, 'If you say I can control everything else also over here, that's fine, but I don't control it. So don't pay me based on that.'" He did concede, though, that Blankfein needed to have—and did have—a larger perspective than just what was happening on Birnbaum's desk. "The way he looks at things on his level is that he's got the $4 billion here and he's got other positions that are being marked down over here," he said. "It's still a multibillion dollar phenomenon. But he's thinking firmwide."

As extraordinary as Birnbaum's 2007 performance was, by the unique combination of chest pounding and double counting that define the Wall Street end-of-year compensation process, he marked himself down—in his personal evaluation form for 2007—as having performed even better. "As a co-head of ABS and SPG trading, my performance in 2007 has been my best ever by any objective measure," he wrote. He claimed his P&L for the year totaled $7.5 billion, rather than $4 billion, including $2.5 billion from synthetic deals, $2 billion from asset-backed securities deals, and $3 billion from his trading—"all #1 on the [S]treet by a wide margin" and "#2 in the world trading subprime risk."

While acknowledging that the "execution" of the trading strategies was a "remarkable team achievement with every member playing a key role," Birnbaum wrote that he considered himself "the initial or primary driver" of the trading strategy.

With slightly more humility than Birnbaum, Swenson trumpeted his own accomplishments in 2007. "It should not be a surprise to anyone that the 2007 year is the one that I am most proud of to date," he wrote in his performance review. "I can take credit for recognizing the enormous opportunity for the ABS synthetics business 2 years ago. I recognized the need to assemble an outstanding team of traders and was able to lead that group to build a number one franchise that was able to achieve extraordinary profits (nearly $3bb to date)."

As examples of his leadership skills, he wrote that "as the stress in the mortgage market starting filtering" out, he "spent numerous hours on conference calls with clients discussing valuation methodologies" for mortgage-backed securities, such as GSAMP-S2, that Goldman had underwritten and sold to investors. He patted himself on the back for withstanding the onslaught from burned GSAMP-S2 investors. "I said 'no' to clients who demanded that GS should 'support the GSAMP' program as clients tried to gain leverage over us," he wrote. A far cry indeed from Goldman's purported top priority: "Our clients' interests always come first."

For his part, Sparks was more modest—at least in print—about his role in the group's accomplishments but conveyed his points just the same. "I delivered the best performance of my career this year to the firm," he wrote. "I led a great team through an incredibly volatile and challenging market[.] [W]e had to change business approaches dramatically and constantly[.] [W]e levered the firm's support, and we didn't just survive—we excelled."

Tourre turned out to be the most understated of all in his 2007 personal professional assessment, perhaps because many of the ABACUS deals he engineered had performed poorly. Indeed, he never even mentioned the ABACUS deal he spent half of 2007 executing. Rather, all he could muster was, "In a difficult market environment, have been persistent and showed patience in executing complex transaction that were involving several financial products including corporate CDS, single-tranche synthetic ABS CDOs, and CDO management technology," he wrote. He is still awaiting his fate at the hands of the SEC as a result of its ABACUS lawsuit, even though Goldman settled the suit, for $550 million, in the summer of 2010. In February 2011, Tourre's lawyers tried to get the case thrown out by claiming the SEC did not have jurisdiction over the matter.

BY MID-DECEMBER 2007, the time had come for the *Wall Street Journal* to follow *Fortune* and the *New York Times* in trying to assess how Goldman had avoided the mistakes of other securities firms in 2007. In a front-page article on December 14, Kate Kelly, at the *Journal*, lionized Swenson, Birnbaum, and Sparks for their gutsy trades that made billions for Goldman and noted that each of them was expected to be paid between $5 million and $15 million in compensation for fiscal 2007. "The structured-products traders were working long hours," she wrote. "Mr. Swenson would leave his home in Northern New Jersey in time to hit the gym and be at his desk by 7:30 a.m. When Mr. Birnbaum arrived from his Manhattan loft, they'd begin executing large trades on behalf of clients. There was no time for breaks. They took breakfast and lunch at their desks—for Mr. Swenson, the same chicken-and-vegetable salad every day from a nearby deli; for Mr. Birnbaum, an egg-white sandwich for breakfast, a chicken or turkey sandwich for lunch. Mr. Sparks, the mortgage chief, climbed into his car at

5:30 each morning for the drive in from New Canaan, Connecticut. To calm his nerves, he'd stop by the gym in Goldman's downtown building to briefly jump rope and lift weights. Sometimes he worked past midnight, arriving home exhausted. He canceled a family ski trip to Wyoming. Although he loved to attend Texas A&M football games and owned a second home near the university, he decided not to join his wife and two children on more than one trip."

A few days after the *Journal*'s story, a Goldman "source" told *The Independent,* a British newspaper, "They are very embarrassed that their names have come out. Until now, nobody had heard of them, including most of the people on the floor where they work." Whether deliberate or not, Kelly's story had humanized at least three of the Goldman cyborgs—an apparent violation of the unwritten rule at Goldman that for the rank and file, no matter how successful, talking to the press is against the rules.

The fact that Goldman did not lose money from mortgages in 2007—when nearly every other major firm on Wall Street did—helped Goldman and its top executives to make a fortune. The firm had record pretax earnings of $17.6 billion in 2007, some $3 billion more than in the previous year. The top five executives at the firm split among themselves nearly $400 million, with Blankfein taking home $70.3 million, Cohn receiving $72.5 million, and Viniar being paid $58.5 million. These breathtaking sums were among the highest compensation ever paid to Wall Street executives in a single year. Still, Gary Cohn liked to pretend with reporters that Goldman did not make nearly as much money in 2007 betting against the mortgage market as people think it did. "We don't disclose segment-by-segment reporting," he said in an interview. "But the market would be really disappointed if they saw our actual mortgage results last year, because they think we made a lot of money." Sparks was much more honest about what happened. "The good thing we did is when we made a mistake we admitted it and did something about it," Sparks said. "We didn't just sit there and close our eyes and pray."

———

A FEW MONTHS after paying out these huge bonuses to its top executives, both Sparks, then forty-one, and Birnbaum, then thirty-five, left Goldman. Sparks had been a Goldman partner since November 2002. Birnbaum was a Goldman vice president, hoping to be made a partner in 2008. Reached at his home in October 2009, Sparks—who had been head of Goldman's four-hundred-person mortgage department for some eighteen months—said in a brief telephone conversation that he does not like to talk to reporters about his experience at Goldman and why it came to such an abrupt end. He had told his colleagues he was "fond of the firm" but that it was "time to move on." He said he had been thinking about leaving Goldman often during the previous six years and the time just became right because his business was changing rapidly—in the wake of the meltdown—and he had had to fire half of his team. He claimed to still be on good terms with Goldman and that it was supportive of him. He is the chairman of Archon Mortgage LLC, a real-estate management company in Irving, Texas, that is affiliated with Goldman. He also appears to have other company affiliations as well. Left unsaid was that, according to the *Wall Street Journal,* in and around January 2008, the SEC had interviewed Sparks about his role in the sale of the Timberwolf CDO. Soon after, a representative of Basis Yield Alpha Fund, an Australian hedge fund that bought $100 million of the deal, and lost money as the deal soured, told an SEC lawyer, "Our belief is the trade was portrayed in a fraudulent manner." In March, a month before Sparks left Goldman, the SEC interviewed the Basis hedge-fund executives further about the Timberwolf deal.

Birnbaum was out the door shortly before Sparks. He is now the founder and chief investment officer at Tilden Park Capital Management, a $1 billion, New York–based hedge fund focused on "opportunities in structured products." Jeremy Primer, the Goldman mortgage-modeling guru, works with Birnbaum at Tilden Park. Not surprisingly, Birnbaum was not shy about setting out his three goals for 2008 at Goldman: "Produce more than $1 billion in trading revenue," "continue to strengthen the GS franchise," and "Make Partner."

It was not to be. Part of Birnbaum's motivation for leaving Goldman seemed to be compensation related. He won't say, but he probably made around $10 million in 2007, apparently less than he thought he should have made. "I guess it depends on your perspective of what's fair, right?" he said. "If you're a steelworker you probably think I got paid pretty well. If you're a hedge-fund manager you probably don't."

Goldman won't say why its two star traders left the firm, although a spokesman said, "We're sorry to see Dan go. He'll be missed," which is of course the typical corporate happy talk dispensed when the real reasons for someone's unexpected departure are too uncomfortable to be discussed publicly. (For instance, had Sparks been leaving unexpectedly to become, say, secretary of the treasury, Goldman might have been slightly more forthcoming.) Goldman said nothing about Birnbaum's departure. There has been speculation that the two men were forced out of Goldman—despite having a profound role in helping to construct a series of trades that may well have saved the firm. Both of them appeared at Senator Levin's famous April 2010 filleting of Goldman Sachs.

CHAPTER 24

GOD'S WORK

Goldman's recent public-relations nightmares began in earnest in March 2009 when the firm appeared at the top of the list of counterparties that had received billions of dollars in payments funneled through AIG by the U.S. government as part of the second phase of the 2008 $182 billion bailout of AIG. The counterparty list had been kept secret for months and was only released after much public outcry. A narrative quickly developed in the zeitgeist that Goldman had somehow received a special benefit along with its $14 billion, thanks to its numerous Washington connections, including Hank Paulson; Steve Friedman, a Goldman board member who was then chairman of the board of the Federal Reserve Bank of New York and a former head of the National Economic Council under George W. Bush; and Josh Bolten, a former Goldman partner who was President George W. Bush's chief of staff. Blankfein later acknowledged as much in a speech he gave to Goldman's 470 partners in January 2011. "Our history of good performance through the crisis became a liability as people wondered how we performed so well and whether we'd received favorable treatment from well-placed alumni," he told his partners. "This was not only a poor place to be, it was a dangerous place to be."

Soon after the release of the AIG counterparties list, Goldman snatched one public-relations defeat after another from the jaws of its financial victory. "I think there are a lot of things, as a firm, we do really, really well," Blankfein said, "but there are other things that we clearly could have been better at for us to be in the position that we were in. I don't think we've done a very good job of explaining what Goldman Sachs does." The opening salvo in this ongoing battle came a few days after the release of the AIG counterparty list, on March 20, when Viniar led an unprecedented—by Goldman's standards—forty-five-minute call with journalists "to clarify certain misperceptions in the press regarding Goldman Sachs's trading relationship with AIG." The gist of Viniar's argument was that Goldman had hedged itself against a collapse of AIG as well as the securities it had asked AIG to insure. "That is why we are able to say that whether it failed or not, AIG would have had no material direct impact on Goldman Sachs," he said.

The call seemed to raise more questions than it answered—among the very people it was designed to pacify: the journalists listening in on behalf of the American people. That frustration—and confusion—showed up first in a July 2009 issue of *Rolling Stone* magazine in a now-classic bit of conspiracy-theory journalism written by reporter Matt Taibbi. "The first thing you need to know about Goldman Sachs is that it's everywhere," Taibbi wrote. "The world's most powerful investment bank is a great vampire squid wrapped around the face of humanity, relentlessly jamming its blood funnel into anything that smells like money." Taibbi blamed Goldman for a multitude of financial sins, including the Great Depression, the Internet bubble, the housing bubble, the explosion in the per-gallon price of gasoline, as well as for "rigging the bailout" to its advantage.

The metaphor of Goldman being a "great vampire squid" soon became so ubiquitous that even Blankfein could not ignore it. "That *Rolling Stone* article oddly enough tapped into something," he said in an interview in August 2009. "I thought it was so over the top that I actually read it as a gonzo piece of over-the-top kind of writing that some people found fun to read. That's how I saw it. But then you had other people sort of taking stuff as if Goldman Sachs burned down the Reichstag, fired on Fort Sumter, shot the archduke Ferdinand, all that kind of stuff."

Goldman's gold-plated image suddenly seemed to tarnish overnight. A few weeks later, Joe Hagan, at *New York* magazine, followed up Taibbi's screed with a more sober analysis of how and why things were going so wrong at the mighty Goldman. In *Capitalism: A Love Story,* the filmmaker Michael Moore, full of vim, vigor, and irony, drove up to 85 Broad Street in a Brinks truck, hopped out, and yelled: "We're here to get the money back for the American people!" before being ushered from the premises without getting inside.

The frenzy seemed to reach what in retrospect looks like a false peak in early November 2009 when the august *Sunday Times,* in London, weighed into the fracas with its own lengthy treatise of how Goldman had become "the best cash making machine that global capitalism has ever produced, and, some say, a political force more powerful than governments." The usual tropes about Goldman were trotted out—including those about it being a collection of the hardest-working, smartest, and richest kids on the block—but questions were also raised about its plethora of conflicts and its ability to manage them. Then there was the question, posed to Blankfein, about whether there can ever be—should ever be—any limit to the firm's ambitions, or the ambitions of the people who work there. "I don't want people in this firm to think that they have accomplished as much for themselves as they can and go on vacation," he answered. "As the guardian of the interests of the shareholders and, by the way, for the purposes of society, I'd like them to continue to do what they are doing. I don't want to put a cap on their ambition." Blankfein's comment seemed to be a direct jab at the ongoing efforts of the Obama administration during its first year to mitigate the growing discrepancy between rich and poor in the country.

As difficult to digest as Blankfein's comment might have been for most readers, it was his off-the-cuff comment on the way out the door that he was just a banker "doing God's work" that set off a new round of firestorms at the firm. Once again, Goldman found itself on the defensive, trying to explain an example of Blankfein's self-deprecating sense of humor, which was ill timed and had fallen terribly flat. Ten days later, Jeffrey Cunningham, of *Directorship* magazine, which would soon name Blankfein its 2009 "CEO of the Year," interviewed Blankfein about the "God's work" comment. "It's nice to be entrapped by you so early in the game," Blankfein quipped. "No, it was obviously a joke. If you asked me now if I wish I hadn't said it, no of course. I'm always warned when I leave, by my handlers, 'Now remember, Lloyd, whatever you do, don't be yourself.' So I walked out and I was talking to a reporter, and the questions were running along the lines of 'How much did your tie cost?' and 'Do you know how much a quart of milk costs?' And I knew where the trend was going, and as I was leaving, we'd gotten into a back and forth on the themes he was projecting, and I was leaving, I said and meant in an ironic way, 'Now I'm off to do God's work.' He laughed, I laughed, but guess what? He got the last laugh. And so, I would say that if anybody has any allergies and you sneeze, and I don't say, 'God bless you,' understand it's because I've learned my lesson."

Despite the gaffe, from other quarters plaudits for Blankfein continued to roll in. How could anyone ignore the firm's extraordinary 2009 profits? *Vanity Fair* named him as its number 1 most powerful and influential person on its annual Vanity Fair 100 list. The *Financial Times* named Blankfein its 2009 "Person of the Year" but made clear, in the accompanying article, that it was grudgingly bestowed. "This is not an unalloyed endorsement of either Mr. Blankfein or Goldman," columnist John Gapper wrote, "which the FT has sometimes criticised in the past year. Instead, it is a recognition that Mr. Blankfein and his bank have taken the leading place in the world of finance, while others have fallen by the wayside."

Like the 2004 Red Sox, though, in the first quarter of 2010, the other Wall Street banks seemingly left for dead began to show signs of life, fueled by a combination of the gift of nearly free money from the Federal Reserve—the rocket fuel of the banking sector—and an economy that had been pulled back from the brink. For the first time since before the 2008 crisis became manifest, other firms, besides Goldman, began to make big money again. Even the beleaguered Citigroup showed a profit—of $4.4 billion—after years of losses. Goldman made $3.3 billion in the first quarter of 2010.

Finally, it seemed, the intense spotlight was no longer focused on Goldman Sachs. Wall Street's sudden return to profitability seemed to signal the return to normalcy that the architects of the TARP envisioned, and no one could have been happier about that than Lloyd Blankfein. By all rights, 2010 should have been Blankfein's triumphal moment. But Blankfein could not catch a break.

In the wake of the SEC's lawsuit and Senator Levin's hearing, a rash of new civil lawsuits were filed against the firm. The SEC was reportedly studying another Goldman synthetic CDO marketed and sold in the fall of 2006: the $2 billion Hudson Mezzanine Funding 2006-1, where Goldman stated in marketing materials related to the deal that its interests were aligned with the buyers—"Goldman Sachs has aligned incentives with the Hudson program by investing in a portion of equity," according to an internal Goldman marketing document—but that, in fact, according to Senator Levin and Goldman documents, Goldman had actually been the sole, $2 billion investor on the short side of the deal, betting the security would collapse. When it did, in September 2007, Goldman made $1 billion. "Goldman Sachs profited from the loss in value of the very CDO securities it had sold to its clients," Senator Levin said. The Justice Department was also said to be investigating Goldman on criminal charges, which if brought would be the firm's death knell, as no financial services firm has ever survived a criminal indictment against it.

In an irony that surely Blankfein can appreciate, the SEC's lawsuit and the Senate hearing emboldened both the firm's supporters, who believe the firm has been wrongly singled out for persecution, and the firm's harshest critics, who believe Goldman embodies all that is wrong with Wall Street and its current mores.

Warren Buffett is among Goldman and Blankfein's most ardent boosters (and the firm's largest individual shareholder). He said he backed the firm "100 percent" and that if Blankfein were to resign, or be replaced, "If Lloyd had a twin brother, I would vote for him" to be Goldman's new CEO. Old hands on Wall Street say Buffett was just "talking his own book," since he has a large financial stake in the firm. On the other hand, Steve Schwarzman, the billionaire founder of the Blackstone Group, competes with Goldman in a number of businesses. So when, a few days after Senator Levin's hearing, Schwarzman told the *Financial Times* that for the twenty-five years Blackstone has been around "we never had any circumstance where there was any question about ethical character or behavior," his words had more resonance. "We are a major client of Goldman's and we will continue to remain a major client," he said.

In an interview recently in a conference room off his office thirty-one floors above Park Avenue, Schwarzman said he thought Goldman was unfairly caught in the crosshairs of Obama's populist, antibusiness rhetoric and the American public's ire at having to bail out Wall Street for its own mistakes, only to watch as bankers and traders—especially at Goldman Sachs—were once again reaping big financial rewards while the economic suffering in many quarters remained palpable. "Goldman became a symbol of prosperity in the time where there was no prosperity," he said. "And Obama ran on a platform to decrease the [disparity] between prosperous people and middle-class people. That's like his touchstone. And so Goldman became the mega-symbol because they outearned everybody, right? I think for Obama this was the nail that was too far out of the board and it was going to get hammered down into the board. They just went out about trying to hammer it down. And from talking with Lloyd at different points during this evolution, it was not clear what would feed this monster." He said that Goldman has become for the Obama administration "either subliminally or purposefully . . . some kind of symbol . . . of the society that Obama wants to change, modify, or destroy." (On the other hand, Henry Kravis, Schwarzman's rival at KKR who once tried to get a job in Goldman's arbitrage department and was a summer intern at the firm, has watched the firm's evolution during the past thirty-five years from one focused almost exclusively on trying to help its clients, for a fee, to one that finds new ways to compete with its clients on almost a daily basis. "That stress between KKR as a principal and Goldman Sachs as a principal was always enormous," said one former Goldman banker. "You should talk to Henry about the firm, too, if you haven't. He has a very, very good view of it. We had a good relationship when I was there. They still have a very good relationship. It goes in and out." Alas, Kravis declined numerous requests to be interviewed.

Others are far less sanguine and forgiving about Goldman and its business practices than either Buffett or Schwarzman appears to be. They hope that Goldman has finally been caught in the web of its own making. There have been long-standing rumors on Wall Street that Goldman engages in "front-running," where the firm becomes privy to a client's confidential trade or interest and uses that information to its financial advantage. Some even think Goldman did this when it put on its "big short" in early 2007, privy as it was to John Paulson's trading patterns, but that it was one example among many. "They view information gathered from their client businesses as free to them to trade on," explained one Goldman competitor. "They don't view that as, 'Hey, that's my client's information. I'm not supposed to be knowing that in terms of trading on my own book.' It's as simple as that." He gave the example of Goldman being hired by, say, a medical supply business on a potential sale or IPO and discovering as part of its due diligence on the company that the demand for the company's services was declining daily and then relaying that information to traders, who would then short the medical supply industry or the securities of companies in the industry.

"They . . . knew as adviser to some of these companies inside information about what's going on in these companies," he said. "And they go and they use this inside information to trade in the market, and they call that 'managing risk.' That's bullshit. That's fucking insider trading. . . . They go, 'Well, that's managing our risk.' What the fuck you mean that's managing your risk? That is the business model . . . to use their clients—and their client relationships—to generate information off which they can trade. They're doing that with countries. They're doing that all the time. It just seems to me that you've got three businesses down there. You've got advisory, securities underwriting, and trading. And they have taken the securities underwriting and advisory businesses away from being separate and important units to being information sources for trading. And I don't understand how that's legal."

Eliot Spitzer, the former New York State governor and attorney general, said in an interview that he has heard these charges about Goldman for years. "Front-running is illegal," he said. "Front-running is a fraud on your client. No question about it. . . . When you have a client, you don't give them bad research, you don't trade in front of them, you don't subvert their bids. It's really simple." But, he noted, neither he nor any other prosecutor has brought such a case against Goldman, in large part because of how difficult it would be to prove in court. "If you had a penny for every person who told you that was what they presume Goldman had done for twenty years, you'd be the richest man in the world," he said. As attorney general, Spitzer was not shy about prosecuting Wall Street. Indeed, in April 2003, he forged a $1.4 billion settlement with a group of ten Wall Street firms—including Goldman, which paid $110 million—after he showed conclusively that the equity research Wall Street was issuing was being unduly influenced by the firms' investment bankers looking to win more business.

But whether the evidence would stand up in court, the anecdotes about Goldman's ruthless behavior abound. One hedge-fund manager recalled the experience his friend, at another hedge fund, had with Goldman during the recent financial crisis when Goldman was the hedge fund's "prime broker," responsible for executing and clearing trades as well as general administrative responsibilities related to the fund. "He had them as a prime broker, where they house all the positions," he remembered. "The people he was trading with at Goldman, they knew exactly what he had and they were basically trying on the trading desk, in conjunction with the prime brokerage business, to squeeze him to make money themselves. Like this sort of front-running the trades that they knew he needed to do to take risk off, because the prime brokers were telling him he had to. They're actively trying to put the guy out of business, because they thought at this juncture, this fund is worth more to us dead. We can mop up the pieces and sort of pick up a bunch of cheap things from them when they're a stressed or a distressed seller. It's worth more to us dead because we can make twenty million bucks more out of this than if it is alive. They had no qualms about making that sort of objective decision. Door 1 or Door 2—which has the highest present value for me? You wouldn't want to be in the door with the lower dollar sign."

Then there is the way the firm handles conflicts of interest, which is at the heart of what Senator Levin found so offensive. One of Goldman's unstated business principles, according to the *New York Times,* is "to embrace conflicts." Goldman "argues that [conflicts] are evidence of a healthy tension between the firm and its customers," according to the paper. "If you are not embracing conflicts, the argument holds, you are not being aggressive enough in generating business." Other firms are far less aggressive than Goldman in this regard. If, for instance, a firm had agreed to represent a seller of a business, it would not also represent the buyer for obvious reasons, even though many firms will also provide financing to a buyer of a company they are selling. Goldman is more willing to try to figure out a way to do both. Although the instances where Goldman represents both seller and buyer are rare, they do occur and are considered investment banking triumphs because the fee potential is doubled.

The pinnacle of what this was about may have been reached in 2005, when Goldman represented both sides of the $9 billion merger between the New York Stock Exchange—then private and led by John Thain, the former president and COO of Goldman—and Archipelago Holdings, a publicly traded electronic exchange in which Goldman was the second-largest investor. Through the complex merger, the stock exchange could both become a publicly traded company and take the crucial steps needed to keep up with other exchanges that did not have brokers on floors but rather computers in offices far from the floor. The merger was all about the future of Wall Street and who was going to control it. In other words, the very kind of deal in which Goldman would be expected to have a prominent role. What shocked people was that Goldman was on both sides and everyone involved seemed to be fine with that outcome. Goldman ended up making a $100 million windfall from the merger, considering its fee for advising on the deal, the increase in the value of its stake in Archipelago Holdings, and the increase in value of its NYSE seats. "Forgetting about the trading stuff, constantly having conflicts and managing those conflicts by just kind of saying, 'Guys, we're above that,'" has always amazed him, one private-equity investor said. "Look what they were doing with the deals with the Stock Exchange, they run every side of the deal. And then people would say, 'You can't do that,' [but for Goldman] it was almost like public service, *they had to do that,* [and then they argued] no one else was as good as they and it would be letting down the mission of furthering tranquility and stability in capital markets if Goldman Sachs didn't actually manage conflicts." In short, the private-equity investor was lamenting the fact that Goldman continues to rely on its tired crutch "Trust us, we're honest."

Goldman has also been invited to partner with one private-equity firm on a proprietary deal, only to decline the offer and then show up in the auction for the company with another private-equity firm by its side. One bank CEO told the story of how he was bidding on a failed financial institution that the FDIC was selling and that Goldman threatened to bid against his company for the bank if he did not let Goldman into the deal. He described Goldman's bare-knuckled approach as "anything to make a buck" and as "a sense of ethics that is not compatible with mine." One former Goldman banker who left the firm and now works at a hedge fund that trades with Goldman continues to marvel at how the firm has changed since it went public. "We trade with Goldman a lot," he said. "I think that they very clearly went to—across all their businesses—the view that what's right for Goldman is what matters. As much as they might say the client's interest comes first here, there, or whatever—

maybe that's still true in investment banking—but it is absolutely not true on the trading side. Like if they could eat your lunch and screw you over, they totally would."

Another private-equity investor put it more bluntly. "What I'm fundamentally saying is that a lot of their basic business model should be illegal," he said. Of course, he has experienced the situation where he has asked the firm to represent him on the purchase of the company, only to be told a week later that the firm "has a conflict" and then showed up bidding against his firm for the company. "I think savvy clients now expect that from Goldman," he said. But he had a larger concern: since Goldman trades on nearly everything these days—from commodities to mortgages to loans—the insider-trading laws, which apply to trading in equities, need to be revised to reflect new categories of trading based on proprietary, nonpublic information that floats around inside Goldman Sachs and then is used to trade. Goldman's proprietary computer risk-monitoring system—SecDB—allows Goldman to think about risk differently from other firms. Bankers and traders actually approach potential clients and discuss the buying and selling of risk. But sometimes, they take this too far. "They view information gathered from their client businesses as free to them to trade on . . . ," the private-equity investor said. "It's as simple as that. If they are in a client situation, working on a deal and they're learning everything there is to know about that business, they take all that information, pass it up through their organization, and use that information to trade against the client, against other clients, et cetera, et cetera. But it might not be insider trading as written by the Forty Act because they might not be trading in the securities of that company. But that doesn't make it less outrageous—and it is outrageous! Doesn't that make it an outrageous business model, where as an adviser to this company, I happen to learn everything there is about the demand for their services ahead of the rest of the market, and then I take that information, I go trade against their competitors, right? If I'm a [widget] company and I'm using Goldman and they're analyzing my business information for a potential sale of it or an IPO of it or whatever, and they see that like my daily orders are declining before that information is released to the public on a quarterly business, well, they take that information and they go, 'Holy shit. We need to go short the [widget] industry.' That is their business model! To use their client—and their client relationships—to generate information on which they can trade. . . . I don't understand how that's legal."

He has decided he won't deal with Goldman anymore, as powerful as they remain. He figured that in the long run, Goldman would be very vulnerable as more and more clients resent their trading on their confidential information. "They keep doing this and over twenty years, people will start to figure it out and stop using them as advisers," he said. "But you have to remember, most companies using them as advisers are really using them for a reason. They're trying to access capital markets. They're trying to underwrite securities. I think at most large companies, the managements are temporary and the banking relationships are temporary. As long as they think Goldman can deliver a high-yield deal or if they think they're best off working with Goldman, they will go with that and worry about the damage later to the extent there is any because they'll probably be gone. So, in essence, Goldman's model takes advantage of the short-term nature of client relationships on Wall Street today. That's something that I don't think people quite get. People will use Goldman if they think that gives them an 'in' with somebody. All these webs of relationships—if you give them plenty of time—might give them an 'in' in the short run. In the short run, to get that 'in,' they'll do that. Then by the time somebody is tipped off about the next thing, it will be a new management team."

NONE OF THIS comes as a surprise to Sandy Lewis, a former Wall Street merger arbitrageur who had many dealings with Goldman during his years on Wall Street and whose father, Cy Lewis, was the senior partner at Bear Stearns and a close friend of Gus Levy. "My take on the whole firm is that it's done a masterful job of integrating various parts of the business, which if you study the rules carefully should not be integrated," he said. "They simply shouldn't be integrated. They can talk about Chinese walls. That might exist in China. I'm not so sure it exists in any of these firms, including Goldman Sachs."

A former Goldman partner said that of course Goldman has changed, and will continue to change as long as it is around. One of the firm's great strengths, he said, is the ability to adapt to changing circumstances with alacrity and still make money. "The firm is not the same now as it was before it went public," he said. "It's, in fact, not the same as it was two years ago or even three years ago. It's constantly changing. The reason for its success is that it has an incredible ability to gauge what's going on in the outside world and respond to it very, very fast. You combine that with a ferocious competitiveness—the competitiveness is astonishing when you see what these people, how much these people want to win, I've never seen anything like it—and that virtually assures that Goldman will continue to be around and continue to excel."

He said that despite "all the negative publicity"—some of which he thought was deserved, some of which he thought was not—"Goldman is being criticized for being successful. If every investment bank in the United States had done what Goldman had done, there would not have been a financial crisis. That's what Lloyd Blankfein should have said up in front of the Senate. If I have any criticisms of Lloyd, it's that Goldman went into the hearing in a defensive mode. What he should have said was, 'Listen, you're criticizing us for making all the right decisions. If everyone had done what we did, we wouldn't be sitting here today. We wouldn't have had a trillion-dollar meltdown.'"

Wondered the former Goldman partner, "Is Lloyd the best person to be dealing with the public, honestly? Probably not. He probably knows that. He's not a natural public face of Goldman. But is he the right person to be running the firm right now? I think probably, because he understands risk profiles better than anybody else. That's what matters the most."

———

FOR HIS PART, Blankfein is not immune to the criticism. "In a crisis, you have to deal not only with how you got there, but you have to deal with the legacy of the past," he said in an interview. "So clearly we have things that we're going to have to work our way through. There's the SEC suit, the hearings, the media scrutiny, and you have to at least say there's certainly a bit of a disconnect between how a lot of people see us and how we see ourselves." In the wake of the Levin hearing, Blankfein appointed an internal fifteen-member committee, headed by Goldman partners E. Gerald Corrigan, a former president of the New York Federal Reserve Bank, and J. Michael Evans, a vice chairman and a rumored potential successor to Blankfein, to review the firm's business practices, particularly relating to client relationships, conflicts of interest, and the creation of exotic securities.

The internal committee released its report during the second week of January 2011; its sixty-three pages reveal an extraordinary combination of chutzpah—in that such a document would be produced at all, as clearly no other Wall Street firm would (or has) undertaken such a project—and an Orwellian beehive, where one official-sounding committee after another has been, or will be, formed to make sure that Goldman, despite its DNA, continues to try to adhere to Whitehead's principles (a complete set of which was featured on the report's first page). According to the report, there are now—or soon will be—at 200 West Street, Goldman's new, $2 billion world headquarters near Ground Zero (tax breaks included), something like thirty separate groups and committees—with names such as "Firmwide New Activity Committee" and "Firmwide Suitability Committee"—that Blankfein and Cohn will use to run the firm. "Goldman Sachs relies heavily on committees to coordinate and apply consistent business standards, practices, policies and procedures across the firm," the report explained. "The firm's committee governance structure should serve to enhance our reputation, business practices and client service. In this way, committees serve as a vital control function." Of course, the "Business Standards Committee," which produced the report, recommended that a new committee be formed—the "Firmwide Client and Business Standards Committee"—that will replace the Business Standards Committee in the future and also have responsibility for "the primacy of client interests and reputational risk." Gary Cohn will head up the new committee, which will "function as a high-level committee that assesses and makes determinations regarding business practices, reputational risk management and client relationships."

If it takes its responsibilities seriously, Cohn's new committee will be plenty busy. One of the few self-critical observations in the report was that, according to an independent survey conducted for Goldman, the firm's clients have been a bit miffed at the firm lately. "Clients raised concerns about whether the firm has remained true to its traditional values and [b]usiness [p]rinciples given changes to the firm's size, business mix and perceptions about the role of proprietary trading," the report explained. "Clients said that, in some circumstances, the firm weighs its interests and short-term incentives too heavily." This led the Business Standards Committee to call for a firmwide rededication to Whitehead's core principles, including a "need to strengthen client relationships which, in turn, will strengthen trust," to "communicate our core values more clearly," and also to "communicate more clearly about our roles and responsibilities in particular transactions." The real question is why Goldman continues to promote a list of principles and behaviors that the firm seems to have abandoned years ago. In the end, is Goldman really all that different from the other firms on Wall Street it believes it is superior to?

Clayton Rose, a former head of investment banking at JPMorgan and now a professor of management practice at Harvard Business School, predicted that regardless of the outcome of the legal process, Goldman will be changed by the current financial crisis. "I think the big challenge for Goldman is internal and it's cultural," Rose said. "They have been, for several generations now, so used to having clients deal with them in an unquestioned way, having access to regulators and government officials in a somewhat unquestioned way, and having played the kind of 'Government Sachs/Goldman Sachs' revolving door and so forth, that having their business ethics, their business culture, their business model challenged at a very core level—and the kind of compensation that results from that as well—is going to cause a bunch of people there to think about whether they're going to want to be part of whatever the new iteration of Goldman is going to be."

That's what Blankfein should be most worried about, he said. "Will it be a great firm?" he wondered. "Probably. But will it be a different firm? Yes, and as we know from the way the markets and capitalism work, Goldman's not guaranteed a place in that kind of pantheon of firms in perpetuity. The biggest danger I think they face is within, not without."

Charles Elson is both a lawyer and the chairman of the John L. Weinberg Center for Corporate Governance at the University of Delaware. Since his think tank is named after one of Goldman's most admired former senior partners, Elson has taken a keen interest in the recent events at the firm. "The fundamental problem [for Blankfein and Goldman]," he said, "is you've made a lot of money when everyone else hasn't, you know? People are angry about it, and frankly, your competitors disappeared, and you were the last person standing, and as the last person standing, you get a bigger piece of, albeit, a smaller pie. But because there are fewer others taking out of the pie, your share gets larger. And you're in a very tough situation where the government allowed the others to fail, yet allowed you to succeed. He is in—they are in—an almost impossible position, and I don't know who could've done it differently. That being said, obviously, the response [so far] hasn't worked out so well."

Jim Cramer, too, is convinced Goldman has flubbed its response so far but also that it is not too late for Goldman to admit to and apologize for its mistakes, to acknowledge the extraordinary lifeline the American people provided to the firm in a time of crisis and then to donate the totality of the 2009 bonuses—$16.2 billion—to a worthy cause, such as to the people of Haiti. "You settle with the SEC at all costs," he said, "at *all* costs you settle with the SEC"—which the firm did during the summer of 2010. "You also say, 'Look, you know, we've been thinking a lot about what happened here and we were very defensive because we thought we did it right. And we thought the people recognized that maybe it was because of our smarts that we did okay, but, you know, as we've reviewed the era and what happened we realized we made some mistakes and what we're going to do—*we* made mistakes, not mistakes were made—and what we're going to do is we're going to review what we did and we're going to forgo those bonuses even though it's going to be at a tremendous cost because we paid taxes on those bonuses. But we're not going to ask for refunds and we've heard what the American people said and we're in this business for the long term and we love our country and we feel very blessed that this country allowed us to make this money so what we're going to do is retroactively make these changes. And you know what? We don't even care if you think it's right. We don't care. We in our hearts know it's right. We look at ourselves in the mirror every day, this is what we should have done—it's never too late to do the right thing. You may think it's deeply cynical—we know it's the right thing.' And then move on." (With the 2009 bonuses long gone, the firm could still follow Cramer's advice for the 2010 bonuses, which were $15.4 billion.)

Others, especially former Goldman partners on the banking—as opposed to the trading—side of the business, agree with Elson and Cramer about Goldman's response to date and wonder whether Blankfein is the right guy to lead the firm through the current morass. What's needed is a wartime consigliere, they argue, and Blankfein is not that guy. "This is not a good role for Lloyd," one former partner said. "It's like having Russell Crowe do a romantic comedy." He said he feared Blankfein was not being well served "by the people around him but, then again, he chose his people." (Some even wondered why the Business Standards Committee included no former Goldman partners, like Whitehead or Friedman or Rubin, who might have been able to convey to the current leaders of the firm how things used to be in the good old days.)

A recurring criticism of Blankfein is that he has surrounded himself with like-minded trader types and that he could benefit greatly from having at the top of the firm a more diverse group of senior partners with different perspectives. "Both Lloyd and Gary are valuable guys, but you also need other guys at the top with a different ethic," another former partner explained. "Then you debate decisions out and you have balance. That has been lost." He continued, "The guys who succeed in this industry are the guys who say, 'I care about the reputation of the firm. I care about my reputation. I care about doing the right thing. I care about having a great firm. I care about attracting and retaining the best people. If I do all of these things and do good business, eventually I'll be fine.' But in this top five, there is nothing about making money. The guys for whom making money is in the top three almost always get themselves into trouble. And this is the essence of how Goldman has changed."

Blankfein has little patience for these arguments, especially from an anonymous group of former partners. He seems inclined to continue to fight his critics. Blankfein thinks Goldman is plenty diverse at the top of the firm and then names one senior executive after another who came to the forty-first floor from areas of the firm other than trading. He said he "reads" more like "a lawyer, banker type" and very rarely did he do any trading, in any event. He laments as "at least ironic, and in some sense disproportionate," the fact that Goldman's mortgage business—which never generated more than 2 percent of the firm's revenues and is much smaller than the mortgage business at other firms—has become such a lightning rod for criticism. But "one of the things you learn in law school is," he said, "and also you learn this being a parent, if you're criticizing somebody's *behavior* they shouldn't be able to defend themselves by saying other people behaved the same way, and get yourself out of it. It's not exculpatory to do that. You learn that it's not a defense in law and it's not a defense by your kids."

The ultimate test of his own and the firm's longevity will be whether Goldman's clients choose to stand by it in its hour of need. So far, so good, Blankfein said. "Look, we're getting great support from our clients," he said, a point conceded by people as diverse in their views about the firm as Schwarzman and Cramer.

But Blankfein said his agita has not diminished one iota. "I feel bad that I need—we're supposed to support *them,* not the other way," he said of the firm's clients. "Nobody puts a gun to your head to take the job. Part of the job evolved in the way it did to deal with the scrutiny of the firm, and it's not exactly what I expected when I became CEO. I want people to come here and feel really, really good about working here and being proud of the firm, which I think they really do. But to the extent that there's a burden on that, that's my responsibility. I want clients to be proud of the fact that they're working with Goldman Sachs, not to explain it. I feel the weight of that, I do. I have a sense of duty about these things, and so I'm in."

All in?

"Look, I have to be," he concluded.

With that, Blankfein put on his suit jacket and a beefy security guard escorted him, via a hidden staircase, to the firm's private dining area one floor above to meet with an unnamed dignitary, whom, he said, "I can't be late for." And then he was gone and the secret door closed behind him.

ACKNOWLEDGMENTS

This book would have been inconceivable—literally—without any number of wonderfully dedicated editors, artists, publicists, marketers, and other professionals at the Knopf Doubleday Publishing Group. At the very top of this list is my friend and editor Bill Thomas, who agreed with me that Goldman Sachs was the next mountain we needed to climb together, treachery, crevasses, and all. I am immensely grateful to him for yet another brilliant edit of yet another large manuscript. I am also extremely appreciative of Sonny Mehta's invaluable support as the visionary leader of Knopf Doubleday.

I would also like to thank, at Doubleday, in alphabetical order (please note the pattern): Maria Carella, Janet Cooke, Melissa Ann Danaczko (my hero), John Fontana, Suzanne Herz, Rebecca Holland, Cory Hunter, Judy Jacoby, Carol Janeway, James Kimball, Beth Koehler, Lynn Kovach, Beth Meister, Nora Reichard (the best production editor in the business), Alison Rich (publicist extraordinaire), Amy Ryan (an amazing copy editor), Vimi Santokhi, Suzanne Smith, Adrienne Sparks, Anke Steinecke, Kathy Trager, and Sean Yule. This is an extraordinary team of talented people who busted a collective gut to publish this book. It apparently does take a village. I would also like to thank my British team at Penguin Press: Helen Conford, Alex Elam, Rosie Glaisher, and Jessica Jackson.

Of course, a book about Goldman Sachs would not have been quite the same without the cooperation of the top executives at Goldman Sachs. At some point my access changed from virtually none to something more than that. For permitting me to interview the six living current and former senior partners of the firm, I suspect I need to thank, first, Lloyd Blankfein, the firm's chairman and CEO (who generously made himself available when asked on several occasions, despite having much more important things to do), as well as John F. W. Rogers, the firm's consigliere, and Lucas van Praag, who may be one of the more resilient men on the face of the earth. Without their approval—although I may never know for sure—I would not have had the chance to speak with John Whitehead, Steve Friedman, Bob Rubin, Jon Corzine, Hank Paulson, Lloyd Blankfein (of course), as well as Gary Cohn, the firm's president, and David Viniar, its CFO. The insights these men provided about Goldman were invaluable.

I would also like to thank others once (or still) affiliated with the firm, including: Cliff Asness, Josh Birnbaum, Geoff Boisi, Craig Broderick, Frank Brosens, Michael Carr, Jonathan Cohen, Jim Cramer, George Doty, William Dudley, J. Christopher Flowers, Bob Freeman, Jacob Goldfield, Jim Gorter, Betty Levy Hess, Bob Hurst, Bob Lenzner, Peter Levy, Bruce Mayers, Tom Montag, David Schwartz, Robert Steel, Alan Stein, the late L. Jay Tenenbaum, John Thain, Byron Trott, Peter Weinberg, Ken Wilson, and Jon Winkelman.

There were, of course, countless others I spoke with—best left unnamed—whose thoughts and wisdom rounded out my understanding of what is an immensely complex firm. Whatever else one thinks about Goldman Sachs, one cannot help but be impressed by the talent, intelligence, and single-minded determination of the firm's top executives and its disciplined army. They—and those who preceded them—have left an indelible mark on what is a singular firm and on Wall Street itself.

Those who are not affiliated with Goldman Sachs but who were also immensely helpful include: Martin Armstrong, Fred R. Conrad, Michele Davis, Chuck Elson, Greg Fleming, Hank Greenberg, Michael Greenberger, Eric Heaton, Peter Kelly, Jeff Kronthal, Nicholas Lemman, Sandy Lewis, Nicholas Maier, Fares Noujaim, Stan O'Neal, Larry Pedowitz, Dan Pollack, Clayton Rose, Wilbur Ross, Steve Schwarzman, Eliot Spitzer, Joseph Stiglitz, Larry Summers, Matt Vogel, Tucker Warren, and Paul Wetzel. Again, there are others I would like to thank, but doing so by name would not serve them—or me—well.

One also must take note of the incredible cache of data that the U.S. Congress and the Financial Crisis Inquiry Commission made publicly available about Goldman Sachs and other Wall Street firms. Without this information—released by the Senate's Permanent Committee on Investigations and its chairman, Senator Carl Levin, Democrat of Michigan—our collective understanding of what happened and why before, during, and after the Great Recession would be much diminished and our nation would be far worse off. While I have had my differences with Senator Levin, he does deserve extraordinary thanks, from me anyway, for making the documents about Goldman public. Senator, I salute you.

Once in a while, during the writing of this book, the Freedom of Information Act actually worked. I found this to be the case with documents I requested from the Federal Reserve Board, and I want to thank Jeanne McLaughlin for her help in getting public information to me. By contrast, the U.S. Securities and Exchange Commission's FOIA office has perfected the art of obfuscation. I will probably be in the grave before that office fulfills my numerous FOIA requests, going back now some six years. (P.S.: The FOIA office at the SEC is seriously broken and needs to be fixed.)

I also want to thank the people at *Fortune*, *Vanity Fair*, the *New York Times*, *The Atlantic*, *Institutional Investor*, the *Financial Times*, *ARTnews*, Bloomberg, CNN, MSNBC, CNBC, the BBC, and NPR, who gave me plenty of opportunities throughout the past eighteen months to divert my attention from writing this book. I am extremely grateful to you all for allowing me to mix it up. Among them are Marilyn Adamo, Deirdre Bolton, Graydon Carter, Robin Cembalest, Laura Chapman, Mark Crumpton, Milton Esterow, Pimm Foxx, Leigh Gallagher, John Gambling, Toby Harshaw, Sylvia Hochfield, Al Hunt, Julie Hyman, William Inman, Bob Ivry, Emma Jacobs, Tom Keane, Andy Lack, Jaime Lalinde, Tim Lavin, Brian Lehrer, Betty Liu, Leonard Lopate, Ian Masters, Matt Miller (both of them), Kathleen Parker, Norm Pearlstine, Don Peck, Ken Prewitt, David Rhodes, Charlie Rose, Andrew Rosenthal, Erik Schatzker, Andy Serwer, Maryam Shahabi, David Shipley, Eliot Spitzer (again), Doug Stumpf, John Tucker, Nicholas Varchaver, and Chitra Wadhwani. A special thanks goes to Mark Pittman, at Bloomberg, who inspired me greatly and, alas, has passed to the next adventure far too soon.

Once again my usual cast of faithful and charming characters sustained me on the lonely eighteen-month trek up the mountainside. They always knew when to administer the proper dose of criticism and encouragement. Among them, in alphabetical order, are: Peter Davidson and Drew McGhee (they insisted on being first and I oblige them happily), Jane Barnet and Paul Gottsegen, Charlie and Sue Bell, Seth and Toni Bernstein, Clara Bingham, Joan Bingham, Bryce Birdsall and Malcolm Kirk, Graham Bowley and Chrystia Freeland, Michael Brod, John Brodie, Mary and Brad Burnham, Jerome and M. D. Buttrick, John Buttrick, Mike and Elisabeth Cannell, Alan and Pat Cantor, Jay Costley, Marc Daniel (and Suzanne Herz), Robert Douglass, Tom Dyja and Suzanne Gluck, Don and Anne Edwards, Stuart and Randi Epstein, the Feldmans (all of them), John and Tracy Flannery, Charles and Patricia Fuller, Al Garner, Ina and Jeff Garten, John Gillespie and Susan Orlean, Alan and Amanda Goodstadt, Jessica and Drew Guff, Christine Harper,

Stu and Barb Jones, Sue Kaplan and David Karnovsky, Michael and Fran Kates, Jamie and Cynthia Kempner, Peter Lattman and Isabel Gillies, Jeffrey Leeds, Les Levi, Tom and Amanda Lister, Patty Marx and Paul Roosin, Dan McManus, Steve and Leora Mechanic, Hamilton Mehlman, Chris and Amy Meininger, David Michaelis and Nancy Steiner, John Morris and Marcia Santoni, Mary Murfitt and Bonnie Hundt, Esther Newberg, Joan Osofsky, Eric Osserman, Jay and Massa Pelofsky, Ron Pillar, Michael Powell, Liz Rappaport, Adam Reed, Stuart Reid, David Resnick and Cathy Klema, Scott Rostan, Steve Rubin (the maestro), Andy and Courtney Savin, Charlie Schueler, Pam Scott and Phil Balshi, Gil Sewall, Robert and Francine Shanfield, Lynn Sherr, Jim and Sue Simpson, Andrew Ross Sorkin, Josh Steiner, Jeff and Kerry Strong, David Supino and Linda Pohs Supino, David and Peggy Tanner, Sarah Twombly, Rick Van Zijl, Silda Wall, David Webb, Andy and Lauren Weisenfeld, Kit White and Andrea Barnet, Jay and Louisa Winthrop, Tim and Nina Zagat, and, of course, Gemma Nyack (last but not least).

I also want to thank my in-laws and relatives, the Futters and Shutkins, in toto, as well as various other Cohans and Hiekens, also in toto. My parents, Suzanne and Paul, as well as my brothers, Peter and Jamie, and their wives and families, continue to be hugely supportive of me, and I thank them, again and again and again (as in every day).

To Joy Harris, my dear friend and literary agent, who has stood by me now for three of these tomes (and hopefully many more to come), I cannot thank you enough. And yet, I still try.

Then there is my amazing, loving, supportive, and nurturing family, Deb Futter, Teddy Cohan, and Quentin Cohan. Once again, I could not have done it without you. I love you all very, very much.

Needless to say, any errors in fact, of omission or commission, are my responsibility alone.

NOTES

Abbreviations

NY   *The New Yorker*

NYT   *New York Times*

SEC   Securities and Exchange Commission

Trust   Securities and Exchange Commission, *Investment Trusts and Investment Companies,* parts I–III (Washington, D.C., 1939)

WSJ   *Wall Street Journal*

WSOH   Walter Sachs Oral History Research Project, Columbia University

Prologue: The Pyrrhic Victory

1. "a cunning cat": Martin A. Armstrong, *Looking Behind the Curtain: The "Real" Conspiracy,* April 9, 2009.

1. "a great vampire squid": Matt Taibbi, *Rolling Stone,* July 9–23, 2009.

2. the "angriest": Jonathan Alter, *The Promise: President Obama, Year One* (New York: Simon & Schuster, 2010), p. 314.

2. "lip-synching capitalism": Ibid.

4. "substantial profit": Letter from Lloyd Blankfein to John Fullerton, April 27, 2009.

6. "I live ninety-eight percent of my time": Lloyd Blankfein's comments at a breakfast sponsored by *Fortune* magazine on October 15, 2009.

7. In a separate interview: Lloyd Blankfein interview with the author.

7. "I try to understand why it is": Senator Levin interview with the author.

9. "People are angry": Letter from Lloyd Blankfein to John Fullerton, April 27, 2009.

9. "[Y]our personally owned shares": Letter from John Fullerton to Lloyd Blankfein, December 31, 2009.

10. "They did not get it": Jim Cramer interview with the author.

11. "Of course I feel a huge responsibility": Lloyd Blankfein interview with the author.

16. "What has been a great awakening": Michael Greenberger interview with the author.

17. The various Goldman Sachs internal e-mails in this chapter were released publicly by Senator Carl Levin (D-Michigan) as part of the April 27, 2010, hearing "Wall Street and the Financial Crisis: The Role of the Investment Banks" before the United States Senate Permanent Subcommittee on Investigations. The testimony from that hearing is taken from the publicly released transcripts of the April 27, 2010, hearing.

Chapter 1: A Family Business

25. "he quickly set off": Stephen Birmingham, *Our Crowd: The Great Jewish Families of New York City* (New York: Harper & Row, 1967).

25. "had supported herself quite nicely": Ibid.

29. Account of the transaction between Frederick Douglas, "A. Cramer," and "Carl Wolff" is from *NYT,* March 19, 1886.

29. Account of the loan to N. J. Schloss & Co. is from *NYT,* December 6, 1893, and December 9, 1893.

30. "well nigh penniless": *NYT,* December 21, 1891.

30. "always charitable to a degree": Ibid.

32. "From the very first moment": Lisa Endlich, *Goldman Sachs: The Culture of Success* (New York: Touchstone, 2000), p. 35.

33. "My boy, you come home and go to work": WSOH, 1956, p. 22.

35. "It was more or less blazing a trail": WSOH, 1964, p. 218.

35. "That Sears business": Ibid., pp. 33–34.

35. "Frank Woolworth": Ibid., pp. 96–97.

36. "commercial banking all over the world": Transcript of the January 6, 1914, public hearing in New York City regarding the establishment of the New York Federal Reserve Bank.

36. "The word 'aid' ": Ibid.

37. "The reserve power": Ibid.

38. "Well, I guess I am out of step": Ibid., p. 39.

38. "I am not in sympathy": Endlich, pp. 42–43.

39. "to give his services": WSOH, 1956.

39. "two or three investments": Ibid.

39. "Being a Jew": Ibid., p. 40.

39. "Henry Goldman was an extraordinary personality": Ibid., p. 41.

40. "suave and polished Southerner": WSOH, 1956.

Chapter 2: The Apostle of Prosperity

41. "tall, slender, unassuming": *NYT*, January 1, 1968.

42. "lack of adequate banking facilities": *NYT*, February 13, 1910.

42. "For the next three years": *Time*, September 14, 1925.

42. "had casually explained": *NYT*, January 1, 1968.

43. "If business is to continue zooming": Ibid.

43. "business cycle was dead": Lisa Endlich, *Goldman Sachs: The Culture of Success* (New York: Touchstone, 2000), p. 44.

43. "Catchings was a brilliant person": WSOH, 1956, p. 43.

43. "such great companies": Ibid, p. 44.

44. "In those days": Ibid.

44. "Our business had grown so": Ibid., p. 45.

44. "there weren't enough": John Kenneth Galbraith, *The Great Crash, 1929* (New York: Mariner Books, 2009, paperback reprint edition), p. 43.

45. "Historians have told with wonder": Ibid., p. 49.

45. "The stock is said to have sold": Ibid.

45. "As a promotion": Ibid.

46. "And the management of the trusts": Ibid., p. 47.

47. "only when the tide goes out": Warren Buffett, "Chairman's Letter," *Berkshire Hathaway 2001 Annual Report.*

47. "[R]arely, if ever, in history": Galbraith, p. 60.

48. "This remarkable premium": Galbraith, p. 61.

49. "sufficient to constitute working control": *Trust,* p. 589.

49. "on the ground that it preferred": Ibid.

49. Information from the GSTC prospectus: Ibid., p. 590.

49. "give the clients and customers": Ibid., p. 591.

49. "other banking houses": Ibid.

49. "Throughout the whole period": Ibid.

50. "build them up": Ibid., p. 592.

50. "might possibly at times": Ibid.

50. "was not even remotely": Ibid.

51. "[A]fter discussing the matter": Ibid., p. 596.

52. "Two of my associates": Ibid., p. 597.

52. "done a great deal of business": Ibid., p. 599.

52. "prestige and standing": Ibid., p. 600.

53. "in connection with the proposed acquisition": Ibid., p. 610.

54. "a tremendous hullabaloo": Ibid., p. 611.

55. "[I]t is apparent that": Ibid., p. 623.

55. "I never regarded that we had": Ibid., p. 625.

55. "The market value for its own stock": Ibid., pp. 626–27.

55. "buying actually improves the market": Ibid., p. 613.

56. "I tell you with great positiveness": Ibid., p. 614.

56. "The spring and early summer": Galbraith, p. 61.

56. "had gone outside its legitimate": *NYT,* April 4, 1929.

56. "Goldman Sachs by now": Galbraith, p. 62.

57. Goldman Sachs Trading Corporation was worth: *NYT*, August 20, 1929, p. 84.

57. "[T]he nearly simultaneous": Galbraith, p. 64.

57. "Well, this is just absolutely crazy": WSOH, 1956, p. 49.

57. "The trouble with you, Walter": Ibid.

57. "I remember that day very intimately": Studs Terkel, *Hard Times: An Oral History of the Great Depression* (New York: New Press, 2000), pp. 72–74.

58. "secure a divorce": *NYT*, February 28, 1930.

58. "beginning, in 1930, to show": WSOH, 1956, p. 46.

58. "Weinberg and I talked together": Ibid., p. 46. Sachs described the entire incident in his oral history.

58. "In those days": Ibid., p. 47.

59. "[We] could hold up our heads": Ibid., p. 48.

60. "the loudest prophet of the New Era": *Time*, August 21, 1933.

60. "Well, that was very nice": WSOH, 1956, p. 49.

60. "There were all kinds of stockholders' suits": Ibid., p. 50.

60. the last one of which did not get settled: *NY*, November 10, 2008.

61. "The margin clerk for Goldman Sachs": Among other sources, *NYT*, July 29, 1969.

Chapter 3: The Politician

62. "great rehabilitation": WSOH, 1956, p. 51.

62. "Don't imagine for a moment": Ibid., p. 53.

62. "In the '29 crash the name Goldman": "Let's Ask Sidney Weinberg," *Fortune*, October 1953, p. 174.

62. "We faced the music": WSOH, 1956, p. 81.

62. "His mind began to fail with age": Ibid., p. 52.

63. "I was perfectly frank": Ibid., p. 82.

63. "that people began": Ibid., p. 53.

63. "kewpie doll": E. J. Kahn Jr., "Director's Director," *NY*, September 8, 1956, p. 39.

63. "hustled his way": *NYT*, July 29, 1969.

64. "half a pint of whisky": *Time*, December 8, 1958.

64. "finding this no strain": *NY*, September 15, 1956, p. 62.

64. "Then he lost": Ibid.

64. "To whom it may concern": *NYT*, July 29, 1969.

64. "for accuracy": *Fortune*, October 1953.

65. "In Sing Sing": *NY*, September 15, 1956, p. 60.

65. "Sometimes you don't know": *Fortune*, October 1953.

65. "feather horse": Ibid.

65. "What's a panic?": *NYT*, December 16, 1967.

65. "had given his heart": Ibid.

65. "Do you need a boy?": *NYT*, February 8, 1942.

66. "Weinberg remained": *NY*, September 15, 1956, p. 65.

66. "Ever try to carry": *NYT*, December 16, 1967.

66. "One course they offered": Ibid.

66. "Paul Sachs was the first partner": *NY*, September 15, 1956, p. 65.

67. "knowing everybody": *NYT*, December 16, 1967. This article also describes his World War I service.

67. "He has since become": *NY*, September 15, 1956, p. 66.

67. "Unless you can make one": *NYT*, December 16, 1967.

68. "It was my own money": Ibid.

68. "I just wasn't very bright": *Fortune*, October 1953.

68. "I guess you must have run": *NY*, September 15, 1956, p. 69.

68. "I'm an investment banker": *NYT*, December 16, 1967.

69. Account of Weinberg in Akron, Ohio, is from *NY*, September 8, 1956, p. 42.

70. "clubhouse Democrat": *Fortune*, October 1953.

70. "The Street was against Roosevelt": Studs Terkel, *Hard Times: An Oral History of the Great Depression* (New York: New Press, 2000), pp. 72–74.

70. "I cannot tell you": Letter from Sidney Weinberg to Franklin Roosevelt, November 9, 1932.

70. "you might wish to have": Letter from Sidney Weinberg to Franklin Roosevelt, January 18, 1933.

70. "He was pleased to have this": Letter from Louis Howe to Sidney Weinberg, February 23, 1933.

70. "intimate friend": Letter from Sidney Weinberg to Louis Howe, December 6, 1932.

71. Paul M. Clikeman's account of what happened at McKesson & Robbins is found in "The Greatest Frauds of the (Last) Century," a monograph in the May 2003 issue of *New Accountant USA*.

71. "I'm for McKesson": *NY*, September 8, 1956, p. 48.

72. "Well, come on, gentlemen": *Fortune*, October 1953.

72. "gave Sidney some uncomfortable moments": Ibid.

72. "pointed out to him": *NY*, September 8, 1956, p. 48.

72. "My partner": WSOH, 1956, p. 122.

73. "Sidney Weinberg has this alchemy": *Fortune*, October 1953.

74. "gourmand's appetite": *NY*, September 15, 1956, p. 49.

74. "an ambassador": *BusinessWeek*, January 27, 1951.

74. "many grimly intransigent": *NY*, September 15, 1956, p. 49.

75. "entirely personal": Letter from Sidney Weinberg to Stephen Early, July 5, 1938.

75. "I don't speak Russian": *NYT*, November 16, 1967.

75. "business and financial monopoly": *WSJ*, February 1, 2010, Amity Shlaes.

76. "FDR saved the system": Terkel, pp. 72–74.

76. "unsound": *NY*, September 15, 1956, p. 49.

76. "I did not support him": Terkel, p. 73.

77. "for a great many years": WSOH, 1956, p. 12.

77. "a man of great charm": Ibid.

77. "in which he thanked me": WSOH, 1964, p. 154.

77. "I remember telling people": WSOH, 1956, p. 14.

78. "Not that I didn't realize": Ibid., p. 15.

78. "maybe it was partly": Ibid.

78. campaign buttons: Letter from Sidney Weinberg to Franklin Roosevelt, January 30, 1942.

79. "Every time I went": *NY*, September 15, 1956, p. 52.

79. "resented": Ibid., p. 54.

81. "stabbing his old friend": *Fortune*, October 1953.

81. "I have just learned": Letter from Franklin Roosevelt to Sidney Weinberg, August 31, 1944.

81. "There was less and less": Charles D. Ellis, *The Partnership: The Making of Goldman Sachs* (New York: Penguin Press, 2008), p. 45.

83. "Jock, if they cut us down": *NY*, September 15, 1956, p. 49.

83. "I didn't have any clear idea": Ibid., p. 50.

Chapter 4: The Value of Friendship

85. "was the greatest outfit": *NY*, September 8, 1956, p. 40.

85. "His lips characteristically pursed": Ibid., p. 39.

86. "Sidney had done his homework": *Time*, December 8, 1958.

86. "That, as Bobby Lehman": WSOH, 1956, p. 56.

87. "flat on his back": *Fortune*, October 1953.

88. "Sidney is a wizard": *NY*, September 8, 1956, p. 47.

89. "The Jew is the world's enigma": Henry Ford, "The International Jew: The World's Foremost Problem," originally published in *Dearborn Independent*, May 1920.

90. "The big problem": *NY*, September 8, 1956, p. 64.

90. he created an alphabet soup of names: Ibid., p. 66.

91. "How could you keep anything confidential": Charles Ellis, *The Partnership* (New York: Penguin Press, 2008), p. 58.

91. "John, John": Ibid.

92. "Without you": Ibid., p. 60.

92. "financial Alexander the Great": *NYT*, September 10, 1958.

93. "ultra-modern": *NYT*, April 1, 1957.

93. The involvement of Goldman Sachs in the antitrust suit is from the Corrected Opinion of Harold R. Medina, United States Circuit Judge, civil action no. 43–757, filed February 4, 1954.

93. " 'the cream of the business' ": Medina opinion, p. 8.

95. "The best description": WSOH, 1956.

95. "the older firms": Medina opinion, p. 170.

95. Medina's chart: Ibid., p. 171.

96. The material on Goldman and Pillsbury is from ibid., pp. 329–46.

98. The material on Goldman and Lehman Brothers is from ibid., pp. 312–16.

105. "in a rather conceited way": WSOH, 1956, p 92.

105. "My own position": Ibid., p. 90.

105. The information on trial costs is from NYT, September 23, 1953.

106. "absolutely firm": Ibid. p. 91.

106. "highly intelligent": Ibid.

106. "I think there's a realization": WSOH, 1956, p. 103.

107. "You have to maintain": Ibid., p. 104.

107. "turned away from": Ibid., p. 105.

107. "It's a wonderful field for young men": Ibid., p. 106.

107. "the next ten years": Ibid.

108. "reason for 1929": Ibid., p. 109.

108. "If you have a lawyer": Ibid., p. 95.

Chapter 5: "What Is Inside Information?"

109. "new brilliant genius": WSOH, 1956, p. 68.

109. "His father was a middle-class doctor": Author interview with L. Jay Tenenbaum.

110. "She wanted to show": Ibid.

110. "He was unsupervised": Judith Ramsey Ehrlich and Barry J. Rehfeld, The New Crowd: The Changing of the Jewish Guard on Wall Street (Boston: Little, Brown & Co., 1989), p. 30.

110. "His mother was a real flake": Author interview with Betty Levy Hess.

110. "I had two dollars in my pocket": Author interview with L. Jay Tenenbaum.

110. "It was the thing to do": NYT, June 4, 1961.

110. "I didn't have any money to lose": Ibid.

111. "With a friend's help": Ibid.

111. "Arbitrage as a form of trading": Ehrlich and Rehfeld, p. 31.

111. "The classic example": Celler Commission Report, Conglomerate Merger Investigations, 1969.

112. "Despite a distinctive lisp": Charles D. Ellis, The Partnership (New York: Penguin Press, 2008), p. 74.

112. "and the opportunities": NYT, June 4, 1961.

112. "had collected a group": Roy C. Smith, Paper Fortunes: Modern Wall Street; Where It's Been and Where It's Going (New York: St. Martin's Press, 2010), p. 86.

112. "None of it was from trading": NYT, November 16, 1967.

113. "The war came": Author interview with Salim B. "Sandy" Lewis.

114. "I didn't have enough experience": NYT, June 4, 1961.

114. "built one of the most active": WSOH, 1956.

114. "Gus was very smart": Ellis, p. 75.

115. "were seeking the assistance": NYT, June 4, 1961.

115. "We've got a policy": Levy interview with Gilbert Kaplan, Institutional Investor, November 1973.

116. "a heap of du——": NYT, May 3, 1973.

116. "The Murchison-Kirby relationship": NYT, May 24, 1961.

116. Information on the Young suicide: NYT, January 26, 1958.

117. "quiet, powerful role": NYT, June 4, 1961.

117. "Pride. Family pride": NYT, July 5, 1963.

118. "I offered the job": Author interview with L. Jay Tenenbaum.

118. Biographical details are from ibid.

118. "I was in combat": Ibid.

120. "But don't forget": Institutional Investor, November 1973.

122. "He was smart, quick": Smith, p. 86.

123. "My mother never got": Author interview with Peter Levy.

123. "Hey you, you": Author interview with Sandy Lewis.

125. "33-man group": NYT, May 25, 1965.

126. "To be perfectly honest": Ibid.

126. "Gus was very proud": Ellis, p. 91.

126. "As long as I am a governor": *Institutional Investor*, November 1973.

126. "I say my prayers": Ibid.

127. "[T]hey were kept short": Ellis, p. 80.

127. "Gus was always": Ibid., p. 78.

128. "I can't say": Author interview with Betty Levy.

128. "Well, we do demand": *Institutional Investor,* November 1973.

128. "The thing about Goldman Sachs": Author interview with L. Jay Tenenbaum.

130. "If you found out": Ibid.

130. "I don't know how I found them": Ibid.

130. "If there were tax cases": Ibid.

131. "That's shooting fish in a barrel": Ibid.

131. "The question is what is inside information": Ibid.

131. "Gus brought him in": Ibid.

132. "L. Jay, I know you're working with Dowler": Ibid.

133. "Gus suddenly becomes furious": E-mail from Robert Lenzner to the author.

134. "Which was *really* good money": Author interview with Bruce Mayers.

135. The description of Mayers's experience in Goldman's arbitrage department: Author interview with Bruce Mayers.

Chapter 6: The Biggest Man on the Block

138. "There's only one problem": Author interview with L. Jay Tenenbaum.

139. "I was an odd choice": Robert E. Rubin, *In an Uncertain World: Tough Choices from Wall Street to Washington* (New York: Random House, 2003), p. 37.

139. "As a young Jew": Ibid., p. 45.

139. "He quickly made a good deal of money": Ibid., p. 46.

140. "a lawyer, an investor": Ibid.

140. "You'd like to dance": Ibid., p. 48.

140. "The people in the town": Ibid., p. 49.

141. "Robbie Rubin": Ibid., p. 50.

141. "My grades were good": Ibid., p. 52.

142. "I looked around": Ibid., p. 53.

142. "seemed a potentially fruitful area": Ibid., p. 55.

142. "with no job": Ibid.

142. "I imagine you track": Ibid., p. 57.

143. "dropping out anyway": Ibid.

143. "perhaps the dean": Ibid.

143. "The trouble with boys": Ibid., p. 58.

143. "I spent most of my time": Ibid., p. 59.

144. "I didn't necessarily want": Ibid., p. 61.

144. "a sense of curiosity": Ibid., p. 64.

144. "it had a more comfortable environment": Ibid.

145. "the pay was slightly higher": Ibid., p. 67.

145. "get on the phone": Ibid.

145. "The first order of business": Ibid., p. 41.

146. "Having Gus Levy": Ibid., p. 45.

146. "took naturally to being": Ibid., p. 44.

147. "More growth occurred": Lisa Endlich, *Golman Sachs: The Culture of Success* (New York: Touchstone, 2000), p. 64.

147. "It was the only firm": Author interview with Robert Rubin.

148. "At some later point": Ibid.

148. "Sidney looked down his nose": Endlich, p. 63.

148. "He preached mandatory retirement": *NYT,* July 11, 1971.

148. "Sidney was a little jealous": Author interview with George Doty.

148. "Gus was much more aggressive": Author interview with Alan Stein.

149. "Sidney and Walter Sachs": Author interview with George Doty.

149. "It was a cause for celebration": Author interview with Sandy Lewis.

149. "became senior partner": Author interview with Peter Weinberg.

149. "Sidney, until the day he died": Author interview with George Doty.

150. "Mr. Weinberg," he said: Charles D. Ellis, *The Partnership* (New York: Penguin Press, 2008), p. 71.

150. "Those are very nice thoughts": Ibid., p. 71.

151. "attitudes about the role": *NYT,* December 1, 1968.

152. "Since Mr. Sidney Weinberg's death": Gustave L. Levy testimony in *Welch Foods Inc., etc. v. Goldman, Sachs & Co.,* September 23, 1974.

152. "assorted crackers": From a copy of the menu for one-hundredth anniversary dinner, December 15, 1969.

153. "There is no gainsaying": *NYT*, April 23, 1969.

153. "Our position is that Goldman": *NYT*, September 23, 1970.

153. "to avoid the time and expense": *NYT*, July 11, 1971.

153. "Everyone hunkered down": Author interview with George Doty.

Chapter 7: Caveat Emptor

155. "Levy is where the money is": *New York*, May 6, 1974, p. 8.

155. "Bob Rubin wanted to get out": Author interview with Sandy Lewis.

155. "I liked what I saw there": Robert E. Rubin, *In an Uncertain World* (New York: Random House, 2003), p. 75.

155. "I never in a million years": Author interview with Robert Rubin.

155. "wasn't happy about": Author interview with L. Jay Tenenbaum.

156. "Gus, Hallingby offered": Ibid.

156. "his pedigree of law": Ibid.

156. "I was, to say the least": Rubin, p. 75.

156. "I thought to myself": Author interview with Robert Rubin.

156. "to what extent are commercial paper dealers": *NYT*, November 17, 1970.

157. "fraud, deception, concealment": Ibid.

157. "For the commercial paper holders": Author interview with Dan Pollack.

157. "[T]here is absolutely no merit": *NYT*, November 17, 1970.

158. "the worst of the paperwork": New York Stock Exchange, *1969 Annual Report*.

158. "topped $20 million": *WSJ*, March 17, 1971.

159. "which rips with action": *NYT*, July 11, 1971.

162. The James Cofield reporting is from *WSJ*, June 1, 1972, plus an author interview with James Cofield and author review of relevant documents, letters, and EEOC filings.

167. Cofield's brother: E-mail exchange between James Cofield and author.

168. "There was real fear": Author interview with Robert Rubin.

168. "As a private partnership": Rubin, p. 71.

168. In his memoir: John C. Whitehead, *A Life in Leadership, from D-Day to Ground Zero: An Autobiography* (New York: Basic Books, 2005), p. 115.

168. "Gus carried it": Rubin, p. 74.

168. The summary of the charges against Goldman in the Penn Central matter is from Securities and Exchange Commission, *The Financial Collapse of the Penn Central Company*, staff report to the Senate Special Subcommittee on Investigations, August 1972. Also helpful were trial transcripts from the *Welch Foods Inc. v. Goldman, Sachs & Co.* lawsuit.

177. "caused people to have a very positive feeling": Author interview with Robert Rubin.

177. "They felt good": Roy C. Smith, *Paper Fortunes* (New York: St. Martin's Press, 2010), p. 85.

178. "This was hard on employees": Ibid.

179. "Within hours": *NYT*, May 3, 1974.

180. "I told him we would not do that": Author interview with George Doty.

180. Information on the Fundamental settlement is from *NYT*, September 6, 1974.

180. "had had a bad harvest": Charles D. Ellis, *The Partnership* (New York: Penguin Press, 2008), p. 104.

181. Pollack's opening statement is from the *Welch Foods Inc. v. Goldman, Sachs & Co.* trial transcript, September 9, 1974.

182. "runs like a brook": Ibid.

182. Piel's opening statement is from ibid.

184. "When the company went under": Pollack's closing statement, October 7, 1974, ibid.

184. "landmark case": *NYT*, October 10, 1974.

184. "epochal": Author interview with Dan Pollack.

185. "This was not a minor event": Ibid.

185. "The value of the paper": Whitehead, p. 115.

185. "He said he felt great": Author interview with Dan Pollack.

186. "L. Jay had *had* it": Author interview with Peter Levy.

186. "He was trying to clear": Rubin, p. 68.

186. "focusing intently": Ibid., p. 81.

187. "Knowing of Levy's habit": Smith, p. 107.

187. "He couldn't be seen": Author interview with Peter Levy.

188. "I didn't go down": Ibid.

189. "After Gus died": Rubin, p. 73.

Chapter 8: The Goldman Way

190. "As you've all heard": Charles D. Ellis, *The Partnership* (New York: Penguin Press, 2008), p. 180.

190. "he'd been able to ignore": Robert E. Rubin, *In an Uncertain World* (New York: Random House, 2003), p. 87.

190. "rummaging through his desk": Roy C. Smith, *Paper Fortunes* (New York: St. Martin's Press, 2010), p. 107.

190. "I'm not saying": Author interview with Robert Rubin.

191. "never was aware": Author interview with Peter Levy.

191. "Gus would *never* have retired": Ellis, p. 180.

191. "Leaderless, the firm was left": Lisa Endlich, *Goldman Sachs: The Culture of Success* (New York: Touchstone, 2000), p. 69.

192. "could tell he was": John C. Whitehead, *A Life in Leadership, from D-Day to Ground Zero: An Autobiography* (New York: Basic Books, 2005), p. 115.

192. "We had a partners meeting": Author interview with George Doty.

192. "We'd often have lunch together": Whitehead, p. 116.

192. "John's face fell": Ibid., p. 117.

192. "My father was a very tough man": *Institutional Investor,* January 1984.

192. "John and I were the logical choices": Ibid.

193. "After we'd decided": Whitehead, p. 118.

193. "I thought that John Whitehead": Author interview with Alan Stein.

194. "a tremendous shock": Author interview with Robert Rubin.

194. "To many people": Whitehead, p. 85. Whitehead's biographical details as well as a description of creating the Goldman business principles and Goldman's new-business coverage model were taken from his memoir, *A Life in Leadership,* along with two author interviews with him.

212. "understatement that has become": *WSJ,* March 20, 1979.

212. "There was a lot of debate": Author interview with Robert Rubin.

212. "When we all first moved in": *New York Observer,* December 8, 2009.

Chapter 9: A Formula That Works

214. "Ahh, I don't want": Robert E. Rubin, *In an Uncertain World* (New York: Random House, 2003), p. 79.

215. "Prices were not transparent": Ibid.

216. "[O]ptions trading turned into": Ibid., p. 81.

217. "Aron's philosophy was": Lisa Endlich, *Goldman Sachs: The Culture of Success* (New York: Touchstone, 2000), p. 92.

217. "I looked at it": Author interview with Steve Friedman.

217. "Whitehead was somewhat annoyed": Ibid.

217. "slightly more than $100 million": *NYT,* October 31, 1981.

218. "While we prefer": Ibid.

218. "I saw huge": Author interview with John Whitehead.

219. "[I]t was something of a shock": Endlich, p. 96.

219. "It was less than six months": Author interview with Robert Rubin.

219. "You had the combination": Endlich, p. 97.

220. "I honestly don't know": Author interview with Robert Rubin.

220. "People thought we had made the sale": Endlich, p. 95.

220. "The three senior people": Author interview with Robert Rubin.

220. "With chest pains": Charles D. Ellis, *The Partnership* (New York: Penguin Press, 2008), p. 263.

220. "I could have said": Rubin, p. 88.

221. "extremely sophisticated": Ibid., p. 89.

221. "which he deserved to be": Author interview with George Doty.

221. "Mark, ten million dollars is not": Ellis, p. 250.

222. "That meant taking risks": Author interview with Robert Rubin.

222. "I took tar and feathers": Author interview with George Doty.

222. "At first I thought": Ellis, p. 264.

222. "most delicate undertaking": Rubin, p. 90.

223. "There is incredible bitterness": *Institutional Investor,* January 1984.

223. "The Pacifist: Goldman Sachs Avoids Bitter Takeover Fights but Leads in Mergers": *WSJ,* December 3, 1982.

226. "Now at Oceanside High School": Author interview with Steve Friedman. Biographical details for Steve Friedman's early life and career are from numerous author interviews with Friedman.

227. "our client won": Ellis, p. 275.

227. "energy of a tightly coiled spring": *Institutional Investor,* January 1984.

229. "It was even harder": John C. Whitehead, *A Life in Leadership, from D-Day to Ground Zero: An Autobiography* (New York: Basic Books, 2005), p. 129.

233. "maintained a remarkably low profile": *NYT,* August 16, 1984.

235. "Can you be in my office": Whitehead, p. 137.

Chapter 10: Goldman Sake

237. "If anything did": Author interview with George Doty.

237. "talking to a guy": Author interview with Steve Friedman.

238. "Our bond business": Charles D. Ellis, *The Partnership* (New York: Penguin Press, 2008), p. 229.

238. "It was a shock": Author interview with Steve Friedman.

238. "The top of that division": Ellis, p. 229.

238. "The business was big": Robert E. Rubin, *In an Uncertain World* (New York: Random House, 2003), p. 97.

238. "Today that wouldn't mean much": Ibid., p. 96.

239. "What happened to us": Ibid., p. 97.

239. "They really got clobbered": Author interview with Steve Friedman.

240. "absolute best year ever": *NYT,* November 3, 1985.

241. "worked day and night": *NYT,* April 13, 1986.

242. "a battered L. L. Bean bag": *Telegraph* (U.K.), September 25, 2005.

243. "Implicit was always": *NYT,* August 8, 1986.

244. "I had to tell him": Ellis, p. 310.

244. "Goldman Sake": Ibid., p. 312.

245. "The negotiations were long": *NYT,* August 8, 1986.

245. "soul searching": *NYT,* September 29, 1986.

245. "lead to Sumitomo influencing": Copy of transcript of the October 10, 1986, hearing at the Federal Reserve.

246. "I may be old-fashioned": Ibid.

248. "The presentation made": Lisa Endlich, *Goldman Sachs: The Culture of Success* (New York: Touchstone, 2000), p. 7.

248. "I always felt there was a terrific risk": Ibid., p. 11.

249. "had a real aversion": Author interview with Peter Weinberg.

Chapter 11: Busted

250. Unless otherwise indicated, the information in this chapter comes from extensive interviews with Robert Freeman and many others involved in the case, plus an extensive review of documents prepared for litigation purposes by Freeman's lawyers and by Goldman's lawyers, as well as the documents filed in the case by the U.S. Attorney's Office for the Southern District of New York.

251. "Bob, you gotta be kidding": Author interview with Larry Pedowitz.

251. "Wall Street went into shock": *Fortune,* May 25, 1987.

252. "I thought he was pulling my leg": Author interview with Larry Pedowitz.

252. "Goldman was super sensitive": Ibid.

256. "They screwed up the complaint": Ibid.

256. "That triggered a truly dreadful period": Author interview with Steve Friedman.

256. "We told the organization": Ibid.

256. "I went to the lawyers": Ibid.

256. "In my daily experience": Author interview with Sandy Lewis.

257. "A number of lawyers": *NYT,* April 10, 1987.

262. "of what it said were difficulties": *NYT,* May 13, 1987.

262. "The tip of the iceberg": *NYT,* May 19, 1987.

264. "Never well conceived to begin with": *New York,* September 4, 1989.

265. "While there was clearly a phone relationship": Author interview with Larry Pedowitz.

266. "They knew our view": Ibid.

268. "As a matter of law": Ibid.

271. "Can you remember any situation": Author interview with Frank Brosens.

Chapter 12: Money

276. "I understand you guys": Charles D. Ellis, *The Partnership* (New York: Penguin Press, 2008), p. 476.

276. "I determined right then": Author interview with Frank Brosens.

276. "On the day of the crash": Author interview with Steve Friedman.

277. "We bought it and we own it": Ellis, p. 366.

277. "It was over very quickly": Author interview with David Schwartz.

278. "They're both capable guys": *NYT,* November 21, 1987.

278. "Think about it": Author interview with David Schwartz.

279. The tale was nothing if not sordid: Dorothy Rabinowitz, "A Cautionary Tale," *New York,* January 8, 1990. The author has also reviewed numerous documents related to the cases and interviewed Gary Moskowitz and Lew Eisenberg.

283. "This worked because": Robert E. Rubin, *In an Uncertain World* (New York: Random House, 2003), p. 99.

284. "Over the years": Ibid., p. 100.

286. "There was a lot": Author interview with Steve Friedman.

286. "No mercy for the yuppies": Anthony Scaramucci, *Goodbye Gordon Gekko: How to Find Your Fortune Without Losing Your Soul* (New York: Wiley, 2010), p. 141. The entire incident is described well in Scaramucci's book.

289. "masses of people": Janet Hanson, *More Than 85 Broads: Women Making Career Choices, Taking Risks, and Defining Success on Their Own Terms* (New York: McGraw-Hill, 2006), p. 24.

289. "All eyes were on me": Ibid.

290. "she was subjected to a hostile": *Utley v. Goldman, Sachs & Co. et al.,* CA 87–6735, Massachusetts Supreme Court. Information about the case can also be found in Goldman's appeal, *Kristine Utley, Plaintiff, Appellee, v. Goldman Sachs & Company, et al., Defendants, Appellants,* 883 F.2d 184, United States Court of Appeals, First Circuit. Heard July 31, 1989, decided August 23, 1989.

290. "were illustrated with nude": Mary E. Crawford, *Talking Difference: On Gender and Language* (Thousand Oaks, Calif.: Sage Publications, 1995), p. 146.

290. The description of Hoffman-Zehner's experience at Goldman is from Hanson, pp. 45–52.

291. The description of Charlotte Hanna's experience at Goldman is from her lawsuit, filed March 2010: *Hanna v. Goldman, Sachs & Co. et al.,* no. 10–02637, U.S. District Court, Southern District of New York.

292. The descriptions of the experiences of H. Cristina Chen-Oster and Shanna Orlich at Goldman is from their September 2010 lawsuit, *Chen-Oster v. Goldman, Sachs & Co.,* 10-cv-6950, U.S. District Court, Southern District of New York.

294. "You're doing everything wrong": Author interview with Steve Friedman.

294. "I'm a huge believer in them": Ibid.

295. "You say to another partner": Ibid.

296. "We were in the chicken camp": Ibid.

299. "led to concerns": *NYT,* May 3, 1991.

299. "The intensity": Ibid.

299. "No star shone brighter": Lisa Endlich, *Goldman Sachs: The Culture of Success* (New York: Touchstone, 2000), p. 83.

Chapter 13: Power

303. "For what it was": Author interview with Jacob Goldfield.

304. " 'Joe' as everyone called Fowler": Robert E. Rubin, *In an Uncertain World* (New York: Random House, 2003), p. 86.

305. "You know, you look good": Ibid.

305. "Bob has a magnetism": Ibid.

305. "Few notions": Ibid., p. 87.

305. "who had made a lot of money": Ibid., p. 91.

306. "Some people like opera": Ibid., p. 94.

306. "first among equals": Author interview with Gene Sperling.

306. "They were hungry": Ibid.

307. "[M]any in the party": Rubin, p. 102.

307. "It's amazing how much": Author interview with Gene Sperling.

307. "Planning for the Next Financial Crisis": Lawrence Summers, in *The Risk of Economic Crisis,* edited by Martin Feldstein (Chicago and London: University of Chicago Press, 1991), pp. 135–58.

308. "Not because of me": *New York,* April 22, 1996.

308. "The gist of it was": Ibid.

309. "For more than three hours": Rubin, p. 102.

309. "Doing that showed": Ibid., p. 105.

310. "well equipped for the job": Ibid., p. 107.

310. "If you don't become": Ibid.

311. "Without any further deliberation": Ibid.

311. "My fascination with Washington": Ibid., p. 106.

311. "How can a wealthy guy": Ibid., p. 107.

311. "same pinstripe suit": *New York,* April 22, 1996.

312. "It was very clear": Author interview with Steve Friedman.

312. The account of Rubin's farewell is from the video of the meeting obtained by the author.

Chapter 14: The College of Cardinals

314. "I don't think John": Author interview with Peter Weinberg.

314. "European currency mechanism": Author interview with Steve Friedman.

315. "I looked on it": Ibid.

315. "a crucial thing to do": Author interview with Jon Corzine.

315. "trading legs": Author interview with Steve Friedman.

316. Goldman's involvement in the Maxwell controversy is taken from the 2001 report "Mirror Group Newspapers plc" (volumes 1 and 2) by the Department of Trade and Industry and from contemporaneous press reports.

317. "a Czech-born Jewish immigrant": *NYT,* December 20, 1991.

318. "never worry about": Lisa Endlich, *Goldman Sachs: The Culture of Success* (New York: Touchstone, 2000), p. 139.

318. "What has happened now": *NYT,* December 20, 1991.

319. "When most of my colleagues": Ibid.

323. "I could see the Maxwell thing": Author interview with Steve Friedman.

323. "I had no desire": Ibid.

324. "Hank would be the first guy": Ibid.

325. "Not because I wanted a promotion": Author interview with Henry Paulson Jr.

325. "I would come to New York": Ibid.

326. "I don't like the feel of this": Author interview with Steve Friedman.

326. "hardly lived up": Steven Drobny, *Inside the House of Money: Top Hedge Fund Traders on Profiting in the Global Markets* (New York: Wiley, 2006), p. 87.

326. "Credit spreads just blew out": Author interview with Henry Paulson Jr.

326. The account of Siva-Jothy's experience at Goldman is from Drobny, pp. 71–103.

328. "Becerra was probably": Author interview with David Schwartz.

328. "When the market went against us": Author interview with Henry Paulson Jr.

329. "I was always very, very careful": Author interview with Steve Friedman.

329. " 'Your job's impossible' ": Author interview with Robert Hurst.

330. "But people weren't as worried": Author interview with Steve Friedman.

331. "We had a really bad dynamic": Author interview with Jon Corzine.

331. "I wanted to avoid": *Institutional Investor,* October 1994.

332. "I had no special call": Author interview with Henry Paulson Jr.

332. "I knew something was up": Ibid.

332. "You can't leave": Ibid.

333. "Mark had turned out": Author interview with Robert Rubin.

334. "Our management committee": *Institutional Investor,* "Inside Goldman's College of Cardinals," October 1994.

334. "You've got to recognize": Author interview with Henry Paulson Jr.

334. The account of the wrestling match between Paulson and Friedman is from author interviews with both men.

335. "I wanted to see as pure": Author interview with Steve Friedman.

336. "Corzine was a given": Author interview with Robert Hurst.

336. "There was no one": Author interview with Steve Friedman.

336. "It was pretty clear": Author interview with Henry Paulson Jr.

337. "They nurtured me all along": Author interview with Jon Corzine.

337. "We came to believe their chemistry": *Institutional Investor,* October 1994.

338. "I really thank you": Author interview with Steve Friedman.

338. "I remember afterwards": Author interview with Henry Paulson Jr.

338. "On the other hand": Ibid.

339. "As a Christian Scientist": Ibid.

340. "I'm not going to tell you": Author interview with Steve Friedman.

340. "the bejeezus out of him": Author interview with Jon Corzine.

340. "My relationship with Mark": *Institutional Investor,* October 1994.

340. Biographical information about Jon Corzine and Henry Paulson Jr. is from extensive author interviews with the two men.

347. "It was a strange place": Henry Paulson Jr., *On the Brink* (New York: Business Plus, 2010), p. 25.

347. "He took us down to the station": Author interview with Henry Paulson Jr.

348. "I did well enough": Paulson, p. 25.

348. "My motive": Author interview with Henry Paulson Jr.

352. "Johnny Weinberg used to say": Author interview with Jim Gorter.

355. "I frequently felt crummy": Author interview with Steve Friedman.

356. "And by God": Ibid.

Chapter 15: $10 Billion or Bust

358. "Jon and I": Author interview with Henry Paulson Jr.

358. "We just cut": Author interview with Henry Paulson Jr.

360. "Winkelman, who has been": *NYT,* November 15, 1994.

360. "If I had known": Author interview with Steve Friedman.

361. "Until you've actually": Author interview with Jon Corzine.

362. "There's no difference": *Fortune,* September 6, 2004.

363. "We were ready to drink": *Financial Times,* November 22, 2010.

363. The accounts of the Arrowwood meetings in November 1994, January 1995, and January 1996 are from documents obtained by the author.

366. "Partners were looking": Lisa Endlich, *Goldman Sachs: The Culture of Success* (New York: Touchstone, 2000), p. 209.

366. "I went through Europe": Author interview with Henry Paulson Jr.

367. "The deal with the titles": Ibid.

367. "if we were the plaintiffs": Charles D. Ellis, *The Partnership* (New York: Penguin Press, 2008), p. 459.

368. "Assigning the costs": *NYT,* April 15, 1995.

368. "Gene, I think you might": Ellis, p. 458.

368. "I have one of these theories": Author interview with Jon Corzine.

369. "There was a psychology": Ibid.

369. "quietly raised": *WSJ,* March 18, 1995.

369. Account of the Bishop Estate: Alix Freedman and Laurie Cohen, "Bishop's Gambit: Hawaiians Who Own Goldman Sachs Stake Play Clever Tax Game," *WSJ,* April 25, 1995.

371. "Jon is inspirational": Author interview with David Schwartz.

372. "What came out of": Author interview with Henry Paulson Jr.

373. "If you did not have this": *Financial Post,* January 5, 1996.

373. "It's not as strong": Ibid.

373. "a shot at the golden carrot": Ibid.

373. "Now would be a good time": *The Independent* (U.K.), January 26, 1996.

378. "You got to be kidding me!": Author interview with Peter Weinberg.

379. "You could have someone": Author interview with Henry Paulson Jr.

380. "I got a little more preachy": Author interview with Jon Corzine.

380. "He isn't going to jam it": *WSJ,* January 22, 1996.

Chapter 16: The Glorious Revolution

381. "just hit me like cold water": Author interview with Henry Paulson Jr.

382. "I remember Sandy Weill": Ibid.

383. "delegation": Author interview with Jon Corzine.

386. "The differences between Corzine and me": Author interview with Henry Paulson Jr.

386. "I said to him": Ibid.

387. "I found people at Harvard": Author interview with Chris Flowers.

387. "He was our franchise": Author interview with Jon Corzine.

388. "It was one meeting": Ibid.

388. "after he was pretty far along": Author interview with Henry Paulson Jr.

389. "I got angry": Ibid.

389. "We concluded": Ibid.

392. "At a multiple of two times book": *NYT*, June 6, 1998.

393. "I went from being the object": Author interview with Jon Corzine.

393. "I believed we were going to need": Author interview with Henry Paulson Jr.

395. "the firm's prospects were steadily dimming": Roger Lowenstein, *When Genius Failed: The Rise and Fall of Long-Term Capital Management* (New York: Random House, 2000), p. 112.

396. "Maybe if we hold": Author interview with Henry Paulson Jr.

396. "Minute by minute": Lowenstein, p. 145.

396. "We've had a serious markdown": Ibid., p. 147.

397. "We aren't getting": Ibid., p. 152.

398. "The end of August": Ibid., p. 151.

398. "Nothing that's happening": *NYT*, September 9, 1998.

399. "It was a very bitter": Author interview with Chris Flowers.

399. "I asked if he had": Author interview with Jimmy Cayne.

400. "Merely informing the world": Lowenstein, p. 172.

400. "appeared to be downloading": Ibid.

400. "If it were true": Jacob Goldfield e-mail to the author.

400. "At the end of one day": Lowenstein, p. 173.

401. "But by 1998": Ibid., p. 175.

401. "did things in markets": Ibid.

401. "He and Buffett": Ibid., p. 183.

402. "the depths of": Ibid., p. 190.

402. "[I]f Long-Term failed": Ibid., p. 194.

403. "It was really a matter": Author interview with Henry Paulson Jr.

404. "The point was to rescue Long-Term": Lowenstein, p. 215.

404. "there is no polite way": Ibid.

404. "One always has to indulge": Ibid., p. 216.

404. "None of us liked": Author interview with Henry Paulson Jr.

405. "I don't think there was": Author interview with John Thain.

405. "This was not a close decision": Author interview with Henry Paulson Jr.

406. "He emerged as the real hero": Ibid.

407. "Politically, it was probably": Ibid.

407. "I decided the best thing": *NYT*, October 23, 1998.

409. "You should be sure, Jon": Charles D. Ellis, *The Partnership* (New York: Penguin Press, 2008), p. 606.

410. "He was more popular": Author interview with Henry Paulson Jr.

410. "I couldn't quite understand": Author interview with Jon Corzine.

410. "I was devastated": Ibid.

411. "Corzine and Paulson fought": Author interview with John Thain.

411. "I may not be the smartest": Author interview with Jon Corzine.

412. "The news that Jon Corzine": *Financial News*, January 18, 1999.

Chapter 17: It's Too Much Fun Being CEO of Goldman Sachs

415. Biographical details about John Thain: Author interviews with John Thain.

416. Biographical details about John Thornton: From press reports.

419. "He is a real dick": *New York Observer*, January 14, 2001.

419. "John Thornton and I": Author interview with John Thain.

423. "Kevin is very smart": *NYT*, October 27, 2001.

425. "There is no equity in the equity markets": *WSJ*, October 3, 2002, which also provides a useful summary of Representative Oxley's report and Goldman's role.

425. "Their conclusion": Ibid.

425. "If an investment bank": Author interview with Eliot Spitzer.

426. Nicholas W. Maier account of "spinning": From his videotaped deposition, May 9, 2005, Brattleboro, Vermont, as a result of litigation in the U.S. District Court for the Southern District of New York, *In Re: Initial Public Offering Securities Litigation.*

430. "Hank, you've been cutting": Transcript of January 2003 Goldman presentation at Salomon Smith Barney investor conference.

431. "News of that comment": Author interview with David Schwartz.

432. "I'm the guy": Author interview with Henry Paulson Jr.

433. "I really liked both guys": Ibid.

433. "You know something?": Ibid.

435. "John will be greatly missed": *NYT,* March 25, 2003.

436. "John A. Thain": Ibid.

436. "He thought it was unfair": Author interview with Henry Paulson Jr.

437. "I actually thought": Ibid.

437. "There's no pretense": Author interview with John Thain.

438. "There were a lot of public policy": Ibid.

438. "didn't say anything for several hours": *Forbes,* November 11, 2005.

438. "I told him I thought": Author interview with Henry Paulson Jr.

439. "These were not easy": Ibid.

439. "We managed the transition": Ibid.

442. "Our bankers travel on the same planes": Boris Groysberg and Scott A. Snook, *The Pine Street Initiative at Goldman Sachs,* Harvard Business School, Case 9-407-053, November 14, 2006.

442. "an interesting blend": Ibid.

444. "I am happy to do business": Author interview with Sam Zell.

447. The account of the NYSE/Archipelago merger was taken from the many public filings the companies made with the SEC as part of the merger.

448. "Wall Street has been buzzing": *WSJ,* April 27, 2005.

448. "We needed someone": Author interview with John Thain.

449. "We kept it from becoming irrelevant": Ibid.

449. "The New York Stock Exchange": Author interview with Henry Paulson Jr.

450. "I questioned whether": Ibid.

450. "magical hold at the summit": "Behind the Brass Plate," *The Economist,* April 27, 2006.

453. "The idea of being Treasury secretary": Todd Purdum, "Henry Paulson's Longest Night," *Vanity Fair,* October 2009.

453. "There are no dress rehearsals": Henry Paulson Jr., *On the Brink* (New York: Business Plus, 2010), p. 39.

454. "I think I surprised and delighted him": Purdum, October 2009.

454. Details from Paulson's confirmation hearing are from the June 27, 2006, public transcript.

455. Biographical details about Lloyd Blankfein: Author interviews with Lloyd Blankfein.

456. "But Lloyd always teased": Author interview with Richard Kalb.

456. "He was brilliant": Author interview with Rabbi Abner German.

457. "He was very personable": Author interview with Richard Kalb.

457. "You survive at either": Author interview with Robert Steel.

458. "We were completely unprepared": Author interview with David Drizzle.

458. "Many of the people": Author interview with Roy Geronemus.

458. "As exam period approached": Author interview with David Drizzle.

459. "became more studious": Ibid.

459. "to keep certain large": Lloyd Blankfein's entry in Harvard University's class of 1975 twenty-fifth reunion brochure, 2000.

460. "We were street fighters": *Fortune,* March 2, 2008.

460. "He was clearly bright and energetic": Charles D. Ellis, *The Partnership* (New York: Penguin Press, 2008), p. 265.

461. "That's probably not": Ibid., p. 266.

461. "It's not about hanging onto": Lloyd Blankfein comments at a breakfast sponsored by *Fortune* magazine on October 15, 2009.

461. "in order to gain credibility": Author interview with Jacob Goldfield.

Chapter 18: Alchemy

466. "It's all about IQ": Rich Karlgaard, "Microsoft's IQ Dividend," *WSJ,* July 28, 2004.

466. Biographical details about Josh Birnbaum as well as his career at Goldman Sachs are from author interviews with Josh Birnbaum.

471. "When securitization arrived": Author interview with Sandy Lewis.

471. "three I's of new markets": *WSJ*, July 5, 2008.

478. Information on the Markit investigation is from Robert Lenzner, *Forbes*, July 14, 2009.

486. E-mails and documents about the ratings agencies are from the October 2008 U.S. House of Representatives hearing by the Committee on Oversight and Government Reform.

Chapter 19: Getting Closer to Home

489. Except where noted, this account comes from numerous conversations with the Goldman traders involved, plus from nine hundred pages of documents released in April 2010 by the U.S. Senate Permanent Subcommittee on Investigations as part of its investigation into the role Goldman Sachs played in the near collapse of the financial system in 2007 and 2008.

491. "When Paulson and [Paolo] Pellegrini": Gregory Zuckerman, *The Greatest Trade Ever* (New York: Crown Business, 2009), p. 154.

492. "If you want to keep selling": Ibid.

492. "heroic": Author interview with Josh Birnbaum.

494. "It was a joke": *Time*, July 27, 1981.

499. "I can give you one hundred": Author interview with David Viniar.

499. "The world was good, right?": Ibid.

500. "One of my jobs at the time": Author interview with Dan Sparks.

500. "We were seeing signs": Ibid.

500. "That was kind of a first sign": Ibid.

502. "The words we used": Author interview with David Viniar.

504. "trade Goldman's own capital": Kate Kelly, "How Goldman Won Big on Mortgage Meltdown," *WSJ*, December 14, 2007.

504. "What you really needed": Author interview with David Viniar.

505. "I had senior guys": Author interview with Dan Sparks.

505. "It was *tough*, okay?": Ibid.

Chapter 20: The Fabulous Fab

508. Unless otherwise indicated, information about Fabrice Tourre and Goldman's involvement in the ABACUS transaction has been taken from the nine-hundred-plus pages released in April 2010 by the U.S. Senate Permanent Subcommittee on Investigations, from e-mails released publicly by Goldman Sachs, and from documents filed in the April 2010 SEC lawsuit against Goldman Sachs and Tourre.

508. "This was the trade": Author interview with Dan Sparks.

524. he "briefly lost his cool": *WSJ*, April 26, 2010.

Chapter 21: Selling to Widows and Orphans

528. Unless otherwise indicated, information about Fabrice Tourre and Goldman's involvement in the ABACUS transaction has been taken from the nine-hundred-plus pages released in April 2010 by the U.S. Senate Permanent Subcommittee on Investigations, from e-mails released publicly by Goldman Sachs, and from documents filed in the April 2010 SEC lawsuit against Goldman Sachs and Tourre.

529. "bright line": Author interview with Dan Sparks.

529. "I don't think": Ibid.

530. "We lost a ton": Ibid.

531. 581-page report: Final report of Michael J. Missal Bankruptcy Court Examiner, February 29, 2008.

533. "In other words": Matt Taibbi, *Rolling Stone*, July 9–23, 2009.

533. "The simultaneous selling": Ibid.

533. "We started marking our clients": Author interview with Dan Sparks.

Chapter 22: Meltdown

547. Unless otherwise indicated, information about Fabrice Tourre and Goldman's involvement in the ABACUS transaction as well as on the effect Goldman's marks had on other Wall Street firms has been taken from the nine-hundred-plus pages released in April 2010 by the U.S. Senate Permanent Subcommittee on Investigations, from e-mails released publicly by Goldman Sachs, and from documents filed in the April 2010 SEC lawsuit against Goldman Sachs and Tourre.

547. "Definitely some people were shocked": Author interview with Josh Birnbaum. Much of the account of the collapse of Bear Stearns's two hedge funds in 2007 comes from William D. Cohan, *House of Cards* (New York: Doubleday & Co., 2009).

560. "Ben shared my concerns": Henry Paulson Jr., *On the Brink* (New York: Business Plus, 2010), p. 63.

560. "All these CEOs": Ibid.

560. "If you had called me": Author interview with Stan O'Neal.

564. "stunning strategy": Peter Eavis, "Questions Arise About Goldman's Blowout Quarter," *Fortune*, October 15, 2007.

567. "For more than three months": *NYT*, November 19, 2007.

Chapter 23: Goldman Gets Paid

571. "interconnected": Author interview with Robert Steel.

571. Except where indicated, much of the detail about AIG, AIG Financial Products, and Goldman's collateral calls on AIG come from William D. Cohan, "Collapse of the House of Hank," *Institutional Investor*, April 2010, and from documents released in 2010 and 2011 by the Financial Crisis Inquiry Commission.

591. "They were one hundred percent right": Author interview with David Viniar.

592. Personal evaluation forms of Josh Birnbaum, Dan Sparks, Mike Swenson, and Fabrice Tourre were found in documents released in April 2010 by the U.S. Senate Permanent Subcommittee on Investigations.

593. "The structured-products traders": *WSJ*, December 14, 2007.

594. "The good thing we did": Author interview with Dan Sparks.

595. SEC interviews Sparks: *WSJ*, May 15, 2010.

595. "I guess it depends": Author interview with Josh Birnbaum.

Chapter 24: God's Work

596. "Our history of good performance": *WSJ*, January 11, 2011.

596. "I think there are a lot of things": Author interview with Lloyd Blankfein.

597. "The first thing you need to know": Matt Taibbi, *Rolling Stone*, July 9–23, 2009.

597. "That *Rolling Stone* article": Author interview with Lloyd Blankfein.

598. "This is not an unalloyed": John Gapper, *Financial Times*, December 24, 2009.

600. "If Lloyd had a twin brother": Warren Buffet, speech at the 2010 Berkshire Hathaway annual meeting, as reported by Reuters, May 1, 2010.

600. "we never had any": *Financial Times*, April 22, 2010.

600. "Goldman became": Author interview with Steve Schwarzman.

601. "Front-running is illegal": Author interview with Eliot Spitzer.

602. "to embrace conflicts": *NYT*, May 19, 2010.

605. "My take on the whole firm": Author interview with Sandy Lewis.

606. "In a crisis": Author interview with Lloyd Blankfein.

607. "I think the big challenge": Author interview with Clayton Rose.

608. "The fundamental problem": Author interview with Charles Elson.

608. "You settle with the SEC": Author interview with Jim Cramer.

610. "at least ironic": Author interview with Lloyd Blankfein.

Index

ABACUS 2006 HGS1, 541–44
ABACUS 2007–AC1—83, 12–16, 23,
    509–10, 511–12, 516–17, 525–26,
    536, 566, 593
Abanto, J. Nelson, 239
ABC, 116
ABN AMRO, 12, 13, 543, 566
Abraham, Kathy, 278–83, 289
ABX.HE, 478–80, 489–91, 492, 501, 504,
    511, 514, 515, 517, 520, 521, 525,
    528, 543, 557, 561, 565
ACA Capital Holdings, Inc., 12, 13, 14
ACA Management, LLC, 12–16, 511–13,
    515, 517, 521, 536, 542, 543–44, 566
Accredited Home Lenders, Inc., 534
ACLI, 218
acquisitions, *see* mergers and acquisitions
Adams, Sherman, 83
Adelphia Pharmaceutical Manufacturing
    Company, 71
adjustable-rate mortgage, 423
Afghanistan, 234
Agee, William, 224
AIG, 383–84, 385, 403, 551–52, 571–76,
    596–97
    CDSs sold by, 542
    financial troubles of, 3, 4, 6, 384, 474,
        571–91
    Goldman Sach's squeeze on, 4, 6, 571–91
    government rescue of, 6, 589–91, 596
AIG Financial Products, 572–91
Aitschel, Arthur, 123
Akamatsu, Shigeru, 578
Akron, Ohio, 69
Albany, N.Y., 102
Alcan Aluminum, 147
Alexander & Baldwin, 153
Alex. Brown Inc., 385

Alger, Horatio, 64, 78
Alien Property Custodian, 102
Aliredha, Yusuf, 566
Allan, John H., 158, 161
Allegheny Corporation, 115, 116–17
Allied Corporation, 224
Allison, Herbert, 403, 404
Alt-A mortgages, 486, 529
Alter, Jonathan, 2
Alterna-Track, 285–86
Altman, Roger, 306, 307, 309, 311
Alton Box Board Company, 185
Altschul, Arthur, 120
Amazon, 428
Amelia Island conference, 485
American Cyanamid Corporation, 161
American Express, 174–75, 179, 218
American Stock Exchange, 125, 421
Amoco, 350, 420
Amstutz, Dan, 216
Anderson, Jenny, 567–69
Anderson Mezzanine Funding, 537–38,
    541
Annenberg Building, 125
anti-Semitism, 81–82, 351
    in Europe, 75
    of Henry Ford, 89, 90
    see also Jews
Aoki, 378
Apple Hill Farm, 188
Araskog, Rand, 379
arbitrage:
    derivatives and, 214
    event driven, 129
    by Goldman Sachs, 111–15, 117–21,
        124, 128–37, 138, 139, 145, 148, 155,
        178, 186, 214–15, 216, 237, 256,
        260–61, 276, 352, 378, 469–70

arbitrage (*continued*):
  merger, 113–14, 129, 214
  of Phillips Petroleum, 214–15
  risk, 111–12, 139
  secret Kidder Peabody department of, 258–59
  and Trading Corporation, 53–54
Archer Daniels Midland, 350
Archipelago Holdings, 447–50, 603
Archon Mortgage LLC, 595
Argentina, 46, 235
Argent Mortgage Company, 483
Arkin, Stanley, 263
Arning, Lee, 158
Aron, Jacob, 216
Arrow, Kenneth, 302
Arthur D. Little & Co., 166
AT&T, 57, 102, 124, 135–36, 195
Athan, Thomas, 579
Atlantic Monthly, 47, 65
Atlas Corporation, 59
auto-loan receivables, 467, 471
Automatic Data Processing, 485
Aranessians, Armen, 371
Aykroyd, Dan, 497

Bache Halsey Stuart Shields, 218
"back-office crisis," 158
Baer family, 27–28
Baker, James, 2
Ballantine, Arthur, 77
Ballantine, Dewey, 77
Ball family, 116
Baltimore American Insurance Company, 50–51
BankAmerica Corp., 385
Bank Clerks' League, 30
Bank One, 342, 343
Bankers Trust Company, 63, 385
Bank Holding Company Act (1956), 245–46
banking, underwriting vs., 245–46
Bank of America, 20
  Merrill Lynch purchased by, 6, 8
Bank of England, 36, 321
Bank of New York, 152
Banque Nationale de Paris (BNP), 445
Barclays de Zoete Wedd, 319
Barkley, Albert, 74
Barofsky, Neil, 590
Barron's, 309

Baruc, Edgar, 111, 114, 117, 118
Baruch, Bernard, 63, 111
Bash-Polley, Stacy, 503
Basis Yield Alpha Fund, 20, 21, 595
Bass, Kyle, 524
B.A.T. Industries, 225
Bear, Dicky, 132, 133
Bear Stearns, 4, 5–6, 177, 399, 507, 510–11, 520, 559
  capital of, 108
  collapse of, 6, 553, 556
  Cy Lewis at, 112–13
  demise of, 3, 4, 5–6, 10
  fixed-income group of, 541
  government rescue of, 5–6, 556, 571
  hedge funds of, 5–6, 20, 54, 522, 529, 532, 547–49, 552, 554, 555–56, 557, 571
  IPO of, 242
  LTCM deal and, 404–5
  mortgage-backed securities of, 482, 541, 543–44, 552, 564
  private-equity fund of, 14
Bear Stearns Asset Management (BSAM), 541, 544, 552, 555–56
Bear Stearns Merchant Banking, 512
Bear Stearns Residential Mortgage Corporation, 541
Beatrice Foods, 259, 269, 270, 272, 273, 274, 378
Becerra, Lawrence, 328
Becton, Dickinson, 145
Bell, Lord Timothy, 418
Bendix, 224
Bentsen, Lloyd, 310, 370
Berkshire Hathaway, 51, 401, 403, 485, 573
Bernanke, Ben, 8, 522, 540, 541, 560, 590–91
Bernanke Doctrine, 560
Bernard, Lewis, 194–95
Bernice Pauahi Bishop, Princess of Hawaii, 300
Bernstein, Sandy, 340
Bethlehem Steel, 102
Bevan, David C., 169, 172, 174, 176, 178, 181, 183
B. F. Goodrich Company, 35, 69, 92, 100, 160
Bhavsar, Avanish, 550
Bieber, Matthew, 542
"big short," 3, 4–5, 6–7, 8, 17, 18–24, 489–95, 496–97, 498–507, 508–27,

528–29, 533–34, 535–36, 539, 540,
544–46, 547, 554–55, 560–64,
591–93, 594
Big Short, The (Lewis), 542, 564
Birmingham, Stephen, 25, 26, 27, 28, 31,
33–34, 35, 37, 38, 40
Birnbaum, Josh, 466–70, 472, 473,
477–80, 508, 556–59, 567, 591,
593–95
"big short" of, 3, 19, 489–95, 496–97,
498, 502, 504–5, 506, 507, 508, 514,
517, 521, 523–25, 533, 535, 539, 540,
544–46, 547, 554–55, 560–61, 562,
591–92, 593
Bishop Estate, 300–301, 354, 369–70,
376, 383, 392, 414
Black, Fisher, 342
Black Panthers, 456
Blackstone Group, 560, 600
Blair & Co., 162
Blankfein, Laura Jacobs, 462
Blankfein, Lloyd, 37, 58–59, 62, 219, 384,
411, 436, 437, 442, 454, 460–61, 499,
519–20, 528, 538, 558, 560, 564–65,
567, 569, 594, 596, 598, 599, 606–7,
608, 609–10
apartment of, 463
appearance and tics of, 10, 22
background of, 455–60
"big short" denied by, 6–7
compensation received by, 3–4, 9–10
on conflict management, 440–41
ignorance of public mood, 9, 24
as law school graduate, 23
made manager of traders, 461
made partner, 461–62
made president, 439
made vice chairman, 434
on "mark-to-market," 4
Obama's criticism of, 2, 8
personality of, 10–11
Senate testimony of, 6–7, 18, 22–234
on strategic planning committee, 389
TARP funds not desired by, 8, 9
"two-percent probabilities" remark of, 6
Blankfein, Seymour, 455
block trading, 113, 127, 134–35, 146–47,
148, 177, 178, 212
of mortgage-backed securities, 491
Bloomberg, 559–60
Blue Ridge Corporation, 56–57
blue sheets, 181

Blyth & Co., 91
B'nai B'rith Foundation, 125
BNP Paribas, 559–60
Board of National Defense, 42
boards of directors, 68–69, 151, 160
Boeschenstein, Harold, 87
Boesky, Ivan, 250, 252, 258, 259, 260, 268
Bohra, V. Bunty, 546
Boisi, Geoffrey, 224, 225, 240–41, 249,
285, 299–300, 416
Bolten, Joshua, 355, 356, 452, 596
Bond Club, 123
bonds, 298
AT&T, 135–36
Eurobond, 351
Ford, 136
foreign exchange trading and, 221
government, 159, 238, 303, 328, 342,
343, 345, 370, 469, 589
high-grade corporate, 238
high-yield (junk), 46, 237, 238, 285, 376
Liberty, 38–39
municipal, 14, 342
railroad, 113, 114–15
utility, 113, 114
Whitehead's work on, 201
bonuses, 71, 177, 178
Booth Newspaper, Inc., 224
Booz Allen, 286
Boston, Mass., 81, 102
Boukhtouche, Fatiha, 514–15
Bouton, Daniel, 444–46
Bowers, Henry S., 40, 67, 96, 104
Bowne Business College, 66
Bradfield, Michael, 245
Bradley, Bill, 417
Branson, Richard, 417
Brattleboro, 428
Brazil, 235
Brazil, Alan, 496
bridge loans, 296
Briger, Peter, 398
British Petroleum, 277, 278
British Printing Corporation, 318
Broderick, Craig, 5, 546, 553, 566, 569
Senate testimony of, 19
Brody, Kenneth, 298, 299, 309
Broeckel, Janet, 552–54
Brook, 81–82
Brookings Institution, 434, 435
Brosens, Frank, 269, 271–72, 276, 358,
461–62

Brown, David S., 250
Browne, John, 417, 420
Brownell, Herbert, 83
Brown Shoe Company, 98, 105
Bryan, John, 420
Buchanan, George, 128
Buffalo, N.Y., 102
Buffett, Warren, 47, 51, 381–82, 471, 591, 599–601
  on derivatives, 508
  Goldman Sachs given loan by, 6, 10
  LTCM investment of, 396–97, 401–3
Bunds, 327
Burgess, Mary, 204
Burnham, Tubby, 126
Bush, George H. W., 306, 356
Bush, George W., 355, 432, 452–54, 596
BusinessWeek, 471
Business World, 268
Butcher, Howard, III, 151
Buzan, Anthony, 285
Byrne, Brendan, 155
Byron, Christopher, 264

Cabot, Paul C., 47, 64, 65, 81–82
Cahouet, Frank, 387–89
Callahan, Jim, 120
Calyon, 586
Cantor, Eddie, 60–61, 73
Capetown, 46
Capital Institute, 9
capitalism, 31, 36, 74
Capitalism: A Love Story, 597
Capital One Financial, 559
Cargill, 216
Carnegie, Andrew, 35
Carnegie Foundation, 310
Carr, Michael, 407
Carter, Jimmy, 305, 306, 348
Cartusciello, Neil, 262
Casey, William J., 176
Cassano, Joseph, 572–73, 574, 575, 578–81, 582–83, 585–88
Catcher in the Rye, The (Salinger), 457
Catchings, Nora Belle Waddill, 41
Catchings, Silas Fly, 41
Catchings, Waddill, 67, 74, 98, 149, 194
  background of, 41
  Blue Ridge constructed and sold by, 56, 57
  on board of Merck, 102
  companies created by, 43–44
  debt-financing scheme of, 58–59
  divorce of, 58, 60
  economic theories of, 42–43
  Goldman Sachs partnership canceled, 59–60, 62, 68, 69, 333
  investment trust created by, 45, 47–56, 68, 97
  made partner of Goldman Sachs, 40, 43
  power grab by, 44
  Shenandoah constructed and sold by, 56
  at Sullivan & Cromwell, 41–42
Caterpillar, 350
Cayne, James E., 399–400, 404–5
CDS IndexCo LLC, 478
Celler, Emanuel, 89
Central Foundry Company, 42
Century Country Club, 119
Cerberus, 534
Chafee, John, 348
Challenger space shuttle, 287
Chamber of Commerce, U.S., 40, 42
Chang, Victor, 344
Charles M. Schott & Co., 64
Charles Schwab, 466
Chase Bank, 78, 404
Chase National Bank, 70
Chen-Oster, H. Cristina, 292–93
Chicago, Ill., 81, 102
Chicago Board Options Exchange (CBOE), 215
China, 324, 353, 394, 432
Cholnoky, Thomas, 589
Christian Science Monitor, 124
Christopher, Warren, 310–11
CIA, 80
CIGNA, 224
Cioffi, Ralph, 522, 541, 547, 548–49, 550, 555, 556, 557
CIT Financial, 39, 104–5, 562
Citibank, 326, 390
Citigroup, 3, 246, 309, 390, 438, 448, 453, 482
Citizens for Eisenhower-Nixon, 82–83
Civil Air Patrol, 114
Clark, Harold B., 96, 97
Clay, Lucius D., 79, 83
Clayton, Dubilier & Rice, 366
Cleary Gottlieb, 138, 144–45
Clemenceau, George, 207
Clikeman, Paul, 71
Clinton, Bill, 155, 246, 309–12, 327, 355

Cluett, Peabody, 99
CNBC, 10
Coakley, Martha, 531
Coburn, Tom, 18
Cofield, James E., Jr., 162–67
Cohen, Harold, 132, 135
Cohen, Jonathan, 283
Cohen, Laurie, 272, 369–70
Cohen, Roger, 317
Cohn, Gary, 10, 358, 362, 437, 499, 502,
    506, 518, 521, 528, 534, 535, 538–39,
    550, 551, 557, 558, 561, 562, 567,
    594, 607, 609
Cole, Christopher, 358
Coles, Michael, 210
collateralized debt obligations (CDOs), 5,
    11–15, 19, 494, 496, 501, 506–7, 508,
    510, 520, 521, 528, 529, 535, 536,
    537–38, 540, 541, 545–46, 550, 553,
    556, 558, 561, 565, 566, 570, 575–76,
    593
  complexity of, 11, 22, 494
  market volatility caused by, 514
  synthetic, 11, 14, 19, 20, 22, 508, 509,
    511–12, 522, 529, 541, 565, 575, 592,
    599
  tranches of, 502–3, 575–76
collateralized debt obligations (CDOs)
  squared, 5, 544, 546
collateralized mortgage obligations
    (CMOs), 467–69, 472
Collins, Timothy, 399
Commerce Department, U.S., 89
Commercial Bank, 27
commercial banks, prevented from
    intermingling with investment banks,
    49, 94, 245–46
Commercial Investment Trust, 104
commercial paper, 26–27, 28, 29, 31, 33,
    34, 124, 157, 161, 168–69, 170, 171,
    172, 174, 175–76, 180, 181, 183, 184,
    223
  see also IOUs
Commodities Corporation, 394
commodities trading, 28, 34, 148, 216,
    218, 296, 326, 394
  see also specific trades
Commodity Futures Trading Commission,
    16, 461–62
Commodore Hotel, 83–84
"Compliance and Reputational Judgment"
    training, 441–44

COMSAT, 150
Congress, U.S., 9
  Joint Economic Committee of, 541
  see also House of Representatives, U.S.
    Senate, U.S.;
Connally, John, 348
Connecticut General Corp, 224
Connor, John T., 150–51
constant maturity mortgage (CMM),
    474–75
"Contagion and Crowded Trades," 566
Continental Can Company, 35, 39
Continental Group, Inc., 268, 272
Continental Illinois National Bank and
    Trust, 342
convergence trades, 395
Conway, Kevin, 366
Cook, Karen, 286
Cooke, Jennie C., 64
Cooperman, Leon, 220
Coopers & Lybrand, 161
CoreStates Financial, 388
Corinthian Broadcasting Company,
    151
Cornacchia, Thomas, 545
Corning Glass Works, 86, 87, 88
corporate raiders, 223, 228, 240–41, 254,
    258, 317–18, 350, 417–18
Corrigan, E. Gerald, 606
Corzine, Joanne Dougherty, 341, 342
Corzine, Jon, 296, 301, 303, 333, 361, 423,
    473
  background of, 340–42
  double role of, 328–29
  early mistakes at Goldman Sachs of,
    343–45
  as Friedman's successor, 336–37, 339,
    354–55
  goals and aspirations of, 374–77
  health problems of, 340
  loyalty to, 385
  LTCM deal and, 395, 396, 397, 402–4,
    405
  Maxwell lawsuit and, 367–69
  mergers desired by, 381–84, 387–89
  and move to go public, 315, 359, 373,
    376, 380, 386, 392–94, 405, 409,
    412–13, 419
  1994 losses and, 328–30, 331, 345, 357,
    358, 369, 397
  "palace coup" against, 410–13, 414–15,
    419

Corzine, Jon (*continued*)
  Paulson's relationship with, 325–26,
    337, 365–67, 381–84, 387, 388–89,
    390, 396, 399, 408, 411, 432
  positive thinking of, 369, 371
Coster, F. Donald, 71–72
cough syrup, 71
Coulson, Frank, 290–91
Council of Foreign Relations, 236
Council on Wage and Price Stability, 305
Countrywide, 468, 480, 483, 559
Coyne, Herbert, 216, 220
Coyne, Marty, 216
Cramer, James, 10, 242, 426–27, 605–6,
  607
C. R. Anthony, 156–57, 180–85
credit-card receivables, 467, 471
credit-default swaps (CDSs), 473–74,
  476–78, 502, 503, 508–9, 510–11,
  523, 535, 542, 578, 586, 588
Credit Suisse Group, 297, 521
credit support agreement, 510
Credit Support Annex, 579
CS-1, 254, 255, 257, 260, 263, 264–65,
  266
Cuckney, John, 368
Cullman family, 28
Cunningham, Bill, 159
Cunningham, Jeffrey, 598
Cunningham, Mary, 224
Curran, Paul, 256, 270
currencies, 389, 394
  see also specific currencies

Daily Mirror, 318
Daily Word, 126
Dauphinot, Clarence, 67
Davies, Gavyn, 327
Davies, Joseph, 75
Davilman, Andrew, 542, 577
Davis, Charles "Chuck," 358
Davis Polk & Wardell, 256
Day, H. Corbin, 156
Dead Poets Society, 365
Dean, Arthur, 100–101, 102
Dean Witter, 412, 460
Dearborn Independent, 89
debt *see* underwriting
De Coppet & Doremus, 64
deficit reduction, 309
Delmar Capital Corporation, 53

DeLucia, David, 239
Democratic National Campaign
  Committee, 74
Democratic National Campaign Executive
  Finance Committee, 70
Democratic National Committee, 74, 304
Demos, Raphael, 144
Denham, Robert, 385
DeNunzio, Ralph, 258, 259
Department of Trade and Industry (DTI),
  U.K., 316–19, 321, 322–23
derivatives, 4, 539–40
  AAA ratings of, 16, 484–85, 488, 532,
    538, 562, 576
  arbitrage and, 214
  Blankfein's defense of, 23
  Buffett's dislike of, 508
  Friedman's worries about, 360–61
  Levin's criticism of, 16–17, 19
Derivatives Week, 541
Detroit, Mich., 102, 229
Deutsche Bank, 378, 423, 482, 487–88,
  489–91, 498
deutsche mark, 314–15, 326
Diamond Rubber Company, 35
Diebold, Inc., 123
Dilday, Clarence, 167
Dillon, Read & Co., 100, 104
Dinkins, David, 271
Directorship, 598
divorce, 231
Dobkin, Eric, 380
DOCOMO, 418
Dodd-Frank Act (2010), 22
Domestic Policy Council, 348–49
Donaldson, Lufkin & Jenrette (DLJ), 218,
  219
Donovan, William J. "Wild Bill," 80, 459
Donovan, Leisure, 459
Doonan, Thomas, 250–51, 253, 254–56,
  257, 260, 263
Doral Arrowwood, 363–65, 369, 372, 373,
  380, 392
Doty, George, 148–49, 153, 161, 162,
  179–80, 191, 192, 193, 229, 237,
  351–52
  and purchase of J. Aron, 216, 217, 220,
    221, 222
Douglas Aircraft Company, 151
Dow Jones Industrial Average, 276,
  391
Dowler, John, 132

Drexel Burnham Lambert, 250, 251, 259, 267, 471, 572
Dreyfus, Ludwig, 29, 40
Drizzle, David, 457–58
Drobny, Steven, 326
drugs, 308
DTI, *see* Department of Trade and Industry, U.K.
Dudley, William, 36
Dukakis, Michael, 306–7, 309
Dun & Bradstreet, 72
Dunbo, Mike, 372
DuPont, 199
Dyal, Gordon, 407

Early, Stephen, 75
Eavis, Peter, 563–64
eBay, 424
Eckert, Alfred "Fred", III, 298, 299
Economist, 319, 320, 323, 450–52, 455
Edelman, Asher, 417
education, 308, 309
efficient market hypothesis, 304
E. F. Hutton, 212, 344
Egol, Jonathan, 495–96, 523, 526, 531, 536, 566
Ehrlich, Judith Ramsey, 110
Ehrlichman, John, 348, 349
Einhorn, David, 475
Eisenberg, Lewis M., 278–83, 284, 285, 289, 315, 324, 352
Eisenhower, Dwight D., 82–83, 84, 150
Eisner, Michael, 424
Elberon, N.J., 31
elections and campaigns, U.S.:
 1932, 70, 74, 77
 1936, 74, 75–76
 1940, 76
 1972, 304–5
 1980, 235
 1984, 305
 2008, 275
Electric Storage Battery Company (ESB), 227
Eli Lilly, 161
Elizabeth Arden, 161
Ellis, Charles, 112, 114, 127, 191, 227, 367, 409
Elson, Charles, 608, 609
EMC Mortgage Corporation, 541
Encore Credit Corporation, 541

Endicott-Johnson, 98
Endlich, Lisa, 191, 239, 248, 249, 299
Engelhard Minerals and Chemical Corporation, 217
England, 46, 47
Engman, Lewis, 348, 349
Enhanced Leverage Fund, 547–49, 555
Enron, 424
Epstein, Edward Jay, 271
Equal Employment Opportunity Commission, 162, 165, 166–67
Equitable Life Assurance Society, 97
equity *see* underwriting
eToys, 424
euro, 314
Eurobond, 351
European Central Bank, 559
Evans, J. Michael, 354, 358, 528, 606
Evans, Nancy, 424
"event driven" arbitrage, 129
Exodus Communications, 428
ExxonMobil, 485

Facebook, 22–23, 60–61
Face the Nation, 268
Fairrie, James, 15
Falcone, Philip, 523
Fanlo, Nino, 551
Fannie Mae, 467, 473
Farrell, Anne Brown, 289
Federal Aviation Administration, 458
Federal Deposit Insurance Corporation (FDIC), 603
Federal Reserve, 245, 246, 307–8, 326, 328, 343, 395, 402, 476, 522, 540–41
 Bear Stearns's creditors rescued by, 6
 design of, 35–37
 as "lender-of-last resort," 307
 in response to European financial troubles, 560
 short-term loans granted by, 8, 10
Federal Reserve Act (1913), 36
Federal Reserve Bank of New York, 8, 36, 246, 400–403, 405, 590, 596, 606
Federal Trade Commission, 129, 130, 349
Federated Investors, 550
Federation of Jewish Philanthropies, 122, 123, 125
Feinberg, Kenneth, 8–9
Feld, Al, 114
Feldman, Albert, 133, 134

FICO, 485, 489
Fife, Eugene, 321, 338, 368
Finance, 146, 147
Financial and Industrial Securities
    Corporation, 48, 49, 50, 52–55, 56
financial crisis (2008), 77, 547
    Goldman Sachs's avoidance of worst of,
        3–4, 7, 9, 17, 24, 466, 569–70, 591;
        see also "big short"
    Goldman Sachs's exacerbation of, 4–5,
        6, 19, 62, 384, 481
    Henry Paulson's fears of, 559
    leverage used in, 47
    see also housing bubble
Financial Crisis Inquiry Commission, 503,
    552–54, 577
Financial News, 412, 513–14
financial system:
    as engine of growth, 20
    evolution of, 11
    gambling analogy of, 11
    government regulation of, 36
    taxpayer bailout of, 8–10
    see also housing bubble
Financial Times, 15, 363, 598–99, 600
First Boston, 105, 210, 225, 296–97,
    471
First Colony Life Insurance, 260
First Franklin Financial Corp., 482
First National Bank of Nevada, 483
First National City Bank, 162, 163
Fisher, Peter, 401, 402
Fiske, Robert, Jr., 256, 270
Fitch, 486, 531
Flick, Jim, 251
Florida land bubble, 139–40
Flowers, J. Christopher, 387–88, 390, 393,
    399, 461
Flynn, Edward, 74
Forbes, 242, 295, 297, 298, 478
Ford, Gerald, 535
Ford, Henry, 89, 90, 203
Ford, Henry, II, 89, 90–91, 92
Ford, Mrs. Edsel, 89, 91
Ford, William Clay, Jr., 417, 424–25
Ford Foundation, 88–89, 90, 203
Ford Motor Company, 136, 148, 151, 164,
    417
    IPO of, 88–92, 124, 125, 203, 297
foreclosures, 487–88
foreign exchange trading, 221–22
Forester, Doug, 413

Forster, Andrew, 577, 580, 581, 582, 583,
    584
Forstmann Little, 475
Fortress Investment Group, 45
Fortune, 62, 64, 68, 72, 73, 81, 82, 87, 88,
    251, 362, 460, 461, 563–64, 567, 593
Foster, William Trufant, 43, 56
Foster Grant Corporation, 185
Fowler, Henry "Joe," 150–51, 210, 235, 304
franc, 315, 326
France, 37, 315
Frank, Barney, 405
Frank, Walter, 126, 189
Franklin Savings Bank, 185
Franks, Bob, 413
Freakonomics (Dubner and Levitt), 514
Freddie Mac, 467, 473
Fredman, Sheara, 535
Freedman, Alix, 369–70
Freeman, Margo, 273–74
Freeman, Robert, 258, 261, 378
    hiring of, 186
    insider trading scandal of, 250–52,
        253–54, 255, 256–58, 260, 261–75,
        276, 278, 284, 315, 324
Fremont General, 534–35, 536
Fremont Investment and Loan, 14–15, 483
Friedman, Barbara Benioff, 226, 325, 332,
    356
Friedman, Richard A., 23
Friedman, Robert A., 245
Friedman, Steve, 186, 217, 219, 232, 241,
    242, 286, 295, 296, 297, 299, 303,
    312–13, 314, 339, 350, 352, 354, 360,
    387, 416, 439, 464, 596
    background, 226–27
    Eisenberg's sexual scandal and, 279
    health problems of, 323, 355–56
    hired at Goldman Sachs, 227
    insider trading scandal and, 256, 265–66
    made co-chairman, 283–84, 285
    made vice chairman, 233, 278
    and move to go public, 243–44, 247–48,
        315–16
    1987 crash and, 276–77
    1994 losses and, 329–30, 331, 360
    as potential head of Goldman Sachs,
        233, 247
    put in charge of fixed-income division,
        237, 238–40
    retirement of, 323–24, 331–40
    as worried about derivatives, 360–61

Friedman & Friedman, 226
front-running, 400–401, 601–2
Frost, Alan, 576–77, 581–82
Fuld, Richard, 560
"full-doc" loans, 481
Fullerton, John, 9–10, 16
Fundamental Investors, 156–57, 180
Funston, Keith, 87, 88
F. W. Woolworth Company, 35

Gadhafi, Mu'ammar al-, 132
Galbraith, John Kenneth, 44, 45, 46, 48, 56
Gang of Five, 120, 122
Gant, Donald, 244–45
Gapper, John, 598–99
gasoline, 597
Gasvoda, Kevin, 501, 517–18
GATT treaty, 306
Gaul, Paul, 290
Geissinger, John, 550
Geisst, Charles, 568
Geithner, Timothy, 8, 560
General Atlantic, 447
General Cigar Company, 151
General Electric, 57, 79, 82, 83, 85–86,
   160, 199, 233
   European bonds underwritten for, 210
   RCA's merger with, 241, 243
General Foods Corporation, 43, 62, 83,
   87–88, 99, 240–41
General Motors, 92
General Re Corporation, 573–74
Gensler, Gary, 461–62, 467
George, Edward, 321
Germany, 37–39, 76, 314–15, 326, 327
Geronemus, Roy, 458
Gerst, David, 543
get-rich-quick schemes, 44–48
Getty Oil, 185
Gilbert, Cass, 35
Gilmour, James, 167
Giuliani, Rudolph, 252–53, 254, 257, 260,
   262–64, 266–67, 268, 269, 270, 275
Glass-Steagall Act (1932), 49, 94, 245–46,
   385
Glauber, Robert, 425
Glengarry Glen Ross (Mamet), 101
Glenn, John, 305
Global Crossing, 424
gold, 74, 218, 221
gold coins, 30, 31

Goldfield, Jacob, 302–3, 304, 400
Goldman, Bertha, 25, 26, 27
Goldman, Henry, 25, 29, 43, 107
   Federal Reserve System designed by,
      35–37
   Germany supported by, 37–39
   Goldman Sachs inherited by, 31
   retirement of, 38–39, 40, 104–5
   as risk-taking, 32
   Sears IPO handled by, 34–35, 39, 40
   underwriting and, 31–32, 39
Goldman, Henry, Jr., 67
Goldman, Julius, 25
Goldman, Louisa see Sachs, Louisa
   Goldman
Goldman, Marcus, 43
   in arrival to U.S., 25
   death of, 31
   gold coins of, 30
   IOUs bought and sold by, 26–27, 28, 29,
      31, 33, 34, 124
   money for Jewish immigrants collected
      by, 30
   Sam Sachs made partner of, 27, 28–29
Goldman, Rebecca, 25
Goldman, Rosa see Sachs, Rosa Goldman
Goldman, Sachs & Dreyfus, 29
Goldman Sachs:
   "Ad Hoc Profit Maximization
      Committee" at, 285, 295
   Administrative Department of, 161
   American Cyanamid Corporation lawsuit
      against, 161
   annual budgeting at, 229–30
   antitrust lawsuit against, 93–106, 201–2
   arbitrage department of, 111–15,
      117–21, 124, 128–37, 138, 139, 145,
      148, 155, 186, 214, 216, 237, 253,
      256, 260–61, 276, 378; see also Levy,
      Gustave Lehmann; Rubin, Robert
   bad news not shared by, 168–77, 180,
      183–84; see also "big short"
   in battles with other companies, 104–5
   board of directors at, 420, 437, 563
   bond department of, 67, 68, 113, 114,
      237–39, 240, 343–45
   Bouton's potential lawsuit against, 444–46
   branch offices of, 81, 102
   Broad Street building of, 93, 109, 148,
      159
   Buffett's loan to, 6, 10
   business department of, 159

Goldman Sachs (*continued*):
  Business Standards Committee of, 607, 609
  Buying Department of, 161, 164, 165
  calling effort of, 159–60
  capital of, 30, 38, 92, 106, 112, 120, 146, 156, 234, 242–43, 244, 278, 295, 300, 330, 351–52, 354, 357, 361, 376, 398
  Capital Structure Franchise Trading Group of, 293
  Catching's company created for, 43–44
  Catching's power grab at, 44
  collusion accusations against, 2
  commercial paper traded by, 26–27, 31, 33, 34; *see also* commercial paper
  compensation at, 2, 3–4, 8, 9–10, 119–20, 177, 178
  competitiveness at, 465–66
  confidentiality and nondisparagement agreements at, 2–3
  conflict management by, 1, 377, 440–41
  Corporate Finance Department of, 162, 163, 184, 415
  Corzine's desire to enlarge, 381
  in crash of 1929, 47, 48, 52, 57–58, 62
  Depression strategy of, 2, 63–64
  discipline at, 3
  85 Broad Street building of, 5, 212–13, 244, 247, 422
  envy of, 1
  ethical code of, 18, 206–9, 397–98, 417
  Executive Committee of, 380, 390–91, 396, 407, 409–10
  factors in prowess of, 230–32
  as family business, 32–33
  fear of, 1
  Financial Institutions Group of (FIG), 358, 359–60, 382, 383, 387, 389, 401, 407
  fine paid by, 15
  Firmwide Risk Committee at, 535–36
  Fixed-Income, Currencies and Commodities (FICC) at, 344, 389, 420, 434, 436, 451, 462, 500
  fixed-income division of, 237, 238, 239–40, 289, 296, 301, 302, 315, 325, 326, 336, 357, 361–62, 373, 408, 460
  Ford IPO handled by, 88–92, 124, 125, 203, 297

  foreign exchange department of, 30, 221, 326, 373, 377, 461
  "great rehabilitation" of, 62, 69–70
  hot IPO's distributed by, 424–30
  hundredth anniversary of, 152
  internal e-mails of, 3, 7, 17–18, 20–22
  International Advisory Committee of, 210
  international expansion of, 209–12, 284–85, 294–95, 316, 324, 325–26, 352–54, 364, 366–67, 377, 384, 418, 440–41
  interview process at, 465
  investment banking of, 15–16, 18–19, 66, 94, 95, 101, 106–8, 121–22, 147–48, 159–60, 178, 193, 200, 204, 229, 232–33, 237, 248, 314, 329, 366, 379, 399, 475; *see also* investment banking
  Investment Banking Services (IBS), 353
  investment trusts of, 45, 47–57, 59, 60, 62, 68, 97, 111, 208, 215
  J. Aron & Company acquired by, 214, 216–23, 344
  as Jewish firm, 34, 194–95, 211, 344, 465
  jokes about, 60–61, 73
  and lack of high-level relationships in Washington, 2
  layoffs at, 430
  leverage used by, 56–57, 357
  liquidity of, 330, 357–58, 398
  major acquisitions shunned by, 214
  Management Committee, 120, 127, 160–61, 167, 190–91, 192–94, 209, 217, 220, 225, 229, 243, 247, 253, 265–66, 276, 278, 296, 315–16, 325, 332, 333, 335–36, 337–38, 345, 352, 368, 389, 393, 399, 409, 419–20, 561
  as "mark-to-market" firm, 4, 5, 6, 19, 498, 553, 566
  Maxwell lawsuit against, 367–69
  mergers and acquisitions (M&A) department of, 186, 223–28, 240, 242, 248, 254, 261, 265, 299, 324, 366, 407, 416, 418; *see also* Friedman, Steve
  modernization of, 285–95
  Mortgage Capital Committee of, 516, 536
  in move to go public, 234, 242, 243–44, 247–49, 250, 315–16, 323,

359, 360–61, 373–74, 376, 380,
381, 383, 385–86, 390–91, 392–94,
397–99, 405–7, 408–9, 410, 411,
412–13, 414, 419, 424, 439, 464,
475
New Business Department of, 161,
204–6, 211
New Business Group at, 285, 353
new skyscraper of, 11
on New York Stock Exchange, 30, 67
1930 debt of, 58, 59
1940s trial of, 2
1987 crash and, 276–78, 360
1994 losses of, 326–30, 331, 335, 345,
357–58, 361, 362–63, 369, 372,
375–76, 397, 472
1998 trading losses of, 408
Owens-Corning IPO handled by,
87–88, 90
"palace coup" against Corzine at,
410–13, 414–15, 419
partner turnover at, 366
Penn Central lawsuits against, 156–57,
161, 168–76, 180–85, 186, 208, 247,
283, 320, 350, 485
phone system of, 93, 109
Pine Street offices of, 43, 70, 93, 109,
200
plans for successor to Friedman at,
331–40
principal investing business of, 379
principal equity business of, 378
private-equity business of, 296, 316,
378, 475, 534–35, 569
profit sharing at, 119, 231, 373
profits of, 1, 3, 4, 9, 17, 19, 24, 30, 158,
159, 177–78, 211–12, 228–29, 230,
233–34, 242, 295, 297, 323, 327, 360,
369, 372, 374, 397, 420, 451, 557–58,
563–64, 567, 569, 599
in proposed merger with AIG, 383–84,
385
public relations fiascos at, 596–610
punishing work schedule at, 288
racial discrimination lawsuit against,
162–67
return on equity of, 30
risk-management committee of, 499
Sears IPO led by, 34–35, 39, 40, 62, 124
SEC investigation of, 10, 11–16, 18, 24,
178, 179–86, 425–30
secrecy of, 1, 2–3, 6, 178

Securities Sales department of, 161,
495, 514
Senate hearing on, see Senate, U.S.,
Goldman Sachs hearing of
seventy-fifth anniversary of, 81
sexual scandals at, 278–83, 284, 285,
289–94, 315, 324
short term loans secured by, 63
in squeeze on AIG, 4, 6, 571–91
stock prices of, 9, 10, 14, 44, 48, 50, 53,
54, 55, 56, 59, 414, 422, 435
strategic planning committee of,
389–90
suicidal clients of, 2
TARP funds given to, 8–10
teamwork at, 242
trading department of, 114, 124, 147,
159, 194, 233, 237–40, 314, 379, 475;
see also Levy, Gustave Lehmann
in turn to bank holding company, 8
valuation of, 391, 394, 397, 405
vulnerability of, 2
Wall Street office of, 43
Water Street Corporate Recovery Fund
of, 296, 298, 299, 300
wave of retirements at, 354
Wells notice received by, 13
World War I and, 37–39, 43
worst of 2008 financial crisis avoided
by, 3–4, 7, 9, 17, 24, 466, 569–70,
591
see also Goldman, Sachs & Co.; M.
Goldman and Sachs; Senate, U.S.,
Goldman Sachs hearing at
Goldman Sachs, deals and underwriting of,
31–32, 34–35, 36, 38, 39–40, 73,
87–92, 93, 96–106, 159–60, 240
of AT&T bonds, 135–36
of bonds, 159, 201
British Petroleum, 277, 278
in business with Lehman Brothers,
33–35, 39–40, 98–100, 105
Facebook stock, 22–23, 60–61
failures of, 102
with General Foods, 240–41
gold coins traded by, 30, 31
insider trading and, 2, 48–49, 56,
129–31, 250–58, 261–75, 276, 278,
284, 315, 324
ITT Corporation sale, 378
KKR, 377
with LTCM, 395, 396, 401–6, 413

Goldman Sachs, deals and underwriting of
(*continued*)
M&A deals of, 160, 186, 223–26, 227,
295, 297, 299, 314, 350, 387, 415,
451
Goldman Sachs, deals and underwriting of
Maxwell and, 316–23, 324, 331, 360,
361, 367–69
May Department Stores, 35, 39, 103–4
Mill Factors Corporation deal, 152–53,
156, 161, 179
in 1970, 158
N. J. Schloss loan of, 29–30
of Penn Central, 153, 154, 156–57, 158,
161, 168–76, 186, 208, 247, 283, 320,
350, 485
Pillsbury's mortgage bonds and, 96–98
with RCA and GE, 241, 243
for Sinclair Oil, 131–33
Studebaker trade, 124–25
with Sumitomo, 243–47, 300, 301
Goldman Sachs, mortgage backed
securities traded by, 237, 238–40, 285,
290, 467–68, 472–88, 533–46, 557,
559–70
"big short" of, 3, 4–5, 6–7, 8, 17, 18–24,
489–95, 496–97, 498–507, 508–27,
528–29, 533–34, 535–36, 539, 540,
544–46, 547, 554–55, 560–61,
562–64, 591–93, 594
CDOs of, 5, 11–15, 494, 496, 501,
503, 506–7, 508–9, 510, 511–12,
520, 521, 528, 529, 534, 535, 536,
537–38, 540, 541, 545–46, 550, 553,
555–56, 558, 560, 565, 566, 570, 593,
599
CDSs and, 473–74, 477–78, 502, 503,
508–9, 510–11, 523, 535, 542, 578
GSAMP deal of, 480–81, 483–84, 485,
487–88, 489, 493, 496, 502, 503, 519,
531
hedging of, 474, 478, 479, 503, 504,
510–11, 519, 526, 529, 536, 558–59;
see also "big short"
marking down of, 547–54, 557–58
Massachusetts's investigation of, 530–31
Mississippi's investigation of, 531–32
residential (RMBS), 495–96, 534, 535,
536, 550, 556, 561, 562
subprime, 477–880
Goldman Sachs Asia, 418
Goldman Sachs Asset Mangement, 443

Goldman Sachs Fellowship, 167
Goldman Sachs Trading Corporation,
47–57, 59, 60, 62, 68, 73, 97, 111,
208, 215
stock prices of, 48, 50, 53, 54, 55, 56, 59
Goldman Sachs: The Culture of Success
(Endlich), 239, 299
Goldman v. United States, 16
gold standard, 68
Gordon, Albert, 259
Gorter, James, 349–50, 352, 367
grain, 296
Grand Central Terminal, 154, 169
Granite Capital International Group, 282
Grannin, Chuck, 120
Grassley, Charles, 454–55
Grasso, Richard, 437, 438
Gray, Harry, 227
Great Britain, 37, 327, 329–30
Great Crash, The (Galbraith), 44, 45, 46,
48, 56
Great Depression, 2, 44, 45, 105, 107–8,
121, 148, 152, 195–96, 214, 307, 340,
597
Goldman Sachs's strategy for, 63–64
Greatest Trade Ever, The (Zuckerman),
491–92
Great Recession, 24
Greenberg, Maurice R. "Hank," 383,
571–75
Greenberger, Michael, 16
Greenhill, Bob, 69, 225
GreenPoint Mortgage Funding, Inc., 483
"green sheets," 181
Greenspan, Alan, 405, 477
Gregory, Hamilton W., III, 134
Gregory & Sons, 134
Greywold Capital, 20
Groysberg, Boris, 443
GSAMP TRUST 2006-S2, 480–81,
483–84, 485, 487, 488, 489, 493, 496,
502, 503, 519, 531
GSAMP TRUST 2006-S3, 487–88
Guaranty Bank, 63
Guggenheim, Peggy, 31
Gump, Akin, 304

Ha, Olivia, 537
Habayeb, Elias, 580, 587
Hagan, Joe, 597
Haire, John, 180

Haiti, 608
Haldeman, H. R., 349
Hall, Perry, 194
Hallingby, Paul, 155–56
Halsey Stuart & Co., 93
Hamilton, Fowler, 138
Hammerslough, Samuel, 34
Hammerslough, William, 99
Hancock, John, 98–99, 100
Hanna, Charlotte, 291–92
Hanson, Lord James, 418
Hanson Trust PLC, 418
Harbinger Capital Partners, 523
Harris, J. Ira, 349–50
Harvard Business School, 67, 101, 107,
    159, 167, 198, 199–200, 202, 210,
    228, 348, 387, 443, 453, 457–58
Harvard Crimson, 77, 131
Harvard Law School, 303
Harvard University, 23, 28, 31, 32, 33, 41,
    42, 47, 64, 141–42, 226, 239, 310,
    486–87
Hasbro, 299
Hawaii, 300, 354
health care, 309
Heckscher, August, 42
hedge funds, 45, 326, 378, 395, 499,
    508–9
    see also specific hedge funds
hedging, 214–15
    against bond prices, 343
    against currency risk, 222
    see also "big short"
Henkel, David, 133
Herrick, Darryl, 503
Hertzberg, Daniel, 267, 268, 270
Hess, Betty Levy, 110
Hewlett-Packard, 379
high-grade corporate bonds, 238
High-Grade Fund, 548
high-yield (junk) bonds, 46, 237, 238, 285,
    377
Ho, Greg, 459
Hoffman-Zehner, Jacki, 290–91
holding company, 45–56
home-equity loans, 529
Homeland Security Department, U.S.,
    456
hostile takeovers, 223, 228, 240–41, 254,
    258, 317–18, 350, 417–18
Hotchkiss, 417, 424
hot IPOs, 424–30

Houghton, Amory, 87
Houghton family, 86
House of Representatives, U.S.:
    Appropriations subcommittee of, 541
    Banking Committee of, 405
    Financial Services Committee of, 424
    see also Congress, U.S.; Senate, U.S.
housing bubble, 476–77, 485
    "big short" and, *see* "big short"
    bursting of, 3, 487–88, 521
Houston, David F., 36
"How Did GS Avoid the Mortgage Crisis?,"
    569–70
Howe, Louis, 70
Hudson Mezzanine Funding, 599
Hu Jintao, 435
Hull, Cordell, 74
Humphrey, George, 83–84
Humphrey, Hubert, 151
Hunt, John, 153
Hunt Foods, 115
Hurst, Robert, 227, 324, 329, 332, 335,
    338, 351, 353, 380, 386, 391, 406,
    409, 410, 411, 419, 420, 434
Hydrox, 43

IBM, 75, 451
ICI, 418
IKB Deutsche Industriebank AG, 12, 13,
    14–15, 515–16, 536
Importers' and Traders' Bank, 27
INA Corp, 224
In an Uncertain World (Rubin), 139,
    155–56, 189
Independent, 330, 418, 419, 594
India, 366, 384
Indonesia, 384
"Inflation and Its Relationship to Economic
    Development in Brazil" (Rubin), 142
Ingram, Kevin, 423–24
Inland Steel, 334, 350, 351
In Search of Excellence (Peters), 230
insider trading:
    Boesky's dealings in, 250, 252, 259, 260,
        268
    Goldman Sachs and, 2, 48–49, 56,
        129–31, 250–58, 261–75
    increasing strength of laws on, 151
    mergers and, 129–30
Inside the House of Money (Drobny),
    326

Institutional Investor, 115, 177, 191, 223, 230–33, 234, 240, 249, 284–85, 295, 306, 340, 373
interest rates, 326, 328, 389, 560
International Jew, The: The World's Foremost Problem (Ford), 89
international markets, 159
  Goldman Sachs's move into, 209–12, 284–85, 294–95, 316, 324, 325–26, 352–54, 364, 366–67, 377, 384, 418, 440–41
International Nickel Company, 227
International Synagogue at Kennedy Airport, 188
Internet bubble, 420, 424, 430, 594
Internet IPOs, 46, 471
Interstate Commerce Commission (ICC), 94, 154, 168, 169, 170–71
investment bankers, on corporate boards, 68–69, 151, 160
investment banking, investment banks, 417
  antitrust lawsuit against, 93–106
  customer service of, 16
  Goldman Sachs's mixing with trade, 159–60
  Levin's criticism of, 16–17, 19, 100
  Medina's judicial decision on, 95–106
  prevented from intermingling with commercial banks, 49, 94, 245–46
  Walter Sachs on, 106–8
  Weinberg's study of, 66
investment trusts, 45–56, 59, 60, 62, 65, 68, 73, 97, 111
Investors Diversified Services, Inc. (IDS), 116–17, 147
IOUs, 26–27, 28, 29, 31, 33, 34, 124, 153
  see also commercial paper
Iraq War, 355
irrational exuberance, 46
IRS, 90, 370, 454–55
ISDA Master Agreement, 579
Ishikawa, Tetsuya, 503
Italy, 315, 328
ITT Corporation, 378–79
Ittelson, Henry, 104–5
iVillage, 424

Jacobs, Eli, 155
Jacobs, Heather, 130
Jamison, Bill, 550
Jamison, John, 162–63, 166

Japan, 246, 327, 345, 353, 418
Jaretzki, Alfred, 102
J. Aron & Company, 214, 216–23, 237, 296, 326, 333, 344, 383, 460–61, 462
Jefferson Islands Club, 74
Jell-O, 43
Jews:
  as bankers, 26–27, 29, 30–31, 123
  Marcus Goldman's collection of money for, 30
  as store owners, 25
Jiang Zemin, 353
Jinro Ltd., 475
John H. Jacqueline, 64
Johns Hopkins School of Advanced International Studies, 464
Johnson, James, 420
Johnson, Jim, 306, 439
Johnson, Lyndon B., 150
Johnson & Johnson, 485
Joint Chiefs of Staff, 80–81
Jonas, Nathan, 49
Jonas, Ralph, 49, 50, 51–53, 54, 55
Joseph, Fred, 259
Journal Company, 299
Journalist and Financial Reporting, 267
JPMorgan, 9, 46, 344, 467, 478, 514, 568
  Goldman Sach's proposed merger with, 381, 383
  investment trust of, 60
  World War I funds raised by, 38, 42
J. P. Morgan building, 58
JPMorgan Chase, 511
  Bear Stearns's merger with, 6, 556
  Glass-Steagall's effect on, 94
  TARP funds repaid by, 9
J. S. Bache & Co., 65
junk (high-yield) bonds, 46, 237, 238, 285, 377
Justice Department, U.S., 87, 129, 130, 138, 167, 478, 597
  Wall Street firms sued by, 93–106, 201–2

Kaden, Lewis, 155, 309
Kahn, E. J., Jr., 63, 64, 67, 90
Kalb, Richard, 456–57
Kamehameha I, King of Hawaii, 300
Kamehameha Schools, 300–301
Kamp, Charlotte, 118–19
Kaplan, Gilbert, 177, 191

Kaplan, Robert, 334, 434
Katz, Robert, 324, 325, 404
  Friedman's succession and, 331–33, 336, 337
Kaufmann, Edgar, 103
Kaufmann, Edgar, Jr., 103
Kaufmann Stores, 103–4
Keenan, John F., 253
Kellogg, 350
Kelly, Kate, 593
Kennedy, Joe, 70
Kennedy, John F., 150
Kennedy, Ted, 416
Kenny, John, 319
Kerouac, Jack, 144
Kerr, Steven, 441
Keynesian economics, 76
Kidder, Peabody & Co., 228, 251, 254–55, 257, 263, 266, 273, 466–67
  secret arbitrage unit in, 258–59
Kim, Anthony, 545
Kimmel, Sidney, 418
Kirby, Allan P., 116, 117, 147
Kissinger, Henry, 210, 236
KKR Financial Holdings, 475, 551, 600
Kleinwort, Sons & Co., 35, 37, 159, 210
Klingenstein, Arthur, 132
Kohlberg Kravis & Roberts (KKR), 255, 269, 378
Komatsu, Koh, 244
Korean War, 74, 82, 192
Kraft Foods, 43
Kraus, Peter, 401, 403, 449–50, 564–65
Kravis, Henry, 188, 259, 278, 282–83, 378, 600
Kravis, Ray, 128
Krimendahl, H. Fred, II, 164, 165, 166, 367
Kroll, Jules, 484
Kronish, Leon, 141, 144
Krugman, Paul, 304
Kuhn, Loeb, 37–38, 95

laddering, 425–30
Lady Ghislaine, 316
Lampert, Edward, 274, 475
Langone, Kenneth, 448
"Larry" (Whitehead's friend), 198
Laser & Skin Center, 458
Lasker, Bernard "Bunny," 269, 270, 271–72, 305

Lautenberg, Frank, 413
Lawson, Nigel, 277
Lazard Frères & Co., 111, 138, 145, 150, 225, 241, 242, 261, 366, 378, 407, 418, 448, 466, 510
  as absent from antitrust suit, 93
  capital of, 108
  gold bullion traded by, 30
  as Jewish firm, 211
  profits divvied up at, 229
  start of, 25
  Sumitomo deal and, 243–45
Leach, Roger, 317
Leasco, 318
lease finance, 159
Lehman, David, 509, 510, 517, 523
Lehman, Emmanuel, 33
Lehman, Herbert, 99, 123
Lehman, Philip, 33, 34, 39, 98
Lehman, Robert, 69, 76, 86, 205
Lehman Brothers, 76, 110, 251, 369, 422, 510, 560
  antitrust suit against, 95
  capital of, 108
  demise of, 3, 4, 8, 10, 589
  Goldman Sachs's squeeze on, 4
  mortgage-backed securities of, 482, 484
  Sears IPO and, 34–35
  start of, 25, 33
  in underwriting business with Goldman Sachs, 33–35, 39–40, 98–100, 105
Lehmans, 25, 27, 28
Lenk, Edward, 424
Lenzner, Robert, 131, 132, 133, 147, 417
Lenzner, Terry, 417–18
Leval, Pierre, 274–75
leverage, 5
  in Blue Ridge deal, 56–57
  in Sheandoah deal, 56–57
leveraged-buyout techniques, 46, 475
Levin, Carl, 19–24, 556, 595, 599, 600, 602
  Blankfein questioned by, 6–7
  complex financial instruments criticized by, 16–17, 19
Levin, Richard, 435
Levine, Dennis, 250, 251, 252, 259, 262
Levis, William, 87
Levy, Bella Lehmann, 109–10
Levy, Betty, 111, 128
Levy, Brad, 478

Levy, Gustave Lehmann, 109–28, 155–56, 158, 223, 261, 282, 289, 305, 318, 343, 437, 446
  alleged letter promoting Weinberg and Whitehead by, 190–92
  in arrangements with Rothschild and Wertheim, 135
  AT&T deal and, 136
  background of, 109–11
  in battle for control of Allegheny, 115, 117
  block trades desired by, 113, 127, 134, 146–47, 148, 177, 212
  Christian Science Monitor article of, 124–25
  civic responsibilities of, 125–26, 128, 154–55, 186, 188, 216
  on corporate boards, 115–16, 123, 155, 185, 186, 187, 188
  death of, 187–89, 190, 191–92, 193, 194, 323, 325, 333
  on Goldman Sachs's pay, 120
  hedging disdained by, 214–15
  Institutional Investor interview of, 177, 191
  Mayers and, 134–35, 137–38
  Missouri Pacific bonds traded by, 114, 115
  options trading approved by, 215
  as parochial, 209–10
  Pennsylvania Central deal and, 154, 157, 168, 169, 172, 179, 180, 181, 183
  placed in charge of arbitrage, 111, 378
  Purchase of J. Aron considered by, 216
  in racial discrimination suit, 165, 166
  religious views of, 123, 126
  schedule of, 126–28
  Studebaker trade of, 124–25
  Tenenbaum hired by, 118
  as tough on subordinates, 121, 122, 127, 128, 131, 133
  UPI piece on, 186–87
  Walter Sachs on, 109
  Weinberg's move uptown engineered by, 148–50, 161, 190
Levy, Jack, 408
Levy, Janet Wolf, 111, 123
Levy, Peter, 111, 123, 187–88, 191
Levy, Rose, 110
Levy, Sigismond, 109–10
Lewis, Michael, 542, 564, 573

Lewis, Robert, 586
Lewis, Salim L. "Cy," 112–13, 114, 122, 123, 128, 605
Lewis, Salim "Sandy," 112, 113, 149, 155, 256, 257, 605
L. F. Rothschild, 132, 133, 134, 135
Liberty Bonds, 38–39
Libya, 131–32
Li Ka-shing, 353, 417
Lincoln, Abraham, 64, 78
Lincoln Center for the Performing Arts, 125
Lindsay, John, 188
Lindsey, Lawrence, 355
lira, 315
Litterman, Robert, 371
Litton Loan Servicing, 482
Loeb, Jeanette E., 247
Loeb, John, 151
Loeb, Rhoades, 108, 151
Loeb, Solomon, 27, 28
London, 46, 210–11
Long Beach Mortgage Company, 483
Long-Term Capital Management (LTCM), 394–97, 399–406, 412, 413
Lott, Trent, 455
Loudcloud, 429
Lowenstein, Roger, 395, 396, 398, 400–402, 403, 404
Lower Manhattan Development Corporation, 282
Loyola University, 185
Lucien Leuwen (Stendhal), 286
Lybrand, Ross Brothers & Montgomery, 153

McAdoo, William G., 36, 37
McCain, Charles, 70
McCartney, Linda, 417
McDaniel, Raymond, Jr., 486
McDonough, William, 401, 402–3
McEnany, John, 262
McGoldrick, Ben, 230–33
McGoldrick, Mark, 378, 475
McGraw-Edison, 351
McGraw-Hill, 234, 236
McGreevey, James, 414
McInnerney, Thomas H., 99
McKesson & Robbins Corporation, 71–72, 86
McKinsey & Co., 243

McMahon, William, 499, 502
Macmillan Inc., 318, 320
McNamara, Jerry, 119
McVey, Henry, 440
Macy's, 240
Madison Square Garden, 169
Madoff, Bernard, 13, 433
Madras, 46
Maiden Lane II, 590
Maier, Nicholas, 426
Malle, Louis, 10
Mallinckrodt Chemical Works, 157
Mamet, David, 101, 350
Maney, Michael, 178
Manhattan, Inc. (Epstein), 271
Manufacturers Trust Company, 49,
    50–51, 52
Marano, Thomas, 541
Markit.com, 478
"mark-to-market," 4, 5, 6, 19, 345, 498,
    553, 566
Marschoun, Michael, 496
Marshall Field, 225
Martin Marietta, 224
Massachusetts, 530–31
Mattel, Inc., 298
Maughan, Deryck, 381, 382, 385
Maxwell, Kevin, 321, 322, 367
Maxwell, Robert, 316–23, 367–68
Maxwell Communications Corporation,
    317, 318–23, 324, 331, 360, 361,
    367–69
Maxwell House Coffee, 43, 316
May Department Stores, 35, 39, 103–5,
    187
Mayer, Jeffrey, 541
Mayers, Bruce, 133–37
Mayfield, Dick, 205
Medicare, 453
Medina, Harold R., 94–106
Mellon Bank, 387–88, 390
Menschel, Bob, 127
Menschel, Richard, 163, 166
Merchant Banker, The (Wechsberg), 227
Merck, 102
Merck, George, 102
Mercy, Eugene, Jr., 156
merger arbitrage, 113–14, 129, 214
Merger Mania, 258
mergers and acquisitions (M&A), 69, 111,
    160, 255, 258, 265, 417, 558
    antitrust procedures and, 138

arbing vs. advising on, 378
    between Archipelago and NYSE, 447–50
    growth of, 397
    inside information and, 129–30
    of NYSE and Archipelago, 603
    of RCA and GE, 241, 243
    of Sinclair Oil and Texas Gulf Producing
        Company, 131–33
    taxes and, 130
    of Travelers and Citibank, 390
Meriwether, John, 395–97, 399–401, 402,
    403, 413
Merkel, Angela, 432
Merkley, Jeff, 22
Merrill Lynch, 151, 227, 320, 342, 391,
    408, 422, 439, 476, 559, 560, 569,
    583–84
    as absent from antitrust suit, 93
    capital of, 108, 242
    European offices of, 210
    financial troubles of, 3, 4, 6, 8, 10
    Goldman Sachs's squeeze on, 4, 6
    LTCM deal and, 403, 404
    mortgage-backed securities of, 471, 482,
        505
    profits of, 212
Merton, Robert, 395
Metz, Tom, 223–26, 227, 228
Mexico, 353, 370, 384
Meyer, André, 69, 205
M. Goldman and Sachs, 28–29
Michigan Bell Telephone, 102
Microsoft, 485
Midway, Battle of, 16
Milken, Michael, 259, 471
milk of magnesia, 71
Miller, Anderson & Sherrerd, 384
Miller, Arjay, 164
Miller, Arthur, 144
Milliken Brothers, 41–42
Mills Factors Corporation, 152–53, 156,
    161, 179
Mindich, Eric, 358, 475
Minsky, Hyman, 307
MIPS, 364
Mirror Group, 320, 321
Mississippi, 531–32
Missouri Pacific Railroad, 114–15, 116
Mnuchin, Robert, 133–34, 136, 161, 190,
    423
Mnuchin, Steve, 423
Mondale, Walter, 233, 305, 306

Money (Cathcings), 40

Money Partners LP, 482

Montag, Thomas, 20–22, 499, 501, 502, 517, 519–20, 521, 525, 539, 556, 558, 561, 562, 565

Montgomery Securities, 385

Moody's, 484, 485, 486, 531, 559, 565

Mooney, Shannon, 486

Moore, Michael, 597

Moot, Robert, 348

moral hazard, 307

Morgan, J. P., 35, 69

Morgan, W. Forbes, 74

Morgan Guaranty Trust, 237

Morgan Stanley, 86, 93, 134, 136, 225, 240, 277, 351, 378, 380, 407, 412, 422, 439, 440, 445, 460, 466, 471, 498, 521, 559
    capital of, 108
    IPO of, 242, 244
    Jew hired at, 194–95
    London office of, 210
    TARP funds repaid by, 9
    in turn to bank holding company, 8
    valuation of, 391, 394

Morgenthau, Robert, 281

Morrison, David, 330

Mortara, Michael, 239–40, 359, 415, 467, 471

Mortgage Bankers Association, 538

mortgage-related securities, 3, 27, 46, 183, 237, 238–40, 285, 528–29, 557, 559–70
    Bear Stearn's losses on, 3, 5–6
    "big short" of, *see* "big short"
    Blankfein's defense of, 23
    CDOs *see* collateralized debt obligations (CDOs)
    CMMs, 474–75
    CMOs, 467–69, 472
    deterioration of, 487–88
    Goldman Sachs's losses on, 3, 5, 6, 62
    Massachusetts investigation of, 530–31
    Paulson's shorting of, 542–44
    ratings of, 16, 484–85, 488, 494–96, 498, 502, 510, 525, 531, 532, 535, 538, 562, 576
    residential (RMBS), 485, 495–96, 534, 535, 536, 550, 556, 561, 562
    subprime, 477–80, 482, 486, 492–93, 501, 504, 511, 514, 518–22, 525, 526, 528–33, 540, 550–51, 557, 560–62, 565
    tranches of, 467, 469, 470, 478, 484–85, 494–95, 502, 576
    underwriting on, 481–82

Morton-Norwich Products, Inc., 224

Morvillo, Robert, 271–72

Moskowowitz, Gary, 280–83, 422

Moszkowski, Guy, 340, 567, 568

Mount Sinai Hospital, 125, 187–89, 192, 216, 355

Mule, Edward, 475

Mullen, Donald, 559, 562–63, 565

Mullins, David, 395

municipal bonds, 14, 342

Murchison, Clint W., Jr., 114, 115, 116–17, 147, 223

Murchison, Clint W., Sr., 114

Murchison, John D., 114, 115, 116–17, 147, 223

Murdoch, Rupert, 418

Murphy, Eddie, 497

Museum of Modern Art, 103

Musica, Philip, 71–72

mutual funds, 146, 455

My Dinner with Andre, 10

NASDAQ, 421–22, 449

National Bureau of Economic Research, 307–8

National City Bank, 63, 163, 482

National City Corp., 559

National Credit Office (NCO), 172–73, 175

National Dairy Products Corporation, 43, 62, 98, 99

National Economic Council, 310–11, 355

National Gypsum, 296

National Liberty Insurance Company, 50–51, 52

National Park Bank, 27

National People's Congress, 435

National Security Council, 310–13, 314, 355, 370

NationsBank Corp., 385

Nature Conservancy, 454–55

Nazis, 39

NC Capital, 483

Nelson, Donald, 77, 79, 80, 81, 82

Newborg & Company, 110

New Business Group, 285, 353

New Century Financial Corporation, 14–15, 467, 480, 483–84, 496, 500, 501, 518, 520, 531, 534, 535, 536, 537, 539, 542

New Crowd (Ehrlich and Rehfeld), 110, 111

New Deal, 74, 76, 77, 304

Newhouse, Samuel I., 224

Newport, R.I., 31

Newsweek, 2

New York, 155, 264, 279

New York Central Railroad, 116, 154

New Yorker, 63, 90, 484

New York Observer, 213, 419

New York Post, 281–82, 569

New York State Division of Human Rights, 166, 167

New York Stock Exchange, 30, 47, 49, 57, 67, 87, 88, 90, 92, 93, 125–26, 147, 149, 158, 164, 165, 188, 212, 269, 414, 421, 437–38, 447–50, 569, 603

New York Telephone Company, 93, 109, 123

New York Times, 30, 31, 41, 56, 67–68, 74, 78, 92–93, 105, 109, 110, 111, 114, 115, 116, 117, 123, 126, 132, 148, 150, 151, 153, 157, 158–61, 168, 176, 179, 180, 184, 188, 194, 201, 217, 220, 233, 234, 235, 237, 240, 241, 242, 243, 245, 257–58, 262–63, 299, 301, 309–10, 312, 314, 318, 319, 340, 360, 368, 393, 405, 407, 411, 423, 436, 437, 439, 463, 567–69, 590, 593, 602

New York Urban Coalition, 164

Niederauer, Duncan, 450, 569

Nietzsche, Friedrich, 37

9/11 United Service Group, 434

Nixon, Richard M., 82, 157, 304, 349

N. J. Schloss & Co., 29–30

Norton Simon, Inc., 179

NovaStar, 522–23

Novotny, Edward, 158–59, 162, 176, 185, 187, 193–94, 220, 223

Nye, Richard, 270

Obama, Barack, 598, 600
Blankfein criticized by, 2, 8

Obermaier, Otto, 271

O'Brien, Michael, 326–27, 328, 330

Och, Daniel, 274, 475

Och-Ziff Management Group, 45

Office of Defense Mobilization, 82

Office of Management and Budget, 311

Office of Naval Intelligence, 67

Office of Production Management (OPM), 76–77, 78–81

Office of Strategic Services, 80

Official Airlines Guide, 318, 320

O'Herron, Jonathan, 170, 171–72, 174, 176, 181–82

Ohio Mattress Company, 296–97

oil, 222, 296, 370

O'Melveny & Myers, 17

O'Neal, Stanley, 560, 569

On the Brink (Paulson), 560

options, 148
on government bonds, 303
illiquidity in market for, 215–16
puts, 255, 559

Orlich, Shanna, 293–94

Osborne, Grace, 574

Ostrem, Peter, 538

Our Crowd (Birmingham), 25, 26, 27, 28, 31, 33–34, 35, 37, 38, 40

Outboard Motor, 334

Overlock, Willard J. "Mike," 324, 338, 353

Owens & Dilday, 167

Owens-Corning Fiberglass, 86–88, 90

Owens-Illinois Glass Company, 86, 87, 88

Oxenberg, Judy, 144–45

Oxley, Michael, 424–25

Pacific Uranium Mine Company, 123

P&Ls (profits and losses), 496, 499, 524, 546, 558, 560–61, 565, 592

Panetta, Leon, 311

Panic of 1907, 33, 34, 36, 41, 65

Pardee, Scott, 246

Paribas, 444–45

Parkinson, Thomas, 97

Pataki, George, 282

Paulson, Henry, Jr., 37, 350–51, 392, 411, 420–21, 438, 439, 452, 511, 540, 596
background of, 345–50
Blankfein praised by, 464
capital put up by, 351–52
on conflict management, 377, 440–41

Paulson, Henry, Jr. (*continued*)
Corzine's relationship with, 325–26,
337, 365–67, 381–84, 387, 388–89,
390, 396, 399, 408, 411, 432
costs cut by, 358–59, 366
employees insulted by, 430–31
financial crisis worries of, 560
as Friedman's successor, 332, 333,
334–35, 336–37, 339
on Goldman Sachs board, 420
as head of Chicago office, 353
health problems of, 339–40
international markets and, 325–26,
352–54, 366–67, 377
leadership abilities of, 421–22
LTCM deal and, 403–4
made partner, 352
made Treasury secretary, 3–4, 452–55
and move to go public, 376–77, 380,
392–94, 405, 406–7, 409, 411
1994 losses and, 357–58, 372
NYSE/Archipelago merger and,
449–50
in "palace coup" against Corzine,
410–13, 414–15, 419
preferred stock of Wall Street firms
purchased by, 8, 9
promoted to head of Goldman Sachs,
391
religious views of, 339–40, 346, 347,
355
retirement considered by, 325,
386–87
salary of, 422
strategic planning committe of,
389–90
Thornton's retirement and, 435–37
Paulson, John, 12, 13, 14, 477, 478,
489–90, 492, 507, 509, 510, 517, 524,
536–37, 540–41, 557, 601
Paulson, Wendy, 325, 335, 347–48, 352,
354, 355, 387
Paulson & Co. Inc., 14, 15, 492–93,
542–43, 545
Pedowitz, Lawrence, 250, 251, 252, 253,
255–56, 265–66, 268–69, 271–73
Peleton, 521
Pellegrini, Paolo, 14, 491, 492, 510
Peltason, Paul, 118
Peltason Tenenbaum Company, 118
Penn Central Transportation Company,
151, 153, 154, 156–57, 158, 161,
168–76, 186, 208, 247, 283, 320, 350,
485
SEC lawsuit against, 178–79
Pennsylvania Railroad, 154
pension assets, 69
pension funds, 146, 367
People's National Fire Insurance Company,
50–51
Perella, Joe, 225
Perella Weinberg, 80
Peretz, Martin, 424
Pergamon Holdings Limited, 316, 317, 318
Pergamon Press, 317
Permanent Subcommittee on
Investigations *see* Senate, U.S.,
Goldman Sachs hearing at
Perry, Richard, 475
hiring of, 186
Peru, 131
peso, Mexican, 370
Peters, Henry, 370
Peters, Tom, 230
Petersen, Bruce, 559
Pet Milk Company, 62
Pfizer, 485
Philadelphi, Pa., 25, 26, 81, 102, 124
Philbro Corporation, 218
Philip Hill Investment Trust plc, 317
Philip Morris, 240–41
Phillips Petroleum, 214–15
Pickens, T. Boone, 254, 263
Piel, William, Jr., 182
Pierre Hotel, 81
Pillsbury, 96–98
Pillsbury, John S., 96
Piper, Jaffray & Hopwood, 96, 97
Pittsburgh, Pa., 41
"Planning for the Next Financial Crisis"
(Summers), 307–8
Plaza Hotel, 122–23
Poland, 76
Polk, Davis, 270
Pollack, Daniel, 157, 173, 176, 181–83,
184–85
Pollack & Pollack, 181
Pollack Foundation for Economic
Research, 43
Poole, William, 307
population growth, 108
Port Authority of New York and New
Jersey, 155, 187, 282
Postum Cereal Company, 43

pound, 327–28
poverty, 308
PricewaterhouseCoopers, 580, 585, 587–88
Primer, Jeremy, 480, 493–95, 496, 555, 595
Primex Trading, 433
Pringle & Company, 111
Procter & Gamble, 205, 240, 432
Profits (Catchings), 40
profit sharing, 71, 119
Program for Global Leadership, 435
Prohibition, 71
Promise, The (Alter), 2
proprietary trading, 3, 243, 247, 261, 326–28, 375, 377, 401, 472–73, 493, 603, 607
Prosecutors, The (Stewart), 271
Prudential Insurance, 218
Public Employees Retirement System of Mississippi, 531–32
Pura, Thomas, 239
Purdum, Todd, 453–54
Pure Oil, 102
puts, 255, 559

Quattrone, Frank, 471
quinine, 71

Raazi, Mehra Cactus, 538, 542–43, 545
Rabinowitz, Dorothy, 279, 282
Racal, 417–18
railroad bonds, 32, 113, 114–15
ramping, 507
R & R Consulting, 533
Ranieri, Lew, 240, 467, 470–71, 486–87, 521
Raynes, Sylvain, 533
RCA, 241
RCM Management, 384
Reagan, Ronald, 232, 235, 304, 306, 349
real-estate finance, 159
recession of 1957, 116
Reed, John, 438
Reed, Philip D., 85
Rehfeld, Barry, 110
Reich, Cary, 234
Reich, Robert, 306, 307, 310
Reilly, David, 580

repos, 5
Republican National Committee, 82–83, 236, 282
Republican National Finance Committee, 232
Reserve Bank Organization Committee, 3
residential mortgage-backed securities (RMBS), 485, 495–96, 534, 535, 536, 550, 556, 561, 562
Resnick, Mitchell, 495, 514
Reynolds Tobacco Company, 102
R.H. Macy, 296
Richardson, Sid, 116
Richardson-Vicks, 240
RICO statutes, 272–73
Rieck McJunkin Dairy Company, 43
risk arbitrage, 111–12, 139
Rivlin, Alice, 311
Road to Plenty (Catchings), 40
Robertson, Jim, 120
Robertson Stephens & Co., 385
Robinson, Joseph T., 74
Rockefeller, John D., 35
Rockefeller, John D., Jr., 58
Rockefeller, Nelson, 125, 155, 188
Rogers, Allan, 172, 173
Rogers, John F. W., 2, 441–42, 528
Rogers, John W., Jr., 452
Rogers, Will, 24
Rohatyn, Felix, 69, 138–39, 205, 225, 241, 366
   on merger arbitrage, 113
   on risk arbitrage, 111–12
   Sumitomo deal and, 243–45
Rolling Stone, 1, 533, 538, 597
Romano, Benito, 271, 272
Roosevelt, Eleanor, 74
Roosevelt, Franklin D., 77, 113, 195
   in 1932 campaign and election, 70, 74, 77
   in 1936 campaign and election, 74, 75–76
   Weinberg's friendship with, 2, 70, 74–76, 150
Roosevelt, James, 74
Root Barrett Cohen Knapp & Smith, 227
Rose, Charlie, 13
Rose, Clayton, 607
Rosenberg, Brad, 545
Rosenberg, David, 476, 492
Rosenblum, David, 496, 516

Rosenfeld, Wendy, 537
Rosenzweig, Robert, 164–65
Rosewald, Julius, 34, 35
Rotbart, Dean, 267–68
Rowley, Worth, 130
Royal Air Force Benevolent Fund of the
    United States of America, 76
Royal Bank of Scotland, 12
Rubin, Alexander, 138, 139, 140
Rubin, Jane, 141
Rubin, Judy, 156
Rubin, Morris, 139–40
Rubin, Robert E., 147–48, 150, 177, 186,
    213, 241, 243, 261, 269, 286, 295,
    296, 297, 303–4, 316, 323, 324, 325,
    329, 335, 337, 339, 350, 352, 359,
    362, 400, 423, 460–61, 569, 609
  background of, 139–45
  Eisenberg's sexual scandal and, 279
  Glass-Steagall repeal and, 246, 385
  hired at Goldman Sachs, 138, 145
  insider trading scandal and, 253, 256,
    257, 265–66
  on Levy's death, 189, 194
  made co-chairman, 283–84, 285, 308
  made partner, 156
  made vice chairman, 233, 278
  and move to go public, 243–44, 247–48
  at National Economic Council, 310–13,
    314, 355, 370, 453
  1987 crash and, 276
  options trading by, 215–16
  on Penn Central lawsuit, 168
  Phillips Petroleum deal and, 214–15
  politics of, 304–7, 308–9
  as potential head of Goldman Sachs,
    233, 247
  and purchase of J. Aron, 217, 220–21,
    222
  put in charge of fixed-income division,
    237, 238–40
  Telmex privatized by, 353
  wealth of, 311
  White, Weld offer considered by,
    155–56
  Young's advice to, 186
Rubin, Rose Krebs, 139
Russell, Faris, 96
Russia, 30, 396, 405
  see also Soviet Union
Russo, Rudy, 120
Russo, Thomas, 404

Ruzika, Richard, 499, 501, 502, 517, 521,
    538
Ryan, Timothy, 585, 587, 588

Sachs, Arthur, 31, 40, 44, 57, 58, 67
Sachs, Harry, 29, 30, 38, 40, 67
  seat on Stock Exchange sold by, 67
Sachs, Howard, 38, 40, 67, 81
Sachs, Joseph, 27–28
Sachs, Julius, 28
Sachs, Louisa Goldman, 25, 27, 28, 31, 39
Sachs, Paul, 31, 32, 38, 66
Sachs, Rosa Goldman, 25, 28
Sachs, Samuel, 40, 66, 67
  as conservative, 32
  death of, 62–63
  Elberon house of, 31
  Goldman Sachs inherited by, 31
  made partner of Marcus Goldman, 27,
    28–29
  marriage of, 28, 39
  World War I and, 37, 38
Sachs, Sophia Baer, 27–28
Sachs, Walter, 28, 32, 33, 35, 38, 39, 40,
    43, 44, 62, 67, 81, 111, 114, 182
  antitrust suit and, 95, 99, 100, 103–4,
    105–6
  on board of May Department Stores
    Company, 103–5
  Catchings disliked by, 57, 58–60
  on investment banking, 106–8
  on Levy, 109
  management of Goldman Sachs by, 77
  in Paris, 33
  political views of, 78–79
  on Weinberg, 72–73, 86
  Whitehead chastised by, 200–201
Sachs Collegiate Institute, 28
St. Denis, Joseph W., 580–81
St. Louis, Mo., 62, 81, 102, 103, 106,
    118
St. Regis Corporation, 268, 269–70
Salem, Deeb, 480, 489, 550–51, 554,
    561
Salomon, William "Billy," 177
Salomon Brothers, 134, 177, 218, 342,
    349–50
Salomon Brothers, Inc., 218, 219, 237–38,
    239, 240, 277, 285, 359, 381–82, 385,
    395, 407, 409, 415, 502
  capital of, 242

Goldman Sachs's proposed merger with, 381–82, 383
securitization by, 467, 470–71
Salomon Brothers, overseas offices of, 210
Salovaara, Mikael, 298, 299
Samuelson, Paul, 302, 307
Sara Lee, 351, 420
Sarbanes-Oxley Act (2002), 69
Saturday Night Live, 60
Saufley Field, 274
Savage, Thomas, 572
Savitz, Jonathan, 475
Sawyer, David, 309
Scaramucci, Anthony, 286–87
SCA Services Inc., 269
Schapiro, Mary, 425
Schelling, Thomas, 142
Schiff, Jacob, 37, 38
Schoenberg, Eric, 344
Scholer, Kaye, 256, 270
Scholes, Merton, 395
Schrader, Edward, 161
Schur, Marvin, 220
Schwartz, David, 277, 328, 371
Schwartz, Harvey, 534
Schwartz, Laura, 14, 511–12
Schwartz, Mark, 363–65, 472
Schwarzman, Stephen, 560, 600, 601, 610
Scotland, 46
Scott, David, 143
Seagram Building, 147–50, 161, 190, 339
Sealy, 296–97
Sears, Roebuck, 34–35, 39, 40, 62, 75, 77, 92, 124
Dean Witter acquired by, 218
securities, *see also* derivatives; "mark-to-market"; mortgage-backed securities
Securities Act (1933), 74, 98
Securities and Exchange Commission (SEC), U.S., 5, 9, 46, 60, 72, 94, 129, 181, 201, 259, 261, 265, 299, 412, 580
American Stock Exchange investigated by, 125
Goldman Sachs investigated by, 10, 11–16, 18, 24, 178, 179–86, 425–30
insider trading laws and, 151
Penn Central lawsuit report of, 168, 169, 170–72, 174, 175, 176–77, 178–79
Securities Exchange Act (1934), 183
Securities Industry and Financial Markets Association, 407
SEC v. Goldman Sachs, 10, 11–16, 18, 24
Seiderman, Samuel, 140
Selby, Beth, 240
Seligman family, 27, 31
Seligson, Charles, 153
Senate, U.S.:
Finance Committee of, 310, 454
see also Congress, U.S.; House of Representatives, U.S.
Senate, U.S., Goldman Sachs hearing at, 6–7, 10, 16–24, 556, 576, 595, 600
"big short" denied at, 6–7, 17, 18–24
Blankfein's testimony at, 6–7, 18, 22–24
Senderra Funding, 482
Senior CDO axes, 556
September 11, 2001 terrorist attacks, 257, 422–23, 432, 560
Serres, Marine, 514, 518, 526–27
7–Eleven, 296
Shah, Rahul Dilip, 486
Shawn, Wallace, 10
Shearson Lehman Brothers, 277
Shearson Loeb Rhoades, 218
Sheehan, Don, 343–44
Sheehan, Robert, 64, 73
Sheffield Farms, 43
Sheinberg, Eric, 156, 317, 318, 319, 321, 322–23, 367
shell company, 45–56
Shenandoah Corporation, 56–57
Sherwood, Michael "Woody," 582, 583, 585
Shinsei Bank, 399
short positions, 395
see also "big short"
Shultz, George, 234–36, 349
Siegel, Martin, 228–29, 250, 251, 252, 253–54, 255, 258–60, 261, 267, 268, 269, 271, 272, 273
as 'CS-1,' 254, 255, 257, 260, 263, 264–65, 266
Silfen, David, 335
Silverstein, Howard, 358, 359–60
Simmons, Ruth, 420
Simon, Norton, 116
"Simple Algorithm to Compute Short-Dated CMM Forwards, A," 474–75
Sinclair Oil, 131–33
Singapore, 46, 366–67
Sinha, Gyan, 520, 522
Siva-Jothy, Christian, 326–28, 406

60 Minutes, 590–91
Skidmore, Owings & Merrill, 212
Sloss-Sheffield Steel & Iron Company,
    40, 42
Smeal, Frank, 237–38, 344
Smith, Bernadette, 250
Smith, John K., 133
Smith, Roy, 112, 122, 177–78, 187, 190
Smith Barney, 381
Smith Breeden Associates, 537
Smithies, Arthur, 143
Social Reponsibilities of Business, The
    (Goldman), 234
Social Security, 452
Société Générale, 444–45, 582, 590
Sokolow, Ira, 251
Soros, George, 132
Sosin, Howard, 572
Sotheby's, 248–49
Southland Corp., 296
South Seas Bubble, 45
Soviet Union, 37, 38, 75, 80, 234, 458
Sparks, Daniel, 479, 508, 531, 538, 542,
    543, 566, 593–95
    "big short" of, 3, 19, 499–500, 504, 505,
        510, 517–18, 521, 523, 525–26,
        528–29, 533–34, 535–36, 546,
        562–63, 593
    Senate testimony of, 19, 20–21
Spear, Leeds & Kellogg, 421, 422, 433
special purpose acquisition corporations
    (SPAC), 46
Special Situations Group (SSG), 378–79,
    475
Spector, Warren, 399
speculators, speculation, 36, 68
    get-rich-quick schemes and, 44–48
    Wall Street crash created by, 58
    Wall Street created by, 1
Sperling, Gene, 306, 309, 311
Speyer, Jerry, 444
Spitzer, Eliot, 401, 425, 428, 573–74,
    601–2
Standard & Poor's (S&P), 484, 485, 486,
    531, 574
Stand House, 316
Stanfield Capital Partners, 538
Stanford University, 162–65
Stanton, Louis, 262, 267
STAR TV, 353
State Department, U.S., 2, 133
Staten Island, N.Y., 41

State Street Bank, 64
State Street Investment Corporation, 47
steamships, 315
Stearns & Foster, 296
Stebbins, Henry V., 100
Stecher, Esta, 358
Steck, Fred, 301
steel, 41
Steel, Robert, 434, 457, 461
Stein, Alan, 149, 193
Steinberg, Saul, 317, 318
Stendhal, 286
Stephanopoulos, George, 307
Stern, Robert A. M., 463
Stetinius, Edward, 42
Stevens, Robert, 87
Stewart, James B., 267–68, 270
Stewart, Jon, 60
Steyer, Thomas, 274, 475
Stifel, Nicolaus & Co., 106
stock market crash (1929), 47, 48, 52, 62,
    110–11, 139, 149, 158, 195, 200
    causes of, 108
    as created by speculation, 58
    Weinberg's memory of, 57–58
stock market crash (1973), 178
stock market crash (1987), 276–78, 307,
    360
StorageNetworks, 429
Storehouse PLC, 417
Storer Communications, 255, 257, 264,
    268, 269
Strauss, Robert, 304–5, 308
Studebaker Corporation, 35
Studebaker-Packard Company, 124–25
subprime mortgage market, 477–80, 482,
    486, 489–91, 492–93, 501, 504, 511,
    514, 518–22, 525, 526, 528–33, 540,
    550–51, 557, 560–62, 565
Sullivan, Joe, 215–16
Sullivan, Martin, 573, 574, 575, 576,
    585–86, 588
Sullivan & Cromwell, 13, 18, 41–42, 60,
    100, 102, 106, 130, 133, 168, 179,
    180, 182, 183, 324, 400, 445
Sumitomo Bank, Ltd., 243–47, 300, 301,
    376, 383, 392, 414
Summers, Anita, 302
Summers, Lawrence, 302, 303–4, 307–8,
    310
Summers, Robert, 302
Sundaram, Ram, 577, 579, 581

Sunday Times (London), 408–9, 416, 418, 597
Super AAA Offering, 556
support tranches, 469
Suskind, Dennis, 460
Swenson, Michael, 479, 480, 565, 593
"big short" of, 3, 19, 488, 489, 498, 502, 505, 510, 511, 523, 533, 554, 561, 593
Switzerland, 326
syndicated bank loans, 377
synthetic collateralized debt obligations (CDOs), 11, 14, 19, 20, 22, 508, 509, 511–12, 522, 529, 541, 565, 575–76, 592, 599

Tabor, Timothy L., 251, 254–55, 257, 260, 261–63, 264, 266–67, 270
Taibbi, Matt, 1, 533, 597
Tannin, Matthew, 522, 541, 547, 548, 555
taxes, mergers and, 130
Taylor, Frank, 58
Telmex, 353
Temple Emanu-El, 188
Tenenbaum, Harry, 118
Tenenbaum, L. Jay, 134, 147, 155–56, 161, 259, 261
Friedman hired by, 227
hired at Goldman Sachs, 118
inside information and, 130–31
Jewish refugee clients of, 119
on Levy, 109, 110
Phillips Petroleum deal and, 214–15
promotions of, 119, 120–21
retirement of, 128–29, 185–86
Rubin hired by, 138
Sinclair Oil deal and, 132
Tepper, David, 404, 475
Tercek, Mark, 455
Terkel, Studs, 57–58, 70
Tett, Gillian, 513–14
Texas Gulf Producing Company, 131–33
Texas Gulf Sulphur Company, 151
Thain, John, 373, 432–33, 434, 435, 438, 447, 448–49, 461, 464, 569, 603
background of, 415–16
on Goldman Sachs board, 420
LTCM deal and, 401, 402, 404
and move to go public, 380, 392, 408, 409, 419
and NYSE/Archipelago merger, 449–50
in "palace coup" against Corzine, 410–11, 414–15, 419
retirement of, 438–39
salary of, 422
Thatcher, Margaret, 418
Thayer, Eugene, 77–78
TheStreet.com Inc., 424
Thiokol, Morton, 224
Thiokol Corp., 224
Thomas, Landon, Jr., 567–69
Thompson, Julian, 71–72
Thornton, John, 366, 373, 424, 432–34, 461, 464
background of, 416–17
on Goldman Sachs board, 420
and move to go public, 392, 408, 409, 410, 419
in "palace coup" against Corzine, 411, 414–15, 419
retirement of, 434–37
September 11 attacks and, 422–23
stock of, 422
Thornton, Margaret, 418
Tilden Park Capital Management, 595
Timberwolf, 20–24, 541, 542, 545–46, 556
Time, 42, 78
Tisch, Laurence, 188
Tonka Coporation, 298–99
too-big-to-fail mentality, 307
Tourre, Fabrice, 183, 508, 510, 511, 512, 515–17, 518, 526, 536, 541, 543–44, 566
affair of, 17–18
SEC's accusations against, 11–12, 13, 14, 15, 593
Trading Places, 497
Trading with the Enemy, 428
Travelers Insurance, 381, 382–83, 390
Treasuries, Italian, 328
Treasury, U.S., 93, 312, 348, 454
preferred stock of Wall Street firms purchased by, 8–9
Trott, Byron, 358
Troubled Asset Relief Program (TARP), Goldman Sachs funded by, 8–10, 599
Truman, Harry S., 74, 81, 82, 150
Trust Company of America, 65
Tsinghua University, 435

Tulane University, 110, 125
Tung Chee Hwa, 353
Turner, Stansfield, 348
'21' Club, 65, 128, 150, 160
Tyco, 424
Tyson, Laura D'Andrea, 306, 307, 310

UBS, 590
Underwood Corporation, 35
underwriting, 31
    banking vs., 245–46
    by Goldman Sachs, see Goldman Sachs,
        deals and underwriting of
    Medina's judicial ruling on, 95–106
    on mortgages, 481–82
    risks of, 32
Union Investment Management, 559
United Aircraft, 227
United Cigar Manufacturers'
    Corporation, 34
United Corporation, 60
United Technologies, 224
University Hill Foundation, 185
Univis Lens Co., 145
Unocal, 254–55, 257, 263, 264, 269
UPI, 186–87
USG Corp., 299
U.S. Steel, 179
utility bonds, 32, 113, 114
Utley, Kristine, 289–90

value-at-risk (VAR) system, 327, 523, 524,
    556–57, 561, 562, 564, 591
Vanderbilt, Cornelius, 315
Vanity Fair, 453, 573, 598
van Praag, Lucas, 425, 446, 564,
    568–69
Venice, 111
Victor, Ed, 417
Vietnam War, 347
Viniar, David, 3, 62, 480, 482, 498–99,
    500–502, 504, 517, 521, 528, 534,
    535, 538, 540, 545, 557–58, 561, 562,
    563, 564, 567, 569–70, 594,
    596–97
    Senate testimony of, 18, 19, 21
Vogel, Jack, 169, 172, 174–75, 181
Vogel, Matthew, 308
Vogelstein, John, 298–99
Volcker, Paul, 307, 476–77, 485, 493

Voltaire, 295
Vranos, Michael, 467

Wachovia, financial troubles of, 3
Wachtell, Lipton, Rosen & Katz, 256, 265,
    270
Waldorf-Astoria Hotel, 85, 154
Walgreens, 350
Walker, Doak, 226
Wall Street Journal, 126, 158, 161, 162,
    167, 180, 212, 241, 299, 369–70, 383,
    385, 436, 448, 466, 504, 517, 521,
    524, 555, 579–80, 593–94, 595
    article on M&A business, 223–26, 227,
        228
    on insider training scandal, 264–65,
        267–68, 269–70, 272
Wall Street Letter, 281
Walt Disney Company, 157, 268, 424
Wambold, Ali, 261
Warburg Pincus, 298
Warner, Ernestine, 485
Warner, Douglas "Sandy," 381, 382, 383
Warner Bros., 62
War of the Spanish Succession, 45
War Production Board (WPB), 76–77,
    78–81
Washington Mutual, 3, 518, 559
Washington Times, 427
Wasserstein, Bruce, 225, 471
Watergate break-in, 348–49
Watson, Edwin, 76
Waxman, Henry, 588
Webb & Knapp, 116
WebEx, 428
Wechsberg, Joseph, 227
Weil, Gotshal & Manges, 576
Weill, Sanford, 381, 382–83
Weinberg, Helen Livingston, 67
Weinberg, Jimmy Weinberg, 86
Weinberg, John L., 67, 160, 161, 234, 237,
    240, 242, 283, 285, 295, 296, 297,
    314, 332, 337, 338, 339, 350, 352,
    355, 383, 446
    BP underwriting and, 277
    Broad Street Building desired by, 212
    Eisenberg's sexual scandal and, 279
    on Goldman Sachs board, 420
    insider trading scandal and, 256,
        265–66, 273–74
    on mergers, 223

and move to go public, 244, 249
Penn Central deal and, 154, 179, 183
promotion to head of Goldman Sachs,
190–94
retirement of, 232, 283
Sumitomo deal and, 244
Weinberg, Peter, 80, 149, 249, 378, 389
Weinberg, Sidney James, 192, 194, 285,
378, 401, 446
and acquisition of J. Aron, 217, 220,
221
and antitrust lawsuit, 94, 99, 105
arbitrage department and, 121
background of, 63–67
on board of investment trust, 52, 55–56
bond trading by, 67, 68
cars of, 92
Catchings fired by, 58–59
Christian Science Monitor article of, 124
corporate board seats of, 68, 69, 70–71,
77, 82, 83, 85–86, 93, 99, 104, 123,
151
corporate management's confidence
in, 69
death of, 150, 151, 152, 323
FDR's friendship with, 2, 70, 74–76,
150
Ford IPO handled by, 88–92, 125
as irreplaceable, 159
as janitor at Goldman Sachs, 66
made partner at Goldman Sachs, 67–68
Management Committee created by,
161
in move uptown, 147–50, 161, 190
Musica's swindle and, 71–72
New York Stock Exchange seat of, 67,
125
on 1929 crash, 57–58
at OPM, 76–77, 78–81
options trading opposed by, 215
Owens-Corning IPO handled by, 87–88
as parochial, 209, 210
partners made by, 119
political views of, 70, 82–84, 150–51,
235
public service of, 73–74, 76–77, 78–81,
82, 459
Scarsdale home of, 67, 73
sense of humor of, 73
surgery of, 87
Trading Corporation stock manipulated
by, 49

Walter Sach's praise of, 72–73, 86
Whitehead's relationship with, 202–4
Weinberg, Sidney "Jimmy," Jr., 67, 149,
161, 249
at Owens-Corning Fiberglass, 86–88
Weinberg & Co., 67
Weinstein, Harvey, 417
Weintz, J. Fred, 206
Welch, John F., 233, 241
Welch Foods, Inc., 156–57, 180–85
Wells Fargo, 523
Wertheim & Co., 108, 132, 135
Westin Hotels & Resorts, 378
When Genius Failed (Lowenstein), 395,
396, 398, 400–402, 403, 404
Whitehall real-estate fund, 296
Whitehead, Eugene Cunningham, 195
Whitehead, John, 91, 147, 190–212, 282,
283, 296, 297, 337, 338, 350
acquisitions and, 225
annual budgeting pushed by, 229–30
background of, 194–200
Broad Street building desired by, 212
calling effort of, 159–60
as deputy secretary of state, 234–36
ethical code written by, 206–9,
397–98
hired at Goldman Sachs, 200
international expansion pushed by,
209–12
New Business Department of, 204–6
Penn Central lawsuit and, 168, 183
promotion to head of Goldman Sachs,
190–94
and purchase of J. Aron, 217, 218, 220,
221
in racial discrimination suit, 166, 167
retirement of, 229–30, 232, 233–36,
237
seersucker suit of, 200–201
Weinberg as mentor to, 202–4
White, Weld, 155–56
antitrust suit and, 96, 97–98
Whitman, Martin, 138
Whitman, Margaret, 424
Whitney, John Hay, 83, 203–4
Whitney, Meredith, 493
Whittle, Reed, 294
Wigmore, Barry, 309
Wigton, Richard B., 251, 254–55, 257,
260, 261–63, 264, 266, 267, 270
Williams, Geoff, 496, 510

Williams, Robin, 365
Wilson, Charles "Electric Charlie," 79–81,
    82, 86, 88–89, 90
Wilson, Ken, 407, 453
Wilson, Malcolm, 155
Wilson, Robert G., 157, 161, 169, 170,
    171–72, 181–82, 183–84
Wilson, Woodrow, 207
Wilson administration, 35–36
Windsor, duke and duchess of, 91, 174
Winkelman, Mark, 221–23, 296, 315, 325,
    344, 460–61
  as dysfunctional, 357, 359–60, 362
  1994 losses and, 328, 330
Winkelried, Jon, 518, 522–23, 528, 534,
    538, 562, 564
Wisenbaker, Scott, 537
Wit Capital, 433
Witco Chemical Corporation, Inc., 123
Witten, Richard, 213
Wolf, Alec, 111
Wong, Richard "Dickie," 370
Woolworth, 39
Woolworth, Frank, 35
Woolworth Building, 35
Worcester County National Bank, 153
World Bank, 221, 310, 344
WorldCom, 424

World War I, 37–39, 42, 43, 66–67, 89,
    108, 207
World War II, 74, 76, 78–79, 82, 85, 86,
    112–13, 114, 118, 140, 192, 198–99,
    283, 459
Wright, Neil, 586
Wu Bangguo, 435
W.W. Sith & Co., 71, 72

Yahoo!, 424
Yamaichi International, 246
Yang, Jerry, 424
yen, 327
Young, Howard "Ray," 161, 186, 217
Young, Owen, 79
Young, Robert R., 116–17
Young Lords, 456
Younkers Inc., 156–57, 180–85

Zeitlin, Jide, 335
Zell, Samuel, 444
Zhu Rongji, 435
Zimmerman, Jörg, 14–15, 536
Zuckerberg, Roy, 325, 333, 391, 392, 407,
    409
Zuckerman, Gregory, 491–92